Themes in Social Stratification and Mobility

Themes in Social Stratification and Mobility

Essays in Honour of Prof K.L. Sharma

Edited by
Ishwar Modi
B.K. Nagla
Arvind Agrawal

RAWAT PUBLICATIONS
Jaipur • New Delhi • Bangalore • Mumbai • Hyderabad • Guwahati

ISBN 81-316-0116-1

Published by
Prem Rawat for **Rawat Publications**
Satyam Apts, Sector 3, Jawahar Nagar, Jaipur 302 004 (India)
Phone: 0141 265 1748 / 7006 Fax: 0141 265 1748
E-mail: info@rawatbooks.com
Website: www.rawatbooks.com

New Delhi Office
4858/24, Ansari Road, Daryaganj, New Delhi 110 002
Phone: 011 2326 3290

Also at Bangalore, Mumbai, Hyderabad and Guwahati

Typeset by Rawat Computers, Jaipur
Printed at Chaman Enterprises, New Delhi

Contents

Introduction

I

Honouring a teacher and researcher by his students and colleagues is an acknowledgement of his contribution to knowledge and learning in general and to some specializations in particular. Since Prof K.L. Sharma has a rare combination of an excellent teacher, a first-rate researcher and an academic administrator par excellence, hence this volume is a tribute to him. Born on November 20, 1941, in a remote village, known as Roopgarh, in Sikar district of Rajasthan, Prof Sharma was deprived of early formal schooling. He joined school in a distant village of his maternal uncles as a student of seventh standard. Up to High School, he received education in rural environs, without sensing waves of urbanization and modernity. The Government College at Sikar, where he spent four years as an undergraduate student, had also rural ethos as most students conversed in local dialect, and generally referred to their social backgrounds in terms of rural/urban origins and membership of Jat/Rajput and other castes. Written and spoken Hindi had the tinge of local words, phrases and idioms. The academic shaping of Prof Sharma began after he joined as a Master's student at the newly established Department of Sociology at the University of Rajasthan in 1961. Two years of post-graduation in sociology transformed him into a budding researcher and scholar with an ambition to teach at the University of Rajasthan.

After Master's in Sociology in 1963, Prof Sharma started doctoral research under the supervision of Yogendra Singh, who was brightest of all the faculty members at the Department of Sociology. The departmental and the UGC scholarships were awarded to Prof Sharma during 1964–68 for Ph.D. He completed his Ph.D. in 1968, and was the first Master's student of the department who had also the distinction of the first Ph.D. degree awardee. His commitment to research was so intense and strong that he even declined lecturership at a government college during his research work. Based on his immense grounding in the discipline during Master's studies and research work, Prof Sharma took up publication of articles and research papers in professional journals. His first article appeared in March 1967, and by 1970, he had published articles in *Man in India, Economic and Political Weekly, Indian Journal of Social Work, Political Science*

Review, Sociology and Social Research (USA), etc. Till date, there is no pause in his zeal for publication.

In 1968, Prof Sharma was appointed as a temporary lecturer at the University of Rajasthan. During 1969–70, he also worked as a fellow at the South Asia Studies Centre of the University of Rajasthan. Due to compelling circumstances at the University of Rajasthan, he decided to join Gujarat University, Ahmedabad, in June 1970, and resigned from there to come back to Jaipur, but again due to the similar reasons he left for Mohanlal Sukhadia University, Udaipur, in July 1971, and finally moved to Jawaharlal Nehru University (JNU) in July 1972, where he taught till February 2003, and on February 7, 2003, took up the vice-chancellorship of Rajasthan University, Jaipur, and remained there till September 30, 2005. During the past four decades, Prof Sharma had opportunities to visit College de France, Paris, as Visiting Faculty, for five times between 1991 and 2006. Besides France, he has also visited and lectured in Poland, Holland, England, Germany, African countries, Brazil and the USA.

Prof Sharma has supervised nearly 100 M.Phil and 35 Ph.D. students, and some of them are holding positions of professors and senior faculty members. Six major research projects and six national conferences and seminars were organized by Prof Sharma, including XXI All India Sociological Conference in 1994. He was honoured with Swami Parnavanand Saraswati Award in 2002 by the University Grants Commission. Twenty books and nearly 70 research papers and articles have been published by Prof Sharma. In addition to these academic achievements, Sharma was chairperson, Chief Proctor, Dean, Director of the Academic Staff College, Coordinator of the Department of Special Assistance, Rector (Pro-Vice-Chancellor) at JNU, New Delhi and Vice-Chancellor at the University of Rajasthan, Jaipur. Currently, Prof Sharma is Vice-Chancellor of Jaipur National University, Jaipur.

Prof Sharma is known for his contribution to the fields of social stratification and mobility, tribal and peasant movements, sociology of law and legal profession, study of small towns, etc. His seminal work *The Changing Rural Stratification System: A Comparative Study of Six Villages in Rajasthan* (1974) has received applaud as a model for doctoral research for more than three decades. In his various studies, caste and caste-class nexus have remained central foci in shaping and re-shaping of social relations. His research work on the Jharkhand movement in the seventies made immense impact not only on academia but also on the leaders and intelligentsia in general. The latest empirical study conducted by Prof Sharma was of Chanderi, a well-known ancient town, famous for weaving of sarees in Madhya Pradesh. Thus, Prof Sharma has conducted field studies in Rajasthan, Jharkhand and Madhya Pradesh.

II

Caste-class nexus continues to remain a means of access to opportunities for employment and for positions of power and authority because of incorporation of purposive rationality and resilience. Caste is no more a fixed entity observed in terms of birth, commensality and connubiality. It has increasingly become a matter of discretion and interpretation. It is also no more an absolute and fixed system of organic relations among different castes – higher and lower, patrons and clients, *jajmans* and *kamins*. Caste, as a system of social relations, is dwindling, but segmentary functioning of caste is, at times, in existence either as a vote-bank mobilizer, or as a force to punish the violators of 'caste ethics' or to promote caste as an interest group.

Inter-caste relations based on birth and traditional bondings are not only ineffective today, but a sort of disliking has also become a stark reality for jajmani-based relations, particularly in the minds of the 'functionary' castes. No one wants to serve their former patrons. Moreover, the patrons also do not depend anymore on the 'service' castes, because the services rendered by them are no more so significant in the present-day context, and there are also alternative ways and means available to the people for gratification of needs, locally as well as in the nearby towns. 'Marketization' of services has become an everyday life reality. Thus, inter-caste relations are no more the bedrock of caste system. *Jajmani* system has become defunct, and statuses of a family and/or of an individual matter a lot more than the status of a caste. Caste is becoming a desideratum, a state of mind, a plastic and malleable institution. K.L. Sharma (2001: 7–8) observes: "No more hyper-symbolization is manifest to express caste differences and typifications on a continuing basis. Though there is a process of delegitimization of the 'essential' of caste, yet the sporadic appearance of caste-based decisions, and articulations of religious and metaphysical interpretations of caste and its divinity, pose a serious challenge to the secularized understanding of social reality."

Sharma has further argued that economic and political aspects have been integral considerations to the caste system. Purity-pollution, economic exploitation, political and social subordination, though apparently seem to be discordant aspects, they have remained basic elements of the caste stratification. The British put emphasis on commensal relations at one point of time, and eulogized functions of caste as positive phenomena at other time. In some contemporary writings, caste has been presented as a unique cultural system by western as well as Indian scholars. The debate on caste has mainly centred around whether it is a structural phenomenon or a cultural aspect of Indian society. It is quite paradoxical to see caste without class and vice versa. For example, a peasant movement could mainly be a mobilization of the people who are dependent on agriculture for their livelihood and also of these who suffer from exploitation and indignities. It may engage the castes and families bearing common sufferings. But, this may not be true always. In the 1930s, in the Shekhawati region, mainly Jats were involved in the peasant movement. Hence, it was named popularly as a Jat movement. The reality was, however, that the agrarian issues, raised in the movement, were also concerned with several other castes and social groups. The smaller groups were overshadowed by the numerically preponderant and strong group, namely, Jat. At times, it becomes quite hazy and difficult to know whether an association is an economic one or an interest-oriented formation, or is it a caste association, despite being named after a caste/clan.

In the late 1960s and the early 1970s, K.L. Sharma argued that social mobility in rural India occurred at three levels, viz., caste, family and individual. All the three levels could reflect social, economic and political shifts in village India, and economic and political changes could be more at the levels of family and individual. But, the point is that mobility is not simply an imitation of cultural ethos of the higher castes by the lower ones. Mobility is social, economic and political, and it could occur at the three levels, namely, group (caste), family and individual. Thus, family and individual have been located, but there is a lot more need to see them historically and contextually as well. Such an understanding and analysis would demythologize the views put forward by M.N. Srinivas (1966) and Louis Dumont (1970) on 'sanskritization' and 'binary opposition', respectively.

Projection of caste as a collectivity on a fixed and regular pattern has created an impression that inequality and discrimination are not so serious matters of India's caste system. Many studies have explained that class functions within the context of caste and caste conflicts are also class conflicts. The issue of honour of the backward, the poor and the deprived has also gained currency, and it is not just a cultural issue. It is about the social space, dignity and freedom which these sections of society would like to have irrespective of their lower caste rank and poor economic status in the past. A new discourse on status and dignity is replacing the conventional criteria of status determination. The 'untouchables' became Harijans, and then they were designated as the Scheduled Castes (SCs), and today they prefer and insist on being called as 'dalits'. Even the classification in terms of forwards, upper backwards, lower backwards, minorities, dalits, etc., devised in the context of Bihar, which was quite expedient politically, is becoming increasingly weak and outmoded. 'Bahujan Samaj' is another model of political mobilization, which has been considerably effective in Uttar Pradesh. Bahujan-Sawaran alliance, known as new 'social engineering' during the recent assembly elections in Uttar Pradesh, has worked quite effectively, surpassing both 'Hindutva' and 'Samajvadi' models of politics.

For an understanding of social stratification, one needs to know about India's social formation in general or social formation of a given region, town, village and area, in particular. One can say that analyses of structure, culture, history and dialectics are the essential methodological features of society, and caste-class nexus is the right approach to have an idea of socio-economic relations. "The caste-class nexus as a framework, goes beyond micro-transactions and alternatively filters down the macro-conceptualizations to the ground reality" (Sharma, 2001: 21). Today, the relevance of the 'nexus' approach has increased because of the extra-caste and extra-class considerations while looking at caste and class situations and contexts. Using André Béteille's idea of 'caste-free areas' (1966: 3) or 'open stratification' system, combinations and permutations of caste, class and power need to be seen in the changing stratification system.

'Caste alone' or 'class alone' sort of perception and understanding are not in tandem with economic status, esteem and power as the evaluative expressions of social stratification. Today, people see themselves as very rich, rich, well-off, not so poor and poor. Another way of seeing is as 'powerful' and 'weak' or as 'superior' and 'inferior' families and individuals. Still one more mode of evaluation implies prestige relating to employment referring to people engaged in lucrative and prestigious government jobs, middle and lower level government services, business, shopkeeping, self-employment, and entrepreneurship, farming, etc. This is the essence of everyday life rather than recognition of caste/sub-caste/clan. References or recognitions of caste are much less today because of its nearly diminished organic character.

Public enchantments of caste were taken as demeaning and narrow-mindedness after independence till 1980s. Only after the Mandal agitation for 27 per cent reservation for the OBCs in 1990–91, a sort of caste war erupted between the 'forward castes' and the 'other backward castes'. Today, upper castes, such as Brahmins and Rajputs, are demanding reservation for themselves and for the poor who have so far remained deprived of the benefit of reservation policy. Identification with castes by political leaders, bureaucrats and intellectuals is no more a matter of shame and shyness. Many see it as an opportunity to help their 'brethren' in the way of casteist atmosphere prevailing everywhere. Some get involved in this game to seek favours and fortunes from the caste patrons, and still the big ones do it to create solid vote banks for themselves. The question is: What happens to our secular national character? Such a situation has brought about one more paradigm shift in the studies of social stratification. Caste and class exploitation, domination, poverty, alienation, distributive justice, social mobility, development as freedom and social constraints are the new concerns of sociological studies and research. What new social relations have emerged and how they are being patterned? What are the norms and practices which have threatened the existence and continuity of the conventional hierarchization and social relations?

Since India's independence, no uniform pattern of social stratification and mobility is visible mainly because of divergent historical and geographical conditions, uneven pace of development, and unequal access to opportunities and lack of distributive justice. The complexity of social disparities and of differences among the people calls for a study of social stratification in the contexts of rural-urban, and urban-industrial settings. Studies of status-relationships with regard to weaker sections and women, new hierarchy, legal and constitutional provisions and social movements would explain the changing patterns of social stratification and mobility (Sharma, 1997: 179–212).

In brief, the significant contributions of Prof K.L. Sharma include a systematic comparative study of social stratification in six villages in Rajasthan, studies of Jharkhand movement, educational problems of the Scheduled Castes in Rajasthan, caste, feudalism/and peasantry in Shekhawati region, and socio-economic profile of Chanderi in Madhya Pradesh. Focus on comparison and historicity of social phenomena, with a view to connect the past with present, are salient features of his writings. His studies of *Jharkhand Movement in Bihar* (1976); *Society and Polity in Modern Sri Lanka* (1988); *Caste, Feudalism and Peasantry* (1998); and *Chanderi: 1990–95* (1999) are evidences of his understanding and analysis of structure, culture, history and dialectics, or in other words, of sociology and history. However, Sharma has consistently shown his interest in the study of caste, class, power and social mobility. In a recent article, D.N. Dhanagare (2007: 3414–21; 3499–3508) acknowledges 'structural-historical perspective' followed by K.L. Sharma in his studies of peasant movements and role of various castes and classes in the princely states of Rajasthan.

III

Thirty contributions included in this festschrift by colleagues of K.L. Sharma are close to his academic interests, such as social stratification, mobility, village community, urban life, tribal and peasant movements, gender relations, etc., and have been arranged on the basis of their thematic similarity.

Yogendra Singh charts out trajectory of sociology from colonial impact onwards till date. The first phase after India's independence (1947–67) describes the democratic social revolution. The Constitution of India itself and the implementation of its provisions made a very basic difference in Indian society. This phase is characterized by national consolidation and balancing acts keeping in view India's cultural, linguistic and social divergences and disparities. 'Motivational approach' is the lead rhetoric of the first phase at all the levels, including individual, family, community and state. This phase is followed by a new phase of economic and social transformation (1968–1988), and it was characterized popularly as the period of green revolution. Several questions relating to the mode of production in Indian agriculture, differentiation of peasantry, caste-class nexus, and unequal benefits accruing from the green revolution were debated and discussed.

Social consequences of the development process were evaluated and examined critically in the third phase. One could see resurfacing of Marxist concepts and ideas in social science studies and analyses. Subaltern studies became quite well known explaining the miserable existence of the forgotten and neglected sections, families and individuals. Enchantment with Marxist concepts and categories became an order of the day against western social sciences and their moorings.

The decade of 1990s was characterized by information revolution and globalization. The English-speaking Indian middle classes were distinctly engaged in this process of change and development. In fact, class character of Indian society has undergone a significant change during the last decade of the 20th century, and the process is still on in the first decade of the 21st century. Globalization, privatization and economism have also cast aspersions on the social welfare policies of the Indian state, particularly concerning with rural-urban poor, artisans, agricultural workers and small and marginal peasants. The current phase of technological change and social transformation has created structural and ideological crisis. Education and health have been made market phenomena, pushing their social gestalt in the background. How do we face such a situation in which the below poverty line people remain deprived of the benefits from the Indian state? We have a 'knowledge society'. The question is: For whom?

Dipankar Gupta reflects on the Indian state and society by analysing the nature of the civil society and communication system as recent modes of ties between the state and society. Civil society has multiple meanings and implications for action by both the state and society. In India, the state has not been able to deliver benefits of modernization and technology, hence, the emergence of civil society in India. Only an elite minority has relished the fruits of modernization. In the western countries, civil society is against overriding dominance of technology, whereas in India technology is scarce, and therefore, it is controlled by the privileged sections. For whom civil society is meant? While referring to the views of Rajni Kothari and Ashis Nandy, Dipankar Gupta explains how according to Kothari and Nandy civil society is for the poor and the indigenous people. However, in contrast, Gupta makes a reference to André Béteille whose opinion is that 'intermediate institutions' should be free of state control and from traditional loyalties. The idea of 'intermediate institutions' is drawn by Béteille from the study of American democracy by de Tocqueville. Gupta also mentions about Partha Chatterjee's view that all modern institutions are instruments of civil society, which is in contrast with both the views held by Kothari and Béteille.

Dipankar Gupta, taking clues from McKim Marriott, observes that 'concentric communication' is in consonance with popular culture. In popular culture, powerful and the subalterns are both included, hence they also share advantages, though not in equal measure. Gupta makes use of 'communication of decipherment' and 'reflexive communication' for making a strong plea for the significance of concentric communication in bringing together unequal participants in civil society. Reflexive communication acts as a medium for realizing citizenship and fraternity.

IV

Contribution on Indian diaspora in Trinidad by R.K. Jain brings out once again the complex question of insiders versus outsiders or that of inclusion versus exclusion based on the notions and reality of ethnicity and race. With vivid details and historical insights, Jain works out a close connection between ethnicity and the political community. But, he also realizes that 'ethnicity' is a vague concept. Despite this, the ideas of 'ethnic boundary' and the 'social organization of difference' in its background help considerably in understanding of multiculturalism. Jain attempts to locate conflicts and dilemmas of the Indian diaspora, particularly labour migration evolving into a middle class in Trinidad.

After providing a plethora of information, which is weaved into nearly three centuries old migration from India to Trinidad, Jain sees to be in agreement partly with Muna Singhe's study Callaloo or Tossed Salad? on the politics of cultural conflict between East Indians and Africans. One can see the moral, political and cultural dimensions of identity through such a conflict between the Indians and the non-Indians. However, Jain disapproves Singhe's view that the East Indians are 'outsiders', and that ethnicity is essentially attached to the ethos of nation-building. 'Emic' perspective is of immense significance, and imposition of a super-academic 'etic' model cannot provide a reasonable solution of the vexed diaspora problem.

The other five papers in this category, by S.M. Michael, S.M. Dahiwale, Shyamlal, Heinz Werner Wessler and Rajiv Gupta, are related to social mobility taking into consideration religious and 'downward' cultural mobility. Michael observes that the phenomenon of conversion is complex because it is related to a person's subjectivity on the one hand, and his socio-cultural status and mornings on the other. Economic, social and religious factors may cause conversion, but Michael states that conversion is seen as a way to gain protection, education and status. A person intends to move up in social ladder by attacking the social constraints. It is a process of gaining social and cultural freedoms and economic and political betterment. With such a framework, Michael looks at various conversion movements and their consequences relating to various tribes, castes, ethnic and religious groups. Initiation, absorption and rejection through conversion are the main trends found among various groups of people. Invitation of Hinduism and conversion to Christianity among tribal people are the main highlights of Michael's illuminating paper.

S.M. Dahiwale pleads for a non-Brahminic perspective on Indian society like some others who have put forward similar views such as use of non-sanskritic (or Buddhist) sources, a view 'from below', etc. While explaining his perspective, Dahiwale writes: "It perceives the practices, which are non-Vedic, non-Shastric, non-caste, non-patriarchal or having equalitarian character, and a number of elements made to bring about change/transformation towards the equalitarian order through protest/resistance/action movements against the Brahminic hegemony." Dahiwale traces dynamics of the history of Brahminic hegemony and exploitation of the non-*dwij* castes and communities in general and of dalits in particular. In conclusion, Dahiwale discusses at length the rejection of the identity granted to the lower castes by the upper caste Hindus and construction/invention of identity by the oppressed castes themselves. Like the oppressed castes, tribal people also claimed themselves as original inhabitants in the regions where they lived for times immemorial.

A very different view is presented by Shyamlal. He pleads that the upper castes have degraded themselves because of the breach of the imposition of the Muslim and British rules in India. The upper castes accepted untouchability or what Shyamlal calls 'Asprashyeekaran'. Like Dahiwale, the analysis presented by Shyamlal is also based on some eclectically chosen instances and episodes. Examples of degradation of upper castes or their social intercourse with the lower castes imply more of given political situations rather than a movement or trend of downward social mobility. Certainly, one can see some fluid aspects in caste system, which also made it a resilient and adaptive mode of social relations.

Heinz Werner Wessler traces the history of the impact of Indology on German Intelligentsia before analysing the Dalit assertion of identity in the Hindi literary world in recent times. He tries not only to explain and analyse from the perspective of the all knowing narrator, but also as an attempt to contribute towards a paradigmatic shift in the perception of India through the Western eye, towards a shift from the Great Tradition and its narration of India to the perspectives of the margins of society.

Rajiv Gupta highlights on the interplay between education and hierarchy in Indian society. Poverty among people, marginalization of the weaker sections, gender inequality, communalization of social relations and increasing food insecurity have hindered education from becoming a means of social transformation. Privatization and marketization of education have further made it a cause of inequality and hierarchy. Gupta advocates introduction of a common school system [on the pattern of (MEP) Marxist Educational Praxis]. He warns against the dangers of 'cultural imperialism' which would emanate from privatization of education.

Another point, boldly put forth by Rajiv Gupta, refers to the prejudices and pride inherent in the textbooks at the school level. The contents of the textbooks, and the use of language and symbols are also a matter of great national concern. Biases, based on caste, gender, religion, economic standing, etc., are already reflected in the textbooks, and the same get expressed in classrooms. 'Communalization of mind' and false understanding of history are the logical offshoots of such textbooks and practice of teaching. Socio-cultural divides are thus further strengthened by the present-day educational praxis. Creativity in the child is the greatest casuality because of such a deplorable condition of our school system. Instead of change, education turns to be a system of stability and status quo. Elitism springs up from privatization and commercialization of education.

V

D. Sundaram explains how significant is the historical perspective to understand hierarchy and power. Individual is the real actor in the historical process. The role of an individual in shaping cultural and social relations at the local level is the essence of Sundaram's analysis of social stratification. Individual is social, hence contextual social space is more important than the textual space. Individual is concrete acting entity. The 'social' dimension of individual members formed a collectivity or a moral order. Caste acknowledged the significance and role played by its individual members. Thus, autonomy/segmentation and interdependence were interlinked aspects of the same system.

A vehement opposition to the application of the functionalist paradigm to the study of Indian tribal society is the crux of the paper by S.L. Doshi. He writes: "We are required to look at the Indian tribals from the perspective of modernity and post-modernity." Because a radical social transformation has occurred in the lifestyle, status and class formation of the tribal people. Tribal people do not constitute a segment of Hindu society, hence, they are not divided into castes and sub-castes. A given approach to the study of caste system, therefore, would not be suitable to study the tribal people in India. However, the ideological and political question relating to 'assimilation' and/or 'isolation' of tribal people remains unanswered even after sixty years of independence, and debate on this vexed issue remains alive.

Doshi observes that tribals have lived in isolation, and Hindus have not been so. Caste-Hindus have exploited them, but they have never become a part of the caste system. Equality among the tribal people could be seen even today in their everyday life interactions. Secular and democratic ethos is built into their values and norms and in behavioural practices. However, Doshi may give more attention to the issue of gender relations from the point of male/female hierarchy and inequality or equality.

The article "Caste, Class and Ecology Movements" by Ranjita Mohanty, a student of Prof K.L. Sharma, highlights on the complex relationship between social stratification (caste and class-based inequalities) and movements (collective actions). Based on the facts of the Chilika movement, Mohanty argues that inequalities provide ground for collective action, and at the same time a collective action or a movement is hindered by inherent socio-economic inequalities prevalent in a society. She writes: "Emergence of mass-based ecology movements against development, in recent times, has heralded a new phase in the history of social movements. Questioning hegemony, dominance and oppression perpetrated by current patterns of development work on an agenda of social transformation which necessitates addressing inequality in all its manifestations, but most importantly social and economic inequality." The role of the state becomes inevitable in taking the benefits of development to its disadvantaged people. The state is under statutory obligation to wipe out the barriers in this act. Caste is one such barrier which forbids people to unite for a common economic goal.

The Chilika Bachao Andolan was led mostly by fishermen against the Tatas who were given the Chilika lake by the Orissa government for commercial venture known as the Integrated Shrimpt Farm Project. Mohanty has clearly demonstrated ties between development (state), ecology, caste and class, through her study and analysis of the Chilika movement. She has also discussed the divides between the fishermen and the non-fishermen and between the poor people, surviving on fishing, and the rich non-fishermen. Thus, caste, class and state need to be seen together in a collective action like the Chilika movement.

In a segmentary society, family is far more crucial unit than the group. P.C. Jain, based on his extensive fieldwork among the tribes of southern Rajasthan, observes that female-headed families are now becoming a new reality, implying weakening of norms of patriarchy, and creation of identity and empowerment of women. However Jain is of the view that this could be done more effectively if civil society could accelerate the process, in addition to the efforts of the state. Women can manage quite well their households provided they do not encounter obstacles from male members.

The next paper in this section by Vinay Kumar Srivastava is based on a case study of the Raika *jati* and its *dharmic* order in western Rajasthan. Raikas are also known as Raibaris and Dewaris. They are an other backward caste. Their traditional main occupation is animal husbandry (camel-breeding, sheep-herding, etc.). They are not a culturally homogeneous community. Despite social and cultural differentiation, the Raikas believe and practise a common religious order. The ten *dharmas,* which the Raikas follow in real life, are the religious lifeline of the community. These *dharmas* are: never swear upon the Lord Shiva; be honest and truthful, particularly with regard to men-women relations; not to axe the banyan tree; worship the *pipal* tree; in ritual feasts the Raika women should eat 'behind the curtain', the married women should always wear the *ati* (head-dress); never sell milk; Shiva's *dhuni* (fire place) should be well-kept; a *bhagwa* flag should be fixed on top of the hut; and Monday should be observed as the most sacred day of the week.

Worship of Lord Shiva is the pivotal around which the life of the Raikas revolve. The caste councils of the Raikas ensure adherence to these religious dictates. However, the Raikas, being a pastoral community, cannot adhere to some of the religious norms. The story of their origin and the mythical history and the duties for the community are being followed quite faithfully. Resilience is also being accepted by the community in the present-day situation.

Based on a discourse on Marxist theory and dynamics of Jharkhand movement, Ajit K. Pandey, also a student of Prof K.L. Sharma, observes that the Marxist theory is inept to explain the socio-economic and political plight of the tribals of Bihar (now Jharkhand). The Jharkhand region is characterized by co-existence of tribal and modern economy, presence of bourgeoisie democracy, alliances of heterogeneous social groups, divergent interests of tribal peasants and urban-industrial workers, statist mode of development, and alien orientation of tribal middle classes. Thus, the Jharkhand region does not present such a picture which can be taken as a platform to examine Marxist concepts and theoretical formulations. Pandey writes: "The central element of the specificity of the Jharkhand case is the fact that the type of economic development that has taken place there has not generated an industrial working class of such a magnitude that it could be a central actor in political action."

However, the questions are: Does Marxist theory not apply to the social formations which have dual modes of economy and polity? To what extent the Marxist theory is grand and macroscopic? One can say that Marxist theory can not be reduced simply to economic analysis. It has a humanistic and philanthropic dimension as its base is quite strong, and therefore, the Marxist theory applies to all the suppressed, oppressed, exploited, subjugated people, irrespective of the fact whether they work in factory or on farm.

Arvind Kumar Agrawal draws our attention for a need to expand Talcott Parsons' formulation of 'pattern variables'. His main argument is that the idea of 'pattern variables' emanates mainly from the experience of modern western societies. Agrawal is of the view that the pattern variables such as hierarchy versus equality, sacred versus secular, and conservative versus liberal could be added to make the Parsonian Action Frame of Reference still more comprehensive and valuable.

VI

Ananta Kumar Giri touches upon the problems of development at the conceptual level. The idea of development today has shaped new forms of political responsibility on a global scale. However, there is a crisis in the very direction of development. A decline is perceptible in commitment to human development on the part of state and global donor agencies. There is also destruction of public space and institutions. On the contrary, state and society have become quite militant with a great deal of cynicism. Further, Giri feels that there is an increasing gap between action and reflection. 'Manageability' and 'results' have become the buzzwords today. 'Reflection' is the main casualty in this shift of focus. After going through a serious thought process on such a knowledge crisis, Giri advocates for a genuine humanistic development anthropology. No process of development can afford to ignore a serious concern with the pathos of human suffering.

New visions of peace, justice and shared suffering can pave a path for hope in a new way. A new global community can do it. Socio-political struggles for global justice and peace can create a paradigm shift in our reflections and actions. We need a structure of activities and relationships commensurating the global hope created for human well-being. Will this create a classless global society?

Can we have all the requisite strength to create a sufferingless and peaceful human society? How do we define global responsibilities in the wake of diversities based on race, ethnicity, caste, language, religion, economic disparities, etc.? These are some of the main questions which may be discussed for better understanding of the underlying human miseries and pathos.

The changing urban-industrial social stratification is the theme of Sanjay Mishra's paper, who is also a student of Prof K.L. Sharma. Mishra, drawing from various studies and approaches, infers that cities are an outcome of political, economic and social arrangements at a given point of time. Resources at the command of power elite are appropriated to shape and re-shape cities, hence distribution of resources becomes a crucial fact in the patterning of urban social life. Of all the factors, economic restructuring or shifts in economy may be a dominant factor. The growth of cities in the post-liberalization period has witnessed an influx of immigrants from rural areas and an unprecedented unemployment due to closure of industries and privatization of public sector establishments. At the same time, over-urbanization has created several problems due to lack of proportionate civic amenities. Uneven growth of cities is another alarming trend in India's urban life. Urban-industrial stratification is having today many anomalies and ambiguities. Despite such a confusing state of urban-industrial life, noticeable changes have occurred. Techno-managers, skilled and contractual workers, new brands of corporate entrepreneurs, workers and helpers characterize today's urban-industrial stratification system.

J.S. Gandhi's paper, "Social-Cultural Construction of Competence and Professional Hierarchy" is also in the category of urban-industrial domain of social life. In this comprehensive paper, based on his field studies in Punjab, Gandhi describes legal practice at the district level. Four categories of legal practitioners are identified: (1) exclusive, (2) semi-exclusive, (3) non-exclusive, and (4) satellite. The degree of exclusiveness decreases in the descending order, from category one to four. Lesser would be specialization among the satellite practitioners compared to those who are above them in this classification. The exclusive lawyers dominate the Bar and the practice at the district courts. These exclusive lawyers are in the three main branches of specialization and practice, namely, criminal, civil and revenue.

Such a structuring of lawyers and practice calls for understanding and analysis of their respective clientele, socio-cultural background, lifestyle, etc. The classification of lawyers worked out by Gandhi is based on the extent of specialization and its realization by clientele and peer groups. For example, the non-exclusive lawyers are divided into young strugglers, late starters and poor performers, and satellite lawyers work generally for senior exclusive lawyers as assistants or on contractual basis. In addition to the professional hierarchization, connections, contacts, network linkages play an important role in legal profession and practice. People's perceptions and particularly that of the litigants add to the status of a lawyer either positively or negatively. Peer group perceptions cannot be undermined. However, objective criteria remain most important in shaping of professional hierarchy.

The last paper in this section by Veronique Dupont is based on a comparative study of two residential colonies, having flats constructed by the Delhi

Development Authority (DDA). Dupont addresses issues such as strategies for acquiring property, constraints of the locality chosen, ownership and tenancy, investment in real estate for income, and perceptions of the people towards government's housing policy and its execution. The two localities selected by Dupont include Mayur Vihar and Rohini. Delhi's fast population growth and unchecked urbanization are the main factors behind the current housing policy. Initially, after independence, housing facility was meant for the benefit of the Pakistani refugees. Since 1960s, the DDA is engaged in various housing schemes in Delhi. The purpose was to facilitate housing for common government and public sector workers/employees. The flats were classified as High Income Groups (HIG), Middle Income Groups (MIG), Lower Income Groups (LIG) and for Economically Weaker Sections (EWS) (Janata Flats).

Dupont provides detailed comparative data about the two localities and the methods by which a person can acquire property from the DDA. The DDA, being a public sector organization, is controlled by certain norms and regulations, but some manoeuvre is always managed. Sociologically speaking, more important point is the purpose of the schemes, and the people who could derive benefit from the DDA's schemes. Selection of a locality and a type of flat determine largely the status of the occupant of a flat either in Mayur Vihar or in Rohini. Today, people prefer to live in flats located in reputed, well-connected and secure localities rather than living in independent houses or in economical, less reputed and inconvenient areas.

VII

A note on rural transformation by Ramkrishna Mukherjee highlights that 'rural' is complementary to 'urban'. Rural can not exist without urban conglomerates and vice versa. Mukherjee draws a clear distinction between change and transformation. Change is both quantitative and qualitative, whereas transformation is not mere change, it refers to change in the primary movers of society. Rural-urban continuum in capital and labour explains rural transformation and also that of urban settlements. Mukherjee denounces the 'sanskritization' thesis and observes that class forces, which were initially feudalistic, acquired colonial-capitalist character later on, have remained always in operation. However, Mukherjee opines that there is less of 'caste' in 'dominant caste', and there is more of 'class' in it. New class forces imply rural transformation. Caste and tribe are more perceptible and evident, whereas class is made consciously visible, and this is generally obstructed by those who get adversely affected by concretization of class-based relations.

Paramjit S. Judge has examined some important theoretical contributions in the context of continuity in Indian villages. Beginning with the ideas of Spencer, Marx and Durkheim, he examines their significance for understanding of social change in Indian society. Was India 'unchanging'? What were the main conceptions of India's villages? Lastly, Judge observes that there is a considerable basis to believe that India's villages have remained static and unchanging. Judge has devoted a good part of his analysis to what Karl Marx says about Indian village. He finds Marx's approach both discursive and dialectical.

Karl Marx exposed the British colonialism for causing misery to the Indian people. However, at the same time, though inadvertently, the British, through their very presence and its effects, brought about social revolution in India by way of socio-political awakening. And Indian village community does not change with increase in population. Marx calls it the dialectical reverse of social change. In view of the Marxian explanation of change in the Indian village community, Judge also looks at the views and explanations given by Sir H.S. Maine, Baden-Powell, Louis Dumont, M.N. Srinivas, F.G. Bailey, B.S. Cohn, André Béteille, Kathleen Gough, Ramkrishna Mukherjee and some others. After sketching the theoretical formulation and their implications for understanding of India's villages, Judge writes: ... "there is not one and the only one explanation or interpretation of a given reality."

In the third section of his paper, Judge describes facts based on his field studies of villages in Punjab. Generally, villages in Punjab are dominated both numerically and economically by given castes. The dominance of a community, for example, namely, that of Jats, hides the social reality of the non-Jat castes and sub-castes. The non-Jat villages have hardly been studied and empirically examined. Specific castes are found in these villages, and these castes have a regional character. Besides the dominant landowning caste in a village, there are a few houses of artisan castes. Such a pattern can be seen throughout the state of Punjab. In conclusion, Judge observes that Marx's views on Indian village communities were comprehensive and significant. Marx described specifically the internal conditions of the village community. The continuity of caste, caste clusters and *khaps,* etc., testifies that village remains an integral and important element of Indian state and society.

The paper by Surinder S. Jodhka and Poul D'Souza on agrarian studies in the 1990s adds further to the enrichment of understanding of rural stratification system. After India's independence, green revolution provided a remarkable impetus to agrarian studies and understanding of new agrarian classes, and their contradictions. With the development of some sectors of rural economy, other than agriculture, agrarian studies have been relegated to the background. A new form of commercialization has substituted the earlier pattern of the green revolution. The fact is that the pre-green revolution, the green revolution, and the post-green revolution – all the phases co-exist, and engage rural people differently in agricultural activities.

Jodhka and D'Souza have surveyed agrarian studies and agrarian regions to discern the post-independence dialectics and differences with regard to agricultural development and emergent relations among various agrarian classes. The last two decades of the 20th century witnessed liberalization and withdrawal of the state from agrarian situation. Such a policy affected adversely the small farmers, the attached and landless agricultural workers. Globalization, agribusiness and contract farming have not benefited the small and marginal farmers. The aspiring middle farmers, who opted for cash crops, have landed into heavy debts, and such a situation has caused suicides by farmers, particularly in states like Andhra Pradesh, Karnataka and Maharashtra. Despite diversification of rural society, agriculture continues to remain a very strong lifeline of the people.

Power politics remains an important factor in rural India along with caste and class as determinants of social stratification. B.K. Nagla, also a student of Prof K.L. Sharma, discusses factionalism and district level politics in Rajasthan, based on his doctoral study of selected villages in Udaipur district. Struggle for power is rooted into social structure. Diversions based on caste and class create cleavages, which, in turn, refer to differential access to positions of power and authority. After presenting a comparative analysis of political power and factionalism, Nagla describes the socio-political situation in Udaipur district of Rajasthan. Based on political events and situations, Nagla discusses factionalism in terms of state level politics in particular, and not so much in terms of caste, class, political parties and ideologies. The present paper does not incorporate the political developments beyond 1977.

VIII

Gérard Fussman and K.L. Sharma have collaborated on an interdisciplinary Indo-French research project on Chanderi town in Madhya Pradesh. Results of their research have been published in the form of books and articles.

The paper by Gérard Fussman is based on a recent inscription. Fully realizing the limitations of historical data to understand the present or to understand the present data or to understand the past, Fussman tries to explain the past with archival evidence and also with knowledge of the present. He also uses the historical materials to understand the present. Based on an inscription found in 1988 near Mathura, Fussman constructs a Brahmin widow and businesswoman in the same person. The woman, whose name is Rahogana, assimilates in her personality all the three statuses and roles. The description about her and her family is quite lucid. Fussman clearly brings out distinct roles of the members of her family. She is the head of the family and the sole owner of the family property. Besides the high status enjoyed by a woman, high juridical status of woman in ancient India is the main crux of the manuscript. Under the control of the woman head of the family some altruistic activities were undertaken. At the same time, male members of the family were engaged in trade.

Another paper on gender is by Nilika Mehrotra who examines how rural women in Haryana manage their disabilities. Mehrotra discusses cultural conceptions of disability and relevance of social factors in its understanding, the social life of physically disabled women and their support system, and state policy or disability in Haryana. Disabled women can be understood both medically and socially. They can be seen also in urban and rural contexts. However, it is necessary to know whether a woman has personal bio-physiological deficiencies or she suffers from 'social constraints'. All sorts of disabilities have some or other cultural conceptions attached to it. Mehrotra refers to some physical disabilities and the cultural notions associated with them, generally in a derogatory or degrading manner.

Another point made by Mehrotra is that women, work and disability are related in a different way than relations between men, work and disability. Not much consideration is given to a disabled woman with regard to her work and responsibilities. However, upper caste handicapped women suffer a little less than their lower caste counterpart. Disability, in general, adds a lot more to the problems of the rural women in Haryana. The state policy on disability is no help in everyday life of the disabled women. They are unable to take advantage of concessions, scholarships and job reservations while being housewives. Pension for the disabled woman goes to family exchequer rather than to the concerned woman.

The last paper in this section is by Renuka Singh, who was also a student of Prof K.L. Sharma, at JNU. Renuka observes that young women are emerging as a vanguard of new sensibility today. They are consciously in pursuit of success, opportunities and power, and aim to take control of their lives. Young women have thus acquired a new value system, and accordingly they re-socialize and recreate themselves. Renuka, after presenting a brief review of literature on young women, describes her observations and impressions based on her recent visit to Kashmir. Financial, legal, psychological, moral and social aspects of women's lives remain pertinent for the developmental issues. Despite education, women in Kashmir remain without their own social space, legal rights and cultural freedom and expression. In some parts of India, women are, however, having certain achievements to their credit. Not only they have education, they are also having employment and modern lifestyle. Feminism is still eluding women in Kashmir. They are deprived of a private world of relationships, marriage, divorce, reproduction and sexuality. Some of them are victims of harassment and violence. A woman as person is yet to emerge in Kashmir.

IX

In the last section, we have papers on social stratification in ancient India, caste, mobility, and social inequalities among children. Shrirama and Indra Deva use *sastric* sources to understand social stratification in ancient India. Aryan supremacy, particularly in terms of colour difference between the Aryans and the natives marked the beginning of stratification. The word 'varna' referred to colour. The Aryan hordes were quite conscious of their cultural and ethnic identity and looked down upon the dark complexioned earlier settlers (referred as Dasas and Panis). The Dasas were made subordinated people by the Aryans. From such a situation emerged the classes of priests and warriors, and the people below them were named as *Vis* or common men. This arrangement transformed itself into the fourfold hierarchy having organic analogy. Shrirama and Indra Deva analyse the traditional pattern of stratification based on *Rgveda, Purusa Sukta,* later *Samhitas* and *Brahmanas, Upanisads, Sutras* and Buddhist literature. The Rgvedic society gave rise to ritualism and the Upanisadic period witnessed revolt against ritualism and Brahminic supremacy. This was followed by efforts for revival of the varna hierarchy and the patriarchal order. Buddhism, as a new ideology, challenged the Brahminical order. However, efforts were made once again to revive the Brahminical system.

The trajectory of such a system of ideas clearly indicates that inequality and equality have existed as dialectical phenomena. There is no consistent and continuous pattern of inequality and equality. The authors conclude that the low position of some people and high position of others lie in the ancient legal system which was influenced by the varna hierarchy. The roots of the present-day hierarchy are in the traditional system of social relations. The traditional legal system, though not in practice, provides today indications for the norms and the patterns of behaviour and attitudes to a large extent.

André Béteille discusses at length about caste in contemporary India, particularly from the viewpoint of its meaning and legitimacy. Caste would not have the same meaning and legitimacy for all the members, being a large and diverse section of society. It is not a uniform medium for its members to act in a similar way. Self-perception and self-deception co-exist regarding caste. Educated people are not clear about its meaning and functioning. Béteille writes: "No one can say that it is easy to give a clear and consistent account of the meaning and significance of caste in India today." Caste barriers are falling, and at the same time one may feel that caste solidarities are rising, particularly in elections. People ignore caste, and at times they look for caste.

Stress on ritual, purity, pollution, etc., is no more a strong feature of caste as it was in the beginning of the 20th century. Caste was projected as a complete system by J.H. Hutton and many others of this period. Today, caste exists, but not as a complete system. It is a truncated system today. Its legal basis has gone. Moral basis of caste has become quite weak and flexible. Rules of marriage are not rigidly followed, particularly in urban India. Political and personal uses of caste have become pronounced. Openly, many politicians grant more preference to their caste than the political parties to which they belong. Shifts in caste have occurred, hence, inter- and intra-caste relations have also changed.

A four-generation study of occupational mobility in a backward caste, known as Padmashi, in Andra Pradesh, is presented in her paper by Sunanda Pande. The study includes migration and mobility among professional groups, semi-professionals, businessmen, ministerial staff, skilled workers, semi-skilled workers, unskilled workers, farmers, and some other people, engaged in different occupations. Pande finds distinctly gradual deviation from caste-based occupations in terms of generational movement. The pattern of deviation is quite remarkable between the first generation and the fourth generation members.

The paper by Madhu Nagla is on nutrition among children in Haryana. Nagla brings out clearly that more than the policies and programmes, social impediments and constraints obstruct proper use of the available health care facilities. The children belonging to the scheduled castes, the other backward castes, and to the general category, are differently benefited from the health facilities because they are unequally placed in the society. This is evident from the data presented in the paper on infant mortality, morbidity and nutritional pattern among these three categories of rural Haryana. In addition to these, social differences, which in effect amount to class distinctions, factors such as rural-urban background, level of literacy and education, standard of living also affect health status of the children. People in Haryana villages suffer from scarcity of food resources. Thus, availability of trained manpower and infrastructure alone are not suffice for proper health care.

Anand Kumar vehemently argues that it becomes a problem when there is growth of 'majoritarianism' beyond 'public interest' and 'imperatives of citizenship' and the state becomes an instrument of discrimination and manipulation in favour of the majority group at the cost of minorities. Inter-group violence and communitarian divides are natural consequences of such a situation. There is a need to discourage such communal divides by invoking and implementing provisions of the Indian Constitution. A democratic society cannot be a repressive society in any way. The story of South Asian countries, despite their democratic ethos, is not supportive of an egalitarian system. Anand Kumar has raised serious questions about the functioning of democracy in the countries of South Asia. His main worry is about recurrence of communal violence.

Cultural diversity should be used as a means to strengthen functioning of democracy and stability of our polity. There is an urgent need to improve the modern statecraft, and to promote role of civil society, human rights, religious freedom, cultural identity and social justice. Media and political parties can play a very effective role in curbing of religious and communal violence and hostility.

References

Béteille, André (1966), "Closed and Open Social Stratification in India", *European Journal of Sociology*, Vol. VIII.

Dhanagare, D.N. (2007), "Practising Sociology through History: The Indian Experience-I and II", *Economic and Political Weekly*, Vol. XLII, Nos. 33 and 34.

Dumont, Louis (1970), *Homo Hierarchicus: The caste system and Its Implications*. London: Weidenfeld and Nicholson.

Sharma, K.L. (1974), *The Changing Rural Stratification System*, New Delhi: Orient Longmans.

—— (1976), "Jharkhand Movement in Bihar", *Economic and Political Weekly*, Vol. XI, Nos. 1 and 2.

—— (1988), *Society and Polity in Modern Sri Lanka*, Delhi: South Asia Publishers Pvt. Ltd.

—— (1997), *Social Stratification in India: Issues and Themes*, New Delhi: Sage Publications.

—— (1998), *Caste, Feudalism and Peasantry: The Social Formation of Shekhawati*, New Delhi: Manohar Publications.

—— (1999), *Chanderi: 1990–1995*, Paris: Edition Diffusion De Boccard.

—— (2001), *Reconceptualizing Caste, Class and Tribe*, Jaipur and New Delhi: Rawat Publications.

Srinivas, M.N. (1966), *Social Change in Modern India*, Berkeley and Los Angeles: University of California Press.

Sociology and Social Revolution in India

Challenges and Responses

YOGENDRA SINGH

In the Indian situation, sociology had its growth, first, through colonial encounter with the West and then normatively and intellectually imbibed the cultural, social and the political discourses of the Indian national movement. And, when India gained independence, it performed both its pedagogic and instrumental functions for the society. As the Indian society is up against new forces of social change brought about by globalization and revolution in the information technology, sociology once again is called upon to take up the challenge. It has now to move ahead with a new pedagogic and pragmatic strategy to achieve the goals both of the promotion of the discipline and the development of the society in the 21st century.

The Democratic Revolution

India, since independence has gone through at least three phases of social revolution: the period between 1947–67 could be broadly described as the first phase of this revolution – we may call it the democratic social revolution. It was marked by the adoption of a Constitution, which enfranchised the Indian people and politically empowered them as the citizens of India, irrespective of the differences of birth, gender, religion, race and class etc. Radical land reforms were introduced which gave the right of ownership to the peasantry. The federal structure of the past was abolished. A national policy of positive discrimination in favour of the Scheduled Castes (SCs), the Scheduled Tribes (STs) and the Other Backward Classes (OBCs) was included in the Constitution. Institution-building for the development of the country was undertaken on a massive scale. A beginning was made for the establishment of the heavy industries, particularly steel and petrochemicals, and the construction of dams and irrigation systems. The Community Development Programmes (CDP) were started throughout the country. Side by side, heavy investment was made in the establishment of a chain of institutions to conduct and promote advanced research and training in the fields of natural sciences, technology, medicine, agro-sciences, management etc. Also, during this period, an unprecedented expansion took place in the number of institutions of art, culture and higher education, particularly the universities and colleges in India. These policies paved the path of radical social transformation. Some changes that these measures brought about could be witnessed immediately, but most others had a revolutionary potential for growth and change, only to bear fruits later.

Consensual Sociology

The Indian sociology played a significant role in planning and implementation of these revolutionary social changes. Despite the debate on the indigenization of their categories, social sciences reflected their universalistic character in theoretical constructions, research methods and generation of data. We find in this period a growing partnership between the research in social sciences and the developmental needs and goals of the state. India adopted a model of import-substitution and welfare planning for economic growth. Within a quasi-federal structure the state occupied a centrality of position in this process. This historicity has significantly influenced the institutional structure of social sciences and sociology in India, its pedagogy, scope and method. Moreover, state remained a major source of funding of research, and most researches were sponsored by its research establishments or through various autonomous institutions which were also its own creation. Sociology, social sciences and its community of scholars reflect, during this period, a spirit of consensus about the state's policies of development and planning. Probably, it was a legacy of the Indian national movement and its ideology of social, economic and political development. The state was not perceived as an adversary but as an enabler to achieve the national objectives of development, nation-building and reconstruction of the Indian society.

Despite this grounding in the national ideology of development and social transformation, sociology and other social sciences did not remain impervious to the normative, theoretical and methodological influences derived largely from the United Kingdom and the United States of America. In sociology and social anthropology, large-scale studies of villages, towns and cities were undertaken; the social and economic impact of the community development, its group dynamics and the contribution of leadership in the adoption of technology and its diffusion of innovation, etc., were systematically explored for their role in the economic, social and political development. In this context, the comparative role of social categories, communities, tribe and caste, etc., were observed and analysed in order to measure the impact of social policies on the processes of development and also to identify the shortcomings in the execution and formulation of these policies. In most of these studies, one may witness a significant level of influence of the Euro-American social sciences, particularly in the choices of methodology and operationalization of conceptual categories.

In political science, the shift from the focus on political theory and the study of its macro-institutions to the study of voting behaviour, the social and institutional structures and processes of the political parties, political mobilization and leadership, etc. introduced a new discourse. The goal of family welfare and balanced population growth being central to the process of planning, the demographers played a key role in the study of family structure, its gender profiles, the occupational mobility and social change. Several studies on the quality of life, health and education etc. were undertaken. The psychologists contributed richly by their systematic studies of the pattern of the Indian 'achievement orientation', and its structure and function. A few studies, using interdisciplinary method, offered insights into the nature of the personality structure in India and its implication to social change and modernization. Among the social sciences, however, economics made the most focused contribution to the process of planning and development, not only by generating benchmark data on significant economic variables but also by systematic studies of the macro- and micro-economic structures and processes of strategic significance for the economic growth.

However, the paradigms of almost all Indian social sciences, including sociology, of this period demonstrate reliance on the 'motivational approach' in planning, rooted implicitly, in the ideology of rational individualism. The primacy was accorded to the unit actor in making choices about goals of development, whether the objective was innovation in agriculture, entrepreneurship, family welfare or voting behaviour. The principle of universal rationality in choice-making was assumed. This assumption, was, no doubt valid for many spheres, such as the enforcement of the legal and citizenship rights, economic choices in matters of trade and investment, etc. But, in the spheres of culture, social structure, politics and political mobilization etc., this assumption was not valid because it neglected the historicity of social forces and their unique initial conditions, needs and experiences. This ideology of rational-individualism, which guided the strategies for the implementation during the first two decades of planning in India, was not only Euro-centric, it was also flawed in its understanding of rationality. It relied heavily upon the social scientist's or the planner's definition of rationality, and neglected the people's or subject's own notion of rationality.

I may illustrate it by one example from the 'family welfare' programme. The studies revealed that the high rate of fertility was most frequent among the poorer sections of society. So, in order to reduce their birth rate, the strategy adopted, during the first two decades of planning, relied heavily upon 'motivating' the people with financial incentives, technical helps and other instrumental measures to adopt small family norm, which was considered to be entirely rational. This approach, however, did not take into account that rationality was operationally altered by social structural conditions of the subjects which may not harmonize with the planner's definition of rationality. In this case, the defining structural condition was the high rate of infant mortality among the poor. It was caused by poor nutrition, health care and illiteracy, etc. So, it was rational for the poor to have larger number of children if only one out of eight or nine infants survived by the age of five! Mere reliance on 'motivation' for adoption of small family norm could not work under these circumstances.

Its realization did come in the following decades when the focus in family welfare programmes began to emphasize improvement in health and nutritional standards of the child and literacy of the mother to reduce the infant mortality rate. We find in Kerala a successful example of this strategy, which is now being adopted in the rest of India as well.

From Democratic Revolution to Green Revolution

The democratic revolution, however, has provided an enduring structure and impetus for social change and transformation of the Indian society. The decades

1947–1967 released social forces of change, which could be defined as "a domain of potentials and high expectations". In concrete terms, economy was not yet powerful enough to support the scale of welfare and employment needs as required or as expected. The country was pathetically dependent on food imports for existential survival. The fissiparous and separatist movements were emerging in several states on the basis of linguistic, ethnic, ideological and other forms of identities. India had to face conflicts with China and Pakistan. All in all, these were the 'dangerous decades' for the country. So, the question arises: what was the nature of the forces and their source which could provide strength and resilience to the country to face up with these challenges? The answer without hesitation is: the constitutional framework of the governance of India and its democratic revolution. The measures undertaken for social, economic and political growth reinforced the social resilience. Although, still in an incipient stage, democracy released hopes and consolidated the aspirations of the Indian people to withstand these challenges. Integrative energies were released which added strength to the nation-building process. The investment in the sectors of industry, agriculture, higher education, research in advanced areas of science and technology, administration and management, etc. resulted into growth of productive energies of the people and consolidation of their national self-awareness.

The political revolution slowly began to expand its potential in the fields of economy and human resources. The decades of 1968–1988 ushered India into a new phase of economic and social transformation. It is epitomized by the green revolution of the 1970s. Apart from making India self-sufficient in food production, the green revolution had major sociological and economic consequences. It activated a modern entrepreneurial and technological ethos which blended with the tradition of joint family mode of production. Apart from production, it involved rational management of resources, credit and market. It necessitated networking with several institutions: the cooperatives, political leadership and development administration. The green revolution, therefore, had deeper economic, social and cultural consequences. It reflected a process of the modernization which was rooted in tradition since the contribution to it was made by the traditional peasant castes. These have also been defined as the backward classes. In most regions of India, they comprise middle-size cultivators, and following green revolution they emerged as a new middle class in the rural society. They increasingly challenged the political and cultural hegemony of the upper castes and classes. It resulted into the countrywide growth of the backward class movement.

The green revolution and the policy of positive discrimination in favour of the SCs, ST and OBCs enlarged the scope and momentum of social mobility and also the size of the middle classes in India, which today comprises nearly one-third of the total population. The 'new agriculture' intensified the scope of the market for the consumer industries and made them increasingly dependent upon the rural market. Today, roughly about 80 per cent of the market for such goods exists in the rural sector and an adverse agricultural productivity puts consumer industries into crisis. In some regions of India, particularly in Andhra Pradesh and Karnataka, the green revolution has not only enlarged the scale of agricultural entrepreneurship, but also led to its linkages with the mercantile and industrial entrepreneurship. Interestingly, linkage has not taken place at the same scale in the North Indian states of Punjab and Haryana, where the green revolution started much earlier. In the other North Indian states, the impact of the green revolution was uneven and localized.

The green revolution mainly benefited the middle-size peasantry. They also took maximum advantage of the reservation policy. The marginal-size peasantry and the lower castes or the working classes did not benefit from it in equal measure. It was soon recognized that the process of social and economic mobility that the green revolution and the reservation policies set into motion favoured the well-to-do castes and classes. The poor and the marginal farmers and working classes did not benefit as much as others. Indeed, in many parts of India, green revolution led to agrarian violence. It set into motion structural contradictions at various levels of society.

The Critical Phase of Sociology

The sociologists and social scientists in India soon realized and their studies increasingly confirmed the fact that state policies of development have so far been advantageous only to the relatively well-to-do sections of society. The overemphasis on the 'motivational approach' to development neglected the need for structural reforms which could empower the economically and socially weaker and marginalized classes in society and could render the benefits of development accessible to them. Their voices and their needs had no centrality in the state policy and strategy of development. Even in the sectors where the state was empathic to their needs, the administration and implementation of policies was flawed. This realization contributed to a break in the 'consensus' within social sciences in India on the approval of the state's development policies. It led to a major shift in the theoretical orientation of social science and the choice of methodology. Social sciences increasingly became 'critical' in their orientation. The uses of the functional theory, or the behavioural approach or the liberal uses of the motivational theory of social action based on the principle of rationality came under sever criticism. The Marxist model of historical or dialectical materialism was increasingly made use of in the studies of agrarian structure, social and political movements and the structure of the rural, urban and industrial economies. The studies now focused upon the role of conflict and alienation in the systems of family, community, industry, polity, caste and class, etc. The dalit and subaltern paradigms for study and research in the social sciences came increasingly into vogue. The institution of state and its organs became a matter of critical enquiry.

From a broader comparative perspective, the shift in the orientation of the Indian sociology from 'consensus' during the 1947–1967 to 'criticism' during 1968–1988 coincides with global shifts in the centre of gravity of the social sciences. It is admitted that after the Second World War, the global supremacy of the United States reached a peak not only in political and economic sectors but also in the domain of knowledge, social science theorizing and methodology. Europe lost its leadership and almost receded into the background. But, this enchantment with the American model of social sciences was short-lived and began to crumble with its involvement in the Vietnam war; a deeper schism in the psyche and value system of the youth in America, Latin America and Europe took place on a large scale. The youth movements of the 1968, which spread all over the world, were prompted by an ideology which rejected the profit-oriented capitalist model of economic growth and its culture of technocracy and consumerism. This movement gave added legitimacy to the critical models of social science theorizing and once again, though slowly, European traditions of theorizing became acceptable. These gained momentum not only in Europe but also the United States of America. The narrow positivism was rejected and the preference for reflexive and phenomenological theoretical paradigms increased. As the legitimacy of state was questioned increasingly, the role of the non-governmental organizations (NGOs) increased not only in the activities related to development but also in social science researches.

These changes left their impact upon the Indian sociology and social sciences. During the early years of this decade India had to get involved into a conflict with Pakistan, leading to the emergence of Bangladesh. It came as a strategic victory but the country had to pay its heavy economic costs, which resulted into political protests and movements later with far-reaching consequence. A national emergency was declared, Congress lost its political supremacy, a political ideology of the coalition politics surfaced, the role of the backward classes in politics emerged powerful as never before, and the government got more and more sensitive to the needs for radical economic reforms. These social and political changes, compounded as they were with a crisis in economy, did set a process of rethinking in the Indian social sciences including sociology. It also oriented the social sciences towards multi-directional theoretical choices. A process of restructuration in the theory and ideology of the social sciences set into motion, but its consequences revealed their potential fully only in the third phase of the social revolution in India.

The Information Revolution and Globalization

The fourth phase of the social and economic revolution was broadly set into motion with the economic reforms initiated since 1991. Its consequences and processes continue to unfold as an ongoing process. Even though, the need for economic reforms was realized from 1978 onwards both by Prime Ministers Indira Gandhi and Rajiv Gandhi, its more focused implementation began from the time of Prime Minister Narsimha Rao. Coincidently, it was the time when the USSR disintegrated and the disenchantment with the state-sponsored model of the planned economy and the import-substitution paradigm of economic growth became universal. Consequently, India began to open its economy to foreign investment, capital and market and also establish linkages with multi-lateral institutions such as the WTO, and entered into a new framework of relationship with the World Bank and International Monetary Fund. It also increased its active involvement with several regional institutions which aimed at multi-lateral economic cooperation. These reforms have exposed India to the forces of globalization whose consequences are not only economic but also political, social and cultural.

The initial condition for the take off of globalization process is provided by the revolution in the technology of information and communication. The space technology, satellite communication, computerization, telephony, internet, etc.

have revolutionized people's mode of communication, the pattern of their social and cultural interactions and the processes of economy. India has, for historical reasons, been relatively more prepared to absorb and take advantage of this information revolution than many other developing societies. Its heavy investment in higher education, particularly in the technological, managerial and scientific education, has not only brought into existence a substantial middle class with rich human resources to take the maximum advantage of the information revolution, but its social and cultural plurality also give it unique resilience to withstand its impact. It also has had the advantage of entering early into the space research programme led by Homi Bhabha and Vikram Sarabhai who had anticipated the significance of space research in leapfrogging over many infrastructural hurdles in India's path of development. A sizeable population of the English-speaking middle classes, containing a substantial pool of the scientific and managerial manpower, estimated as the world's largest, has helped augment and absorb the positive impacts of information revolution and globalization.

No doubt, both information revolution and globalization have augmented employment opportunities, rendered it possible for the Indian entrepreneurs in the information and many other sectors of economy to go global. It had made the reach of telephony available to far-flung villages, to fishermen, farmers and the trading communities, and they tend to profit from its rather effectively. It enlarges the possibilities of making best educational resources and expertise available to people living in the remotest and most backward areas. It expands the scope of health care, management of natural resources, protection of environment, rationalization of the cropping pattern, social forestry and fishery, etc. to an optimum scale. Its benefits have revolutionary potentials for the future. It is also an irreversible process.

Nevertheless, globalization remains a cause for universal anxiety and discontentment. There are many substantial reasons for this. First, globalization is driven by market mechanism and quest for optimization of profit. Privatization of economy draws capital into sectors which yield maximum profit. Thus, the social and welfare sectors of investment, such as education, health, nutrition, ecology and infrastructures, etc., which primarily serve the needs of the poor, marginalized and less empowered sections of society, are neglected. Secondly, the main sponsors of globalization, such as the International Monetary Fund, World Bank, World Trade Organizations, etc., often put pressure on states to withdraw from the administration and investment in the sectors of social welfare. This is disruptive in societies where a large population remains below the poverty line. Thirdly, globalization also implies massive mobility of capital from the multinational corporations, located mainly in the developed economies, to the developing economies in search of profit and cheap labour, on a global scale. This brings money and jobs to the developing economies. To a certain extent the poor and the marginalized sections may also benefit from it as it creates employment. However, it favours only those who are educated and socially empowered. But, even for these, the employment that globalization offers is perpetually subject to structural displacement due to the flight of capital as it is in perpetual search of more lucrative markets for investment. It leads to massive unemployment and recurrent retrenchment. Devoid of welfare-insurance, globalization can compound the miseries of the poor and the marginalized people, more particularly in a developing society such as India. It may also create a crisis of cultural identities and constitute a threat to the local cultures and value system of the people. The social and cultural inequalities already existent in society are compounded by a 'digital inequality' by structural regimentation of access to information technology.

Crisis in Sociology and Social Sciences

This third phase of social revolution has brought a 'crisis' in sociology and the social sciences in India. The social science ideologies of 'consensus' and 'criticism' are now faced with a deeper crisis, which is structural as well as ideological. The structural threat to sociology and the social sciences arises due to the random shifting of priorities in these disciplines. These priorities are no longer governed by the long-term visions of social and economic transformation of the Indian society or the creation of values, knowledge and skills to achieve those objectives. On the contrary, it is governed by the market forces which tend to fluctuate. Education, anchored on the market, promotes profit-driven areas of teaching and research. It is devoid of the long-term vision and is partial to fundamental researches which in the social sciences are essentially ideological. From a different perspective, the same ethos in sociology and social sciences is also the guiding principle in the researches by the NGOs who now have a sizeable presence in India. Moreover, globalization and market economy prompt the state to withdraw more and more from its commitment to the promotion of higher education, and particularly in the social sciences. The market forces and private investment in education favour applied research. The liberal, humanistic and critical aspect of education is secondary to its goals. Market-governed education is oriented to gain skill and 'information', rather than 'knowledge'. This ethos in education, which is driven by market, has arrived in college and university premises on a large scale. The short-term job-oriented courses are launched and taught, which are governed by the opportunity of the moment rather than an enduring perspective and value system.

There is a cleavage at present within the worldview of the Indian sociology, social sciences and humanities. The 'market worldview' of these disciplines does not always integrate with the 'knowledge discovery' worldview of the social sciences. In many parts of India the enrolment in the social sciences is declining and very few students opt for research degree in social sciences. Even in the management schools and the IITs, doctoral research no longer attracts students. The crisis in the normative principle of knowledge is compounded by a crisis of values in pursuit of higher education.

In India, we are at the crossroads of a revolutionary transition. Our history, civilization, and social and ethnic plurality have given us resilience to face up with all challenges. It is urgently required that we evolve a systematic strategy to overcome the crisis that sociology and social science teaching and research encounters today. Some pointers in this regard are obvious. State has to continue its involvement actively not only with primary and secondary education but also with higher education. Institutionalized mechanisms should be evolved to bring about a synergy between the contending two worldviews of the social sciences that I have mentioned above. The role of the corporate sector and private agencies in the field of social science and sociological researches has become limited by the arrival of market force, but it cannot be ruled out altogether. The need is to formulate an enduring perspective and vision of teaching and research in sociology and the social sciences as a part of the national agenda of social, economic and cultural ideology of development which could provide an integrative principle to determine the future planning and investment in sociology and social sciences. The Indian business houses and corporate groups should, as in the USA, come forward for investment in higher education not only in the sectors such as business management, information technology, engineering and medicine etc., where they are drawn by market forces, but also in the field of advanced researches in the social sciences and humanities. The need today is for investment at much higher scale. This cannot be achieved without the pooling of all resources and the Indian social scientists themselves rising up to the challenge of this historical and revolutionary moment. Along with higher investment there is also an urgent need to revive the process of professional development of the faculty involved in teaching and research in sociology and social sciences. The existing listlessness and ambiguity in the policies of the state towards promotion of sociology, social sciences and humanities would retard our competitive ability in the international realm and would render us vulnerable as members of the future 'knowledge society' for which all of us aspire. A future knowledge society cannot attain stability based merely upon material or technological gains. It has to be anchored deeply in culture and values which optimize the emotional and spiritual well-being of the members of the society. For this, and also in order to resolve a string of institutional problems that the future 'knowledge society' in India is likely to be confronted with, major and continued investment in sociology, social sciences and humanities is indispensable.

2 Civil Society, State and Communication

DIPANKAR GUPTA

Till recently the concept of civil society led an incognito classroom life. Political philosophers routinely passed it down from generation to generation. It aroused no passion nor called out for a second look. From Locke to Hegel civil society meant the establishment of institutions by a constitutional democratic state which would guard and enlarge the principles of liberty. Civil society was to the classicists a celebration of' freedom from tradition and from hierarchical and absolutist orders. Civil society and the state came together, not as one against, or independent of, the other. Of course. in a subject as large as this, there were bound to be many ambiguities, but few bothered too much about them.

Now, quite suddenly, all that has changed. Distinguished academics lead eager acolytes to delve into the subtleties of civil society. In most quarters discussions on this subject have taken on an urgent and practical dimension as well. It is now also linked to social movements, cultural assertions and to affirmative action as well. Even social activists, who generally sneer at anything with a remotely academic provenance, have been rumoured to use it. Consequently, the term has taken on a variety of connotations. As it means different things to different people, it can often be an embarrassment of clichés.

There is therefore the temptation to knock down the revival that civil society is now enjoying as yet another misguided obsession by attention-seeking academics. To yield to it would be unfortunate for the contemporary debates around this term tell us a great deal of the sociology of our times in terms of the options now available to citizens in constitutional democracies. This concept also allows us to reflect on the limits of liberalism in an age when focalized state politics have lost much of their shine.

Like elsewhere in the world, civil society's allure in India has also become of the general disenchantment with the state. In developed western democracies this disenchantment is largely because of the surfeit of consumerism leading people to wonder what happened to certain natural simplicities. Even so, it must be admitted that the alienation from the state can also be an outcome of being overburdened by too much technology. The attention has thus turned to the limits of technology and to its more unsavory aspects. This is where new social movements make their presence felt. In their view, peace, environment and gender harmony are all under threat because technology dominates both the commanding heights and every nook and cranny. Indeed, the state itself is the biggest purveyor of technology what with its gigantic instrument of domination coercion and surveillance. The way out is to resurrect civil society and free it from the clutches of the state. The civil society thus becomes autonomous of the state. It is now urged to generate alternative meanings which would enrich lives by making freedom more than just a legal token (see, for instance, Touraine, 1992).

In contrast to the western experience, the reason for the interest in civil society in India is because the state has not been able to bring the fruits of technology and modernization to the average citizen. A majority of Indians have only experienced the downside of technology while the state calmly abets in the aggrandizement of an elite minority. This minority has access to the state of the art in technology and use it to dominate the many. The acquiescence of the state in this process is often too blatant to be overlooked. Thus, while both in India and in the west, the call of civil society is anti-technology, the reasons for this are quite different. Civil society in India, according to some leading experts, resides among the poor and the downtrodden. Rajni Kothari, the foremost exponent of this position, argues that the crisis of governance in contemporary India is because the state tries to stifle the initiatives of the poor and the marginalized by relying on a techno-managerial structure. This has led to the emergence of two Indias – one urban and the other rural (Kothari, 1988a: 2227). Kothari sympathies are clearly with the latter, for it is in the village and in submerged civilizations (ibid., 1988b: 3) that the impulses for civil society lie.

Ashis Nandy, another important figure in this field, endorses Kothari's position very forcefully in a number of widely read and quoted pieces. According to Nandy, the western educated elite in India first look to the state and adjust their culture accordingly. This is why, the state is hostile to those with indigenous cultural moorings (Nandy, 1984: 2078–80; see also Nandy, 1989: 9). Civil society is, therefore, supposed to protect the many precious diversities between communities and oppose the state's grand homogenization project which is carried out in the name of modernization (ibid.).

Civil society thus gets identified with tradition and ascriptive bonds. This is yet another difference between this conception of civil society and the dominant trend in the west. Civil society in the west is not nostalgic about the past. It does not seek to go back to tradition, as it is fully aware of its many iniquities. In the Indian case there is indeed quite a romantic revivalism under the aegis of civil society. It has even encouraged a species of interpretation of traditional Hindu texts like the *Yagnavalkyasmriti* and the *Manusmriti,* which is surprising to say the least. These texts are the staple of Hindu chauvinists as they justify caste hierarchy and the subordination of women. Now, quite suddenly, from self-professed secularist quarters, they are being upheld as models of harmony and uncomplicated goodwill (see Kishwar, 1994).

It is this position, I believe, André Béteille is primarily reacting against. His is a lone voice, but his vast academic reputation more than compensates for it. With Béteille once against the classics from Locke, to de Tocqueville to Hegel and Gramsci are recalled, Béteille, however, takes a non-tradition approach opting for a Tocquevillean notion of civil society. Though Tocqueville did not directly contribute to this subject, his study of American democracy led him to develop the concept of intermediate institutions which are free of the church and the state. Béteille takes his cue from here. In the Indian context, argues Béteille, these institutions should be free from state control and traditional loyalties, which have a strong presence in the subcontinent. The institutions that Béteille has in mind in this context are universities, hospitals, judicial courts, economic corporations, and the like (Béteille, 1991, 1996). These institutions take forward civil society as they centralize citizenship.

This is not hard to imagine for economic and entrepreneurial institutions. In a constitutional democracy corporates are managed by executives who are constrained to act as citizens. In the case of those institutions that are supposed to contribute to basic social welfare, efficiency can best be obtained by factoring in citizenship in a meaningful way. On the other hand, in India, we have many instances of private hospitals and educational establishments coming up having no concern for people as citizens. Their attention is turned to those with money. These institutions, would not meet with Béteille's standards as they do not administer to citizens but cater to a very small minority. In a country with scarce resources, the diversion of such vital services away from the public is surely a retrograde development.

In Partha Chatterjee we have a clear espousal of civil society without citizenship. For Chatterjee all modern institutions, even if they have been set up by the colonial regimes, are instruments of civil society (Chatterjee, 1997). Quite like Kothari and others discussed earlier, and unlike Béteille, Chatterjee is averse to modern institutions. But, unlike Kothari, who sees the civil society residing outside the state, Chatterjee locates it right there in the heart of the beast. Yet, Chatterjee's civil society has nothing to do with citizenship, only with modernity and with the elites who have benefited from it.

When civil society is thus separated from citizenship, it effectively lets the state off the hook. There is no longer any pressure on the state to deliver and be responsible to the people. The state is now conceptually free to roam about capriciously. Kothari and Nandy would like to protect traditional solidarities and primordial ties by turning a blind eye to their many repressive attributes. For Chatterjee, as civil society has nothing to do with citizenship, but only with modern institutions, he would like to separate the realm of the political from that of the state and its apparatuses. Only Béteille takes seriously the inevitability of the modern state. As Marx once said in the *Grundrisse* it is impossible for us to return to ancient Greece as we can no longer be so naive.

This is a very serious issue, especially in a developing country like India. Unlike developed societies, where some can indeed afford to scoff at technology and state-centred developmental programmes, in poor countries, such an attitude seems quite anachronistic. Even, the 'new social movements' in the west do not run away from involvements with the state. They simply have no ambitions of capturing power. They are content instead to influence the state from the outside with strong demonstrations of protest derived from modern democratic sensitivities. Looked at this way, the conceptions of civil society in India seem to have gone further than in the west in denying the validity of the state altogether, and in this process allowing the notion of citizenship to languish. This is surely surprising given India's backwardness where the state is expected to act as a mobilizing agency. To distance citizenship and the constitutional democratic state is conceptually risky and in practice fraught with many dangers. If the state is now no longer expected to perform, then why should it? People cease to be citizens and instead turn their attention either to grassroots organizations and voluntary agencies, or to privatized institutions which run on the principles of profit. If current form holds, then, the crass myrmidons of the state in countries like India have a world go gain free from all kinds of countervailing pressures from all active citizenry.

The understanding of civil society can be fleshed out further if one considers the mode of communication that is appropriate for it. This is necessary if the notion of civil society is to be more than merely a normative one which sets out an ideal, with little thought as to how that ideal is to be accomplished. Accordingly, let us consider the modes of communication best suited for each of the various conceptualizations of civil society considered above.

Concentric Communication

In the communitarian version of civil society, communication is easy and well established. The rules and units of communication are already in place. Innovative methods of communication, or fresh interpretations of norms are generally not entertained. At this point McKim Marriot's understanding of the dense interactional nexus of community relations is very helpful (Marriot, 1991). In this interactional situation, there is no scope for altering the terms of reference. The ground rules are so completely assimilated and broad-based that the form of communication is not outward-looking, but instead concentric in character.

This concentric form of communication is akin to what Roland Barthes would call a 'readerly text' (Barthes, 1970: 156). In such a text, the reader is meant to participate in authorial intentionism, and no innovative reading, or open communicative reading, is really called for. On the face of it a readerly text and community-based concentric communication are somewhat different, but nevertheless one should not overlook the underlying similarity between them. It is true that a readerly text privileges the authorial mood to which the reader must orient oneself, and that in concentric community-based communication there are no real authors but only participants, nevertheless in both cases the text is not a fresh creation. Communication is based on a given horizon of meaning which makes for a very limited repertoire of interpretations.

McKim Marriot has been able to show with the case of caste that an interactional system of the village inhibits caste mobility and the freedom to extravert for the subjugated castes (Marriot, 1991). A person is not known by one's attributes, but relationships are built on the history of interaction of the village. Status and styles of communication are known well in advance which eventually constricts both the dominated and the dominator. In the case of the former, the room for manoeuvre is much more restricted, though conceptually the subaltern and the powerful are locked in a form of communication that can only be called concentric.

This kind of concentric communication is in consonance with what is known as popular culture. Stuart Hall is, in my opinion, is the most forthright in this matter. According to him, in popular culture, there is both containment and resistance (Hall, 1981: 238). This implies that pop culture is based on tradition, in the knowledge of a pre-given community (or fraternity), and essentially closed beyond a limited set of stylized interpretations (Hall, 1981).

In popular culture, like in concentric communication, the powerful and the subalterns are both included, though with different levels of advantage. This allows the subaltern people scope to undermine the advantages that accrue to the powerful, but only within the limited range of possibilities already available within the system. In other words, the text is really a readerly one for the range of options is limited in advance.

It is quite to be expected then that any communication that attempts to subvert the advantage of the power bloc is seriously constrained. As these attempts still function within the horizon of meaning of a concentric form of communication nothing new is ever really articulated. DeCertau believes this to be a kind of everyday resistance though I do not agree with his analogy of guerilla struggle in this connection (1984: 30), as the scope of meanings in any language is already given and weighted in a certain direction. As Paul Ricoeur said, while explaining polysemy, multiple meanings emerge only in the background of the literal meaning which is never elided (Ricoeur, 1974).

The significant issue here is that in this form of concentric communication the subalterns and the powerful are involved as participants. Though there are tactical manoeuvres on the part of each to outwit the other, a strategic overthrow of the system is never really contemplated or even conceived. This is what makes concentric forms of communication inimical to the development of free citizenship, though undoubtedly it connotes security and predictability, and everybody probably knows where they belong.

Communication of Decipherment

In a pure rational-legal organization, which is either meritocratic or market-oriented, or a combination of the two, the form of communications is weighted in favour of decipherment. Decipherment is opposed to reading to the extent that the language of another has to be comprehended according to rules given from the outside. In rational-legal organizations, regulations, terms and conditions of interaction are laid out by the bureaucratic elite and they have to be deciphered and imbibed by all those who are involved in such organizations. Membership into a rational-legal institution, or structure, is open, but every new entrant must be willing to decipher what is given out to be read. The form of communication that is appropriate to such organizations is therefore one of decipherment.

In the decipherment mode of communication the range of meanings is further constricted if it is not actually univocal. The fact however remains that there is no ascriptive criterion to be fulfilled in order to enter into this mode of communication. It is open to all and its only condition is that the form of communication should not be concentric or participatory, but one which is sanctified by rational-legal imperatives and not open therefore to other kinds of considerations. There is little security here, no pre-established community given by birth, residence, or family and economic background. The decipherment mode of communication welcomes all so long as the communication is really one way and univocal in character.

Reflexive Communication

A reflexive communication is of a different order. This form of communication is one that is best suited for enhancing the character of citizenship. If' citizenship is, as we have argued throughout, the most important aspects of civil society, then, the form of communication that is most relevant for it cannot be either concentric or based on decipherment.

In the case of concentric communication, the pre-condition is that one must abide by a readerly text where meanings are limited in advance. It is a closed system of communication which only promotes surreptitious attempts to carve out sectional advantages without questioning the moral order. The moral order in which concentric communication is based in one where citizens are not central, but community members and blood brothers are.

The decipherment of communication is not conducive to citizenship though it does not formally endorse either the community or give value to accidents of birth. It is an open system in the sense that everybody is welcomed to decipher the code that is given in advance. This code, as was mentioned earlier in the context of' rational-legal organizations, may not encourage citizenship as it might deepen a certain understanding of efficiency.

Citizenship is realized best in a reflexive form of communication. To go back to Barthes, one might say that this reflexive communication favours a 'writerly text' where the reader is encouraged to open the text and give it meaning as a free writer. At this point, however, it is necessary to add an important rider. It is not as if such writerly imaginations are free flowing and unconstrained. When there is a certain constraint only then can communication be reflexive – indeed only then can communication he communication at all.

Reflexive communication provides the citizen the freedom to develop socially valued assets but only as a citizen, that is, as a member of a collective. But, this collective is not a community, but rather a fraternity that has to be established. This is where the contract theorists score over those who talk purely in terms of evolutionary development. In a civil society fraternity must be established between equals. This is a fraternity of citizens. This one aspect is inviolable. In other words, reflexive communication cannot trample upon the rights of citizens, and the citizens are held back by duties so as not to trespass over rights of other citizens.

Given this constraint, which is different from the ties of blood brothers or of rational-legal colleagues, communication tends to be open ended and writerly in its text. Reflexive communication must respect citizenship and the status is accorded to individual even as it allows writerly interpretations. Ricoeur is relevant once again in the sense that the polysemy of the writerly text must not forget that original literal meaning of citizenship which cannot be sublated, undermined or deflected. If the original meaning is overwhelmed, it will no longer be true polysemy but random diachrony, floating allusions and homonymy, all of which can only please post-modernists and nihilists.

In reflexive communication citizens are ever alive to their rights and duties which is why there is the need for constant communication. Individualism is encouraged to develop differential talents which have no preordained value connotations. If one were to use Pierre Bourdieu's colourful vocabulary, then one could say that in reflexive communication there is the freedom to acquire cultural capital without the constraints of symbolic capital coming in the way. As symbolic capital valorizes certain lifestyles, tastes and nodes of authority, it constantly tries to freeze the open spaces around which differential kinds of cultural capital call be acquired.

Fortunately, the only kind of symbolic capital which is status laden in the case of reflexive communication relevant for civil society is that of citizenship. This is one status that is common to all, and as was mentioned earlier, it tends towards equality (T.H. Marshall). Further, reflexive communication need not remain an abstract ideal but can easily be put into practice. It can be realized in pressuring the state to deliver to its citizens the freedom to acquire socially valued assets. As the common factor is citizenship, the arenas where reflexive communication works best is when the state is asked to live up to its commitment to provide education, medical care, and housing to all so that regardless of accidents of birth citizens can acquire public goods with equal ease.

It is sometimes argued that the best place where such a communication can take place is in universities arid educational institutions. Jurgen Habermas is of course a great champion of this point of view. Habermas' limitation is that he takes public space of the university for granted and does not adequately distinguish between a rational-legal public space and a public space constituted of citizens. Nor, is it that communication is a free for all where anything can be said in a state of pure equivocality.

Reflexive communication is a communication between citizens which keeps the state in the forefront – not as an object veneration, but medium for realizing citizenship. This makes for a democratic fraternity, and the communication between members of this fraternity should be one that enhances commonalities between them before they can differentiate in their individual ways. It is this dual task that reflexive communication addresses itself to. This dual task is accomplished best when the state is pressured to deliver to citizens the basic conditions for a free and unprejudiced development of conditions for acquiring socially valuable assets. It is not in schools and universities alone that such communication takes place most effectively. There are no privileged sites as such. The important point is not the place, but the discourse – who is addressing whom and for what. Reflexive communication can be put in practice when citizens address the state for providing them with education, health services and social security. This deepens the commitment that citizens have to each other and to the state that is the source and the ultimate repository of freedom.

References

Barthes, Roland (1970), *S/Z*, London: Jonathan Cape.

Béteille, André (1991), "Distributive Justice and Institutional Well-being", *Economic and Political Weekly*, Annual Number (26), pp. 591–600.

—— (1996), "Mediating Institutions", First Fullbright Memorial Lecture delivered in Calcutta on February 22, Reproduced in *The Telegraph*, March 12 and 1–3.

Chatterjee, Partha (1997), "Beyond the Nation? Or Within?", *Economic and Political Weekly* (32), pp. 30–4.

De Certeau, M. (1984), *The Practice of Everyday Life*, Berkeley: University of California Press.

Hall, S. (1981), "Notes on Deconstructing 'The Popular'", in R. Samuel, (ed.), *Popular History and Socialist Theory*, London: Routledge and Kegan Paul, pp. 227–40.

Kishwar, Madhu (1994), "Codified Hindu Law: Myth and Reality", *Economic and Political Weekly* (32), pp. 2145–61.

Kothari, Rajni (1988a), "Integration and Exclusion in Indian Politics", *Economic and Political Weekly* (23), pp. 2223–27.

—— (1988b), *State Against Democracy: In Search of Humane Governance*, Delhi: Ajanta.

Marriot, McKim (1991), "Multiple Reference in Indian Caste Systems", in Dipankar Gupta, (ed.), *Social Stratification*, Delhi: Oxford University Press.

Nandy, Ashis (1984), "Culture, State and Rediscovery of Indian Politics", *Economic and Political Weekly* (19), pp. 2078–83.

—— (1989), "The Political Culture of the Indian State", *Daedilus* (18), p. 1026.

Ricoeur, Paul (1974), *The Conflict of Interpretations*, Evanston: North Eastern University Press.

Touraine, Alaine (1992), "Beyond Social Movements?", in Mike Featherstone, (ed.), *Cultural Theory and Cultural Change*, London: Sage.

3 Exclusion and Inclusion

Ethnicity and Race Relations in Trinidadian Indian Diaspora

RAVINDRA K. JAIN

Max Weber was among early sociologists to devote attention to the phenomenon of ethnicity. He observed that "... ethnic membership does not constitute a group; it only facilitates group formation of any kind, particularly in the political sphere. On the other hand, it is primarily the political community, no matter how artificially organized, that inspires the belief in common ethnicity" (Weber, 1978: 389). "... All in all, the notion of 'ethnicity' determined social action subsumes phenomena that a rigorous sociological analysis ... would have to distinguish carefully ... . It is certain that in this process the collective term 'ethnic' would be abandoned, for it is unsuitable for a really rigorous analysis. However, we do not pursue sociology for its own sake and therefore limit ourselves to showing briefly the diverse factors that are hidden behind this seemingly uniform phenomenon. The concept of the ethnic' group ... dissolves if we define our terms exactly" (ibid.: 394–95).

Two features which Weber perceptively uncovers about ethnicity deserve attention: first, the close connection between ethnicity and the political community, and, second, ethnicity as a bundle of factors, which render this concept unsuitable for a strict definition. Later authors, especially those working in multi-cultural societies, have built upon these early insights of Weber. Barth's (1969) conceptualization of ethnic boundary rather than the cultural stuff it encloses and his insistence on the social organization of difference that this boundary signifies, capture both the remarkable conceptual difficulties as well as the evanescent quality of ethnicity in social life. Furthermore, the existence of ethnicity in the subjective consciousness of social actors – the 'us' and 'them' dichotomy – as situationally located in the subjects – is a feature which later sociologists and anthropologists have honed into the concept of identity. Both politics and belongingness and the interface between them inform the sociological analysis of ethnic identity and conflict in the universe of discourse about ethnicity. Besides this 'universal' rendering of the concept of ethnicity there is in the sociological literature today an insistence on carefully recording the historical trajectory and the material-ideological particularity of ethnic situations. Especially in the study of multi-cultural societies all over the world a great deal of attention is being paid to the triangulation between ethnic identities, process of nation building and 'nationness' and state power (Borneman, 1992). Finally, in the current phase of globalization (sometimes written about as 'post-nation', cf. Appadurai, 1997) ethnicity is being seen in a paradoxical mode: the simultaneous existence of transnational and sub-national identities and conflicts of citizens as social actors. This paper aims to locate the above conflicts and dilemmas in one situation of the Indian diaspora – the predominantly labour migration, evolving into a middle class composition, of the people of Indian origin in Trinidad.

East Indian Exclusivity in Trinidad

How does a numerical majority of middle class Indians gets excluded from the socio-political mainstream in the new nation of Trinidad? I begin with a brief outline of the demography, origin, socio-economic mobility and present status of the Indian[1] community in Trinidad. Of a total population of 1,213,733 in 1990, the ethnic composition of Trinidad and Tobago was the following: African descent, 39.6 per cent; East Indian descent, 40.3 per cent; White, 0.6 per cent; Chinese, 0.4 per cent; mixed, 18.4 per cent; other 0.2 per cent; and not stated, 0.4 per cent (central statistical office 1997 and 1998). On May 30, 1845, the Fatel Rozack arrived in Trinidad with the first Indian immigrants: 225 men, women and children. Except for a brief period between 1848 and 1852, when emigration was suspended, labour continued to be supplied by India until indenture was abolished in 1917. Approximately 143,939 East Indians came to Trinidad during the indenture years, with the number of male recruits consistently outnumbering that of females. The immigration ordinance of 1854 set the main parameters for the system of indenture. The immigrants signed contracts in India that bound them to certain terms for the period of indenture. On arrival in Trinidad the Indians were assigned to a plantation, where they had to work for three years. Then, they had the option of choosing their employer for the following two years to complete the total of five years of mandatory industrial residence, the pre-requisite for becoming legally 'free'. To qualify for the free return passage to India, the immigrants had to reside in the colony for a total of ten years. After completion of the industrial residence they were again free to choose their occupation and employer for the remaining five years. The law regarding return passage was revised in 1895 and 1898 so that immigrants who arrived in the island after 1895 had to pay a proportion of their return passages. Only 33,294 immigrants (22.47% of the total) eventually opted to return to India; the majority of Indians gradually abandoned the hope of one day returning to India. For many it was not a conscious decision, and only practical circumstances precluded any possibility of return. Yet others, who chose to re-indenture themselves or even to return to the West Indies after they had repatriated to India, showed a commitment to Trinidad as their home. By and large, East Indians, believing their situation in Trinidad to be only temporary, displayed little enthusiasm to integrate with the wider community. To be fair, the conditions imposed by the colonial government to confine the East Indians to the plantation environment of the sugar belt, together with the black population's hostile attitude towards them, left the East Indian little alternative but to remain exclusive.

The vast majority of Indians who settled in Trinidad came from the densely populated central plains of the Ganges – the United Provinces, Oudh, Bihar and Orissa. Since they embarked from Calcutta, they came to be known as Kalkattiyas. They were not a homogeneous group. There were religious differences among Hindus, Muslims and Christians; there were caste distinctions and there were linguistic distinctions and regional differences. Some South Indians, 9,133 in all, also arrived in Trinidad as indentured labourers; they were all called Madrasis. Although popular opinion in Trinidad claims that most immigrants belonged to the lower castes, the academic community continues to debate this issue. Between 1876 and 1885 the Hindu immigrants had the following caste composition: Brahmans and other high castes 18 per cent; artisan castes, 8.5 per cent, agricultural castes, 32 per cent; and low castes, 41 per cent (Wood, 1968: 144–45). Although such figures tend to substantiate the hypothesis that the majority of immigrants were low-caste members fleeing the grip of the upper castes, caution is needed in accepting these records because, on the one hand, there is a strong likelihood of the immigrants representing the normal range of castes found in India and, on the other, the premium placed on the agricultural castes in recruiting could have led Brahmans and other high castes to register themselves as agriculturalists. It is true, however, that despite heterogeneity in the derivation of indentured immigrants – not only along provinces but also within the districts and villages of origin – they were looked upon by others and also forged consciously an identity that was homogeneous. The mixing up of castes, language and region in the course of journey to Trinidad as well as common proletarian living conditions on the plantation must have worked in that direction. However, the historical perspective should not be ignored: there is evidence that caste and other distinctions were restored when the East Indians settled in villages in Trinidad (Jha, 1985: 10) and even to this day the distinction between Brahman (the highest priestly caste) and Chamar (which designates all untouchables in Trinidad) is quite pervasive (Vertovec, 1992: 95–100).

We need not go into the details of the legal differentiation and spatial isolation of the early Indian immigrants to Trinidad (Munasinghe, 2001: 73–76) but can note that these factors along side the occupational segregation which was endemic to their status as sugar labourers, contributed to making the East Indians an exclusive and excluded group in the new setting. In this milieu not only did the other non-Indian ethnic formations look upon the Indians as outsiders but also the 'coolies' themselves considered their stay as a sojourn. I shall soon return to the social and ideological representation of Indians as outsiders in Trinidad but let me first note the 'objective' conditions, which make these representations a problematic to be resolved. We have already noted the demographic parity, if not numerical superiority, of the East Indians vis-à-vis other races or ethnic groups. Also, unlike in Malaysia, for example (cf. Jain, 2003) the majority of Indians were quite early knocking at, if not actually entering, the door of the 'middle class' status.

East Indian Upward Mobility: A Mixed Picture

"During the last quarter of the nineteenth century the acquisition of land and education constituted the primary means of mobility for East Indians. Yet it is a testimony of Trinidad's ethnic situation that this mobility, which continues today, did not fulfill its potential to integrate East Indians into Creole society.

Rather, the very circumstances governing East Indians' mobility served to enhance their alien ness, many achieved success through landownership and education, but this prosperity acquired the peculiar veneer of an East Indian style of success" (Munasinghe, 2001: 89).

The author of the above quote is right about the failure of the Indian integration into Creole society, but her overall conclusion about upward mobility through landownership and education paints an over-optimistic picture of the East Indians' status in Trinidad society at the end of the 19th century. Elsewhere (see Jain, 1988: 129–33) I have argued that the increasing number of Indian immigrants in farming after 1884 was a reflection, firstly, of unemployment and retrenchment of free labourers from sugar estates. This factor was closely related to the planter policy of renting out or contracting abandoned estate land to 'free' labourers with the stipulation that they plant cane in a certain manner (frequently under estate supervision), growing subsidiary crops only in certain years, and assume responsibility for tax payment if a house was built. Indeed, the continued employment of indentured labour for estate work, the widespread practice of renting and contracting rather than owning property among ex-labourers, the preponderance of extremely small holdings of Indian 'farmers' contrasted with the large and medium-size properties of Creole farmers with whom they competed (unfavourably) for the cultivation and sale of cane. The resultant necessity of these largely tenant-farmers to supplement their earnings by regular or irregular work as agricultural labourers on estates, the rise of an Indian peasantry and their possible rise as a vanguard 'middle class' was an absolute chimera. The figures cited by Munasinghe both for the large number of cane farmers among Indians and the labourers' progressive abandonment of residence on estates has to be placed in this perspective. Table 1 (Occupations of Indian Immigrants, 1891) tells its own story, with 38,889 agricultural labourers and 720 peasant proprietors in a gainfully employed population of 49,401. Laurence (1985: 111–12) cites cases of two labourers who became big property-owners but describes them as 'most exceptional'. As the *Mirror* of 13 April 1901 remarked: "Comparison is often made between our cane farmer and the peasantry in other countries, but there is not the slightest similarity. The cane farmer is simply a labourer the exigencies of the sugar industry have placed in his present position. As a rule he has no means and lives from hand to mouth" (cited in Johnson, 1972). In sum, following from Beckford's conclusion (Beckford, 1985: 413) that "the dominance of the plantation mode of production is the single most limiting factor inhibiting peasant development and the associated necessary economic and social transformation in the Caribbean", it is obvious that in Trinidad the Indian population mainly involved in this 'mode of production' must be adversely affected by hindrances to peasant development.

Land was the initial basis for East Indian mobility, but for a few. Very few East Indians also sought mobility through education in the late 19th century. Colonial authorities failed for the most part to provide adequate educational facilities for East Indians because they were perceived as transients. Although government 'ward' schools established in 1846 were available to children of East Indian labourers for primary education, however, enrolment was low on account of the fear of mixing with those of an alien race and faith. Yet, the resistance on the part of the East Indians was not the only factor; from the very beginning there has been a running battle between denominational and state sponsored schools in Trinidad ending with the decisive triumph of the former. From the 1890s onwards until as late as 1950, the only Indian-friendly schools available were the Canadian Presbyterian missionary schools, which aimed as much for conversion as for education. "The East Indian in Trinidad ... was prepared to use the mission schools as levers for upward economic mobility, but was unwilling to forsake his ancient faith" (Samaroo, 1975: 51). The separation of Indian pupils in Canadian missionary schools fostered exclusivism and the curriculum content, based primarily on the Canadian model, far removed from the local situation, did little to bridge the racial divisions. Samaroo also suggests that the propagation of East Indian exclusivism might have been part of a deliberate strategy to keep the two non-white races apart (ibid.: 55). The only genuinely Indian 'middle class' at this time comprised of "the pariah and commercial groups" (Rex, 1978) of shopkeepers, Sirdars and *pandits* (priests).

According to Vashti Singh, "the revolt of the East Indians in the education sphere was fully initiated around 1928 to 1930" (Singh, 2002: 33). This was the period during which the reformist Hindu sect of Arya Samaj was introduced in Trinidad. The East Indian concern for education under their own management was greatly influenced by liberal intellectuals of the Arya Samaj sect (Vertovec, 1992). The Arya Samajis instituted the Arya Pratinidhi Sabha in Trinidad in 1934. The Tackveeyatul Islamic Association (TIA) was the first Muslim body incorporated by government in 1931. However, just as in India, the leaders of the Sanatan Dharma community attempted to form organizations to resist controversies instigated by the Arya Samaj. The post-1930 period witnessed a great deal of argument, and factionalism among Hindus in Trinidad. For the next two decades Indian (Hindu and Muslim) organizations in Trinidad engaged in a kind of infighting with the eventual victory of the Hindu organization, SMDS (Sanatan Dharma Mahasabha), under the leadership of Bhadase Sagan Maraj as President General. In 1953 Maraj formed the People's Democratic Party (PDP), primarily as an Indo-Trinidadian Hindu political body that drew its support from the Indo-Trinidadian rural masses led by "a conservative group of East Indian businessmen and professionals" (Hintzen, 1989: 44, cited by Munasinghe, 2001). He consolidated the religious and political position of leadership by becoming the President of the major sugar union, the ATSEFWTU (All Trinidad Sugar Estates and Factory Workers Trade Union). With his control over three important political and cultural bodies, Maraj was a formidable force in the upcoming 1995 elections.[2] Here was a perfect case of someone combining religious and political leadership of the 'minority' (since 'outsider') East Indian community; however to understand this alliance of politics and religion we must look at the major activity of Bhadase Sagan Maraj, his dynamism in creating East Indian educational institutions, something inevitable in the special configuration of denominational education in Trinidad.[3]

Before the advent of this strident non-Christian leadership among East Indians, non-Christian schools were struggling for their existence. In 1938, an SDBC memorandum to the West India Royal Commission, under the chairmanship of Lord Moyne, outlined the pitiable condition of almost two dozen non-Christian schools. No action was taken. In the general election of 1950, Bhadase Sagan Maraj won the parliamentary seat in the constituency of Tunapuna as an independent. He intended to transform the Hindu community from one of cane cutters and grass cutters to one with opportunities available for educational advancement. His prime objectives were to bring all Hindus under one organization and to build primary schools in areas where there were no schools (Seetahal-Maraj, 1991). His first act as a Member of Parliament was the consolidation of the SDA and SDBC to form one Hindu organization, what is known today as the SDMS (Sanatan Dharma Maha Sabha) of Trinidad and Tobago Inc (Ordinance 41 on June 26, 1952). The SDMS was accorded recognition as a School Building Authority on July, 25 1952. Foresight and personal commitment led Bhadase without any government assistance to undertake and complete the construction of the first six Hindu primary schools by September 1952 (for details, see Vashti Singh, 2002: 50 passim). By the end of 1953 the SDMS had built 31 schools; in 1954 two more SDMS schools were opened, and by the end of 1956 there were 41 SDMS primary schools. These schools had a dual role as envisaged by the founding father: the achievement of academic education and the propagation and dissemination of Hinduism. The curriculum of Hindu schools was modelled on the English educational pattern operative in the society but Bhadase was firm in his conviction that teachers in Hindu schools should teach their religion as well. During the period under review, Eric Williams, founder of the People's National Movement (PNP), was the main adversary of Bhadase's PDP. As we have seen, through no fault of their own, East Indian leaders of the SDMS were keeping Hinduism and politics hand-in-glove. Williams's critique of this connection was bitter. He labelled Bhadase's political party – now graduated from PDP to Democratic Labour Party (DLP) – as comprising of Trinidad Indians who were "a recalcitrant and hostile minority masquerading as the Indian nation, and prostituting the name of India for its selfish, reactionary political ends" (Williams, cited in Ryan, 1974: 192). "Bhadase retorted, "Williams would have to destroy every East Indian in Trinidad because we do not intend to sit with our arms folded and let him do what he wants" (ibid.: 194). Some agreed that the Indians were indeed clannish, but believed that their behaviour had to be viewed as a natural urge on the part of the minority group to preserve its religion and culture for advancement. As Vashti Singh puts it, "Bhadase was outraged that PNM had selected the Indians as their social target rather that the Europeans who had rejected them completely. The East Indians elicited strong protests via the press and Williams was accused of using "race to maintain his slipping power", of "soiling other people's clothes while licking his wounds" and of "unleashing the mad dogs of racial strife" (Singh, 2002: 69).

Recent East Indian Mobility and Exclusivism

I have so far delineated the conjoint processes of limited mobility through landownership and education on the one hand, and East Indian exclusivity, on the other, as the initial objective or infrastructural conditions of the immigrant group's adaptation in Trinidad society. The socio-economic mobility of the East Indian community, along with that of the other ethnic sections of Trinidad, was accelerated during periods of the so-called American 'occupation' of these islands during the Second World War and, more recently (1974–83), with the oil-boom. In fact, the petroleum sector had begun to expand during the former period. Oil accounted for only 10 per cent of exports in 1919 but by 1932 it had increased to 50 per cent and by 1943 had reached 80 per cent. Of course, the unprecedented increase in oil prices and consequent emergence of the

Indo-Trinidadian rural masses "as the nouveaux riches par excellence in the 1970s" (Munasinghe, 2001: 148) meant their increasing participation in mainstream sectors. According to Vertovec (1992: 134–35), by most measures Indo-Trinidadians constituted the most depressed group in Trinidad during the 1960s and early 1970s. In 1960 Indians had an annual per capita income of £195, whites of £1,250, and blacks of £260; nationally, East Indians represented the highest proportion of the poor. In 1964, 83 per cent of Indo-Trinidadians lived in rural areas in comparison with 51 per cent of Afro-Trinidadians. In 1970, Indo-Trinidadians also had the lowest level of education; only 7.5 per cent had post-primary education, and 26.1 per cent had no education at all (Dookeran, 1985). As we have seen, an incipient Indo-Trinidadian middle class (primarily Christians and Muslims) had begun at the turn of the 20th century to enter the higher echelons of society through education and business, but the most of Indo-Trinidadians were rural, poor, and had little education before the oil-boom. The situation in the late 1980s were markedly different. In her analysis of social mobility experienced by different ethnic groups between 1960 and 1989 Reddock concludes that according to the three indicators of occupation, education and employment, "Indians in general have been experiencing the most significant degrees of mobility" (Reddock, 1991: 232).

There is disagreement between anthropologists who have described changes which conspicuous consumption among Indo-Trinidadians introduced in the late 1970s and early 1980s. Joseph Nevadomsky (1980 and 1983), who studied the same East Indian village in 1972–73 in Trinidad, which Morton Klass had described in 1961, contended that there was acculturation. On the other hand, Vertovec (1992) and Munasinghe who also conducted research on East Indian villages after the oil-boom suggest that traditional patterns did not die out in the face of new ones but were instead rejuvenated with the influx of wealth. Thus, we are presented with a picture where socio-economic mobility among Indo-Trinidadians is accompanied by exclusivity and perceived marginalization as much as in the initial period. Further, based on an account of village trends as well as macro-level developments in Trinidad, Munasinghe decisively asserts that in the very recent times East-Indian culture has made a bid to enter the socio-political mainstream of Trinidad. The most striking evidence, according to her, is the election in 1995 of Basdeo Panday, the East Indian leader, as the Prime Minister of Trinidad and Tobago, an eventuality unforeseen in the country at any other time.

Explanations

Munasinghe's monograph, *Callaloo or Tossed Salad?* is a historical and ethnographic study of East Indians in Trinidad with an emphasis on the politics of cultural conflict between East Indians and Africans, the nation's two traditionally subordinate ancestral groups. She argues that East Indians in Trinidad seek to become a legitimate part of the nation by redefining what it means to be a Trinidadian, not by changing what it means to be an Indian. In her view, Indo-Trinidadians' recent and ongoing struggle for national and cultural identity builds from dissatisfaction with the place they were originally assigned within Trinidadian society. The author examines how Indo-Trinidadian leaders in

Trinidad have come to challenge the implicit claim that their ethnic identity is antithetical to their national identity. Their political and cultural strategy seeks to change the national image of Trinidad by introducing Indian elements alongside those of the dominant Afro-Caribbean culture. Munasinghe analyses the moral, political and cultural dimensions of identity, the relation between ethnicity and the nation and details how principles of exclusion continue to operate in nationalist projects that celebrate ancestral diversity and multi-culturalism. Drawing on the insights of theorists who use 'creolization' to understand the emergence of Afro-American cultures, Munasinghe argues that Indo-Trinidadians can be considered Creole because they, like Afro-Trinidadians, are creators and not just bearers of culture.

The manner in which Munasinghe develops her analysis of the East Indians being considered 'outsiders' in Trinidad and, secondly, the argument abut ethnicity (ethnic identity, awareness and patrimony) of the various groups in multi-cultural and multi-racial society as being attached to the ethos of nation-building, leaves much to be desired. To take the 'outsider' status of East Indians first Munasinghe claims to take into account both the "material" and discursive factors but her clinching argument is based on the latter set, especially on the lexical analysis of the terminology used by Trinidadians in respect of race, colour and ancestry. It is claimed that while the Afro-Trinidadian and European identities as also those of the 'mixed' groups are based on colour (black and white continuum), there is no counterpart of 'colour' for the East Indians. Besides colour the Afro-Trinidadian and European identities are also based on ancestry. Further, the Afro-Trinidadian identity is based also on phylogeny ('Negro' identity). The East Indian identity according to Munasinghe is based only on ancestry (their origin from India). What is missing in this characterization is, firstly, a realization that colour is only a signifier of 'race' and that the three criteria of a race relations situation as defined by Rex, for instance (cited in Jain, 1990), applies to Trinidad. The three elements, which are necessary and sufficient to characterize a situation as a race relations situation, are:

(1) a situation of abnormally harsh exploitation, coercion or competition between groups,
(2) an individual in these groups could not simply choose to move himself or his children from one group to another, and
(3) that the system should be justified in terms of some sort of deterministic theory, usually of a biological sort.

Secondly, the analysis remains incomplete, being oblivious of the strong racialist opposition between 'coolie' and 'Kirwal' (the former term being used universally for the East Indians and the latter by the East Indians for Creoles (perhaps only for the Negro and 'mixed' excluding 'local whites'). Breman and Daniel (1992: 268–95) have shown how 'coolie' both etymologically and contextually is a racist-cum-class term. My principal disagreement with Munasinghe is that she fails to include in her lexical analysis the East Indian representations.[4] If these representations were given their due place, the result will be to reinstate in our analysis the emic points of view of 'coolies' and 'creoles'.

Munasinghe's second argument is that the Creole narrative for nation-building in Trinidad is keyed as that of a mixture (for which she uses the metaphor of Callaloo) whereas the East Indian narrative emphasizes the cultural landscape of Trinidad as a 'miniature United Nations' or a plural society (for which she uses the metaphor of tossed salad). The East Indian narrative, obviously, is cast in terms of exclusivity whereas the Creole narrative is inclusive of the culture of all ethnic groups in Trinidad *minus* the East Indians. Given Munasinghe's explanation of East Indian exclusivity and exclusion in lexical terms, their very late entry in the political process of nation-building is seen as a turnabout in the sense that they wish to contest and change the very definition of 'Trinidadian' by adding on (but not changing) the Indian cultural element. In other words, it is not acceptable to the East Indians that the nation-building process in Trinidad would be only in Creole terms. And this is possible because factually, if not in perception, the East Indian culture in Trinidad has also been *creative,* incorporating Creole elements.

I think there is a circularity in the above argument when the concept Creole is being used simultaneously as the exclusive patrimony of non-East Indian culture as well as of the historically created heritage of all Trinidadians including the Indians. In an earlier article (Jain, 1986) I have argued that for conceptual clarity the 'creolization' of East Indians in Trinidad should be termed as interculturation. Further, this interculturation – a symmetrical process of give and take – should be distinguished from acculturation – an asymmetrical process – whereby the Afro-Saxon model of 'respectability' had been emulated both by the 'mixed' and 'black' populations in Trinidad. The exclusivity of the East Indian ethnicity in Trinidad would then be a reflection of social stratification of the race-cum-class structure (Jain, 1986, also 1988).

The diversion, on the other hand, to the nation-building process, which is something without a beginning or an end (as contrasted with ongoing political processes), is unhelpful in the present context (cf. Verdery, 1994 for the distinct valence of ethnicity in relation to 'nation' between European and 'third world' contexts). In a paper dealing with Tamilians in Malaysia (Jain, 2002) I have demonstrated how the framework of 'nation' and the omnibus 'Indian' identity are neatly subverted in actual political processes. Ethnicity and racerelations need to be viewed conjointly to unravel the historical trajectory of cultural politics in Trinidad.[5]

Conclusion

Where do these 'narratives' arise from? The infrastructural conditions lead us to the causes of these stereotypes and conflicts. In this dialectical relationship between reality and ideology the 'emic' perspectives of the social actors are of paramount importance. We may try and split hairs by distinguishing between the lay, the political and the academic perspectives on ethnicity but the battle may be won while the war will be lost by imposing a super-academic 'etic' model. A discourse analysis, while certainly useful to analyse the surface reality, needs to be supplemented, if not dominated, by a material one. For example, the underlying economic interests of the big business – British and US – in the forest resources of Fiji were not the least among reasons for the triggering and still suppurating wounds of Indo-Fijian and native Fijian ethnic conflicts.

Notes

1. I have used the terms 'Indian', 'East Indian' and 'Indo-Trinidadian' throughout the text interchangeably to denote the same community but to suit the context.
2. How the colonial state in Britain sabotaged the 1955 election when the Indo-Trinidadian leaders appeared poised to assume control of the state is a fascinating story in itself. Britain postponed the elections to the following year, providing Eric Williams and his supporters an opportune moment to forge a 'legitimate' national party to contest and win the 1956 elections with the help of colonial authorities (for the manipulation, especially by Governor Beetham, cf. Brereton, 1981: 237; Oxaal, 1968: 115).
3. The point is illustrated by the fact that the two rival Hindu organizations (apart from the third, Arya Samaj) SDA (Sanatan Dharma Association) and SDBC (Sanatan Dharma Board of Control) had their origin in the controversy between the Presbyterian and Catholics who, respectively approved and disapproved Divorce Legislation. The pioneering leader of the SDA was a Presbyterian and of the SDBC, a Catholic!
4. We may ask the question as to why she researched on lexical terms from a white or European perspective only? What about the 'agency' and proactivity of East Indians in controlling their identity?
5. In this respect, see Roger Sanjek's approach to the understanding of intermarriage and the future of races in contemporary United States of America. He writes, "Both repressive processes of exclusion (race) and expressive processes of inclusion (ethnicity) must be accounted for on our analytic ledgers" (1994: 110).

References

Appadurai, Arjun (1997), *Modernity at Large: Cultural Dimensions of Globalization*, Delhi: Oxford University Press.

Barth, Fredrik (1969), *Ethnic Groups and Boundaries: The Social Organization of Cultural Difference*, London: Allen and Unwin.

Beckford, G.L. (1985), 'Caribbean Peasantry in the Confines of the Plantation Mode of Production', *International Social Science Journal (Food Systems)*, 105: 401–14.

Borneman, John (1992), *Belonging in Two Berlins: Kin, State, Nation*, Cambridge: Cambridge University Press.

Breman, Jan and E.V. Daniel (1992), 'Conclusion: The Making of a Coolie', *Journal of Peasant Studies*, 19 (3 and 4): 268–95.

Brereton, Bridget (1981), *A History of Modern Trinidad, 1783–1962*, Kingston: Heinemann.

Dookeran, Winston (1985), 'East Indians and the Economy of Trinidad and Tobago', in J. La Guerre (ed.), *Calcutta to Caroni: The East Indians of Trinidad*, St. Augustine: Extra Mural Studies, University of the West Indies, pp. 63–76.

Jain, Ravindra K. (1986), 'The East Indian Culture in a Caribbean Context', *India International Centre Quarterly*, 13:153–64.

—— (1988), 'Overseas Indians in Malaysia and the Caribbean: Comparative Notes', in Howard Johnson (ed.), *After the Crossing: Immigrants and Minorities in Caribbean Creole Society*, London: Frank Cass, pp. 123–43.

—— (1990), 'Race Relations, Ethnicity, Class and Culture: A Comparison of Indians in Trinidad and Malaysia', *Sociological Bulletin*, (38: 1): 57–70.

—— (2002), 'South Asian Diaspora: A Global Perspective from India', in Hase Yasuro, et al. (eds.), *South Asian Migration in Comparative Perspective*, Osaka, National Museum of Ethnology, pp. 1–17.

—— (2003), 'Culture and Economy: Tamils on the Plantation Frontier in Malaysia Revisited, 1998–1999', in Bhikhu Parekh et al. (eds.), *Culture and Economy in the Indian Diaspora*, London and New York: Routledge, pp. 51–80.

Jha, J.C. (1985), 'The Indian Heritage in Trinidad', in J. La Guerre (ed.), *Calcutta to Caroni: The East Indians of Trinidad*, St. Augustine, Trinidad and Tobago, Extra Mural Studies Unit, University of the West Indies, pp. 1–20.

Johnson, Howard (1972), 'The Origins and Early Development of Cane Farming in Trinidad: 1882–1906', *Journal of Caribbean History*, 5 November, pp. 46–74.

Laurence, K.O. (1985), 'Indians as Permanent Settlers in Trinidad before 1900', in John La Guerre (ed.), *Calcutta to Caroni*, St. Augustine, Trinidad Tobago, Extra Mural Studies, University of the West Indies, pp. 95–116.

Munasinghe, Viranjini (2001), *Callaloo or Tossed Salad? East Indians and the Cultural Politics of Identity in Trinidad*, Ithaca and London: Cornell University Press.

Nevadomsky, Joseph (1980), 'Changes in Hindu Institutions in an Alien Environment', *Eastern Anthropologist* 33: 39–53.

—— (1983), 'Economic Organization, Social Mobility and Changing Social Status among East Indians in Rural Trinidad', *Ethnology* 22: 63–79.

Oxaal, Ivar (1968), *Black Intellectuals Come to Power: The Rise of Creole Nationalism in Trinidad and Tobago*, Cambridge Mass: Schenkman.

Reddock, Rhoda (1991), 'Social Mobility in Trinidad and Tobago: 1960–1980', in S. Ryan (ed.), *Social and Occupational Stratification in Contemporary Trinidad and Tobago*, St. Augustine, Institute of Social and Economic Research, University of the West Indies, pp. 210–33.

Rex, John (1978), Introduction in UNESCO, *Race and Class in Post-Colonial Societies*, Paris: UNESCO, pp. 11–52.

Ryan, Selwyn (1974), *Race and Nationalism in Trinidad and Tobago*, Toronto: University of Toronto Press.

Samaroo, Brinsley (1975), 'The Presbyterian Canadian Mission as an Agent of Integration in Trinidad during the 19th and early 20th Centuries', *Caribbean Studies*, 14 (4): 41–55.

Sanjek, R. (1994), 'Intermarriage and the Future of Races in the United States', in Steven Gregory and Roger Sanjek (eds.), *Race*, New Jersey: Rutgers University Press, pp. 103–30.

Seethal-Maraj, B. (1991), *Master and Servant, Bhadase Sagan Maraj*, St. Augustine, Trinidad: Publications Committee of the SDMS of T&T Inc.

Singh, Vashti (2002), Denominational and State Conflict: The Experience of the SDMS (Sanatan Dharma Maha Sabha) Board of Education, 1952–1996, A Thesis for the Master of Arts in Education, The University of the West Indies, St. Augustine.

Verdery, Katherine (1994), 'Ethnicity, Nationalism and State Making', in Hans Vermeulen and Cora Govers (eds.), *The Anthropology of Ethnicity: Beyond 'Ethnic Groups and Boundaries'*, Amsterdam: Het Spinuis, pp. 33–58.

Vertovec, Steven (1992), *Hindu Trinidad: Religion, Ethnicity and Socio-Economic Change*, London: Macmillan Education.

Weber, Max (1978), *Economy and Society: An Outline of Interpretive Sociology* (2 Vols.) in Guenther Roth and Clauss Wittich (eds.), Berkeley: University of California Press (first printing 1968).

Wood, Donald, (1968), *Trinidad in Transition*, Oxford: Oxford University Press.

4 Religious Conversion and Social Mobility in India

S.M. MICHAEL

The phenomenon of religious conversion is immensely complex and varied. Accounts of individual and group conversions that have come down to us from early days are repeated even today. All the same, this topic of religious conversion is an emotional and a sensitive one in the given political scenario of contemporary India. Hence, it is important that social scientists approach this area of research with an objective judgement on the subject in order to avoid the biases of emotion and prejudice.

Methodology of Study: Anthropological Approach – Holistic and Comparative Approach

The 'scientific' study of religious conversion has been approached from various perspectives: historical, sociological, psychological and phenomenological. Factors preceding conversion, as identified by these approaches, include socio-political upheavals, psychic factors of anguish, turmoil, despair, conflict and guilt and self-realization. No single approach is adequate for a comprehensive view of the complex nature of conversion.

Here, we look at the phenomenon of religious conversion from an anthropological perspective. An anthropological approach is multidisciplinary and comprehensive consisting of historical and comparative methods. Human beings have been migrating from place to place and they have been building cultures through invention, discovery and diffusion. An anthropological view of humanity is holistic in nature, i.e., anthropologists seek generalizations about man and his behaviour from all dimensions – economic, social, political and religious. An anthropological approach is in some respects a synthesizing field of knowledge (see Keesing, 1958: 2–3).

There is thus need to study the phenomenon of conversion from an anthropological perspective because in India this has been looked at partially either from political or economic or social dimension. While the above aspects of human behaviour may shed light in understanding the complex process of conversion in human history, this knowledge will only be partial if it is not viewed holistically or in its totality. An anthropological approach to a reality tends to be holistic. It also takes into consideration both the temporal and spatial dimensions of human beings in a culture.

Hence, our methodology of studying religious conversion in India will be one of holistic and comparative in nature.

Conversion in India Through the Ages: Towards Brahminic Hinduism (Towards the Process of Sanskritization)

Usually, when conversion is discussed in India, it is in the context of conversion to Islam and Christianity. In reality, however, conversion has been going on all through the history of India. In other words, there have been cultural and religious encounter and interaction over the ages.

India is a subcontinent with a vast population of very diverse levels of culture. Indian society, economy and politics from ancient times until the 12th century displayed a great deal of dynamism that does not accord well with stereotyped images of India's changeless tradition. The very cultural assimilation of influences emanating from a succession of new arrivals – Aryans, Greeks, Scythians, Parthians, Shakas and Huns before the 8th century, as well as Arabs, Persians, Turks, Afghans and Mongols between the 8th and 12th centuries – was a vital and dynamic process. Indigenous tribal groups also played a creative role in processes of state formation (see Bose and Jalal, 1998: 21–22).

Among the different migrants to India from ancient days, it was the Aryans who vigorously tried to establish a hierarchical order – *varnashrama dharma* – as a universal social system in India. They have succeeded to a large extent by placing people in one or the other *jati* (caste) categories and incorporating their gods and customs and manners. Hence, from the beginning, the Brahminic Hinduism was a missionary endeavour without claiming to be one. Dr Ambedkar expressed his views that if Hinduism was not a missionary religion it could not have spread over the face of India (see Valiamangalam, 1996: 129–46). The renowned historian Dr Mujumdar stated that Hinduism in the form of Brahminic religion flourished in the Malay Peninsula, Cambodia, Sumatra, Bali and Borneo moulding the lives of the people of this vast region (Raj, 1988: 14). Jawaharlal Nehru has also opined that Hinduism was propagated by the Hindu colonizers in the East and South-East Asian countries. Though the term 'conversion' may not have been used in the sense in which we use it today, we cannot deny the presence of the fact of conversion in the past. This may further be elaborated by looking into some of the anthropological data on India.

Anthropological knowledge of the people of India reveals that all known racial groups have migrated to India at different times with their own language, religion and culture. All these racial groups have been organized into the caste system. The caste system in the past helped to keep the diverse racial, social and cultural groups apart, for it prevented them effectively from mixing with one another. The population of India is thus very heterogeneous and this diversity penetrates the whole sub-continent, every state and district, every town and village (Fuchs, 1979: 1). Through a process of absorption and assimilation, a process of Hinduization was taking place all through the history of India (Kumar, 1967). With all its different shades, Hinduism has been adopted by the major part of Indian population, especially by its upper and middle classes.

In India Adivasis or tribals have been absorbed into the dominant religion from ancient days. Various elements in the ancient civilization of India were contributed by the tribals. It is believed that they were the earliest among the present inhabitants of the country, even before the entry of Aryans into India. There are four distinct racial families of Adivasis existing today in India. They are: (1) the Negritoes, the Kadi-speaking Jarawa stone-agers in Andaman and the Pulayans and Irulas in the Western Ghats and the plains of Kerala and Tamil Nadu; (2) the Australoids of the Austro-Asiatic and Indo-European language groups, which include the Khasis of Khasi Hills, the Nicobarese of Andaman Nicobar, the Santalis of Bihar and Bengal, the Mundaris of Bihar and Orissa, the Hos of Bihar, the Bhils and the Meenas of Rajasthan and the Kuknas, Varlis, Vasavas, Gamiths and Chaudhuris of Gujarat and Maharashtra; (3) the tribals of Dravidian origin, which include the Tulus, Kodagus, Todas, Kotas and Badagas of south India, the Kuis of Orissa, the Kolams of Maharashtra, the Gonds of Madhya Pradesh, the Orans of Bihar, Orissa and Bengal; and (4) the Mongoloid group of tribals, which include the Tibetans, Baltis, Ladakhis, Sherpas, Lepchas of the Indo-Himalayan region and the Bodos, Garos etc. of the Assam-Burmese family (Vidyarthi and Rai, 1977: 237; Sharma and Sharma, 1998: 96).

When the Aryan immigrants entered the country, they found in the land *Dasyus*. The word *Dasyu* was used to denote the people other than themselves, i.e., the Aryans. In the early historical period of India, the Aryan invaders began to superimpose their superiority over the other racial people of India. This led the non-Aryan tribals to either compromise with the Aryan social order or to run away to deep forest (Sharma and Sharma, 1998: 100). All through the long centuries, the Sanskritic Hindu rule absorbed and assimilated the non-Aryans into different gradations of caste social structure. The observations of Baine (1891: 118), Risley (1901: 98), O'Malley (1911: 235), Shoobert (1931: 403), Elwin (1941: 35), etc., also suggest the absorption of the tribals with the Hindu culture.

During the long Hindu period of Indian history, when the Brahmins and other upper castes had so much influence over the lower castes, untouchables and tribals, the culture and history of the lower castes, untouchables and tribals was submerged with that of the Brahminic Hinduism. Jayant Lele explains this process as follows: "The Brahminic worldview had succeeded on several occasions in the past in capturing the diversity of cults, deities, sects and ideas (by making many compromises) under the rubric of *sanatana dharma*. It had thus stabilized existing practices and subjected them to the supervision and patronage of a brahmin dominated economic and political order. Many of the tribal, low caste deities to which Brahminism had to adapt ended up as consorts or local incarnations of the pan-Indian patriarchal gods, thus investing these pan-Indian symbols with unprecedented power and potency for popular mobilization" (Lele, 1995: xviii). The history of the lower strata of Indian society cannot be traced exactly and here only the Historical Anthropology which includes the popular beliefs, legends, myths, tales, short history of the locality or region, etc., of the folk people can help us know about the unrecorded past (Sharma and Sharma, 1998: 101).

N.K. Bose also observes that "even in ancient times, Hindu lawmakers were clearly conscious of the fact that various *jatis* were coming within their organization and it was necessary to teach them Brahminical morals and

Brahminical religious ceremonies in order to bring them closer to the rest of the population" (Bose, 1967: 211). Bose further says: "Hindus hardly left any economic freedom to the *jatis*, but they left intact the original social and religious culture of the tribes in so far as that was possible. Their policy was not to eradicate the old beliefs and practices where they were not inconsistent with Brahminical moral ideas. But it was nevertheless necessary to do something in order to bring the tribal cultures in line with Brahminism, as we have seen in the quotation from the Mahabharata. So they made a rule that each caste, on becoming a part of Hindu society, was to be served by Brahmin priests during marriage, birth, initiation and funeral ceremonies. A close and living connection was thus established between the priestly class and the new recruits, and a means of direct infiltration of culture was thus successfully organized. The Brahmins modified the old culture where it went against the grain of their own ideas and left the rest intact. They added to tribal ceremonies certain items of their own, which were to be performed by Brahmin priests on behalf of their new clients" (ibid.: 212).

Explaining this process of Brahminic incorporation, reinterpretation, appropriation and assimilation of tribal and other cultures, Bose says: "Once a tribe came under the influence of the Brahminical people and was converted into a caste enjoying monopoly in a particular occupation, a strong tendency was set up within it to remodel its culture more and more closely in conformity with Brahminical way of life" (ibid.: 214).

Jayant Lele traces the origins of Brahminism as a hegemonic project. He explores some of the subaltern struggles against that project and the resistance shown by diverse, self-conscious communities against its attempts to homogenize, reinterpret and control their diverse origins and identities. According to him, "Popular memories of tribal, egalitarian communities and of aspirations for an enriched and expanded life of thriving interdependence, kindled during the early years of the Mauryan empire, were subsequently subjugated, reinterpreted and employed to justify a new hierarchical social order" (1995: ix). Lele also studied the resilience of Brahminism, during centuries of challenges and counter-movements through the dual strategies of appropriation and exclusion (ibid.: 81–103). This is done by the Brahmins through a process of reinterpretation of tribal and other communities' histories, distortion of their folktales and disembodiment and rearrangement of their rituals and symbols. According to Lele, "An important step in ensuring the viability of this sort of exercise is to monopolize the institutional mechanisms through which information comes to life as knowledge and is validated as officially acceptable and true" (ibid.: x).

Jaiswal (1981) has thrown light on two processes that have contributed to the resilience of Brahminism: (a) the incorporation of immanent critical impulses through their hegemonic reinterpretation, and (b) marginalization of counter-cultural threats through their designation as permissible but quarantined deviance (*vama marga*). These processes seem to repeat themselves in subsequent periods.

A few instances of Hinduization of tribals will confirm the state of affairs. In middle India, the Nagbansi Raja of Chotanagpur, who was the head of the Oranons and the Mundas, seeing the pomp and show of the Hindu rajas (kings) of northern India, changed his surname of Rai into Shah or Shahi (around 1628 AD). He assumed the title of Maharaja and began to imitate the ideal of royalty of Hindu rajas. A suitable palace was constructed. And Shahi Maharaja soon gathered Brahmin priests, Rajput courtiers and *amlahs* and palace-hunters. The Oraons and the Mundas resisted this and, as a consequence, more and more outsiders were called in by the successive Maharajas and the heavy cost had to be borne by the villagers. This period is also remarkable as the period of erection of a number of temples like Jagannath Mandir, Ram-Sita Mandir, etc. The Bhils of Western India also came into direct conflict with the local rulers and Maratha invaders (see Sharma and Sharma, 1998: 106–10).

Even today, many of these tribal groups have been Hinduized through organizing festivals, and using other Sanskritic symbols and rituals. This has been explained by N.K. Bose as "the Hindu method of tribal absorption" (Bose, 1967; also see Valiamangalam, 1996: 129–46). After giving several examples for the Hindu method of tribal absorption, Bose observes: "But besides all these it is absolutely certain that some *jatis* are undoubtedly of tribal origin; and this has been the result of a conscious plan of Hindu society to dominate over and absorb tribal groups within its economic and social framework. It may be recalled in this connection that some of the untouchable castes have cultural traits which clearly show their original affiliation and indicate their tribal origin" (ibid.: 208).

In spite of these efforts, because of the geographical isolation enjoyed by the tribals, some of them were still able to preserve to a great extent their socio-religious identity, faith and practices. But, when the British introduced roads, postal system and civil government, easier transport and communication was made possible within the tribal areas. This attracted the traders and moneylenders into the area. They were followed by Hindu missionaries. This led to the subsequent Hinduization of the tribals. Before that the tribals had kept up the purity of their blood because they did not intermarry with non-tribals. Since they did not practise untouchability among them, they were saved from the loss of self-image.

The sacred orders of the tribals were too far removed from the Vedic dharma of Hinduism. But, the Hindu traders, moneylenders and landlords, who became resident in the tribal area, were able to introduce elements of Hinduism into the tribal religions, paving the way for their assimilation into Hinduism (Bose, 1975).

Another way of assimilation of the tribals into Hinduism is through close contact with lower caste Hindus, since they intermingle with tribals easily and adopt Hindu religious beliefs and practices (Bhuriya, 1992: 17). The dominant Brahminical religions during its evolution through the past centuries subjugated and absorbed many tribal groups with their gods, religious rituals and customs (Bose, 1975). The priests and poets of the Brahminical traditions succeeded in identifying the tribal gods with one of the deities in the Hindu pantheon. For example, the tribal god of Orissa, Lord Jaganath, became identified with Vishnu; and Murugan of Adi-Dravidians became identified with Skanda of the North Indian Hindu traditions. However, the biggest number of conversions was effected through the Hindu census enumerators. They were persuaded to return the religion of the tribals as 'Hindus'. G.S. Ghurye, an eminent sociologist, addressed tribals as 'Backward Hindus' (Ghurye, 1963: 19). He promoted the idea that the tribals of India must refer themselves as part of Hindu society and should not claim an autonomous culture of their own. According to him, "the only proper description of these people is that they are the imperfectly integrated classes of Hindu society" (ibid.).

Like the tribals who were assimilated into Hinduism, the non-Aryan, i.e., the *Sudras* and *Ati-Sudras*, were also assimilated and sanskritized into Hinduism. The powerful upper castes of a particular area exercised such an influence on the lower castes and outcastes that they also wanted to be integrated into the caste hierarchy by adopting the values and practices of the upper castes. This process is described as 'sanskritization' by the eminent anthropologist M.N. Srinivas (1989: 56). He defines sanskritization as the process by which a 'low' caste or tribe or other group takes over the customs, rituals, beliefs, ideology and style of life of a high and, in particular, a 'twice-born' (*dwija*) caste. Orthodox Hindus frequently assert that dalit Buddhists are really Hindus because the Buddha is a reincarnation of Lord Vishnu. Just as putting a snake over the head of the Buddha transforms him into an icon of Lord Vishnu, so too clothing statues of the Buddha's five first companions in the Mahabodhi temple compound allows them to be identified as the five Pandavas, Hindu heroes of the great epic, the Mahabharata (Lynch, 1998: 11).

Conversion Movements to Christianity

The seed of Christianity was laid in India (Kerala) in AD 52. It is the ancient tradition that Saint Thomas, one of the twelve Apostles of Christ, came to India in AD 52 and established Christian communities in seven places (Cranganore, Palayur, Parur, Kokkamangalam, Niranam, Quilon and Nilackal) and finally died a martyr at Mylapore near Madras (Chennai). This tradition is shared by the non-Christians as well (see Koodapuzha, 1995: 3).

Though Christian presence in India is from the first century, the extensive diffusion of the message of Christ began only after the discovery of the sea route from the West to India in 1498. The conversions that took place since then could be classified into four types, that is, of individuals, group movements, Christian dalit conversion and Christian tribal conversion. A number of case studies on individual conversion are recorded by Wingate (1997: 9–14). Most of them are from Brahmin castes. The reason for their conversion seems to be the unsatisfactoriness of Hindu religion (ibid.: 13).

By far the majority of South Indian Christians in Tamil Nadu, Andhra Pradesh and Karnataka have become so because either they, their parents or their ancestors converted in what have been called mass movements. Such movements have also taken place in other religions, to Islam, Sikhism or Buddhism. Grafe lists thirteen movements in Tamil Nadu (Grafe, 1990 as quoted by Wingate, 1997: 15). An example is the Nadar/Sambavar movement in South Travancore and Tirunelveli areas (see Hardgrave, 1969).

When we study the significant conversion movements in Indian Christian missionary history, we understand the manifold factors which are operative in them. Conversion is never an isolated event. One may discover the reality of God through one's everyday experiences in the socio-economic reality of life. Before we go further on the study, let us concentrate on some of the conversion movements in India.

Conversion to another, often well-developed, hence powerful religious meaning systems, had always been an aspect of the local caste resistance struggles even in pre-modern times. The presence of such a large number of Muslims in the country can have no other explanation. With the advent of the Europeans, however, the different forms of Christianity presented themselves as the major opportunity to equality and equal social treatment. The profession of Christianity that God being the father of all, men, despite differences are but brothers to each other, had obvious pull with the lower caste masses, often treated inhuman by the dominant castes. The missionary efforts in spreading literacy and their assistance in times of material crises, added the necessary existential dimension. Mass conversions started in different parts and among widely separated communities of the country: the Mangs and Mahars of Bombay, the Chuhras and Mazahabis of Punjab, the Doms of Benares, Kumaon and Garhwal Hills, the Dhusiya Chamars of Shahabad (Bihar) and Ballia (U.P.), the hill tribes of North East, the Karta Bhojas of Bengal, the Bhils of Central India, the Mallas and Madigas of Andhra, the Sambavars, the Shanars and Parayars of Tamil Nadu.

Studies on mass conversions to Christianity by Aloysius (1998) and Chatterjee (1994) and others "clearly indicate that these emerging communities did not 'accept' Christianity in 'cow-like' obedience, as the upper caste nationalists claimed, but indeed consciously and deliberately moved away from one set of religious symbolism, now perceived as sectarian and unjust, to another, again perceived as universal and egalitarian and hence suitable for the situation" (Aloysius, 1998: 19).

Julian Saldanha (1996) has also summarized the different studies on Christian conversion movements in India. He begins with those mass movements to the Catholic and other churches which commenced in various parts of India from around the 1870s. It is estimated that about half of India's Christians are drawn from the dalit and tribal sections of the population.

Tribal and Dalit Efforts for Social Mobility

While the Hindu fundamentalist organizations through their assimilation policy claim the tribals and dalits to be Hindus, the tribals and dalits on the other hand reject this superimposed identity. For the sake of maintaining power in the changed circumstances, the Hindutva forces claim a cultural affinity with dalits and tribals as vote banks. The upper caste Hindus, while trying to get the services of the dalits and tribals, paid little attention to alleviate their deprived conditions. They are addressed as 'Backward Hindus'. Rejecting this identity, the tribals and dalits have found their own ways to move up in the social ladder of Indian society.

The tribals, though greatly diverse, share a dependence on the land and forests for their very survival. "Even today, tribals form around 70 per cent of the forest dwellers in India. Traditionally, their dependence on the forest was total. From it they got about 80 per cent of their food, which included cereals and pulses harvested from shifting cultivation. They depended on the forests for fuel, organic manure, fodder, medicinal herbs, and other needs" (Fernandes, 1992: 13; also see Fernandes, Menon and Viegas, 1988: 151–57).

"To them land is not a purely economic asset, but a part of their spiritual as well as economic heritage. The importance tribals attach to the land that sustains them is much deeper than mere economic utility would indicate. All agree that the problems of land and tribals' rights on lands they cultivate are fundamental for a more efficient use of land resources" (Reddy, 1987: 14–15).

Given the extent of their dependence, tribals ensured that forests and land were treated as renewable resources that catered to the needs of their community and were preserved for posterity. Through an egalitarian community they served the needs of every family. They also had in-built social control mechanisms meant to discourage any family from appropriating to itself a large share of the resource than was its due (Sharma, 1976: 13–14). Conservation was ensured also by developing myths, traditions, and a whole culture geared to treating land and forest as community resources meant to be preserved for posterity and not as property to be destroyed at the owner's will (Fernandes, Menon and Viegas, 1988: 159–70). Briefly, land and forests were the very centre of tribal life; tribals built their religious, cultural, social, economic and political life around them. Consequently, any interference with these resources was bound to result in a total crisis in their whole society.

Such an intervention took place with the coming of upper caste people to the tribal areas. The British colonial administration together with the upper caste *zamindars* and *thikedars* (merchants who supplied luxury goods) exploited the tribals. In addition, the forest policy of the British turned the tribal's life support system into state property and a source of revenue for the colonial administration. Initially forest dwellers were given some rights. These were slowly turned into privileges and eventually into concessions (Fernandes, 1988a: 84–94).

As for the tribals, their very independence, self-respect and human dignity were closely linked to their forests and land. Consequently, loss of these resources jeopardized their family, cultural, religious and social life. Their very identity was under attack. Protests against this marginalization and efforts to recover their lost identity were inevitable. Being a more cohesive group than the untouchables, there were more organized movements among them than among the dalits. Religious conversion was one such effort to recover the security and identity lost through colonial and upper caste interventions (Fernandes, 1988).

Dalits who tried to adapt first to the Hindu social structure of India, later experienced the burden of untouchability, unseeability and other oppressions of Hindu society. They gradually realized that they would never be able to attain their humanity in the Hindu Dharma. Hence, they also began to search for an alternative identity. Their search took the form of two types of cultural movements aimed at freedom from oppression (Shah, 1985: 175). The first is reformative, that is, change within the Hindu system. It included the *bhakti* movement, sanskritization, and the non-vedantic dalit movements, in Maharashtra, Tamil Nadu, and elsewhere. The initiative in a few of these movements came from the upper castes, but it was a response to pressure from below (see Fernandes, 1996: 15).

The second type of movement includes alternatives from outside the Hindu fold. In some cases these took the form of conversion to Christianity, Islam, Sikhism, and other religions that preached equality (Sharma, 1976: 219). Pickett (1933) sees one of the motives, and a quite legitimate one, in dalit conversion, as the desire for social liberation. Webster (1992) argues that conversion to Islam and Christianity represented a rejection of a hierarchy which kept dalits down. The untouchable converts are often accused of being "rice Christians," i.e., persons who embraced Christianity "for a plate of rice", that is, material incentives. But is it so simple? It is true that in many cases the missionary offered material help with humanitarian considerations. However, Forrester (1980: 74) and Fernandes (1996: 17) point out that a deeper analysis of the conversion movements, made not from the missionary or upper-caste point of view but from that of the convert, shows that to the untouchables change of religion was not primarily a mode of economic an social improvement. It was, more than anything else, an effort to change social status, a search for freedom from caste oppression. Oddie asks, "If the desire for material advantage and protection was the only consideration, how does one explain the tenacity and perseverance of some converts who, in spite of material losses and persecution, still adhered to the mission?" (as quoted in Wingate, 1997: 19).

The conversion movements among the dalits and tribals have shown the potential of social change in religion. The religious movements initiated by the dominant communities like the Arya Samaj, Brahmo Samaj, Theosophy, to mention only the most prominent ones, were intended to revitalize the traditional ideology-religion, effecting the necessary minimal modifications, so as to make it an effective vehicle for hegemony and a weapon for dominance under the changed circumstances. The lower caste-led movements, on the other hand, as a continuity of their pre-modern egalitarian struggles, stood for abolishing the principle and practice of hierarchicalism, altogether within society as a whole, failing which at least to carve out a respectable niche for themselves in society. Their new religious symbolism in this context was a vehicle of social protest and a protecting shield in struggles towards emancipation (Aloysius, 1998: 15). The dalits and tribals have sought a religious response of conversion as a mode of upward social mobility. This interaction was inevitable because of the close link between their cultural, economic, religious and social life. In that sense conversion was not merely a religious act but also a search for a new social identity. But, later, the deeper dimensions of Christian theology reinforced by instruction to foster a new interior life began to shape the lives of these tribals and dalits.

Thus, the mass conversion of tribals to Christianity is related to the tremendous socio-economic and cultural changes brought about by westernization and modernization (Natarajan, 1977). Snaitang, a Khasi, in his *Christianity and Social Change in North East India (1993)*, finds that Christianity provided a means through which the tribals could accommodate themselves to the changes that were imposed through British administration and the process of modernization it brought with it. In a situation where radical changes were taking place Christianity provided institutions, a new lifestyle and ideology which protected the tribal society from the danger of de-tribalization and loss of identity. A new sense of tribal solidarity, which transcended the traditional fragmented order, was created. This was founded over the maintenance of the traditional kinship code, which was the only feature common to the tribals prior to the coming of the British. Saldanha (1996) explains this by citing several examples. He shows that the prohibition of head-hunting alone, among the Nagas, Kukis, Garos and others, caused a most severe disruption, because it was connected with social status and with rites for the welfare of the family, village and fields. The Second World War, which extended into a furious battle at Kohima, left no doubt in the minds of the tribals that their centuries old isolation was at an end, and the old lifestyle was no longer viable.

The old order could not provide an ideology or worldview giving meaning to their new experience. They were searching for a sense of identity, of belonging and for self-determination in the new social order. They found in Christianity a new sense of identity, as well as a worldview and tools (a script, literature, education) to make the transition with self-respect. They were not converted easily; they took their own time to come to a decision. Thus, these brave and self-reliant people were able to adapt to the new society while remaining masters of their own destiny. Their acceptance of Christianity has been enthusiastic and their commitment to it firm.

Saldanha concludes by saying: "A sincere analysis of these conversion movements reveal that they were not the result of material inducements, nor were they exclusively religious events. They might better be described as socio-religious movements" (ibid.: 79). Forrester comments on motives: "The search for material improvement or enhancement of status is seldom if ever the sole or even the dominant motive in a mass movement. Dignity, self-respect, patrons who will treat one as an equal, and the ability to choose one's own destiny – all these are powerful incentives to conversion" (1980: 75). He adds that, within the caste affected, the first to convert are the more prosperous and independent families. Others follow when they see progress. What was important to the converts was the "sociological or practical meaning of religion" (Matthew, 1982: 1032). Here, social and religious motives blend into a complex whole, making it impossible to determine where one ends and the other begins (cf. Saldanha, 1984). Group conversion especially corresponded to the mentality of the people, for they were accustomed to act in groups already determined by caste or tribe (see Michael, 1980: 112–23). According to Picket (1933), mass movements protected the converts from social dislocation and reduced the danger of westernization.

On the positive side, these movements represented an effort on the part of the dalits to gain dignity, self-respect and the ability to choose their own destiny for themselves and their social group. There was a growing restlessness among them to have a fuller life of dignity for themselves and their children. Webster (1992: 71–76) observes that the mass movements constituted the first stage in the modern dalit movement; they were initiated and led by them, and sustained by their heroism in the face of persecution. These were group decisions to belong to a new community which not only had a religious tradition comparable to that of the caste Hindus, but which also began to distinguish itself from the traditional caste community. On the negative side, they were a revolt against a socio-religious system, which failed to provide a meaningful response to their needs and aspirations (Boel, 1975). It is in this sense that we must understand the observation of Dewan Bahadur Srinivasa Rghava Iyengar in his Forty Years' Progress: "Indeed, the best thing that can happen to them is conversion ... for there is no hope for them within the pale of Hinduism" (Travancore Law Reports, Vol. 22, 1929: 253, as quoted by Saldanha, 1996: 81).[1]

Some Hindu leaders are of the opinion that Christian conversions are only due to famines, poverty and starvation (see Jordens, 1977: 150). But, the above proposition is too simplistic and does not want to admit the complex phenomena of Christian conversions. Saldanha points out that, "It is true that India was racked by terrible famines between 1866 and 1901. However, we must remember that most dalits were admitted to the Church, not during, but before or after these famines and epidemics; many had been touched by the loving service of the missionaries, who treated them as equals. The missionaries lacked the resources to alleviate the poverty of those who approached them. The dalits were persecuted with physical violence and economic deprivation. Nevertheless, these converts persevered in the new faith and formed new Christian communities" (1996: 81).

Related to the above charge of the Hindu leaders that conversion to Christianity is due to famine, J.E. Clough found that large numbers of Madigas still wanted to be baptized (1877–78) even though no famine aid could be given. Furthermore, the first individual and families to enter the Church were among the more prosperous, they had greater independence of decision and action. In fact, the leadership provided by certain individuals in the early stages was a crucial factor in these movements (quoted by Saldanha, 1996: 81). Also, in recent years, the lead in conversions of dalits to Islam was given, at least in some cases, by the educationally and economically advanced sections of the dalits. "A certain level of economic independence and critical awareness through education has been a necessary condition of conversion" (Matthew, 1982: 1032). Hence, their conversion cannot be explained as the result of purely material inducements.

B.N. Banerjee, a Bengali Hindu, asks: If poverty was the reason for their conversion, then why did the poor brahmins not do the same? Rather, the dalits "pushed to the wall, are asserting a sense of dignity and self-respect, very peacefully, by conversions ..." (Banerjee, 1983: 393, as quoted by Saldanha, 1996: 81). B.D. Forrester describes the conversion movements as a kind of 'group identity crisis' in which the group affirms a new social and religious identity. However, especially in the early stages, these movements did include many individual and family decisions (cited in Oddie, 1977: 43).

All these factors are well illustrated by J.W. Gladstone (1976, 1986) in his case study of the conversion movements among the lower castes in Travancore, during the second half of the last century. The educational endeavours of Christian missionaries played an important role in the social renaissance among them. Furthermore, the missionaries strove to secure equal rights for them. Thus, a Christian was the first (1851) low caste to walk on the public road near the temple at Tiruvalla. They did much to free them from slavery and unjust taxation. Around 1859 they sided with the Nadars for the right of their women to wear the upper cloth. Thousands became Christians in the midst of these struggles (see Saldanha, 1996: 79–97). Christianity became a socio-religious movement, which indirectly gave birth to neo-Hindu reformist movements (see Jordens, 1977: 145–61). The above observations confirm that the phenomenon of conversion is of great complexity, and that is its attraction as well as its mystery, since we are touching the depths of the human heart.

Today, it is no longer advantageous for a group to convert, since power has changed and, to be a Christian, is to be politically and economically disadvantaged. Hinduism is resurgent, and in a way threatening, something that has never been felt before. Though Christian institutions remain, they are not able to be as free in their policies as before. In this situation, it is not surprising that some who converted earlier are reverting to Hinduism. "What is perhaps surprising is that these remain a comparatively small number. There is widespread loyalty to Christ that will stand a great amount of disruption and this indicates that the spiritual element should not be underplayed with conversion" (Wingate, 1997: 3).

Religious Conversion and Social Mobility

Sociologically, conversion is a process of change from one religion to another. The motive for a change of religion may be due to economic, social or religious reasons. Our study indicates that conversion could be seen as a way to gain protection, education and status. It is used by the individual to move forward in society, above all through education, and by a group to free themselves from inherited shackles, to better themselves and their children. These shackles might be those of caste, of illiteracy, of economic slavery, of psychological apathy, of disease, or of a religion of fears and taboos (see Wingate, 1997). But all these factors are always interlinked and no one of them should be considered in isolation (Michael, 1983: 40–52).

Religious conversion movements are towards equalitarian religions like Christianity, Islam, Sikhism and Buddhism. For example, in 1929, Ambedkar advised the untouchables to embrace any other religion that would regard them as human beings and give them an opportunity to break off from oppressive structures and enable them to act, eat, walk, and live like men (see Wilkinson and Thomas, 1972: 33; also Michael, 1996: 305–7). Following this, twelve untouchables embraced Islam and a group of untouchables from a village near Nasik decided to embrace Islam (Matthew, 1982: 1031). In 1935, at a conference attended by 10,000 untouchables at Yeola, Ambedkar declared: "I solemnly assure you that I will not die a Hindu." He found in Hinduism the cause of his people's wretched condition because, he argued, it was Hinduism's sacred texts that defined dalits as lowest of the low, untouchable and polluting the non-untouchable castes. In addition, it was Hinduism's sacred texts that mandated the degrading, humiliating, and unjust treatment from which his people had suffered for centuries. Under the inspiration of Ambedkar there was a mass movement of conversion. Ambedkar and a half a million untouchables (dalits) embraced Buddhism on October 14, 1956 at Nagpur (Zelliot, 1977: 119–44).

In reality, Buddhism and Jainism were widespread in India, but today they are reduced to small minority religions because of the missionary activities of

Brahminic Hinduism. Hence, a deeper study will show that the idea of conversion is part and parcel of the Indian tradition. The Arya Samaj and other Hindu organizations like the Vishva Hindu Parishad promote conversion and reconversion in their programmes not only in India but all over the world (see Jorden, 1977). The *Ghar Vapsi* (Home Coming) movement of conversion of Christian tribals and dalits to Hinduism initiated by Dilip Singh Judev, a BJP Member of Parliament from Jashpur targeting Chotanagpur plateau in Madhya Pradesh and portions of Bihar, Orissa and West Bengal is well known (see *The Asian Age*, 1997: 4). The Sikhs and Buddhists believe in a process of conversion towards human dignity and emancipation. All this point out the complex nature of religious conversion in India, but they are linked to social change, political, cultural and economic emancipation and very much interlinked to social mobility.

Note

1. Quoted by the Chief Justice of the Travancore High Court, Sadasiva Aiyar, in a judgment in 1905, Travancore Law Reports, Vol. 22, 1929: 253.

References

Aloysius, G. (1998), *Religion as Emancipatory Identity: A Buddhist Movement among the Tamils under Colonialism*, New Delhi: New Age International Publishers.

Andersen, W.K. and S.D. Damle (1987), *The Brotherhood in Saffron: The Rashtriya Swayamsevak Sangh and Hindu Revivalism*, New Delhi: Vistaar Publications.

Asian Age (1997), "VHP Plans Ghar Vapsi to Reconvert Christian Tribals", *The Asian Age*, 25th October, p. 4 (Calcutta edition).

Baine, Sir A. (1891), *Census of India*, Report.

Banerjee, B.N. (1983), "A Hindu Attitude to Conversions", *International Review of Missions*, No. 287, pp. 393–97.

Basu, Tapan et. al (1993), *Khaki Shorts Saffron Flags*, New Delhi: Orient Longmans.

Bhuriya, Mahipal (1992), "Reconversion of Tribal Christians to Hinduism in Madhya Pradesh", *The New Leader* (June 16–30).

Boel, J. (1975), *Christian Mission in India: A Sociological Analysis*, Amsterdam.

Bose, Nirmal Kumar (1967), *Culture and Society in India*, Bombay: Asia Publishing House.

—— (1975), *The Structure of Hindu Society*, New Delhi: Orient Longmans.

Bose, Sugata and Ayesha, Jalal (1998), *Modern South Asia: History, Culture, Political Economy*, Delhi: Oxford Publications.

Chatterjee, Partha (1994), *Nation and Its Fragments*, Delhi: Oxford University Press.

Chattopadhyay, Dhiman (2001), "Two volumes on freedom movement were snuffed out to prevent RSS expose, claims historian", *The Times of India*, Mumbai, January 6, p.1.

Dalmia, Vasudha and H. von, Stietencron (eds.) (1995), *Representing Hinduism: The Construction of Religious Traditions and National Identity*, New Delhi: Sage Publications.

Elwin, Verrier (1941), *Loss of Nerve: A Comparative Study of the Contact of Peoples in the Aboriginal Areas of Bastar State and the Central Provinces of India*, Bombay: Wagle Press.

Fernandes, Walter, Geeta Menon, and Philip Viegas (1988), *Forests, Environment and Tribal Economy: Deforestation, Impoverishment and Marginalization in Orissa*, New Delhi: Indian Social Institute.

Fernandes, Walter (1988a), "The Draft Forest Policy 1987: The National Water Policy 1987", *Social Action*, 38.

Forrester, D.B. (1980), *Caste and Christianity: Attitudes and Policies on Caste of Anglo Saxon Protestant Mission in India*, London: Centre for South Asian Studies, University of London.

Fuchs, Stephen (1979), *Anthropology for the Missions*, Allahabad: St. Paul's Publications.

Ghurye, G.S. (1963), *The Scheduled Tribes*, Bombay: Popular Prakashan.

Gladstone, J.W. (1976), "19th Century Mass Movement in South Travancore: A Result of Social Liberation", *Indian Church History Review*, No. 1, pp. 53–66.

—— (1986), "Christian Missionary Work and Socio-Religious Movements in Kerala: 1850–1910", *Indian Church History Review*, No. 1, pp. 30–42.

Grafe, H. (1990), *The History of Christianity in Tamilnadu in the 19th and 20th Centuries*, Vol. 4, Part 2 of the Church History Association of India, History of the Indian Church, Bangalore: CHAI.

Hardgrave, Robert L.Jr. (1969), *The Nadars of Tamil Nadu*, Bombay.

Jaiswal, Suvira (1981), *The Origins and Development of Vaisnavism*, Delhi: Munshiram Manoharlal.

Jha, D.N. (1997), *Ancient India: An Introductory Outline*, New Delhi: Manohar.

Jordens, J.T.F. (1977), "Reconversion to Hinduism, the Shuddhi of the Arya Samaj", in G.A. Oddie (ed.), *Religion in South Asia*, New Delhi: Manohar, pp.145–61.

Keesing, Felix M. (1958), *Cultural Anthropology: The Science of Custom*, New York: Rinehart.

Koodapuzha, Xavier (1995), "Catholic Mission in the Region of Kerala", in Augustine Kanjamala (ed.), *Integral Mission Dynamics: An Interdisciplinary Study of the Catholic Church in India*. New Delhi: Intercultural Publication.

Lele, Jayant (1995), *Hindutva: The Emergence of the Right*, Madras: Earthworm Books.

Ludden, David (ed.) (1996), *Making India Hindu*, New Delhi: Oxford University Press.

Lynch, Owen M. (1998), "Dalit Buddhism: The Liberate Bodh Gaya Movement", *Dalit International Newsletter*, Vol. 3, No. 1, February, 1998.

Matthew, G. (1982), "Politicization of Religion: Conversions to Islam in Tamil Nadu", *Economic and Political Weekly*, No. 25, pp. 1027–34; No. 26, pp. 1068–72.

Michael, S.M. (1980), *The Cultural Context of Evangelization in India*, Indore: Satprakashan.

—— (1983), "Sociological Perspectives of Conversion in India", *Indian Missiological Review*, January, Vol. 5, No. 1, pp. 40–52.

—— (1996), "The Cultural Context of the Rise of Hindutva and Dalit Forces", *Vidyajyoti: Journal of Theological Reflection*, May, Vol. 60, No. 5, pp. 294–310.

—— (2000), "Real Issues Behind the Violence", *Mission Today*, January-March, Vol. II, No. 1, pp. 9–22.

Natarajan, Nalini (1977), *Missionary among the Khasis*, New Delhi: Sterling Publishers.

Oddie, G.A. (ed.) (1977), *Religion in South Asia*, New Delhi: Manohar Book Service.

O'Malley, L.S. (1911), *Census of India*, Report.

Panikkar, K.N. (1995), *Culture, Ideology, Hegemony: Intellectuals and Social Consciousness in Colonial India*, New Delhi: Tulika Publishers.

Picket, J.W. (1933), *Christian Mass Movements in India*. Lucknow: Lucknow Publishing House (2nd Indian Edition).

Raj, Sunder (1988), *The Confusion Called Conversion*, New Delhi: TRACI.

Reddy, Prakash G. (1987), *Politics of Tribal Exploitation: A Study of Tribal Unrest in Andhra Pradesh*, New Delhi: Mittal Publications.

Risley, H.H. (1901), *Census of India*, India Report.

Saldanha, Julian (1984), "Conversion and Development of the Weaker Sections", *Indian Missiological Review*, No. 3, pp. 239–42.

—— (1996), "Patterns of Conversion in Indian Mission History", in Joseph Mattam and Sebastian Kim (eds.), *Mission and Conversion: A Reappraisal*, Mumbai: St. Paul's Publications.

Shah, Ghanshyam (1985), "Anti-Untouchability Movements", in I.P. Desai et al. (eds.), *Caste, Caste Conflict and Reservation*, Delhi: Ajanta Publications.

Sharma, S.P. and J.B. Sharma (1998), *Culture of Indian Tribes*, Vol. 1, New Delhi: Radha Publications.

Sharma, Ursula (1976), "Status-Striving and Striving to Abolish Status: The Arya Samaj and the Low Castes", *Social Action*, 26.

Shoobert (1931), *Census of India*, C.P. and Berar Report.

Snaitang, O.L. (1993), *Christianity and Social Change in North East India*, Shillong: Vendrame Institute.

Srinivas, M.N. (1989), *The Cohesive Role of Sanskritization and Other Essays*, New Delhi: Oxford University Press.

The Times of India News Service (2001), "Amartya hits out at Sangh Parivar for trying to 'rewrite history'", *Times of India*, January 3, p. 6 (Mumbai).

United News of India (2001), "RSS attempts rewrite history", *The Indian Express*, January 1, p. 4 (Mumbai).

Valiamangalam, Joseph (1996), "Conversion in Indian Religions", in Joseph Mattam and Sebastian Kim (eds.), *Mission and Conversion: A Reappraisal*, Mumbai: St. Paul's Publications.

Vidyarthi, L.P. and B.K. Rai (1977), *Tribal Culture of India*, Delhi: Concept Publishing Co.

Webster, John C.B. (1992), *Dalit Christians: A History*, Delhi: ISPCK.

Wingate, Andrew (1997), *The Church and Conversion: A Study of Recent Conversions to and from Christianity in the Tamil Area of South India*, Delhi: ISPCK.

Wilkinson, T. and M.M. Thomas (eds.) (1972), *Ambedkar and the Neo-Buddhist Movement*, Madras: CLS.

5 Non-Brahmanic Perspective on Indian Society

S.M. DAHIWALE

In contemporary literature on social and religious movements, the word, *non-Brahman*, is often used. The Phuleian (after Mahatma Phule) or the Ambedkarian approach has been followed for having adopted the analysis of the non-Brahman/backward classes/dalit movement in India. Since the 1980s, Sharad Patil became well known for his use of the trilogy of Marx, Phule and Ambedkar in his historical analysis of Indian society. His trilogy is termed as the non-Brahmanic interpretative methodology. According to Patil, the non-Brahmanic stream means the end of the slavery of class, caste and women. Following Patil's perspective, the Women's Studies Centre at the University of Pune organized a seminar on Non-Brahmanic Feminist History Writing on September 24–25, 1998, and published the presented papers in the form of a book (Bhagwat and Pardeshi, 1998). The scholars in the book have been critical of Indian history from the non-Brahmanic perspective and reiterated the observations made by Patil, Phule and Ambedkar in their writings. They affirm that the notion of purity worked in exercising the dominance of Brahmans in the hierarchies of caste, gender and culture. But, the understanding of the larger Indian society, which is made of several religious groups, castes, gender, and is full of dynamics, requires a comprehensive definition of the non-Brahmanic perspective. It perceives the practices, which are non-Vedic, non-Shastric, non-caste, non-patriarchal or having equalitarian character, and a number of attempts made to bring about change/transformation towards the equalitarian order through protest/resist/action movements against the Brahmanic hegemony. In this volume, since T.K. Oommen's paper deals with the perspective 'from below', it is necessary to give some clarification about his construction/use of the term, *below*, and my standpoint on using the 'non-Brahmanic perspective'. Oommen's construction is largely based on empirical observations comprehending the localized religious practices, prevalent gender equalitarian practices and social justice in the Dalit-Bahujan society. It is certainly non-Brahmanic in its formulation. The use of the term, below, denotes the western influence, especially that of Marxian literature. Considering the history of change from Vedic religion to Hindu religion, the growth of caste, the adapted patriarchal practices amongst lower caste Hindus, etc., on one hand, and the history of both egalitarian religious movements in ancient and medieval India and social reform movements in British India on the other hand, the term 'non-Brahmanic' is used in opposition to the Brahmanic and differentiating from it. As the ex-untouchable castes were regarded outside the *varna* (caste) society, these were kept away from the process of sanskritization and have not been made free from their age-old disabilities in the countryside even today. And how the peasant/intermediate castes (dominant today) had to struggle in medieval and British India for claiming Kshatriya status and for performing Vedic rites is a well-known historical fact, but these are sanskritized today. In post-independent India, because of the power politics, the peasant castes have become the agents of Brahman *dharma*. This is to say that the term, below, connotes a class category, while the term, non-Brahmanic, signifies the historical categories of religion, caste and gender. Accordingly, attention is focussed here on the important aspects of both early and later religions, religious movements, untouchability, social movements, gender and identity.

Indian society is composed of people of a variety of religions, sects, castes and tribes. It has a preponderance of 82.72 per cent Hindus (Census, 2001), who belong to the Hindu religion having a history of about 2,000 years. Hinduism has no monolithic character of having a single founder, a single sacred text, a single god or a well-defined doctrine. It has a caste system in which one's superior/inferior status is determined by birth. Historically, the outsiders have used the word, Hindu, to refer to the people living in the Indus valley. Since the pre-Vedic times, the history of Indian society has been a history of wars, oppositions, protests, conflicts and movements in various forms. Many tribes from outside invaded India, but the Aryan tribe culturally, socially and politically dominated the indigenous tribes.

The Aryan Invasion and the Rise of the Vedic Religion

Sources in Vedic literature lead to the inference that the original home of the Aryans was the Arctic region (between North Germany and Scandinavia/north of Siberia), but they later settled down in the plains of Central Asia (Tilak, 1956: 275, 380, 388, 390). The names of both Iran and Ireland signify them as the lands of the Aryans (Trautmann, 1997: 13). From the linguistic viewpoint, the Indian languages (Sanskrit and its descendants in North India and Sri Lanka) are studied as closely related to the Iranian languages (ibid.: 6). Archaeologists, such as John Marshall, R.E. Mortimer-Wheeler, Ramprasad Chanda, S.K. Chatterjee and R.D. Banerji, have argued that in struggles/wars with the Dravidians, the Aryan invaders destroyed the Indus valley civilization (Ramaswamy, 2001: 105–45). Such references in ancient Indian literature establish the fact that the Aryans entered the northwest of India around 1500 BC. According to the Vedic scholar, Malati Shendge, the Aryan invaders entered through the northwest crossing the Indus and its tributaries ... met with continuous opposition from the Asuras and the Raksasas (Shendge, 1977: 181). Prior to the Aryan emigrants, amongst the non-Aryan aborigines were the Dasyus, the Nishadas and the Dravidians. Among the Dravidians were the Tamilians, the Tulus, the Koorgs, the Gonds, the Oraons, the Khonds, the Todas, the Kols, the Juangs, the Santals, the Mundas, and the Hos.

During the *Rig Vedic* times, there were wars between the Aryan invaders (nomads) and their opponent non-Aryans, viz., the Asuras (agriculturists), the Raksasas (demons/warriors), the Yaksas (fearful beings), the Pisacas (architects/carvers), the Dasas (fishermen/sailors), the Dasyus (village folk), etc. After several attempts, Indra and Vishnu defeated the Asuras. Indra was the leader of the Aryans, the killer of the Dasas/Dasyus. In the *Rig Veda*, there are references to the forts of the Dasas (Jaiswal, 1998: 146). The Dasas and the Dasyus had armies of women warriors (Shendge, 1977: 145). Indra killed the non-Aryan enemies, Sambara, Pipru, Arsasanas, Sushna and Namuci, who are described as black and short-nosed (Kosambi, 1964: 78–79). Indra defeated and killed 30,000 Dasas, the dark skinned, who were settled in the land of the seven rivers, using a cunning strategy (Shendge, 1996: 29). Another Aryan hero, Vishnu, had battles with the Asuras, the Dasas, etc. After the defeat and looting of the wealth of the Dasas by the *Rig Vedic* Aryans, they were made slaves (Jaiswal, 1998: 146, 157). The lower classes of Hindus consist of ... aboriginal inhabitants (Trautmann, 1997: 175). The aborigine Dasyus/Dasas are described as the Raksasas/Mlechhas, the barbarians (ibid.: 197). They had no practice of sacrifices or performing rites and they were phallus worshippers (ibid.: 208–9).

For obtaining victory over the Asuras, the Devas appropriated the rites of sacrifice, i.e., fire worship, from the Asuras (Shendge, 1977: 92–94). After the victory of the Aryans over their enemies, certain events of transformation took place. One, the practice of fire rites was created. Two, the heroes, namely, Indra and Vishnu, of the Aryans became gods, and the enemies, viz., the Asuras, the Raksasas and others, became demons. And Vishnu was placed as the highest of the gods. Third, the defeated enemies were given the lowest status in the Aryan social structure by forbidding their participation in *yajnas,* the newly created religion of fire (ibid.: 283). Krishna, the dark-skinned hero of the Yadu tribe, a protector of cattle, who never invoked at a fire sacrifice where animals were offered, is a demon, an enemy of Indra in the *Rig Veda* (Kosambi, 1964: 115). Thus, the Dasas/Dasyus and the Panis suffered loss of social status because of their resistance (Shendge, 1977: 284). The historicity of Dipavali, the festival of lights, is that it was introduced by the Aryans as a mark of victory over the destruction of Asura Bali and Naraka, the non-Aryan leaders. But, unfortunately, the non-Aryans also joined the celebration because of their ignorance.

We find the appearance of the word 'Aryans' in the *Rig Veda* text (1400 BC). They were divided into three social classes, viz., the warriors, the priests and the commoners (Thapar, 1966: 37). They composed the hymns of the *Rig Veda.* In the *Rig Veda,* the word 'Brahman' is used as one of the seven priests and it evolved gradually as a class of priests in the *Rig Vedic* period itself (Misra, 1978). The Brahmans are "the repositories both of the divine word, and of the spirit of devotion or prayer" (Monier-Williams, 1877: 12). In the second division of the *Veda,* called *Brahmanas* (1000 BC), we find the idea of sacrifice and rituals. The Vedic divisions of the *Brahmanas* have the *Aitareya,* the *Taittiriya,* the *Satapatha,* and the *Gopatha,* etc. The Brahmans developed ritualism when they settled in the northwestern part of India (ibid.: 24). For attaining immortality, three objectives of sacrifices were agreed upon: (i) to nourish the gods as a necessity of their being, (ii) to expiate for sins committed, and (iii) to acquire superhuman power. Initially, humans were offered in sacrifices. Later, animals – horses, oxen, cows, sheep and goats – substituted for them. Sacrifices of all kinds increased in the *Brahmana* period (probably from 800 to 500 BC) (Monier-Williams, 1877: chapter III). D.D. Kosambi adds one more object – of getting victory in war (Kosambi, 1964: 87). King Janamejaya III performed a great sacrifice for the total destruction of the Nagas (ibid.: 92). King Dasarath performed an Aswamedha (horse sacrifice) for obtaining a son (Wheeler, 1973: 10). The sacrifices were enclosed between the two upper castes, viz., Brahman and Kshatriya. The Raksasas alluded to the different tribes of aborigines which had opposed the Brahmans and their sacrifices (ibid.: 38). J. Wheeler cites that the Raksasas once rushed to defile the Brahmans' sacrificial altar with bones and blood, but it was prevented by Rama (ibid.: 44). Perhaps this could be the reason for excluding Shudras in the Brahmanic sacrifices in Vedic India.

The Rise of Buddhism and Jainism

The above stray mention shows that there was opposition to the practices of Brahmanic sacrifices. The revolt against the Vedic religion of sacrifices (*yajnas*) by Gautama Buddha, the Shakya (532–487 BC), and Vardhamana Mahaveera, the Licchavi (539–467 BC), and their teachings, developed later as independent religions, in the form of Buddhism and Jainism, respectively. Both religions uphold non-violence and ethical practices in personal as well as social life. Buddha prohibited Bhikkus from holding private property and from remaining householders, contrary to the practices of the Brahman priests of the Vedic religion. Upali, a barber, Sunit and Svapak, scavengers, were admitted as monks to the Bhikku Sangha. Women were also admitted to the Sangha. Mahaveer did the same, but with strict rules of austerity and non-violence. The Licchavis and the Mallas did not follow the Vedic practices (Monier-Williams, 1877: 130).

According to B.R. Ambedkar, "The history of India is nothing but a history of a mortal conflict between Buddhism and Brahmanism" (Ambedkar, 1987: 267). Ambedkar defines Brahmanism in terms of the spirit: "the idea of high caste and low caste – which implanted the idea of pollution from human beings and implanted social privileges and inequality" (Keer, 1971: 89) and "the negation of the spirit of liberty, equality and fraternity" (ibid.: 303). Also, the effects of Brahmanism have been elaborated further mentioning "not confining only to social rights such as interdining and intermarrying. It denied them also the civic rights. So omniscient is Brahmanism that it even affects the field of economic opportunities" (ibid.: 304). He notes certain facts of the triumph of Brahmanism in the history of India. Sisunag, the aboriginal Nag, founded the kingdom of Magadha in Bihar in 642 BC. Nanda, who ruled the Magadha empire upto 322 BC, replaced the Sisunag dynasty. Chandragupta Maurya, who was related to the Sisunag dynasty, and restored the Naga empire of Magadha, dethroned the last Nanda king. The Mauryan empire extended its boundaries by a number of conquests. Ashok Maurya succeeded in 270 BC. After large-scale killings of animals and men in the war of Kalinga, Emperor Ashok realized the horror of what he had done and converted to Buddhism. We find the Buddha's *Dhamma*, which Ashok promulgated on his rock edicts, is as follows:

1. No animal should be slaughtered for sacrifice.
2. Performing rites or ceremonies for luck on the occasion of sickness, weddings, and childbirth, or starting a journey, are worthless.

3. Honour should be paid to all belonging to other sects.
4. The *Dhamma* is doing benefits to others; compassion; liberty; truth; purity.

Since Ashok made Buddhism the official religion of his great empire, the Brahmans lost their chief source of living, performing sacrifices. This lasted for nearly 140 years during the Maurya period, which, according to Ambedkar, was the greatest blow to Brahmanism (ibid.: 268). Therefore, Pushyamitra Sung (180–151 BC), the Sam Vedic Brahman, and the believer in animal sacrifices, took up the cause of destroying the Buddhist state and reinstating the Brahmanic religion. After ascending the throne, Pushyamitra not only performed the horse sacrifice, but also launched a violent persecution of the Buddhists. He proclaimed a price of 100 gold pieces on the head of every Buddhist monk (ibid.: 269). The *Smritis* and *Puranas* were written during Gupta period (2nd c. BC 4th c. AD), after triumphing over Buddhism.

The point of conflict between the Brahmans and the Shudras or between the Brahmanic followers/protectors and the Buddhists is reflected in the epic, *Ramayana*. During the *Ramayana* times (400 BC–400 AD), great stress was laid upon caste distinctions (Wheeler, 1973: 8). The conflict between Rama and Ravana is interpreted as "local conflicts between the agriculturists of the Ganges valley and the more primitive hunting and food-gathering societies of the Vindhyan region" (Thapar, 1966: 33). The character of Rama is depicted as a protector of the Brahmans and an opponent of Buddhism. The known example is that Rama beheaded Shambuka, who did penance for the acquisition of merit. Rama had the purpose of destroying Ravana, who was a Buddhist sovereign (Wheeler, 1973: 347) and Buddhist (ibid.: 233). Ravana is also believed to be a Dravidian king, the chief of the Raksasas, the aborigines, and the protector of his subjects. In the conflict, although Brahmans conquered the Buddhists, there is evidence of revering Ravana. Ravana is still worshipped in the Dravidian country and in a few villages in the North. On Vijayadashmi, the festival symbolizing the victory of good over evil, the villagers in Ravana, a village named after Ravana in Netaran taluka of Vidisha district in Madhya Pradesh, worship the nine-feet tall stone idol of Ravana installed there in the 12th century. People from the villages around Ravana assemble for the celebration (*The Times of India*, October 27, 1993, and *Loksatta*, Pune, October 25, 2001). An idol of Ravana is also worshipped in Mandsor of Madhya Pradesh, in Devadha near Sultanganj of Bihar and in Fattehapur district of Uttar Pradesh (*Maharashtra Times*, Mumbai, October 22, 1985).

For the emergence of Buddha, Ambedkar draws attention to a few of the social evils of the Aryan community of the pre-Buddhism days. He mentions drinking Soma and Sura, gambling of honour and dignity, the drinking and dancing of the Aryan women, sexual immorality (e.g., Vashishta and Manu who married their own daughters, Shatrupa and Ila, respectively), the Yajna Bhumi (place of sacrifice) becoming an open ground for cohabitation and sexual intercourse, the practice of renting out women to others for a time (e.g., King Yayati gave his daughter, Madhvi, to his teacher, Galav, and thereafter to the kings), and, allowing women to have sexual intercourse with the Devas and Aryans of superior status and prowess for good breeding (Ambedkar, 1987: Vol.3,

Chapter 6). These social practices of the Aryans reveal that the Aryan religion was never concerned with a righteous life (ibid.: 176). Buddha, therefore, emerged as a reformer. He laid down five precepts for the laity: (i) not to kill, (ii) not to steal, (iii) not to lie, (iv) not to be unchaste, and (v) not to consume intoxicants. He denounced the *yajna* as a form of religion as well as the caste system and admitted low-caste men to the rank of Bhikku (priest).

Buddhism spread across several parts of India, but disappeared gradually. Ambedkar offered two main reasons for the fall of Buddhism. One was the invasion of the Muslims, who used their swords to massacre the Buddhist priests, and the other was the persecution of the Buddhist laity by the Brahmanic rulers, namely, Lalliya who founded the Brahmin Shahi dynasty (880–1021 c. AD) in Punjab, Jayapala (960–980 c. AD), Anandpal (980–1000 c. AD) and Trilochanpal (1000–1021 c. AD), who belonged to the Brahmanic faith (ibid.: 229–31). He cited the source of Vincent Smith for instances of persecution of the Jains in southern India in the 7th century and in Gujarat in the 12th century by Ajayadeva, a Saiva King (ibid.: 238).

The Revival of Brahmanism

The downfall of Buddhism is seen to coincide with the revival of Brahmanism in the post-Mauryan period. If Emperor Ashok promoted Buddhism as the religion of the state, Pushyamitra Sung (180–151 BC) ended the degradation of the Brahmans by destroying the Buddhist state (ibid.: 268). During the reign of Pushyamitra, the *Manusmriti* was promulgated, stated Ambedkar. Ambedkar regarded the *Manusmriti* as the institution of Brahmanism (ibid.: 271). He held Manu responsible for upholding the principle of gradation and rank in the caste system (ibid.: 25). It is through the prescriptions in *Manusmriti* that the religious, ritualistic and social life of all castes was governed.

In Ambedkar's view, Brahmanism brought about the following changes:

1. It established the right of the Brahman to rule and commit regicide.
2. It made the Brahmans a class of privileged persons.
3. It converted the *varna* into caste by making status and occupation hereditary.
4. It brought about a conflict and anti-social feeling between the different castes.
5. It degraded the Shudras and women.
6. It forged the system of graded inequality.
7. It made legal and rigid the social system, which was conventional and flexible.

Interestingly, Ambedkar stated facts contrary to the view that the Hindu civilization is *sanatan* (unchanging). Brahmans have always changed things to suit their interests. The Vedic gods – Indra, Vishnu, Varuna, Mitra, Brahma – whom they worshipped in the Vedic times, were abandoned when they started worshipping non-Vedic gods, including the Muslim Pirs (Ambedkar, 1987: Vol. 4, 5–6). Brahmans became temple priests, household ritual performers, etc., because they received offerings/gifts. He described this characteristic as faithless. This is why the Brahmans made priesthood their privilege. Hinduism is polytheistic unlike Islam, Judaism and Christianity, all monotheistic religions, "because the Hindu society has been formed by the conglomeration of many tribes and many communities each of whom had their own separate Gods" (ibid.: 79). Absorption has been a characteristic of Hinduism. The protest traditions of Buddhism, Jainism, the Bhakti movement, etc., and the traditions of little communities have been absorbed into it. For that, the idea of incarnation was also evolved, making Buddha, Krishna, etc., incarnations of Vishnu. According to Indologist, R.G. Bhandarkar, the *avataar,* incarnation, has always been assumed for destroying all the demons (Bhandarkar, 1982: 50).

In his paper, 'Castes in India: Their Mechanism, Genesis and Development' (1917), Ambedkar stated the thesis of the *superimposition of endogamy on exogamy* towards the creation of caste and observed the role of customs, viz., (i) *sati*, the burning of the widow on the funeral pyre of her husband, (ii) enforced widowhood, and (iii) child marriage, in preserving the caste endogamy. Ambedkar noted two socio-psychological characteristics of the hierarchical organization of the caste system, which produced (i) a spirit of rivalry among the different castes for dignity, and (ii) an ascending scale of hatred and descending scale of contempt (Ambedkar, 1987: Vol. 4, 48). The segmentation of Indian society into castes has been brought about with a view to prevent united action by non-Brahmans to overthrow Brahmanism (ibid.: 304).

Ambedkar classifies Hindu society into four classes. The broader division he classifies into two, i.e., (i) caste Hindus, and (ii) non-caste Hindus. Class I constitutes the privileged castes of Dvijas (i.e., Brahmins, Kshatriyas and Vaishyas), Class II, the low castes of the Shudras (i.e., peasants and artisans), Class III, the primitive as well as criminal tribes/castes and Class IV, the segregated untouchable castes (Ambedkar, 1989: 167). In *The Untouchables* (1948/1990) Ambedkar advanced the Broken Men Theory, tracing two roots of untouchability: (i) contempt and hatred of the Broken Men as of Buddhists by the Brahmans, and (ii) continuation of the eating of beef by the Broken Men after it had been given up by others. In support of his argument, he cited the source in *Mricchakatika*, a Sanskrit drama written in the 4th century AD, and evidence of Chandragupta II (412 c. AD) who made cow killing a *Mahapataka*, a mortal sin. But his theory lies outside the consideration of the mainstream historians. For more details, in this volume, consult the chapter, The Broken Men Theory of Untouchability.

Besides religion and caste as categories of grouping in Indian society, gender is also an important category. Gender discrimination has been one of the distinctive features of Hindu society. In the later Vedic period, i.e., 900–500 BC, women were not allowed to recite or listen to Vedic hymns. In the Buddha's time, the status of women was elevated by admitting them in the community of Bhikkus (priests) and allowing them to gain and impart religious knowledge. In ancient Hindu society, the injunctions of devotion, virtuousness and subordination to her husband were imposed on the wife, especially during the *Sriti* and *Smriti* periods. In the *Smriti* period, they had no right to make offerings in a *yajna*. Also, they had no life as an ascetic. A woman was treated as untouchable due to her menstrual cycle. *Manusmriti* denied her the right to property. A woman was put in subservience to a man. For marriage, a woman had to be a virgin and, after marriage, she had to be loyal to her husband. In the notion of *kanyadaan*, giving away daughter as a gift in a Hindu marriage, a woman is conceived of as an object, like property. In the traditional Hindu order, a woman is not viewed to be independent because she is protected in her childhood by her parents, after marriage by her husband and in her old age by her son. In Ambedkar's view, women have been seen as a means to preserve caste endogamy and, so, the Brahmans have introduced the practices of child marriage, *sati* and enforced widowhood. These practices are the characteristic features of a Brahmanic society.

The rules of endogamy, hereditary occupations and commensality within the social group are universal characteristics of any traditional society. As regards the Hindu society, the question is that of understanding the basis of social distinctions and the privileges enjoyed by the high castes and the number of social disabilities imposed on the lower castes. Indologist G.S. Ghurye attributes the idea of ceremonial purity to an exclusive social stratification (Ghurye, 1969: 171). According to him, the first regulations began with the exclusion of the Shudras, the aborigines, from the religious worship developed by the Aryans. They forbade their presence in their sacrificial hall (ibid.: 172). To preserve their fair skin and cultural integrity, the Brahmans regulated endogamy (ibid.: 173). As Ghurye says: "Caste in India is a Brahmanic child of the Indo-Aryan culture, cradled in the land of the Ganges and the Jamna and thence transferred to other parts of the country" (ibid.: 176). Thus, the rules of purity and impurity were not only applied to treat the social groups of different physical, cultural and vocational traits hierarchically, but also to put restrictions on marital, social, occupational and other such relations also. In the *Rig Veda*, three classes, viz., Brahma, Kshatra and Visha, are mentioned. In Vedic times, there were no restrictions of commensality, marriage and following/adopting a vocation. We, therefore, find a number of mentions in pre-Buddhist literature of sages, namely, Vyas, Vasishtha and Valmiki, who were born in the lower classes. In Buddhist India, people could change their vocations. A Kshatriya could work as a potter, basket-maker, reed-worker, garland-maker or cook (Rhy-Davids, 1903: 54–55). A Jain source informs that Sovaga, a Chandala by birth, visited the sacrificial enclosure of a Brahman teacher and lectured to him on certain values of life (Sharma, 1958: 134).

In the *Manusmriti*, which came only in 200 AD, the clear distinctions of the caste and regulation of the caste system are found manifested. But, ancient history scholar, Suvira Jaiswal pushes it to a much later period. According to her, "The emergence of endogamous subcastes within the brahman varna is a post-Vedic, presumably early medieval phenomenon" (i.e., 600 AD) (Jaiswal, 1998: 157–58). Besides priestly activities as a source of the Brahmans' livelihood, many provisions were made in the *Manusmriti* for strengthening their economic position. Brahmans were exempted from taxes (X. 79), taking away property by the king was made impossible (IX. 189) and they were given the right of recovering their fees (X. 85). Being the lawgiver class, they recommended the gift of land to Brahmans as being a *Mahadana*, a great gift, for attaining spiritual merit and they became a class of landowners (Nath, 2001: 23–24). And so they were landlords till the implementation of the land reform laws in post-Independent India.

Ambedkar perceived Hinduism as the modified form of ancient Brahmanism. He said that in Hinduism, there was no difference between law and ethics. Both are concerned with "regulating the conduct of the low class Hindus to *subserve* the ends of high-caste Hindus" (Ambedkar, 1987, Vol. 3, 84). In this way, Ambedkar summarized Hinduism as serving the interests of the Brahman class at the centre. In the interest of the untouchables, he denounced Hinduism, which stood for inequality and oppression, and embraced Buddhism, which promoted knowledge, love, compassion, equality and morality. In the historical background, he justified conversion for the "self-respect and honour of the untouchables" (Ambedkar, 1989: 412). For the emancipation of the untouchables, he did not see conversion as the only remedy and so he launched a struggle for obtaining for them social rights, educational attainment, and places in government administration and political power.

Movements against Brahmanism

To counter the dominance of Brahmanism, some religious and social traditions were developed in India. We have seen the emergence of Buddhism and Jainism as protest movements against the Vedic religion and practices of sacrifice. According to M. Monier-Williams, in the post-Buddha period, the founders of Vaishnavism and Shaivism and their followers imitated Buddha in requiring their followers to drop caste distinctions (Monier-Williams, 1877: 57). Interestingly, the Rudra-Shiva is assumed to be the great God of the pre-Aryan settlers of the Indus Valley (Daweewarn, 1982: 6). The Shaivites worship both the bull and the phallus. The tradition of worshipping both is non-Aryan and inherited from the Harappans (Wheeler, 1968: 109). It is seen even today in South India. The revolt of the Brahman prime minister of Bijjala against Brahmanism in 1160 AD in the north Karnataka and south Maharashtra region is prominent. Basava (1131–67 AD) founded Veershaivaism, which rejects the authority of the *Vedas* and the doctrine of rebirth, objects to child marriage, approves of the remarriage of widows, and nurses an intense aversion to the Brahmans (Daweewarn, 1982: 17). Basava not only preached equality of caste and sex, but also brought it into practice. He treated equally all Shaivaite untouchables. He did not believe in the Brahmanic notion of impurities. Veershaivaites, therefore, do not accept the impurities of birth, caste, menstrual cycle, death and remnant food. Basava considered women fit for entering the temple and worshipping the 'linga'. The 'linga' is not regarded as an idol. Basava criticized idol worship. He helped in bringing about an intercaste marriage between the daughter of a Brahman and the son of a cobbler. Basava gave dignity to labour and offered the freedom to follow any occupation to all individuals (including women). This is why, the Veershaivaites have taken up enterprising activities, rather than spiritual ones. Veershaivaism emphasized non-violence. The followers, therefore, are vegetarian. Basava approved of widow remarriage and he organized such marriages. A Lingayat widow could participate in all religious as well as social ceremonies and festivities. In his time, Basava gave women the freedom to form an association for spreading education and awakening political interest. Under his leadership, Nagalambika and Gangambika started a political movement. Veershaivaite women are also given the freedom to contribute earning to the household income by taking up any productive/industrial activity. Basava founded an association of individuals of different occupations (including untouchables' jobs) and professions. All these practices show how Veershaivaism developed distinctly from the Brahmanic religion of believing in caste based on birth, gender inequality, sacrifices (*yajna*), ritual purity, predetermined action (*karma*), etc. (Ghugare, 1995). On the whole, Basava was a social revolutionary of his times.

A long tradition of the Bhakti movement advocating social equality is widespread both in South and North India. The Bhakti concept is found in the *Bhagavad Gita* (about 467 AD) and is a movement of saints who emphasized the equality of all devotees, irrespective of caste and gender. The movement originated especially as a popular movement of protest against Brahmanism and the rigours of the caste system (Jaiswal, 2000: 14). The Tamil Alvar saints belonged to the 6th century AD (ibid.: 15). They had non-Brahmanic origins, namely, from the Appar, the Vellala and the peasant caste, and one amongst them was a Nandanar, a Parayan/Panar, an outcaste (ibid.: 18). It is noteworthy that most of the saints of the medieval and modern times belong to the Bhakti movement. They emerged from non-Brahman communities. Namdeo (14th c. AD) was a tailor from Maharashtra. Kabir (1440–1518 AD), the son of a Brahman widow, was nurtured and brought up by a Mohameddan weaver family. Kabir condemned the rites, ceremonies and other practices of the Brahmans (Bhandarkar, 1982: 101). He is known for rejecting the caste system. He did not believe in the concepts of god, soul, reincarnation and rebirth. While comparing a donkey and a dog with a Brahman, a donkey carries a load and a dog serves its master honestly, but a Brahman does nothing, says Kabir in a couplet. There are references to Buddha, Mahaveera and Charvak in his couplets. Kabir had followers from all castes. In 1463, Kabir's disciple, Dharam Das, a Bania, distributed eighteen lakh rupees in charity (Prakasam, 1998: 60). Meerabai (15th c. AD), a Sisodia Rajput rebel, accepted Saint Ravidas, a cobbler, as her guru (teacher). She intermingled with male devotees and associated with lower caste people. Besides Namdeo, Kabir and Meerabai, the other non-Brahman saints were Dhana (a Jat peasant), Sena (a barber), Tukaram (a Maratha), Savata Mali (a gardener) and Chokhamela (a Mahar or untouchable). Among the saints, there were women too, viz., Andal in the Tamil country, Akkamahadevi in the Kannada country, Janabai and Soyarabai in Maharashtra, and Meerabai in Rajasthan. In the words of M.N. Srinivas, "The Bhakti movement of medieval India was really pan-Indian attracting a large number of men and women from the lower orders and it even crossed the religious divide between Hindus and Muslims as with Kabir and, much later, Shirdi Sai Baba" (Srinivas, 2003: 459).

Guru Nanak, the founder of Sikhism, had come under the influence of the egalitarian philosophy of the 16 Hindu and Muslim saints and he incorporated their couplets in his *Guru Granth Sahib*. Guru Nanak was against idol worship, Brahmanic rites and caste distinctions. Brahmanic ideology undermines manual labour. Guru Nanak encouraged his followers to take up enterprising activities. The Sikh movement in the 16th century was initiated to bring about changes in the Brahmanic values. A tradition of *langar* (free community meals) and *pankit* (a line without caste distinction) at the Golden Temple in Amritsar is an example of practising equality. The temple is open to all, irrespective of caste, religion and gender. In Sikhism, there is absence of a priestly caste and the performers mostly belong to the middle castes. Women can also become priests. Guru Amar Das trained 146 persons to go out as priests and missionaries and of those, 52 were women. Sikhism facilitated a change in the character of caste structure, for instance, the Jats started practising intercaste marriages by accepting girls from lower castes (Judge, 2002: 180–81).

Various religious movements continued their struggle against social inequality from the ancient times of the Buddha through the medieval and modern times of saints such as Kabir and Gadge Baba of Maharashtra, respectively. The leaders of these movements reacted against the notion of caste and gender hierarchy at the ideological level and tried to be equalitarian in practice at the individual level. But they faced the limitations of their times. The saints of the Bhakti movement, while rejecting Brahmanism, emphasized humanitarian and egalitarian values in their preachings, but they appealed to god. Since they had no action programme, it did not help much in bringing about a social change.

About the egalitarian order of Hindu society, the Hindus believed that it was ordained and so, unalterable. It was in the British regime that some non-Brahmans could have modern education, especially in the Christian missionary schools, and under the impact of rational thinking, a few rebels emerged to question birth-based inequality, offering the opinion that it was man-made, particularly by the Brahman priestly class in their self-interest. The non-Brahman leaders of the social reform movement, therefore, started not only attacking the Brahmans' authority and their *Shastras* in public meetings, but also adopted the action programme of breaking several rules of caste and gender customs.

The 19th and 20th centuries witnessed social protest/reform movements in various parts of India. The movements of Ghasi Das in Chattisgarh, the Mahima Dharma in Orissa, Sri Narayan Guru in Kerala, Jotiba Phule and B.R. Ambedkar in Maharashtra, the Ad Dharam in Punjab, and the Namshudra in Bengal and the Adi Dravida and Periyar in Tamil Nadu are some examples. These movements in the real sense have helped in elevating the social status of the non-Brahmans, especially intermediate and depressed castes. So it is necessary to take an overview of protest and reform movements launched by the leaders/revolutionaries of the times in their regions.

To improve the social status of the Chamars (cobblers), Ghasi Das, an ex-untouchable, initiated a movement between 1820 and 1830 in the Chattisgarh region. He was against idol worship. He threw away the idols of Hindu gods and goddesses. His followers gave up their traditional caste jobs, rejected the authority of the Brahmans, ignored Hindu festivals and resisted high-caste domination (Prakasam, 1998: 69–70). Ghasi's son, Balak Das, challenged the privilege of the high caste by travelling on elephants and horses (ibid.: 72). The Mahima Dharma (1826–76) in Orissa resisted the *varna* order and was developed as a counter to the Hinduization of the upper-caste domination (Pati, 2001: 4207). The Chamars in Punjab launched the Ad Dharm movement in the 1920s, rejecting their Hindu roots, and as many as 4,18,789 persons reported themselves as Ad Dharmis in the 1931 Census of Punjab. The conversion to Buddhism by B.R. Ambedkar and a million of his followers in Nagpur on 14th October, 1956, is an epoch making event in the history of the conversion movement. The conversions of a large number of ex-untouchables to Christianity and Sikhism are other examples of rejection of Hinduism. Religious conversions are described as redemptive (Omvedt, 2002: 294). These conversions helped not only in registering a protest against Hinduism, but also in the formation of a distinct identity for obtaining freedom for development. However, it did not help end the age-old discrimination or assist the converts in entering the government administration and positions of power.

Jotirao Phule (1827–1890) was regarded a revolutionary thinker/activist who propounded non-Brahmanic thinking in the modern period. He viewed Brahmanism as a powerful system of oppression of the Shtrishudratishudra, i.e., women-peasants-untouchables. He reacted vehemently against the ordination of caste and the performance of rituals by Brahman priests, labelling it an occupation of mendacity, and their devised system of Hindu mythology. Prior to the spread of the Aryan culture of sacrifice, patriarchy and gradation of Hindu society on the basis of the purity-impurity notion, there were the cults of worshipping Jotiba, Khandoba, Mhasoba and such other idols, which Phule calls the Assyrian culture of the earlier natives. He, therefore, expressed a desire for the reign of Mahabali, the Asura king, who ruled over the Malayala Nadu. Mahbali is revered as an icon of social justice and equality in Kerala even today. Thiru Onam, the festival of flowers, is celebrated in the spirit of Mahabali's reign of justice. Phule offered Sarvajanik Satyadharma, the universal religion of truth, a proclamation of equality of all men and women, as an alternative to Brahmanism. Besides, Phule saw education as the key to solve many socio-economic ills and adopted a programme of imparting education, especially to women and untouchables in the 1850s.

Chhatrapati Shahu (1874–1922) of the Karveer (Kolhapur in the southwest of Maharashtra) state is known as a great social revolutionary who spearheaded the struggle against Brahman bureaucracy. He was denied his claim as a Kshatriya for a Vedic recitation and was treated as a Shudra by his royal priest in October 1899. The incident shocked him. He decided to fight against the domination of Brahmans in education, administration and politics. He is known for his anti-untouchability crusade and regarded as the originator of the reservation policy for backward classes (including Muslims and native Christians), introduced on his birthday, 26th July, 1902, in his state services. In 1913, to end the monopoly of the Brahman priests, Shahu encouraged the Satyashodhak ideology of Phule by founding a Satyashodhak School to train non-Brahman priests in performing religious rituals. As a result, in the Karveer state, as many as 5,161 religious events were performed by non-Brahman priests in 1913 itself (Suryawanshi, 1984: 473). Shahu abolished several ill practices, viz., untouchability, slavery, and the daily appearance of persons of criminal castes before the village police officer, bonded labour and dedicating girls to god. The caste system is characterized by the restrictions of marriage, occupational mobility and commensality. He took steps to remove all these. For social and national integration, in February 1918, he issued the order for intermarriages and took the initiative in bringing about intermarriages. He issued the notification permitting widows to remarry in July 1917. To end the exploitation of the peasants, he abolished the monopoly of the Kulkarnis, who were Brahmans and the village revenue officers. Shahu realized the importance of education and so he made primary education compulsory in his state. For girls' education, he founded separate schools for them. He encouraged girls in medical education as well. In the Karveer state, the number of educational institutions increased from 224 in 1894 to 559 in 1922 and the number of non-Brahman students both in college and high school increased five-fold (Pawar, ed., 2001: 597–98).

To demolish the domination of Brahmans in politics, Chhatrapati Shahu gave support to the non-Brahman movement and encouraged it in the Deccan in the early 1920s. A similar movement was started in southern India around 1892. There was not a single non-Brahman legislator in the Madras Legislative Council. In Madras, the Justice Party was founded on 20th November, 1916. Although the political representation to non-Brahman communities, including women, was the main item on the agenda of a non-Brahman movement conference held about then, other issues of education, including of women, intermarriage, forging a fraternity between non-Brahman communities, including Muslims, Christians, Adi Dravidas and other depressed classes, for both political and social purposes, were also discussed.

E.V. Ramasamy Periyar separately launched the Self-Respect Movement in 1925. He was an atheist, an upholder of Buddhism and a critic of Brahmanism. The Self-Respecters launched a movement against the sacred texts of Brahmanism, especially the *Ramayana*, an Aryan text, because it signified the Aryan conquest over Ravana and the *Raksasas*, who were the earlier natives. Periyar and the Self-Respecters considered atheism, Buddhism and Islam as alternatives to Brahmanism. They conceived of a new community, which they described as a Samadharmic society, where rights, claims and responsibilities would be equal. To devalue the status of Brahman priests, they called for a boycott at non-Brahman weddings and evolved a simple ritual to be performed either by a community elder or a Self-Respecter or a distinguished non-Brahman. They deliberately conducted marriages on days considered unholy by Hindus and at inauspicious hours. They also conducted intercaste marriages. For instance, a landlord married a woman from a *devadasi* family. To fight Brahmanism, Periyar emphasized a new relationship of mutuality and reciprocity of the Shudra non-Brahmins and the Adi Dravidas. The Self-Respecters redefined their gender concern. Penn-ina-nallar wrote an article entitled, 'Women's Depressed Status', in the *Kudi Arasu* of April 22 and 29, 1928. In 1929, Periyar started an informal organization for women in his house in Erode and ran a sort of home for deserted wives. In his article, 'Masculinity Must Be Destroyed', Periyar stated that the term 'masculinity' degraded women. He considered marriage a symbol of womanhood and the burden of motherhood, which made woman a property, a slave. He perceived the liberation of woman from the Brahmanic patriarchal dominance, in equal rights to property and authority in the household and outside, in motherhood as a choice and in granting divorce. He advocated birth control and opposed abortion. Periyar was critical of the wasteful expenditure on rituals, festivals and pilgrimages. Regarding the temple priest, the Brahmans had their hereditary claims. The practice of appointing a temple priest on a hereditary basis was done away with by passing an amendment to the Hindu Religious Act in 1970 by the Dravida Munnetra Kazhagam under Chief Minister K.

Karunanidhi, the inheritor of Periyar's ideology (for details, see Geetha and Rajadurai, 1998).

In the non-Brahmanic religious traditions, viz., Buddhism, Jainism, Veershaivaism, Sikhism, etc., gender equality was not only normatively advocated, but also practised in certain spheres of life and relations. Some instances of the practised equality between men and women have already been given earlier. In the social reform tradition of the 19th century, reformers such as Raja Ram Mohan Roy, Justice M.G. Ranade, Maharshi Karve and Gopal Ganesh Agarkar took up the issues of the abolition of *sati*, allowing widow remarriage and banning child marriage. But, in practice, Justice Ranade married a young girl and Maharshi Karve did not give admission to the sister of social reformer Maharshi Vitthal Ramji Shinde in his home for widows at Hingne near Pune because she belonged to the Maratha caste, lower than Brahmans. These instances show how their programmes of reform were narrowed down for their caste group (i.e., Brahmans). Justice Ranade had not become free from the impact of conservatism. But Mahatma Phule observed the roots of evil customs as the impact of Brahmanism and so he gave the call of unity of the Shtrishudratishudra, in which women, as a class of Shudras, were included, and appealed to the oppressed to reject Brahmanism. Like Phule, E.V. Ramasamy Periyar also deplored Saw women's oppression in the Brahmanic society. Thus, both Phule and Periyar rejected Brahmanism and its practices.

In Maharashtra, some activist scholars who were influenced by the ideologies of Phule and Ambedkar developed the non-Brahmanic feminist perspective. It rejects the rule of caste, class and patriarchal domination and believes in the independent status of women. The perspective is developed to reinterpret the history of the institutions of caste, marriage, family and property. From this perspective, the bipolar notions of purity-impurity and superiority-inferiority have been seen as Brahmanic (Bhagwat and Pardeshi, 1998).

After independence, the intermediate/peasant castes dominated the state and other institutional power. This new elites started playing the role of Brahmanism in their areas by doing injustice, inflicting atrocities and observing discrimination in distributing the benefits of government policies and programmes to the members of SCs, STs, OBCs, nomadic tribes and Muslim minority. This experience has caused the rise and growth of the Bahujan Samaj Party in Uttar Pradesh and other states (see Pai, 2002).

Issues of Identity and Conversions

The notion of identity is important for several reasons. One, it involves the sense of belongingness of people to a territory/country and, hence, it becomes a matter of right over means/resources. Two, it relates to the culture which a group represents. Three, a group may have a linguistic identity. In this way, identity is associated to several things. So far as India is concerned, her identity is seen changed a number of times in the past. India in the past was known as Vedic India, Buddhist India, Hindu India and, today, Secular India. It shows that the identity of India was/is known by the religion/culture of her people. Thus, we do not find continuity of any one identity. The point is that social groups, which were 'given' a particular identity by others, were/are in quest of their identity.

Since the identity of the people has changed, it calls for re-examining their history. Thus, the issue of identity is not important to those who belong to the dominant religion/society, but it is important to those who are 'broken' in their struggle. Ambedkar called untouchables 'broken men'. There are several such social groups in India, e.g., the denotified tribes in post-independent India, who were/are branded the 'criminal tribes'. A brief account of both rejecting the identity given by the upper-caste Hindus and constructing/inventing an identity by the oppressed/suppressed/ depressed is given in this section.

The people living in India have been called Hindus since the middle of the 6th century BC (Chaudhuri et al., 2003: xii). It is both in social and religious senses. For Hindus, Muslims and Christians are 'other'. But, amongst the Hindus, since the Hindu religion has not created a feeling of brotherhood, caste is considered important for identification. Each caste group has its distinct identity and a distinct way of life determined by the Brahmanic system. Since the members of several thousand castes were called Hindus, they were supposed to be entitled to the right to worship Hindu gods and goddesses in temples, the right to recitation of hymns, the right to Vedic performances, etc., and several civil rights besides. Although the members of the underprivileged castes were called Hindus, they were not allowed to enjoy religious and civil rights and they had to suffer from their caste disabilities, including such prominent figures as Shivaji Chhatrapati and Shahu Chhatrapati, who were denied their Kshatriya claims to the Vedic rites. The issue of caste identity was triggered for discovering the roots of those who were denied their rights and the rights of those earlier inhabitants, especially untouchable and Adivasi communities.

The earlier attempts of Shudra-Atishudra castes were to find their place within the Hindu social order. For that, there have been attempts for upward mobility by asserting claims to get the status of Kshatriya. Also, the untouchables had to fight for temple entry as well as for civil rights both in pre- and post-independent India. In post-independent India, the Shudra castes gave up the idea of assertion of Kshatriya claim since those have become the ruling castes in their regions. And, the powerless castes and Adivasi communities sought the path of conversion. Lancy Lobo, in his paper, 'Brahmanical Social Order and Christianity in India', attributes the large-scale conversion of untouchables and Adivasis to the ill-treatment that they received at the hands of the upper castes. When they met with failure in their attempts, they had to seek a solution in conversion to other religions, namely, Christianity, Islam and Buddhism. For instance, Ambedkar took the path of conversion because he saw no opportunity for liberation within Hinduism. Through his conversion to Buddhism on 14th October, 1956, the revival of Buddhism was seen as a protest to Hinduism. Interestingly, Ambrose Pinto describes 'conversion as subversion of hierarchy' and so he views the attacks on egalitarian religions from insecurity and imagined threats to the economic and social interests of the Hindutvavadis. After conversion, naturally, they adopted a new religious identity. The self-respecting untouchables objected then to being called Harijans and Dalits. Those who embraced Buddhism were proud of being identified/recognized as Buddhists.

But, the Hindutva activists, rejecting their aboriginal status, call the Adivasis as Vanvasis, forest dwellers. The tribals adopted the identity of Adivasi with the formation of the militant Adivasi Mahasabha in 1938. In this identity, there is an assertion that they are the original inhabitants of the country.

Apart from the attempts at developing alternatives to Hinduism, the development of independent religious ideologies helped many others find a religious identity of their own. The followers of Jainism held the Jain identity. The development of Sikhism culminated in Kahn Singh Nabha declaring in 1899 that "we are not Hindus" and formed the identity of the Sikhs as distinct from the Hindus. There are status groups among the Sikhs, but Sikhism does not grant those by birth. To undermine caste distinctions, between 1880 and 1920, the leaders of the Singh Sabha Movement encouraged the people to replace clan names with village names.

Thus, when the identity given to them by others within the Hindu framework is not seen as acceptable, self-respecting members of the non-Hindu communities have developed a self-constructed identity for themselves. The new identity held by the members of caste/tribe/religion group represents a new spirit of egalitarian values.

The above discussion on the course of history since pre-Vedic times reveals that there have been conflicts in intermittent or in silent form between the proponents and the opponents of Brahmanism. The Vedic religion is characterized by sacrificing animals to the fire to maintain the purity of the altar, the chanting of Vedic hymns by the Brahman priests and the perpetuation of graded classes. In the Vedic times, the earlier inhabitant Raksasas, the Licchavi Mahaveer and the Shakya Gautama opposed the sacrifices. During Ashok's time, Brahmanism was paralysed. But Pushyamitra Sung revived Brahmanism and a lot of literature was produced to rule over the Shudratishudra classes. We have a long tradition of the Bhakti movement preaching equality till yesterday. Today, the role of social reform movements in social transformation has been recognized. And, since Phule's time, the resistance has taken a shape and the representation of lower castes in national politics, especially the rise of the Bahujan Samaj Party of the Bahujans in the northern states, has been described as 'India's silent revolution' (Jaffrelot, 2003). This struggle is continued with the adoption of new identities such as Dalit, Buddhist and Adivasi, which contain both a sense of egalitarian values and a spirit of assertion. In the essay, 'Decoding Dalitism: Reflections on Dalit Literature in Maharashtra', S.P. Punalekar perceives the dalit as a category "to dismantle hegemony of the ruling ideas of the socially entrenched groups and classes".

Prominent in the movements of Phule, Shahu, Periyar and Ambedkar against Brahmanism were the issues of caste and gender discrimination as well as the issue of representation in government. From the early decades of the 20th century, as the non-Brahman movement viewed power politics as being on top of its agenda, the real issue of fighting against Brahmanism was relegated to the background, resulting in the disunity of non-Brahmans. Consequently, the dominant castes gradually joined the Hindutva politics in post-independent India and the sole section of untouchable castes were left fighting against the discriminatory practices adopted by both the upper as well as intermediate castes in social life, politics and administration. The problem is that the peasant, artisan, untouchable and adivasi communities belong to the oral tradition and they have become the victims of the written tradition.

The Relevance of the Non-Brahmanic Perspective

The present knowledge of history, religion, culture and society, which has been produced and disseminated, is quite one-sided. In this respect, some observations can be mentioned here. S.M. Michael's paper, 'Conversion, Empowerment and Social Transformation', draws attention to the Brahmanic/Sanskritic world-view of G.S. Ghurye, N.K. Bose and RSS historians, who captured the diversity of cults, deities and practices of the Shudratishudras and Adivasis under the rubric of Hinduism and termed them the Sanskritic Hindus and the biggest converters in India. Surinder Jodhka, in his paper, 'Nation, Anthropology and the Village' (in this volume), has undertaken a review of 'mainstream Indian sociology', which, produced by the Brahmans, offers a biased view emphasizing the unity and solidarity of all social groups within a village, and adds Ambedkar's realistic view of a village as the site of caste oppression. Some social scientists broadly categorized Indian traditions as great and little. For example, the Mother Goddess, which is worshipped by all in every village, has been regarded a part of little tradition. It means the scholars of Indian religions and social history perceived the development of Buddhism and such other sects, the Bhakti traditions and local traditions of the masses as parts of the broader Hinduism and ignored the dimension of opposition in a variety of forms and a history of value conflict. It shows that what is practised by the upper castes becomes a matter of great tradition and the rest, of little tradition. Padma Velaskar, in her paper, 'Educational Stratification, Dominant Ideology and the Reproduction of Disadvantage in India', argues that the dominant ideology of the upper castes and classes have restricted the hopes of equal opportunity of the socially oppressed people and maintained the heights of elitism in education. In his paper, 'Confronting Caste Inequality', Satish Deshpande is critical of joining the anti-Mandal stance by sociologists and the failure of Indian sociology to address the issue of caste inequality in terms of policy perspectives. And based on the data of the NSSO 55th Round and Santosh Goyal's study (1992) on social inequality, Deshpande argues that the sharp caste inequalities have continued in contemporary India. Thus, the hegemony of the upper and the dominant caste Hindus is a challenge to both scholars and socio-political activists of radical ideas to thwart the mainstream ideology.

The distinctive features of the non-Brahmanic perspective can be summed up as under:

1. The perspective has a basis in the philosophy of humanitarian and egalitarian religions such as Buddhism, in the preachings of the saints of the Bhakti movement, Phule's Sarvajanik Satyadharma (universal religion of truth) and the like.
2. It helps in understanding social forces in the struggle against Brahmanism.
3. It focusses on the examination and analysis of social inequalities and the impact of practices on the continuity/marginalization of social groups in other fields of life.

4. It is useful to identify the oppressed/depressed sections of society as the result of the creation and maintenance of hierarchical order based on caste and gender.
5. It seeks the binary domains of knowledge of the Brahmanic and the non-Brahmanic traditions.
6. It provides the framework for understanding the participation of actors across caste, religion, gender in an action and the programme of anti-caste, the programme against gender discrimination, etc.
7. It assumes the continuity of relatively non-discriminatory/egalitarian practices.
8. It believes in the truth of age-old myths, oral traditions also as sources for interpreting history.
9. It believes in the unity of oppressed untouchables, Adivasis, Muslims, Christians, denotified and nomadic communities.

References

Ambedkar, B.R. (1987), *Dr Babasaheb Ambedkar, Writings and Speeches*, Vol. 3, Mumbai, Government of Maharashtra.

—— (1987), *Dr Babasaheb Ambedkar, Writings and Speeches*, Vol. 5, Mumbai, Government of Maharashtra.

—— (1989), *Dr Babasaheb Ambedkar, Writings and Speeches*, Vol. 4, Mumbai, Government of Maharashtra.

—— (1990), *Dr Babasaheb Ambedkar, Writings and Speeches*, Vol. 7, Mumbai, Government of Maharashtra.

Bhagwat, Vidyut and Pratima, Pardeshi (eds.) (1998), *Abrahmani Strivadi Itihaslekhanachya Dishene* (Marathi), Pune: Women's Studies Centre, University of Pune.

Bhandarkar, R.G. (1982), *Vaisnavism, Saivism and Minor Religious Systems*, Pune: Bhandarkar Oriental Research Institute.

Chaudhuri, Nirad C., Madeleine Biardeau, D.F. Pocock and T.N. Madan (2003), *The Hinduism Omnibus*, New Delhi: Oxford University Press.

Daweewarn, Dawee (1982), *Brahmanism in South-East Asia (From the Earliest Time to 1445 A.D.)*, New Delhi: Sterling Publishers Pvt. Ltd.

Geetha, V. and S.V., Rajadurai (1998), *Towards a Non-Brahmin Millennium: From Iyothee Thass to Periyar*, Kolkata: Samya.

Geetha, V. (1999), 'Gender and the Logic of Brahminism: Periyar and the Politics of the Female Body' in Kumkum Sangari and Uma Chakravarty (eds.), *From Myths to Markets: Essays on Gender*, New Delhi: Manohar Publications.

Ghugare, S.B. (1995), *Veerashaivaism in India*, Gadhinglaj (Kolhapur district): Veerabasappa Balasaheb Ghugare.

Ghurye, G.S. (1969), *Caste and Race in India*, Mumbai: Popular Prakashan.

Jaiswal, Suvira (1998), *Caste*, New Delhi: Manohar Publications.

—— (2000) 'Change and Continuity in Brahmanical Religion with Particular Reference to Vaisnava Bhakti', *Social Scientist*, Vol. 29, May-June.

Jaffrelot, Christophe (2003), *India's Silent Revolution*, Delhi: Permanent Black.

Judge, Paramjit (2002), 'Religion, Caste, and Communalism in Punjab', *Sociological Bulletin*, 51 (2), September.

Keer, Dhananjay (1971), *Dr Ambedkar: Life and Mission*, Mumbai: Popular Prakashan (Reprint 1991).

Kosambi, D.D. (1964), *The Culture and Civilisation of Ancient India in Historical Outline*, New Delhi: Vikas Publishing House Pvt. Ltd. (Reprint 2001).

Misra, Padma (1978), *Evolution of the Brahman Class*, Banaras Hindu University, Sanskrit Series, Vol. VIII.

Monier-Williams, M. (1877), *Hinduism*, Calcutta: Susil Gupta (India) Ltd. (Reprint 1951).

Nath, Vijay (2001), 'From Brahmanism to Hinduism: Negotiating the Myth of the Great Tradition', *Social Scientist*, Vol. 29, March-April.

Omvedt, Gail (2002), 'Ambedkar and After: The Dalit Movement in India,' in Ghanshyam Shah (ed.), *Social Movements and the State*, New Delhi: Sage Publications.

Pai, Sudha (2002), *Dalit Assertion and the Unfinished Democratic Revolution: The Bahujan Samaj Party in Uttar Pradesh*, New Delhi: Sage Publications.

Pati, Biswamoy (2001), 'Identity, Hegemony, Resistance: Conversions in Orissa, 1800–2000', *Economic and Political Weekly*, November 3.

Pawar, Jayasingrao (ed.) (2001), *Rajarshi Shahu Smarak Grantha* (Marathi), Kolhapur: Maharashtra Itihas Prabhodhini.

Prakasam, Gnana (1998), *Social Separatism: Scheduled Castes and the Caste System*, Jaipur: Rawat Publications.

Ramaswamy, Sumathi (2001), 'Remains of the Race: Archaeology, Nationalism and the Yearning for Civilisation in the Indus Valley', *The Indian Economic and Social History Review*, 38(2).

Rhy-Davis, T.W. (1903), *Buddhist India*, Delhi: Motilal Banarasidas (Indian Reprint 1997).

Sharma, R.S. (1958), *Sudras in Ancient India*, New Delhi: Allied Publishers Pvt. Ltd.

Shendge, Malati J. (1977), *The Civilized Demons: The Harappans in Rigveda*, New Delhi: Abhinav Publications.

—— (1996), *The Aryans: Facts without Fancy and Fiction*, New Delhi: Abhinav Publications.

Srinivas, M.N. (2003), 'An Obituary on Caste as a System', *Economic and Political Weekly*, February 1–7.

Suryawanshi, K.G. (1984), *Rajarshi Shahu Raja va Manus* (Marathi), Pune: Thokal Prakashan.

Thapar, Romila (1966), *A History of India*, Vol. 1, New Delhi: Penguin Books (Reprint 1990).

Tilak, B.G. (1903), *The Arctic Home in the Vedas* (Reprint 1956), Pune: Tilak Bros.

Trautmann, Thomas R. (1997), *The Aryans and British India*, New Delhi: Vistaar Publications.

Wheeler, J. Talboys (1973), 'India of the Brahmanic Age: With Reference to the Ramayana', Vol. II of the *History of India*, Part I, New Delhi: Cosmos Publications.

Wheeler, Sir Mortimer (1968), *The Indus Civilization*, London: Cambridge University Press.

6 Asprashyeekaran-Dalitization through Ages

SHYAMLAL

The history of the degradation of the upper castes into lower castes (untouchable castes) is very old and dates back to the time of the Vedas. The real social degradation in India, one could say, began with the imposition of the Brahminical code in the country. We shall, therefore, confine our analysis of degradation primarily to the consequences of the breach of the Brahminic code and later on to the imposition of the Muslim and British rules in the country. In the light of theses processes, it is being endeavoured to find out the general pattern of degradation in the Mughal and British periods in India. The major cultural processes which have been already recognized by sociologists and anthropologists are sanskritization, Islamization, westernization and modernization. Many of these processes have been analysed in the context of heterorganic growth in culture. Apart from these processes, however, one major process which was unfortunately never caught the eyes of any sociologist or otherwise is that of 'Asprashyeekaran'. This process, therefore, now needs to be seriously probed into.

I have explained in my two earlier papers the two processes by which the transformation of higher castes into lower untouchable castes is effected. In one of these papers "De-Sanskritization and High Caste Converts into Bhangis"[1] an attempt was made to assess the process of Bhangiization in Rajasthan, according to which a high caste person accepts the membership of the Bhangi (untouchable) caste and thereby lowers his social as well as ritualistic position in the Hindu social order. The study illustrated the radical changes which came about in the style of the life and values of the converts. After giving a detailed account of Bhangiization of the converts, the motivating factors in the Bhangiization, the process of Bhangiization and socio-religious and cultural changes. we had concluded that changes of identity from an upper to lower untouchable caste status explains the course of the social change in the history of Rajasthan.

In another article 'Conversion of Upper Castes into Lower Castes: A Process of Asprashyeekaran (encompassing Untouchability)"[2] again, an attempt was made to assess the process of Asprashyeekaran in India. Accordingly, members of the higher castes individually or in groups became Bhangis, Chamars, Bhambhis, Jatavs, Bairwas, Balahis and so on, losing thereby their high caste names and memberships. The examples of Maru Bhambhis, Jata Bhambhis and Charnia Bhambhis of Rajasthan were cited in this connection in the paper. They were originally Rajputs, Brahmins, Jats and Charans, but have been incorporated into Chamar caste-folds. Similarly, the Pariahs, the Mal Paharis, and the Karagas of South India, Jatiya/Chamars of Uttar Pradesh and Bihar, the Kadars of West Bengal were reduced to the status of untouchables because of their poor economic conditions, landlessness and dependence on others for their livelihood. They were originally tribals.

Indian sociologists and anthropologists today take much interest in studying family, religion and also caste politics, but not in the process of the Asprashyeekaran (or Dalitization). The following observations of Prabhati Mukherjee on untouchables may be noted in this regard:

> It is only from the beginning of the twentieth century that serious attempts are being made to study scientifically the position of untouchables. While some readily come forward to study their contemporary position (to name only a few like Bailey, Bose, Briggs, Cohn, Freedaman, Fuchs, Lynch, Mancher, Moffat, etc.). Some amount of hesitation and reluctance is noticed among Indologists and historians to study the past history of the untouchables. It seems as if the volume and magnitude of the task acts as a deterrent to a systematic study of the issue involved. [3]

With this view in mind, the present study attempts to assess the process of Asprashyeekaran in Hindu society.

Objectives of the Study

The phenomenon of conversion from higher castes to the lower untouchable castes and the change of the caste identity provided this author an important field of research so far unexplored by sociologists, anthropologists or ethnographers. The broad objectives of the present study may by laid down as under:

(i) To examine the factors responsible for degradation and the socio-religious principles involved.
(ii) To give a historical review, accompanied by the sociological analysis, and provide a comparative and critical study of the degraded castes.
(iii) To evaluate the process of degradation as to what activated Asprashyeekaran (which may also be termed as 'Dalitization') in India.
(iv) To present the issue to serious sociologists, anthropologists and cultural historians for analysing social change with the help of the concepts like Bhangiization and Asprasheyeekaran in India.

Cultural Rigidity of the Caste System and Asprashyeekaran

Since the present study deals with the phenomenon of Asprashyeekaran, it is better to state at the very outset as to how untouchability has been defined. According to Mukherjee,[4] the primary attributes of the untouchables are: (i) they are asprasyas (untouchables) to the caste-Hindus, and (ii) their segregation into the distinct hamlets, non-commensality and non-connubiality with the caste-Hindus. The term 'untouchability' however is somewhat confusing as it may be temporary or permanent. For the present study, it has been treated as a permanent phenomenon.

The socio-historical genesis and development of untouchability in India has been studied by Mukherjee and we shall be relying mainly on her writings in our discussion of the degradation of the 'Dwijas' (twice-born) from the times of Rigveda. Mukherjee has given very authentic description of the degradation of the Dwijas and her study is based on the materials collected mainly from the Brahminical sources, covering a period of about 2,500 years. Apart from those texts which are primarily sacred in character, greater reliance was placed on the evidences obtained from lexicons like Nirukta, Grammars of Panini and Patanjali, the Arthasastra of Kautilya, accounts of Greek travellers and epigraphic materials.[5] Besides the Brahiminical sources, Mukherjee has also made use of the Jain and Buddhist sources. The Buddhist ideology was a serious challenge and posed a greater threat than the Jain ideology to Brahminical viewpoint.

The Brahminical literature, although of the immense historical importance, may prove too much to the cope with, at this stage of the study. Moreover, the main purpose of the study is to trace the origin of degradation. On the basis of the Brahminical literature, one has to ask the question: Who writes for whom? Furthermore, it is always uncertain whether the texts portrayed the 'ideal' or the 'real' situation existing in the society.[6] While dealing with these issues, Mukherjee concluded: "Nevertheless, one can probably draw a valid inference regarding the real situation by accepting the 'ideal' situation as maximizing the trend of a particular phenomenon. The limit thus indicated may refer to the positive or the negative aspect of the phenomenon. What, however, is not easy while studying the degradation of Dwijas for describing the process of Asprashyeekaran is to arrange the available information under well-demarcated phases."[7] What we have done, therefore, is to arrange the incidents according to landmarks in the accounts of untouchables as recorded in these texts. We have collected as much material as is available and have relied more on the recorded development of the untouchables than on otherwise.

We shall make efforts to find out whether any instances of degradation of Dwijas were at all in existence during the ancient period. Instances of degradation of higher castes during the ancient period have been many. Mukherjee reports such cases. She writers: "... not only with regard to the candalas, but some other groups also, which enjoyed a better position previously, there was a general downward movement in the social hierarchy."[8] She further adds: "For instance, the Nisadas were regarded by some as belonging to the Vaisya varna ... and the Rathakaras (or Ugra) were Dwijas, i.e., they belonged to the cluster of the first three varnas ... . Eventually, the two groups went even lower down in the varna hierarchy."[9]

Thus, the degradation of Dwijas from ancient period onward depicts the life of degraded peoples as untouchables. Referring to the castes in this context, Mukherjee says:

> What, however, is not clear is why sutas, magadhas, vaidehkas and ayogavas lost their erstwhile prestigious and independent status in the society. A suta, while following almost similar occupations like those of ksattr, was downgraded as a candala. In some respects, suta enjoyed a better position in the sense that he was closely linked up with the court that also had reputation of being a brave warrior.

> Similarly, from being traders, the magadhas and the vaidehkas now became the same as canadalas. One may probably explain their downward movement in the social hierarchy from the antipathy to the traders from the time of the Rgveda. And possibly the other job of a vaidehka as a harem-attendant was not a very honorable one either. For the ayogavas, again, is hard to account for their degradation … . In any case, now, all of them were reduced to the category of candalas.[10]

Thus, we find from the foregoing literature that the number of degraded persons mingling with the untouchables category increased gradually.

According to the varna model, untouchables are outside the caste system and contact with them pollutes members of other four varnas. Under Manu's code, these people must eat the half-chewed food of the caste-Hindus. The words "Nichiohta-mann bataryam (x125)" convey the sense of the remnant of food.[11] The higher-caste Hindus are prohibited from taking food with the people affected by institution of untouchability. But, if the cases of breach of socio-religious norms by upper-caste persons are taken into account, one can easily understand how people were punished for violating them.

With these realities, Mukherjee rightly stated about the degradation of the Brahmins in India:

> The Vindhya forest is mentioned as the dwelling place for the kiratas, sabaras, pulindas, candalas and matangas. Once upon a time the people living there were referred to as kiratas only. The name of the son of a pulinda was Matanga who seams to have been their leader. The same source also reveals the presence of several Bhahmanas among them, because they accepted cooked rice from the pulindas which probably degraded them to the same status. These Brahamanas gave up the study of the Vedas, pious and upright life befitting Brahmana, and took the life of the kiratas instead. Therefore, in that secluded, fearful and dense forest infested with wild beasts lived the kiratas and those 'fallen Brahmanas' Matangas, their leaders roamed the forest, cruel and arrogant.[12]

Thus, the degradation of Brahmins, as described in Dasa Kumar Charita and Jatakas, supplies some information about the location of where different categories of degraded peoples lived and what factors were responsible for their degradation. In this way, we may be able to find out who the degraded untouchables were and where they lived. The Buddhist birth stories, called 'Jatakas', written in Pali, reflect mainly the degradation of the Brahamins to Mlechha (i.e., low untouchable caste). Mukherjee also narrates an incident from the Jatakas in which 16,000 Brahmins had to leave their own country and go to Medya desa (Madhya desa or Mlechha desa), because they took leftover food from the candalas.[13] Not only the Brahamins, but also Kshtriyas were reduced to the status of the untouchables.[14] And, therefore, we can safely draw a conclusion that many historically known untouchables were at one time Brahmins and the Kshatriyas.

In order to support the above conclusion from the Brahminical and Buddhist sources, we can in addition examine other evidences also. In his book, *India: From Primitive Communism to Slavery* (1949), S.A. Dange has mentioned that the Brahmins were also reduced to the status of untouchables under the following circumstances:

> In places where there was famine and the drought, the proud ruling class Brahmins turned to the hated Chandalas in their forest retreat to ask for food, and it had become the privilege of conquered enslaved Chandalas, to preach morality to the holy Vishwamitra of conquering Aryas not to resort to eating the carcass of a dead dog to preserve his own life.[15]

Other studies have also revealed that degradation is not just a recent phenomenon in India but was also present in ancient time. The predominance of the ritual pollution and purity in social and religious life, which were characteristics of the traditional society, introduced the element of degradation. Rights and liberties against the violation of Varna Dharma were not allowed to groups and to individuals. The system was rigid rather than the flexible. Of this system, R.B. Tripathy writes:

> Gradually as the Hindu varna system grew fashionable, strong strict measures were also adopted to enforce it. Social inter-course and inter-marriages were prohibited. Society became strictly endogamous and was divided into water-tight compartment. Those who violated the law of endogamy were ex-communicated and were forced to live outside the community. In consequence they had no option other than the low and degrading occupations.[16]

To the question as to why the upper caste people were degraded in the traditional society, Tripathy answers:

> In Puranic period, i.e., 3rd century A.D. to 1000 A.D., due to certain economic forces the people belonging to higher castes indulged in lower occupations and naturally they were declared as the outcastes and once they lost their position it was not possible for them it regain it.[17]

Thus, it is evident that there are several factors to explain as to why these groups of people became untouchables. One of the most important factors was ritual purity and pollution. Haimendorf has supported this factor when he says: The reasons put forward as to why these particular upper castes became untouchables, is usually that of ritual purity and pollution. The untouchables are ritually impure because they follow an unclean profession or the vice versa."[18] It is clear that such changes have been taking place right from the Vedic times, the process known as Asprashyeekaran in the contemporary socio-religious realities existed in traditional India as well.

Impact of Muslim Invaders and Rulers of India: Historicity of Asprashyeekaran

We have attempted to understand the degradation from traditional value system, namely, the Brahminical viewpoint. We should probe further into Sanskrit literature alone. We have, therefore, made maximum use of historical findings. In Indian history, foreign invasions, local waves of conquest famines, epidemics, floods and other natural man-made calamities added to the number of the untouchables. Due to this, a new era of social degradation began. During the course of centuries, degradation of high-caste Hindus increased all over India. This degradation was fairly common and presents some curious features. There were interesting developments, which show that the Hindu society had reached the crossroads. It will suffice to quote here some historical instances and authoritative comments in order to show that high-caste persons were reduced to untouchables at the beginning of the Muslim and British eras.

S.V. Ketkar,[19] for example, while analysing the caste systems and social life of the people in India, during the 3rd century, found that a person could not go into higher castes but could move down from his high status. He could lose his caste status and could mingle with persons of the lower castes. He further says, there were many castes, which suffered in status on account of their mixing with the low castes or neglect of sacred rituals. Ketkar's statement indicates that Ashprashyeekaran is not just a recent phenomenon in India. On the contrary, if was present during all the ages of Indian history.

From the day India became a target of the Muslim invaders, its people began to be enslaved in droves to be sold in foreign lands or employed in various menial or lowly jobs within the country. Indeed, from the days of Mohammad bin Qasim in the 8th century AD, enslavement, distribution and sale of Hindu prisoners was systematically practised by the Muslim invaders and rulers of India. In these years and centuries of oppression, they (Hindu prisoners) were reduced to the status of untouchable castes. We get the following account of degradation of Rajput zamindars, peasants, etc., during the medieval era in K.S. Lal's book *Muslim Slave Systems in Medieval India*:

> To be brief, many zamindars and peasants escaped into the forests because of fear of defeat and enslavement, but in course of time, they were reduced to the position of Scheduled Castes, Scheduled Tribes and Backward Classes. For example, many Parihars and Parmars, once belonged to the proud Rajput castes, are now included in lower castes. So are the 'Rajputs' counted as Backward Classes in South India. Take the case of the Thaaru women in the Tarai region as described by Hugh and Colleen Gantzer.[20]

To the question, why the untouchable population increased all over India, Lal answers:

> 'One has to travel through the country like Hugh and Collen Gantzer to meet such types, almost everywhere. Today, the SC/ST and OBC (Other Backward Classes) all account 50 per cent of the population of India. This staggering high figure has been reached because of the historical forces operating in the medieval times primarily. Muslim rule spread all over the country and resistance to it by the Hindus also remained wide spread, jungles abounded throughout the vast land from Gujarat to Bengal and Kashmir to Kanyakumari and flight into them was the safeguard. That is how the SC/ST people are found in every state in large numbers.[21]

The review of the position of slaves in the neighbouring countries – Nepal and Bhutan – from historical perspective, reveals that they are counted among the untouchables. Bhagwan Das writes: "Slaves doing impure work gradually merged with the Chandalas. Descendants of slaves in Nepal and Bhutan are counted among the untouchables."[22]

Thus, a potent source of degradation in the pre-British India was demotion of the defeated warrior castes into low untouchable castes. Such a situation was not limited to any particular part of India, but characterized the system everywhere. In order to humiliate the captives, they were employed in despised occupations like sweeping, latrine cleaning, tanning, shoemaking, weaving, washing clothes, etc. Once, they did so or accepted these unclean occupation, they were no longer accepted by their castemen. The captive groups, then, had socialize their ritual and lifestyle and be known as the untouchable castes.

A few studies and reports, which have been undertaken to study this process tend to substantiate this trend of Asprashyeekaran. The origin of the Bhangi caste is described by B. Pathak as follows:

> The Muslim had brought with them some women who used the Burqua (veil) to cover their faces and they did not like to defecate in the open. The bucket privies were, therefore, designed and constructed for their defecation in Purdah. Those made captives were forced to clean the latrines like bucket privies and throw the night soil at places. After those captives were released, they were not accepted by their castemen and, hence, they formed a separate caste of Bhangis who were renamed as Mehtar by emperor Akbar.[23]

Similarly, according to D.D. Chaturvedi,[24] Kshatriyas and Bhangis have descended from the same source. For, he says, one notices a marked similarities between them. He has cited the following similarities: Bhangi: Vas, Vasvar, Bir Gujar, Bhadwaris, Bisen,, Mehtar: Bundelia, Chandal, Chauhan, Nado, Yaduvanshi, Kachhwaha, Kinwar, Thakur. Rajput: (99) Bundela (48) Bargujar Panna (222) Pann (295) Dajoha or Yaduvanshi Gujar Panna (248) Raut.

The first phase of sanskritization started with the census operations in the last quarter of the 19th century. In some sections, census was also considered to be an excellent opportunity for the improvement of a caste's social standing. On the other hand, Mead and Macgregor, O'Malley, Desai and others also have referred to the process of Asprashyeekaran in census reports. It was the natural for an ICS ethnographer to be struck by this peculiar social phenomenon. There was separate account of degradation in the census reports. The merger of the upper castes into lower castes was termed as 'degradation' or 'admission of outsider into lower castes'.

Some ideas of social degradation, change of identity and admission of higher caste into the lower castes may be obtained from the following statement given by O'Malley in the Census of India report (1991, Bengal, Bihar, Orissa and Sikkim) about the Bhangi caste of India. O'Malley writes:

> Obviously, the castes engaged in the disposal of human excreta were not at all divergent of a single caste."[25]
>
> Regarding the same problem, Stanley Rice writes:
>
> Therefore, not only Kshatriyas, but also those who were engaged in cleaning night soil since ancient time ... and also those who were made captives in wars ... . In India ... are Bhangis and Mehtars of today.[26]

This has also been realized by M.R. Malkani, who writes: "The Bhangis of today are those people who were warriors and made captives after they fell to the enemy."[27]

If these views of scholars are accepted, we can draw conclusion that Bhangis were at one time Kshatriyas.

Processes identical to those mentioned above have also been pointed out by Ghanshyam Shah, Jwala Prasad Mishra and Kesington. A reference to social degradation of Rajputs in Gujarat in the 16th and 18th centuries during the Mughal period quoted from the Gazetteer of the Bombay Presidency, 1879 by Ghanshyam Shah says:

> ... during the Mughal period, Bhils gave asylum to some defeated Rajputs rulers. During their stay, the guests married their hosts' daughters. Therefore, their generation, a mixture of Bhils and Rajputs, is considered as half caste, called Kolis.[28]

J.P. Mishra reports a similar case of degradation of Rajputs to a low untouchable caste in Orissa. He writes:

> In 1272, during the thirteenth century (Samvat-1284) Mohd. Gajnavi attacked on 'Anhalwada' Gujarat. Chandra Rao was the ruler. Chandra Rao was badly defeated by Gajnavi. Even then, Gajnavi continued his attacked. Under these socio-political conditions the defeated Solankis had to move to some other places. In Orissa, they were settled down permanently near the historical temples – Jagannath. The Jagannath area of Orissa was now for it's making of cotton cloth. The stranded people were forced to take to accept weaving occupation, as a means of earning their livelihood. In course of time, Solanki Rajputs assumed a new low caste designation 'Weaver' (untouchable caste) and the original caste name 'Rajput' disappeared in practice.[29]

We also get the following account of the degradation of Rajputs in the Hoshiarpur district, Punjab in report by Kesington, published under Authority of the Punjab Government in 1883: "Ethnologically, the most interesting of the people are the Mahtons, who were originally Rajputs, but have long since degraded in the social scale, owing to their customs of making Karewa marriages with widows.[30]

Many similar instances could be reproduced from the studies of sociologists, historians and the ethnographers on various aspects of caste, which also substantiate the process of the Aspreashyeekaran.

Breach of Traditional Norms and Asprashyeekaran

We have commented at some length various ways through which higher-caste Hindus were degraded to low untouchable castes in the traditional Indian society. We have stressed the point that within the traditional systems there was an increase in the untouchable population and we shall pursue this further in this section.

The laws framed by Brahmin law-makers like Manu, Narada, Vasistha and Yajnvalkya were strictly enforced by the Hindu rulers who ruled through caste and village heads. Even persons who had taken water from the hands of certain discarded persons lost their caste status. Ghanshyam Shah, quoting from the Gazetteer of the Bombay Presidency, 1879, refers to such instances of Asprashyeekaran in Bombay Presidency. He writes: "Those Rajputs who had taken water from the hands of Bhil women in Gujarat, had been outcaste and lost caste status."[31]

Not only the daily livelihood means, namely, water and food, even the touch of an untouchable caste person caused degradation. Quoting Barbosa, on this point, Hutton writes: "... women touched by a Pulayah, i.e., of the lowest untouchable caste, was outcaste and had to leave her house, for fear otherwise of polluting her family."[32] Such instances are quite common in the Indian society, and it is presumed that no caste would be an exception to this rule.

The association of higher-caste Hindus with the Muslims lowered their prestige, position and caste status. In some castes, it also led to their being outcaste and eventually merging with untouchable groups. Throughout the

Muslim regime, Hindus continued to suffer from the disabilities and difficulties imposed in the name of the Dharmic (religious) law. These practices of upper-caste Hindus led to an increase in the untouchable population all over India. Bhagwan Das summarize the causes for this rapid growth as follows:

> After the fall of Buddhism, those who continued to follow their religion were also treated as untouchables. Any Hindu associating freely with the Muslim was also considered an outcaste and joined the ranks of lower caste and untouchables. Wars, famines, epidemics, floods and other natural and man-made calamities added to the number of untouchables.[33]

We learn from Srotriya Pandit Chhote Lal Sharma's book *Jati Anvensan* (1914) that when the Brahmins of Central India breached the sacred rituals, rites and deeds, their actions roused the wrath of the entire Brahmin caste. In Madhya Pradesh and Maharashtra, for instance, the Brahmins who breached the code of Manu, resulted in their being outcaste. Those outcaste Brahmins were known as 'Klanki Brahmins'.[34] They had no connection with the parent caste and formed a new separate lower caste of their own. In this connection, one scholar has described eight possible reasons for degradation. These are as follows:

(i) On the suspicion that a new-born child was the result of illicit relation with a Muslim.
(ii) Has mingled with untouchable castes.
(iii) Received offering made at public place of all castes – high and low.
(iv) Took alms from prohibited castes.
(v) On committing heinous crime.
(vi) On suspicion about the caste origin of a new-born child or born by rape.
(vii) Solely engaged in the cultivation of heinous agricultural product and plantation.
(viii) Engaged in degraded low occupations.

These instances support the view that degradation to lower castes was caused by the cultural rigidity of the caste system. A major cause behind degradation, therefore, might have been the violation of the social and religious norms. Though there might also be other factors like economic constraints and crises, etc. However, the groups degraded were from upper castes for whom the psychological appeal of belonging to the upper strata of society must have been very strong. The main structural deprivations here were those of the rights and liberties against the dharmic (religious) law. In all the traditional societies, where the system of social stratification is closed and there are legimate structural means to move down in social hierarchy, the breach of norms or of customs and rituals could lead to such move downwards.

With some variations, the process of Asprashyeekaran continued during the British rule in India. Even today, we may observe the process in Indian society. In Gujarat, Audhich and Nagar Brahmins are sociological cases of Asprashyeekaran. Govind Bhai H. Desai[35] (1911), the then Superintendent of Census Operations, Baroda, observed that Parajia Brahmins were originally Audhich Brahmins and were living in village known as Ismaliya. Later on, they moved to the another village, namely, Paroj near Junagarh. Here, they became the priests of Ahirs and Charans. Not only this, they started eating with them, which were totally antithetical to their own group. As a result, the Parajia Audhich Brahmins were degraded. In course of time they became a distinct 'endogamous group'.

Of the Nagar Brahmins, Desai[36] (1911) writes that they accepted the low caste jobs like acting as fiddlers of female singers. The norms of not allowing the Brahmins to do polluted and degrading work resulted in the lowering of the high social position of Nagar Brahmins. They were reduced to the status of musician (untouchables) and segragated from the Nagar caste. In this connection, the observations made by M.N. Srinivas may be noted: "... throughout history of caste new caste groups arose as a result of such fission from the parent group body."[37]

Sharma's and Desai's instances illustrate the degradation which occurred in the social position of the Brahmins when they breached the mores, rituals and beliefs of their own groups. Socio-religious factors were responsible for the degradation of a large number of Brahmins in Madhya Pradesh, Maharashtra and Gujarat to untouchable castes as it had happened among Bhangis, Balahis, Meghwals, Bairwa and so on.

A caste has its own image and identity on the basis of which it considers itself distinct from other castes – historically, socio-culturally and nominalistically. It tenaciously sticks to and justifies this identity in spite of various changes taking places. It is this sense of identity which is the basis for survival of the caste. However, during times of hardship, distress and economic crisis, caste members may be forced to do unpleasant work. The Rajasthani Gancha, from Nagaur, Didwana, Ajmer and Pushkar (all in Rajasthan), for instance, are another case of Bhangiization. As degraded Bhangis (untouchables), they offer a unique example in Rajasthan. In this connection, when we talked to some of the old Gancha Bhangi informants about their conversion, they narrated that nearly four of five centuries ago their forefathers converted Gancha by caste and their main traditional occupation was to prepare baskets and other domestic articles for bamboo.

Among the major problems of Gancha, special mention may be made of their poor earning from the traditional occupations which seems to be too small to maintain a family of five or six persons. This was one of the most serious problems which their forefathers faced. Thus, they were forced by economic constraints to do dirty, unpleasant polluted and degrading work like scavenging. As a result of this, they were reduced to the status of Bhangis. In course of time, they became a distinct endogamous caste group. At present, along with the Bhangis, the Gancha Bhangis, both men and women, are employed in various Nagar Palikas of Rajasthan. They are engaged to sweep and clean roads and drainages. They are also engaged privately to remove garbage and to clean latrines.

The Gancha Bhangis are not found at all in many towns and are very few in other towns. According to 1971 census, the population of Gancha Bhangis in Rajasthan was 2,076. Out of these, there were 1,063 males and 1,013 females. The Gancha Bhangis and their family members are treated as Bhangis both by caste-Hindus and non-Hindus. They are not allowed to sit, dine or mix with clean castes or occupational groups. They do not have social interaction with their Bhangi counterparts except at the job site. The Gancha Bhangis, do not invite the Bhangis on the occasion of marriage, festivals, etc. Nor are they invited on such occasions by the Bhangis. The Gancha Bhangis do not eat from the hands of Bhangis but Bhangis eat from their hand. The Gancha Bhangis too have not developed any socially recognized commersal relation with Bhangis. This situation had led to occasional quarrels among them.

As social scientist we have also heard and observed such situations minutely and have found that Gancha Bhangis demonstrate a sense of superiority although they are in a minority. We think this prevailing situation of conflict among the Bhangis and Gancha Bhangis is unique and needs a detailed scientific study for a full picture of their cultural complexities.

Not only the Gancha caste, but even the tribals have also engaged in sweeping roads etc. The tribals were formerly not connected at all with cleaning the roads and drainage, as the description of tribals in anthropological literature shows. Jha supplies some important information about the tribal scavengers in Bihar, where different categories of tribal groups sweep and clean the roads. From that we may be able to find out why they accepted this lowest type of work.

The city of Ranchi was a small tribal village before 1834. After the establishment of the British administration, Christian missionaries came to India, and in 1845 arrived in Ranchi and in less than 50 years they turned it into the Cathedral headquarters of Christian churches. The history of the Ranchi city took a new turn when the Ranchi Municipality was established in 1869. It is pertinent to mention here that the forefathers of the Bhangis of Ranchi came from Rajasthan along with their masters and settled down here along with them. They had been brought by their masters to serve at their houses, clean the night soil and remove the garbage from the streets and courtyard. This is why, when the Ranchi Municipality was established in 1869, there was not a single Bhangi in the Municipality. In 1883, some of the migrated Rajasthani Bhangis were employed as scavengers to carry the night soil and to clean the service latrines.

In the meantime, the government agencies wanted to appoint tribal men and women to work as scavengers in the government offices as well as in the Ranchi Municipality, but the tribals refused to serve as Bhangis or Mehtar to carry the night soil. Thus, the tribals maintained a social distance from the Rajasthani Bhangis and considered themselves above them. But, the situation took a new turn after India's independence when some tribals were appointed by Ranchi Municipal Corporation (RMC) to clear the drainage and roads. M. Jha, describing the problems of the Bhangis in Ranchi, Chotanagpur found that "It is very interesting to note that being a tribal city, located in the midst of tribal population of Chotanagpur, the strength of the tribal scavengers in Ranchi Municipal Corporation presently is only 227 out of the 661 scavengers."[38]

When we look at the scavengers of the Municipal Corporation of Patna, the capital of Bihar, the composition of the scavengers is different. The present strength of scavengers (category I, Rs 775–1,025) under PMC is 4,208.[39] Out of this, there are 2,118 scheduled caste male and 1,225 female scavengers. Besides this strength of SC scavengers, there are nine tribal scavengers (all male), 600 other backward classes scavengers (584 male and 16 female) and 226 general caste scavengers (221 male and 5 female) respectively.

Unemployment among both educated/uneducated Indian youth, overgrowth of population, economic crisis, hardships and constraints, limited number of job opportunities in government sectors – are all significant factors in contributing to decline in prestige of purely traditional occupations. Similar conditions exist in other developing countries but what is unique to the Indian situation is that all those higher castes/tribes, which have accepted scavenging jobs as the primary source of their income, for instance, the Adivasis of Bihar, are poor and their condition is hardly better than that of the Bhangis. A scavenging job provides not only a source of livelihood but economic security also. It would be significant to add here that in sweeping work particularly, no skill is required and this appears to have attracted the tribals, other backward classes and even higher-caste Hindus to accept this work in Nagar Palikas, Railways and some other government organizations.[40]

From the above the picture that emerges is that Asprashyeekaran has been a major process of social change in Indian history and it has occurred in every part of the Indian subcontinent. It may have been more active at some period than at others and some castes are more mingled than the others, but there is no doubt that the process has been universal.

Notes

1. For details, see my article, "De-Sanskritization and High Caste Converts into Bhangis", *Indian Journal of Social Work (IJSW)*, Vol. VLLII, No. 2, April 1992. Also see my book, *The Bhangi*, Popular Prakashan, 1992, p. 59 and "Conversion to Lower Caste Common in Rajasthan". *The Times of India*, New Delhi, May 16, 1994, p. 9.
2. For details, also see my "Origin of Bhangis: A Hypothesis" in *Eastern Anthropologist*, Vol. 44, No. 2, 1991 and "Conversion of the Upper Castes into Lower Castes: A Process of Asprashyeekaran (Encompassing Untouchability) in *IJWS*, Vol. 57, No. 2, 1996.
3. Prabhati Mukherjee, *Beyond the Four Varna: The Untouchables in India*, Delhi: Motilal Banarsidas, 1988, p. 12.
4. Ibid., p. 14.
5. Ibid.
6. Ibid., p. 15.
7. Ibid.
8. Ibid., p. 41.
9. Ibid., pp. 41–42.
10. Ibid., p. 62.
11. P.T. Borale, *Segregation and Degradation in India: A Sociological Study*, Bombay: Manaktala, 1968, p. 212.
12. Mukherjee, op. cit., p. 67.
13. Ibid.
14. Borale, op. cit., p. 37.
15. S.A. Dange, quoted by Borale, p. 61.
16. R.B. Tripathi, *Dalits: A Sub-human Society*, New Delhi: Ashish Publishing House, 1994, p. 7.
17. Ibid., p. 4.
18. Haimendorf, quoted by Mukherjee, p. 13.

19. S.V. Ketkar, *The History of Caste in India*, Vol. I, Ithaca: Mesoers Taylor and Carpenter, 1909, p. 108.
20. K.S. Lal, *Muslim Slave System in Medieval India*, New Delhi: Aditya Prakashan, p. 64.
21. Ibid., p. 66.
22. Bhagwan Das, "Socio-Economic Problems of Dalits" in *Dalit Solidarity* by Bhagwan Dass and James Massey (eds.), Delhi: ISPCK, 1995, p. 78.
23. Bindeshwar Pathak, *Road to Freedom: A Sociological Study of the Abolition of Scavenging in India*, New Delhi: Motilal Banarsidass Publishers, 1991, p. 38.
24. D.D. Chaturvedi, quoted by Amritlal Nagar, *Nachyo Bahut Gopal*, Delhi: Rajpal and Sons, 1990, p. 9.
25. L.S.S.O. Malley, quoted by Bindeshwar Pathak, p. 38.
26. Stanley Rice, quoted by Amritlal Nagar, p. 9.
27. M.R. Malkani, Report of the Scavenging Conditions Enquiry Committee, Delhi: Ministry of Home Affairs, Government of India.
28. Ghanshyam Shah, *Caste Association and Political Process in Gujarat*, Bombay: Popular Prakashan, 1975, p. 10.
29. Jwala Prasad Mishra, *Jati Bhaskar*, Bombay: Venkteshwar Steam Mudran Yantralai, Samvat 1829, p. 200.
30. Gazetteer of Hoshiarpur District 1883–84. Compiled and published under the authority of Punjab Government, Lahore. The Civil and Military Gazetteers Press, Chapter III, D. Tribes and Castes, Mahtons, p. 60.
31. Ghanshyam Shah, *Caste Association and the Political Process in Gujarat*, Bombay: Popular Prakashan, 1975, p. 11.
32. J.H. Hutton, *Caste in India*, II Edition, London: Oxford University Press, 1951, p. 78.
33. Bhagwan Das, op. cit., p. 46.
34. C.L. Sharma, *Jatil Anvensan*, Part I, Phulera, H.D., V.V. Mandal, Samvant 1971, p. 156.
35. Govind Bhai H. Desai, *Census of India*, 1911, Vol. XVI, Baroda, Part I, Report Bombay, printed at the Times Press, 1911, p. 245.
36. Ibid., p. 245.
37. M.N. Srinivas, *Social Change in the Modern India*, New Delhi: Orient Longman, 1977, p. 30.
38. Census of India, 1971, Rajasthan Series 18, Rajasthan Part V, Special Tables and Notes on Scheduled Castes and Tribes, p. 2, S. No. 36.
39. M. Jha, "Problems of Scavengers of a Tribal City: A Case Study of Ranchi, Chota Nagpur", *Man in Asia*, Vol. VII, No. 2, 1994, pp. 3–9.
40. Ibid., p. 5.

7 The Hindi Literary World and Dalit Assertion

A Western Perspective

HEINZ WERNER WESSLER

Kalidasa and the Pariah

Even a common taxi driver in some of India's fast growing metropolitan cities knows something about the strange German occupation with indology and often interprets it in terms of a somehow natural affinity between India and Germany. Max Mueller's contributions to his field of research, particularly to Vedic studies, may actually be studied only exceptionally, but Mueller's national identity and his background in German indology – even though he was employed in England most of his academic life – are widely perceived as such and sponsor the extraordinary reputation of German indological studies in India.

The sacrilegious and sinful act of publishing the mantras of the Rigveda, kept secret for thousands of years from anyone considered not twice-born, is long forgiven by the great majority of the keepers of this tradition, the Brahman orthodoxy. Remains Max Mueller's undisturbed fame – a philologist, born outside of the holy continent of *Bharatavarsa* (i.e., the Indian subcontinent), therefore by definition a *mleccha*, which means "foreigner" or "Indian outcaste"[1] according to classical religious law (*Dharmasastra*), whatever good he may have done – who never touched Indian soil – Max Mueller, a non-Hindu highly respected in Hindu society, who has made public the most auspicious piece of sacred literature for any Hindu, whatever creed he may follow and whatever ritual tradition may be his own within the multitude of creeds and religious practices within what is widely perceived as a single religion, called Hinduism.

The tremendous impact of translations of classical Sanskrit fine literature on the German intelligentsia before and after the year 1800 is well known – starting with Kalidasa's *Shakuntalam* into English (by William Jones) and then into German (by Georg Forster) in the 1780s, continuing to Arthur Schopenhauer's reception of the *Oupekhnat* – the Latin translation of a selection of Upanishads first translated into Persian on Dara Shuko's incentive, elder brother of the famous Moghul ruler Aurangzeb. German romanticism with its India-oriented undercurrent was particularly deeply influenced by Friedrich von Schlegel's book *On the Language and the Wisdom of the Indians* published in its original German version 1808 – the language of Sanskrit and the wisdom it is supposed to preserve from a bygone glorious past.

Academic scholars started to perceive the riches of classical Sanskrit and its literature and the relation between India and Europe through this language and the culture it once incorporated. The study of old Indian languages – including Pali and Prakrit – soon became institutionalized on the academic level in the reactionary epoch following the final defeat of Napoleon during the battle of Waterloo and the following conference of Vienna, which paved the way to a restoration of the multitude of kingdoms and fiefdoms in Germany. Even though politically reactionary, it was an epoch open to the discovery of new fields of knowledge and research, of the founding of universities and chairs, particularly in the state of Prussia.

Even though institutionally unrelated to colonial ambitions as of the then East India Company rule, it can hardly be successfully argued that the 19th century German indology was not part of an imperialist approach to the East aiming at mapping the orient, defining and owning of its cultural heritage. The growing awareness of the conditioned nature of oriental research has to be kept in mind, particularly the strong Brahmanical orientation of German indology as a result of its occupation with Sanskrit text sources.

Friedrich von Schlegel's brother August Wilhelm became the first-ever Professor for Oriental Languages with special regard to Sanskrit in Europe in 1818, when the University of Bonn – the small town going back to a Roman military camp at the shores of the Rhine river – had become part of the Prussian state in 1815 – was founded in the same year. Berlin and other universities followed soon after. The year 1818 therefore marks the beginning of the tradition of German indology. Most of the about 15 small departments and institutes of indological learning existing today in Germany go back to the 19th century with their still strong focus on Sanskrit, Pali and Prakrit literature. In the meantime, modern Indian languages and their rich literature have also been introduced and studied at almost all these places, but usually Sanskrit comes first – with few exceptions to this rule.

The enthusiasm of one of the most renowned German men of letters, Johann Wolfgang von Goethe, after reading the translation of *Abhijnanasakuntalam natakam,* is well known. It is also known, how the Indian conception of drama and particularly the role of the *sutradhara* stimulated his addition of the first scene in his most famous drama "Faust".

It is however less known that the same Goethe has also worked on an issue that was hardly known even then, at least not in the 1820s, the outcast issue. The result of his recognition of untouchability as a feature of Indian society led him to the creation of his ballad "The Prayer of the Pariah" *(Weimarer Ausgabe I,3;9).*

Edel sind wir nicht zu nennen.
Denn das Schlechte, das gehort uns,
Und was andre todlich kennen,
Das alleine, das vermehrt uns.

[We are not to be called noble.
'Cause the evil, this is ours,
And what others know as deadly,
This alone, this continues us.]

The fascination of the untouchable is so strong, because untouchability is somehow unparalleled in the European tradition and therefore alien to occidental consciousness. What is alien is attractive, particularly when it relates to the Orient, which since antiquity was perceived as a perfect space for projection of all sorts, including the projection of an Aryan civilization representing an original and somehow ideal state of mankind and society. Untouchability is, as Goethe's poem may demonstrate, a kind of anti-projection to the Brahman focus on purity.

Nevertheless, it was not at all Goethe's bad will, but an honest effort to internalize an imagined Paria's identity in his ballad, probably inspired by Michael Beer's (1800–1833) tragedy *The Paria*, which was performed in the Prussian King's Theatre in Berlin in 1823.

Anyway, in the 1820s, even though not in detail, the peculiar hierarchical character of Hindu society with its ritual and sacral dimensions was already known and perceived. And, together with this, the state of the outcast as an untouchable together with the term *Paria*, which was already well established and used as metaphor in early 19th century German. By the way, *Paria* is one of the few loan words going back to Dravidian origin – through Portuguese mediation – in European languages.

A New Paradigm

The following remarks on the genre of Dalit literature in Hindi may be understood as a kind of workshop report. My personal interest in Hindi Dalit literature started off from my occasional reading of Dalit short stories, particularly in the famous Hindi literary monthly *Hans*, under its senior editor Rajendra Yadav. I soon started to appreciate some of these stories and to realize not only the authenticity of experiences expressed in literary form in these stories, but also the literary potential in this genre, which was not as well developed in Hindi as in Marathi until some years ago. The group of authors centred around and patronized by one of the living doyens of Hindi literature, Rajendra Yadav, were the first I became acquainted with, particularly Om Prakash Valmiki. Gradually, I became aware of others, who publish elsewhere.

Beyond that, I became aware of the hidden link between Dalit issues and an indologist from Bonn University. Dr B.R. Ambedkar (1891–1956), the undisputed Dalit leader during the fight for independence and after independence the father of the Indian Constitution, had enrolled himself at Bonn University in 1921 and 1922, and his application letter in fluent German and some other documents have survived in our archives until now. Besides economics, the subject he was enrolled in, Ambedkar appears to have intended to learn Sanskrit under Hermann Jacobi, the then holder of the indological chair in Bonn.[2]

Representation

For Goethe and his middle-European contemporaries, the question of the Paria's literary self-representation was something like a non-question, as it might still be a non-question for many in India and Germany even today. This perception was already true for the then contemporary Hinduism. Contemporary religion and society in India was widely perceived as irrelevant for the understanding of the Sanskritic tradition, whose academic study followed the guidelines of the study of Roman and Greek antiquity. Sanskritic tradition was a matter of antiquity, surviving only in letters. If perceived, the presence was usually interpreted as a form of decadency of a glorious but bygone past. And, the knowledge of the social reality of the untouchable contributed to this European understanding of the Indian presence as a decline from a great past.

The image of the untouchable as a backward, and at the same time an illiterate or at least less educated person, as somebody ascribed to and stubbornly absorbed by a subaltern manual occupation, perceived as his traditional and original profession according to some kind of dharma, is still dominating. A survey in some Western countries would beyond doubt uncover that the image is somehow similar to the image transported by the Indian middle class, which ascribes *jhadu-lagana* (sweeping) without further comment to castes like *Bhangis* and *Chamars*, and somehow at least implicitly support the Brahmanic definition of identity as caste-bound and denying social and cultural identity beyond this occupation.

I understand my own effort in reading and translating Dalit literature predominantly to a Western audience as my own contribution not only to explain and analyse from the perspective of the all-knowing narrator, but also as a contribution towards a paradigmatic shift in the perception of India through the Western eye, towards a shift from the Great Tradition and its narration of India to the perspectives of the margins of society.

Representation and Self-awareness Drive

After women's literature, Dalit literature appears to be the second most vibrant genre in contemporary Hindi writing. The number and quality of literary works in Hindi by Dalit writers has been steadily increasing since the early 1990s. Several autobiographies have been composed and published, being the first step towards a full development of Dalit literature in Hindi as a genre of its own, separate from the world of Hindi writing as a whole, and at the same time related to the world of Hindi language and literature. Among the autobiographies I would like to mention are Mohandas Naimishray's *To each his own cages* (published in two volumes), Om Prakash Valmiki's *Joothan* (translated into English) and Suraj Pal Chauhan's *Deprived*. Not to forget a text like *From the hut to the governor's office* by the prominent Indian National Congress leader Mata Prasad, who also comes from a Dalit background.

Most of the prominent authors stem from small towns or villages in the countryside, and as "untouchables" many carry their personal experiences of the extremely crude forms of discrimination with them. Often they have been among the first in their extended families who have gone through a form of higher education, sometimes the first to have learned to read and write. And they have made it to the rather anonymous big towns – mostly to Delhi, where the cast background dominates social life less and discrimination is less crude. Many have been able to procure government jobs, and write during long evenings and holidays. They belong to the few examples of Dalit assertive action. The fact that they live in the big cities is not only the proof of their upward mobility, for them it is also an escape from the mostly traumatic experiences in the countryside of their childhood.

From Autobiography to Fiction

Almost all kinds of fiction are covered in contemporary Hindi Dalit writing, starting with the short story as the most important tool of literary production in

Hindi. There are some interesting novels, even though their number is yet rather small. There are few theatre works – mostly sketches for lay groups, but there is a lot of poetry, essay writing and literary criticism.

Suraj Pal Chauhan has recently (2004) brought out a volume of the already published short stories of 22 prominent Dalit authors. Most of these have started to publish back in the 1980s or early 1990s – some of them in Dalit magazines, but there are also many who started publishing in well-known daily newspapers. Literary magazines seem to have accepted their works only later. This volume attempts to look back and to shape the memory the beginnings of the movement and clearly demonstrates how Dalit Hindi literature presently enters a new phase, in which the attempted direct communication between writer and readership is bound to turn into historically mediated literary reflexivity.

Marginalization and Mainstream

"How long can India's Dalit literature, recently attracting the interest of researchers in America, England and Canada, continue to be suppressed in its own country?", says Shyauraj Sinh 'Becain' in his editorial of the recent Dalit literature special issue (August 2004) of the famous Hindi literary monthly *Hans*.

In spite of this constant complain, it is at least not very difficult for a Dalit writer to get his writing published. Dalit organizations have their own networks, their publication houses and their distribution networks. In respect to high literature, there is the high ranking literary and cultural magazine *Apeksha*, edited by Tej Singh. Then, there has been the Dalit Literature Yearbook since 1999, edited by Jayprakash Kardam.

Authors often consciously address a Dalit readership instead of a general public and interpret their identity as authors and their writing as a part of the social and political Dalit awareness movement. Some authors engage themselves in the production of political pamphlet literature – which can reach a much wider readership than the somehow elitist Hindi literature – and join political campaigns, particularly in support of Kanshi Ram's majority society (*bahujan*) project and party politics with the Bahujan Samaj Party (BSP) as political party representative of genuine Dalit interests. Some Hindi Dalit authors are political activists at the same time, mostly related to the BSP, and they relate their literary activity very much to the movement, the *andolan* identified with the party. I do not want to argue that this is bad from a purely literary point of view. But on the long run I think the development will be similar to what we have witnessed with Marathi Dalit literature. For creative writing, a certain degree of detachment from party politics is essential

Nevertheless, the discovery that rejection is not an individual, but a collective experience, is often a painful but inspiring discovery for many authors. I am however not sure about the readership of Dalit literature. Printing is cheap in India, there are a lot of publishing houses, and at the same time it is prestigious one's works published and printed. As everyone knows, reading contemporary literature, particularly in Hindi, is normally confined to a very limited number of people. The distribution of Hindi fictional writing and literature is also very limited. Financial loss is often avoided only because government institutions decide to distribute books free to their employees on certain occasions. Others make it into some BA Hindi curriculum and get some fee for reprinting in textbooks designed for students.

Contributing to the self-awareness rally is an essential part of their identity. I am however not sure, whether they actually reach a broader Dalit public, even if their works are to be considered as engaged literature in the strict sense of the term. Any student of Hindi, who starts working on modern Hindi literature, very soon has to observe that contemporary Hindi literature is somehow esoteric, since its readership is confined to small circles. There is no proof that Dalit literature is different – that the developing genre of modern Dalit literature is much read in Dalit middle class households.

At the same time, Dalit literature enters the curricula in schools, colleges and universities. This can be taken as an indication of an ongoing process of mainstreaming Dalit literature in Hindi. It is well possible that some pieces of Dalit literature will become canonical, similarly to what happened with Marathi Dalit literature of the 1970s. The interaction between creative Hindi Dalit writing and other forms of creative writing becomes more and more intensive, particularly through literary magazines and the discourses they inspire. Particularly the experiments with literary forms may be taken as hints for this development.

The Dalit literary representation is related to the Dalit awareness drive in politics and society. Dalit autobiography as well as fiction is full of stories of discontent. Autobiography and fiction are close to each other, sometimes the gap is hardly felt. The focus is naturally on the dark side of Hindu society, where human beings are in more or less crude forms rejected according to their imagined impurity. Naturally, the immediate focus of Dalit authors is on literary self-representation (*pratinidhitva*).

The collective search of identity is perhaps best illustrated by a remarkable peace of literature, a kind of narrative literary recovery of Dalit history composed by Bhagwan Das originally in the 1950s, published in a first version in Urdu in 1957, in a first Hindi edition in 1981 and in a largely revised edition in 1998 under the self-conscious and provocative title *Main Bhangi Hun*. Das says explicitly in his introduction: "To be brief, this is the history of the untouchables of India."[3] And, it indeed contains most of the elements that can be found in the creations of the younger generations: The collective *bhangi* and his history of suffering and injustice, but also a history of Dalit religiosity expressed in *nirgun-bhakti* and Buddhism as its proprium, the modern self-awareness drive and the appeal for collective resistance and assertive action.

The therapeutic function of this writing and reading as well is beyond question. I have heard from many Dalit intellectuals, how important the reading about the experiences of rejection made by others was in the development of their consciousness, and how this sharing of experiences turned into an incentive for their own writing or political activity or both, for their conscious identification with being Dalit. I would also like to mention the authobiography *Jhonpari se Rajbhavan* of the Congress leader Mata Prasad in this context, published 2002. Even though this is not a strictly literary but a political biography, it contains a lot of reflections and experiences that are very similar to the other ones written by men of letters in the proper sense, even though Mata Prasad is regarded as a traitor by some. He somehow represents a generation of Dalit intellectuals before the advent of Kanshi Ram's *bahujan* project and the electoral success of the BSP. Definitely, his alliance to the Congress somehow filters his Dalit emancipation agenda. For example, much of the responsibility for the experiences of apartheid goes to the responsibility of a pre-1947 colonizers-zamindari coalition, even though Mata Prasad condemns *Brahmanvad* like any other Dalit activist.

As is well known, many Dalits prefer names which are not supposed to indicate their caste identity directly. Others, like Suraj Pal Chauhan for example, take the name of their clan name (*gotra*) as personal name – Chauhan is an untouchable *bhangi* and not a *thakur* (warrior), as his surname Chauhan may indicate. There is a wonderful story in his collection *Hari kab-aega* on the intricacies of his pretention of being a Chauhan by caste – a Kshatriya, when he follows the proposition of a rikshaw-driver in Rishikesh to turn to a temple for an overnight stay with his family, when he finds that all the hotels are already occupied because of the ongoing religious festival of *Ardh Kumbhmela* the family had not been aware of. Since the temple priest understands, they are *thakur*, he offers them shelter for the night. One of the two professors for Hindi at Mumbai University is Prof Madhav Pandit – not a Brahman (as the name may indicate), but a Dalit. He has simply decided to take up the Brahmanic name Pandit, because he is a man of letters and professor at a well-known university. However, Om Prakash Valmiki, one of the most prolific Hindi Dalit authors and intellectuals, has consciously decided to stick to Valmiki as a family name, which directly indicates his Churah identity, much to the trouble of his wife, as mentioned in his autobiography *Juthan* (*mere nikammepan ki gintiyom men ata hai*, 1997, New Delhi).

Compassion and Experience

Literary magazines and other publications sponsor the trend and create important spaces for Dalit literature and its discourse. Rajendra Yadav, senior editor of *Hans*, has been publishing Hindi Dalit literature on a more or less regular basis since the early 1990s and keeps commenting and inspiring his authors in his much disputed editorials. One can easily come across prominent Dalit authors at Rajendra Yadav's small office with its big desk in a narrow lane in Delhi's Darya Ganj locality.

Hans has recently come out with the Prem Chand anniversary special issue on the "Discourse on Power and the Dalit" (8/2004). This 242-page volume covers not only 21 originally published short stories by some of several well-established authors, but also a large number of other items such as commentaries, essays and some interesting interviews. Of special interest is an interview with Ramanika Gupta, writer, editor and activist for Dalit, Adivasi and women issues for almost four decades. About modern Hindi Dalit literature she says: "I think that, at this moment, a lot more of refinement is required. In poetry, Dalit literature has gone much forward ... In prose writing, an arguing intellect dominates .... There is definitely intellectual reflection in Dalit literature, but creative writing is comparatively not as much there as it should be" (p. 233).

This argument – crudeness or lack of refinement – is sometimes used maliciously in a generalizing mood based on the usual anti-Dalit resentment so often encountered in Indian society. But even though literally "crude", this literature conveys unique experiences, argues Surajpal Chauhan: Non-Dalits can of course write on Dalit issues, their sentiment being based on compassion (*sahanubhuti*). But this compassion is always momentary (*kshanik*), while Dalit experience (*anubhuti*) is never just momentary (interview with me in September 2003). Rajendra Yadav argues against this position: "Do we have to become thieves and murderers to write on a thief and a murderer?" (*Hans*, 8/2004, p.7). As far as can be assessed, the literary contributions in this special issue are by Dalit authors only.

Aryan or Non-Aryan

Even if some critics are not accepted by the authors themselves, their articles are printed in the same magazine as the work of authors that they criticize. This is particularly true for a respected magazine like *Kathakram*. Guest editor Mudrarakshas of the Dalit special issue of *Kathakram* (11/2000) views the whole issue from a long-term perspective of the oppressed non-Vedic sub-text in the history of Indian culture and religion, relating it to a Marxist interpretation of literature. Among the many articles focusing on a Marxist interpretation of Hindi Dalit literature I would like to mention Sada Kanhade's *Marxism and Dalit Literature* in *Vasudha* (58/2003).

Another author who devotes much of his analytical writing to discussing the recovery of Dalit tradition from the clutches of twice-born Aryan society is Dr Dharmvir. Apart from his many articles on a large number of historical Dalit issues, he is particularly respected and criticized for his deconstruction of Hazari Prasad Dwivedi's "Brahmanic" interpretation of the medieval saint Kabir. Dharmvir has argued in several books and numerous articles that Kabir and other classical poets of the lower class *sant* tradition contain genuine Dalit experiences and have to be interpreted solely on their caste background. Rajdev Singh argues similarly as he compares the mainstream devotion to Rama as a personalized god and the *sant* poets reverence for a 'formless' Rama.

These efforts to reinterpret Indian history with the purpose to recover the history of the Dalits are inspired by the intellectual heritage of B.R.Ambedkar, the undisputed leader of Indian Dalits. His formal conversion from Hinduism to Buddhism in 1956, shortly before his death, is a topic for a intense debate: can one be an Ambedkarite Dalit without being Buddhist? Because of the fear that this debate could harm the unity of the movement, this topic is not written about often, it rather the subject of an oral discourse.

Ramanika Gupta's *A Collection of Dalit Short Stories*, published in 2003 by the national agency for Indian literature, the Sahitya Akademi, in New Delhi, includes short stories in Hindi (20), Marathi (9), Telugu (5), Gujarati (8), Panjabi (5), and Malayalam (1). This volume somehow illustrates that Dalit literature is genre literature in various Indian languages, and this literary "unity in diversity" fits well not only into the Dalit or *bahujan* ("majority") awareness drive, but also into the Sahitya Akademi's harmonist publication policy that focuses on national unity rather than existing oppositions. Other publications, like the yearly bulletin published by Jayprakash Kardam, follow similar lines by translating from other languages, and particularly Marathi, into Hindi. Similarly, the Dalit special issue of *Vasudha 58* (2003), the magazine of the progressive writers union in Madhya Pradesh, contains stories that were translated from Marathi.

Similarly, the Dalit literature special issue of *Uttar Pradesh 30,1* (2002), a publication of the official UP state government, sponsored by the then governing Dalit party BSP under its Dalit Chief Minister Mayavati, contains a mix of translations from Marathi and recent and original Hindi stories. Marathi literature is well read by Dalit Hindi authors, though mostly in translation.

Dalit and Non-Dalit Perspectives

Compassion with Dalits and the support of the social reform agenda is an old issue in Hindi literature, starting with Bharatendu Harishchandra of Benares (1850–1885). Let us have a brief glance at his famous drama *Bharat Durdasa*. Among the evils, general "death of the truth" (*satyanas*) reveals in the third act during an outbreak of demoniac dance, belongs his fame to have encouraged untouchability.[4] The hierarchical split of the Indian society along caste lines is already in Bharatendu's age understood as an obstruction to modernization and the nationalistic agenda of the Indian elites. The religious reformers too, particularly from Vivekananda onwards, were in favour of a homogenous Indian citizenship, national unity and spiritual egalitarianism, offering the same religious opportunities to everyone. Hindu reform was advocated first in correspondence with the British, and then, after World War I in a growing opposition to the colonial order.

The value of literature of non-Dalits on Dalit issues is a hot and often discussed subject. Specimens of Dalit literature are extremely rare in pre-independence literature. One of few exceptions in Hindi literature often referred to is *Ek achut ki sikayat* by a certain Hiradom, published in the famous literary journal *Sarasvati* in 1914. There is however a certain amount of non-Dalit literature on Dalit issues. I have however not heard or read a complete refusal of the value of this *gair-dalit* literature (unlike the refusal of "whitey literature" by some Afro-American authors). During my interviews with authors during September 2003, *sahanubhuti*-based literature of non-Dalits and *pratinidhitva* – compassion versus self-representation – was on several occasions understood as a difference of *jati* (class), even though the two may sometimes come close to each other.

As is well known, the *Aesthetics of the Ugly* plays a crucial role not only in Dalit literature itself, but also in the literature on Dalit issues written by non-Dalits. Mulk Raj Anand's *The Untouchable*, an early masterpiece of Indian literature originally written in English (published in 1935), is the key for this genre. Towards the end of the novel, which also appeared twice in German translation, the initial aspiration of the main character Bakha to live a respectable life is reduced to a rather vague hope for the introduction of a technical innovation the introduction of water closets, which would make the manual latrine cleaning irrelevant. Neither will the society change nor appears Bakha's willpower strong enough to overcome his pitiable status on his own without any support from anyone, and not even from his own community. Compassion-based literature appears not less pessimistic as experience-based literature.

Jayprakash Kardam's novel *Chappar*, published in 1994, delivers a completely different and optimistic message. As a student of Hindi literature, I am much aware of critical Indian statements one can hear on modern Hindi literature in general. Even some of my Indian friends have occasionally argued that for example the *Nai Kahani* is particularly pessimistic and somehow un-Indian because of this feature. I am not convinced of this view, but anyway, Dalit literature in general is hardly less pessimistic than for example the *Nai Kahani*. *Chappar*, however, is somehow different from the mainstream.

The main character of the novel is Chandan, the first son of village Mayapur, who makes it to the town to go for a college education. Chandan is a Dalit, and becomes a Dalit activist while being in the town. Not only in the town, where he opens a day school, but also in his village the situation changes to the better, particularly through education. The local feudal lord changes over sides, and, inspired by his daughter, gives the land away to its tillers, while the local Hindu priest leaves the place. Towards the end, Chandan becomes ready to marry a young woman, daughter of his landlord, who had been gang-raped in her youth and delivered a son because of this.. She, however, renounces to marry, and she is killed shortly afterwards. In the last scene of the story it becomes clear that Chandan will marry Rajni, the daughter of Mayapur's former feudal landlord, and at the same time they agree that they will adopt the child, son of the martyred daughter of Chandan's landlord in the town. The two know each other particularly through the letters between Chandan and his parents, which because of his parents being not able to read and write, were communicated by her over the years.

Is this utopia of a just enclave – the village Mayapur – in an unjust society a reflection of an original Dalit experience? Usually, Hindu or Indian society is widely perceived as unchangeable, and even if the more drastic forms of discrimination may disappear from the surface in the towns, discrimination continues – the subject of much of the Dalit literature written on the life in the growing towns in India. In Kardam's novel, however, it is the village that changes, and not the town. The experience of Dalit solidarity in the town is only one of the facets of the perception of town life in the novel. The most striking experience in the town life is the murder of Kamla, while the village goes through a highly fictional process of change, an imagination beyond reality and in opposition to reality.

My personal impression is that this highly imaginary development has to be read on the folio of the opposition of town and village in Prem Chand's famous novel *Godan* and its inherent pessimism of the Prem Chand of the 1930th on development in Indian society. The author positively means it as an example of the highly idealistic Dalit humanism (*manavta*), an egalitarian and explicitly anti-Hindu ideal of a secularized society. As the *thakur* himself comments, when he demands not to be called by his caste identity, but by his surname in future: "*Keval manusyata ka rista ho hamare bic. Manusyata hi hamara gotr ho, hamari jati aur manusyata hi hamara dharm ho*" (Kardam 2003: 112). "There should be nothing but our relationship through humankind between us. Humankind only should be our kinship, humankind only should be our caste and humankind only should be our religion." This is a play with words and their meanings, since *manusyata* means humankind as well as humanism, and *jati* means caste as well as people in the ethnic sense.

Creating Space for Dalit Awareness?

While Marathi Dalit literature goes back to at least thirty years of a powerful tradition, with the backbone of the strong, and largely Buddhist Dalit movement and its immediate Ambedkarite inspiration through the Marathi language, the political, religious and literary unity of the Dalits in the Hindi-speaking area faced more difficulties and more diversity than in the comparatively more homogenous climate of Maharashtra.

Many Hindi authors easily agree with a statement by the Marathi author Sharan Kumar Limbvale, who sees his books as "weapons" in the fight against the caste system and its ideology under the name of "Brahmanism": Literature is largely perceived as an essential tool of the ongoing Dalit awareness drive.

The rising Dalit voice in Hindi literature is primarily an essential tool for the expression of an authentic social experience. Experiments with broken forms of narration as in the works of authors of the younger generation, such as Ajay Navariya, hold a promise for the future of fictional Dalit writing. There is no doubt that the increasing quantity and quality of Dalit writing, either in journals or in independent publications, is important not only for its authors themselves, but also for future Hindi literature in general. It is becoming more difficult to ignore the Dalit voice in mainstream Hindi literature.

Notes

1. The term *mleccha* was used both for foreigners and for the outcastes within Indian society. Comp. Halbfass (1990: 172) and Gandhi (1999: 69). Halbfass (1990: 177): "The *mleccha* ... do not always appear as foreigners *per se* in their undifferntiated otherness. Occasionally, the term also refers to a specific group of outsiders among other groups in India."
2. Compare Bellwinkel-Schempp, Maren, "Ambedkar Studies at Heidelberg". *SAI Report 4/2003*, p. 3–4 (http://www.sai.uni-heidelberg.de/saireport/2003/ambedkar.pdf).
3. "*Samksipt mem yahi bharat ke achutom ka itihas hai*" (Das, 1998: iv).
4. *Bharatendu Granthavali I*, p.138.

References

Ansari, Dagmar (1970), *Die Frau im Modernen Hindi-Roman Nach 1947*, Berlin.

Aston, N.M. (2001), *Dalit Literature and African-American Literature*, New Delhi: Prestige.

'Becain', Syauraj Singh; 'Minu', Rajat Rani [ed.] (2001), *Dalit Dakhal*. Ghaziabad.

Chauhan, Suraj Pal (2001), *Chu nahim Sakta (tin laghu natikaem)*. New Delhi.

—— (2002), *Tiraskrt*. New Delhi.

Das, Bhagwan (1998), *Main Bhangi Hun*. Dvitiy samsodhit tatha samvardhit samskaran Lakhnau (first ed. 1981).

Deliège, Robert (1999), *The Untouchables of India*. Translated from the French by Nora Scott. Oxford [etc.] (French original 1995).

—— (2004), *La religion des intouchables de l'Inde*. Villeneuve (Collection "mythes, imaginaries, religions" ; 3).

Dharmvir (1998), *Kabir ke Alocak*, Delhi.

Gandhi, Rajmohan (1999), *Revenge and Reconciliation: Understanding South Asian History*, New Delhi: Penguin.

Gnanadason, Aruna (1993), "Dalit Women: The Dalit of the Dalit". A.P. Nirmal (Hrsg), *A Reader in Dalit Theology*, Madras: Gurukul Lutheran Theological College and Research Institute, pp. 129–38.

Gupta, Ramanika (ed.) (2001), *Hindi sahitya mem dalit-samghars ke unnayak Do. En. Simh.* Ghaziabad, 2001.

—— (2003a), *Dalit kahani samcayan*, New Delhi, 2003.

—— (2003b), "Bhasaem marne se imkar karti haim", *Hans* 10, 2003, pp. 39–41.

Halbfass, Wilhelm (1990), *India and Europe: An Essay in Philosophical Understanding*, New Delhi: Motilal Banarsidas (First German edition 1981).

Hawthorn, Jeremy (1998), *A Concise Glossary of Contemporary Literary Theory*, London: Arnold (3rd ed.).

Horstmann, Monika (2001), "Whose Kabir?", in *Hindi: Language, Discourse, Writing 1*, Vol 1, Delhi, pp. 177–187.

Ilaiyah, Kancha (1996), *Why I am not a Hindu: A Sudra Critique of Hindutva Philosophy, Culture and Political Economy*, Calcutta: Samya.

Inkinen, Magdalena (2003), *Mobilising the Lower Castes: The Rise of the Bahujan Samaj Party in India., Uppsala.*

Jaffrelot, Christophe (2003), *India's Silent Revolution: The Rise of the Low Castes in North Indian Politics*, Delhi: Permanent Black.

Kardam, Jayprakash (1994), *Chappar*, New Delhi.

Keer, D. (1971), *Dr. Ambedkar: Life and Mission*, Bombay (3rd ed.).

Khare, R.S. (1984), *The Untouchable as Himself: Ideology, Identity, and Pragmatism among the Lucknow Chamars*, Cambridge (Cambridge Studies in Cultural Systems: 8).

Mandelbaum, David G. (1970), *Society in India*, University of California Press, Berkeley.

Mata Prasad (2002), *Jhonpari se Rajbhavan*, New Delhi.

Omvedt, Gail (1995), *Dalit Visions: The Anti-caste Movement and the Construction of an Indian Identity*, New Delhi: Orient Longmans (Tracts for the times ; 8).

Orenstein, Henry (1965), *Gaon: Conflict and Cohesion in an Indian Village*, New Jersey: Princeton University Press.

Pachauri, Sudhish (2001), "Kabir ke Alochak: Deconstructing, Reconstructing Kabir", in *Hindi Language Discourse Writing 1*,1, pp. 208–17.

Pandey, Indu Prakash (1989), *Romantic Feminism in Hindi Novels Written by Women*, New Delhi: House of Letters.

Ram, Dines (2002), *Dalit Mukti ka Prasna aur Dalit Sahitya*, Ghaziabad.

Shah, Ghanshyam (ed.) (2002), *Caste and Democratic Politics in India*, New Delhi: Permanent Black.

Singh, Rajdev (1998), *Nirgun rambhakti aur dalit jatiyam*, New Delhi.

Singh, Shukdeo (2002), "The Sants and the Struggle Against Brahmin Dominance", in *Images of Kabir*, ed. by Monika Horstmann, New Delhi: Manohar (South Asian Studies; 40).

Spivak, Gayatri Chakravorty (1988), "Can the Subaltern Speak?", in Cary Nelson and Lawrence Grossberg (eds), *Marxism and the Interpretation of Culture*, London: Macmillan.

Sumanakshar, S.P. (chief ed.), Parwana, L.R. (ed.) (1995), *Who's Who of Dalit Writers in India* (Vol. I), Delhi.

Valmiki, Om Prakash (2001), *Dalit sahitya ka saundaryasastra.*, Delhi.

Weber, Jurgen (2003), "Dalits zwischen Bildungschancen und Diskriminierung (Teil I)", *Sudasien 23 (1/2003)*, pp. 28–32.

Pride and Prejudices[1] in Education

The Shaping of Hierarchies

RAJIV GUPTA

It is uncommon these days to find people who have achieved highest positions in academic world and yet continue their academic pursuits with a deep sense of honesty. Professor K.L. Sharma is one of such rare persons. Thus, to write an article in honour of Professor Sharma is, in fact, an honour to academic scholarship of liberal nature. I have known Professor Sharma since 1980 when I met him at the residence of the late Professor N.K. Singhi. The kind of affinity which Professor Sharma possesses is enough to accept him as one of the most lovable members of the family. I have also got several academic opportunities to work with Professor Sharma in numerous workshops organized for writing and evaluating textbooks. In these academic discourses, I have always found him innovative, constructive, deterministic and friendly. These attributes of his personality make him an assertive person. His academic depth always acts as a source of aspiration to those who wish to understand what social life is. As a scholar of international repute, Professor Sharma always prefers to live in the 'world of social sciences'. He has always given importance to social science perspective to expose the systems and sub-systems of exploitation and oppression. His thought-provoking understanding of social stratification and social change has tempted me to construct my thought on an interplay between education and hierarchies in Indian society.

I

Education, health and public distribution systems in a developing society like India are prerequisites to inclusive development. In fact, standard of living, quality of life, real living and democratic ethos of socio-political life become one-sided if education, health and public distribution systems do not reach the people. Since these systems are yet to reach the people, the process of social development in India is still an 'imperfect and incomplete project'.[2] The process of social development in general and educational development in particular, for the author, are always ideological concepts because state (and now international organizations also) directs and regulates the processes of development in such a way that dominant sections of society monopolize the benefits. Educational development can be examined with this logic. Since education makes people 'enlightened mass', the state promotes those apparatuses of education intentionally[3] which undermine 'questionable mindset' – an essential attribute of critical consciousness. Education content, i.e., syllabus and pedagogy are prepared with the design that ideology of individual achievement dominates the mindset of young people. Critical consciousness and sense of collective conscience as values are at loss in education. This is known as class character of education to my mind. Educational development in different social spaces proves this logic of class character of education.

The performance of the Indian state in several sectors is not encouraging much. The United Nations International Covenant on Economic, Social and Cultural Rights, in an evaluation, made in 2008, reports that "progress on all social fronts is deemed unsatisfactory".[4] It is pointed out that nearly 50 per cent of Indian children are dropped out of schools before they turn fourteen. Educational development is further weakened due to economic crises in rural sector, socio-economic exclusion of marginalized sections of population, gender inequality, communalization of social relations and increasing food insecurity. As a result, education is not making effective contribution to the expansion of creative labour amongst marginalized sections of Indian society. Education, thus, appears as one of the sources of hierarchy. At this stage, an important issue can be raised: "What role does education play in social development?" The minimization of the systems of hierarchies should be the role of education, otherwise, the sustainability of democracy, equality and secularism as values can be questioned as well as threatened at any stage. Since education has been accepted as one of the fundamental rights, the organized efforts of the state should be rational and logical. Adequate increase in number of government schools and proper financial support to existing government schools are necessities. Support of the state to private schools and encouragement to private-public partnership in operation of the schools make 'right to education' discriminatory. Privatization and marketization of education at early stage makes education divisive. Encouragement to privatization of school education or private-public partnership in school education goes contrary to the interest of disadvantaged sections, such as SCs, STs, minorities and other backward classes. In private schools, the participation of children of these social categories is marginal. The children of non-disadvantaged groups, the teachers of private schools, the parents of students and the management of these schools lead to such academic environment in the schools that the children belonging to disadvantaged groups face 'social exclusion' both directly and indirectly. In other words, the efficiency quotient of disadvantaged groups cannot be improved because of the 'socio-cultural environment' constructed by private schools in support of upper caste class groups. The formation of such hierarchies can never be challenged because of legitimacy to discrimination. The acceptance of common school system, where all children, irrespective of their ascriptive and achieved identities, study with the sense of belongingness, is the only alternative to implement right to education with the ethos of equality, democracy and secularism. India as a knowledge society can be advanced in desired direction only if common school system is introduced. Knowledge becomes people's power only when such institutional arrangements are established. It will be an attack on the presence of 'prejudices' and 'pride' which children and their parents have developed about government schools and private schools respectively. If such efforts are not made at the earliest, then the view of the Planning Commission that "education and health are desirable because improved levels of health and education as critical inputs determine the growth potential in the longer term"[5] becomes debatable. The absence of common school system will perpetuate educational hierarchies in those eleven states where rural female literacy rate is below 50 per cent.

The process of globalization and dominance of international financial capital have introduced private schools in metro cities or in nearby 'supportive space' which serve the interest of corporate ruling class, upper and middle-upper classes and social categories of elites in Indian society. It is a kind of 'cultural imperialism'. India as a knowledge society with the help of such private schools will legitimize culture of consumerism and commodification of social relations. 'Prejudices' and 'pride' as notions will appear with a different meaning of neo-marginalized culture and neo-privileged culture respectively. Education imparted in such private schools, in other words, will keep alive further the divide of dominant and subjugated culture and validate global capitalism. Common school system can become an instrument by which such private schools as elements in cultural control can be challenged.

Constitutional provisions of democratic Indian society establish all structural organs of education, ranging from early education to higher education, as part of concurrent list. Thus, educational development in desired direction is the joint responsibility of union government and governments of provinces. Central schools and state schools are those two types, which provide education to children at an affordable price. With the directives of ruling class, caste and religious organizations and numerous interest and pressure groups, provincial governments have been supporting (quasi) privatization of education. In these private schools, fee structure cannot be afforded by the large segment of rural mass, scheduled castes, scheduled tribes, other backward classes, minorities (particularly the Muslims) and middle-middle to lower-lower urban classes. Thus, there is a qualitative and institutional discriminatory differentiation (in the classrooms) as far as social base of students in private and government schools is concerned. Such differentiation is extremely complex because typologies exist within the structures of private schools and of government schools. Such hierarchical division of schools and social base of students support the continuance of India as a discriminatory society. On the basis of reports which newspapers publish, it can be said that even lower class parents do not wish to send their children in schools operated by provincial governments, whereas in central government operated schools and private schools getting admission is a difficult task. It is also found that in the schools operated by the union government and provincial governments, the teachers are qualified and experienced. They are also given approved salary. In private schools, the norms of qualifications and salary are violated. The concept of 'meritocracy' at this juncture becomes highly debatable. 'Merit' as achievement of students ('best' out of qualified or eligible) is by and large associated with private schools because in these schools teachers devote their time in classroom interaction and co-academic/extra-curricular activities under authoritarian control of school management. Aggressive propaganda (sometimes on the basis of falsehood) of qualities of private schools has reached to the families of various classes through the institution of mass media. Thus, these private schools have became 'reference structures' for all classes. Several families now make drastic cut in the expenditures relating to basic needs so that at least one child, preferably the male child, could get admission in such private schools. As a result, neo-liberal education system legitimized by market forces is becoming successful in Indian society because it is now accompanied by neo-liberal changes taking place in other spaces also. This is one of the sociological apprehensions of the author that various sectors of people of India, particularly the rural people, will not be able to enter into the world of 'inclusive development' by using education as one of the instruments. The state of India should discuss the perspectives associated with people's interest centric change and models of governance, otherwise 'unrest' can lead to threat to democratic polity. Privatization of education and private-public partnership in education do not necessarily lead to quality education for those pupil who wish to have advantage of right to education alongwith the values of equality and social justice. Privatization of education in one sense is the commercialization of education which (re)defines excellence as per the normative patterns of ruling (dominant) class and its principal allies which intentionally overlook the notion of 'inclusive education' and inclusive growth. Social sciences and humanities as well as indigeneous languages are ignored in private schools due to institutional prejudices. Since private schools are mainly English speaking, the communication skills with western styles create a sense of pride. Disciplines like physics, chemistry, biology, mathematics and commerce are continuously encouraged. A large number of (un)academic organizations regularly organize competitions in which competence, excellence and logical presentations of pupil are assessed. Certificates, revealing the performance of the competitor, are distributed. These certificates are produced, with a sense of pride, by students on several occasions. The development and expansion of scholarship and personality of students are not the purposes of these competitions. "Privatization of education has developed quality" is the message, which is always legitimized by these competitions. Education in this sense becomes a commercial activity in private schools which also produces prejudices and pride. This production has led to deep-rooted hierarchies amongst schools.

II

My second argument associated with how 'prejudices' and 'pride' are constructed is based upon the content structure of the textbooks. Teachers communicate the content in such a way that 'prejudices' and 'pride' become organic features of the culture. The content structure of the textbooks, the use of language and symbols by teachers during classroom interaction and the nature of pedagogy are those indicators which stimulate anybody to examine the roles and responsibilities of teacher. These aspects can also be given importance when educational objectives and policies are evaluated. The critical analysis of textbooks, thus, from knowledge and culture perspectives, become important. Classroom prejudices and classroom pride are institutionalized because of the continuance of subjective content in the textbooks. Explicit discrimination in classroom by the teachers and upper categories of the students is directly and indirectly associated with the text structured by teacher(s) as author(s). Caste biases, gender biases, religious biases, class biases and other forms of biases can be located when content of the textbooks is analysed. Up to a large extent, the present textbooks, published by National Council of Educational Research and Training (NCERT), are free from biased content structures.[6] As a result, the phenomenon of social discrimination is being attacked in an effective manner. But, the provincial governments have intentionally encouraged the authors to institutionalize biases so that segmentization of society could become the part of mindset of students. The biased text leads to disintegration of (i) learning to know, (ii) learning to do, (iii) learning to live together and (iv) learning to be – the four bases of learning framed by UNESCO.[7] Textbooks construct national character at early stage of learning. Unfortunately, market of parochial interests dominate over the textbooks prepared by provincial governments. The parallel books recommended by schools to their students have further perpetuated the world of (mis)information and (contra) culture amongst students in a decisive way. The textbooks and parallel books in Rajasthan at all levels of school and college education act as those instruments which give rise to 'communalization of mind' and 'myths-based historical understanding' of society.[8] It is a fact that content structures of books, prepared by provincial governments, cannot be identical across country but mythical structures for imparting knowledge and values can be restricted because such content structure negates the constitutional value of scientific temper. In my opinion, such narrow content structure in the textbooks and parallel books lead to alienation and marginalization in the large section of students also. Sociologically, we accept that content structure is not an end in itself, it is a mode by which students are encouraged to think. Prejudices and pride appear in that thinking process of students which, at any stage, can direct to initiate those activities which are of parochial character. Such kind of education becomes a particular mechanism by which exploitation and social exclusions are either developed or reproduced. At this juncture, one can discuss the relationship between the expectations of students and the role playing of teachers.

The roles performed by teachers in classroom interaction are not always in accordance with democratic liberties. Their attitude in rural areas in particular possesses all forms of biases. I am reminded of the statement of Mrs Ramsree of Surothi (Dholpur) village of Rajasthan in which she says, "The teachers only teach upper-caste children. They use our children to do odd jobs in the school. They do not teach them one thing that all pupils should be taught equally".[9] It is 'casteization of pedagogy' which one can find in all schools (with variations), whether private or state owned. Thus, both the pedagogy and the content structure of the textbooks and parallel books form prejudice and pride, which shape and institutionalize discrimination and inequalities in the mindsets of the students with the direct and indirect help of teachers. It is also a fact now that interplay between local knowledge/understanding and global knowledge/understanding is well established in NCERT books. Such interplay is missing in the textbooks published by boards governed by provincial governments. Since flux, uncertainty and insecurity are features of India's socio-economic change, education system needs special attention from both the political society and the civil society. Unfortunately, privatization of education and communalization of society have restricted the critical roles of education by which peoples could understand what alternative institutions do they need at this juncture. The notion of 'effective learning' based on scientific rationality is lost. Stigmatization of various religious and caste categories as anti-national and non-intelligent categories has led to social division amongst students which in my opinion is negation of effective learning. Krishna Kumar rightly comments that representations of the past, dispersed by institutions like schools and the state media, ultimately serve as mental maps which guide large multitudes of people in shaping their responses to present-day situations. The textbooks of provincial schools have failed to undermine military-industrial complex which is the root of poverty and inequality. In my opinion, without undermining military industrial-complex, no textbook of social sciences and humanities can establish the logic of democracy. The teachers, who support cultural orthodoxies, military-industrial complex and biases in textbooks as author(s) and use aggressive language in support of above mentioned connotations, distort the entire teaching process. These aspects of teaching and learning process lead to the formation of 'selective tradition'[10] – a concept introduced by Raymond William. These selective traditions construct the dominant culture (cultural practices of ruling class) in textbooks in such a way that child strats protecting ruling class interests with a sense of pride. The use of violent acts by students in the schools and rejection of value of social justice by students are indicators of their support to ruling class. Connell's concept of 'curricular justice' becomes significant in this context. According to him, curricula should be designed with this perception that interests and perspectives of subordinate groups in meaningful manner are there. This 'counter-hegemonic curricula' can initiate an ideological attack on both the prejudices and pride if content-structures associated with the textbooks are prepared incorporating these counter-hegemonic realities. Teachers can built, preserve and popularize these counter-hegemonic realities amongst students and other members of social groups because teachers as one of the social categories possess enormous influences on society and its developmental direction. Thus, there is a need to create structural breakdown in existing socially and culturally determined consciousness which provides legitimacy to prejudice and pride. The recent books published by NCERT, to a certain extent, initiate this structural breakdown and, thus, act against repression of children's talent.

III

The notions of 'prejudice' and 'pride' constructed as ideas of 'they' and 'we' respectively constitute the interdependence between consciousness, content structure, curriculum and nature of politics. The presence of 'prejudice' and 'pride' based informations (facts?) and narratives (knowledge) can never generate the skill for analysing and rejecting (if needed) history, culture and polity. Ethnocentric understanding makes students a part of close-minded people. Krishna Kumar, in a study associated with histories of the freedom struggle in India and Pakistan taught in the respective schools, argues that in the school textbooks of India and Pakistan one can find two prototypes (master narratives) of story of freedom which make India and Pakistan 'in group' and 'out group' in the cognitive maps of respective students. "For India, the end of freedom struggle signifies a great achievement, along with a terrible sense of loss and sadness whereas for Pakistan the end signifies a remarkable achievement, somewhat mitigated by a sense of injustice" (Krishna Kumar, 2001: 73).[11]

These master narratives with several happening taking place during freedom struggle shaped religion-based hierarchies and inter-religious rivalries as secular versus communal. Religious fundamentalism, as ideology of some of the political parties, is continuing in both India and Pakistan because of such master narratives which communicate the logic of religious concept of nation. In the textbooks of social studies prescribed in Rajasthan,[12] religious fundamentalism as one of the ideas find important place. Issue of conversions is projected as anti-patriotic act and as a result 'Hindutva' comes close to the concept of nation. Since caste/jati is the most significant institutional arrangement, the functional roles of caste are parts of the content structures of textbooks. These positive roles of caste lead to caste-based community consciousness. Anti-caste consciousness, thus, is not a product of education which is needed if the state is committed to develop India as secular and democratic society. The realities of 'oppressed life' and their fall out in context of marginalized sections of India are not given significance in the textbooks. In my opinion, the absence of such 'life stories' in the textbooks has developed opposition of value of 'social justice' amongst students. Anti-reservation psyche and its manifestation in forms of agitations are products of non-acceptance of social justice. Media has also formed public opinion against 'social justice' by giving importance to individual achievement and merit as basic objectives of education. Almost in all textbooks of history and social studies in Rajasthan, the oppression of Hindus by Muslim rulers has been presented as if it was a religious oppression. This presentation gives rise to communal consciousness. Rightist organizations support this presence of communal consciousness so that they could manufacture a debate between 'real secular' and 'pseudo-secular'. The tensions between majority and minorities are consequences of this support which is discussed in family and other informal groups and become prejudice and pride in classroom also. These roles of 'selective traditions' incorporated in textbooks attack on socio-cultural diversities of India. This kind of knowledge and information incorporated in textbooks become constraint to the process of rationalization and cultural modernization.

Another important 'selective tradition' incorporated in the textbooks legitimize patriarchy. The glorification of joint family in all textbooks can be presented here as an example. The submission of wife before her husband, values of obedience and loyalty and acceptance of gender hierarchy so that joint family could continue are given central importance in the textbooks of sociology. The sacramental character of Hindu marriage is glorified and contractual character of Muslim marriages are produced in such a way that satisfaction of sexual needs becomes the only important (rather most important) purpose of such marriages. The glorification of Hindu social institutions as Indian social institutions has been presented in these textbooks. Early marriages, restrictions on widow remarriages, caste endogamy and confinement of women in domestic world have also been appreciated in the textbooks with the logic that these institutional arrangements are indispensable for the continuance of sexual morality. Cultural policing and moral policing also find legitimacy after socialization of the students through these textbooks. The advancement of education in both the urban and the rural space is now a reality. These educated persons will, in future, be able to take effective participation in all forms of decision-making process. With sectarian mind set, developed through the present content structures of textbooks, these persons cannot generate Indian society with constitutional norms. Misguided and parochial actions and decision cannot perpetuate cultural modernization conducive to democratic, secular and socialist Indian society. The world of knowledge and cultural formed by selective traditions based content structures of textbooks should be critically evaluated and rejected (if needed) because it incorporates biases against (i) minorities, (ii) lower castes, (iii) tribes, (iv) women, (v) agriculturalists, (vi) groups involved in lower occupations, (vii) working class, (viii) neighbouring countries, and (ix) secularism, socialism, social justice, tolerance and human rights. In other words 'neo-colonization' of education is still a dominant Indian reality which marginalize disadvantaged groups in such a way that 'social exclusions' as necessary conditions become the organs of mindset of the people. Tolerance and human rights. In other words, 'neo-colonization' of education is still a dominant reality in India, which marginalizes disadvantaged groups in such a way that 'social exclusions' as necessary conditions become the organs of mindset of the people.

IV

Let us initiate our concluding remarks with a question: why educational inequality persists in India? The answer to this question is not simple but rich India and poor people, to a certain extent, is a fact. It has happened because of discriminatory and non-scientific education system on the one hand and multiple hierarchies of school systems on the other. Probably state firmly believes that segmented society always needs segmented education so that neo-liberal development logical religious beliefs caste identities, orthodox customary practices and parochial perceptions are powerful forces within education. As a result, conservatism exists both inside and outside the education. The outlook of child due to conservatism gives importance to 'prejudices' and 'pride' and shapes hierarchies as sets of ideas. In India, education has failed to challenge the informal-domestic space which does not provide legitimacy to constitutional norms and social interaction based on institution of law. Educational divide in form of elitist (private) schools and people (government) schools create obstacles to social justice which does not advance democracy as mode of associated learning (Salsey and others, 1997: 4).[13] Education does not make child creative because in classroom interaction he/she is controlled by teachers and in family experiences authoritarian control of parents and entertainment control of media. Child at the early stage is forced by market to become conscious about career and merit. But, at the same time, textbooks produce or reproduce mythical or quasi-mythical world of knowledge and information by which the values of democracy, social justice, gender equality and the rule of law as indicators of modernization are threatened (Thapar, 2000: 85).[14] The market of education is based on 'competition of unequal', which continuously proves that there is no alternative to elitist (private) schools which communicate quality education to children by charging fee up to the extent of Rs 75,000 per annum. These elitist schools employ teachers belonging to various social categories of elite. Essential qualification required for appointment as teacher does not matter much. Thus quality education is a finished product manufactured by 'elitist workers' in a global industry of formal learning. 'Knowledge society' of a particular kind is the purpose of privatization of education created and governed by multinational and transnational industries which have entered in the field of education through the infrastructural support of state. Teachers in these schools are elitist (un)workers who belong to upper and dominant sections of society. Both the students and the teachers represent almost the same socio-economic background and support those 'selective traditions' which legitimize neo-liberal model of development and culture associated with it. Thus 'education by the elites for (potential) elites' shapes hierarchy in Indian society. These elites, to a large extent, do not oppose conservatism and sectarian outlook (religious beliefs making orthodoxies appropriate) so that they could establish hegemony on all forms of markets. They understand that even if dogmatic perceptions are produced as ruling class ideas, they can use such perceptions for profit making.

The second structure in hierarchy is developed by semi-elitist private schools which serve the interests of one section of middle class (particularly the middle-middle and middle-lower class). This class possesses aspiration to have equal status with 'neo-rich' and 'super-rich' whenever opportunity is found. Central Schools and Navodaya Vidyalayas, to a large extent, are also choice structures of these sections of society. Selective traditions, orthodoxies and conservatism are found in classroom interaction of semi-elitist private schools. Such kind of sectorian learning hardly possesses any space in Central Schools and Navodaya Vidyalayas. Unfortunately, learning in family and other informal institutions along with media make this generation quasi-orthodox. As a result, this generation also accepts 'selective traditions' and manifest them so that they could claim closeness with corporate class, upper class and social category of elites.

The third structure in hierarchy is composed of schools controlled and regulated by provincial governments. These structures educate pupils belonging to lower classes, scheduled castes, scheduled tribes, other marginalized groups and girls associated with middle-lower class. Provincial governments are least interested in generating infrastructural facilities and supporting structures for making educational activities children-friendly. Private-public partnership for smooth operation of these schools has been initiated which, in future, will convert these schools into 'small' educational shops. Provincial governments introduce 'selective traditions' based education in these schools and convert teachers into government employees whose basic goal is to produce cheap 'workforce' (academic proletariat). These students are almost fully imitative. They reveal commitment towards orthodoxies and search satisfaction in those activities which are alienated culturally. These students in future can be converted into that 'force' which can be used as pressure or interest groups by political parties (in power) and aggressive crowd for certain (hidden) intentions. These children of lower classes lack quality skill and skill of communication. They accept 'selective traditions' mentioned in the textbooks as 'mainstream cultures'. In communal and caste violence, political parties try to use these educated people as their force. These students develop faith systems in what constitutes prejudice and pride and organize their actions mechanistically on the basis of prejudices and pride.

Thus education system in India by incorporating content structure of books as 'identity of prejudices' and 'identity of pride' shapes complex hierarchies within students (potential workforce) which institutionalize segmentization, parochialization, communalization and discrimination as processes. There is thus a need to critically examine textbooks from the viewpoint of language, content structures and selection of the topics. 'Selective traditions' serving the interests of ruling class make education a part of indoctrination. Democratic and secular Indian society needs only and only democratic and secular education – a prerequisite to socially desired development. Educational inequality legitimized by selective traditions and structures of schools persists because ruling class and its allies are interested in neo-liberal development – an antithesis to socially desired development.

Comments

The University Grants Commission has given research award to this author to complete research work on 'Sociology of Textbooks: Culture and Knowledge(as) Perspective'. As part of this research, the author is trying to identity 'selective traditions' in the textbooks prescribed up to senior secondary level by governments of U.P., Gujarat, Rajasthan and M.P. In this article the arguments relating to textbooks of Rajasthan are based on: (i) textbooks of political science of senior secondary level, (ii) textbooks of sociology of senior secondary level, (iii) history books of senior secondary level, and (iv) textbooks of social studies prescribed for the students of class tenth.

Notes

1. The terms 'pride' and 'prejudice' have been used by Prof Romila Thapar and Prof Krishna Kumar in the contexts of evaluating historical phenomena. Their perceptions stimulated me to use these terms for evaluating biases in the field of education.
2. Development and change as processes are always incomplete and imperfect because of presence of antagonistic forces which interact under the pattern of dialectics. For detail see Anthony Giddens (2003) *The Progressive Manifesto*, Cambridge: Polity.
3. Education as organ of super-structure (Karl Marx), non-coercive ideological apparatus and roles of restricted codes in learning (Louis Althusser and Basil Bernstein respectively) are important theoretical constructions to understand this issue in detail.
4. These facts were produced in a news published by national daily *Hindu* in the month of May 2008. The exact date is not remembered.
5. The observations of Planning Commission about health and education have been examined in the magazines, *Teacher of the World* and *Teachers' Movement*.
6. The books published by NCERT on the basis of National Curriculum Framework 2005 represent the realities of cultural diversity in an objective but critical manner. These

books in classroom will be able to generate live interaction between teachers and students.

7. These four bases of learning, according to K.N. Panikkar, are guide-posts for preparing the Kerala State Policy on Higher Education. For detailed understanding, see *Teachers of the World*. Vol. 8, No. 4. April-June 2008.
8. The analysis of these books is published by me in a monograph entitled 'Shiksha Ka Sampradayikikaran Aur Sampradayikikaran Ki Shiksha' (Communalization of Education or Education of Communalization) (1991), Jaipur: Janwadi Lekhak Sangh.
9. See *Public Report on Basic Education in India* (1999), New Delhi: Oxford University Press, p. 51
10. See Lois Weis and others (2006), *Ideology, Curriculum and the New Sociology of Education*, New York: Routledge.
11. Krishna Kumar (2001), *Prejudice and Pride*, New Delhi: Viking.
12. For details, see, Rajiv Gupta (1999), 'Shiksha Ka Sampradayikikaran Aur Sampradayikikaran Ki Shiksha', Jaipur: Janvadi Lekhak Sangh. Articles published in *Vimarsha*, Year 8, Vol. 6 (2006) and Year 9, Vol. 1, (2007).
13. A.H. Halsey and others (1997), *Education: Culture, Economy, Society*, Oxford: Oxford University Press.
14. Romila Thapar (2000), *India: Another Millennium?*, New Delhi: Viking.

9 Culture of Hierarchy and Power

Local Socio-Historical Perspectives – Indian Case Study

D. SUNDARAM

In all discourses on inequality, there is an uncritical assumption on (a) nature of hierarchy, power and thereby (b) on the socio-economic and cultural co-ordinates of hierarchy in local historical situations. With this assumption, this study through the description of Indian social structure and institutions within a specific time and space in socio-historical perspectives considers the significance of the cultural tradition on which Indian society and the nature of hierarchy and power was based. This descriptive focus on the cultural tradition of Indian society marked by a form of social structure is to have a selective incorporation of cultural elements constructing a general civilization process within a specific historical event.

The need for giving pre-eminence for such approach to inequality/equality could not have been clarified much better than Alexis de Tocqueiville, who compared the two historical situations, namely, France and America in 18th and 19th century along with the respective socio-cultural co-ordinates. Though, he has not deliberately intended with the perspectives as we seek, the case is an illustrative significance of the dynamic nature of equality/inequality under the given local socio-cultural conditions characterized with ranking, hierarchy and difference (Tocqueville, 1946). The issue of social equality versus social inequality by Tocqueville under the two distinctively different structured conditions of society, namely, France – the aristocratic and US – the democratic, is a point of reference here. The conditions where equality was minimized or maximized are socio-culturally different and separate. Tocqueville's exposition of how the aristocratic society in France in a given historical situation has eroded the principles of equality while in contrast how democracy in U.S. in a given historical time influenced the principle of equality is significant. The social and cultural conditions that have generated ideas and social outlook on equality in these two historically different situations are his basic approach (Tocqueville, 1945).

This paper is revised version of the report on the project on Life Thought and Culture for the Indian Philosophical Sciences Research Council, March 1994 and also of the presentation (in absentia) at the second international conference on Hierarchy, Power and Civilization, Institute of Oriental Studies, St Petersburg, Russia, July 4–7, 2002.

Similarly, the inequality eradication programme in India through affirmative action, i.e., the backward classes development, is another case in point. The criteria of identifying individuals for social, educational and economic development through the social group to which they belong to as individuals was more on cultural factors rather than on economic dimension. And, it is nothing but dismantling the hierarchical ranking and status due to social backwardness of the social group to which they belong to as individuals. This version of social backwardness is explicitly stated more as a historical disadvantage and thereby, the caste/class as socially backward has been seen in a historically conditioned socio-cultural context and background where the issue of hierarchy was more deterministic in arriving at the backward class status. André Béteille (1981) has stated that the problem of the backward classes in achieving equality in a world permeated by inequality, i.e., the significance, lies not only in its size and content but also in the uniquely Indian way of defining the boundaries, i.e., the hierarchical boundaries. This uniqueness is a reflection of specific social and historical conditions, which may be formulated as culture of hierarchy.

Dipankar Gupta (1991), in his work on stratification, has elucidated the extent in which the hierarchies have inherent characteristics of inequalities by virtue of social enforcement at a particular point in time and by the contingencies, which strive for imposed order to ranking the human differences as a dynamic structure. His version of bracketing the hierarchy of Brahminical version as capricious as non-Brahminical version and also the need to give cognizance to the fact that they should also hierarchize differently and separately in as much as castes are different and separate is the point to be pondered over. Gupta, while acknowledging further on the variety of the form and shape of hierarchies – an inevitable component in the study of inequality and stratification – has noted that the different hierarchies are contextualized through the different socio-economic and cultural co-ordinates.

Indian society through the historical dynasties is an abundant source to state that hierarchy is not a static concept. It is as dynamic as the culture of tradition in Indian society. The social structure and institutions were in fact subordinating the cultural tradition of hierarchy in Indian system to such an extent that subsumption of power into status took place more by an act of individuals, and not through the textual prescription of the social order. Thereby, the form and shape of hierarchy got transformed over the cultural bases. I.P. Desai (1988) joined the Dumont version of hierarchy in the context of the real and apparent differences in the caste system in India, which have internally of multiple identities and tensions. Also, in this context, the precedence of the difference over hierarchy or hierarchy preceding difference – the concern of Desai are the other points of view on hierarchy

Thus, the understanding of the issue of inequality through the culture of hierarchy is of how the hierarchy as a component of inequality is a locally variant one with the potentials of continuity and change. The knowledge and scholarship on such local variant of the hierarchy within a historical and cultural context will be an added input into the inequality dimensions of the development paradigm. The current inequality eradication programmes of development paradigm are of income generation and of delinking the occupation from the traditional characteristics with symbolization towards material advancement. The cultural connections of hierarchy, particularly of the culture at the local dimensions of inequality, is to be given due significance as is in the case of the development and welfare of backward classes and weaker sections in Indian society. The issue of culture in relation to inequality has to be analytically taken up not necessarily within the framework of modernization. The determinist model of Marxism and views of host of scholars like Sahlins, Frank, Wolf, Laclaw and Wallerstein, Banaji and Hindess also do not explain adequately culture of hierarchy. Rather, it is on the other side, i.e., beyond the determination model. The issue is not in contesting, rebutting, challenging or social action groups practising negotiating the issue of culture as meaning of human practice but it is within the framework of continuity and change of the form and shape of culture connections over several social dimensions of society, which include inequality, hierarchy and social stratification.

With this background, an analytical study of Indian social structure and institutions within a specific time and space has considered the significance of the cultural tradition on which Indian society and the hierarchy was based. The emphasis of this approach is through the description of the issues in the given consciousness of the historical period and also has been on the context and content of the process.

The knowledge, in this context, to be derived is supposed to be the one on the 'historical consciousness' of social institutions rather than on the dynastic chronicle alone. In this context, social significance is on the consciousness of the event, process or act. No specific methodology of the traditional scientific outlook could be effective because the social framework of Indian society through time and space cannot be looked through the holistic tradition without its variants, namely, religion, culture, values and political contexts. Also, to see them through text and theory without reference to context and practice will be an academic fiasco. Therefore, the methodology was in departing from a mere chronicling Indian cultural history. An attempt is made to look into the state and society in a specific historical space and time to analyse how the ideological interests of hierarchical socio-cultural order of the period are fostered by social structural conditioning. In the process, the social reality of Indian society has been discussed in a sociological ethnography of persons as individuals in a group, community and society through the social structure of the state. Thus, the dynastic chronicle of the state is analysed along with the social chronicle of society. The dominant trend of caste analysis is reversed with a specific period, i.e., 300–1000 AD through the history and through the approach of individuals in their umbilical card relation with the social group to which he belongs to. Thus, the methodological understanding of this process was through description of the issues. The traditional methodological approaches appear to be an excessively reductionism one in terms of style and process rather than that of the context and content of the process. This descriptive focus is a modest one to study the culture and society in India marked by a form of social structure, which has a selective incorporation of cultural elements constructing a general civilization process within a specific historical event.

The kings and dynasties during this classical age in India were not bound by the rigid legitimization of caste-right even when society was ridden with caste-based social relationship. For example, Chandragupta married a princess from the great aboriginal tribe of the Lichchhavis; the Parthiharas were said to be descendants of a Gujara tribe from Central Asia; Pallavas were said to be aboriginals, while the Chola, Chera and Pandya rulers were of Kshatriya origin. From this, it is clearly evident that in the quest for political power and also to sustain themselves in it, by certain individuals, there was an element of desire for mobility and social change to seek socio-economic opportunities. Although normative prescription of scared scriptures disallowed the Brahmins to be a king, the Brahmins with their superiority in Sanskrit language and literature remained on top by holding themselves strongly in a higher ranking in ritual hierarchy. They ignored ethnic fission and fusion in the social order and continued to patronize the exclusive social authority of power. As far as south is concerned, the dynastic history of the classical age during this period reveals a long march of Samudragupta to the south reaching as far as Kancheepuram. To sustain his rule in the far-off south, he devised a method by arranging the marriage of a Gupta princess to Vakataha prince of the Deccan dynasty. During the same time, the Pallava dynasty was extending its boundaries in Tamil Nadu in south. Of the greatest kings of Pallava was Mahendra Vikrama Varman I, and Narashimha Varman III ruled Pallava kingdom. Southernmost India had a division of Pandya, Chola and Chera kingdoms, which bore the history of small kingdoms and principalities. Imperial Cholas were the exception for a short period. They had a great empire with suzerain authority over the largest geographical area crossing nautical boundaries.

During this period, the tradition of Indian social organization had a unity of purpose among the different social groups. There were differences in tradition without assimilating with the other, although they co-existed together. There was non-assimilative nature of the caste features based on inter-cultural autonomy, which flourished through the ages. In a way, work done by every one and their every nature was occupationalized with hierarchical authority as described in Hindu 'jajmani' system. Although this system is described as reciprocity, it depicted exploitative reciprocity. With such cultural and structural characteristics of the groups, people were working in different occupations with an autonomy in their social space of their occupational skills by maintaining inter-cultural autonomy but co-existing with a dependency relationship with each caste-based socio-occupational forces. The fundamental relationship between culture and social structure in Indian society is manifested abundantly in the form of the caste system. There were the number of tiny groups with distinct culture, occupation and systems of belief with which these tiny social groups lived side by side. The autonomy of each tiny group has been respected while, at the same time, cooperation has been ensured between them. This kind of theoretical standpoint of the Indian tradition about man and society within a matrix of the relationship between culture and structure and within the context of king, state and social order in organizing the society has several issues like 'individuality' to name one among few.

Accordingly, the individual's consciousness within the then existing framework of political power, economy and society/social group was one of the frameworks, which was purely a functional element. Here, the quest of individuals and groups as intermediaries between kings and subjects appeared to be a functional one cutting across caste. The social structures and institutions played a significant role in absorbing the tradition of cultural features of caste in an adaptive sense.

The system of a leader or feudal lord or intermediary or local chieftain and so on mostly characterized the angle of individuality without individualism for the maintenance of the group life being Indian values. They were fostered mostly by the power of the state and not by the sacred prescriptions of theoretical social order. This was one of the hallmarks of the institutionalized social power away from the power of the king and his authority. It was the social power circle vested by the king to wield his authority from a distance. In this context, the principle of hierarchy within and between castes did not shape the form of individuality. It emerged from the Indian values of individuality without individualism, i.e., from the culturally stipulated attributes of an individual for being the leader for the sustenance of the group or village or region. These were the principles that highlighted the co-existence of group mind and individuality. All these denote the meaning of the social bases of power to regulate the mechanism of people's interest. They were fostered from the point of view of land, social control and the maintenance of the economic organization of society. The social division was not purely a caste-based one, i.e., based on the practice of social power vested among the individuals. But, the social relationships were on caste lines. It was mainly because of the possible economic interests that certain individuals in the society and village were forced to be the holders of socio-political power positions. Thereby, the groups and the castes in the villages had to accept these individuals as persons of social authority but not of the ritually determined hierarchical authority and thus these individual persons acted as intermediaries between the king and subjects.

The person as individual in Indian context is in his interaction through the 'group mind' in essence unlike in West where it depicts personal liberty and freedom. Rather, the individuality in Indian social organization was characterized with the values of dependency of the group or the compulsions for the group to look towards someone who was socially powerful/tall and locally influential with willingness to meet the group demands and also to fulfil the needs and aspirations of the people in the social group irrespective of caste, kin or class in a given region. So, the group's quest for someone among the group as individual to lead and to give direction was the hallmark of the Indian social organization. Accordingly, social institutions of Indian social organizations were not as depersonalized as that of the west either by way of power having a meaning of coercion over others or remaining apart from the group from which the individual transforms into a leader. The group functioned at the level of personalized social interaction by reposing faith and confidence among those 'individuals' who were believed to be above everyone else in the social group. Accordingly, Dumont's paradigm of 'individuality' in Indian social organization may be reformulated on the fact that he superimposed the western values of individualism and tried to evaluate it in the Indian context.

In this context, the existence of such a relationship of people with social groups needs to be seen in historical consciousness of Indian society. There is no dearth of academic exercise on 'individual and group' among the Indian academia who used the framework of 'caste and hierarchy'. They have, at the same time, tried to see the need for co-existence of 'individuality with the groups' in caste, clan, kinship and village. In reality, the emphasis of caste hierarchy used to be only partial even though the scholars of Indian civilization has enunciated the issue of 'cultural holism'. To put it differently by borrowing the existing academic versions on the subject, the version of individual and his relationship within the caste as that of the one occurring in social space seems to be only a cognitive reality very much different from the existential reality. It may appear that the caste as an insular social space of an individual reflected in the restriction of the hierarchical relationship to certain specified areas of social needs. The transition from *varna* to *jati* framework was essentially a transition from the form and shape of existential reality conditioned by the necessities of certain social situations. There, the divisions of interest of certain social elements of groups within the larger groups had a quest for a separate social identity. The dissonance of cognitive reality of the social reality to that of the existential reality is not only a transition as is in the case of *varna* to *jati*, but also, an inevitable existence of individuality with group mind in Indian social organization.

Certain individuals in society emerged into a socially nodal point of the group/caste (to which the individual belongs) based on "the supremacy of the accumulative and distributive potential of individuals". It was considered as a significant socio-genesis of power relationship in Indian society. In terms of social history of a person and group, the Indian civilization is replete with the occurrences of such 'accumulative and distributive' relationships between the king and his subjects as is elucidated by the South Asian scholars on the social structure, caste and the persons in the social relationship. The social salience of dominance of individuals either single or as group apart from the hierarchical features of the caste was visible among the analytical contributions of Indian society by Gloria Raheja (1988a), Carol A. Breckenridge (1977), Nicholas Dirks (1987) and Arjun Appadurai (1981). These scholars have observed that there were several community level agents and agencies that had "distributional social power and status among them cutting across social relationships at the caste level. Therefore, the emergence of individuality without individualism in Indian social organization was legitimized by the forces of social obligation of individuals for the social group comprising several castes and not of one caste in which he was socially located although he belonged to a particular caste. This social obligation was, besides his self-interest, with no quest for personal freedom and equality.

In reinventing such social salience of 'individuality' in the classical age of our Indian history, without in any way discarding the existence of caste hierarchy, an analysis of the prevalent social economy and the socio-political order may be relevant. Thus, the evolutionary form and type of state control over its subjects in terms of the right over the land forms a piece of social history. The form and shape of the state control over land, right from the Gupta period to the emergence and consolidation of empires, was not a simple 'land and state' relationship. It was the mechanism of enforcing economic relationship through a kind of social formation of peasantry.

For example, land was the primeval source of economy, society and polity. Such land, with all its wealth potential to maintain the army and the subjects for the kings of a given region in India had the features of the system of land tenure and also associated features like land grant and revenue system. Unlike in Europe where land feudalism prevailed with all its private potential, i.e., private landlordship, the kings in India merely provided rights of power over the land to some select subjects in various regions to collect the revenue purely within the framework of land as a property of the state. The king and the state had discretion to remove this right and power over the lands among the subjects and thus the private ownership of land was absent. To cite an example, the Gupta empire under the classical age of India, like other empires in India, was primarily relying on revenue share from the lands that Indian peasants had to part specified amount out of every harvest to the kingdom. It was often said that there has been a crystallization of feudalism, i.e., over the land and its products during this historical period. A survey of land control and kings' relationship with the subjects revealed that there was a system under which lands were transferred to local feudal lords. There were two different ways of controlling the land tenure. One way was levying tributes in kind from local leaders and tribal chiefs without an intermediary class. The other was to locate intermediaries and give them the responsibility to collect tax and remit it to the feudal hierarchy.

It is said that "in the course of time, it was the intermediary structure between king and society which emerged into a ruling class whose function was to appropriate the surplus of the peasantry". An incisive analysis of land tenure relationship under this semi-feudal system demonstrated the development of 'accumulative and distributional' power having been vested among the intermediaries between the king and his subjects. Mattison Mines, in his exhaustive social analysis of the structure and tradition of the grounded social relationships, assumes this kind of dependency-dominance syndrome as a 'significant man-centred individuality' as is conceptualized elaborately in a different context. This explains that this 'power of wealth and resource' did not have economic significance alone without having the features of the 'power of ruling' vested in the leaders by the kings during their conquest of a region. The real issue was the social dependency of the 'subjects' on these 'feudal lords'. This ultimately results in the debate whether there was feudalism. Much more than the argument on the existence of feudalism, the issue is beyond the social formation of peasantry and is in the cultural forms of peasantry. The cultural forms, in this context, were in the co-existence of political, economic and social power at the level of peasant society. The social power in the form of caste hierarchy remained so constant. But, it continued as a structural tradition limited to a functional element of greater social mobilization and identity. But, the equilibrium between the political power and economic power at the peasantry level was in the form and shape of culture of individuality, which should be a subject of debate in the context of the question of hierarchy.

Contextually, this issue, i.e. the position of 'land' may be taken up for an analysis. The account of pilgrims during the fifth and sixth century AD provided an indication that there was no land register in terms of household allotments at the hands of king's authority. It only showed that the state was not directly operating the land tenure system, although the lands with mineral value were at the command of the state. Also, there were records of land grants to guilds and Brahmins. Essentially, the intermediaries between the king and subjects directly operated lands. The statements of Fa-hsien during the Gupta period show that their officials and the conquered princes were granted lands. These princes and petty officials were more visible with their economic power over the merchant and professional guilds. During the Gupta period, these princes who commanded the various groups including merchants and professional guilds and demonstrated their political power vested in them as individuals. The political power of these individuals was restricted within the vicinity of space and regions to which the kings have given them authority. These individuals through their 'individuality', i.e., social individuality, played a significant role in shaping cultural and social relationship at the local level. The subjects under the different dynasties including Pal lava and Chola were both inside and outside the caste groups. This is a complex tradition with a culture of hierarchy in Indian society.

To sum up, the social order during the classical age was of continuity and change in the cultural features of hierarchy. The framework of the person's 'individuality' without individualism represented how the hierarchical concept could undergo change or transformation in a given context. By narrowing this discussion to the nature and characteristics of hierarchy, an endeavour is made to capture the cultural forces of hierarchy in the Indian social order.

The Indian social system and institutions in the classical ages did represent a situation where the features of hierarchy were located within the dynamics of change in the structural features for a functional necessity more determined by the contextual social space and not by the textual space based ritual hierarchy. The knowledge and scholarship on hierarchy in the Indian context, by their explanatory endeavour invoke the concepts of tradition, changing dimensions of power, economic arrangements, and social reward and also of moral values and ideas. In the textual clarification of the Indian social system, there was a description of moral obligations on the part of the individuals and groups to stay within the hierarchy of the social order. The significance of such moral obligations was in the inflexible attitude among the mobility of individuals from one status to another in the social order. These features were effectively institutionalized also in various forms of social categories. The issue is whether these textual prescriptions were practised in the social contexts.

Here, a brief survey of commentaries of the hierarchy in Indian society may be relevant. Attempts were not made to look into the conditions of hierarchy in an exclusive manner. Instead, there were attempts to know as to who were actually advocating and practising the principles of hierarchy as per the texts. Also, it was seen in which contexts these people advocated and practised. It is concluded that all the people entered into the hierarchical relationships, i.e., obligations emanating from the cultural structure of hierarchy. From the point of view of the four-fold stages of Hindu way of life, a system of hierarchical ways of life was enunciated in the forms of stages of Brahmacharya, Grahastha, Vanaprastha and Sanyasa. In reality, the absoluteness in the practice of passing through all these four stages for every individual or group in the society was not there. There were clear-cut deviations that a majority of the masses did not adhere to this in the strict tradition. Many of them remained purely ideological referents with certain elements of motivational force. Such motivational force was impelling some individuals in society to translate the precepts into practice. In this context, the institutionalization of the ideology was not total resulting in the nature of culture that mediates the structure of the social relationships for various individuals in variously different ways.

In terms of conformity to the ideological aspects of Hindu divisions of life featuring a form of hierarchical orientation, there was the least rigidity and thus they remained purely a hierarchical culture without rigid institutional roles. In this context, if one goes to the extent of saying that the Indian caste society is holistic and hierarchical and the expressions of individualism and is subordinated to collectivism, it may not match perfectly as there was no proper fit between ideology and fact, or precept and practice. The absence of such a fit between ideology and fact or percept and practice of hierarchical features either in the ways of Hindu division of life or in the *jati* system could not be explained by the lack of institutional complexes alone. The basic features of hierarchy in the Indian social order are in the co-existence of separation and interdependence as far as the formulation of social relationships is concerned. The *jati* model of caste and its transition from *varna* (although it is yet another cultural subordination of the structure) has been seen in practice during the Gupta dynasty and their counterparts in south at the time. There was flexibility in the practice of the behavioural norms, which differed from the text. It was evident in the pursuit of power by some people or clans. They located themselves in institutionalized forms like monarchy as in the case of kings and princes who have their marriage alliances from the caste other than their own as stated elsewhere in this paper. This is a situation where there was a chance for a clan or a group to move away from the hierarchical restrictions provided by the caste-based social relationships.

Similarly, the features of individuality as located among the chieftains or local persons in the name of intermediaries through the system of land grants and power to collect the revenue were yet other forms of lack of Fit between the hierarchical ideology and fact, although it may look like performing the royal function by the local chieftains. These persons sustained themselves in a social power that raised them to a status of position; the groups and castes in the region and locality looked towards them. Then, these persons became dominant individuals cutting across the caste-based hierarchical relationships. Dumont and others discuss this issue of dominant individuals at the local level within the framework of power and status. Differentiating the levels of power and status into primary or non-segmented level, Dumont discovered that the power is subordinated to status at the former level and the same becomes equal to the status at the latter level. M.N. Srinivas, in his commentary on the position of Dumont about the relationship between power and status at these different levels, has stated that there is a different legitimatized exercise of power. The differentiated levels like kings getting coroneted and the local chiefs not getting coroneted and the usage of Brahmin priests in the process are the classic situations of relationship between 'individuality' and 'hierarchy' within the cultural features in defining the individual and his status.

The separateness and interdependence of caste-based hierarchical relationship at the social level was also replicated at the level of individuality and hierarchy. The local chieftains get grouped into individuality not by subordinating the power, both social and political, to the status determined through the contextually prescribed hierarchy. The person's 'individuality' obtained by the local chieftains during the periods was not within the textually prescribed hierarchy.

Thus, the question of uncritical assumption of the nature of hierarchy is a subject for a critical debate both in its conceptual framework and on the culture as a base of hierarchy.

References

Appadurai, Arjun (1981), *Worship and Conflict under Colonial Rule: A South Indian Caste*, New York: Cambridge University Press.

—— and Carol A. Breckenridge (1976), 'The South Indian Temple: Authority, Honor and Redistribution', *Contributions to Indian Sociology N.S.*, Vol. 10, pp. 187–211.

Basham, A.L. (1975), *A Cultural History of India*, Oxford: Oxford University Press.

Béteille, André (1981), *The Backward Classes and the New Social Order*, New Delhi: Oxford University Press.

—— (1986), 'Individualism and Equality', *Current Anthropology*, Vol. 27, pp. 121–34.

Desai, I.P. (1988), *Division and Hierarchy: An Overview of Caste in Gujarat*, Delhi: HPC, p. x.

Dirks, Nicholas B. (1987), *The Hallow Crown: Ethno History of an Indian Kingdom*, New York: Cambridge University Press.

Drekmeier, Charles (1962), *The Kingship and Community of Early India*, California: Stanford University Press.

Dumont, Louis (1970), *Homo Hierarchicus: An Essay on the Caste System*, Chicago: University of Chicago Press.

Gupta, Dipankar (1991), *Social Stratification*, New Delhi: Oxford University Press, p. x.

Sundaram, D. (1994), *Indian Social Structure and Institutions: A Social History in Retrospect, A.D. 300: 1000: Culture of Hierarchy*, paper presented at the seminar on Society and Culture for Indian Philosophical Research Council, March.

Tocqueville, Alexis de (1945), *Democracy in America and Old Regime and French Revolution*, Winkle Book edition, page 14, 338–339 and XII.

—— (1946), *Democracy in America (1835)* and *Old Regime and the French Revolution (1856)*.

10 Class, Status and Gender

Social Stratification among Tribes of India

S.L. DOSHI

Indian sociology has earned a great deal of notoriety by writing on the tribal social stratification found in the forms of class and caste. What is worse, the literature on social stratification is characterized by the ideology and methodology of functionalism. What applies to Indian sociology equally applies to Indian social anthropology. Historically, sociology and anthropology in India have mixed up so much that even for analytical purpose, it is difficult to separate one from the other. They are the two sides of the same coin. Social stratification has remained a taboo for social anthropology. What is written by social anthropology in India is immensely ethnography. Even K.S. Singh, who is editor of *People of India,* has fallen victim to the theme of ethnography of the various communities. It is argued by most of the sociologists and anthropologists that the tribals are a lot of people who deny social change, particularly modernization. The tribals in all respects are a 'savage' people who have been given the benefits of protective and development safeguards. The image of tribals given by sociologists and anthropologists is that of the people who still suffer from ecological romanticism and are anti-modernists.

We contest all these theoretical and methodological notions. Let us refer to the volume of research material, which is available with us to draw some generalizations about the conditions of social stratification among the tribals of India. To make these generalizations, we adopt an approach, which is beyond the disciplinary boundaries of sociology. Such an approach helps us to understand the condition of tribal class, status and gender. But, before we take up the theme of tribal social stratification, let us argue that so far sociologists have not done any 'social justice' to tribals. Tribals are represented mistakenly in social sciences, particularly sociology and social anthropology, as Hindus. No effort, however, has been made to provide an authentic portrait of the tribal society. There has been so much of discrimination against the tribals that their age-long identity has been merged with the caste society. If the tribal society is undifferentiated from the caste society, what made our constitutional framers to give certain privileges to the tribal society? Why this society is not identified with the scheduled tribes? Obviously, the tribal society is not characterized by any kind of untouchability. It has its own identity, its own ethnicity, and its own history of pain and pleasure.

Why do our sociologists not identify this reality of grassroots? The fault with our sociologists is that they are highly influenced by functional ideology. Functionalism entered India through British social anthropology. M.N. Srinivas, who was a follower of British sociologists, has found functionalism inbuilt in Indian society. The influence of Srinivas on Indian sociology is so fantastic that no analysis is complete without reference to sanskritization and westernization – the concepts which emerged from his study of the *Coorgs of South India.*[1] Srinivas is not all alone. His company of followers includes a large number of sociologists, such as T.N. Madan, Ashis Nandy and André Béteille. These functionalists have developed the notion that secularism has failed to ensure inter-religious harmony. They provide a critique of the modernist nationalist historiography approach to understanding the nation-building process. They hold that "the very logic of modernity and its variant attributes such as centralized state power, industrialization, nationalism, democracy (elitist) and secularism are responsible for society's ills, particularly the growing violence reflected in caste, communal and rural-urban conflicts."[2]

For Indian sociologists of social stratification, the remedy to the societal ills remains with the social change returning to caste society. Perhaps, sanskritization ensures all consensus to the cohesiveness of Indian society. Sanskritization, westernization, dominant caste, little tradition and great tradition, caste ranking and a few more contributions are claimed to be the theoretical capital of Indian sociologists. But, the objective of these concepts is to establish that all sections, of society including tribals, are adopting Brahmanism as their course of social change. A kind of Brahmanical sociology has developed in India during the post-independent period. In one of his articles published in the *Times of India in* 1993, M.N. Srinivas argued that India needs a new philosophy to solve the grave cultural and spiritual crisis facing the country, and that philosophy cannot be secular humanism.[3] It has to be firmly rooted in God as creator and protector.

Value-free Sociology and Ideology in Sociological Theory

Indian tribal society has been studied quite extensively. It must be admitted that ethnographic data on Indian tribes is the richest one in social anthropology. But, the methodology of ethnographic studies is functionalism. The ethnographic theory of sociology in India is characterized by the status-quo of social structure. The study of tribals beyond the disciplinary boarders of social anthropology is difficult to find.

Functionalism, as a theory and method, is a part of value-free sociology debate in social sciences. In the US, it was George C. Homans (1964), who for the first time criticized the structural functional perspective that had been dominant for the living generation of sociology in the US. He observed:

> Functionalism had run its course, done its work and now positively gets in the way of our understanding of social phenomena.[4]

Homans argued that structural-functional explanations were not in fact scientific, largely because they failed to provide explanations for empirical relations and, therefore, functionalism never worked as a theoretical perspective. Later on, Lewis A. Coser and Alwin W. Gouldner criticized the theoretical mindlessness of statistical research and the limitations of structural functionalism as well as ethnomethodology.[5] Actually structural functionalism came into vogue in the US in the 1940s. It was argued that sociology as a scientific discipline should not take sides. It should be "statistically-oriented, empirical and positivistic". Structural-functional methodology drew its inspiration from value-free sociology. At a later stage, it was found in the US that functionalism had its interests identified with the capitalist US and the state power. Sociologists like Edward Shils supported America's attack on Vietnam. The functionalist sociologists worked as academic imperialists in the colonial countries. The Britishers also used functionalism as a method of colonialism in Africa and India.

What we argue is that whatever we have in the tribal studies is all characterized by functional theory, methodology and ideology. Indian sociologists are very 'cleaver' to promote the cause of functionalism in India. It is said that Indian sociology has no theory. It is all ethnomethodology. Of recent studies is the publication of *People of India*[6] which argues in its introductory volume that Indian tribal studies are basically ethnomethodological studies.

Our argument is that the tribals of India are not only ethnomethodological entities. Like any other social structure, they have also witnessed fantastic social change, for example, Malinowski[7] made meticulous recording of social life of Trobriand Islanders of New Guinea in 1915 to 1918. Another British anthropologist Radcliffe-Brown[8] studied the Andaman Islanders in 1922. These two tribal groups are not the same today. They have not remained unchanged. They have come at the doorsteps of post-modernism. If the Trobrianders have reached to this stage, should we not think that the Bhils of Rajasthan and the Gonds of Madhya Pradesh have today attained the status of a people characterized by modernity and post-modernity?

We are required to look at the Indian tribals from the perspective of modernity and post-modernity. It would be our mistaken notion to think that the Indian tribes have not witnessed a radical social stratification in the field of their lifestyle, status and class formation. The tragedy of Indian social anthropology and sociology is that our patron sociologists still argue that sociology has the ideology of functionalism. In a broader way, sociological theory has taken two theoretical methodological directions: functional and dialectical, the latter being put to marginality. We have in hand the latest writing of Yogendra Singh.[9] His preface to the *Ideology and Theory in Indian Sociology* runs as below:

> Sociology, like most social sciences, is embedded in ideology … . In publishing these essays our intention is to put across to the readers the ideological challenges which have overwhelmed sociology in India in the past and also continue to assume a great deal of relevance today.

Tracing the history of ideology and theory in sociology, Singh says that the earlier ideology of sociological theory was enlightenment. It took history as a progressive ideology. The progress was not without its challenges. There emerged social anomie, impoverishment and exploitation of the working classes, women and children by the rapacious industrial capitalism. It was Karl Marx who for the first time demonstrated the significance of ideology in social science and sociology. Emile Durkheim, another founder sociologists, also established the relationship between ideology and theory. He is said to be the pioneer of functionalism in sociological theory. Max Weber talked about the notion of 'rationalization' in bringing about social change in society. Weber explained class, status and polity with his concept of rationalization. Yogendra Singh makes all efforts to bring home the fact that ideology has always been integral to sociology. His thesis of ideology and sociological theory is concluded as under:

> The debate on ideology in the sociological discourse of the Western sociology assumed importance during the entire period from 1889 to 1930. It was on account of two basic reasons: first, due to the limitations of positivistic theory in failing to explain the negative social and cultural consequences of the early 19th and 20th century industrial and capitalist social order. The extent of poverty, social and cultural anomie and social conflict, which followed in the wake of capitalist- industrial growth in Europe, could not be explained by the rationality paradigm on which the positivistic sociology was founded. Secondly, in the writings of sociologists of this period, of which Marx was precursor, we find an attempt to offer theoretical and methodological alternatives.

The alternatives in the western sociology came through the emergence of Frankfurt School, which gave rise to critical theory. New critical theory and structural-functional studies took to empiricism as a popular method of enquiry. But, gradually, there emerged discontent from the structural-functional sociology. The sociology of Talcott Parsons in USA "became an iconic symbol of the ideology of conservatism". Scholars like C. Wright Mills and E. Gouldner made Parsonian sociology as the central piece of their critique of the functional sociology.

As we find today, functionalism has become outdated in Europe and USA. But, in Indian context, the things are altogether different. We still have our older and younger sociologists practising functionalism as a major theoretical and methodological tool. As discussed earlier, M.N. Srinivas who brought functionalism to India through his mentor Radcliffe-Brown made Indian tribes as Hindus. His concept of sanskritization is so pervasive that it explains all cultural change occurring in various ethnic groups of the country as a wider process of Brahmanism and Hinduization.

The history of sociological studies that we have in India shows that Indian sociologists have contributed immensely to the study of village communities, tribe, caste, family and religion. In addition, many studies of planning and development constituted specialized concerns by a considerable amount of sponsored research. Village studies have offered a few conceptual tools such as dominant caste and parochialization. The caste studies discussed about mobility and hierarchy. Indian sociologists cling on to functionalism in such a way that they do not find social change in the areas of development and modernization. Yogendra Singh says that there is social change in India but this change is not radical, it is adaptive. Adaptive social change is the core characteristic of functional change. Our hypothesis is that the Indian sociologists' and social anthropologists' blind love for functionalism has kept the tribals away from the reality with which they have been struggling. We reject functionalism, we reject value-free sociology. Our effort is to understand the tribals in terms of the present-day theoretical ideology of modernity and post-modernity. We further argue that the tribal society is not a Hindu society as is being argued by the *Hindutva* ideology. At best, the tribals are one of the distinct ethnic groups in the country who are willing to allow change in their social stratification and at the same time struggling hard for the survival of their ethnic identity. Any social change, which is brought to the doorsteps of the tribals, is irrelevant if the identity of the tribals as an ethnic group is jeopardized.

Is the Tribal Society a Caste Society?

The issue of relationship between tribes in India and the Hindu caste system has received a new dimension in contemporary India where fundamentalism and communalism have raised their ugly heads. The massive destruction of human life in post-Godhra violence in Gujarat brought the tribals to the problem of their relationship with the caste society. The caste-Hindus argued that many of aggressors in the violence were outsides and these outsiders were tribals. It is reported that many of the acts of violence were done by the tribals. Nearly 60,000 tribal labourers migrate to Baroda every year in search of employment. From the third day of the riots these tribals returned to their villages and in the villages they burnt the Muslim shops. The Hindu fimdamentalists triggered the Gujarat violence in 2002 instigating the tribals. The involvement of the tribals in violence has recently given a new edge to the relationship between the tribal society and the Hindu caste system. These happenings raise the question: Is the tribal society a caste society? The Hindu fundamentalists have started a network of NGOs who are working in the interior parts of tribal country. *Vanvasi Kalyan Parishad* and a host of other educational institutions instigate the tribals for adaptive change. In fact, the problem of relationship between these two communities is embedded in the ideology of social research.

Historically, anthropologists have tried to analyse the relationship between tribes and castes. For instance, with the exception of Hutton, who maintains that caste system and many cultural traditions of Hinduism have organic links with the tribal cultures, and of Ghurye who holds similar views, all other Census Commissioners and anthropologists, such as Risley, O'Malley, Elwin, etc., hold the tribal and the Hindu traditions to be separate. D.D. Kosambi also maintains that many cultural items of existing peasant Hindu culture in India have their origin in the aboriginal cults and cultural patterns.[10]

The functionalists strongly believe in conservatism and capitalism. Yogendra Singh argues at length that even the Indian traditions adopt modernization in the country's history. In one of his latest publications, Singh observes:

> The attributes of functional analysis in Indian sociology are in popular image associated with this phase of village and caste studies. In the caste system it was assumed through the universal dominance of the pollution-purity values and in the village context the integrative relationships of caste, *jajmani* and family and kinship and social ecological distinctiveness ... . The second aspect of these studies relates to their treatment of the social change. The notion of change in most of these studies is that of systematic adaptations.[11]

We have referred to Yogendra Singh at length only to support our view that tribe and caste in India have been studied with functional perspective, that is, *change is not radical but adaptive.* In fact, functionalism applied the axioms of

Hinduism to understand tribal social change. For these functionalists, Srinivas' *Religion and Society Among the Coorgs of South India* might be cited as the best sociological study of this period. It has obvious links with structural notions, especially in the analysis of rituals. Srinivas earlier gave the concept of Brahmanization. He argued that lower castes tried to imitate the ideology of high caste Hindus. The practitioners of functionalism have simply to the look at tribals with the ideology of Hinduism which has today become pervasive in the agenda of parties having fundamentalism as their agenda.

The debate on the relationship between tribals and caste-Hindus has also been analysed by K.S. Singh in his *People of India* (PoI) project. It must be observed here that the basic difference in caste and tribe is that the former is hierarchical while the latter is autonomous. Each tribal group has its own autonomy. There is no hierarchy between the Gond, Baiga, Muria and the Bhil. Each tribal group has also its own distinct ethnic identity. This does not apply to caste system. A caste – may it be Brahmin or Rajput – is a part of the wider caste system held together by purity-pollution and ranking.

K.S. Singh says that despite wider social change the tribals even today have not become a part of the caste system. His findings run as below:

> The tribes have generally remained outside the varna system ... . A major finding in terms of religion has been the continuance of the autonomy of the tribal religious system in spite of the tribes' close interaction with Christianity. The hierarchy of the clan and the village deities is intact. There are more sacred specialists among the tribals from their own communities. There are only a very small number of sacred specialists from other communities. The calendar of festivals and festivities is also relatively intact.

The condition of tribals, as we find them today, is mixed with controversies. The sociologists and also social anthropologists have tried to establish the fact on the strength of ethnic data that the tribals of India are Hindus. They have made all efforts to established ritual, religious, functional relations between the caste and the tribe. G.S. Ghurye who is described as the doyen of sociology, defines tribals as backward caste Hindus. N.K. Bose thinks that Hindus have a historical method of absorbing the tribes. It appears that sociologists have taken a position to present the tribals as Hindus. They argue that the tribals are ever ready to imitate the model of Brahmins and Rajputs. We argue that such an approach to the study of tribals is a mistaken one. They have their own history and it is the history of their isolation which has kept them away from the Hindu mainstream civilization.

Before we close this discussion, we would refer to the analysis made by Verrier Elwin. How does he look at tribals, that is, Baiga, Gond, and Muria?

Freezing the Tribal Social Stratification

Thus, there are two streams of ideology concerning with the tribal social stratification. One stream of social anthropologists advocates the incorporation of tribals into Hindu society, while the other one is characterized by the ideology of freezing the social stratification of tribals. It says that class, class consciousness, production relations and things of this kind did not affect the tribals. Mention may be made in this connection of Elwin. It was between the 1930s and mid-1940s that Elwin emerged as an influential voice on the question of tribal social stratification. He was critical of tribal development. He was a tribal activist par excellence. Ramachandra Guha comments on the status of Elwin in the field of Indian tribals:

> Most of all, Elwin must be distinguished from other primitivists, he actually lived with the communities whose culture be vigorously celebrated .... There is a poignant and heroic logic that distinguishes Elwin's brand of activist anthropology with academic anthropology.[12]

Elwin elaborated his thesis and thought that the impact of modern capitalism would be negative on the tribals in the long run. He argued that homogenous tribal social stratification based on their customs and traditions need not be polluted by Hindu castes. The tribals have been living in harmony with nature since the ancient times. This meant that they were the original inhabitants of their lands, and their practices were regulated by institutions that gave their society a certain social coherence and stability. Following this was the assumption that tribal practices were ecologically friendly in character. And, this was also reflected in the cultural and social life of tribal societies. Elwin writes:

> The life of a true aboriginal is simple and happy, enriched by natural pleasures. For all their poverty, their days are spent in the beauty of the hills. A woman carrying a load to the hill-top pauses a moment to see the scene below her. It is the "sweet forest", the "forest of joy and sandal" in which they live.[13]

Elwin advocated a policy of 'partial isolation' of tribal people. The Gond, the Baiga, and the Agaria, all believed that societal harmony, that is, absence of caste, class and gender stratification made their past life happier. When his *Aboriginals* was published, it created a storm among the sociologists. G.S. Ghurye came out with his classical work *Caste, Class and Occupation*[14] and contested the theory of Elwin. The controversy raised by Ghurye was a matter of debate in social sciences. He argued that the future of Indian tribes was closely linked with the caste hierarchy. The tribals, according to him, were destined to be a part of backward caste Hindus.

It is interesting to note that Elwin always shifted his position on the social stratification of tribals. His theory of tribal isolation later on came to be known as the theory of tribal integration in the caste society. He found that the tribals were caught between the Hindus and Christians and all these organizations tried to convert them into their respective folds – Christian or Hindu. This made Elwin to change his position:

> In particular I urge all Hindu organizations interested in this problem to pass resolutions accepting the major aboriginal communities as Kshatriyas which is what they are and what they claim to be .... I appeal, therefore, to the great Hindu community of India, who have executed the wonder and administration of men in every part of the civilized world, to awaken and rouse yourselves.[15]

In his later life, Elwin was influenced by Jawaharlal Nehru. When Elwin became advisor to North-East Frontier Agency (NEFA), he advocated the theory that the tribals should be left to their genius and nothing of the caste Hindu culture should be imposed on them. This ideology is known as *Panchasheel,* that is, five principles of the theory of social stratification of tribals.

A review of the approaches taken by social anthropologists, sociologists and activists for the incorporation of tribals in the Indian society indicates that the problem of the isolation of tribals is very much related to their social stratification. The theory of stratification has never been ideology-free. The functionalists as they would like to maintain status-quo want to take the tribals to the road of Hindu castes. The Hindu fundamentalists have a belief that tribals can be useful when bargaining with the political leaders. Obviously, the Hinduization or Brahmanization of tribal social stratification has taken a new paradigm of exploitation. Violence can be (as in the case of Gujarat) put to the accountability of tribals; votes can be bargained with the tribals. There is need today to explain the tribal stratification in terms of democracy, capitalism, state power and above all with reference to the challenges given by globalization, market, privatization and modernization. The argument is simple: sociologists and social anthropologists cannot misrepresent the tribals as their caste-Hindu brethren who can be always relied upon to work for the cause of the high-caste Hindus. It would be mistaken all the time that the tribals have a blind faith in nature and they should not be brought to modernity. Admittedly, the Baigas of Madhya Pradesh had earned notoriety for practising shifting cultivation. All such tribal practices have now become the things of the past. Like any other ethnic group of the country, the tribals of India are ready to accept the challenges of democracy, capitalism, market and globalization. They have developed a vigorous self-consciousness, which accepts that change has brought to them more inequality and more exploitation. Sanskritization, dominant caste and conceptual things of this kind cannot keep the tribals anymore in good humour. They have proved themselves to be the competing partners on the road to modernization and globalization. The sociologists, who have analysed tribal social stratification on the pattern of Hinduism or Brahmanism, have now proved to be wrong for their biased ideology. They cannot interpret tribals as Hindus, who have their own ethnic identity and history.

Tribals and their Condition of Stratification

The tribal social stratification is different from the caste-Hindu stratification. They are known for their autonomy. Each tribal group has a distinct ethnic identity. It is not a part of wider tribal system. What is defined as a scheduled tribe in our Constitution is only an administrative definition. For our day-to-day concern, each tribal group is different from other group. It is in India that we define tribes as scheduled tribes. And, these groups are those, which are included in the scheduled list of tribals given by the President of India. Outside India, in other countries, tribals are known as indigenous peoples. Actually, indigenous peoples in Asia are now referred to officially by a number of designations. For instance, in India, they are defined as scheduled tribes; national minorities or minority nationality in China and Vietnam; and hill tribes in Thailand. What is common to these communities is that they have generally been outside the ambit or only loosely incorporated under the pre-colonial stages. Generally populating hill-forest regions, they have often been on the boarders.

K.S. Singh in the *People of India (PoI)* project reports that the population of the scheduled tribes comes to about 8 per cent. They are spread over all the states except Punjab and Haryana and over all the union territories except Chandigarh, Delhi and Pondicherry. They are basically a rural people. The largest concentration of tribals is in Madhya Pradesh (23.22%), followed by Orissa (11.46%), Gujarat (9.30%), Rajasthan (8.10%), Andhra Pradesh (6.15%) and West Bengal (5.95%). The smallest population comes from Goa, Daman and Diu (0.02%). There are more than 400 tribal groups in the country, the largest being the Gond, the Bhil, the Santal, the Mina and the Oraon. It is difficult to identify the exact racial identity of these groups. However, the tribals in India belong to four racial stocks, viz., Negrito (the great Andamanese, and the Onges and the Jarawas), the Proto-Austrotoid (the Munda, the Oran and the Gond), the Mangoloid (tribes of the north-east), and the Caucasoid (the Toda, the Rabari, the Gujar). There has been so much of intermingling of these racial traits that it is difficult to identify any pure race. K.S. Singh, while admitting this difficulty, writes:

> The concern with racial typology has now given way to the study of morphological and genetic traits of tribal population. Two observations may be made in this regard. First, that the existing data is too meager to permit any generalization; and second, that there is a homogeneity in the traits shared by different population groups of a particular region. An analysis of blood groups among the tribals in general exhibits preponderance of gene B over A, and B is represented in varying proportions. The tribals of the northeast show allele A in greater value and also the presence of the hemoglobin variant Hb E (frequency range 0.3 to 0.5).[16]

If an attempt is made to find out the racial stratification of the tribals of India, it will not lead us to any dependable conclusion. However, it must be observed that the tribals of north-east are a different racial stock of Mangoloid trait. In the same way, the Negritos of Andaman come out as a distinct racial group. The rest of the tribal groups found in the heart of the country have a racial affinity with the local people. This kind of racial stratification strikingly keeps the north-east and Andaman as a separate entity. The stratification pattern of north-east and extreme south thus is simple. The problem of these tribals is more of political nature than cultural. They are not concerned with caste phenomenon. Nor have they anything to do with sanskritization. More than 90 per cent of them are Christians.

Yet another variable of stratification is the linguistic structure. In the central part of the country tribal groups are different from caste-Hindus as the variable of language. K.S. Singh provides information on languages/dialects spoken by the tribals:

> We collected information on languages/dialect spoken within a family or kin group and those spoken outside them. The picture that emerges from an analysis of our data is an interesting one. Firstly, though Indo-Aryan languages are spoken by a vast majority of the tribal community, those speaking Dravidian and Tibeto-Burman languages are not few in terms of communities, though the 1981 Census indicates a relatively small number among the tribes. According to our study, the tribal communities speaking Indo-Aryan languages are 163, Dravidian 107, Tibeto-Burman 143, Austro – Asiatic 30 and Andamanese 04.[17]

What is interesting is that the incidence of bilingualism, even trilingualism, among the tribal communities has become pervasive. The tribals living on the borders of Maharashtra and Gujarat are mostly bilingual. Social stratification on the speaking of language has brought the tribal closer to caste-Hindus, Muslims and Christians. Bilingualism helps them to establish marriage alliances.

Yet another aspect of social stratification is ranking on the basis of food habits. The caste-Hindus leaving some exceptions of Rajputs and lower castes are vegetarian. On the other hand, the tribals are non-vegetarians. They eat pork and beef. The three vegetarian tribal communities are the Toda, the Rabari and the Bharwad. The caste-Hindus look down upon tribals because of their habit of beef-eating. K.S. Singh argues that the three tribal groups, who are vegetarians and come closer to high-caste Hindus, make it easier to adopt to Hindu social stratification. Giving reasons for tribal vegetarianism, K.S. Singh writes:

> It is interesting to observe that the three vegetarian communities are pastoral … . Vegetarianism in India has so far been associated with Jainism and Vaishnavism, which witnessed the transformation of pastoral god Krishna into incarnations of supreme godhood (Brahma). Here, the point to be noted is that the pastoral communities, which were involved in the growth and development of Vaishnavism, were all vegetarians like the Jats, Ahirs, etc.[18]

The prevalence of vegetarianism, which is a recent one, has brought about a significant change in the stratification of tribals. Bhagatism, that is, religious reform on the lines of high-caste Hindus, has influenced tribal stratification to a great length. It is common to find social strata among tribals who are based on vegetarian food. There are Santhals who have accepted Vaishnavism; likewise, there are Bhils, Gonds and Kawars who have accepted vegetarianism as a criterion of social ranking.

Tribal Isolation and 'Limited' Social Stratification

As stated earlier that tribals in India have been studied extensively both by Indian and British anthropologists. The British are of the view that the tribals are a 'savage' people and they could use them for colonial rule in India. The rulers of medieval period – Rajputs and Marathas – also 'used' the tribals in the battlefield. In such a historical situation the anthropological shift on social stratification did not emerge. The tribals were described as an ethnic identity having nothing to do with the wider caste society. At this level of discussion, it must be emphasized that the tribals lived in hills and forests and their isolation did not bring them closer to the caste-Hindus. They had limited contacts with the Rajputs when they were engaged in war against the Mughals. It was the functional ideology, which never induced sociologists to find out the nature of social stratification, which the tribals enjoyed.

Who are the tribals? Officially, their status is clear. They are included in the scheduled tribe list issued by the government. But, popularly, the tribals are known by a number of terms. Verrier Elwin and Ghurye described them as aboriginals. But, such an identification of tribals has run into difficulties in contemporary, India. The caste-Hindus refer them as Vanvasi, that is, groups of people living in forests. They do not consider the tribals as original settlers to this country. For these fundamentalists, Aryans are the original settlers to this land. The status of tribals, therefore, was that of hills and forest people. Archana Prasad argues that the tribals lived in this country in the plains and were routed by the Hindu rulers to hills and forests. In fact, for Archana, tribals are the original settlers to this country. She writes:

> ... the term 'Adivasi' has been used by people's movement to suggest that the tribals were the first inhabitants to their habitat, which is usually the forests. Though the Hindu Right does not use the term 'Adivasi'. It modifies this expression to 'Vanvasi' and essentially denoting the ancient origins of tribal people. And, the fact that they have been living in forests since the ancient times and were the original inhabitants of this habitat. 'Vanvasi' has been used by the Hindu Right to mobilize public opinion in a way that suggests that tribal people were not only part of the Hindu society, but they were also the first Hindus.[19]

What Archana Prasad wants to say is that the tribals were the original settlers to this land and were pushed to forests by the high-caste Hindus, particularly Rajputs and Marathas. What the Hindu Right people have been establishing today is that the tribals in the past were not only part of the Hindu society but they were also the first Hindus. If the thesis of Vanvasi, which is propagated by the Hindu Right people, is accepted, it obliges the tribals to demand for their rights on forest, land and water. These days, the tribals are making violent claims for *jal, jameen and jungle,* that is, water, land and forest.

The history of tribal habitation has remained a history of isolation. During their period of isolation, the tribals did not have any functional relationships with the caste-Hindus. Their only relationship with the caste-Hindus during the medieval period was with the Rajputs and the Marathas. When the battle was over, the tribals returned to their country of hills and forests. They did not have agriculture as their source of livelihood. Elwin informs us about the Baiga and Gonds of Madhya Pradesh. The Baigas took to cultivation only recently. They had shifting cultivation which was their only source of income. Archana Prasad writes:

> Thus, it is telling that in Gond mythology the origins of Garb Mandala, the land of the Baigas, is associated with the spread of plough cultivation rather than shifting cultivation. The Baigas are considered to be the original inhabitants of Chhattisgarh along with the Gonds.[20]

During the period of their isolation, the Baigas, Gonds and Bhils of Rajasthan and Gujarat had a very limited pattern of social stratification. The western and eastern regions of Rajasthan had Bhil rulers. These rulers only provided protection to the high-caste Hindus. The Bhils of Mewar and of Kota, that is, Hadoti region, had experience of fighting in the battlefield; they, therefore, provided safety and protection to the high-caste Hindus during peace times. The pattern of social stratification during this period was very elementary. There was minimum division of labour. Both males and females had free exchange of their roles. If the wife had gone to bring water, the husband would grind the corn. However, the tasks, which required hard labour, were done by the males. Such a society was characterized by kinship relations. In hours of crisis the kins provided assistance. Thus, during the period of isolation, the tribal social stratification was very elementary.

A new stratification pattern emerged among the tribals migrated from hills and forests to the plains. Shifting cultivation was denied to the Baiga. The Bhils took to settled agriculture. They lived in settled villages. Their migration to plains brought them in close association with the Rajputs and Baniyas who have elaborate social stratification in their society.

Feudal Social Order and the Shift in Stratification

With the coming of feudal period and the end of battles between the Rajputs and the Marathas, the tribals got a radical shift in their stratification. The ideology of stratification was to increase the sources of livelihood by the tribals. This provided opportunity to the NGOs, particularly Christians and Hindu organizations, to work among them. The original Bhils, Baigas, Gonds or Santals, who had migrated to plains took agriculture as their sole source of livelihood. The tribals were new to agriculture. They had to learn from the Hindu peasants the skills of cultivation. Among the high-caste Hindus, the Baniyas came as a source of providing easy loans for agricultural development.

The shift in social stratification brought about a radical change in the status of women. In fact, the new pattern of stratification influenced the traditional institutions of the tribe. The 'Muriya Gotul' system and the polygyny found among all the tribal groups of Bihar, Orissa and Central India received a tremendous change. There was 'limited' promiscuity among the tribals. This turned into monogamy. The women aspired to be 'Pativarta' on the model of high-caste Hindu women. There appeared also some kind of division in the family. The male acquired domination in the distribution of household work. The men worked in the fields and forests and women were required to clean the cattle, upbring the children, bring water and collect fuel. The kind of division of labour, which the tribals had acquired, was common to the general peasantry of the country.

The historical change that we see among tribals of India during the medieval period is that for the first time the tribals got stratified into the hill and forest tribal society and the society of plains. These two segments of tribal society also became culturally separate as they did not have marital relations. The highland tribals considered the tribals of the plains as polluted and given to the cause of high-caste Hindus. On the other hand, the Bhils of the plains characterized the highland tribals as backward, savage and given to excessive drinking. This shift in the stratification also brought a change in the division of labour. The tribals of the plains took agriculture as their main source of livelihood whereas the highlanders did not have any sophistication in agriculture. They took only rainfed crops and depended on forests as their source of livelihood. The tribals of the plains began to take commercial crops of sugarcane, tobacco and cotton.

In their initial interaction with the tribals, the caste-Hindus considered the latter a savage, addicted to the flesh of dead animal and beef. The opportunity also encouraged the high-caste Hindus to exploit the tribals. Though the tribals did not change much but they identified themselves with the future of high-caste Hindus. Baniya and Rajput became their model of imitation. Such a situation of introductory social stratification can be explained by the dominance of traditions and the ideology of stratification. The anthropological researches, which were conducted among the tribals by the middle of 1940s, were all characterized by functionalism. A massive change in tribal stratification came with the onset of modernization.

Challenges of Modernization and the Ideology of Sociological Theory

With the attainment of independence the traditional isolation of tribals was broken in a massive way. The Constitution gave the tribals certain privileges in the form of protective and development safeguards. Reservation in government services disturbed the isolation substantially. The cultural restrictions pertaining to marriage between the highlanders and the plains people got disturbed. The highlanders came to the plains and the people of the plains got their placement in highlands. Meanwhile, the central government services which the tribals got put them to far-off places in the country. The protective legislation provided the tribals with the implementation of several schemes.

The tribals, social stratification received challenges from two sets of forces. One is consisted of special privileges granted to the tribals and the other included modernization and development. The government came with a large number of schemes through the institutional network of Tribal Sub-Plan Area and Modified Area Development Approach (MADA). The objective of the government schemes was to make the tribals self-reliant in the field of agriculture. The modernization forces also threw new challenges to the people. It must be mentioned that the first shift in the tribal stratification came when the tribals migrated from hills to plains. They adopted agriculture and thus a new wave of stratification emerged. The tribals had to bear a lot when they came in contact with the high-caste agriculturists. In the beginning they had had no paucity of land. They could cultivate anywhere, there was enough space for cultivation. Or, they could easily burn the forest and make new lands for cultivation. But, with the spread of modernization, the high-caste Hindus made encroachment on the tribal land. In this process of land transformation, a new strata of tribals emerged. These tribals worked on the field of big Hindu farmers, for instance Patidars in Gujarat and Rajputs in Rajasthan and Madhya Pradesh. The tribals worked as bonded labourers and were known as 'Halis'. The 'Sahukars', that is, Hindu traders advanced loan to the cultivating tribals. It was the beginning of exploitation of the tribals at the hands of Sahukars. These tribals were known as 'Asamis', that is, dependent cultivators of the Baniyas or Sahukars. The relationship between the Baniya and the tribal remained, all through the feudal and modern period, quite smooth, though in states like Maharashtra, Gujarat and Rajasthan cooperative movement started to combat the exploitation of Baniyas. But it did not work well. David Hardiman informs on the strength of data collected from Gujarat that the "tribals did not take any initiative to start cooperatives. The cooperatives always came from the government and not from the peasants". As a result, the peasants tended to view this as a new system of government credit, in which loans were provided at lower rates of interest. They regarded themselves as clients of the government Sahukar.

The tribals now became a status group of Asami, that is, economically depended segments of tribals. This was another substantial shift in the stratification of tribals. In Bihar, the 'Dikoo', that is, the Sahukars exploited the Asamis on the pattern of Maharashtra and Gujarat. The homogeneous kin-based tribal social structure became more stratified and heterogeneous. The bonded labourers and the Asamis now became new strata of stratification. Hardiman observes:

> On the whole, the peasant-usurers in Gujarat were Patidars, and in some cases Brahmin peasants, while their victims were poor Kolis, Dhed untouchables, adivasis or Muslims. Patidars and Brahmins were everywhere in a minority in the peasant population, and as a lot of land was owned by these poor groups, they could appropriate land by these means without alienating members of their own community .... In Maharashtra similar developments were seen at the time in Khandesh where there were many adivasi peasants. This was another region in which land-grabbing by rich peasant-usurers became marked during the late 19th century.[21]

What is Tribal Stratification?

We would reiterate that we do not want to employ any sociological theoretical ideology of Hindu fundamentalism to understand tribal social change. We have taken a position by asserting that in most of the part sociologists have employed structural-functional ideology, which is capitalistic and conservative. We define tribal social change in terms of theoretical stratification. Anthony Giddens considers social stratification as social inequality. For Giddens, existence of structured inequalities between groups in society, in terms of their access to material or symbolic rewards. While all societies ... "social stratification is the existence of structured inequalities between groups in society, in terms of their access to material or symbolic rewards. While all societies involve some forms of stratification only with the development of state-based systems do wide difference in wealth and power arise. The most distinctive form of stratification in modern societies involves class divisions."[22]

Indian Modernization: The Challenges Emerged

When the tribals of Central India, Bihar and Orissa crossed the hill lands, their society received a new pattern of stratification. This newly emerged stratification was characterized by modernization, industrialization and capitalism. The concept of modernization is very complex. Emile Durkheim, for the first time, defined modernization as elaborate stratification. He proposed that more there was industrialization and modernization, more there was stratification. Max Weber looked at modernization in terms of rationality and for Karl Marx modernization was identified as commodification. In fact, modernization has received several modifications in its definitions in developing countries such as India. Anthony Giddens is said to be an authority on the trends of modernization in developing countries of Asia and Africa. He argues that modernization is multi-dimensional. It is oriented to capitalism. When a Gond or a Bhil cultivates crops for sell in the market, it is a clear trend of capitalism. Thus, modernity is capitalistic, that is, *production for market*. It is also democratic and finally it identifies state as a potential power.

The social change that we witness in the field of social stratification among the tribals indicates that these indigenous people have now become conscious about their democratic power. Even, the Baigas who were once upon a time excited about Burra, that is, shifting cultivation, now claim to be modern skilled agriculturists. It may be argued that even today there are tribals, who are below poverty line (BPL), have developed a symbolic power among themselves. The poorer tribals have now become self-conscious about their constitutional and reservational rights.

The tribals, who suffered isolation for a protracted period of history, are now under the spell of modernization, democracy and state-sponsored development programmes. It is unhistorical to find a class system among the traditional tribals of Central India, Bihar and Orissa. Class formation is the result of modernization, and surely not Hindu fundamentalism. The status groups and the gender relations, which have resulted from modernization, have given new dimension to the tribal social stratification.

Emerging Tribal Class Structure

Although 'class' is a widely used concept in sociology, there is no clear agreement about how it should best be defined. For Karl Marx, a class was a group of people standing in a common relationship to the means of production. Weber saw class as an economic category but stressed its interaction with social status and the affinities of party. When we look at the tribal class stratification, we find that middle class has emerged among these people. In fact, there is no capitalist or upper class among the tribals. They do not have any control over investments or money capital; they do not have enough land which could provide employment to additional members besides the members of the family. In other words, the tribals do not have control over labour power.

The middle class, which has cropped up among the tribals, is employed in government service. Recently, the middle class amongst tribals has acquired skills and expertise in technology. This class is now in demand in the labour market and also exercises a specific form of power in the capitalist system. The parts of Jharkhand and Rajasthan, which are rich in mineral wealth, have large number of tribals, who have acquired skills in mining. Mining today has become a technical job. In a technologically developed mine, unskilled labourers are almost absent. These mines are mostly manned by the middle class tribals in Orissa, Madhya Pradesh and Rajasthan. Thus, the middle class, which has come up among the tribals, has acquired salaried jobs and is technically competent. Tribal middle class is also pervasive in big towns and cities where tribal migrants reside. Ranchi, Ahmedabad, Surat and Mumbai are such metropolis where migrant middle class members make their livelihood.

Some sociologists locate class structure in the arena of lifestyles. It is said that we should evaluate individual's class location not only or even mainly, in terms of economics and employment, but also in relation to cultural factors, such as lifestyle and consumption patterns. According to this approach, the tribals are associated to lifestyles, symbols and market-related consumption. Among the Bhils of Jhabua and South Rajasthan, the constraints of market are so overpowering that the lifestyle of the tribals has undergone change. In the interior villages, it is common to find a Bhil, Gond or Baiga purchasing Johnson's baby powder or the cosmetics of Pond's and Fair and Lovely. In a weekly market one could easily find crowd in the beauty parlours. It is surprising to find even tribals of interior villages to own a motorbike. Adopting the current lifestyle of the region is a prevalent idiom of the tribals. It is now not unusual to find electronic gadgets in a tribal middle-class member. Earlier, *gur* (jaggery) was the only sweet dish for the tribals but now middle class tribals enter into a hotel and enjoy a variety of sweets.

Members of tribal middle class more than often migrate to big towns and cities close to their hinterland. There are villages where all the adults, except the aged and the children, migrate to big cities in search of earning a livelihood. The migration, admittedly, not only brings good amount of money to village but it also encourages cross-cultural interaction. The village social stratification redefines itself in terms of the stratification found among the urban people. Education becomes popular, tribal women assert their rights and the rural tribal life steadily but surely moves towards the stratification pattern of the urban life. A Gond or a Santhal is as particular to cast his vote in general elections as is a caste-Hindu.

Move Towards Secular Modern Society

It is unfortunate that the sociologists and anthropologists have conspired against the Indian tribals to identify them as Hindus. As a matter of fact, one has to be very cautious to label the tribals with a particular sect. The tribal history all over India is the history of isolation. When they migrated to plains or when the non-tribals from the plains enter into the tribal hinterland, it really bewilders the isolated tribal. He becomes a victim of exploitation. He subordinates himself to caste society and the latter identify them as Hindus. Even, the Dutch social anthropologist Jan Breman[23] terms the tribals like Halpatis as tribal castes. The Halpatis are never a caste. What has happened with the tribals is that their interaction with the caste-Hindus has put them in a queer position. The tribals nourish the notion that if they have to improve their lifestyle, they should acquire as much power as possible. It is the search for power, which makes them Hindu, Christian, Muslim or tribal. The bewildered tribals today are like a bull in the China shop. In their acquisition of power they worship the Jain Tirthankar, the temple of Mahaveerji, which is found in the Kaurali district of Rajasthan. At Mahaveerji temple the 'Palki' or the chariot of the Lord, which is only taken out once a year, is shouldered by the Minas only, not even the Jains. Does it mean that Minas are Jains. Again, the Bhils of South Rajasthan work as *Halkara,* i.e., messengers in the Tazia festival. This should not tempt us to identify them as followers of Islam. The Hindu fundamentalists label the tribals as Hindus when the latter are found participating in Hindu festivals. Actually, the tribals of India are neither Christians, nor Jains, Muslims or Hindus. While participating in the wider activities of the region, they want to corner as much power as possible. This, however, should not mean that they have compromised their autonomous ethnic identity.

The 73rd Constitutional Amendment gives reservation to tribal women in the different Panchayat Raj tiers. Sociologists and political scientists analyse the amendment as empowerment of tribal women. In fact, the so-called empowerment has ended up in tribal women's disempowerment. What has really happened at the grassroots level is that more and more women have begun to follow the Hindu women's way of life. The constant interactions, which the tribal women have with the non-tribal women in the activities of Panchayat Raj, make them imitators of Hindu way of life. There are studies which show that widowhood which was unknown to tribals has crept into their society. The gender relationship, which used to be based on egalitarian base, now has become hierarchical. The gender freedom is now no more visible. Women are now required to follow a restricted life.

The social stratification that we find today among the tribals of India is not on the pattern of caste-Hindus. The tribal social structure is not hierarchical. It is based on the idiom of secularism, democracy and modernization. Equal interactions characterized the tribal way of life. The notion that tribal social stratification is Hindu social stratification is mistaken. It appears that there is a deep-rooted conspiracy to identify the tribals as Hindus so that democratic battles could be won on their numerical strength. In reality, as recent comers from isolation, the tribals are a secular, democratic lot of people. Their economy is increasingly oriented to modern capitalistic economy. More and more tribal people now produce for the market.

[The author is obliged to P.C. Jain, Rajendra Upadhyay and Dinesh Shah for collecting field data.]

Notes

1. M.N. Srinivas (1952), *Religion and Society among the Coorgs of South India.* Oxford: Clarendon Press.
2. Quoted in Alam Anwar (2002), "Secularism in India: A Critique of the Current Discourse", in Paul R. Brass and Achin Vanaik (eds.), *Competing Nationalisms in South Asia*, Orient Longman, New Delhi.
3. Quoted in Joseph Tharamangalam (1995), "Indian Social Sciences and Critique of Secularism," *Economic and Political Weekly,* XXX, No. 9, March 4, p. 459.
4. George C. Homans (1964), "Bringing Men Back", *American Sociological Review, 29,* pp. 809–18.
5. See Lewis A. Coser (1965), "Two Methods in Search of Substance", *American Sociological Review,* 40, pp. 69–70 and Alwin W. Gouldner, "Anti-Minotaur: The Myth of a Value-Free Sociology", in Maurice R. Stein and Arthur Vidich (eds.) (1963), *Sociology on Trial.* Englewood Cliffs, NJ: Prentice-Hall.
6. K.S. Singh (1992), *People of India: An Introduction,* Calcutta: Anthropological Survey of India.
7. Malinowski, *Trobriand Islanders, 1912.*
8. A.R. Radcliffe-Brown (1964), *The Andman Islanders,* New York: Free Press.
9. Yogendra Singh (2004), *Ideology and Theory in Indian Sociology,* Jaipur: Rawat Publications.
10. The relationship between these two societies has been discussed in a summary form by Yogendra Singh. See Yogendra Singh (1994), *Modernization of Indian Tradition,* Reprinted, Jaipur: Rawat Publications.

11. Yogendra Singh (2004), *Ideology and Theory in Indian Sociology*, Jaipur: Rawat Publications, p. 176.
12. Ramachandra Guha (1999), *Savaging the Civilized: Verrier Elwin, His Tribals and India*, New Delhi: Oxford University Press, p. 123.
13. Verrier Elwin (1944), *Aboriginals: So Called and Their Future*, New Delhi: Oxford University Press, p. 29.
14. G.S. Ghurye (1961), *Caste, Class and Occupations*, Bombay: Popular Book Depot.
15. Verrier Elwin (1944), *Aboriginals: So Called and Their Future*, New Delhi: Oxford University Press.
16. K.S. Singh (1997), *The Scheduled Tribes, People of India*, National Series 111, Anthropological Survey of India, New Delhi: Oxford University, p. 5.
17. Ibid.
18. Ibid., pp. 5–6.
19. Archana Prasad (2003), *Against Ecological Romanticism*, New Delhi: Three Essays Press, p. 2.
20. Ibid., p. 8.
21. David Hardiman (2004), *Feeding the Baniya*, New Delhi: Oxford, p. 278.
22. Anthony Giddens (2001), *Sociology* (Reprinted), New Delhi: Polity.
23. Jan Breman (1985), *Of Peasants, Migrants and Paupers*, New Delhi: Oxford University Press.

11 Caste, Class and Ecology Movements

RANJITA MOHANTY

Emergence of mass-based ecology movements against development, in recent times, has heralded a new phase in the history of social movements. Questioning hegemony, dominance and oppression perpetrated by current patterns of development, the movements work on an agenda of social transformation which necessitates addressing inequality in all its manifestation, but most importantly social and economic inequality. In this endeavour it becomes imperative for the movements to interface with the state to democratize the relationship between the state and its disadvantage populace; simultaneously, the movements also have to address the inequalities in the social sphere so that relationship among unequally placed people can be equalized.

However, ironically, the inequalities which ecology movements strive to wipe out act as barriers in realizing this goal. This takes place in two ways. Caste differences make it difficult to mobilize people along class lines.[1] That is poor people belonging to hierarchically placed caste groups often find it difficult to come together to pursue a common goal. Coalescing unequal class positions for strategic reasons may help the movements to meet their immediate goal, but they, in fact, further strengthen the differences between groups and the inequalities continue. That is, to strengthen the collective voice and put pressure on the state, ecology movements may sometime have to make the difficult choice of forging solidarity between groups which are historically placed in relationships of domination and subordination.[2] But this very strategic alliance prevents the movements to address the structural inequalities of caste and class.

The paper sets out to examine these aspects of caste, class and the transformative agenda of ecology movements mentioned above by specifically discussing the fishermen struggle which took place around the Chilika lake in Orissa in the 1990s.

The paper is based on a study I conducted as part of a global comparative project on civil society and governance. The global project, in which my institution was the partner from India, was located at the Institute of Development Studies, UK. An earlier version of the paper titled "Save the Chilika Movement: Interrogating the State and the Market" is published in the book *Does Civil Society Matter? Governance in Contemporary India,* edited by Rajesh Tandon and Ranjita Mohanty and published by the Sage Publications.

Chilika Bachao Andolan (Save the Chilika Movement) was a movement by the people, mostly fishermen, who posed a successful resistance in the early 1990's to the Integrated Shrimp Farm Project (ISFP) – a joint venture agreed upon by the Tata Iron and Steel Company and Government of Orissa for intensive prawn cultivation and export. The project was a direct threat to the livelihood of fishing communities living around the lake. The movement, which was wedged against the Tata's commercial prawn project, was successful in pressurizing the Orissa government to withdraw the project. But, the movement could neither address inequalities between the low-caste and high-caste fishermen, both reeling under poverty, nor could it address the material inequality and antagonism between the poor and rich fishermen. As such, the paper argues that despite achieving its immediate goal of stopping the Tata project, the movement's larger social transformation agenda remained incomplete.

Development, Resource Use and Ecology Movements

Mobilization by the marginalized groups to protect their livelihood resources against commercial use is not new in India. During the colonial regime, there were tribal and peasant uprisings against the state intervention in the customary practices of the people. The replacement of customary management of the common property resources by the state management led to conflict of interest and it manifested in people asserting their claim, right and control over their subsistence resources. After independence, the developmental ideal prompted the state to pursue a path of economic growth through optimum utilization of the natural resources. Thus, economic growth through industrialization and commodity production became the core of Indian economy and industry, mining, and giant irrigation projects took shape in quick succession to change the economic and social landscape. The developmental path of a democratic state was ideally designed to benefit the disadvantaged and promote equity and social justice. Ironically, the democratic developmental agenda of the state was subverted by the dominant forces as they appropriated the benefits of development much to the disadvantage of the marginalized who had suffered social and economic vulnerability in the past and who the developmental projects were designed to bring benefit (Kothari, 1986; Bardhan, 1984, 1988; Kohli, 1987, 1988; Dhanagare, 1987). Not only developmental projects did not benefit them, they added new dimensions of disadvantages to their already disadvantaged position. As the technocentric economic growth took off and huge irrigation, hydel projects and heavy industries took shape, thousands of people were displaced from their original habitat and without a comprehensive resettlement and rehabilitation policy displacement became the inevitable fall out of development. As the natural resources were put into commercial use a large number of people directly dependent on nature for their subsistence lost their access and control over their resources. It is no surprise then that they have resisted the policies formulated to bring benefit to them.[3]

The conflicts over natural resources as I pointed out earlier are not new, but the contemporary ecology movements have added a new dimension to the struggle by articulating the issues in terms of survival of the majority dependent on nature and the related issues of unequal distribution of developmental benefits, sustainable development and poor people's involvement in decision-making. Hence, while on the one hand the movements critique the state and pressurize it to follow a developmental path based on the democratic principles of equity, on the other hand they strive to promote social justice and equity in local resource distribution.

Chipko movement, which heralded people's struggle to gain control over their sustenance resources, was a movement by the local people, particularly women, in the hills of Garhwal, Uttaranchal (the then Uttar Pradesh) to save their forest from commercial felling. It was the continuation of the old peasant struggle, but it added new dimension to the struggle by raising the issue of survival, dependence and control of people over their resources. The struggle was also new in the way it articulated its target – it was directed not against any class *per se* but against the state (Guha, 1991). It happened in the early 1970s – a period significant for the Stockholm Conference on Environment. Chipko brought home the truth that environmental degradation and social inequalities are intrinsically linked in more than one way (Guha, 1991; Bhatt, 1991). The overuse of natural resources for commercial purposes not only deprives people from their resource base and widens the gap between the elites and the impoverished masses, it does not leave any choice for the people to use their resources sustainably, because the people dependent on the dwindling material base for their sustenance cannot be asked to be prudent users of nature. The success of Chipko was followed by resistance against big dams, mines and industry. In Tehri, Narmada valley, Western Ghats, Kaiga and Baliapal people started raising voices against the developmental policies of the state, against the loss of their productive resources like forest, water, land and against the large-scale displacement, which has become a common feature of all the big developmental projects. However, the success of the movements has more often than not accessed on the basis of their successful interface with the state. Undoubtedly, this is an important dimension of ecology movements critiquing development. Nonetheless, the internal conflicts arising out of structural inequalities of caste and class also need to be paid attention to. Since the movements' agenda of social transformation essentially rests on creating conditions for social and economic justice, the way the movements address the structural inequities of caste and class is as important as the way the movements deal with the state.

Ecology, Caste and Class in Chilika

Chilika, located in the Puri, Khurda and Ganjam districts of Orissa, is the largest brackish water lake in India. It is home to large varieties of fish and plants that thrive in the brackish water. The lake is separated from the Bay of Bengal by a long sandy ridge varying between 100 to 300 yards in width with one natural opening near Arakhkuda, which permits the flow of water and migration of fish from the sea to the lake. The lake maintains a sweet-saline ecosystem during the year. It becomes sweeter (less saline) between July and December due to inflow of floodwater and becomes more saline between January and June due to the ingress of seawater. Chilika has been identified as a wetland of international importance at the Ramsar Convention, held in Iran in 1971 to which India was a signatory. The Government of India has also declared Chilika as a bird sanctuary for facilitating the migration of nearly 132 species of birds from Siberia every winter.

A large number of villages in and around the lake are inhabited by a heterogeneous population comprising both fishermen and non-fishermen belonging to different castes. Fishing and agriculture are the two primary sources of livelihood for these people. The fishermen belong to the lower castes and most of them are either landless or posses tiny landholdings. They, therefore, are completely dependent on fishing. The non-fishermen belong to higher castes and are engaged in agriculture. A large number of them, however, have taken to fishing to supplement their income because the productivity of the land is low due to salinity, erratic monsoon and lack of irrigation facilities. Many non-fishermen are now engaged in fishing, particularly after prawn became a lucrative market commodity. Ever since the white prawn and the tiger prawn became lucrative export items many non-fishermen such as traders and rich and influential people from outside the lake have taken to shrimp farming thus displacing the fishing communities from their resource base.[4]

Since fishing is done by the lower castes, in earlier times it was looked down upon as a lowly occupation and higher castes in the past shunned fishing. Now that the higher castes are themselves engaged in fishing, the stigma attached to the occupation is removed. Nevertheless, for social purposes, the upper castes still maintain their distance from the lower castes. The low social status of the fishermen gets intensified by their low economic status. They live in conditions of poverty, there is not much education among them, and many of them are in debt, taken from moneylenders, middlemen and traders for household expenses and for buying fishing equipment. The caste and class differences are thus very sharp in the area.

Traditional Fishing Grounds

On the basis of general slope of land and the depth of water in the lake, the fishing grounds can be grouped as follows:

Jano: Jano fishing grounds are mostly located around the various islands of the lake. *Jano* fisheries are barricaded fisheries (barricaded with split bamboos) in sallow water and are operated from October to February.

Khati: Khati fisheries are shrimp fishing grounds in which fishing is done with traps. *Khati* fishing is done mostly with the help of bamboo traps set in shore areas and are operated between March and September.

Bahan: Bahan refers to net fishing, which is done in the deeper portion of the lake. It is done throughout the year but to a lesser extent during October to December.

Dian: Dian fishery ground is confined to upland areas and is operated during September to January.

Uthapani: Uthapani refers to shallow water fishing during monsoon.

The fishing practices differ for the fishermen belonging to different caste groups.

Keuta (also known as *kaibarta* or *khatia*) form 68 per cent of the traditional fishermen and they fish with nets. *Kandara,* the second largest group, use traps – *dhaudi* and *tata* – for catching crabs and prawns. *Tiar* people use bamboo traps called *baja. Karatias* use both traps and nets for fishing. In the past the castes were required to follow their respective fishing practices and any violation of the rule was considered as a serious social offence. The *Kandaras* and *Tiars* thus could use only bamboo implements like traps and the rest used nets. The fishermen had to go to their prescribed fishing grounds even if it was at a distance from the village.

Fishing Rights of the People

The traditional fishing communities claim their fishing rights to the British period. When Chilika fishery sources were in the hands of the kings of Parikuda and Khalikota, the fishermen used to obtain most of the fishery sources by paying royalty to the king. In order to protect the interest of fishermen and eliminate the non-fishermen and traders encroaching on the rights of the fishermen, the first co-operative society, Balugaon Fishermen Co-operative Store, was established in 1926 at Balugaon, in the Puri district. It brought 24 fisheries under it. After the abolition of the estates and with the fishery sources coming within the purview of the Orissa government in 1953, they were leased out by the Anchal Adhikari through open auction to the fishermen. The non-fishermen were allowed to take a limited number of *dian* fisheries and in some cases a few *jano* fisheries. Besides, the unleased *bahani* areas were open for the non-fishermen to catch fish by paying a nominal fees to the government. This practice continued till 1959 when the Central Co-operative Marketing Society was established in Balugaon. This was designed to act as an apex body that would take lease from the government and sublease them to the primary fishermen co-operatives. A dual co-operative structure was thus established to protect and regulate the fishing rights of the people. The Central Society was to take lease from the revenue department through the Collectors of Puri and Ganjam to sublease them to primary co-operatives at that time numbering 48. Most of the important fishery sources were subleased to the primary societies. In case there was no primary society *dian* fisheries were subleased to villages dominated by fishermen. Those sources which were not taken on lease by the Central Society were auctioned. The tehsildars (government officials from the revenue department operating at the block level) of Puri, Krushnaprasada, Banpur and Ganjam had the right to settle the unleased fisheries through auction. The Chilika reorganization scheme thus made a clear-cut distinction between fishermen and non-fishermen and gave non-fishermen limited right on the lake.

Till 1988, however, there was no clear-cut demarcation of fishing sources, type of net to be used, and barricades to be set up to catch prawn. This resulted in considerable difficulty for the primary societies to operate. There was a dispute in 1986 between two primary societies relating to the fixing of barricades for catching prawn. It was a dispute between fishermen inhabiting the upper and lower region of the lake. The fishermen in the upper region had fixed very lengthy barricades which obstructed the flow of fish to the lower region. Following this dispute the 1988 policy demarcated the fishery sources; it also increased the annual lease of fisheries to three years.

In 1991, the Government of Orissa issued an order which divided the fisheries in Chilika into two categories, viz., capture and culture, without however, adequately defining the meaning of the terms. Capture rights were confined to the fishermen and culture was opened to the non-fishermen and those villagers which were not members of primary societies. Since the government order did not lay down any guidelines for the operation of capture and culture fisheries, the Collector was free to act according to his discretion. This policy created further confusion and conflict. The fishermen feared that their traditional rights were being curtailed by leasing out culture sources to the non-fishermen.

Despite the repeated reiteration by the government that the policies were meant to safeguard the traditional rights of the fishermen, the policies did not yield the desired effect for various reasons. They were ill-defined, there was lack of rational and equitable distribution of fisheries. As a result, there was widespread illegal subleasing of fisheries and there was no mechanism to prevent it. The Central Society was given limited power and it acted merely as a body between the revenue department and the primary societies. The Central Society itself made erratic distribution and illegal subletting. Most primary societies bypassed the Central Society and marketed directly through commission agents. The very purpose of a dual co-operative structure designed to protect the interests of the fishermen was thus vitiated.

Initially, the culturing of prawn began in the peripheral landmass of Chilika. The leased out *dians, uthapani,* and upland *jano* fisheries were converted into prawn culture ponds with mud embankment. Later, the lake, deeper Chilika, was also enclosed with bamboo poles and net for prawn culture.

Since 1980s the lake is witnessing widespread subletting of leased out fisheries by the Central Society, primary societies and illegal encroachment by non-fishermen and outsiders.[5] This culturing of prawn on a big scale has resulted in the widespread conversion of traditional fisheries into prawn culture ponds or net enclosed *gheries* (barricaded space). Culture fishery requires heavy capital investment but ensures big profit. Hence, many primary societies have found it a source of making money by leasing it out to resourceful persons.

This widespread culturing of prawn has threatened the livelihood of traditional fishermen as well as the ecosystem of the lake. Thousands of fishermen and non-fishermen families have lost their livelihood due to conversion of traditional fishing sources into culture fishery. Cases of litigation and 'prawn politics' now define the lives of the people in Chilika.

It is in this socio-economic and political background that the Government of Orissa made an agreement with the business house of the Tatas for a joint semi-intensive prawn culture project called the Integrated Shrimp Farm Project (ISFP) and allowed them an advance possession of 400 hectares of land in Chilika for the project.

The Integrated Shrimp Farm Project

In 1986 the then Congress government of Orissa entered into a contract with the Tata Acquatic Farms Ltd. to lease 1400 hectares of land in Chilika for prawn cultivation for a period of 15 years. The government had 10 per cent share in the deal. The Janata Dal had opposed the project then. When it came to power in 1989, it merely changed the name of the farm into Chilika Acquatic Farms Ltd. and increased the share of the government to 49 per cent. In December 1991, the Government of Orissa leased a landmass of 400 hectares in advance (from Barakudi village in Brahmagiri block to Gamhari village in Krushna Prasad block in Puri district) to Tatas for the prawn culture.

The project envisaged the creation of an artificial lake inside the Chilika by enclosing the landmass with a 13.7 km long ring embankment. This artificial lake was to be divided into a number of ponds in which the prawns are to be nurtured and reared commercially. The entire output of the farm was to be processed and exported. The annual turnover from the farms was to be of Rs 30 crore which was to be in foreign exchange.

As a part of the extension service to small farmers and co-operatives in Chilika region, the project mentioned that about 70 million larvae would initially be made available to them along with technical advice. As the requirement for feed increases due to increase in farm areas and production, a captive feed mill would be established in due course. The project stated that the shrimp produced by the farmers would be brought by the project at fair market price. The training, technical assistance and services would be imparted to the framers free of cost and the Government of Orissa would render any infrastructural help required in this regard. The project emphasized that the direct as well as indirect employment of people in the project and opening of new farms would elevate the socio-economic status of the people around the farm.[6]

The Movement: *Chilka Bachao Andolan*

Though the fishing communities had been resisting the commercial use of the lake and their consequent loss of control over their resources, never a mass mobilization could take place in Chilika till the ISFP took shape and the threats became more visible, imminent and gigantic. The people of the villages adjacent to the project were aware of it but there was little awareness about the threats it would pose to their livelihood. In fact, people anticipated a good bargain for their fish catch and employment in the project. Initially, a few educated people in these villages became sceptical about the project. Later, *Meet the Students* (MTS) group, an informal group of students from Utkal University, Bhubaneswar (the capital city of Orissa) took initiative to visit the villages and discussed the issues with the villagers. Later, a provincial level students forum *Krantadarshi Yuva Sangam* (KYS) was formed to mobilize the youths against the Tata project. Its core group was formed by the students who were former members of MTS and as they passed out of the university they joined the KYS. Thereafter, it was decided that MTS would function at the university level and KYS would function as a forum to mobilize the youths against the project.

Gradually, the students also realized that the local organizations could be an effective vanguard for carrying the resistance against the project. Their grounding on the local issues and the trust local people have in their own organizations would help the local organizations carry the resistance forward more effectively. Steps were thus taken to involve the *Chilika Matsyajibi Mahasangha (CMM)*, a mass organization of 122 revenue villages in Chilika which works towards the protection of interests of the fishermen. CMM, which was fallen to the politics of rivalry between political parties, was revived to take up the cause of the fishermen vis-à-vis the Tata project. The *Chilika Bachao Andolan* (CBA) was formally launched in January 1992 to work as an extension of CMM in the areas adjacent to the project to spearhead the movement. Sri Govind Behera was nominated as the convenor of the movement. CBA was extended support by many other civil society organizations like *Ganatantrik Adhikar Suraksha Sangathan,* an organization based in Bhubaneswar and working towards the protection of the democratic rights of the people, and *Orissa Krushak Mahasangha* (OKM), also based in Bhubaneswar, which works for the cause of the farmers.[7]

All these initiatives gave the local people's protest the form of a movement which raised economic, social, legal and environmental issues related to the project. The followings were some of the prominent issues raised by the movement:

1. The land allotted to the ISFP was traditionally being used by the neighbouring 26 villages for harvesting prawn. The shallow water collected during monsoon was ideal for the natural breeding of prawn.
2. The threats of flood and waterlogging due to the construction of the embankment on the Bhubania canal which forms the outlet of the lake into the sea.
3. The embankment would obstruct the movements of the fish and prawn from brackish water to the sea during the breeding season. This would obstruct the natural regeneration of the prawns.
4. Long-term availability of fish within the lake would be adversely affected due to the pollution caused by protein feed chemicals and pesticides.
5. The project had moved ahead without the mandatory Environment Impact Assessment.
6. The land given on lease to the ISFP was classified as reserved wetland and community pasture land. Hence, the leasing of the lake was illegal as the lake was not classified under leasable property.

The above immediate issues were linked by the movement with the central question on development and resource use. As the movement put it: "The Tata project is not the central point of attack of this people's movement. The prime focus of opposition is the policy of the government towards Chilka and its people, and the Tata project is only an instance of this policy" (Chilka Bachao Andolan and Kantadarshi Yuva Sangam).

The movement articulated the issues in the three questions it posed:

1. Whom does Chilika belong to – the people or the state?
2. If the big business houses enter into prawn culture, what will be the fate of the people for whom fishing has been the only source of livelihood?
3. What should be the priority of the state in a situation where the commercial use of resources comes into conflict with the livelihood pursuit of poor people?

Initially, the mobilization against the Tata project was confined to a few villages adjacent to the project. On September 20,1991, the date on which the three-year lease to the Central Cooperative Society was expiring, thousands of fishermen gathered at the state capital – Bhubaneswar – and protested in front of the Vidhan Sabha (provincial assembly) which was in session. A written memorandum was given to the Fishery Minister who in turn assured people that not even an inch of Chilika would be leased out to the business house of the Tatas. Demonstrations, meetings, dharnas and rallies at the project site and in the state capital summarize the activities of the movement during this phase.

In its second phase the movement became more broad-based and adopted a somewhat militant tone when the people broke the embankment of the project.[8] The bureaucracy and the police tried brutal measures to suppress the resistance at the local level. Nevertheless, the protest continued and the broader environmental issues pertaining to the project began to be addressed by the movement along with the livelihood issues. The fragile ecosystem of the lake and the threat to the livelihood of fishermen were articulated to put pressure on the government. In advocating the environmental aspects of the issue emphasis was given on India's commitment to the international community to preserve the lake which was declared as an endangered wetland in the Ramsar Convention and to which India was a signatory. It was reiterated repeatedly that preserving the environment was the fundamental duty of the citizen.

At this stage, disagreement appeared regarding the leadership of the movement between the Chilika-based *Chilika Bachao Andoaln (CBA)* and Bhubaneswar-based *Orissa Krushak Mahasangha (OKM)*.[9] There was a strong resistance to the leadership of Mr B.B. Das, President, *OKM* as it was felt by the local leaders that by overemphasizing on the Ramsar Convention he was diverting attention from the livelihood and survival issues. The movement at the local level time and again gave emphasis on the local leadership and saw the movement as a reflection of the initiatives taken by the people and a manifestation of their strength – *gan udyam avam gan sakti* (people's initiative, people's power).

Thereafter, the CBA continued its activism at the village level and OKM operated at the provincial capital and national level. People at the village level raised issues pertaining to the loss of their livelihood resources, loss of their control over these resources and kept the resistance confined to the local area. OKM articulated the issues in environmental terms linking the threat from the project with the fragile ecosystem of the lake and livelihood of the fishermen. As a strategic move it also emphasized on the Ramsar Convention. At the same time, the government was interrogated on the ground of legality of the issues by invoking the Land Settlement Act according to which Chilika is a 'reserved wetland' and therefore cannot be leased to any individual or company.

Unlike the advocacy campaign, which was carried out by the OKM at the provincial and national level away from the villagers, and therefore, was not affected by the inequalities and power equations prevalent at the local level, the local struggle had not only to constantly negotiate with the local power equations among various groups, it also had to struggle hard to keep the spirit of the resistance alive. This had significant bearing on the nature of the movement. The movement was primarily a resistance by the fishermen. As a strategic choice to make the mobilization broad based the non-fishermen were persuaded to join the movement. Since the Tata project was perceived as a threat by both, the poor non-fishermen engaged in fishing as a source of livelihood as well as the rich non-fishermen engaged in prawn cultivation for commercial purposes, they eagerly joined the struggle. Nevertheless, this solidarity was confined only to resistance against the Tata project. In the day-to-day living the fishermen and non-fishermen continued with their traditional rivalry. The poor low-caste fishermen historically exploited by the rich powerful and dominant upper-caste non-fishermen were suspicious of the latter's motive. However, in reiterating their claim over the fishery resources, the fishermen also alienated those poor non-fishermen for whom fishing has become a source of livelihood. The caste differences thus kept the poor fishermen and non-fishermen separate and the conflicts could not be resolved, though for temporary purpose they joined hands. The strategic alliances between poor fishermen and rich non-fishermen hid the tensions and rivalries between groups having differential access to local resources and power. The leaders of CBA tried to keep the resistance against the Tata project shield from the local conflicts between the groups. They assured the fishermen that their priority was to fight the bigger enemy, the house of the Tatas, and once that battle was won, the other exploiters of the fishermen's resources (which were called mini-Tatas) will be dealt with.[10] With all the internal strategic alliances, the movement in Chilika continued as fishermen's struggle against the Tata business house and the Government of Orissa.

While the Orissa government and the business house of Tatas kept ignoring the movement, the then Union Minister for Environment and Forest, Mr Kamal Nath intervened and the Ministry issued an order putting ban on further work on the project till an environmental impact assessment study was conducted. While the rift between the Government of Orissa and the Union Ministry was going on and the movement was advocating vociferously against the project, the judgment of the High Court of Orissa in 1993 relating to the fishing rights of the fishermen in Chilika clearly put a stop on intensive or semi-intensive prawn cultivation in the lake.[11] The High Court verdict was not directly related to the Tata project, but by putting a ban on intensive and semi-intensive prawn cultivation; it also barred the Tata project.

It may be argued that the verdict of the High Court was not a direct response to the movement. Nevertheless, the very fact that the resistance to the project was grounded on same issues which the report of the Fact Finding Committee (known as Das Committee) substantiated and that the government by recognizing the negative impact of intensive prawn cultivation on the ecosystem of the lake and on livelihood of people did recognize the validity of people's voice against the project, speaks about the triumph of the Chilika movement.

The battle with the corporate house was won, but the battle with the mini-Tatas was soon forgotten. The temporary alliance between the poor fishermen and rich non-fishermen was broken with this victory and the illegal encroachment on the lake continued. The conflicts of interest between fishermen and non-fishermen created considerable damage to the movement. Though for strategic purpose the movement was to engage the rich non-fishermen in the struggle, it was their involvement which limited the scope of the movement. It could not address the issues of illegal encroachment on the lake and widespread prawn cultivation by these dominant non-fishermen from outside the lake. Due to the inability of the movement to address these issues, it could not be sustained once the victory over the common enemy, the house of the Tatas, was achieved.

Conclusions

Inequalities in society provide context for collective action, but collective action is also hindered by these inequalities. It was the existing socio-economic inequalities and their further perpetuation as a consequence of wrong developmental priorities of the state which gave rise to the Chilika movement, yet these inequalities also limited the agenda of the movement. The traditional caste antagonism, which the fishermen in Chilika have towards the non-fishermen, limited their vision to the fact that fishing is also a livelihood pursuit for poor non-fishermen. That is, while movements concerned with livelihood issues and poor people's right and ownership over their natural resources raise critical questions regarding 'public good/collective good' among unequally placed marginal groups, there may not always be an unanimity of opinion and interest with regards to 'collective good'. This conflict of interest between two equally deprived groups has significant implication. How can their everyday existence be democratized when the poor and resourceless people, due to their traditional caste differences and rivalries, cannot come together to question dominance and oppression? Secondly, when the movements, in their attempt to strengthen their mass base, bring together people, who otherwise have no common purpose in their everyday existence, they merely project a temporary collective goal. This undoubtedly helps the movements to achieve their immediately gaol and save poor people from losing their livelihood resources as happened in Chilika. The Chilika movement was successful in the resistance it posed to the Tata project. Yet, by not addressing the exploitation which poor people, surviving on fishing, are subjected to by the rich non-fishermen, who abuse the lake for commercial purposes, the movement could not address the inequities in local resource distribution. By alienating the poor non-fishermen dependent on fishing for livelihood, the movement succumbed to the antagonism which mark the relationship between the low-caste fishermen and upper-caste non-fishermen, both equally poor and resourceless. These restricted the movement from addressing the structural inequalities of caste and class. Hence, while it became successful in saving people from an outside enemy, namely, the Tatas, it could not save them from everyday exploitation, dominance and conflicts. The contexts of inequalities in which collective action such as Chilika movement takes place, therefore, demand that the movements must strive to democratize the state and society at the same time if the larger goal of social transformation is to be met.

Notes

1. As new social movements (Offe, 1985; Touraine, 1985; Scott, 1990; Cohen, 1985), the ecology movements address new issues of ecological degradation. Hence, it is a green agenda that the movements follow than the traditional red agenda of class struggle. However, in a country like India, where a large number of poor people depend on

natural resources of land, water and forest for survival, the ecological movements, in their articulation of interest of survival of poor people, can not but address the issues of material inequality. In their attempt to address inequality, the movements, therefore, have to bring poor people on a common platform, even when it is, in the conventional sense, not a struggle of the proletariat against the bourgeoisie.

2. Such strategic alliances are made from time to time by ecology movements. The Narmada movement, for instance, brings the rich farmers and landless agricultural labourers in its struggle against the Sardar Sarovar Project (Mohanty, 1995; Baviskar, 1995).
3. There is a growing body of literature available on people's resistance to environmental consequences and loss of subsistence natural resources in different regions in India. See Agarwal, 1985; Baviskar, 1995; Bhatt, 1991; Fernandes, 1991; Gadgil and Guha, 1994; Guha, 1989, 1991; Omvedt, 1993; Mohanty, 1995; Pathak, 1994.
4. Besides there are *Nolias* – the Telegu immigrants who fish mainly in the sea and partly in the lake mouth and in some parts of the outer channel with drag nets and cast nets and a lrge number of refugees from East Bengal who have taken to fishing as their means of livelihood though they do not posses any legal right to fish in the lake.
5. See the report of the Fact Finding Committee on Chilika Fisheries, submitted to the High Court of Orissa, Cuttack on 16th August 1993, for an extensive account of the government policies relating to fishing in Chilika, the ambiguities inherent in these policies and the consequent illegal subletting of the fishery sources and illegal encroachment on the lake by outsiders.
6. See the Integrated Shrimp Farm Project Report of Chilika Aquatic Farms Limited, July 1991, for a detail account of the project.
7. Mr B.B. Das, the president of OKM, played an important role in highlighting the environment hazards of the project and persuaded the government to undertake an environment impact assessment study relating to the project. He was also instrumental in inviting the attraction of the international community to the issue by campaigning that the Government of India must honour the Ramsar Convention in which Chilika lake was declared as one of the endangered wetland which needed to be protected.
8. For a chronological account of the movement see "Chilika: Voice of the People", published by *Chilika Bachao Andolan* and *Krantadarshi Yuva Sangam,* the date of publication is not available.
9. Personal interview with the leaders of the movement. This aspect also is briefly mentioned in *Maa, Mati, Chilika,* published by *Chilka Bachao Andolan and Krantadarshi Yuva Sangam,* 1993.
10. This aspect of the movement was gathered from the personal interview with the people involved in the movement and from the leaders.
11. Some primary fishermen societies had filed a case against the 1991 policy of the Government of Orissa and the subsequent encroachment on the rights of the fishermen. The report of the Fact Finding Committee (popularly known as Das Committee) constituted to study the situation in the area reported widespread prawn cultivation and its adverse effect on the livelihood of people and the ecosystem of the lake.

References

Agarwal, Anil (1985), 'Ecological Destruction and the Emerging Patterns of Poverty and People's Protest in Rural India', *Social Action,* Vol. 35.

Bardhan, Pranab (1984), *The Political Economy of Development in India,* New Delhi: Oxford University Press.

—— (1988), 'Dominant Proprietary Classes and India's Democracy', in Atul Kohli (ed.), *India's Democracy: An Analysis of Changing State-Society Relation*, NJ: Princeton University Press.

Baviskar, Amita (1995), *In the Belly of the River: Tribal Conflicts over Development in the Narmada Valley*, Delhi: Oxford University Press.

Bhatt, Chandi Prasad (1991), 'Chipko Movement: The Hug that Saves', Survey of the Environment, *The Hindu*.

Chilika Aquatic Farms Limited (1991), Integrated Shrimp Farm Project Report.

Chilka Bachao Andolan and *Krantadarshi Yuva Sangam*, Chilika, Voice of the People (n.d.).

—— *Maa, Mati, Chilika* (in Oriya language), 1993.

Cohen, Jean and Andrew, Arato (1992), *Political Theory and Civil Society*, Cambridge: MIT Press.

Cohen, Jean L. (1985), 'Strategy or Identity: New Theoretical Paradigm and Contemporary Social Movements', *Social Research*, Vol. 52, No. 4.

Das, B.B.(1996), *Chilka: The Nature's Treasure: Will it be Allowed to Die?*, Bhubaneswar: Orissa Krushak Mahasangh.

Dhanagare, D.N. (1987), 'Green Revolution and Social Inequalities in Rural India', *Economic and Political Weekly*, Vol. 22.

Fernandes, Walter (1991), 'Power and Powerlessness: Development Projects and Displacement of Tribals', *Social Action*, July-September.

Gadgil, Madhav and Ramachandra Guha (1994), 'Ecological Conflicts and the Environmental Movement in India', *Development and Change*, Vol. 25.

—— (1989), 'New Social Movements: The Problem', *Seminar*, No. 355, March.

Guha, Ramachandra (1991), *The Unquiet Woods: Ecological Change and Peasant Resistance in the Himalaya*, Delhi: Oxford University Press.

High Court of Orissa (1993), Report of the Fact Finding Committee on Chilika Fisheries.

Kohli, Atul, (1987), *The State and Poverty in India: The Politics of Reform*, Cambridge: Cambridge University Press.

—— (ed.) (1988), *India's Democracy: An Analysis of Changing State-Society Relation*, NJ: Princeton University Press.

Kothari, Rajni (1986), 'Masses, Classes and the State', *Economic and Political Weekly*, Vol. 21.

—— (1987), 'On Humane Governance', *Alternatives*, Vol. XII.

—— (1988a), *State against Democracy: In Search of Humane Governance*, Delhi: Ajanta Publications.

Meluci, Alberto (1988), 'Social Movements and the Democratisation of Everyday Life', in John Keane (ed.), *Civil Society and the State*, London: Verso.

Mohanty, Ranjita (1995), 'Environmental Movement in the Context, of Development: A Sociological Study of the Movement against Sardar Sarovar Project', unpublished Ph.D Thesis, New Delhi: Jawaharlal Nehru University.

Offe, Clause (1985), 'New Social Movements: Challenging the Boundaries of Institutional Politics', *Social Research*, Vol. 52, No. 4.

Omvedt, Gail (1993), *Reinventing Revolution: New Social Movements and the Socialist Tradition in India*, New York: M.E. Sharpe.

Pathak, Akhileswar, (1994), *Contested Domains: The State, Peasants and Forests in Contemporary India*, New Delhi: Sage Publications.

Scott, Alan (1990), *Ideology and the New Social Movements*, London: Unwin Hyman.

Touraine, Allain (1985), 'An Introduction to the Study of Social Movements', *Social Research*, Vol. 52, No. 4.

12 Tribal Family

Towards Structural Mobility

P.C. JAIN

Enough literature on tribal social stratification is available. The tribals have witnessed decades of planned development. They have been late-comers to agriculture. Despite this drawback, they have made great strides in the field of economy. They started cultivation through hoe and have now reached to plough and mechanical cultivation. Some of the tribal belts of Maharashtra and Gujarat have made the tribals active participants in the field of green revolution. The recent forces of modernization, democratization and globalization have brought to them some new cultural changes, which have remained unreported in the field of social stratification. Admittedly, sociology has studied elaborately ethnomethodology of the tribals. Their new economy has also been studied. It has also been reported that the tribals have taken to political changes. But, in the field of culture, the tribal social institutions have also witnessed substantial change. There has come mobility in the tribal social structure.

Mobility is, in fact, social movement, usually of individuals or the groups between different positions within the system of stratification. The tribal marriage, kin and clan have undergone the process of mobility. Mobility is more obvious in the field of family. It must be argued here that tribal family is not a joint family. When I.P. Desai[1] says that Indian family is basically joint, does not apply to the tribals. In the case of the Bhils of Rajasthan, Maharashtra, Gujarat and Madhya Pradesh, it can be safely said that the tribal family has witnessed structural mobility. Although it is difficult to say whether this structural mobility is upward or downward, it can be said in certain terms that the traditional tribal family is moving towards female-headed family. The tribals of Central India have great regard for matriarchal family. Even today, the Bhils of Western India give due status to the sister of the father – *Bhua*. In all ceremonies, beginning from birth marriage to and death, *Bhua* is accorded a prior position. The status of *Bhua* in the tribal family indicates the importance of matriarchy.

The female-headed family system is on the ideology of matriarchy. In the absence of husband who is on migration in search of new pastures, the women who are left behind continue to nurture the family. What we want to stress here is that female-headed families create a new dimension for the tribal family. The families show the abandoning mobility among the tribals. In the present paper we shall discuss the female-headed family, which is the new form of stratification among the tribals.

Traditional Tribal Family

Tribal family is not a joint family. It is a mix of nuclear and joint family. As soon as the son of a Baiga or a Bhil gets mature and ploughs his field with his own hands, the father asks him to live separately. He is given a portion of land in consultation with the village elders – *Bhanjgaria*. And, now, the economy is separated. Though the son ploughs the field independently, the land is not in his name. He does not have any ownership entitlement. He also erects his own hutment, prepares food from his hearth and lives with his wife. This is the first phase of his mobility. It could be called upward mobility in sociological sense. For the purposes of village, the separated son has his independent identity as a household owner. However, the father has control over the produce of the field. He takes a part of produce for his own consumption but socially and culturally the son is independent. This kind of family mobility has taken a new shift. Now, there is emergence of female-headed family – a new movement in mobility. This has affected considerably the social stratification of the tribal institutions.

New Forces of Social Change

The tribals are basically agriculturists. But, the division of land among family members has been so forceful that the average landholding of a Bhil is two to three bighas. And, then, there has been encroachment of non-tribals on tribal land. This has compelled the tribals to take to other occupations. Jan Breman[2] refers to his study of Bardoli, Palsana and Valod of Surat and says that in absence of economically viable land the tribals have become proletariats. This has obliged them to give up agriculture. In such small patches of land it is not possible to adopt any measures of agricultural improvement. This compels the tribals to depeasantize. They have come out in search of new occupations. And, this ends up in the migration of the tribals.

Besides paucity of land, proletarianization and depeasantization, the tribals of Madhya Pradesh and Rajasthan are increasingly facing the challenges of directed social change, modernization and mechanization. It appears that migration is a strong force to effect mobility in the tribals. In the new situation, they have ceased to be peasants. They have new statuses – cart pullers, mill wage earner, technician, truck driver, and wage earner. These new statuses are the indicators of mobility. Admittedly, the tribals have now received new opportunities of wage earning, their cultural formations at the family level have undergone tremendous changes. There have emerged female-headed families. In their absence, at the parent village, the females work as heads of the family. The migrated tribals occasionally visit the parent village and intervene in the functioning of the family. Thus, there has been mobility of migrant worker and also the female head. These two positions could be termed as upward mobility. But, in a sense, the upward mobility proves to be downward mobility for the migrant worker. He now ceases to be the head of the family and satisfies himself as wage earner.

Form of Female-headed Family in the Wake of Mobility

The Bhils are a patriarchal stock of people. When the male head of the family goes out for work, he leaves place for his wife. In a way, it gives matriarchy to manage the family in the tribal setting. Thus, for the purpose of this essay, a female-headed family is that where in the absence of tribal male, the tribal female runs the family. The female head has a new role now as the head of the family. She has to take the decisions about the family at her own level.[3] Some of the problems with which the female head in a tribal family is concerned are given below:

1. *Sowing and harvesting of crop*: Normally, the head returns to the parent village at the time of sowing and harvesting, but if he fails to come in time, the job is done by hiring labour. Payment for this work is done immediately but if cash money is not available, it is given in a couple of days.
2. *Keeping vigil*: It is the responsibility of the female head to arrange for the vigil of the crop. Normally it does not require any manual labour and, therefore, the female head herself or her family members perform this work.
3. *Borrowings*: The female head in times of need borrows money from the trader of the nearby town. For the trader the family is his client, that is, permanent customer. He knows it well that whenever the female head would receive remittances from the migrant, his dues would be paid. In the absence of man it is the responsibility of the female to establish her credit worthiness. She is required to keep the creditor in her confidence. If he is not satisfied with the mode of due payments, credit could any time be scrapped. A successful family head is supposed to be that who can mobilize the trader to any extent she wants.
4. *Exchange transactions*: The crop is harvested normally with the help of the migrants. But it is not sold immediately. The market rate determines the sale. Though the tribal peasant has hardly any capacity for holding his produce, efforts are made to get reasonable return from the market from the produce. This decision is taken by the female head. She would also decide as to the quantity of commodity which has to be kept in store for the daily consumption of the family. Consumption and exchange are determined on the basis of the farm output received for a particular crop. It is here that the female head has to exercise her skillfulness. The migrant himself, who is away from the family, does not have any idea about the commodity which could be sold in the market as a surplus.
5. *Resolution of conflict*: Crises are several in a tribal family and in the absence of man, they multiply. There are a few crises relating to agriculture: it is the female who has to decide when to irrigate the crop; it is she who has to decide whom and what terms for hire. Then, there are conflicts regarding marriage and death. All these conflicts require on-the-spot decision. There are also some sensitive issues relating sex relations. She does not know, any time a drunken tribal can knock her door at midnight. This has to be tackled by her in total isolation from the relatives and members of the village.

The female head of the family in the absence of male is vulnerable to large number of difficulties. Though the female head makes effort to handle the remittances, satisfies the trader and manages agriculture, there are always some gaps. Her skillfulness lies in how she handles the family in the absence of her male counterpart. It must be admitted that the tribal female head has been empowered to take decisions regarding her family in the absence of man. If the female headship makes a successful story, naturally, the status of female is elevated not only in the village and kinship groups but within the cluster of tribal village also. The 73rd and 74th Constitutional Amendments have given statutory powers to women, but the power which she has got when her husband is absent from village, has definitely enhanced her social status. This is precisely empowerment of tribal women in the field of social and economic life of the community. The social empowerment of tribal women in the capacity of head of the family is not absolute. She is always in contact with her husband. And, in his absence, whatever decisions she takes are okayed and approved by the husband. This approval is invariably received whenever he returns home. We have not come across any dispute, which has arisen out of the decisions taken by the female head. And, therefore, it would be safe to infer that the female head is *de facto* head of the family though approval is always sought from the head.

The Migrant in the City: His Pleasure and Plight

On a broader base the migrants of South Rajasthan work in the cities of Ahmedabad and Surat. Our focus here has been on the migrants to Ahmedabad city. These migrants are classified into two categories one, the household workers of Rama and two, the wage earners working in trade, factory, road construction, etc. The earnings of the Rama and the ordinary migrants are not very high. Normally, a migrant is expected to remit Rs 500 to his family but the risk with the non-Rama migrants is great. They have to remain unemployed for a couple of days during a month. Sometimes, the are also compelled to leave the host community and resume work at his parent village. Such tragic cases are not few. It is found that the recent employment situation in Gujarat is quite discouraging. The textile mills in Surat and the looms also are not working to their full capacity. The trends now in Ahmedabad are moving towards increasing unemployment. It appears that in the years to come more and more migrants of South Rajasthan would return empty-handed. That would be a tragedy for the tribals.

Those who have been staying in Ahmedabad as migrant labour do not carry their females with them. However, there are some exceptional migrants who work in Ahmedabad with their females. There are migrant studies of Kutch and Orissa which show that in course of time the migrants shift their families also to the workplace. This might happen with the Bhils of South Rajasthan also.

Returning the Migrant to his Parent Village

When a migrant returns to his parent village, he resides with the host community for a couple of months in a year. During this period, he is obliged to participate in this society, which is essentially a caste society. He adapts to new patterns of accommodation. He is exposed to elements of modernity. He is introduced to a large number of technological items. He becomes familiar with a large number of secondary institutions. He becomes part of an anonymous society. He is also a participant to the family celebrations with which he is intimately associated. He is also a party to the celebrations of community festivals such as Garba, Ganesh Mahotasava, Holi and Diwali. This has an impact on the tribal's ideology of food and nutrition. He is also influenced by the lifestyle of the host community. His notions about health, hygiene and sanitation also get transformation.

When the tribal visits his village, he is a new culture man. He has learnt enough about the way of life which the Gujaraties live. When he reaches his house he takes a long session familiarizing his family members about the host community. Though he cannot effort to spend on his breakfast of balanced meals quite like Gujarat, but he does display his appreciation for the way of life which the people live. There is definitely a deep impact on the family. Small size family is propagated by him. Education is stressed by him. Though there can not be immediate achievement in terms of new lifestyle, but it is guessed that in course of one or two generations his family would attain some improvement in its lifestyle.

The parent village of the migrant also receives a transformation. In a single tribal village there are about a dozen migrants and in some cases each household in the village has one or more migrants to Ahmedabad and other places. The migrants make all effort to give new shape to community festivals. In fact, new ceremonies are begun by them in the village. Community temples are erected by collecting contributions from the migrants. There are always some households in a village where 'Katha-Kirtans' are organized during festival days when the migrants are expected to be in the village. The old deities of the village are brought to limelight and some new deities alien to the village are also created.

The parent village becomes an arena where there is a close interaction between the indigenous culture and the borrowed host culture. There are limitations of funds also which come in the way of accepting the alien culture. Despite the limitations, in the villages of migrants, the host culture becomes an ideal model for imitation. The ideal model is a mix of caste-Hindu culture and the secular culture of city. In this total impact, the migrant's local culture increasingly losses its identity. Some of the traditional functions of the village are becoming oblivious. For instance, on the festival of Holi, all the villagers including women used to go to the neighbouring town for singing and dancing to their respective traders. The traders on their part used to give some presents in cash or kind. However, such a visit of village people has now become exceptional. "Why should we go and pamper the trader on the day of our festival? It is we who give business to the trader, not he." It must be stressed that the host culture brought by the migrants has challenged the age-old traditions and mores of the village life.

Civil Society in the Parent Village

The migrants know it very well that the civil society in the towns and cities of Gujarat is very strong. They also know that whenever the state fails to provide civic needs of the people – may it be water, electricity or road – there is always some agitations. People do not march to the government offices. Political rallies, demonstrations, strikes and bandhs are common in the city life. All this in Ahmedabad is possible because the civil society there is much conscious of its rights. At the village level the civil society is very weak. It is almost absent here. In fact, the civil society in the migrant's village only insists to follow the community mores and traditions.

In the tribal context too, the relations between civil society and state are almost inactive. For the tribals, historically, the state has always been repressive. It is the state, which is constitutionally accountable to the welfare of the female-headed family. Why an adult male is compelled to leave his village and work at a place which is alien to him? Had civil society been awakened among the tribals, the female-headed families would not have emerged at all. Which woman would like her husband to remain absent from village not for a day or two but for months together without minimum interaction? If the resources of earning had hijacked by the state, the tribal family would have lived peacefully. It is the force of traditions, which has the female head to survive in a village, which is isolated and settled in a scattered way.

Our understanding of the tribal society, which has come out of our prolonged fieldwork, shows that the female-headed families could be strengthened, if the civil society becomes stronger. As a matter of fact, the civil society can work as an alternative to the state. For instance, the civil society should create certain institutions which could facilitate the survival of the female-headed family. For the strengthening of civil society there is always need for social movement. This will make the journey of the female head smoother.

Female-headed family is a new dimension of tribal family. The concept needs to be thoroughly investigated on empirical grounds. The basis of female-headed family is residence. The man who is the head of the tribal family does not share residence with other members of the family including his wife. In other words, both his residence and hearth are separate from rest of his family members. Viewed this way he does not make a family. He remits his earnings to his family. Yet another criticism is that though the male member has separate residence, his actions are oriented to his own family. The basic idea of female-headed family can further be questioned: the female surely takes decision in the absence of man. But all these need to be approved as soon as the male returns. If final decision rests with the migrant head, how is female the head of the family. Such a kind of argument makes a sense. But, the fact remains that whatever has been independently decided by the female head is fully approved by the male. And, this makes the female head more powerful and successful.

Feminists usually rejoice on the emergence of female-headed family. They argue that the tribal women have very successfully taken over the charge of family head from the males. It has also been amply demonstrated that given proper opportunities the females are fully capable of taking independent decisions. They are empowered. Such an analysis of the female-headed family is worthwhile but there is yet another aspect of this new pattern of family. The females are not without their hardships. As a matter of fact, migration is never without its social costs. The highest cost that a woman has to pay is her long interval of isolation. Her empowerment needs to be applauded but at what cost. She too has her own libido. What happens to her and for what period?

Notes

1. I.P. Desai (1964), *Some Aspects of Family in Mahuva*, Bombay: Asia Publishing House.
2. Jan Breman (1985), *Of Peasants, Migrants and Paupers*, New Delhi: Oxford University Press, p. 55.
3. Empirical information for the present essay is taken from author's recently completed project on the Female-headed Family among the Tribals of Rajasthan, Gujarat and Madhya Pradesh.

13 Raika Jati and Its Dharmic Order

VINAY KUMAR SRIVASTAVA

In his writings on social stratification, K.L. Sharma observes that in India, caste as a socio-religious system (comprising the notions of purity and pollution, hierarchy and hereditary callings, endogamy and hypergamy, etc.), has visibly weakened, and has turned into a 'politico-economic formation' (1999: 15). Those aspects of caste that were outside its purview have now come to the centre stage. Economic and political power is gradually replacing ritual power. However, in this reworking, the ideological distinctiveness of caste has come to acquire a pivotal place. There are several instances where the diacritical signs (the 'identity markers') of a caste that had largely faded, or were being relegated to the back seat, have now been vigorously rejuvenated with explicit instructions from the councils of castes and their leaders to observe them closely and fastidiously. More and more discourses on the glorious origin of a caste and its valorous ethno-history are being held. A cursory look at caste periodicals, whose number is multiplying every year, will tell us that they carry articles on the magnificent traditions and pasts of their respective caste-folks. The exemplary deeds of their caste persons are described repeatedly, and they are deified in course of time. In other words, caste is on its way of becoming a 'sociological entity' *for* itself.

Against this background, a study of the respective ideological orders of different castes has become extremely important. This paper provides an account of the ideological order that lies at the base of the caste of the Raika of Rajasthan.[1]

Introduction: The Pastoral Raika

Just as human beings have founded a hierarchy for themselves, so do they have also created one for the animals that live in and around their territory. The species of animal a caste domesticates, has a bearing on its social status. In Rajasthan, in addition to the pan-Hindu concept of the sacred cow, the camel was placed high in animal hierarchy, although it did not evoke the same kind of sacredness that is associated with the cow. When modern transport did not exist, the camel was the mode of conveyance in the desert (and is still even today). The princely lineages had their camel armies. In almost all the love stories of Rajasthan – for instance, Dhola Maru, Mahendra Mumal, Nihalde Sultan, Amala Khimvaji, to name some prominent ones – the role of the camel is eulogized. A religious text called *Goraksha Samhita* records that Kalakarni, a female deity, has a camel as her mount. Some prefer to call her Ustravahini Devi (the goddess that rides the camel) (Srivastava, 1981: 182).

Royal lineages and rich peasants generally owned the camel herds.[2] Small peasants often aspired to own a couple of camels. Besides serving as a traction and draught animal, its ownership raised, and even today raises, the status of a family. However, only rich peasants can afford to buy camels today, as each camel costs on average not less than five to six thousand rupees.[3] While other peasant castes (viz., Jat and Bishnoi) do own camels, the tasks of camel-tending and breeding, keeping camel herds and taking them out for grazing, training them for various services, and looking after their health, are the traditional duties of the Raika, a 'herding caste', now classified in the list of the Other Backward Classes (OBCs) (Srivastava, forthcoming). The Raika are also called and call themselves Rebari and Dewasi. They not only manage the camels owned by others, but also have their own herds. There may be individual camel specialists in other castes, but the Raika have the reputation of being the foremost camel-breeders of Rajasthan, even when they have kept the flocks of sheep from time immemorial, or have switched to sheep-herding in recent years. The love lyrics of Rajasthan that praise the camel also pay tribute to its traditional rider, the Raika.

Besides being presently concentrated in Rajasthan and Gujarat, the Raika also inhabit some villages in the states of Haryana, Punjab, Uttar Pradesh and Madhya Pradesh. In Gujarat, these people call themselves Rebari, although they know that their caste is also known as Raika. Although no department (government or otherwise) has any knowledge of the total Raika population in India, a general estimate is that they number not less than four hundred thousand.

Besides the Raika, the other pastoral communities of Rajasthan are the Gujar, Ahir, and Sindhi Muslim. The peasant castes (such as Jat, Sirvi, Bishnoi) keep sheep and goats, but never so many as to constitute a herd. They mainly invest in milch animals. However, the Raika graze (on payment in cash) the camels that peasant castes own. Other castes (martial as well as artisan) also cultivate land, and keep some animals, which are grazed by one of their family members.

Internal Distinctions

According to the Raj Marwar Census (1891: 571–72), the Raika are divided into two 'types' (*bhed*): Maru and Chalakya. Let us first summarize the findings of this report that became the basis of several other writings (both colonial and post-colonial) on the Raika.

The Maru inhabit parts of Marwar, the Chalakya, regions of Godwar, that is the southern area of Pali.[4] According to this report, the Maru consider themselves superior to the Chalakya – a claim supported by a combination of two factors. First, they do not domesticate sheep; they are true camel-breeders. A Chalakya herd predominantly comprises sheep, though it may have a couple of camels for transporting the camp on migration.[5] Second, the Maru think that the Chalakya are dirty, do not observe the norms of hygiene and purity and pollution, and are basically non-vegetarian.

Further, the Raj Marwar Census distinguished these two groups in terms of certain cultural traits. The Chalakya women wear brass (*pital*) ornaments; that is why this group is also known as Pitalya. The married Chalakya women do not wear the head-dress (locally called *ati*), as is customary with their Maru counterparts. The Maru men wear a long loin-cloth (*dhoti*) stretching up to the toe; the Chalakya have a shorter loin-cloth. As the Maru consider themselves superior to the Chalakya, they can accept women from the lower group (hypergamy); the opposite practice (hypogamy), however, is non-existent.

Although the term 'Chalakya' was used later in the entries on Raika in several compendia on castes and tribes by administrators and ethnologists in the early 20th century and as recently as 1975 by S. Westphal-Hellbusch, I did not come across its popular usage in the villages where I did my fieldwork. With an aim to clarify certain points, I introduced my key respondents to both words – Chalakya and Pitalya. The genealogists (called the Rav) of the Raika knew the existence of these terms, but they were not a part of the popular vocabulary. However, these genealogists did not rule out that their caste-fellows in other parts of Rajasthan might have used these terms in their descriptions of the Raika inhabiting south Rajasthan. It may be inferred from this that the source of information for the Raj Marwar Census officials and others, and also of Westphal-Hellbusch, was the genealogists of a particular region.

Contemporary Raika distinguish between three of their groups according to the region each one of them inhabits. There are, thus, Maru, who are from Marwar, the Godwara Raika, who live in Godwar, and Kutchis, the Raika of Kutch in Gujarat. It is true that the Maru regard themselves as superior to the other two groups. Some of them also say that the lower categories of Raika should abstain from using the honorific title of 'Dewasi'. I also heard that, as said before, the Maru can accept women from lower groups, but hardly any case existed in people's memory to substantiate this. On the other hand, in my fieldwork in Godwar, I found that the Raika of this region also make a similar claim; along with this, they attack the distinction between Maru and Godwara by saying that the latter have also dispersed from Marwar. This also indirectly implies that the Godwara Raika accept (if only implicitly and reluctantly) that they are inferior. The differing claims of these territorial groups are supported by their respective genealogists.

Cultural distinctions also exist between the Maru and Godwara, and the diacritical marks (such as the head-dress, the length of the loin-cloth) taken up in the Raj Marwar Census are not entirely incorrect. That the Maru and Godwara do not eat from the same plate is also true. But my submission is that the fact of belonging to the same caste (the idea of *jati bhai*, 'caste brother') transcends these cultural differences, and the Raika see the others of their caste inhabiting different geographical areas as having the same 'essence' (*ansha*). The Raika know that the differences in *khana* ('food') and *pani* ('water') bring about differences in *rahna sahna* (the 'style of living'), and therefore various groups of their caste have adopted different characteristics because of the fact of living in different ecological zones and states. Consequently, their marriage ties have also been broken.

There is no substance in the distinction between the Maru and Godwara in the types of animal each group domesticates. The Maru have flocks of sheep and the Godwara have camel herds. A distinction between these groups with reference to their respective food habits is also incorrect as both of them regard themselves as vegetarian. But, it is true that the Maru, Godwara and Kutchi are not intermarrying groups. The spouses are invariably sought from a circle of neighbouring hamlets. It is rarely the case that the Maru of Pali-Marwar have marital relations with those in Bikaner, or other farther districts. In other words, there are differences which the Raika themselves recognize between their different territorial groups. These differences are upheld in relations of commensality and marriage, but they are transcended by the unity of *jati bhai*. Thus, any Raika from any part of India can seek shelter in any of his caste hamlets by simply announcing his caste and identity. The local caste council (*panchayat*) has the right to punish its members for denying general hospitality, food and temporary shelter to any other person from their caste. This is an important factor in the formation of Raika identity.

The Story of the Raika Origin

Let us begin with the hypothesis that the story of Raika origin not only defines what is central to their popular religion but also forges a unity between the Raika all over Rajasthan. In present times, when Raika leaders are working towards the unity of their caste, they, in addition to emphasizing the problems faced by all of them, also draw attention to the fact that all Raika (irrespective of their sub-castes, geographical areas, variation in dress patterns and dialects, restrictions on marriage, conviviality and commensality) are *one* because of their descent from the first Raika who was created by one of the three Hindu gods, Lord Shiva.[6]

Once, the story of Raika origin tells us, Shiva goes into meditation for twelve years near a pond (*nadi*) in Mount Kailash, where he lives with his wife, Parvati. While he meditates, his consort engages herself in various playful activities. Using clay, she makes objects in the shape of various bodily parts – torso, legs, eyes and face. When Shiva emerges from meditation, she requests him to infuse life (*jivit karo*) into the clay objects. One by one, each object awakens, and that is how the animal world is created.

Finally comes the turn of an object that has five legs, the fifth one stuck to its belly. Shiva points out the grave difficulty this animal will have in walking, but, at Parvati's insistence, he says *utha,* meaning 'get up'. From that day, this animal comes to be known as *untha,* or the camel. But, as expected, it has difficulty in moving, so Parvati requests her husband to 'make the fifth leg disappear'. Shiva tries to convince Parvati that once the camel has four legs it will create problems for them, but she is unconvinced and reiterates her request. So, Shiva pushes the fifth leg upward; it now emerges as a hump (*thumbi*) and its base forms the boss (*aidar*). He also makes some marks (called *chugli*) on the upper part of the posterior side of the camel's hind legs, which the Raika say are still found. The *thumbi, aidar* and *chugli* are, according to this story, Shiva's 'stamps' (*nishan*) on this animal.[7]

Once the camel has only four legs, it starts running swiftly, often disappearing into the wilderness. It is difficult for Parvati to keep it under control, and she once again requests Shiva to create a man to look after the camel. Shiva had already created a man called Nando Charan of the Kachela sub-caste, to look after his bull (*nandiya*); and he had also created a Suthar (the carpenter), of the Vishkarma sub-caste, to take care of the "renouncer's fire" (*dhuni*) and to bring water from the pond. For grazing the camel, he now creates a man from the 'dirt (*mail*) of his thighs (*pinda*)'; the camel-grazier is named Pinda and is assigned to the Samar sub-caste.

Pinda's duty is to take the camel out to graze. Once, on his way home from the forest, he runs astray into a cremation ground. It is already dark, so he decides to spend the night there. After a while, he feels hungry, and looks around for a vessel in which he could collect the camel's milk and drink. He finds an earthen vessel, chipped on the rim (*khanda*) lying near a burning corpse. Pinda picks it up and begins milking the camel using the vessel to catch the milk. A drop of that milk falls on the ground. As a result, the ghost of a Maheshwari Brahmin awakens, whose corpse is also burning there. This happens because the divine camel's milk is sacred and its touch has a life-giving quality. The ghost manifests its desire to pay obeisance to Lord Shiva. So, in a state of fright, Pinda brings him to Mount Kailash. The ghost falls at the feet of Shiva and requests him to release it from ghost-hood (*bhut juni*) as its last rites are yet to be completed. Shiva 'showers compassion' and the ghost transforms into a human being (*manushya*). He is called Jamra and the divine couple keeps him with them as an errand boy.

In contrast to the other 'sons' of Shiva, Jamra is from the mortal world (*mrtyulok*). He has passed through the different vocations (*asrama*) of life, and knows the inevitability and significance of conjugal relations. He advises his three brothers (Pinda Samar, Kachela Charan and Vishkarma Suthar) to approach the divine couple to ask for matrimony, so that they might be blessed with progeny. Parvati requests Shiva to find suitable spouses for them.

At this point the story provides a detailed account of how Shiva begins the search for his sons' prospective spouses, and finally finds the pond where the sixty-four celestial nymphs (*pariyan, joganian, saktan*) come to bathe. He asks Kachela Charan to collect their clothes, which they usually leave under a tree near the pond, and bring some of them back to him. On the way, he is advised to drop a couple of them after every step or two; those *pariyan* who get their clothes back return to the pond, whereas the rest keep on chasing the thief. When Kachela Charan reaches Mount Kailash, he has the clothes of five nymphs, but by the time he arrives at Shiva's hermitage, one of the nymphs called Kinka succumbs to death. The clothes are handed over to Siva who promises to return them to the nymphs on the condition that they marry his four 'sons'. The nymphs consent to marry provided the name of their dead friend Kinka is made immortal. Shiva transforms the dead nymph into a goddess (called Gaur) and his 'sons' and the entire world are advised to worship her.

Pinda is married to the celestial nymph named Rai, and their progeny, one son and twelve daughters, come to be called Raika (meaning, "of Rai's"). The second nymph, Sanwari, marries Vishkarma Suthar. They have eight daughters.

Chanwri becomes the wife of Kachela Charan, and they are blessed with five daughters. The children of Sanwari constitute the Suthar caste, whereas those of Chanwri are the Charan. The 'ghost' Jamra marries Rambha, and sixteen daughters are born to them. The Rav of Maru Raika say that the descendants of Jamra and Rambha are called Rebaris.

Thus, for these Rav, Raika and Rebari are two different castes. To quote from the narration of the Lambiyan Rav: "The Rebari are the people who live in Godwar and Kutch; they are the children of the ghost. The Maru have no relations with them, except for the similarity in occupation." This, however, is not the view of the Rav of Godwara Raika. The story of the ghost, they say, is not in their texts, and they think that it is an addition made by the Rav of Maru Raika not only to give an erroneous and derogatory explanation to the origin of Godwara Raika, but also to provide a textual support to the self-acclaimed superiority of the Maru. According to them, Shiva's camel-grazier is married to two *pariyan,* Avri and Gavri, and the purported distinction between the Raika and Rebari, as held by the Rav of Maru Raika, is wrong and misleading.

Now, the story of origin enters into the realm of segmentation within the Raika caste. The problem of marriage surfaces again when the children of Pinda and Rai are of marriageable age. Since there exists no other Raika family in the entire universe, the premise of caste endogamy is ruled out. Once again, Pinda seeks the help of the divine couple in finding spouses for his children. Consequently, Shiva appears in the dream of Sesna Arjun, the mythical king of Patangarh, and orders him to spare twelve of his warriors (of Rajput caste) for Pinda's daughters. The king complies and the Raika girls are married to twelve different Rajput sub-castes. But what happens to Pinda's son? In which caste group is his marriage arranged? The Rav of both the Raika groups (as well as the published account in the Raj Marwar Census) do not have an answer to this question. When I posed it before the Lambiyan Rav, he said that perhaps Pinda's son was also married into the Rajput, most probably its high-ranking Solankhi sub-caste.

The twelve Rajput families agree to marry their sons to Raika women under the imperial command. As these marriages are against the principle of caste endogamy, the Rajput bridegrooms are excommunicated from their caste. Now, they merge with the Raika identity. However, their Rajput caste names continue, and for these, the Raika as well as their genealogists use the term *nakh.* Furthermore, it is believed that different Raika sub-castes (Bar, Ulva, Khatana, etc.) are named after the names of the sons born to Rajput fathers and Raika mothers. There is a common belief in Rajasthan that all the 'thirty-six castes' (*chatris quam*) have emerged from Rajputs; this, however, does not imply that they all have an equal status. It is relevant here to remember Tambiah's (1985) demonstration of the relationship between *varna* and *jati.* According to him, the numerous castes found in India "arose from the unions of males of different varnas with women belonging to varnas differing from their own" (ibid.: 214).

Central to the segmentation of the Raika caste is the distinction between *nakh* and *jat.* The Raika know the term *gotra* (or *got,* as they call it), meaning 'exogamous particlan'. Some of them remember their *gotra* names they learnt from their ancestors.[8] But *gotra* has no functional relevance in the local perception of their organization, marriage ties, corporate, and inter-group relations. In contrast, *nakh* and *jat* are crucial for understanding their organization. As other observers of Indian society (such as Béteille, 1964; Davis, 1983) have also noted, the term *jat* (or *jati*) is used for many levels of segmentation; in other words, there is no separate indigenous term for sub-caste. However, this does not mean that people lack the idea of segmentation, fission and fusion. For a Raika, his Raika identity is in relation to other structurally equivalent identities, such as the Gujar, Nayak, Sunar, etc. Moving downward on the model of segmentation, his *jat* is Maru in relation to the Godwara or Kutchi.

Thus, the word *jat* is used for the Raika (the encompassing group) as well as Maru or Godwara (the encompassed group). But, at the following level of segmentation, a terminological distinction occurs, and the word *nakh* is introduced. The Maru Raika have twelve *nakh* because the first Raika's daughters marry twelve Rajput men of different sub-castes. As mentioned earlier, each *nakh* is the name of the Rajput sub-caste, and after the sons born to each of these twelve marriages, the Raika sub-castes came into existence, for which again, the term *jat* is used. According to the Rav, in total thirty-six sub-castes resulted. If closely inspected, it means that the sons of these daughters did not acquire any sub-caste, either of their father or mother; on the contrary, they founded the sub-castes.

Let us now take up the case of Pinda's son. Pinda's sub-caste, to recapitulate, is Samar, assigned to him by Shiva. His son also acquires his father's sub-caste, which is not the case with his sisters. He marries a Rajput woman (?), and as the system is patrilineal, his sons continue to remain within the Samar sub-caste. The Rav say that the Samar do not have *nakh*. Including him, the Raika have thirty-seven sub-castes, thirty-six from Pinda's daughters and one from his son.[9]

Against this background, let us examine the concept of *nakh*. It may be difficult to find a word in English which properly conveys its meaning. The Raika say that *nakh* refers to the 'seed' (*bij*), and it is an implicit indication of the male procreative function. In the case of Pinda's son, it is the Samar 'seed' which procreates the group, hence there is no separate *nakh;* in other words, *nakh* merges with *jat*. So, the fact as to whether or not he marries a Rajput woman is inconsequential. But in the case of his sisters, the 'seeds' come from the Rajput; the descent however, is not traced in the father's line (or, the sons born to Raika sisters do not become Rajput) because the role of these Rajput warriors, who are excommunicated from their caste, is to procreate the Raika progeny. Thus, the sons of Raika sisters and Rajput warriors are neither Samar, their maternal grandfather's sub-caste, nor do they inherit their father's sub-caste. They found their own Raika sub-castes; but, since the system is patrilineal, they remember their respective father's sub-caste, which comes to be conceptualized as *nakh*.

Like *got*, *nakh* is not the basis of any corporate function. But unlike *got*, it is remembered and the Raika talk about it while exploring their relations with the Rajput. A few of the educated Raika who now live in cities have started using the *nakh* names, instead of their caste (Raika or Dewasi) or sub-caste (such as Bar, Jhuan, Sukel, etc.) names, as their surnames. This may be because using Rajput surnames is still a source of respect in the cultural tradition of Rajasthan.

Finally, these thirty-seven sub-castes are not arranged in any hierarchy. No norms of separation or exclusion operate on them. Observing the prohibition on sub-caste endogamy, marriage is permissible between all. It may be relevant here to quote Ellis (1991: 87): "the greater the degree of segmentation, the less the stress upon hierarchy as a principle of social interaction." However, the Samar are 'respected' (and distinguished from the others) because they are the descendants of the first Raika, and also their sub-caste name was coined by Shiva. The report on the 1891 Census (1894: 157) notes: "the descendants of Samar alone claim a pure extraction while the others comprise a combination of several Rajput tribes." A Raika teacher of Bikaner told me that if you meet a Samar, you must immediately fold your palms before him, because he has the 'essence' (dirt of the skin, or locks of hair, or sweat) of Lord Shiva in him. The local kinship concepts (such as who contributes the 'seed', proximity to or the progeny of the creator, the system of descent, etc.) are used to generate and explain differences. Thus, the Samar are respected because they represent the pure patrilineage. But, this 'respect' (or, 'pure extraction') does not entitle them to any special favours; they are neither the most sought after for marital alliances nor are they allocated any religious role. Even in the past, they did not have precedence in any of the social roles. As is the case with other castes (and sub-castes) in India, stereotypes are attached to some of the Raika sub-castes as well; for instance, Piswala are known for their affection, Bar are praised for being the most reliable, and so on.

Duties for the Raika

This section gives an account of the duties (*dharma*) prescribed for the Raika by their creator. As the Rav of Maru Raika narrate, when the primeval founders of the four castes married the celestial nymphs, Shiva announced twenty moral maxims for them. Of these, ten were ordained upon the Raika, six on the Suthar, and four on the Charan. No moral maxims were pronounced for the Rebari, perhaps because their ancestor was not created from Shiva's body. These rules were essential for the *devaputra* ('sons of the god') as each one of them was destined to live after his marriage in the mortal world rather than Mount Kailash, and thus should know how to lead his life. Shiva advised his 'sons' to live according to their respective maxims if they wanted a happy and glorious life, and prosperous posterity.

As we saw in the case of *jati*, the term *dharma* is used for the whole as well as its parts. Each of these twenty maxims is called *dharma* and following this connotation, the Ravs say that the Raika have 'ten *dharmas*'. The set of these individual *dharmas* is also referred to by the same term; thus, the twenty *dharmas* constitute *bisotri dharma*. In addition, *dharma* also designates the broad religious category, in this case Hinduism, in which the Raika classify themselves. It seems to me that of all the Indological concepts, *dharma* is perhaps the most multivalent and polysemic. It is constituted of three meanings – religion, duty, and morally correct, righteous, danger-thwarting, and merit-accumulating behaviour. Further, the occupation pursued by a caste is also termed *dharma*.

All these meanings of *dharma* are couched broadly in a religious idiom. The pivotal meaning given to it depends on the context of its usage. Distribution of gifts (*dan*) to 'serving and occupational castes' (*kamin*) at the time of solar or lunar eclipse is a dharmic action to avert any ensuing danger; feeding beggars is for gaining merit; wearing bracelets on both arms is morally correct for a *suhagan* ('married woman'); keeping camels is a duty of the Raika; and classifying one's group as Hindu is to adhere to the broad religious category, and in this context, *dharma* refers to religion.

The ten *dharmas* of Raika are supposed to be original. Since then, the Rav tell us, many more *dharmas*, the commands of other gods and goddesses, have been added to this list. The people, however, keep a distinction between the maxims assigned to them by Shiva and those that have the legitimacy of other divine powers. The distinction is also kept while performing rituals and thanking the deities for help. For instance, when a she-camel delivers a calf, it is imperative that sugar-wafers (*batasha*) and coconut (*naryal*), and, if possible, some money, are offered to the caste- and the area-specific god, Balinath-ji, because he is believed (in Bikaner) to have issued a set of commands regarding the use of camel products. Moreover, on this occasion, the transcendental and supreme deities (of whom Shiva is one) can always be approached for any help. But it will not happen that Balinath is ignored and only Shiva is approached for a she-camel's safe delivery. The Raika remember the god (or goddess) who has assigned a particular *dharma* for them, and he (or she) must be remembered while adhering (*palan*, 'nurturing') to it. The Rav also point out that because of the ten *dharmas* (*das dharma*) that the Raika follow, their caste is also known as Dewasi.

Let us have a look at the ten *dharmas* and their explanation by the Rav as well as the Raika.[10]

Pehlo dharma Dewasiyan ra Shiva saugandha nahin khaye

The first *dharma* of the Dewasi is that they should never swear upon Lord Shiva, irrespective of whether the oath is true or false (*sachchi*, or *jhuti saugandha*).

The Rav explain that sometimes the people have to swear upon the names of the deities in order to prove their innocence or to make others accept the truth of what they say. Swearing adds a tremendous moral force to the claim, along with exposing the oath-taker to unknown dangers. In the council meetings, it is quite common for the contending parties to swear upon the deities and also upon their close kin (children, parents and the spouse) in urging their claim (*hak*) or version (*bat*). All know that whosoever swears falsely might either be a victim of divine wrath or that his kin (particularly the one sworn upon) may succumb to grave illness or even death. Although swearing is not as serious a matter among the Raika as it is in some other communities, for instance, the Angami Naga (Hutton, 1921: 144–48), they are always afraid of taking an oath on false matters. But, irrespective of the truth of the matter, the first Raika *dharma* is not to implicate their creator in the business of oath-taking.

Duja dharma Dewasiyan ra sham dharma rakhaya

The second *dharma* of the Dewasi is to be honest and truthful, and this has reference to the relations of Raika men with women in general.

In explaining this *dharma*, the Lambiyan Rav emphasized that a Raika is famous in Rajasthan for never 'casting a dirty (passionate) eye' (*buri nazar dalna*) on any woman. Except for his own wife, he regards all other women as mothers, sisters and daughters. He is (and was) employed by dominant castes and princely lineages for accompanying their women to their husbands' or natal villages because he represses his passions and has tremendous control over his senses. This is not only what the Raika say about them; the other neighbouring castes also have the same opinion about the Raika.

A common belief in Rajasthan is that a lonely woman should have no fear of the Raika. He will not only be nice to her, but in case she has lost her way, he will accompany her to her destination. It is imperative for the Raika, as I see it, to uphold this image. Otherwise, in a sexually segregated society where both pre-marital and extra-marital sex are completely prohibited, and strangers, whether from towns or villages, are suspected as threats to local women, the Raika grazing expedition, in which they have to depend on the help of people in other villages, would get into serious difficulty. Perhaps this is one of the reasons why the Raika council (*panchayat*) deals very strictly with any laxity in sexual norms. The offenders are levied enormous fines, and in some cases are also punished corporally, particularly in matters of serious sexual deviations.

Tijo dharma Dewasiyan ra badlo katan naye

The third *dharma* of the Dewasi is not to axe (or fell) the banyan (*Ficus bengalensis*) tree. Although the term used in this verse is *badlo*, meaning banyan tree, the people interpret it to mean all trees. In contemporary situation, this *dharma* is also used for external consumption to defend their claim of never indulging in illegally cutting trees.

Throughout my fieldwork, the Raika (inhabiting different hamlets) confided in me that they have been wrongly accused by the Panchayat Samitis (statutory councils) of different villages for cutting down trees. In Sadri (Pali-Marwar), they held the Grasia responsible for felling trees in collusion with forest guards. According to them, the Grasia men fell trees for firewood, and their women sell it in nearby towns. The income from this is divided equally between the Grasia and forest guards. Though they are not the culprits, the Raika are blamed and penalized by the forest department.

The Raika say that they (meaning, their animals) depend on green leaves and grasses rather than wood. Animal droppings are used as fuel and supplemented with dry branches obtained from shrubs (*jhar*). "If trees disappear, how would we feed our animals?' In these words, one may summarize the Raika view.

Chautho dharma Dewasiyan ra Pipal pujan jaye

The fourth *dharma* of the Dewasi is to worship (*puja*) the Pipal (*Ficus religiosa*) tree. The day of worship is not stated in the verse but the Rav say that it can be performed in the morning hours of any day in the week. However, the most auspicious day for this worship is Monday, because Pipal is regarded as the abode of Lord Shiva in local folklore, and Monday happens to be his day.[11] One of the funeral rituals, performed on the ninth day after the day of death, is called *Pipal chokha karno,* on which this tree is worshipped.

The Pipal *puja* consists of the following ritual acts: (a) offering plain water, or if one can afford it, water mixed with a pinch of sugar and grains of rice; (b) standing with folded palms before the tree and then, touching (or pressing) its stem (or the base of its stem); the fingers (and the palm) which have touched the tree are brought to caress one's forehead. Here, the stem stands for the legs of the god and its base symbolizes his feet. This ritual action is central to all *pujas* whether for local deities, or renouncers, or deities without a stone platform dedicated to them. In the latter case, the right hand is just waved in air and then brought back to touch the forehead. And (c) circumambulating the tree, sometimes, as happens in the case of *Pipal chokha karno,* a cotton thread is wrapped all around its stem – an act that symbolizes the offering of clothes to the deity.

There are no gender distinctions on the worship of Pipal; this *dharma* is for all. The sacredness of Pipal multiplies because temples and platforms dedicated to deities are founded in its neighbourhood or shade. However, the absence of a religious place in its vicinity does not reduce its holiness. Any attempt to defile the place where Pipal stands (by urinating or defecating), even if done inadvertently, infuriates the divine force.

In the absence of a Pipal tree in the vicinity of a hamlet, the people offer *puja* to the Khejri tree. The switch from Pipal to Khejri does not pose any conceptual problem because both these trees are sacred. However, Khejri is not believed to be the abode of Lord Shiva. More properly, it is the 'Tulsi (Basil) of the Thar desert'.[12] Both Pipal and Khejri are gendered; the former is male, the latter, female. As we noticed for Pipal, there is no gender restriction on the worship of Khejri.

Although the worship of Pipal also embraces the worship of Shiva, how does one explain its substitution by Khejri which is not believed to be Shiva's abode. It puzzled me in October 1989 when I observed the last rites of an old Raika. The tree chosen for the ninth-day purificatory ritual, *Pipal chokha karno,* was Khejri (and not Pipal as the name of the ritual suggests) because that particular hamlet did not have a Pipal tree. Perhaps, more important among the Raika is their attitude towards trees in general. In this light, the third and the fourth *dharmas* can be seen as related – the former prohibits them from cutting trees, the latter, advises the converse, that is, worshipping the idea of trees. The third *dharma* prohibits them from cutting any trees; however, the fourth does not advise the worship of every tree. Why Pipal and Khejri are worshipped may be understood in terms of the general proposition: the idea of sacred is crucial for ritual expression. The sacredness of Pipal is a pan-Indic idea, while that of Khejri is mostly confined to Rajasthan. In the Raika case, I think, the worship of these two trees guides us to their attitude to vegetation in general.

Panchva dharma padman tano parde jiman jaye

The fifth and the sixth *dharmas* of the Dewasi are related to their women. The fifth one proclaims that in ritual feasts, the Raika women should eat 'behind the curtain'.[13]

Let me note here a few observations on ritual feasts. On such occasions, the place where the guests eat is always the backyard of the host's house, and it is close to where the temporary kitchen (*bhatti*) is set up. In front of the main entrance to the house, canopies are erected for guests. On being invited by the hosts to join the feast, the guests from each hamlet (men, women and children)

Map 1

Rajasthan District Map

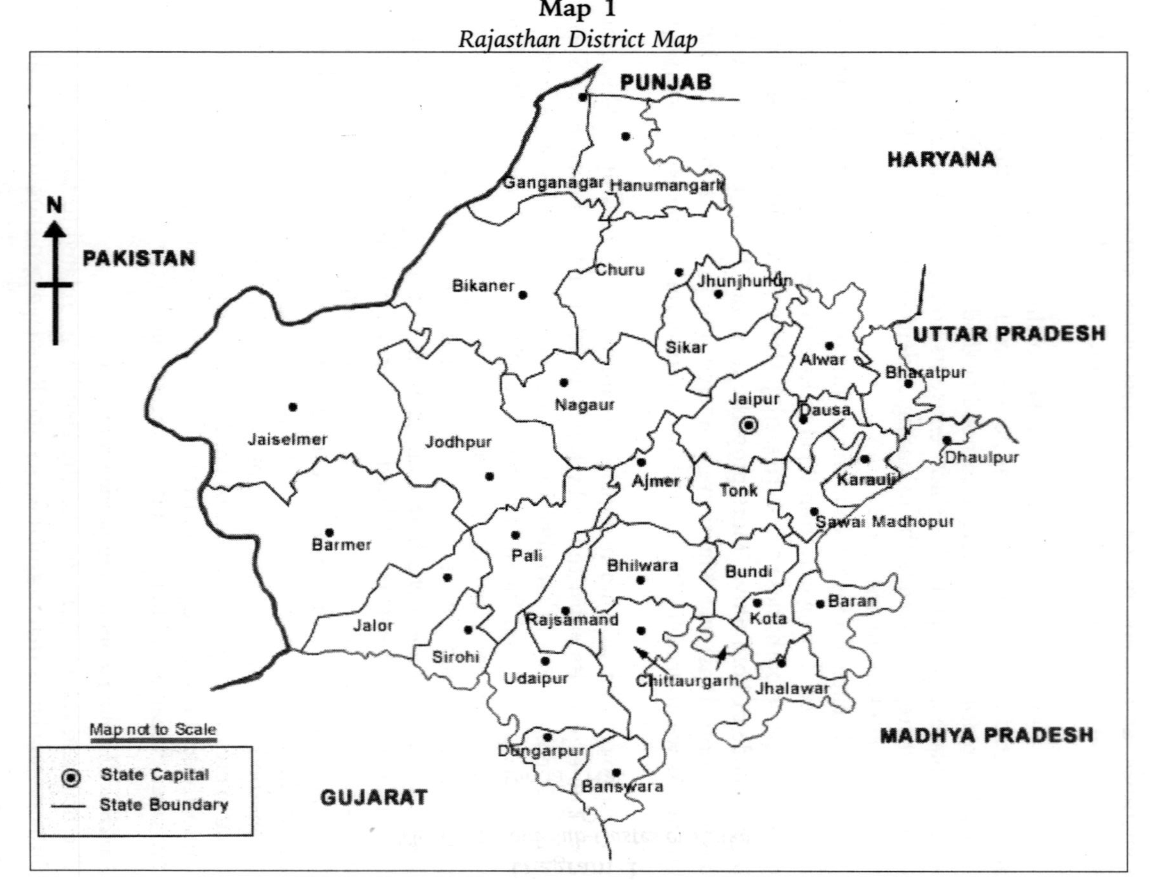

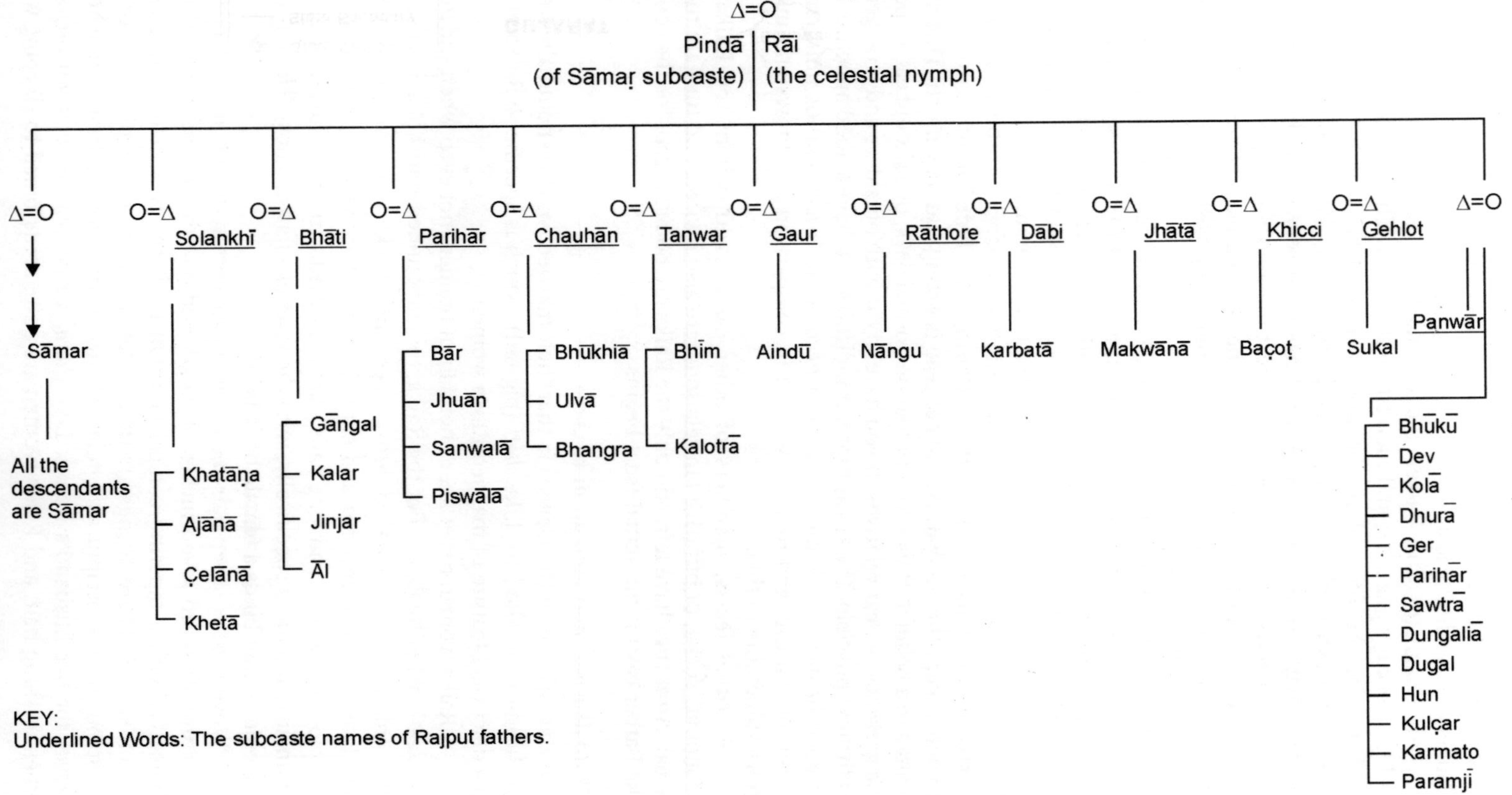
Diagram 1
The Caste and Sub-Castes of Raika
Δ=O
Pindā
(of Sāmaṛ subcaste)
Rāi
(the celestial nymph)
Δ=O
Sāmar
All the descendants are Sāmar
O=Δ
Solankhī
Khatāṇa
Ajānā
Çelānā
Khetā
O=Δ
Bhāti
Gāngal
Kalar
Jinjar
Āl
O=Δ
Parihār
Bār
Jhuān
Sanwalā
Piswālā
O=Δ
Chauhān
Bhūkhiā
Ulvā
Bhangra
O=Δ
Tanwar
Bhīm
Kalotrā
O=Δ
Gaur
Aindū
O=Δ
Rāthore
Nāngu
O=Δ
Dābi
Karbatā
O=Δ
Jhātā
Makwānā
O=Δ
Khicci
Baçoṭ
O=Δ
Gehlot
Sukal
Δ=O
Panwār
Bhūkū
Dev
Kolā
Dhurā
Ger
Parihār
Sawtrā
Dungaliā
Dugal
Hun
Kulçar
Karmato
Paramjī
KEY:
Underlined Words: The subcaste names of Rajput fathers.

go together in a procession, led by men. The women sing, and are seen carrying blankets to the dining space.

An imaginary line halves the dining place: women, along with their children, occupy one side; and men sit on the other. Then, those given the duty to distribute the food place the brass-plates (*thali*) before the people. Five persons are expected to eat from one plate, but in case of women, a couple of children may also join in.[14] After food has been served, the hosts, who stand there to supervise the distribution, request the guests to eat well. At this time, the women spread the blanket on their heads; one blanket covers five women (and children, if any) and one of them holds it up with her left hand to create space within the cocoon.

Though enough food is served in the first instance, if the women want some more, one of them stretches out her right arm, and the food-server has to bend considerably to place more food in the plate. Once they have eaten, they take off the blanket, fold it, and leave singing in praise of both the food and the hosts.

It is not easy to explain how this practice came into existence. The respondents said that women are shy of eating in the presence of others, and on ritual feasts, since they have to eat with a gathering, they hide behind a curtain so that no one, except the co-sharers, can see who is eating and how much. This may be related to a belief in Raika society that on normal days, one should eat alone or in the presence of near relatives. If you have to eat with outsiders and strangers, eat as little as possible. If you eat more, it indicates you have a good appetite, a sign of good health, which means you can become an intentional or unintentional victim of evil eye, and married women in comparison to widows and men are more vulnerable to this.

At ritual feasts, members of other castes, with whom the Raika have economic, social, or putative kin relations, are also invited, and they are the first to eat. After they have left, and only the Raika are home, except for the cooks (of the Barber caste), the actual feast begins.

Chato dharma sakti lano ati di baksaya

The sixth *dharma* of the Dewasi is that their married women should always wear the head-dress called *ati*. Like *choti* (pig-tail), which is specific to Raika men, *ati* is a diacritical feature of married Raika women.

A Raika woman never keeps her hair unbraided, not even when she mourns the death of her husband. For the Raika, the unbounded states of a female body – like unbraided hair, 'naked arms, legs, and neck' (meaning arms without necklaces), uncovered head and chest [meaning, not wearing the wrap (*odhni*) and blouse (*kanchli*)] and long nails – are identified with the inauspicious state of liminality, and more specifically, with the state of a female ghost (*bhutni*). One of the objects that binds a female body is *ati*.

Woven out of sheep hair and covered with cotton thread, an *ati* is a pen-like structure, of six to seven inches of length and one to one and a half inches in diameter, with a tapering conical end. On its base are stitched three or four cotton strings. These strings are tied to the upper end of the plait, and thus the *ati* stands on the occiput as a pole.[15] A girl wears it for the first time when she leaves for her husband's house. Like *chura*, *ati* is also never taken off, except when washing hair, and Raika women are quite accustomed to sleeping with it.

It is discarded, like *chura*, by a widow on her husband's twelfth day of the funeral ritual.

According to the Rav, of the Hindu goddesses, Parvati is the only one adorned with *ati*. Citing the myth of Raika origin, the Rav say that the celestial nymphs were advised by Shiva, after they had married his 'sons', to live like Parvati, a woman devoted to her husband. Of all Parvati's attire, Shiva asked Rai, the wife of the first Raika, to keep *ati*, and since then, the Raika women have been wearing it. For this reason, some Raika hold that Rai was the daughter of the jewel-bearing serpent king, and *ati*, which is like a snake, stands for her primordial status as a snake-daughter (*nag kanya*).

Satwan dharma Dewasiyan ra dudh bechan nahin jaye

The seventh *dharma* of the Dewasi is that they should never sell the milk of their animals.[16]

Both camels and sheep are milked twice a day, which is an exclusively male duty.[17] The sheep milk is for domestic use, and women process the surplus into clarified butter (*ghi*). When on migration, if the migratory group does not have women, it is the men's duty to make *ghi*. Like milk, *ghi* is also for household consumption. Though there is no sanction on its sale, hardly any surplus is left for marketing.[18] This is primarily because of the value placed on *ghi*. Not only considered as the source of instant energy and good health, its generous distribution is also tied to status consideration. One who generously distributes *ghi* on ritual occasions, or offers a couple of its *adulis* (spoons) to one's guests gains in respect and prestige. One of the major expenses in *mausar* (marriage-cum-death feast) is on *ghi*, this is the reason why these feasts are also called *kharcha* (meaning, expenses).[19]

Sheep milk is processed to make curd and *ghi*. But, there are taboos against processing camel milk (which have recently been challenged by a voluntary organization). In this context, the Raika of Bikaner say that Balinath-ji Maharaj, an ascetic, ordained upon them certain *dharmas* regarding the utilization of camel products. In some areas, these prohibitions are said to have been imposed by Pabu-ji, another Raika deity. Camel milk should never be sold; in this context, Köhler-Rollefson (1992: 78) writes: "Selling milk is sometimes equated with selling children." The milk must be used for domestic consumption, for drinking or making rice pudding. To the needy ones, it should be freely given. "Camels help you to sail through the times of famine", the Raika say, and there are stories of Raika helping people with milk in years of extreme drought.

Camel milk should not be processed into curd, butter or *ghi*. This *dharma* is taken so seriously that even a suggestion to the Raika to try churning the milk is viewed with suspicion. Two additional reasons are offered for following this *dharma*: (a) howsoever hard one tries, camel milk would never curdle; on the contrary, it will putrefy;[20] and (b) its medicinal properties remain if consumed fresh, or with minimum boiling. The Raika ethno-veterinarians claim that many deadly and incurable diseases are cured by consuming fresh camel milk.[21]

Camel hair should not be sold. There is some ambiguity regarding this *dharma*. Some believe that it was pronounced by Balinath-ji, while others say that it was a later addition, mainly because of the inferior quality of camel wool (ibid.). It is coarse and hard, and is used mainly for making rugs and carpets (*bhakal*), ropes (*damna*), strings for charpoys (*khat*), and blankets (*kambal*). Sometimes it is mixed with other wool, if the latter is in short supply. Like camel milk, camel wool is given freely to anyone asking for it.

Of these three aforementioned restrictions, the first two are faithfully observed in many areas where the Raika live. There is no taboo on the sale of camel-dung and camels as work animals. Camel-dung is usually collected by the herdsmen when the herd rests for the night. It is mostly used as fuel for domestic purposes. There are certain elements of subsistence economy in camel pastoralism: for instance, camel milk, hair and dung are all used for domestic consumption. As the Raika are vegetarian, there is no question of killing their animals for food. The main source of earning of Raika camel-breeders is either from the wages they get by grazing the animals of other owners (Raika included) or selling their own camels.[22] A few Raika have also bought camel-carts and work as transporters of goods.

Athwan dharma Dewasiyan ra Shiva ri dhuni sajaye

The eighth *dharma* of the Dewasi is that they should 'keep', tend, arrange, and decorate (*sajaye*) Shiva's *dhuni* ("renouncer's fire"). As I have discussed elsewhere (1993), a *dhuni* is associated with ascetics and not with householders. Himself being an ascetic *par excellence*, Shiva is believed to tend *dhuni*, and to recapitulate, he created Vishkarma Suthar to look after it. The Rav's interpretation of this *dharma* is that a Raika should keep faith in the renouncers who look after the *dhunis*. He should take some fuel, or offerings of food (like coconut and sugar-wafers) for the *dhuni*. A *dhuni* must not be defiled by spitting or approaching it in an impure state.

Nauvan dharma Dewasiyan ra bhagvi jhandi lagaye

The ninth *dharma* of the Dewasi is that they should always put up a flag or banner (*jhandi*) of ocher (*bhagva*) colour. But where? The aforementioned verse does not specify it, however, the Rav say that it should be fixed on top of the hut (*jhunpa*), or in its animal enclosure (*bara*), and in the case of a migratory herd, wherever it rests for the evening, or for a few days.

The ocher colour is identified with Shiva, and, by implication, with Saivite renouncers. A flag of this colour, the Rav submit, constantly reminds the people of Shiva and the *dharmas* that he has pronounced for them. In addition, *bhagvi jhandi* is a sign of auspiciousness. Except for some, the Raika generally do not erect *bhagvi jhandi* on their huts. But this *dharma* is punctiliously followed by the leaders of migratory herds who carry not one but many such flags which are fixed all around the camp. Being a sign of auspiciousness, it portends the welfare of both the animals and their herdsmen. The other reason for putting them up is that they become the emblems of a Raika herd. Other herdspersons or travellers passing through the same area can ascertain the identity of the resting herd from distance.

As with migratory herds, the *dhunis* tended by Raika renouncers always display a *bhagvi jhandi* on the roof of their hermitage and near the fire altar.

Daswan dharma Dewasiyan ra som akta rakhaye
The tenth *dharma* of the Dewasi is that they should observe Monday as the most sacred day of the week. It was noted earlier that Monday is Lord Shiva's day, and the Rav strengthen this *dharma* with an additional piece of information: the first Raika was created on a Monday (*utpatti ro din*, the day of the origin). Therefore, on this day, the Raika should keep fast, visit Shiva temple and offer water, flowers, and, if nothing else is available, *aka* (*Calotropis procera*) leaves to the deity.[23] If possible, they should organize devotional singing and give alms (*bhiksha*) to beggars and donations (*dan*) to poor. Also, the Raika have been asked to observe some taboos on Monday, such as

(a) do not kill a black snake;
(b) do not go to search a lost camel;
(c) do not give the cauterization treatment (*dam dena*) to sick animals (oral medicines may however be administered); and
(d) do not visit the house where a death has occurred (*kan mein jana*).

Although a full and complete account of the Raika *dharmas* – the sequence in which they are presented – is available from the Rav, the Raika know about all of them. In fact, I came to know of their existence in the initial phases of my fieldwork with the Raika, before I collected their systematic account, and the exact verses in which they are presented, from the Rav. However, the respondents often faltered in remembering the verses and their correct order. The people often refer to these *dharmas* in their daily life, and explain the rationale of their practices in their terms. The Raika *dharma*, as a whole, draws the boundaries between its followers and the outsiders, the neighbouring groups. As we shall see later, their caste council plays a significant role in reinforcing these religious precepts, and regulating the daily life according to them.

The Raika *Dharma* and the Hindu *Dharma*

The Raika see themselves as adhering to their own *dharma* as laid down for their caste by Shiva, as well as the Hindu *dharma*. The pigtail (*choti*) the Raika men keep is a reminder of their Hindu *dharma*. But Raika *dharma* is not separate and independent from Hindu *dharma;* on the contrary, it is contained, as the Raika say, within Hinduism. Being caste-specific, it does not conflict with the *dharmas* of other castes.

The Rav also reinforce the Hindu identity of the Raika. Giving a condensed account of the Raika 'history', they say that the first Raika couple moved to the 'mortal world' from Mount Kailash and started living in Kutch. Many generations passed before the new rulers of Kutch, the Muslim kings, began forcibly converting the local communities to their faith. Some Raika did embrace Islam, but most of them fled to Jaisalmer where they founded three villages, viz., Brahmsara, Kodumba and Ladarva. Although Jaisalmer, the Rays say, was also ruled by Muslim kings, they were more benign than those in Kutch, and did not impose their religion on their Hindu subjects.

A Raika family of Aal sub-caste lived in the village of Ladarva. One of its daughters named Hira was a bosom friend of the Muslim king's daughter. When the latter was going to her husband's house (the ceremony called *gauna*), she requested her parents to send her Raika friend as part of her dowry. The king called Hira's father and ordered him to bring his daughter to the fort the following morning.

Hira's father pleaded before the king to have mercy on his daughter and his status, but his plea fell on the deaf ear. Back in the village, he called the elders for advice, who unanimously resolved that sending a Raika girl as a 'wedding gift' would not only lower their caste status, but also mean disposing of one's daughter to the life of a slave girl (*dasi*). Hira's father was in a state of consternation; if he failed to comply with the king's order, he would be in great difficulty. And, if he carried out the imperial command, the caste council would excommunicate him.

Hira understood her father's dilemma and thought that by committing suicide, she would succeed in saving her own honour as well as that of her family and caste. Seeking pardon from Bayan-sa, the goddess she worshipped every day, she jumped into a well. The news of her death spread, and the entire area became accursed for the Raika. All of them from different villages left (*gada rop diya*) Jaisalmer before the crack of dawn.[24] According to the Rav, this event took place in 678 AD (Vikram Samvat 735), and since then the Raika have been living in Marwar.[25]

This story of deserting Jaisalmer and finding an almost permanent abode in Marwar is an important aspect of the Raika's construction of their own community and religious identity. Instead of relating their migration to the search of fertile grazing grounds, they see it as a result of the oppression unleashed by Muslim kings.[26] But they could retain and further their primordial religious identity once they were in a Hindu kingdom.

The Caste Council and the Observance of the Ten Duties (*Das Dharma*)

Of the above ten *dharmas*, the first, the fourth, and the last three deal in one way or another with the worship of Lord Shiva. Two *dharmas* – the fifth and sixth – are for Raika women. The third *dharma* brings the Raika closer to the Bishnoi, a sectarian group in Rajasthan and Haryana, whose love for plants and animals is unequalled (Bishnoi and Bishnoi, 2000). Sexuality is restrained by the second *dharma,* which, as we saw, gives Raika an image of trustworthiness and chaste people. The seventh *dharma* defines the Raika occupation, which is not to make their livelihood by selling milk; it, thus, helps in the retention of several pastoral products for domestic use; for generating cash, they have to depend on the sale of animals, sheep wool, and dung (if possible). The dead animals of the Raika are left to be removed by an ex-untouchable caste called the Sansi.

The *dharmas* concerning Lord Shiva (henceforth, Shiva *dharma)* are devotedly followed. A few deviations may occur (such as the placing of the ocher flag on their huts), but they do not lessen their faith in the principal deity. The taboos listed in the tenth *dharma* are observed, even by the migratory group. On Mondays, the number of Raika visiting the Shiva temple is the largest. If there happens to be an ancient Shiva temple in their area, rich with a folklore of miracles and the stories of famous renouncers who practised austerities, the Raika spend the entire Monday there.

Shiva *dharmas* have an inbuilt sanction. The idea is not that if these *dharmas* are defiled, divine displeasure will follow, because Shiva is not classed as a punitive deity. He is the progenitor of the Raika, the guardian of their long-term welfare, and his commands must be followed. Deviating from these commands amounts to expressing doubt in one's welfare. It is not fear, but respect, which constitutes the core of these inbuilt sanctions. If unknowingly, a taboo is broken, and the mistake is realized, one must throw oneself at the deity's feet for pardon. The norms of purity and pollution are strictly followed with regard to divine places (*devasthan*). In other words, the caste council has no role in enforcing the Shiva *dharmas*. It is for the individual to see that he (and his family) adhere to them. However, with regard to other *dharmas*, the *panchayat* takes a decisive role in their enforcement.

Of the ten *dharmas*, the caste council strictly enforces the second, the third, and the sixth. If a Raika violates the norm of restraint on sexuality, he is severely punished, although such cases are quite rare. Attempts to fell trees are equally uncommon, and the *panchayat* takes a serious note of any such actions. Similarly, a woman refusing to wear the traditional dress and *ati* invites the elders' displeasure. In one case, a prominent Raika, who had set his eyes on a political position, decided to start reforming women's traditional costumes. He sent his sister to her husband's house without the *chura* and *ati*. Her in-laws refused to keep her in their house; not only did they send her back, but also reported the matter to the *panchayat*. The Raika was fined, and escaped from the humiliation of being excommunicated when he promised never again to interfere with the *dharmas* laid down for women. Concerning women, the only *dharma* on which the *panchayat* of some areas has taken a lenient view is eating behind the curtain. I was told that the elders realize the terrible problem women have while eating with one hand and holding up the blanket with the other, and thus have softened their view.[27]

To sum up, on the whole, the ten *dharmas*, as well as the others that supplement them, are faithfully followed by the Raika. Their caste council reinforces those *dharmas*, whose violation threatens the caste identity. However, in those areas where Raika population is sparse, some of these *dharmas* have started changing, or are not adhered to so strictly. In much of north Rajasthan and Haryana, for example, Raika women have excluded *ati* from their day-to-day costume, and wear it on ritual and festive occasions only. Eating behind a blanket is also rarely seen. Those households that have acquired milch animals are not reluctant to sell milk. In such areas, caste council is also weak, and here, the sort of discipline it imposes in western Rajasthan, where the Raika are in large number, is relatively unknown.

Conclusion

This paper provides an introduction to the community of the Raika of Rajasthan in terms of the ideological factors that purport to give it a sense of unity. The Raika are facing tremendous economic problems because their primordial occupation is threatened by ecological despoliation, and the worsening of relations between pastoralists and peasants (Srivastava, forthcoming). Many programmes of development do not lay emphasis on pastoralism (Srivastava, 1987, 1991). The agricultural bias of these programmes has been pointed out by many studies. Against such a background, the identity of the Raika is acquiring a greater importance. The primordial elements of their identity such as the story of their origin, the mythical history, and the duties for their community are being reinforced. This would explain why a meeting of the Raika caste councils of Marwar (held in Balganga, Bilara, Jodhpur, on 10 October 1991), ordered that all Raika would unfailingly follow their identifying cultural elements. Anyone defying the codes of conduct laid down by the caste council was liable to be heavily fined and even excommunicated from caste membership. Instead of dying out, cultural traditions adapt to new situations; and are extremely potent in all the movements of social identity.

Notes

1. See the map of Rajasthan.
2. According to one estimate of 1982 (Khanna et al., 1988: 31), there were 1,16,000 camels in Sri Ganganagar district which is dominated by peasant castes (such as the Jat, Bishnoi).
3. Male camels fetch more money than the females (Köhler-Rollefson, 1992: 78).
4. Literally, the word 'Chalakya' means "one who grazes goats". The term *god* means foothills, and thus the area at the foothills of Aravali range in south Pali is called Godwar. The Maru Raika use this term not only for their counterparts in south Pali, but also the neighbouring districts of Jalore and Sirohi.
5. Kothari (in Bharucha, 2003: 57) says that the sheep-breeding Raika are called Chavandia.
6. For the first detailed version of this story, see Raj Marwar Census (1891: 567–8); this version, as well as the Raika interpretation are analysed elsewhere (Srivastava, 1991). Structurally, this story as recorded in the 1890s from the Rav of the village Bijapur by the Marwar census officials, and as it was relayed to me in 1990 and 1991 by the Rav in Lambiyan, Sadri. and Mundara, remains the same, although some important differences exist in details, as we shall see. The version in the Raj Marwar Census was collected from the Rav of Godwara Raika. Here, I present the version recorded from a Rav of the Maru Raika who lives in Lambiyan. The Rav of this village are said to be the most authentic.
7. The camel created by the divine couple is of the female sex.
8. For instance, the Aal are divided into four *got*, viz., Mewaria, Siyadia, Rampa, and Alaut. Except for a few of my respondents, most of the Raika do not know their *got* names. Their Rav also do not talk about these. On ritual occasions, the Brahmin priest is supposed to use the *got* name of his clients, but instead of using any separate names, he uses what I am calling here the sub-caste names. Thus, Bar, which for the Raika is a *jat* name, is used by the Brahmin priest as a *got* name. The Raika do not object to such a usage. For the *gotra* names of the Parihar sub-caste, see report on the Census of 1891 (1894: 157).
9. See Diagram 1 for the sub-castes of the Raika.
10. These ten *dharmas* are presented in the form of a verse. The exact verse of each *dharma* is quoted here.
11. Also refer to the tenth *dharma*.
12. Powlett (1894: 94) writes: "In Rajputana, the 'Khejri' has a certain sanctity, owing to its figuring in the history of Ramachandra, and it is worshipped at the Dasahra festival." Khejri has a special meaning for the Bishnoi. Three centuries ago in 1731 AD, in a Jodhpur village (now called Khejarli after the name of this tree), more than 350 Bishnoi men and women sacrificed their lives saving Khejri trees from being felled by the then

Emperor's axemen (Weber, 1988: 91–94). Khejri leaves are extremely nutritious for animals, but its wood is of inferior quality (Powlett, 1874: 94 also notes this). This tree can withstand extreme aridity, although its growth may remain stunted. The Government of India issued a postal stamp in 1988–89 to honour Khejri and the communities that have a ritual relationship with it.

13. This practice has however died out in those areas of Rajasthan where the Raika are fewer in number. See further reference to this custom later in this paper.
14. First of all. each Raika man feeds a morsel of the food to all the others who have joined him in the same plate.
15. Educated and urban Raika women have however given up this costume.
16. Rao (1988: 198–99) observed the same practice amongst the Bakkarwal of the western Himalayas.
17. Similar taboos have been reported from other societies (Wilson, 1984). For instance. the Gabbra of Kenya believe that camels should be milked by uncircumcised boys or men in a state of sexual abstinence (Torry, 1971).
18. The Rebari of Gujarat, on the other hand process a lot of *ghi*, because they keep milch animals as well. One can see Rebari women in Bhuj (the capital town of Kutch) moving from house to house selling *ghi* (Elson, 1979: 91). In Sadri, it is mainly processed for the market by the Sirvi.
19. One who has organized a *mausar* has the right to distribute *ghi* on ritual occasions, a practice called *chari ghumana*. A *chari* is like a kettle; *chari ghumana* means "distributing clarified butter with this kettle". An *aduli* is a small brass vessel with a long handle used for measuring the quantity of *ghi*. Its capacity varies, starting from 10 gms. Individual Raika families buy this measuring equipment, generally of the lowest capacity, and when guests (or council members) arrive, two or sometimes three *adulis* of *ghi* are offered to each of them. Some prefer to drink it raw; others may mix *khand* (powdered sugar of brown colour) with it. The Raika have a tremendous capacity to consume *ghi*. For *mausar* feasts, they buy *ghi* from the market.
20. Köhler-Rollefson (1992: 78) reports the case from a Jaisalmer village where around the time of 1937 drought, people tried to curdle camel milk without success. However, a Raika woman in Pali told me that once she inadvertently processed camel milk thinking that it had come from the goat. When she realized her mistake, she rushed to throw it away. To her utter surprise, it had coagulated. But, as she was extremely upset for breaking the taboo, she immediately went to the Shiva temple in her area and apologized for her mistake.
21. A recent study that the Indian Council of Medical Research (ICMR) commissioned found not even a single case of diabetes among the Raika of Rajasthan. One of the hypotheses this study has proposed is that it could be because they consume camel-milk. It is this practice which distinguishes them from the other neighbouring communities (*The Indian Express*, 13 March 2005).
22. The Raika caste council has prohibited the sale of female animals but without success. In all cattle-fairs, female camels are brought for sale. It also prohibits the gift of female animals to the traditional singers (called *dhadhi)* because of the fear that the latter might kill or sell them.
23. This shrub is supposed to be one of Shiva's favourites. Its leaves are used by Raika for drinking camel milk directly from the animal (Srivastava, 1987). The Raika observation is that the camel eats the leaves of every plant and tree except those of the *aka*, and this further strengthens their belief in its sacredness.
24. When the members of a caste decide to leave a village permanently, they erect a stone-tablet [with the figure of a donkey (*gadha*) embossed on it] at some public place. Their caste name (and sometimes the reason for deserting the village) is engraved at the base of this tablet. This practice is called *gadha ropna*. No members of that caste, present or future, will ever settle down in a village divorced in this manner. In recent

years, however, some Raika families have settled down on the borders of Jaisalmer contiguous with the other districts.

25. This date given by the genealogists roughly coincides with the entry of Islam in India. Although Islam came to India with the first Muslim invasion of Sind in 711 AD, there were earlier several small pockets in this part under the rule of the Arab tribal chiefs (Allan et al., 1934: 205; Rizvi, 1975: 245–46; Madan, 1991: 18). Spear (1967: 31–2) notes that the "first Muslims appeared in India within a few years of the Prophet's death in 632 AD."
26. On this point and the probable route of migration the Raika took before reaching Kutch, see Mankad (1939), Westphal-Hellbusch (1975), and Westphal (1976: 223–25), Elson (1979).
27. But, in the October 1991 meeting of all the caste councils of Marwar, this principle (*niyam*) of eating behind the curtain has been strictly reinforced by the elders.

References

Allan, J., T.W. Haig and H.H. Dodwell (1934), *A Cambridge Shorter History of India*, Cambridge: Cambridge University Press.

Béteille, André (1964), 'A Note on the Referents of Caste'. *European Journal of Sociology*, V: 130–34.

Bharucha, Rustom (2003), *Rajasthan, an Oral History: Conversations with Komal Kothari*, Penguin Books.

Bishnoi, Kishnaram and Narsiram Bishnoi (eds.) (2000), *Religion and Environment*, Volume 1 (in Hindi), New Delhi: Commonwealth Publishers.

Davis, Marvin (1983), *Rank and Rivalry: The Politics of Inequality in West Bengal*, Cambridge: Cambridge University Press.

Ellis, Christine M. Cottam (1991), 'The Jain Merchant Castes of Rajasthan: Some Aspects of the Management of Social Identity in a Market Town', in Michael Carrithers and Caroline Humphrey (eds.), *The Assembly of Listeners: Jains in Society*, Cambridge: Cambridge University Press (pp. 75–107).

Elson, Vickie C. (1979), *Dowries from Kutch: A Women's Folk Art Tradition in India*, California: Museum of Cultural History.

Hutton, J.H. [1921 (1969)], *The Angami Nagas*, Bombay: Oxford University Press.

Khanna, N.D., S.N. Tandon and A.K. Rai (1986), 'Studies on Quantitative and Qualitative Genetic Parameters in Indian Camels', *Annual Report*. Bikaner: National Research Centre on Camel, (pp. 26–42).

Köhler-Rollefson, Ilse (1992), 'The Raika Dromedary Breeders of Rajasthan: A Pastoral System in Crisis', *Nomadic Peoples*, 30: 74–83.

Madan, T.N. (1991), 'Introduction' in T.N. Madan (ed.), *Religion in India*, Delhi: Oxford University Press (pp. 1–22).

Mankad, B.L. (1939), 'Rabaris of Kathiawad: A Social Study', *Journal of the University of Bombay*, 7: 31–71.

Powlett, P.W. (1874), *Gazetteer of the Bikaner State*, Bikaner: Government Press.

Rao, A. (1988), 'Levels and Boundaries in Native Models: Social Groupings Among the Bakkarwal of the Western Himalayas', *Contributions to Indian Sociology* (n.s.), 22 (2): 195–227.

Report on the Census of Marwar and Mallani (1891), Jodhpur: Government Press (1894).

Report Mardumshumari Raj Marwar (Raj Marwar Census) (1891), Jodhpur: Census Press.

Rizvi, S.A.A. (1975), 'The Muslim Ruling Dynasties' in A.L. Basham (ed.), *A Cultural History of India*, Oxford: Clarendon Press (pp. 245–65).

Sharma, K.L. (1999), 'Introduction' in K.L. Sharma (ed.). *Social Inequality in India, Profiles of Caste, Class and Social Mobility*. Jaipur and New Delhi: Rawat Publications (pp. 15–25).

Spear, Percival (1967), 'The Position of the Muslim, Before and After Partition' in Philip Mason (ed.), *India and Ceylon: Unity and Diversity,* London: Oxford University Press (pp. 30–50).

Srivastava, V.K. (1987), 'Some Issues in the Anthropology of Development', *Man in India,* 67 (4): 317–34.

—— (1991), 'Who are the Raika/Rabaris'? *Man in India,* 71 (1): 279–304.

—— (1993), *On Religion and Renunciation: The Case of the Raika of Western Rajasthan.* Ph.D. Dissertation, Department of Social Anthropology, Cambridge: University of Cambridge.

——, Forthcoming, 'The Raika of Rajasthan', in H.S. Verma and Nadeem Hasnain (eds.), *The Other Backward Classes in India,* New Delhi: Serials Publications.

Srivastava, V.S. (1981), 'The Iconography of the Ustravahini Devi' in: V.S. Srivastava (ed.). *Cultural Contours of India,* New Delhi: Abhinav (pp. 178–87).

Tambiah, S.J. (1985), 'From Varna to Caste Through Mixed Unions' in S.J. Tambiah. *Culture, Thought and Social Action,* Harvard: Harvard University Press (pp. 212–51).

Torry, W.I. (1971), *Animal Husbandry and Social Organization among the Gabbra, with Notes on the Rendille Tribes,* Nairobi: Ministry of Agriculture.

Weber, Thomas (1988), *Hugging the Tree: The Story of the Chipko Movement,* New Delhi: Viking.

Westphal-Hellbusch, S.: 'Changes in Meaning of Ethnic Names as Exemplified by the Jat, Rabari, Bharvad and Charan in North Western India' in L.S. Leshnik and G.D. Sontheimer (eds.), *Pastoralists and Nomads in South Asia,* Weisbaden (pp. 117–36).

Westphal-Hellbusch, S. and Heinz, Westphal (1976), *Hinduistische Viehzuchter im nordWestlichen Indian II. Die Bharvad und die Charan.* Berlin, Duncker and Humblot, (Summary on the Rabaris in English, pp. 214–44).

Wilson, R.T. (1984), *The Camel,* London: Longman Group Limited.

14 Jharkhand Movement, Tribal Social Structure and Marxist Theory

AJIT K. PANDEY

The relationship of Marxist theory to social movements in industrialized societies cannot be disputed. The issue becomes polemical when one analyses the tribal situation. The pattern of development that has taken place in Jharkhand area contradicts in many ways what Marxism considered to be its starting point: the development of capitalist society. Indeed, the way in which capitalism is developing in Jharkhand is highly specific and does not follow the orthodox model. This paper attempts to reflect on this specificity in the light of two types of evidences: one, the contributions of some sociologists and social anthropologists supporting conclusions that ilustrate this particularity to Jharkhand and, two, a very summary presentation of different factors causing Jharkhand movement in Chotanagpur-Santalpargana (C-S) region of undivided Bihar during British and post-British period. Finally, the paper will engage in a general consideration of the problem of the relationship between Marxist theory and social movements in the light of the evidence presented.

I

A coherent analysis of the process of social development in the C-S region was formulated by Jyoti Sen (1972), K.L. Sharma (1976), Sen Gupta (1980, 1983), Pathy (1982, 1988), A.P. Sharma (1988), Devalle (1992) and Pandey (1997). Perhaps these scholars being familiar with the method of Marxism were able to produce an interpretation of the economic and social structure of the C-S region. In their analysis, the interpretation of feudal and capitalist modes of production seems to be the central characteristic of what was happening in this region in the 19th and 20th centuries. Capitalism in this region was the result of British colonial as well as *Dikus* penetration in the mining and agricultural sector. Nevertheless, capitalism coexisted with the feudal sector predominant in the Chotanagpur region where the tribal population was exploited by the *Dikus* even after the independence of the country. The interpretation of these elements, as per their analysis made it possible for Jharkhand to undergo a process of bourgeoisie movement that would result in the formation of Jharkhand state. Socialism had to be the objective of social revolution, given the imperial character of capitalism and its relations with the feudal social formation. These scholars drew this conclusion on the basis of an analysis in which the dominant section of tribal population were not national in their social and economic commitments during British period and ethnic during post-independence period. These sections were subordinated to British capital till the independence of the country and they could not develop politically independently from their ties to it. After the independence, they came under the spell of utilitarian politics. The dominant classes, in which the tribals had the important place, had to assume their historical role and put forward the necessity of socialist movement as spelled out by tribal leaders from time to time because, in spite of being majority, they feel excluded from any participation in political life. In this sense, one could say that the tribal population may be identified with the universal class in the Marxist sense and it can be made the essential instrument of the movement in Jharkhand. This perspective appears to run counter to any model of phased political development and to contradict the image of a linear type of social process. This framework strongly supports a discontinuous model of social development. It also runs counter to analysis where the role of the particular classes (such as adivasi – moneylenders) was central essentially as a buffer between tribal and non-tribal.

Between the early phase of Jharkhand movement and the formation of so-called Jharkhand state in the year 2001, many events took place in the C-S region of undivided Bihar, the formost among which is the appearance of BJP-led tribal regime. This regime, in spite of many differences and contrasts, claimed to fantastically share the common characteristics of having been governed by a state supported by an alliance of tribal and capitalist political ideoogies. Political figures such as Sibu Soren, Suraj Mandal. N.E. Horo – all tribals – on one hand and A.K. Roy, Sadanand Jha. Binod Bihari Mahato on the other, in spite of belonging to different political ideologies, succeeded only in constructing political Jharkhand state in which the various tribal populations as will as non-tribal ones appear to be a part of it. It is expected to last as long as the economic progress associated with industrialization by import substitution will continue to deliver some economic and social benefits. This period, which may be characterized as a process of democratization through authoritarian means where some degree of institutionalization of the political system occurred (in contrast with previous and later periods), can be very difficult to interpret in terms of Marxist theory. Indeed, the degree of class struggle that appeared as a result of intensified process of industrialization and the consequent formation of segments of tribal working class was never as acute as it had been in Europe in corresponding periods. On the contrary, between 1930 and 1960, tribal organizations, trade union organizations, entrepreneurs and the Bihar state were driven by the essential priorities. This explains the relative absence of confrontation among all classes and the difficulties of adapting historical events to a rigid scheme such as that applied by some communist organizations during that period. In many ways, the application of Marxist theory by communist parties operational in Jharkhand area supported an interpretation which followed closely a model of historical stages where the subordination of the working classes to the dependent bourgeoisie was a necessary phase of the process of transition from feudal to capitalist society and a precondition for the development of a socialist revolution. In an area like tribal Bihar, where the populism was less clear, it was argued that the working class had to support the bourgeosie's programme of industrialization through import substitution, leading to a differentiation of the occupational structure. Thus, the formation and increase of the working class would contribute to the development of progressive political organization. This position, deriving from an objective alliance with the dependent bourgeoisie which included the right to organize unions, declare legal strikes and participate in political life through the presentation of legitimate demands within the provisions of the 'social law', was successful in some degree. Indeed, the tribal movement was able to push for bread and butter benefits for the tribal workers and also in spite of the demagogy involved, some political consciousness appeared among tribals working in mines, industrial organization and agriculture. But, at the same time, a process of subordination of the tribal movement to the Bihar state took place. Those social laws and those bargaining rights did not go without obligations and very often was taken away through inflation or outright repression by the dominant partners in the alliance. And last but not the least, tribal leaders became a part of the decision-making structures of the state without having much autonomy to represent the legitimate and particular interests of the tribal workers. The whole process was tacitly and implicitly supported by various tribal political organizations as necessary steps or phases through which social development had to take place. It also reflected the climate which favours tribal political alliances to fight against the exploitation but which was divorced from the specific conditions of Jharkhand at that time where this problem was not as central as in other parts. Thus, popular fronts and other varieties of political alliance resulted in subordinating tribal working class objectives to those of other classes in Jharkhand society.

II

Notwithstanding the particular relations between the tribal political organizations having left leaning and the BJP populist regime, they are not the only perspective through which tribal revolutionary organizations analysed the process of social development in Jharkhand. The moment when the real questions began to be asked and when the application of Marxist theory becomes an important issue was when the Jharkhand movement was successful in getting the statehood in the name of Jharkhand without the explicit and implicit support of the communist organizations operational in this area. This event changed the terms of the analysis of the Jharkhand situation on the part of left organizations. Questions are being asked now about the subordination of the political programme of the tribal working class to that of the dependent bourgeoisie. Tribal populations now have begun to question the analytical and historical assumptions on which political alliances were made and to ask why the tribals in general were following the leadership imposed from an utilitarian party such as BJP. This has the result of provoking a series of splits within organizations of left orientations. It becomes evident that answers have to be given to these questions – the entrance of BJP leaders into Jharkhand was a political earthquake which had a profound resonance all over the tribal areas. That is why, the decade of 1990s and 2000s are characterized by the so-called debate between the capitalists and socialist. This debate implies that new strategies have to be formulated for the action of working class within tribal population. In terms of the problems we are addressing here, i.e., to say the relationship between social movements and the development of Marxist theory, the issues of the theoretical and political consequences of the Jharkhand movement are central.

What are the implications of this historical event for the Jharkhand for the development of Marxist theory in India ? Can one say that it changed the parameters within which theoretical analysis took place and that, since then a new period in this process be identified? All these questions and others can be addressed through the consideration of the following facts in regards to the Jharkhand situation. First of all, Jharkhand can be considered a dual society where a modern sector coexists with a traditional sector without having connections. Instead of this being an adequate characterization of Jharkhand, it experiences a process of internal colonialism where the modern sector is in fact living off the traditional sector. There, the two sectors are intertwined in a similar way as feudal and capitalist forms of production were related. At this juncture, it is important to discuss the development in Jharkhand. Development in Jharkhand is, in fact, the political project of some modernizing elites among tribes, entrepreneurs, professionals which, allied with some popular sectors, succeeded in obtaining political power. The typical example of the triumph of this process is identified with the tribal government. The problem with state sponsored development programmes in Jharkhand is that it took for granted a bourgeoisie which could undertake a process of tribal development when in fact the overall pattern of development in Jharkhand area was directly subordinated to the expansion of imperialist capital, especially in raw material sector. The failure of this development strategy to grasp this situation explains why the strategy of industrialization through import substitution failed to provide solutions for the economic problems of the region. This critique of developmental perspective is also a critique of the analysis that the left-oriented political parties was making of the situation in the area. The left argued in favour of two-step process of social development which could first entail the bourgeois-democratic revolution and only after that occurred could one struggle for socialism. The Jharkhand movement challenged this view first by succeeding in continuous protests developed outside 'democratic institutions' and secondly by brining into question (since its social base was essentially composed of tribal peasantry) the dogma that movement is necessarily the product of working class mobilization that may be questioned by the negative evaluation of a possible alliance between tribal peasants and workers in a revolutionary movement.

In subsequent years, this development framework may be questioned from another theoretical perspective by the dependency approach which was successful in making it clear that an autonomous, independent capitalist development was a dream that historical reality would not support. On the contrary, events in Jharkhand area are much related to capitalist economic relations that the aforesaid development framework would admit. The dependency approach argues that Jharkhand is dependent not only in terms of high level of indebtedness but also in terms of the perspective that its dominant groups adopt in relation to the development of themselves particularly their close ties to the strategies of capitalist theory. In this respect, in spite of the weight of internal factors in the explanation of political life, external penetration and its assimilation by internal social elements can be seen in Jharkhand. Dependency is thus identified with the internal presence of external factors within the Jharkhand social formation. Development is therefore a function of national economy and cannot be conceived as an autonomously defined process in which tribal groups, centred around the state, play a central role. In this perspective, one can say that dependency analysis corresponds to the analysis of externalism as seen from the periphery, that is from the angle of the internal social structure of Jharkhand. That is why, the approach stays very close to a Marxist perspective but it does so without doing violence to the specific conditions of Jharkhand.

The aforesaid analysis questions a series of truths concerning social development in Jharkhand. By reflecting on historical process and on the social structures prevailing in the area, they provided perspectives through which to interpret historical events. From our focus in this paper, we can say that their appearance was a function of the process of social development and that they were not mere intellectual exercises. Some conditioning factors that explain their relevance were failure of the state sponsored development perspective, the increase in the direct influence of both central as well as the erstwhile Bihar state government on internal politics, armed insurrections as well as the influence of modernization on economic development. These factors, and perhaps specific state-centre influences, shaped their thinking and contributed to the questioning of old and static formulations.

The various perspectives analysed in this paper try to interpret social reality globally without losing contact with its dynamics. The answer given by these perspectives will provide the starting point of a discussion leading upto some unorthodox conclusions about Marxist theory in Jharkhand. Schematically, the following propositions derived from them are relevant for considering the relationship between Jharkhand movement and Marxist theory:

1. Dualism, that is to say, the coexistence of a modern and tribal sector or of a capitalist and feudal sector side-by-side without any interconnections cannot be sustained as a correct characterization of Jharkhand social formation.
2. Bourgeoisie democracy is not viable in Jharkhand because the dominant groups are dependent upon external capital and cannot formulate a programme of development for their societies; that is why the struggle for socialism precedes the achievement of democratic institutions.
3. Class conflict is mediated by the establishment of populist structures of domination which reflect alliances of heterogeneous social groups, both dominant and dominated.
4. Tribal peasants and tribal industrial and urban workers do not possess common interests, especially because the latter are incorporated into the model of economic development, while the former are excluded and remain outside the populist structures of domination; therefore, it is difficult to focus revolutionary movements in which both social categories act together.

5. State development strategy where tribal economic priorities are established around industrialization through import substitution and central as well as state control of natural resources failed to produce the expected results in term of income equality, economic diversification and growth, especially because foreign interests would mould the formulation of economic policy through external investment, multilateral and bilateral lending, scientific and technological dependency.
6. Middle classes among tribals in Jharkhand are neither progressive nor nationalistic and dynamic, and are related to external influences, both economically and culturally; they do not constitute a potential basis for social mobilization in conjunction with tribal peasants or urban tribal workers.

The image that one can derive from these propositions is quite divorced from the traditional orthodox Marxist perspective. If we consider this perspective to be identified with the view whereby the development of capitalism (associated with industrialization) as the starting point for the formation of a tribal urban working class which through trade union and political organization can achieve a degree of social participation enabling it to struggle for the abolition of exploitation and for political control of the state, then the image that we obtain from the analysis presented for Jharkhand is quite different. From the very beginning of the process of industrialization, the C-S region was dependent upon external sources for investment to exploit the raw material posited in the huge amount in this area, so that an autonomous development was frustrated and blocked. In addition, the type of industrialization that took place, highly concentrated in terms of supply in sectors of so-called conspicuous consumption items and highly capital intensive, did not favour the formation of a large tribal working class. On the contrary, as various studies have shown the relative weight of the active population in the secondary sector has stagnated and what has grown beyond expectations is the population employed in the tertiary/service sector. Therefore, in terms of the occupational structure of Jharkhand, we do not obtain the preconditions that orthodox Marxist theory had established as a necessary consequence of the process of industrialization. Also, if we consider the problem of the relative autonomy of the tribal working class to develop its own political strategy, we observe that contrary to expectations, dependence upon state apparatus has been the typical case.

Therefore, the working class has not been able to act independently of other social classes, but has allied itself with its theoretical enemy, the bourgeoisie (*Dikus*). Alliances, such as the populist ones that were typical of 1980s, 1990s and 2000s, result in diminishing the space of poor tribals (the working class) and accentuating its subordination to the political dominance of other social classes. In this sense, we have a situation where the role prescribed by orthodox theory to the proletariat is put seriously into question by the type of social, economic and political development of Jharkhand. In one way or another, these problems have presented serious difficulties for the application of the Marxist framework of analysis in Jharkhand. Additional difficulties appear when we consider the characterization of this revolutionary movement.

The Jharkhand movement first started with unity over ethnic cleavages in 1912. Later, in 1928, the Chotanagpur Unnati Samaj, an organization of Aglican and Lutheran educated Christians and a few non-converts demanded the upliftment of Chotanagpur from the backward state and improvement of the social, political and economic conditions in the tribals. It sought to secure the employment for educated tribals, reservation in services and legislative bodies and formation of a sub-state to Bengal and Orissa. Though, it sought to spread its activities among the villages, it remained essentially an urban movement. The members of the Samaj however differed among themselves on some issues and could not remain united for long. As a result, a parallel organization known as Kishan Sabha was established to focus attention on the problem of the peasants (Vidyarthi, 1967b; Sachchidanand, 1976; Guha, 1983). After sometime, it was visualized that unless denominational differences among the tribals were overcome and they stood united on a common platform, they could not shed their social economic and political backwardness. Consequently, the Chotanagpur Adivasi Mahasabha was convened in 1938. It was led by the professional political workers. Some of them were highly educated and articulate. It involved tribals other than Mundas and Oraons and extended to both urban and rural areas. It was during the later part of the first phase of the movement during 1930s, the demand for a separate state was presented before the Simon Commission and the Cripps Mission (Vidayarthi and Sahaya, 1976).

The year 1939 saw the beginning of the active phase in the Jharkhand movement. Jaipal Singh, a Munda convert and as a prominent leader in the adivasi Mahasabha, later became its chairman. Though he was politically much skilled and articulate but carried a bad image as a leader because of his inability to forge a solid front by bringing together the different leaders, the suspicious of corruption against him and the alliances he sought (Devalle, 1992: 139). Jaipal Singh was never involved in the Indian National Movement, rather he dismissed more than a century old tribals' anti-colonial struggle (Singh, 1972). The Mahasabha under his direction launched a struggle not against the British Raj but against the 'Diku Raj'.

The formation of the Jharkhand Party, as a political wing of Mahasabha in 1950, brought a new turn in the Jharkhand movement. The separatist movement was now transformed into a party-based movement and a new secular model emerged which symbolized the aspirations and needs of the local and regional people. The party led a demonstration before the States Reorganization Committee in 1955 for a separate state but was reconciled on being assured by the State Government of special measures for tribal development. From 1952 to1957, the Party dominated the electoral politics in the region. In the 1962 elections, its performance was very poor, as a result it merged with Congress in 1963. This led to the formation of a new Jharkhand Party under the leadership of N.E. Horo. Devalle rightly points out the reason of the debacle of Jharkhand Party in 1962 elections:

> "The change in electoral preferences was due to the activity of several all India parties in the area and also to the increasing gap between the rising elite and the rest

of the adivasi. The class interests that guided the party started to come more sharply into light. The party did not have any agrarian programme as is still the case and failed to redress the needs of the growing adivasi individual working force. Furthermore, it accepted landlords and money-lenders as members as they come to hold important executive positions. This was understood by the electorate as an alignment of the Jharkhand Party – with the Diku interest. Moreover, the party failed to win its own explicit and widely accepted demand: the creation of a separate state when India was being geographically reorganized along linguistic and regional lines". (Devalle, 1992: 140)

In the period since 1964, which was the beginning of the revival phase in Jharkhand movement, the continuous splits fragmented the Jharkhand Party. The splintered groups did not have differences in their programmes and mostly emerged out of the personal differences among their leaders. The All India Party was formed in 1967 in opposition to the Jharkhand Party's merger with the Congress Party, and was in turn divided as a consequence of alliances with the various Indian parties. In 1968, the Santal Hul Jharkhand Party was formed from which the Progressive Hul Jharkhand Party emerged in 1972 (Sachchidanand, 1976: 19). The late sixties and early seventies witnessed the emergence of other organizations like the Birsa Seva Dal, All India Sido-Kanhu Basie and the Adivasi Socio-Educational and Cultural Associations. The last two were mostly concerned with cultural revivalism and took up a verbal deference of adivasi land rights (Gautam, 1978b: 114–115). The Birsa Seva Dal formed in 1967 as an urban pressure group, concentrated on the industrial complexes and on the demands for jobs and educational reservations for the tribals. It had links with the CPI (ML). Until 1964, the Birsa Seva Dal was radical and militant. It was directly involved in the re-appropriation of urban lands in Jamesedpur which ended in police repression in 1968 (Vidyarthi and Sahaya, 1976). The Birsa Seva Dal then ceased to carry out direct actions retaining only an intermittent influence at Jamshedpur. One would agree at this stage with the following Devalle's analysis of the political formation in the Jharkhand area:

"In the formation of fragmentation of the Jharkhand Party and the proliferation of sectional groups, the ethnicity has been variously used in the political area. These uses depend on the class situation alliances and interests of those who appeal to the ethnic factors in their ideological discourses. In Jharkhand, there never has been just one discourse of ethnicity but several following socio-economic cleavages. In the 18th and 19th centuries, ethnic assertion responded to a situation of conquest and was an expression of the adivasi peasantry. In the 1940s, the rising indigenous petty-bourgeoise resorted to ethnic politics to place itself in a better position and to gain benefits from an established colonial system whose end was mistakenly not perceived as being imminent. Apparently, this elite saw itself as Jharkhand's national leadership. It took up the task of directing the rest of their communities on the basis of its class position, 'superior' western education and in many ways – alleged 'superior' religious ascription through conversion to Christianity. By stressing adivasi backwardness and not acknowledging existing structural socio-economic problem, this elite fostered inferiority complex" (Devalle, 1992: 140–41).

In 1963, Jharkhand movement had a new shape and direction. Tribals in the C-S region started taking action independently of the elite and political parties responding to a critical situation aggravated by drought and famines. Forcible harvesting and violent confrontation between landlords and peasants engulfed almost the entire C-S region. It was the period (1972) which gave birth to Jharkhand Mukti Morcha (JMM) as a new political party. This party led an already mobilized tribal mass. At the end of 1972, the Shivaji Samaj was formed among the Kurmi peasants. The JMM and the Bihar Colliary Kamgar Union (BCKU) made an alliance and operated under a triple leadership comprised of the Kurmi lawyer Binod Bihari Mahato, the Santal leader Sibu Soren and the Dhanbad Trade Unionist A.K. Roy of the Marxist Coordination Committee (MCC). In 1973, the Shivaji Samaj was replaced by the Morcha led by Binod Bihari Mahato, Sibu Soren and Sadanand Jha. Sadanand Jha, a young trade union leader in Dhanbad hailing originally from North Bihar, was unfortunately murdered in 1973, probably by the collieries' muscle-men. It was then the 'Kurmies' of the Shivaji Samaj and the tribals came under the direct leadership of JMM on the issue of the restoration of land alienated by landlords and money lenders. The JMM moved to Santhal Pragana, Giridih and Hazaribagh. The years between 1973 and 1975 were the most violent in the struggle carried on in the form of forcible harvesting Dhan Kato Andolan (Recover Your Paddy), which involved adivasi peasants and other rural poor. This unrest witnessed colossal loss of lives and property (Devalle, 1992: 142).

In 1978, during the Janata Government, the demand for a separate Jharkhand state was put forward as a United Front basis. Nine professional organizations formed the Front Committee – the Jharkhand Party (led by N.E. Horo), the MCC (led by A.K. Roy), the JMM (led by Sibu Soren), the CPI (ML) the Birsa Seval Dal, the Jharkhand Muslim Morcha the Hul Jharkhand, the Revolutionary Socialist Party of India and the Congress-I. Unrest in Santal Pargana in 1979 was characterized by demonstration against land eviction, CPI (ML)'s demands for a better share for sharecroppers and minimum wages for the agricultural labourers, harvest clashes, JMM's protests against atrocities on adivasis, incidents of rape of Santal and Harijan women by policemen and landlords, and CPI (ML)'s demand for implementation of the Act against moneylending (Dhan, 1980a; Devalle, 1992).

III

All the considerations discussed above, point to the necessity of an overall revision of some fundamental assumption made by Marxist theory in its analysis of the dynamism of social and political change in relation to Jharkhand. Both on general and abstract levels, where we reviewed the contributions of sociologists and social anthropologists and the concrete historical level where we considered the characteristics of the revolutionary movements in Jharkhand, we are led to conclude that the conditions in Jharkhand are far from satisfying the criteria that Marxist theory has presented in its more orthodox versions for the generation of revolutionary movements. How should we focus this revision? How can we enrich the development of Marxist theory on the basis of the concrete experience of Jharkhand movement? While this revision is certainly beyond the possibilities of this paper, we will try to present some element of it drawn from the points already made above.

The principal issue in such a revision takes account of the specific characteristics of the process of social, political and economic development in Jharkhand. The central element of the specificity of Jharkhand case is the fact that the type of economic development that has taken place there has not generated an industrial working class of such a magnitude that it could be a central actor in political action. In addition, the working class that has appeared is very much subordinated to state control and cannot develop autonomous action. Until very recently, this has been the case and with very few exceptions in some economic sectors, this will continue to be the case. As a consequence, there is no central social actor in the constitution of revolutionary movements in Jharkhand. On the contrary, the social basis of revolutionary action is very heterogeneous and does not include one single social group alone. Although tribal peasantry has played an important role in Jharkhand movement, it is not sufficient to say that there are predominantly agrarian or tribal revolutionary the movements. It is not possible to draw this conclusion because movement was very much centred on developing political strategy that coincided with the critical struggle that had to spread in urban areas, where power centres were located. Also, economic stagnation typical of most of the parts in India and its correlates – unemployment, decreasing real wages and general popular unrest – explain why so many social categories support the movement. We could even add that this heterogeneity in the social composition of the revolutionary movement is one of the principal difficulties that revolutionary leadership has to face after the triumph of the struggle. As it does not have a single constituency to answer to and as it has only a vague notion of the people for which to develop revolutionary initiatives, it is very difficult to satisfy demands on the part of each and all of the social categories that initially supported the Jharkhand movement for a separate state. This is very far indeed from the elements necessary for a dictatorship of a proletariat in the orthodox sense of the Marxist theory.

The political programmes of the movement in Jharkhand are also important to the revision of Marxist theory. In this respect, the revolutionary movement in Jharkhand focussed on democratization and separate state as their central demands. There was no well-defined model of industrialization or of a general economic programme. Indeed, the experience in Jharkhand over the period that has implemented agrarian reform in a radical manner has been negative from the point of view of food production – one of the main stumbling blocks for post-movement governments.

Perhaps, one could also mention that a model of participative politics is part of the revolutionary programme. To a certain extent, Jharkhand state developed political participation, through organizations that grouped social categories according to their age group (youth organizations) or occupational location (workers or peasants), instead of developing democratic institution within the political system. These are the instruments through which political life was structured after the revolutionary governments begin the exercise of power. This can be taken to imply a non-class system of representation whereby interest groups are a part of the decision-making structure instead of class-location. This corresponds in some measure to the concept of popular democracy that prevailed in the post-movement period in north-eastern states in India.

These considerations point to the necessity of developing much more elaborate research on the characteristics of movements in Jharkhand and on the context within which they have taken place. In many respects but perhaps essentially because they are so important for concrete political activity both in the revolutionary and post-revolutionary periods, such studies should contribute to the formulation of new alternatives for making Marxist theory relevant to the solution of the problems confronting the people of Jharkhand. If Marxist theory does not incorporate those specific elements that characterize the process of the development of capitalism in Jharkhand, it will be very difficult for any social movement to make political analyses and to tackle the problems of actions. Among those elements is the fact that the weight of the industrial proletariat instead of increasing within the occupational structure, of consolidating itself as a homogeneous class and thereby becoming a revolutionary actor is diminishing, both in numerical terms and as a political agent. For example, the tribal movement is increasingly composed of social categories with very different origins and locations. Also, labour action, as manifested in protests, strikes, takes place outside the industrial sector, in the service sector. These specific elements imply, in one way or another, that the orthodox theory about the place of the proletariat within the revolutionary movement has to be revised. A new position must be elaborated which should include the specific traits of the Jharkhand situation and spell out revolutionary strategies in which revolutionary action is based not on the industrial proletariat but on the other social categories with very different work situations and possibilities of developing a class consciousness. The same could be said in relation to the characterization of the dominating sectors. What is a revolutionary strategy going to be if the bourgeoisie is really a dependent sector of the multinational establishment without much autonomy in deciding independent economic development? The problem of correct characterization of Jharkhand social formation in 21st century is undoubtedly a most important issue for both social science and revolutionary strategy.

References

Devalle, Susana B.C. (1992), *Discourses of Ethnicity: Culture and Protest in Jharkhand*, New Delhi: Sage Pubications.

Dhan, H. (1980a), 'Split in Jharkhand Mukti Morcha', *Economic and Political Weekly*, XV (31) 2, August, 1299–1300.

Guha, Ramachandra (1983), *Elementary Aspects of Peasant Insurgency in Colonial India*, Delhi: Oxford University Press.

Gautam, M.K. (1978b), 'Tradition, Modernization and the Problem of Identity among the Santal' in R.R. Moser and M.K. Gautam (eds.), *Aspects of Tribal Life in South Asia-I: Strategy and Survival*, Berne: University of Berne, 105–21.

Pandey, A.K. (1989), 'Traditionalism and Modernity among Mundas and Oraons', *The Eastern Anthropologist*, Vol. 44, No. 3, July-September.

—— (1997), *Tribal Society in India*, New Delhi: Manak Publications.

Pathy, J. (1982), 'An Outline of Modes of Production in Tribal India' in B. Chaudhary (ed.), *Tribal Development in India: Problems and Prospects*, Delhi: Inter India Publication, 23, 24.

Paul, M. Sweezy (1978), 'Karl Marx and the Industrial Revolution' in Donald Mcquarie (ed.), *Marx: Sociology, Social Change, Capitalism*, London: Quartet Books Ltd.

Sachchidanand (1976), *Tribal Voter in Bihar*, Delhi: National Publishing House.

Sengupta, N. (1980), 'Class and Tribe in Jharkhand', *Economic and Political Weekly*, XV (14), 5 April: 664–71.

—— (1983), 'Beyond Mark's Capital: Sons of the Soil in Particular Ethnic Upsurges in General' in A.N. Das, N. Nilakant and P.S. Dubey (eds.), *The Worker and the Working Class: A Labour Studies Anthology*, New Delhi: PECCE.

Sen, Jyoti (1972), 'The Jharkhand Movement' in K.S. Singh (ed.), *Tribal Situation in India*, Shimla: Indian Institute of Advanced Study: 432–37.

Sharma, A.P. (1988), 'The Jharkhand Movement: A Critique', *Social Change*, 18 (2), 60–62.

Sharma, K.L. (1976), 'Jharkhand Movement in Bihar', *Economic and Political Weekly*, 11 (1–2).

Singh, K.S. (1972), *Tribal Situation in India*, Simla: Indian Institute of Advanced Studies.

Vidyarthi, L.P. (1976b), 'Aspects of Tribal Leadership in Chotanagpur' in L.P. Vidyarathi (ed.), *Leadership in India*, Bombay: Asia Publishing House.

Vidyarthi, L.P. and K.N. Sahaya (1978), *The Dynamism of Tribal Leadership in Bihar*, Allahabad: Kitab Mahal.

Vineri, A. Schlomo (1968), *Karl Marx: On Colonialism and Modernization*, New York: Doubleday and Company.

—— (1970), *Marx's Socialism*, New York: Lieber-Atherton.

Zdravanyslov, A.G. (ed.) (1986), *Development in Marxist Sociological Theory*, New Delhi: Sage Publications.

15 A Note on Talcott Parsons' "Pattern Variables"

ARVIND KUMAR AGRAWAL

Every society is characterized by certain specificities and unique features. Indian society, too, is known for its caste system with its myriad forms of hierarchy, rituals, customs and taboos. In fact, it is not possible to understand Indian society without accounting for its caste system and its hierarchy-dominated cultural system. Talcott Parsons tried to formulate a general theory of action to provide a single theoretical system having a general and an all-inclusive character. However, Parsonian theory lacks the provisions to understand any hierarchy-dominated society as evident from his scheme of pattern variables.

1. It attempts to show that a few more pattern variables can be fitted into this framework of pattern variables for structural analysis. These additional pattern variables would be logically essential to understand and undertake structural analysis of various societies. Also, these additional pattern variables point out the existing gaps in the Parsonian framework and these newly coined pattern variables fill up these gaps successfully.
2. It also attempts to demonstrate that without a few more pattern variables, Parsons cannot achieve his ideal of general analytical theory. As "the whole point of a social theory, for Parsons, is that it should be a general analytical theory, permitting systematic comparisons of all societies and the development of general laws about them."[1]

The contribution of Talcott Parsons in Sociological Theory after 1937, the publication of his first major work, *The Structure of Social Action,* has been awesome. In fact, most of the sociological scenario for next four decades remained focussed on *pro- and anti-Parsons debate.* As stated above, Parsonian attempt to formulate a general theory of action is to provide a single theoretical system having a general and an all-inclusive character. How significant was this work for rest of his writings has been highlighted by Parsons himself in these words: "... the book, *The Structure of Social Action* ... is the basic reference point of all my subsequent theoretical work."[2]

In an attempt to construct a general, all-inclusive single theoretical system, Parsons analysed the works of Weber, Durkheim, Pareto and Marshall. In the divergent theoretical positions, Parsons has attempted to seek a point of convergence. This infers that the goals sought after by the actors in the society are socially derived and it is the society that socializes individuals in a manner they pursue these socially determined goals. This inference was radically contrary to the then prevailing utilitarian view. Parsons deals with the dilemma of positivistic-utilitarian approach on one hand and idealistic-historic on the other, Parsons claims that in both these approaches "positions from different starting points move and converge into a voluntaristic theory of action."[3]

Parsons claims that has successfully converged these different approaches in a manner where their strong points are retained and weaknesses are eliminated in the voluntaristic theory of action.[4] Virtually, all of his subsequent work has been devoted to the systematic development and elaboration of this theory.[5]

This point of convergence inferred by Parsons has helped him in formation of his action theory. The convergence of pattern variables schema is his major contribution which is developed step-by-step. In order to suggest more pattern variables for understanding society, it is imperative to first understand the Parsonian framework of pattern variables.

The Action Frame of Reference and the Pattern Variables: A Framework for Structural Analysis

Parsons has based his theory on action frame of reference wherein he refers to the action of actors in a 'situation'. According to him, every action is behaviour but not every behaviour is action.[6] The distinction between action and behaviour is that of subjective motivational process of orientation. Every action essentially involves subjective motivational process of orientation whereas behaviour may not involve it. The minimum frame of reference for action[7] must include the following: (i) actor; (ii) situation; (iii) goals; (iv) norms; and (v) subjective processes of orientation.

The first four constituents of the frame of reference for action are objective aspects. The minimum frame reference signifies: What constitutes any social action?

An *actor* is a socialized human being, who has internalized the value system, various role-system and social relationships in the process of socialization. An actor has organismic characteristic of energy and sociological characteristic of self or ego. He can think and coordinate past, present and future. An actor has the capacity for symbolic communication.[8]

All actions take place in a situation. According to Parsons, *a situation* cannot be defined independently of actor's orientation towards it. Situation consists of three types of objects in his immediate surroundings: (1) physical; (2) cultural; and (3) social. Physical objects include objects and organisms other than man. Cultural objects include language, beliefs, artifacts and values, etc. Social objects could be either other individuals or collectivity.[9]

Goals are desirable and hence an actor orients his action towards a goal. "Goals or ends, in the Parsonian schema, are simply the actor's pictures of future states of affairs regarded as desirable and worth living towards, or in the negative case, as undesirable and worth guarding against. They may be immediate or remote, highly specific or vague and general, objective, subjective, or even transcendental.[10] Goals motivate actors for undertaking action and therefore the action involves subjective process of orientation. Goals are always chosen with reference to values. Thus goals are desired, exist in future and their attainment necessitates efforts.

Norms are socially given in any society. Norms are the core principles for behaviour in a particular situation. Norms provide guidelines, direction and procedure to behave in accordance with the institutionalized expectations of society. These norms are part of the individual's socialized self (personality), i.e., actor himself. Goals are also determined by societal values.

Subjective processes of orientation are related to the need dispositions of every actor. Every actor acts because of these subjective processes of orientation. There are two aspects of this orientation: (i) gratification aspect; and (ii) orientation aspect.

The gratification aspect of subjective process of orientation indicates: Why any social action takes place? Gratification aspect means actor wants to maximize gratification (achievement) and avoid deprivation. Deprivation could mean three things:

(i) withdrawal of a gratifying object possessed by the actor;
(ii) the obstruction in accessing a gratifying object for which actor is striving; and
(iii) the enforced relationship of the actor with the object which is not gratifying and it can be physical or psychological.

The orientation aspects specify: How a social action takes place? The orientation aspect plays a central role in action theory, the way in which the relationship of the actors is organized with the objects. It involves cognitive, cathectic and evaluation modes of orientation.

The cognitive mode means knowledge of the object: How an actor defines the object? It helps the actor in determining goals and means to achieve them. The cathectic mode refers to the psychological dimension of the actor whereby he feels negative or positive, repelled or attracted towards the object. The evaluative mode refers to the stage where actor has to decide between available alternatives. It involves the various processes by which an actor allocates his energy among the various actions with respect to various cathected objects in an attempt to maximize gratification.[11]

Pattern Variables: A Framework for Structural Analysis

In order to undertake structural analysis of different societies/situations, Parsons gave a set of five mutually exclusive, polar opposite and dichotomous variables. Discussing the nature of these pattern variables, Parsons writes that "variables as we have stated them are dichotomies and not continua".[12] These variables constitute the universal and basic dilemmas confronting any actor in any social situation. Each variable represents a fundamental problem of orientation. Parsons seems to have deduced these variables from Ferdinand Toennies' dichotomy of *Gemeinschaft* and *Gesellschaft*. These variables are supposed to provide resolution to the dilemmas and are associated with definite role expectations and types of social systems. The one set of variables is supposed to be present, predominantly, in *Gemeinschaft* type of social system and other set is supposed to be present in the *Gesellschaft* type of social system.

Devereux[13] has given three criteria as guidelines for these variables:

1. These variables should be completely general and permit all sorts of comparisons.
2. These should be relevant for the action frame of reference, which means when applied to actors (when applied to personality system), these should yield classification of types of orientations; when applied to cultural system, these should deal with types of normative patterns and when applied to social system, these should deal with types of orientations (statuses, relations and roles).
3. These should be relevant for the analysis of the functional problems about which system differentiation occurs. This means any change in any variable should have important consequences in terms of system functioning.

These pattern variables are as follows:

(i) *Affectivity vs Affective Neutrality:* In certain roles and situations, affectivity is normative expectation whereas certain other roles and situations demand affective neutrality as part of normative expectation. Any shift in such roles and situations would be a deviant act.

(ii) *Specificity vs Diffusiveness:* Specific type of relationship concentrates only on one dimension of the actor's life whereas in diffusive type of orientation there is a total involvement with all the dimensions of life of the actor.

(iii) *Universalism vs Particularism:* In universalistic orientation the object is judged in terms of universal or rational or general frame of reference. In particularistic orientation, the object is judged in terms of particularistic, affective or non-rational consideration.

(iv) *Quality vs Performance:* When the primary consideration in defining a relationship or orientation is ascriptive, the quality variable is in operation. In performance variable, the consideration is the performance or achievement of the individual.

(v) *Self-Orientation vs Collective Orientation:* In self-orientation, an individual's main concern is his personal interest, whereas in collective orientation the individual's main concern is collective interest.

Later on, Parsons added one more pattern variable to the set of these five dichotomous pattern variables with a view to make these exhaustive. This is:

(vi) *Long-Run vs Short-Run Focus of Valuation:* The long-run focus of valuation takes into account the long-term goals compared to short-term goals addressed in the short-run focus of valuation. However, he has not used this dichotomy in his subsequent works.

Parsons categorically affirms that these pattern variables are essential and exhaustive in nature. He wrote: "On the question of the pattern variables, I think it can now be said that they are essential (if they are not used, essentially the same concepts under different names would have to be introduced) and that are exhaustive, though not so in the 1951 formulation".[14]

It is imperative for the convergence thesis of Parsons that the pattern variables are exhaustive in nature in terms of *The Structure of Social Action.* Contrary to the then prevailing utilitarian view, Parsons contends in this book, that the goals are socially determined and internalized into an individual through the process of socialization in such a manner that actors pursue these socially given goals. Therefore, there is a fair degree of consensus about these goals in society. For example, in a modern society, there is a heavy emphasis on material success and hence most of the actors want to achieve material success (unlike traditional and other non-modern societies where material success is not socially enforced).[15] In the light of this convergence thesis of Parsons, the pattern variables as part of general theory of action should be compatible and capable for a comparative analysis of modern, non-modern or traditional and other such societies like India, not just confining to *Gemeinschaft-Gesellschaft* or mechanical solidarity-organic solidarity comparisons only. This is only possible when some more logically compatible pattern variables are added to it.

Similarly, Max Black has listed criticisms about the pattern variable schema of Talcott Parsons. In this list, his *sixth criticism* refers to the same point as mentioned in the above paragraph by the author of this research paper that a few more pattern variable could be added to this scheme. Black writes: "For it is easy to think of any number of other ways of classifying the selected attitude of the 'actor' to his object. Why not introduce the 'choice' between treating the object as a person or as a member of some social system or between taking account of or ignoring another person's 'evaluative' aspects or to instance an altogether different type of choice, between considering short-term factors and long-term ones?"[16]

Robert Bierstedt, too, has criticized Parsons for his claim that these pattern variables are exhaustive. Bierstedt writes: "It is difficult to take seriously his contention that his pattern variables exhaust the possibilities both because of his own uncertainty as to their number and because he has both subtracted from and added to the list as his scheme developed. Since they occur in sets of two whose terms appear to be contraries, one can also ask whether we have a dichotomy or a continuum. Parsons[17] insists that the two terms in his sets of variables are dichotomies but in response to criticism that at least one set represents a continuum, says, with a fine disregard of the law of contradiction that a mutual exclusiveness is not incompatible with continuity of variation".[18]

Bierstedt also offers examples of personal vs impersonal orientation and interested vs disinterested orientations. To these examples, the author of this paper is in disagreement as these two examples are sufficiently subsumed in Parsons' affective vs affective neutrality orientation and universalism vs particularism orientation. However, the author of this paper has already talked of proposing some additional pattern variables which are listed later in the discussion. Philip Selznick also wrote, "where does Parsons get the particular pattern variable he chooses to stress when, on abstract grounds, so many others might be chosen".[19]

Bierstedt further writes: "To these criticisms many other could be added, two in particular merit mention. The first is that despite the complexity of the scheme, it is in fact not a noticeably sharp instrument of discrimination. Clearly, business relationships and family relationships are different in character. The former are impersonal; the latter, personal. But if we concede that the doctor-patient relationship is characterized by affective-neutrality, specificity, universalism, performance and collectivity-orientation, so also are such relations as teacher-student, minister-parishioner, coach-player, foreman-worker, tax collector-tax payer, conductor-orchestra member, captain-crew, and vice-president – secretary, to mention only a few. Some of these are arguable but so, as I have mentioned, is Parsons' characterization of the doctor-patient relationship. Parsons himself says that in all cases where authority is involved we have a collectivity-orientation".[20]

Hence, in the light of the foregoing discussion, this paper is undertaking an effort to present a few additional pattern variables that are strictly formulated according to the guidelines implied in Parsons' writings for the nature and formulation of these pattern variables, so as to understand Indian society and its caste system.

Additional New Pattern Variables

The set of six pattern variables available so far in Parsonian schema does not really serve the purpose of analysis of the *Gemeinschaft-Gesellschaft* dichotomy, the mechanical solidarity-organic solidarity dichotomy or the traditional society-modern society dichotomy. It also does not solve all the dilemmas of value orientations facing an actor. This can be exemplified by the following pattern variables:

(i) *Hierarchy-Oriented vs Equality-Oriented:* Since hierarchy is one of the principal features of the caste system, therefore, it is imperative for Parsonian scheme to have a pattern variable to explain hierarchy-oriented action. This dichotomy is not a continuum, rather it represents polar opposite value-orientations. Hierarchy and equality at the level of actor involve value orientation and at the level of social system involve different statuses and social relationships such as friend-friend (equality orientation) and *master-servant* or jajman-kamin (hierarchy orientation). At the level of culture systems, they yield different types of normative patterns prevalent in modern-traditional societies: societies with *mechanical organic solidarity* and in *Gemeinschaft-Gesellschaft* type of systems.

(ii) *Sacred-Orientation vs Secular-Orientation:* Traditional societies have generally a sacred-orientation reflected through its various rituals, taboos and customs. Therefore, there has to be pattern variable that can express the dilemma of sacred-orientation vis-à-vis secular-orientation. This dichotomy refers to the dilemma of value orientations on the part of *the actors*. Also, it signifies the different social relationships and statuses at the level of social systems. For example, in the traditional system, the social relationships between Dalai Lama and the laity, in Tibetans between Pope and the laity, in Catholic Christians between ulemma and the laity in Muslims and between monk/seer/saint and the laity among Hindus, Jains and Buddhists signify sacred orientations. In the secular-orientation, all contract-based relationships such as doctor-patient and lawyer-client are included. At the level of cultural systems this dichotomy typifies the dilemma of normative patterns between traditional and modern societies.

(iii) *Conservative Authoritarian Orientation vs Liberal Democratic Orientation:* A tradition society reflects the dilemma of conservative authoritarian orientation vis-à-vis liberal democratic orientation. This dilemma refers to the dilemma of *polar opposite value orientations* on the part of actors. Also, it can involve different statuses and social relationships such as the relationship between the *dictator-people* or the *Taliban-like ruling elite-commonman* (conservative authoritarian orientation) and mass leader-followers (liberal democratic orientation). At the level of cultural systems they yield different types of normative patterns prevalent in traditional-modern societies. For example, the former orientation could be seen in the Taliban-ruled Afghanistan and the latter can be seen in any modern democratic society, such as the USA, India or Canada.

Similarly, in order to compare a traditional society, with a modern one, one can use Yogendra Singh's formation of a traditional society.[21] He has given the values of holism, hierarchy, continuity and transcendence signifying a traditional society in contrast to a modern society characterized by individualism, equality, change and this-worldliness. In this context, other pattern variables could be formulated.[22] These additional pattern variables demonstrate that many more such similar dichotomies can be formulated in order to fill up the gaps in Parsonian theory.

Pattern variables focus on dilemma of choices within bipolar dichotomies. Thus, it standardizes action into conformity or deviance. It excludes the possibility of degrees and levels of conformity and deviance. The dilemma itself is superimposed. Several choices do not present dilemmas. Similarly, the personality system, cultural system and social system are congruent only ideally, not empirically. Society is an empirical reality, so are actions in their objective manifestations. It does not deal with the question of distinction between empirical-self and real-self, the invisible aspects and the visible aspects of social system and the diversities of cultural system within the same cultural system. Thus, Parsons' *theory* cannot be general and grand if it misses the *nuances of details of systems*, in which the actor lives, matures, alters, conforms and deviates.

Notes

1. Edward C. Devereux (1961), "Parsons' Sociological Theory", in Max Black (ed.), *The Social Theories of Talcott Parsons: A Critical Examination*, Englewood Cliffs: Prentice Hall, p.18.
2. Talcott Parsons (1961), "The Point of View of the Author", in Max Black (ed.), *The Social Theories of Talcott Parsons: A Critical Examination*, Englewood Cliffs: Prentice Hall, p. 316.
3. Wolfgang Schluchter (1989), *Rationalism, Religion and Domination: A Weberian Perspective*, Berkeley: University of California Press, p. 64.
4. Edward C. Devereux (1961), "Parsons' Sociological Theory", in Max Black (ed.), *The Social Theories of Talcott Parsons: A Critical Examination*, Englewood Cliffs: Prentice Hall, p. 19.
5. Ibid.
6. Ibid., p. 21.
7. Arvind Kumar Agrawal (2000), *Max Weber and Modern Sociological Theories*, Jaipur: Rawat Publications, p. 138.
8. Ibid., pp. 138–39.
9. Ibid., p. 139.
10. Edward C. Devereux, op. cit., p. 23.
11. Arvind Kumar Agrawal, op. cit., p. 140.

12. Talcott Parsons and Edward A. Shils (eds.) (1951), *Toward a General Theory of Action*, Cambridge: Harvard University Press, p. 91.
13. Edward C. Devereux, op. cit., p. 26.
14. *Supra* at Note 1, p. 336.
15. Irving, M. Zeitlin (1973), *Rethinking Sociology: A Critique of Contemporary Theory*, New York: Appleton Century Crofts, p. 41.
16. Black Max (ed.) (1961), *The Social Theories of Talcott Parsons: A Critical Examination*, Englewood Cliffs: Prentice Hall, p. 288.
17. Talcott Parsons (1953), "Some Comments on the State of the General Theory of Action", *American Sociological Review*, 18 (December): p. 624a.
18. Robert Bierstedt (1981), *American Sociological Theory: A Critical History*, New York, Academic Press, p. 421.
19. Philip Selznick (1961), *American Sociological Review*, 26, (December): 935.
20. Robert Bierstedt, op. cit., pp. 424–25.
21. Yogendra Singh (2002), *Modernisation of Indian Tradition* (Reprint), Jaipur: Rawat Publications, p. vii.
22. *Orthodox Fundamental Orientation vs. Secular Humanist Orientation:* Just like the example given above, this dilemma of value orientations, too, can be explained. Particularly after witnessing Taliban's Afghanistan, the specter of Osama Bin Laden, the regime of Saddam and the event of September 11, 2001 this pattern variable can be easily explained. In fact, many more such pattern variables can be formulated.

16 Reflections and Mobilizations

Development as Global Responsibility

ANANTA KUMAR GIRI

I
The Problem: Crisis of Interventionist Development and the Calling of Global Responsibility

The discourse and practice of development is at a critical juncture now. The idea of development, in its present interventionist mode, had originated at the end of the Second World War as a new vision of hope against the backdrop of the devastating experiences of the war and the rising process of decolonization. At this juncture, the idea of development shaped new forms of political responsibility on a global scale. It gave rise to many applications. Now, after more than fifty years of application, development has gradually lost its appeal and vitality. We are facing a crisis, not knowing how to move on in a meaningful way. We now face a crisis in a foundational way and in terms of major transformations at the macro level as well as in our daily routines in the world of development. This crisis is manifest in many fields – in the declining commitment to human development on the part of state and international donor agencies, destruction of public space and institutions without parallel efforts to reconstitute them, a growing militarization of state and society, and the growing cynicism among all concerned.

One major aspect of our contemporary crisis is the growing gap between action and reflection. Within the world of action we witness a transition from development interventions as expressive of specific political responsibility towards a notion of development in which the issue of manageability has taken central stage. The focus of moral and political reasoning has shifted from goals to results. In the world of reflection we have seen a shift from modernist faith in development towards the post-modern, de-constructive critiques of it. But both these shifts are within the frames of 'liberty', 'rights' and 'justice' discourses of modernity and lack a transformational engagement with the emergent discourse and practice of responsibility. But this constitutes a foundational problem which contemporary shifts in development – either from the political masters to managers, or from development as hope-generating machine to development as dystopia – are completely unreflective about. For example, when the neo-liberal advocates propound a market redefinition of development or deconstructive critics, a Foucauldian critique of development as hegemony (cf. Escobar, 1995) we are still operating with development as rights and justice but what needs to be understood is that the rights and justice frames had emerged in specific historical circumstances and now these frames need to be radically and transformationally supplemented by a practice and perspective of responsibility.

The crisis in daily routines and paradigms of development that we now face can be better illumined if we relate this to our clinging to only 'rights' and 'justice' frames of modernity and lack of willingness to accept the calling of responsibility. In his provocative work, *Discourse and Knowledge: The Making of Enlightenment Sociology*, Piet Strydom (2000) helps us understand this foundational problem. For Strydom the rights frame had emerged in the early modern revolutions, e.g., the Revolt of the Netherlands, the English Revolution and the French Revolution. The justice frame had arisen in the wake of industrial revolution in "late eighteenth century England and continued unabated yet in a sublimated form until the second half of the twentieth century, focused on the problem complex of exploitation, pauperization and loss of identity [...]" (ibid.: 20). These two discourses have inspired and influenced socio-political movements in the modern world including interventions of development but they have now their limits to come to terms with the emergent challenge and calling of responsibility. For example, to come to terms with environmental crisis and the attendant calling of responsibility discourses of rights and justice and politics and policies revolving around these have their limits. In face of such challenges, in Strydom's pregnant formulations, "The theory of justice is today making way for another, still newer semantics in the form of the moral theory of responsibility which is crystallizing around a number of intertwined debates about the problem of risk" (ibid.: 20).

Thus, the calling of responsibility constitutes a critical juncture, one which is heightened by the rise of a risk society, both locally and globally. In fact, problems of poverty, rights, injustice and now the valorized problem of terrorism can be looked at as part of our risk condition but our approach to such risks has to be one of responsibility, a responsible engagement. The calling of responsibility here is a broad-based one in which all the relevant actors – state, market, social movements/voluntary organizations, and self – have a role to play and in fact are called upon to embody their responsibility in a spirit of autonomy and interpenetration. In this there is a need for transforming development as freedom to development as responsibility because freedom discourse, as important and indispensable as it is, is still incapable of undertaking the suffering that the self needs to undertake in order to fulfil its responsibility to other (cf. Levinas, 1974; Sen, 1999). But this plea for reconstitution of development as responsibility is neither a plea for locating responsibility outside nor colluding with the contemporary neo-liberal politics of irresponsibility in which the downtrodden and the victims of the systems are singularly blamed for their miseries but a plea for a multi-dimensional transformation in which all concerned actors in the field of development are engaged.

But responsibility here does not mean only political responsibility but also ethico-moral and spiritual responsibility, embodying co-responsibility.[1] At the same time, modes of responsible engagement do not emerge only from the public sphere, as Strydom (1999) seems to suggest in a Habermasian mode but involves practices of self-cultivation including spiritual mobilization of self and society. In fact, it is the perspective and practice of responsibility emerging from multidimensional practices of care of self, looking up to the face of the other, and being part of conversations and civil labour in the public sphere, that constitutes the moral critique of development that constitutes development as responsibility that this essay wishes to present.

The field of development has been subjected to a Foucauldian critique in the works of scholars such as Escobar (1995) which valorizes political criticism but this now needs to be radically supplemented by a moral critique and perspective and practice of reconstructive responsibility. A moral critique however does not proceed with an opposition between politics and morality but contains interpenetrative critical moments and possibilities between politics and morality acknowledging the limits of an either-or-approach, and always inspired by a beyond, a transcendence that exists within these immanent domains. With this perspective of reconstructive responsibility, the paper asks whether the contemporary redefinition of development in terms of Amartya Sen's 'functioning' and 'capability' is adequate to challenge of developing one's mind and heart (cf. Sen, 1999).

It is important to bring this perspective and practice of responsibility in our critical interrogation of the logic of interventionist development. This is emerging in various contemporary movements of reflections and mobilizations. The simultaneously engagement with reflections and mobilizations in this essay emanates from a basic realization that reflection is not the work of an isolated ego but emerges from appropriate inter-subjectivity, and participation in social, cultural and spiritual movements. But, while critical reflections on development, like the post-war articulation and subsequent application of it, suffer from an Euro-American bias, the critical mobilizations we refer to and valorize are primarily socio-political movements. But, in this essay, with an emphasis on reconstructive responsibility, I discuss both socio-political and socio-spiritual movements and the way critical reflections on human development now need to go beyond its Euro-American binding and take part in a trans-civilizational dialogue on the meaning, process and telos of development.

The paper outlines two domains of responsibilities that reflections and mobilizations in the field of development face: (a) the challenge of a trans-civilizational dialogue on development; and (b) the challenge of realization of global justice and the striving for peace. It also discusses socio-political and socio-spiritual movements providing glimpses of reconstitution of development as a global responsibility. The paper further discusses the contours of the emergent moral critique of development in the face of globalization, i.e., the marketization of the globe by the forces of corporate world. It discusses how development as a global responsibility now faces the challenge of both a cross-cultural and trans-civilizational dialogue on the meaning, process and telos of development as well as socio-spiritual and socio-political struggles for justice and peace. Without presupposing a dualism between socio-spiritual and socio-political movements, it describes the significance of the socio-spiritual mobilization of Swadhyaya and the socio-political movements such as Attac (Association for the Taxation of Financial Transactions for the Aid of Citizens) in Europe and the anti-mining struggle in Kashipur, India fighting against corporate globalization. Swadhyaya brings a new cultural and civilizational perspective on development than offered by the Enlightenment model of human development which interventionist models of development are now striving to globalize with the force of money and power. The paper describes the violence in such a globalization of world-view and pleads for a trans-civilizational and transcultural dialogue on development. It submits that such a trans-civilizational dialogue calls for mutual interrogation and open-ended learning where we are concerned not only with issues of application and justification but also prepare ourselves to undertake suffering for peace, justice and renewing development as practices of hope. This, the paper argues, is essential to rethinking and reconstituting our responsibilities in and to the world after the violent turbulences of 9/11.

II

Broadening and Deepening the Meaning and Practice of Development: Socio-spiritual Mobilizations and the Calling of a Trans-civilizational Dialogue

Swadhyaya is a socio-spiritual movement in contemporary India which also works globally in England, Caribbean, USA and Africa (Giri, 2000a). 'Swadhyaya' means study of self but both these are understood in broad terms, and here efforts in self-study and self-development are intimately connected with being with others in many experimental ways. Swadhyaya does not believe in an interventionist mode of development. It has varieties of activities which can be called community development projects but that would be an externalist representation of the vision and practice of Swadhyaya. Swadhyaya calls these *prayogas* which means experiments – experiments which facilitate self-development of participants in an experimental ground of working and being together where self is attuned both to the higher self within and the other self standing laterally. *Bhaktipheri* – devotional travel – and *Shramabhakti* – devotional labour – are the foundation of Swadhyaya. Swadhyaya believes that one of the greatest contemporary challenges is to overcome the distance between man and man and for this people should meet with each other without any profit motivation. In *Bhaktipheri* Swadhyayees go from one place to another and spend time with each other. In *Shramabhakti*, Swadhyayees offer their devotional labour in experimental grounds of self-development and collective well-being. For example, in villages where Swadhyaya is active, there is a *prayoga* called *Yogeswara Krishi* or Lord's farming in which Swadhyaees cultivate a piece of land taken on lease on a co-operative basis and through their own labour. The produce of this experiment is treated as impersonal wealth or *apoureshaya laxmi* and this is utilized for addressing the needs of the community. Through such generation of impersonal wealth from varieties of experiments some of which exist at a supra-village level (for instance, the experiment of Sri Darshanam and Brukha Mandir brings people together for offering of devotional labour from more than twenty villages), Swadhyayees also learn to overcome the bindings of a narrow economic reason and learn to relate to wealth in a non-possessive way, a learning which can transform the contemporary discourse of social capital (cf. Putnam et al., 1993). In the contemporary discourse, social capital is primarily thought of in rational terms but rationality is not enough in tackling the problem of individualism, atomism and the tendency to free ride in contemporary societies. In Swadhyaya trust is a value in itself, a value which is generated and strengthened in networks of relationships and here a dialogue with Swadhyaya can help us to understand the significance of spirituality, namely, practical spirituality, in the generation and renewal of social capital (cf. Dasgupta and Serageldin, 2000; Dore, 1997).

For its work, Swadhyaya says that it does not accept any grant from either multilateral donor agencies, like the World Bank or IMF, or from the state, and the philanthropists. Swadhyaya generates wealth and well-being from the time and labour that participants bring to these experimental grounds of mutual nurturance. Here, we witness a new attempt to realize value from our own time and labour without passing through the media of money and market and without standing with folded hands in the corridors of international and national donor agencies for starting rural and tribal development work in one's vicinity. Many efforts in contemporary West such as the LETS (Local Employment and Trading Systems) network in Netherlands and Canada (cf. Offe and Heinze, 1992) and what Ulrich Beck (2000) calls varieties of civil labour where one works for the common good also embody such a spirit of realization of value from our own free time and free labour – an art which we have lost in the logic of organized modernity. Realizing development as a shared global responsibility calls for a new relationship to time and labour – a time which is not just what Heidegger calls a "clock time" but a lived time and labour which is not teleologically geared only to earning money for oneself but becomes a means of taking part in a shared world of working together for a new hope, for a new beginning (Dallmayr, 2000b). We find glimpses of a new relationship to time and labour in Swadhyaya which has been made possible by a spiritual mobilization of tradition. Swadhyaya does not believe in the post-traditional telos of modernity – the telos which guides the discourse of development too, that tradition is necessarily a barrier to be overcome in development; rather there are many spiritual resources in traditions which can be creatively mobilized for alternative development at the contemporary juncture (see Dhanagare, 2003). In such mobilizations, unlike Giddens (cf. 1999) and Habermas (cf. 1993), justification of faith is carried out not through rational argumentation alone but also through one's participation in concrete projects of practical spirituality which are embodiments of aesthetic and ethical projects of love. Love for God as simultaneously love for self and love for the world is at the heart of such an initiative in development which helps us to understand the calling of a new dialectic of transformation that Roy Bhaskar has recently presented to us: "The dialectics of de-alienation (of retotalization) are all essentially dialectics of love, of love of self (Self), of each and all (Totality) and in both inner and outer movements, both as essentially love of God. [...] and God, we could say, is not essentially love but essentially to be loved" (Bhaskar, 2000: 44).

In Swadhyaya, practical work of development and spirituality is not separated from each other but here combining love for God with love for the world is not free from ambiguity, tension and contradiction (cf. Touraine, 2001).

Followers of Swadhyaya make a distinction between God's work and social work; for them contributing to development of human mind and heart through various life-elevating projects is an aspect of God's work, while building new roads is an aspect of social work. This distinction has not enabled Swdhyaya to come to terms with concrete challenge of social development in local communities such as repairing dilapidated roads, building cowsheds, and stopping the encroachment of village common lands by influential landlords, not to mention its hesitance to publicly denounce communal carnage carried out in the name of religion. But here followers of Swadhyaya appeal us to rethink the very meaning of development. During one of my fieldwork journeys to Gujarat in Western India – the state where Swadhyaya is most active – I was once asked a question. I was walking with Pappot Bhai, an inspiring leader of Swadhyaya, and his fellow co-walkers in a village near the coastal town of Veraval. Pappot Bhai asked me: "Is building road the only meaning of development? Developing mind, intellect and heart of human beings – is it no development?" This question of Pappot Bhai could be asked to the project of development which, despite its shift from economic development to human development, does not have within itself any striving for development of human heart.

In fact, Fred Dallmayr, the preeminent philosopher of our times for whom philosophy is an experiential embodiment of cross-cultural dialogue, asks such an important question: should development participate in what he calls "Enlightenment Blackmail" and globalize modern Western models of economic development and rationality or be a critical hermeneutic effort in understanding the limitations of such a philosophical and historical starting point and undertaking efforts to create new spaces of self-development and mutual flourishing (Dallmayr, 1998). Dallmayr tells us that in Europe itself there was also another tradition of *Bildung* which emphasized self-cultivation in talking about development, a cultivation which simultaneously aimed at authentic humanization and divinization.[2] The ideal of *Bildung* is not confined only to the classical German period but found virtually in all cultures of the globe which have stories or mythical-religious narratives which emphasize the "process of divine human formation" but "how much of these older stories of formation, culture (*Bildung*), and self-development still leaves in contemporary conceptions of social development?" (ibid.: 245). Thus, cross-cultural dialogue on the meaning of development where we seek to understand the contingency of not only our social locations but also our values is an important task here. Applying the insights of self-cultivation, Dallmayr tells us: "With specific reference to global development, formation (*Bildung*) postulates an open-ended encounter between societies and cultures, a reciprocal learning process animating a 'global village' continuously in the throes of formation" (ibid.: 14). And, in such an engagement with development as a cross-cultural striving for human flourishing we need to build on alternative traditions of spiritual humanization but bringing these voices to the contemporary discourse of development requires a memory work, an act of courageous remembrance and contemporary restitution. In the words of Dallmayr, "This path of humanization [as charted by Confucius and Herder] offers the potential for renewal that is never cut loose from historically sedimented moorings and situated vernacular beliefs. To avoid rupture, what is needed along this path is memory work, attention to the still untapped resources of the past; in our time of rapid globalization with a bent toward global amnesia such memory-work emerges as a crucial requisite for the preservation of critical humanness" (ibid.: 11).

Thus, in order to take part in development as a global conversation, we cannot ignore the task of cross-cultural and cross-civilizational dialogue on development. Such a dialogue should not be another exercise in imposing the dominant conception of human development as propagated by contemporary triumphal capitalism but an engagement in "mutual interrogation and interpellation" where "a distinct life-form – a concrete mode of 'being-in-the world' – opens itself up to the challenge of otherness in a manner yielding a deeper, transformative understanding of self and other" (ibid.: 6/7). And, in this dialogue, we should also overcome the contemporary tempting logic of clash of civilizations (cf. Huntington, 1996) and take part in various attempts in overcoming their situational, valuational and historical contingencies and arrive at spaces of mutually created co-beings. But, in this cross-civilizational dialogue on development, we should not be confined only to the horizontal dimension of self-other relation but should be open to the vertical dimension as well. This vertical dimension refers to how a civilization or culture relates to Nature and Divine. For Dallmayr, "On the level of civilizational discourse, horizontal openness means attentiveness to other civilizations, but also to civilization's corollaries (nature and the divine) [...] which speak or intervene in human discourse, but do so in recessed and 'non-informatic' ways. The question is whether we allow ourselves to be addressed in this fashion" (Dallmayr, 2001a: 16).

But the Enlightenment model of development self-confidently cuts itself off from the world of nature except as an object of domination and the world of transcendence except as an idle superstructure or a collective hallucination. Here, a widening of our universe of discourse is urgently called for in both axes. On the first axis, we need to engage ourselves with a much more radical critique of anthropocentrism and go beyond the contemporary rethinking of development as 'anthropocentrism with a human face' (cf. Nederveen Pieterse, 2001). Here, a cross-cultural experience of nature would be helpful, for example, the experience pointed to by the Indian spiritual traditions where all life is sacred and human beings do not have any right to dominate the non-human world. The emergent developments in technologies such as the rise of cyborgs (virtual people with artificial intelligence) may also force us to rethink our anthropocentric models of development as "for the first time in their history, human beings would have to cooperate with a different species" which takes all sentient beings, not only humans, seriously (Hamelink, 2000: 36). And, in so far as the axis of transcendence is concerned, contemporary development discourse is an unreflective participant in the Enlightenment dichotomy of the human social world and the world of transcendence and the task for us here is to realize the harm such a dissociation does to relationship between humans here on earth itself. As Jean-Luc Nancy tells us: "It is precisely the immanence of man to man, or it is man, taken absolutely, considered as the immanent being par excellence, that constitutes the stumbling block to a thinking of community" (quoted in Dallmayr, 1998: 281; also Unger, 1987).

It was Ralph Dahrendorf (1968) who more than thirty years ago had characterized development as 'Applied Enlightenment' but in the meantime much water has flown in both Rhine and the Ganges and many critical commentators point to the difficulty in thinking about development as Applied Enlightenment. But these critical reflections do not call for a fundamental transformation in our modes of being and modes of relationship along these two axes – the natural world and the transcendental. Both the critics and defenders of Enlightenment leave unproblematic these oppositions and here Foucault's much drummed about reconstitution of Enlightenment along "people's knowledge" is also part of the same Enlightenment privileging of the human social world. The proposal of a third enlightenment or practical enlightenment offered by enthusiastic Anglo-American philosophers such as Hilary Putnam (2001) and Richard Rorty (1999) also seems to be very much a family quarrel rather than a radical, global interrogation of the presuppositions of Enlightenment. Here, Putnam's proposal of practical enlightenment and Toulmin's call for return to reason via reasonable human practice does not explore the spiritual ontology of human practice. John Dewey is a hero to the American pragmatists and they are now out in the world preaching everywhere his virtues but unfortunately in a missionary way. Surely, all over the world, we have lot to learn from the democratic and educational experiments of Dewey but in this age of global conversations while talking about Enlightenment, can we beat the drums of Dewey in an uncritical manner without relating the democratic enlightenment of Dewey to the spiritual enlightenment of experimenters like Gautama Buddha and Mahatma Gandhi? In fact, both Buddha and Gandhi combined spiritual seeking with reason, democratic and spiritual enlightenment in their own ways, Buddha spending his post-Enlightenment days in teaching the excluded sections of society and exhorting them not to abandon reason in the name of custom (Carrithers, 1983). Thus, as we make development a part of global conversation, we would have to proceed cautiously vis-à-vis the contemporary American proposal about third enlightenment as there is a one-sided globalization of John Dewey here which is not delinked from the globalization of Coca-Cola.

The dualism between universalism and particularism is another legacy of Enlightenment which determines our modes of development and embodiment of responsibility. In order to rethink development as an embodiment of global responsibility, we have to transcend the boundaries between the two. Here critique of universalism as offered by Foucault and others is not enough, what is called for here is an understanding of and participation in the work of what Wallerstein and his colleagues call 'particularistic universalism' – a proposal which has close affinity with the one of 'situated universalism' recently submitted by Sheldon Pollock, Homi Bhaba, Carol Appadurai Breckenridge and Dipesh Chakravorty (Pollock et al., 2000; Wallerstein et al., 1996). This in turn calls for a multi-valued logic in place of the either-or-logic of particularism and universalism and an ethics of non-injury and non-violence. Philosopher J.N. Mohanty (2000: 24) brings a cross-culturally sensitive philosophical reflection to bear on this pathway of multi-valued logic:

> The ethic of non-injury applied to philosophical thinking requires that one does not reject outright the other point of view without first recognizing the element of truth in it; it is based on the belief that every point of view is partly true, partly false, and partly undecidable. A simple two-valued logic requiring that a proposition must either be true or false is thereby rejected, and what the Jaina philosopher proposes is a multi-valued logic. To this multi-valued logic, I add the Husserlian idea of overlapping contents. The different perspectives on a thing are not mutually exclusive, but share some contents with each other. The different 'worlds' have shared contents, contrary to the total relativism. *If you represent them by circles, they are intersecting circles, not incommensurable, [and it is this model of] intersecting circles which can get us out of relativism on the one hand and absolutism on the other.* (emphasis added)

III
Beyond the Violence of Corporate Globalization: The Challenge of Global Justice

From a philosophical perspective J.N. Mohanty presents us the picture of intersecting circles to transcend the opposition between universalism and particularism and David Harvey presents us the picture of multiple theatres from the perspective of emancipatory political practice. Harvey writes: "The metaphor to which I appeal is one of several different 'theatres' of thought and action on some long frontier of 'insurgent' political practices. Advances in one theatre get ultimately stymied or even rolled back unless supported by advances elsewhere. No one theatre is particularly privileged [...]" (Harvey, 2000a: 234). Harvey's meditations can help us have a turning point in this reflective journey, and encourage us to combine the widening of the universe of discourse of development with concrete socio-political and spiritual struggles. But, as we undertake this task of combination, development as humanization meets with specific and often violent challenge now in the contemporary effort to turn the world into a global market place. True, markets have their own place in enabling continued socio-economic development in the planet but the contemporary marketization of the globe has no sense of limit and is a narrowing of our conceptions of self and the world and shrinks our sense of responsibility (Sachs, 1999). In this context, it is helpful to keep in mind what Jean and John Comaroff write about our contemporary predicament: "Life under millennial capitalism is neither a game nor a repertoire of rational choices. [...] Already there are signs of altered configurations, of fresh efforts to challenge the triumphal reign of the market [...]" (Comaroff and Comaroff, 2000: 334–35; also see Bourdieu, 1999).

There are anti-systemic and alternative movements everywhere on the rise now and while the advocates of corporate globalization including their media spokespersons dismiss these anti-globalization movements, they are in fact striving for an alternative globalization, i.e., globalization as humanization. For these movements marketization of the globe is not an inevitable destiny and they strive to shape the unfolding contours of globalization in favour of primacy of the human rather than market or corporations. Thus, one of the slogans I heard in the demonstrations against the EU summit meeting in Gothenburg in June 2001 is: "People, not Profit: Our World is not for Sale". On the final day of this gathering, twenty-five thousand people marched peacefully in the streets of Gothenburg chanting "International Solidarity, International Solidarity". The battle of Gothenburg was continued just a month later in Genoa, Italy where 150,000 people took part.

In both Gothenburg and Genoa there was violence though an overwhelming majority of protesters were non-violent and do not believe in violence as a mode of contestation. In reflecting on this violence, the mainstream global media such as CNN holds protesters responsible. But this is a systematically biased reporting. I had taken part in the Gothenburg summit and I have seen how police riding on galloping horses and with dogs first jumped into the marching crowd. In the ensuing confrontation while police had the most sophisticated weapon, protesters even did not have stones to throw at. But, as the confrontation intensified, protesters with black masks started digging stones from the ground and started throwing stones at the police. So, what we witness here is a fight between the defenders of the system who have the most advanced technologies in their command and the protesters (here referring to only those protesters who do not feel shy to use violence) have only stone age tools such as stones and chairs. Despite this, police in Gothenburg shot at the volunteers of the 'Reclaiming the Street' group who were having their anti-corporate street rally in the night, critically wounding three people which included a journalist. On the second day of the summit, in the garden near the canal where protesters had set up their tents, I met a young man who showed me his bleeding hand – blood coming out of the bites of the police dog. Despite this he and his friends were charting the slogan 'Love, Love' and flying balloons, not stones, towards the police.

But the violence during the G8 summit in Genoa, Italy was even much more and here police killed one demonstrator. Carlo Juliani whose place of assassination in Genoa I visited in November 2002 is the first martyr from Europe in the struggle against corporate globalization but while his martyrdom has recently inspired demonstrations in many parts of Europe, especially among the young, he still remains unnamed to most of us. In this contestation, the defenders of the system are engaged in a one-sided condemnation of violent protesters and even use the name of Mahatma Gandhi for this.[3] But Gandhi is not a purist proponent of non-violence, especially non-violence of a cowardly kind, and though he himself would give his life in truthful non-violent (*satyagrahic*) fight against the oppressive forces of the system, he would never pass an apriori moralizing judgment on those who use violence to protest against the inhumanity of a system – a system which has shut its doors and windows of perception. A Gandhian engagement with dramas of contestation at both Gothenburg and Genoa also needs to ask this question: what prevents the assembled world leaders to invite the protesters into a roundtable conversation and listen to them?

Thus, as we reconstitute development as a global responsibility, there is no way we can dissociate our duties from taking part in this violent confrontation between corporate globalization and globalization as humanization. For students of development studies it calls understanding the emergent new logic of violence where forces of multinational capital and state power join hands in suppressing rights of people. Such a development scenario is ethically problematic and morally wrong in the first place, not to mention that it violates the spirit of democratic constitutionalism (cf. Habermas, 1996). To understand this, let us acquaint ourselves, albeit briefly, with another struggle. Kashipur in the state of Orissa is one of the most backward tribal areas of India. For the last eight years, the people of Kashipur have been waging a fight against multinational mining companies bent on establishing mines in their area. With the might of the state these companies have also acquired land from many people in the affected villages. Neither the multinational companies nor the State Government has ever discussed with the local people what they want to do in their area and what is going to be their fate after being evicted from their homelands. Agragamee, a local voluntary organization, which has not been afraid to support a dialogue between these contending parties, has been subjected to attacks and the state of Orissa under the leadership of a tyrant chief minister even banned it for two years. Local people themselves have been subjected to numerous violent attacks and in some cases villagers have also kidnapped the functionaries of multinational mining companies. But, when all this did not deter the spirit of the local people, a platoon of police descended on the village of Maikanch on 16 December 2000 where people had just completed their communal lunch together and started firing at them. The police killed in cold blood three people who were running to the hill top for their lives and before leaving the village burnt its own vehicle and told the world that it resorted to firing in self-defence.

The multinational Hydro company of Norway is one of the parties in this contestation and the voluntary organization named Norwach which is based in Oslo has brought the struggle of Kashipur to the public sphere in Norway. Tarjei is one of the activists of Norwatch and he has provided support to this struggle. On his own experience about this participation in an emergent movement of global solidarity, Tarjei says: "I am struck by the fact that our own organization Norwatch is such a small group, we are only two people, but we are able to create a public opinion here against the mining activities of Hydro. I feel that as the system is becoming increasingly more and more powerful, it is also becoming more and more vulnerable where a single individual can challenge and transform it in concrete ways."

Attac is one of the fast growing transnational social movements at present which is struggling for embodiment of global responsibilities in concrete ways. Starting in France, it has spread quickly into many parts of Europe and the world and in countries like Sweden and Finland it has taken the character of a multi-dimensional grassroots mobilization involving both non-violent public protest as well as critical study of the contemporary dynamics of globalization. It conducts study circles on both the logic of corporate globalization as well as democratic alternatives in economy and society. Young and old cutting across ideological and party lines are now joining the space of global solidarity that a movement such as Attac creates. I had a discussion with Bjorn and Gunnar, two young volunteers of Attac, Sweden in Stockholm in June 2001 and they told me that members from Social Democratic Party of Sweden are leaving their old party home and joining Attac because they find it providing them a democratic space for self-expression that is not available in the party spaces. Attac also provides them a space to think about issues of global justice in a more concrete and personal way. One of the demands of Attac is that multinational companies should pay a certain amount of tax to the local community where they are working, what is called now the Tobin Tax. The volunteers of Attac are responding to the calling of global responsibilities at the contemporary juncture in multiple modes of contestation and creativity, reflection and action. They were at the forefront of the peaceful demonstration on the final day of the EU summit in Gothenburg in June 2001. When one talks to the animating volunteers of Attac one realizes that the global community is "not simply an empirical reality or presence, but matter of an advent, a calling [...]" (Dallmayr, 1998: 282).

But, in this global fight over life and death, the issue of concrete human suffering is an elusive one and it requires a sensitive development anthropology to record this beyond the representation of movements themselves. In this context, Upendra Baxi, a sensitive scholar of contemporary globalization and social suffering, writes: "The 'analytic' standpoint fails to see the logic of social movements from the perspective of those violated?" (Baxi, 2000: 39). But, what Baxi does not realize is that leaders of social movements themselves can fail to identify themselves with the suffering faces and bodies of men and women whose lives they represent. Here it is helpful to come back to the story of the anti-mining struggle in Kashipur. Abhilash Jhodia is one of the three people killed in the police firing in Maikanch last year, and he hails from the village of Maikanch itself. He was a young man, only twenty-five when he was shot dead leaving behind his pregnant wife, two children and ageing parents. During my visit to Maikanch I felt that leaders of the anti-mining struggle in the village are in a way happy that the firing took place because police firing and the unintentional martyrdom of these three people have provided new momentum to the struggle and has contributed to people's loss of fear. But, the experience of Subarna, Abhilash's wife, and his children is different. When I went to the house of Abhilash along with some young people of the village, Subarna was not at home. She had gone to a distant forest, even at this advanced stage of pregnancy, to collect woods which she would sell for her livelihood. Abhilash's father who was holding his young son told us: "In the night it is difficult. The young boy is asking when would his father come home?" And when I was finally able to meet with Subarna, she was silent as a statue. Words and tears have run their course in her life and her vacant eyes embody a different experience of struggle compared to the leaders in the village for whom Abhilash has quickly become a dead somebody whose martyrdom has contributed to new energies of the movement. There is an erasure of concrete faces in such a movemental representation as well and here the calling responsibility calls for a vigilant awareness which refuses to be trapped even in the logic of anti-systemic movements and in a spirit of continued seeking of solidarity brings the untold suffering of women such as Subarna Jhodia to our consciousness.

Thus, there are many ethical sides to globalization and global responsibility than meets the eye. Along side globalization, cosmopolitanism is another regnant discourse today with which it is helpful to have a brief encounter as a prelude to our following reconstitution of development as an undertaking in suffering and hope. Here again, we witness two contending forces: cosmopolitanism as an elitist globalism which wants to be cosmopolitan in its lifestyle (not in life-politics) and cosmopolitanism which represents the force of global democratization – a fight for cosmopolitan democracy from within local societies and nation-states. About the first kind of cosmopolitanism, Sheldon Pollock and his colleagues write: "The discriminatory perspectives of an older form of globalization – colonization – seem to have revived themselves at the point at which we readily consider ourselves to be worldwide citizens forever 'hooked up' (connected) on-line. All the derring-do between the local and the global in the dialectic of worldly thinking should not conceal the fact that neoliberal cosmopolitan thought is founded on a conformist sense of what it means to be a 'person' as an abstract unit of cultural exchange" (Pollock et al., 2000: 581). And about the later, Urlich Beck tells us: "[...] cosmopolitanism means global interrelationships and a transnational vocabulary of symbols, but it also means a deep engagement in local activities, local consciousness, connection to local people. It means having wings and roots at the same time" (Beck, 2001: 2). Beck goes on to argue: "[...] globalism is a basic enemy of democracy and therefore be supplemented by the cosmopolitan principle of recognizing the otherness of the other" (ibid.).

Responding to the calling of global responsibility at the contemporary juncture requires development to participate in this contested field of cosmopolitanism, the struggle between cosmopolitanism as a global elitism and cosmopolitanism as a yearning for cosmopolitan democracy which parallels the struggle between globalization from above and globalization from below (Appadurai, 2000; Das, 2001a). And here as David Harvey argues, "A meaningful cosmopolitanism does not entail some passive contemplation of global citizenship. It is, as Kant himself insisted, a principle of intervention to make the world (and its geography) something other than what it is" (Harvey, 2000b: 560).

IV
New Dimensions of Realization of Justice: Self-Cultivation, Hope and Suffering

But Harvey is not alone in invoking the memory of Kant in radical ways for helping us come to terms with the contemporary challenge of global responsibility. Notable here is the passionate reflections of anthropologist Keith Hart who writes: "Kant saw that the world was moving towards war between coalition of nation-states; yet he posed the question of how humanity might construct a 'perpetual peace' beyond the boundaries of state, based on principles we all share [...] Kant held that the last and most difficult task facing humanity was the administration of justice worldwide" (Hart, 2000: 3). As we have seen with the case of movements such as Attac, the Kantian question of a global justice is now at the heart of many movements for a humane globalization and has gone beyond the speculative world of Kantian philosophers of justice of our times such as John Rawls (see Rawls, 1999, 2001). For Hart, "In order to pursue this goal, the world has to be imaginatively reduced in scale and our subjectivity expanded so that a meaningful link can be established between the two" (Hart, 2000: 3).

In this praxis of establishing meaningful linkage, Hart says: "We need to feel more at home in the world, to find the means of actively resisting alienation" (ibid.). The task of resisting alienation can be enriched now by creatively embodying the spirit of both Marx and Heidegger. Marx spoke about the need to overcome social alienation and Heidegger, the alienation of our authentic self. At the contemporary juncture, there is a need to combine these two aspirations of overcoming alienation (cf. Harvery, 1996). But here Heidegger also challenges us to understand the fragile character of our being in the world and urges us not to cling to our secured homes and undertake a journey of homelessness, a travel in the world. We of course have to come home but the home we come back is not a secured abode: "[...] the 'home' sought and found in homecoming is not a place located somewhere else in empirical space-time, but rather something like a promise [...] – a promise which also does not point simply to a no-place or a place outside of space-time, but rather inhabits the journey from beginning to end" (Dallmayr, 2000a: 8). In our effort to resist alienation in the world at presen,t we need to understand and take part in this dialectic between homelessness and homecoming.

This need for a simultaneous effort in overcoming self-alienation and social alienation calls for an interlinked simultaneous engagement in self-cultivation and democratic public participation. Sadly in critical theorists of public sphere and human development of our times such as Jurgen Habermas and Amartya Sen we miss any acknowledgment of need for appropriate self-cultivation. In their recent work, *India: Development and Participation*, Jean Dreze and Amartya Sen tell us about both the instrumental and intrinsic significance of participation for 'value formation' and for democracy and development (Dreze and Sen, 2002). Dreze and Sen's agenda of democratic participation is definitely of great significance for all of us concerned, especially in India, which is still feudal in its temperament and social arrangement in many ways and where even spiritual movements have hard time in overcoming their feudal past. But, in Dreze and Sen, there is no recognition of the need to radically supplement public participation with appropriate self-engagement and self-participation including nurturing appropriate self-cultivation for value formation. But radically supplementing democratic public participation with self-cultivation is now an epochal challenge. Ramshroy Roy presents this need for simultaneous engagement in his characteristic evocative manner:

> [Public order is threatened by the split between] man's concern for his own good and that for the good of others. But can this threat to the public order be mitigated, if not completely eliminated, by the installation of the Polis? [...] For Aristotle, transcendence of self-interest is consequent upon participation in public affairs [but] the shortcomings associated with personal character cannot be expected to be rectified by the public realm, if it lacks necessary support from individuals reborn as citizens. To be reborn as a person who, rising above his self-interest, becomes attentive to and actively seeks to pursue collective good, is, then, to willingly accept a life dedicated to the cultivation of *dharma*. (Roy, 1999: 5)

But taking part in the dialectic of homelessness and homecoming, self-cultivation and public engagement is not a smooth affair; it calls for us to be able to undertake suffering for the sake of our journey. Kant and Kantians such as Hart and Habermas forget this issue of suffering and here it is helpful to realize that for the sake of embodying a life of justice as "subjects in history," we have to prepare ourselves to undertake suffering, in fact embody the pains of a groaning humanity. For this we have to go beyond Kant as in the Kantian world we find little preparation for undertaking suffering for the sake of justice, an inadequacy which continues to haunt us even now despite the glorious chanting of Kant's name by many of us. For this we may need to befriend Gandhi. Gandhi presents us a passionate call for undertaking suffering for the sake of establishing peace and justice. Gandhi urges us to understand the link between morality and martyrdom, as he, following a long line of martyrs – Antigone, Socrates, Jesus Christ – lays down his life for the sake of peace and justice (Giri, 2002; Uberoi, 1996). Without mentioning the name of Gandhi, Edward Said also provides us a similar path of engagement. For Said (2000), the conflict between entrenched rivals such as Palestenians and Israelis cannot be resolved unless both the parties understand the suffering of each other rather than inflict suffering on the other and through such shared suffering lay the foundations of peace.

Thus, shared suffering is a key challenge now and the challenge for a morally sensitive development anthropology here is not only to describe the suffering of those who are violated by the logic of corporate globalization but also share this suffering in an embodied mode. Such embodiment of justice has its own mode of justification as well. Neo-Kantians like Habermas who are now celebrated heroes of a politics of inclusion of the other tell us that we must justify our beliefs to others through a process of rational argumentation. But rational argumentation has its limit in convincing the other about the soundness and significance of our moral beliefs and convictions. And here suffering – in fact, suffering undertaken for the sake of love – has the power to unlock the minds and hearts of others.

The need for such a mode of engagement which feels identified with the suffering of others and approaches one's own not from a position of valorized strength but from acknowledgment of human vulnerability has become urgent after the violent turbulences of September 11. On September 11, the twin towers at New York city were destroyed and thousands killed by the so-called terrorists. But what has to be our response to this? A key issue here, as heart-touching Indian anthropologist and philosopher Veena Das tells us: "Might we be able to mourn with the survivors of September 11 without the needing to appropriate their grief for other grander projects" (Das, 2001: 111). And, the grand project in the global order now is the war on terrorism but those who are leading this war do not want to acknowledge that their war on terrorism is itself a campaign in terror and posing a great threat to human security and global peace.

Thus, there is a need for a different response to the so-called problem of terrorism. The first thing is to realize that this problem cannot be solved through war especially when those who are fighting this war on terrorism are themselves terrorists in killing innocent children, women and men whenever they feel like doing it. They are enabled in their terrorism in the now triumphant ideology of just war (Hardt and Negri, 2000: 12). Now war has become part of the ideology of an imperial formation and here "Just war is no longer in any sense an activity of defense or resistance. It has become rather an activity justified in itself" (ibid.: 13). This new imperial mode of justification is now beginning to create new modes of justification for development. Now, the emerging new justification for development is: we must have development so that we would eliminate social situations of poverty and underdevelopment which breed terrorism. But development as global responsibility has to go beyond such instrumental and violent justifications. A humanistic development anthropology has to go beyond such instrumental and violent justification for development. A humanistic development anthropology concerned with the pathos of human suffering has a greater role to play in creating self-awareness that the key challenge here is not terrorism but the establishment of peace and help us remember what Erasmus had urged us to realize in his epochal work, *Complaints of Peace,* more than five hundred years ago:

> Peace speaks: If it were to their advantage for men to shun, spurn and reject me, although I have done nothing to deserve it, I would only lament the wrong done to me and their injustice; but since in rejecting me they deny themselves the source of all human happiness and bring on themselves a sea of disasters of every kind, I must shed tears rather for the misery they suffer than for any wrong they do me. I should have liked simply to be angry with them, but I am driven to feel pity and sorrow for their plight. (Erasmus, 1516: 293)

By putting forward visions of peace, justice and shared suffering development can contribute to reconstitution of hope in a new way as the global community is now at a turning point parallel to the catastrophic decades of 1940s when development had emerged as a new hope. Both socio-spiritual mobilizations in providing a new aspiration of human development and socio-political struggles for global justice and peace and the attendant preparation in undertaking suffering can provide a substantive content to development as hope in the present context. At present, we talk about development as hope only in an archaeological manner, characterizing the history of development in its formative years. But now we have to renew development as multiple practices of hope by undertaking multi-dimensional political and spiritual struggles all of which call for some amount of undertaking of suffering from all of us concerned. There is an intimate connection between suffering and hope and this is mediated through our concrete activities and relationships in the world.[4] But, at the contemporary juncture, there is a decline of hope especially as it relates to improving the quality of relationships in the world and in our readiness to undertake suffering for realization of social hope. Hope persists, if at all, mainly in our individualistic domains confined to issues of a rising income and one's own security. Now many of us cannot even hope that "someday we shall ever have a classless global society; one in which there are now vast differences open to children in one nation and another, or between those open to children in one section of a city and those in another section of the same city" (Rorty, 1999: 230; also see Wilfred, 2000).

In this context, to be able to hope requires courage – courage not only of the intellect and will but also of the whole being. But here we have to learn to hope in a new way different from the past modes of certainty. We would have to learn to hope in the concretes spaces of our socio-political and spiritual struggles but at the same time proceed with an acknowledgment of contingency and a sense of human finitude and fragility. But in coming to terms with the calling of global responsibilities neither contingency nor human finitude should be an excuse for not undertaking concrete activities which contributes self-development, reduction of human suffering and transformation of the world. As Chitta Ranjan Das urges us: "One liberates oneself by collaborating with a liberating process and that is perhaps how we collaborate in the march of this world of ours" (Das, 2001b: 179).

[I am grateful to Dr Philip Quarles van Ufford for his comments on this essay which is part of our larger collaborative work on development ethics and to Professor Fred R. Dallmayr for helping me with many of his unpublished papers. I also thank Professor N. Jayaram for his interest and the anonymous reader of *Sociological Bulletin* for his comments.]

Notes

1. Like Strydom, we owe the idea of co-responsibility to philosopher Karl-Otto Apel. Apel (1993, 2001) argues that to come to terms with ethical and moral challenges of our times neither indiviudal-centred micro-ethics nor society-centred macro ethics is enough. What is required is a planetary ethics of co-responsibility where all of us consider ourselves responsible to each other as member of a planetary community. Apel makes clear that this does not mean that all of us share the responsibility in the same manner. In a recent discussion, Apel also makes clear that "even if Iwas not the one who had ordered the war in Kosovo still I am not totally absolved of my responsibility" (personal communication).
2. Dallmayr, like Dumont (1994), is sensitive to the elitist bias in the historical manifestation of *Bildung* in Germany but for Dallmayr reviving the spirit of *Bildung* now is not to perpetuate elite culture or class privilege but to embrace popular culture with openness to learning.
3. This was the position of Jim Clancy, the CNN anchorman hosting the discussion on damage caused by violent protest in Genoa: "Who is Going to Pay for the Loss of Property?"
4. As philosopher Jayne M. Waterworth (2001) tells us: "[...] hope is an anticipatory activity; hoping is primarily something that people do, not something that just happen to them. Its significance is shown especially in contexts of suffering ... hope sustains the humanness of human beings ... ."

References

Apel, Karl-Otto (1993), 'How to Ground a Universalistic Ethics of Co-Responsibility for the Effects of Collective Actions and Activities', *Philosophica,* 52 (2): 9–29.

—— (2001), 'Globalization and the Need for Universal Ethics', *European Journal of Social Theory,* 3 (2): 137–55.

Appadurai, Arjun (2000), 'Grassroots Globalization and the Research Imagination', *Public Culture,* 12 (1): 1–19.

Baxi, Upendra (2000), 'Human Rights: Suffering between Markets and Movements', in Robin Cohen and Shirin M. Rai (eds.), *Global Social Movements,* London: Althone Press.

Beck, Ulrich (2001), 'Cosmopolitanism and Risk', Manuscript, University of Munich.

Bhaskar, Roy (2000), *From East to West: The Odyssey of a Soul,* London: Routledge.

Bourdieu, Pierre (1999), *Acts of Resistance,* Cambridge: Polity Press.

Carrithers, Michael (1983), *Buddha*, Oxford: Oxford University Press.

Clammer, John (2000), 'A Critique of 'Cognitive' Development Anthropology', *Anthropology Today*, 16 (5): 1–3.

Comaroff, Jean and John Clammer (2000), 'Millennial Capitalism: First Thoughts on a Second Coming', *Public Culture*, 12 (2): 291–343.

Dahrendorf, Ralph (1968), 'Der Geist der Aufklaring: die machbare Welt und ihre Grenzen', in Die angewandte Aufkarlung, Muncen: Fischer Bucheri.

Dallmayr, Fred (1998), *Alternative Visions: Pathways in the Global Village*, Lanham, MD: Rowman and Littlefield.

—— (2000a), 'Homelesseness/Homecoming: Heidegger on the Road', Manuscript, University of Notre Dame.

—— (2000b), 'Future of Tradition', Keynote Address presented at the International Seminar on 'Future of Tradition', Forum for Contemporary Theory, Aurangabad, December.

—— (2001a), 'Dialogue of Civilizations: A Gadamerian Perspective', Manuscript, University of Notre Dame.

—— (2001b), *Achieving Our World*, Lanham, MD: Rowman and Littlefield.

Das, Chittaranjan (2001a), 'Jagatikarana: Sanskruitka Atmaparichiti [Globalization: The Question of Cultural Idenity]', The text of a memorial lecture delivered in Sambalpur, India.

—— (2001b), 'Integral Education: The Vision and the Experiment,' in Ananta K. Giri (ed.), *Rethinking Social Transformation: Criticism and Creativity at the Turn of the Millennium*, Jaipur: Rawat Publications.

Das, Veena (2001), 'Violence and Translation', *Anthropological Quarterly* 75, (1): 105–112.

Dasgupta, Partha and Ismail Serageldin (eds.) (2000), *Social Capital: A Mulitifaceted Perspective*, Washington, DC: World Bank.

Dhanagare, D.N. (2003), 'Globalisation: Towards an Alternative View', *Sociological Bulletin* 52 (1): 4–31.

Dore, Ronald (1997), 'Trust and the Workings of Market Capitalism', Working Paper, International Social Science Institute, The University of Edinburgh.

Dreze, Jean and Amartya Sen (2002), *India: Development and Participation*, Delhi: Oxford University Press.

Dumont, Louis (1994), *German Ideology: From France to Germany and Back*, Chicago: The University of Chicago Press.

Escobar, Arturo (1995), *Encountering Development*, Princeton: Princeton University Press.

Erasmus, D. (1986 [1516]), *Querila Pacis: A Complaint of Peace Spurned and Rejected by the Whole World, The Collected Works of Erasmus*, Toronto: University of Toronto Press.

Giddens, Anthony (1999), *A Runaway World: How Globalization is Reshaping our Lives*, London: Profile Books.

Giri, Ananta (2000), 'Globalization of Hinduism: Swadhyaya in England and Sai Baba in Bali', *IIAS Newsletter*, 23: 10–11, October, 2000.

—— (2002), *Conversations and Transformations: Towards a New Ethics of Self and Society*, Lanham, MD: Lexington Books.

Hamelink, Cees (2000), *The Ethics of Cyberspace*, London: Sage Publications.

Habermas, Jurgen (1993), *Justification and Application: Remarks on Discourse Ethics*, Cambridge: Polity Press.

—— (1996), *Between Facts and Norms*, Cambridge: Polity Press.

Hardt, Michael and Antonio Negri (2000), *Empire*, Cambridge, MA: Harvard University Press.

Hart, Kieth (2000), 'Reflections on a Visit to New York', *Anthropology Today*, 16 (4): 1–3.

Harvey, David (1996), *Justice, Nature and the Geography of Difference*, Cambridge, MA: Basil Blackwell.

—— (2000a), *Spaces of Hope*, Edinburgh: University of Edinburgh Press.

—— (2000b), 'Cosmopolitanism and the Banality of Geographical Evils', *Public Culture* 12 (2): 529–64.

Huntington, Smauel P. (1996), *The Clash of Civilizations and the Remaking of World Orders*, New York: Simon and Schuster.

Levinas, Emmanuel (1974), *Otherwise than Being, or Beyond Essence*, Dordrecht: Kluwer Academic Publishers.

Mohanty, J.N. (2000), *Self and Other: Philosophical Essays*, Delhi: Oxford University Press.

Muthu, Sankar (2000), 'Justice and Foreigners: Kant's Cosmopolitan Right', *Constellations* 7 (1): 23–45.

Nederveen, Pieterse (2001), *Development Theory: Deconstructions/Reconstructions*, London: Sage Publications.

Offe, Claus and R.G. Heinze (1992), *Beyond Employment*, Cambridge: Polity Press.

Pollock, Sheldon et al. (2000), 'Cosmopolitanisms', *Public Culture*, 12 (3): 577–89.

Putnam, Hilary (2001), The Spinoza Lectures, Lecture 1: Three Enlightenments, The University of Amsterdam.

Putnam, Robert et al. (1993), *Making Democracy Work: Civic Traditions in Modern Italy*, Princeton: Princeton University Press.

Quarles van Ufford, Philip and Ananta K. Giri (eds.) (2003), 'A Moral Critique of Development', in *Search of Global Responsibilities*, London: Routledge.

Rawls, John (1999), *The Laws of Peoples*, Cambridge, MA: Harvard University Press.

—— (2001), *Justice as Fairness: A Restatement*, Cambridge, MA: Harvard University Press.

Rorty, Richard (1999), *Philosophy and Social Hope*, London: Penguin Books.

Roy, Ramashroy (1999), *Beyond Ego's Domain: Being and Order in the Vedas*, New Delhi: Shipra Publications.

Sachs, Wolfgang (1999), *Planet Dialectics: Explorations in Environment and Development*, London: Zed Books.

Said, Edward (2000), 'Invention, Memory and Place', *Critical Inquiry Winter*: 175–92.

Sen, Amartya (1999), *Development as Freedom*, Oxford: Oxford University Press.

Strydom, Piet (1999), 'The Challenge of Responsibility for Sociology', *Current Sociology*, 47 (3): 65–82.

—— (2000), *Discourse and Knowledge: The Making of Enlightenment Sociology*, Liverpool: Liverpool University Press.

Toulmin, Stephen (2001), *Return to Reason*, Cambridge: Harvard University Press.

Touraine, Alain (2001), Foreword to Ananta K. Giri, *Building in the Margins of Shacks: The Vision and Projects of Habitat for Humanity*, Delhi: Orient Longmans.

Uberoi, J.P.S. (1996), *Religion, Civil Society and State: A Study of Sikhism*, Delhi: Oxford University Press.

Unger, Roberto M. (1987), *False Necessity: Anti-Necessitarian Social Theory in the Service of Radical Democracy*, Cambridge: Cambridge University Press.

Wallerstein, Immanuel et al. (1996), *Open the Social Sciences*, Stanford, CA: Stanford University Press.

Waterworth, Jayne M. (2001), *Living in the Light of Hope: An Investigation into Agency and Meaning*, Department of Philosophy and Linguistics, Sweden: Umea University.

Wilfred, Felix (2000), *Asian Dreams and Christian Hopes*, Delhi: ICPCK Publishers.

17 Urban Crisis in Post-Liberalization Period

Implications for Urban Industrial Social Stratification

SANJAY MISHRA

The growth of modern cities and that of urban sociology is rooted in the history of industrial revolution. The founders of the discipline, such as Emile Durkheim[1] (1858–1917), Ferdinand Tonnies[2] (1855–1936) and Georg Simmel[3] (1858–1918), took keen interest in the study of the processes of urbanization and their immense impact on European societies. Cities grew rapidly in European societies, which provided the scope for the emergence of the concepts such as migration, industrialization, secularization and modernization, to name a few. The classical theories of city also came into existence and were widely applied. In short, the transition from traditional village life to urban modern life was the dominant concern of the earliest theorists. The perspectives evolved by them were based on their own wide-ranging experiences. They emphasized the social order, social cohesion and community ties in an environment of social differentiatio,n which was on increase in social life.

The classical theories were applied by the American sociologists in their study of North American cities. But, they had to go beyond the reaches of classical theories. Mainly two reasons were pointed out by them. first, the classical theorists had provided little empirical evidence. A bottom-up perspective was also lacking in early classical theorists. Hence, detailed information was needed to have a comprehensive view on how specific cities worked rather than emphasizing only on broad historical nature and process of the cities. Second, the classical theories could not explain the various possibilities associated with the process of changing economic order. For instance, how was it possible to distinguish the effects of urbanization from those of industrialization? Which characteristics of urban life are specifically attributed to the processes of urbanization and industrialization? A simple cause and effect method was practised in most of the early writings. Thus, the classical theorists could not visualize the impact of diversity and apparent fragmentation of city life.

The Chicago School, led by Robert E. Park[4] (1864–1944), emphasized the regular patterns along with hidden aspects of city life such as the life associated with ethnic ghettoes; the Chicago School was both empirical and interdisciplinary in borrowing concepts and methods from a wide range of sources. Park labelled his approach to urban life as human ecology or the "web of life" to show

how the different parts of a city depend on each other. Park encouraged his students and collaborator, e.g., Zorbaugh[5] study of 'Gold Coast and the Slum', Chicago, 1929, Burgess[6] thought of the city as concentric zone model, 1925, to find the regularities and patterns in social life of urban areas. Subsequently, researchers developed 'sector model[7] and 'multiple nuclei model'.[8] Thus, the search for uniform model to describe and explain the city was not possible through the complexity at the global level.

Besides location and growth of different areas of cities, the Chicago School also made an attempt to study the social life. Louis Wirth[9] did the widely quoted work "Urbanism as a way of life" in 1938. He found three factors the size, density and heterogeneity of the population – which were instrumental in shaping the social relations form in the cities.

After 1950, the Chicago School branched out in several new directions, such as social areas analysis, community ethnography and so on. Though, ecology remained an important paradigm to study urban social life.

Another paradigm of political economy was influenced by the theories of Karl Marx,[10] Friedrich Engles[11] and Max Weber.[12] These theorists observed the same phenomenon 'urban' and developed different understandings and interpretations of their underlying causes. Although Marx did not focus directly on cities, some concepts that he introduced in other contexts were used to analyse urban phenomena. His most famous contribution is the recognition of urban industrial working class or proletariat.

Weber set out the idea that a single dimension, such as population size, cannot define a city. He says that the existence of city lies not in its size alone but also in its economic and political functions. Weber's successors used his contribution to study urban patterns of inequality and conflict based on social divisions, such as race, ethnicity and religion as well as those based on class divisions.

Two factors contributed to the growth of political economy paradigm – the limitation of human ecology paradigm to explain varied urban patterns and the ever-changing conditions of urban life during 1970s which was markedly different from the 1920s when ecologists developed their theories. The factors related to the accelerated sub-urban growth in relation to city population raised several issues which could not be scientifically addressed by the ecologists. Thus, the political economists argued that it is necessary to look beyond the growth patterns of the city to examine the factors that made it possible to sub-urban areas to grow. Increasing polarization in terms of race and income also assumed the focal point for political economists. The changing role of the government in urban affairs and the changing nature of economy and its impact on cities laid the groundwork for the emergence of political economy approach to study urban issues. In short, the political economists held a consensus view that:

(a) Cities are the outcome of political, economic and social arrangements of their times rather than products of natural resources:
(b) Cities are shaped by the decisions made by powerful actors who control resources.
(c) Distribution of resources helps shape urban patterns and urban social life.

(d) Economic restructuring, or a pattern of widespread shifts in tile economy is one of the main factors affecting local communities.

Numerous studies on the third world urbanization are rooted in political economic orientation, which critically analyses the subordinate role that less developed countries play in the world political and economic system to contribute to their patterns of city growth. Analytically, proponents of political economic paradigm have identified three types of urban unevenness. First, demographic and economic balances occur between the urban and rural set-up. This imbalance is usually referred to as 'overurbanization' or 'urban bias'. Second, skewed patterns of population distribution are characterized by concentration of people and resources in largest places, leading to debates over 'optimal city size' and 'urban primacy'. Third, material disparities within cities are reflected in dualistic patterns of housing, consumption and access to political participation. This helped produce literature on slums, squatter settlement, urban poverty and informal sector

Immanuel Wallerstein's[13] image of the world system is hierarchical and is composed of three layers of countries: the core, the periphery and the semi-periphery. The core is the 'advanced' nations promoting imperialism. The periphery has been exploited by the core nations and suffers from underdevelopment. The semi-periphery is an in-between layer which is characterized as the prosperous industrial southern European nations.

Historical case studies and cross-national researches have revealed that dependent cities (periphery) are characterized by unevenness of all three types. The role of the peripheral cities can be explained by saying "peripheral primate cities are nodes on the conduit which transmit surplus values to the core and dominate the periphery, while primate cities in the core receive surplus value and transmit domination".[14] These suggest that contrary to the historical experiences of the western nations, there is no natural link between urbanization, on the one hand, and industrialization and economic growth, on the other. In fact, rapid uneven city growth and relative economic stagnation are likely to occur together in the third world countries, since both are associated with high levels of international economic dependence. Moreover, patterns of urbanization, migration and urban economic and social structure are affected by the changing contexts of industrialization and the power of the elite. That is why, different countries and cities have experienced divergent path of development.

Urban Crisis in Post-Liberalization Period

The growth of cities continued unabated in post-independence India as has been revealed by census reports and other governmental and non-governmental surveys conducted from time to time. Most of the socio-economic surveys of cities are descriptive in nature which could be used for further analysis.

Very little attention is paid to the methodological problems of urban studies. Though, various studies conducted on the subject were confined to urbanization, city and region, urban function, urban internal physical structure, urban social organization, urban community, urban social problems and urban planning. These studies have failed to apply rigorous standards to find out the causal relationship to the problem under investigation. Some of these studies also suffered from inconsistencies with regard to the objective of the study, methods and theoretical framework. Moreover, these studies have not developed any useful theoretical perspective and generalization which could be applied to other urban centres. Thus, the studies on urban India lack a theoretical perspective, which can be applied to contemporary urban issues which have emerged in the post-liberalization period.

The post-liberalization period has witnessed unprecedented events in urban industrial centres (metros, medium and small), such as an influx of immigrants both economically and occupationally better-off and landless labourers from rural areas and an unprecedented unemployment in urban industrial centres due to the closure of small and medium size industries and privatization of large public sector industries. These reasons have been assigned to the obsolete technologies of small and medium-sized industries and attempt to improve dwindling financial bottom line of the public sector units located in urban centres. Industrial units of both organized and unorganized sectors have been exposed to the tremendous challenges to cope with the wave of liberalization of Indian economy. Shedding and becoming slim at every human cost is the buzzword of both sector. Consequently, a large number of small and medium-sized units were closed forever. In the post-reform era, the shrinking employment in PSUs, organized sector jobs share dips to 14 per cent. The growth rate of public sector employment has fallen by almost 56 per cent.[15] Thus, the number of jobless has grown as organization cuts flab to survive.[16] The capability of the state to create job opportunities is extremely limited in the process of liberalization. As a result, the employment in organized sector has not grown in any significant manner. On the other hand, a steady decline in the proportion of regular salaried workers is more likely in future as observed in the past decade. This trend is gaining momentum in contemporary period. Much of the employment growth in the economy is taking place through a process of sub-contracting, using casual and self-employed workers. As a result, city is exposed to unorganized sector and non-regular salaried workers that have a high incidence of poverty.[17] Apart from this, these types of workers are included in tertiary sector, which has resulted in a steep decline in the percentage of manufacturing employment in urban areas.

The decrease of industrial employment in urban areas is also partly attributed to relocation of large units outside the municipal limits due to environmental concern.[18] In some cases owners have consciously shifted the industrial units for better use of high valued urban land for residential complexes. Furthermore, the capacity of unorganized sector to absorb rural migrants seems to be drying up in post-liberalization period. Thus, the growth of cities depending on migrants on rural areas seems a remote possibility. The real differences in wage rates and person days of employment, etc., in urban and-rural areas, have gone down in the 1990s. Therefore, the decline in the inflow of migrants at the margin of rural economy certainly shall depress the rate of urbanization. This will place rural poverty at par with urban poverty. Also, the rate of unemployment in urban areas will be higher than in rural areas.[19]

The accelerated growth of urban industrial centres in the situation of overurbanization has far outpaced the ability of the state and municipal governments to meet the growing civic amenities particularly of the rural migrants and low skilled industrial displaced workers. Restricted land use and all kinds of zoning restrictions have further affected the expansion of metro cities. Apart from this, tendency to institutionalize disparity and availability of civic amenities within the large cities and strengthening of the process of segmentation have been noticed with the empowerment of local government. Furthermore, privatization of the land and civic services in general is likely to push up their prices, particularly in metro cities. These growing situation of scarce civic amenities will further depress immigration of the poor people. The socio-economic consequences of this will be seen in the increase of crime, violence, depersonalization, alienation and increased economic inequality. As a result, it will give a setback to recent efforts to promote social justice and ensure human rights. The physical condition of cities is characterized by overurbanization, pollution, congestion, ugliness and so on. As a result, nobody can be satisfied with the form of city life today.[20] It is an accepted cliche that we live in an age of urban crisis.[21]

Urban unevenness in India has increased over past decade. Cities which have introduced state-of-the-art technology in their production system have maintained the momentum of growth in comparison to cities which have failed to introduce such technologies. In this era of cut-throat competition, it seems that the principal of 'survival of the fittest' is applicable to the survival of at least small and medium size cities. Therefore, shrinkage, in city size is inevitable in post-liberalization period. The old industrial cities have been shaken by an over all decline in manufacturing jobs. Large organizations providing long term employment for workers are on the decrease.

The availability of low education at entry level of jobs in cities have dropped sharply. Therefore, mismatch between people and jobs is growing. It seems that cities are moving as 'dual cities' because of tendency towards income polarization. The reason may be assigned to the growth of informal and unorganized sectors, which have depressed the wage levels. Finally it seems that a fundamental restructuring of cities, which involve the physical restructuring of central business district as well as economic and social restructuring, is taking shape in post-liberalization period. This wide-ranging transformation of the characteristic of the cities has created a situation of urban crisis.

Implications for Urban Industrial Social Stratification

The changing economic reality has necessitated the delayering and reconstitution of urban industrial social stratification. There is a mad rush to flatten, delayer, downsize and to deal with surplus manpower. Both private and public sector units are in the process of modernizing their production technology to meet the challenges of liberalization. Consequently, a large number of workers (both managerial and non-managerial) were asked by their respective management to accept voluntary retirement scheme under their structural adjustment programme. As a result, a large number of workers have lost their jobs. In some cases, they were even forced to accept the voluntary retirement scheme. In addition to this, the changing economic reality has prompted industries to focus on their core competencies and hive off non-profitable and non-synergetic business leading to the reduction in the number of jobs.

The market conditions, coupled with considerations of cost of production and technological dominance, are such that the nature of jobs is changing. Several traditional jobs are loosing importance with the introduction of new technology. Even existing jobs, which require skill inputs from outside as well as exposure to different areas, will have to be done differently. Technical changes have increased the proportion of skilled workers. It may lead to qualitatively new type of composition of workforce resulting into a new urban industrial social stratification.

A perceptible change is taking place at all levels of urban industrial social stratification. At the upper echelon of the stratification, the techno-managers are replacing the traditional managers. The changing needs have redefined the managerial roles to a large extent, making reinvention even more necessary at the lower layers. The importance of middle-level supervisory layer is vanishing because of the introduction of capital-intensive technology which significantly reduces the number of workers. Furthermore, restructuring exercise to suit the new technology is reinforcing the concept of team-based management from the shop-floor to the upper layer, which again undermines the position of supervisors.

It also appears that technological changes have increased the proportion of skilled and contractual workers and the proportion of semi-skilled and unskilled workers are decreasing in the composition of the workers. It may lead to the emergence of qualitatively new type of composition. Moreover, the restructuring exercise of human resources has created new biology and chemistry at the workplace. Changing organizational structures by hiving, combining, sell off or disinvestment, privatization, and introduction of state-of-the-art technology have become common phenomena in post-liberalization period. The restructuring exercises have induced changes in the constitution of each layer of urban industrial social stratification. To conclude, the above mentioned reflections are the indicators of a process of change in the existing urban industrial social stratification, which will crystallize in due course of time.

Notes

1. Emile Durkhiem (1964), *The Division of Labor in Society*, New York: Free Press.
2. Ferdinand Tonnies (1969), *Community and Society*, New York: Harper and Row.
3. Georg Simmel (1905), "The Metropolis and Mental Life", reprinted in the *Sociology of Georg Simmel*, edited by K. Wolff, New York: Free Press, 1950.
4. Robert E. Park (1936), "Human Ecology", *American Journal of Sociology*, 42: 1–15.
5. Harvey Zorbaugh (1929), *The Gold Coast and the Slum*, Chicago: The University of Chicago Press.
6. Ernest W. Burgess (1925), "The Growth of the City", in *The City*, edited by R.E. Park, E.W. Burgess, and R.D. Mackenzie, pp. 47–62, Chicago: The University of Chicago Press.
7. Homer Hoyt (1939), *The Structure and Growth of Residential Neighborhoods in American Cities*, Washington, DC: Federal Housing Administration.
8. Chauncey Harris and Edmand Ullmen (1945), "The Nature of Cities", *Annals of the American Academy of Political and Social Sciences*, 242: 7–17.

9. Louis Wirth (1938), "Urbanization as a Way of Life", *American Journal of Sociology,* 44: 1–24.
10. Karl Marx (1971), *The Grundrisse,* edited and translated by D. Mclellan, New York, Harper and Row; 1970, *A Contribution to the Critique of Political Economy,* New York, International Publishers.
11. Friedrich Engles (1958), *The Condition of the Working Class in England,* Stanford: Stanford University Press.
12. Max Weber (1958), *The City,* edited and translated by D. Martindale and G. Neuwirth, New York: Free Press.
13. Immanuel Wallertein (1976), *The Modern World System,* New York: Academic Press.
14. Christopher Chase-Dunn (1992), "Urbanization in the World System: New Directions for Research", in J. John Palen, *The Urban World,* New York: McGraw-Hill Inc., Fourth edition.
15. Sanjukta Mitra (2000), "Organized Sector Job Share Dips 14 Percent", *The Economic Times,* New Delhi, 26 October, p. 6.
16. Gubir Singh (1999), "Corporate India's Load Shedding Comes with a Very Heavy Human Cost", *The Economics Times,* New Delhi, 20th January, p. 6.
17. Amitabh Kundu (2000), "Trends and Structure of Employment in the 1990s: Implications for Urban Growth", in Uma Kapila, ed., *Indian Economy Since Independence,* New Delhi: Academic Foundation, p. 923.
18. Ibid., p. 923.
19. Ibid., p. 234.
20. Lewis Humford, "The Urban Prospect", quoted in J. John Palen, op. cit., p. 251.
21. J. John Palen, op. cit., p. 251.

18 Socio-cultural Construction of Competence and Professional Hierarchy

J.S. GANDHI

Point of Departure

Professions, as viewed in the context of sociology of professions, are located in a secular domain, and are also subject to the principle of achievement, meaning thereby that hierarchy in a professional fraternity is performance-based, and is not guided by the criteria of generational elitism, or any other particularistic parameters. Accordingly, it would mean that the son or daughter of a professional need not benefit from the level of professional achievement represented by his or her father or mother. It would also imply that one does not benefit from one's social network in building one's position in the professional fraternity. Notwithstanding an occasional dilution of this principle in actual practice, this is supposed to be the guiding principle governing professional hierarchy as stated ideal – typically in the theory of professions.

However, as against this simplistic paradigm, what is sought to be argued here is that the hierarchy in a professional setting, i.e., hierarchy among the lawyers in a district court setting, is constructed very significantly through particularistic factors as well such as those ensuing from one's family connections and intimate social network. The data used here is indeed outdated, i.e., two decades old or even more, but since the author has been constantly writing and researching in this field, more particularly in Delhi now, no compulsive evidence has come to the fore to change this perception of professional reality. It would look appropriate to argue, therefore, that the traditional character of Indian society, i.e., its *gemeinschaft* character continues to weigh heavily even on the professional (secular) domain and significantly determines the professional stratification or the system of professional hierarchy. But, we shall revert to this theoretical assertion later after we have presented some discrete data.

Brief Description of the Overall Nature of the Professional Work Available at the District Court

As a part of the overall scenario in which we are attempting to locate our main argument, it seems logical to start by outlining, legal practice of Gobindgarh courts[1] can be categorized into three main areas distinct from each other: criminal, civil, and revenue. As reported by the Bar members and also objectively speaking, these three fields of activities cover the entire gamut of legal practice in which the lawyers at Gobindgarh courts are engaged. *Criminal practice* refers to all such cases as are triable under the Indian Penal Code and/or under various statutory legislations passed by the state to meet the requirements of security and 'law and order' objectives. This includes all criminal offences – both major and minor – classifiable, respectively, as cognizable and non-cognizable offences. All these cases are tried according to the latest revised Criminal Procedure Code of April 1974. *Revenue practice* refers to such litigation as relates to any one or more of the juridical aspects of agricultural land or such land as is charged land revenue. Disputes here may be related to partition, sale, inheritance, or revenue on an agricultural land. All such litigation as is not covered under the above two categories falls under *civil practice*. This may include a whole range of issues from rent or sale of urban property to those covered under the personal and social laws. In other words, it includes a wide range of issues and problems of civil life, which are justifiable in a court of law. Both revenue and civil cases are governed by Indian Civil Procedure Code.

Some of the questions which we shall try to answer in this study are: What is the incidence of 'specialized' versus 'mixed' practice at the courts, i.e., what segment of the Gobindgarh Bar takes to any one of these three practices exclusively, and what segment engages in more than one type of practice; we shall also try to account for this situation? Besides, we will see whether success achieved by a lawyer in practice can be related to the degree of his specialization.

One general impression carried by both the lay as well as informed observers is that the legal practice becomes specialized only at High Courts and Supreme Court while it is of a *mixed* and *omnibus* variety at the District Courts. An obvious corollary to this impression is that the process of specialization starts at High Courts and reaches its apex at the Supreme Court. Furthermore, the practice at Supreme Court may be confined not only to one of the above noted three categories of practice but to a sub-category or even to a sub-sub-category of practice, such as employer-employee relations instead of the general category of labour cases, and writ petitions instead of the general category of civil cases. Based upon this generalized impression rather than on sound empirical facts, Charles Morrison (1969) reports from his study of a District Court in Haryana that, "there is little specialization in Indian district practice ..." Contrary to this, Gobindgarh study reveals a significant degree of specialization at the District Courts. We also find, as discussed in subsequent sections of this chapter – and this is also because the tendency to specialize is rooted in the nature and dynamics of legal practice as well as in the social milieu of its location, from where it is drawn. There is also a strong and positive relationship between the degrees of specialization in practice and the level or degree of professional achievement in one's career. As a result, specialization in practice comes to function as a dynamic process of professional standing and achievement.

Practice Specialization as the Sub-structure of Professional Hierarchy

In all, we have identified four categories of legal practitioners in our study: (a) exclusive, (b) semi-exclusive, (c) non-exclusive, and (d) satellite practitioners. The first three categories may be seen to constitute a continuum of descending order of specialization in practice. As we move from category (i) to category (iv) through category (ii) and (iii), the degree of 'exclusiveness' decreases. In other words, the practice becomes increasingly 'mixed' in the same order of continuum. Therefore, the downward polar end of the continuum, i.e., category (iv) represents almost evenly matched proportion of two or more varieties of practice.

The fourth category of satellite practitioners, as we shall see, does not fit into the continuum of specialization indicated, since this category has hardly any distinctive characteristic of its own, except that the lawyers of this category are placed in a different set of career opportunities than those characterizing the earlier three categories. From the standpoint of specialization, which is the hallmark of the earlier three categories and even distinguishes them mutually, the satellite lawyers may thus be said to constitute a residual category.

The fourfold classification of lawyers is derived from the information furnished by our respondents about their own practice as well as about the practice of their colleagues. The veracity of the information was confirmed through an initial test check of twenty cases. This could be explained in terms of respondents' awareness regarding researcher's access to the entire bar. As such, we elicited from the practitioners themselves, most of the basic information needed about his practice and subsequently sought its corroboration as the work progressed.

For analysing the data regarding practice and career of the four categories of lawyers, we have used a broad framework comprising of three sub-divisions: (a) nature of practice and clientele composition, (b) social background, and (c) lifestyle.

Exclusive Lawyers

By exclusive lawyers we refer to those lawyers who confined themselves exclusively to one type of practice to the almost complete exclusion of the other two. This does not imply that the practitioners so identified did not accept cases from outside their own area of specialization. They did accept such cases when offered but it happened only occasionally, and then more often than not, they traded these cases by passing them on to their colleagues who needed to put in less of the preparationti me, since the cases fell in their routine area. Hence, generally, they stuck to their own area of specialization. From amongst the whole of the Bar we identified only twelve lawyers answering this descriptions – six from criminal practice and three each from civil and revenue practice.

It was corroborated by all the respondents interviewed at Gobindgarh Bar that a significant chunk of the total practice at Gobindgarh District Courts was handled by only a handful of the exclusive lawyers. To quote a typical response:

> Ten per cent of the Bar monopolizes ninety per cent of the total business and the remaining ninety per cent of the Bar members fight among themselves for mere 10 per cent of the total business.

This may be an overstatement but none of our respondents, including the exclusive lawyers themselves, disputed the view that the few lawyers identified as exclusive lawyers handled among themselves at least 50 per cent or more of the total business available at the District Court. It is not possible to determine the exactitude of the professional monopoly on account of the highly sensitive nature of the required information and also because the magnitude of the practice might refer to any of the two dimensions, namely, total fee charged from the clients and the number of cases handled by these lawyers. All the same, without discounting the usefulness of the inquiry in this direction, we present below some perceptual evidence of the professional monopoly:

Table 1

Extent of Concentration of Practice among Exclusive Lawyers as Perceived by Exclusive Lawyers and Other Bar Members

Category of Practice	*As perceived by other lawyers*		*As perceived by exclusive lawyers*	
	Lower range of practice concentration	*Highest range of practice concentration*	*Lowest range of practice concentration*	*Highest range of practice concentration*
Criminal	70	85	55	65
Revenue	75	85	60	65
Civil	60	70	50	60

Table 1 presents cross-sectional data on practice concentration among exclusive lawyers. As this table shows, the phenomenon of heavy concentration of practice in a few hands is affirmed by all the Bar members. A comparison of the lowest and the highest range of practice concentration for the exclusive and the non-exclusive lawyers shows that there is a marked difference between the versions of the two categories of lawyers. There may be two explanations for this trend. The comparatively higher degree of concentration projected by other lawyers may be related to their personal grudge and relative deprivation they suffered.[2]

At the hands of the exclusive lawyers, it implies that they tend to overemphasize the cleavage between themselves and the exclusive lawyers on account the latter's cutting into their business interests. On the other hand, a comparatively lower assessment of practice concentration as projected by the exclusive lawyers by way of an understatement of professional reality may be with a view to counteracting the general impression of near-complete monopoly of legal business by them and putting up a more humane public front.[3] It is also relevant to record here that, in the informal interviews, both the biases of 'under' and 'over' emphasis on the practice of monopoly of legal business were imputed to each other by these two respective categories of lawyers in unmistakable terms. In any case, both the versions taken together support the broad inference regarding the monopoly in the legal business enjoyed by the exclusive lawyers.

The comparatively lower magnitude of practice concentration perceived in civil practice as against criminal and revenue practice is on account of the higher degree of variations in the nature of this practice as against the latter two. As mentioned earlier, litigation cases under this category are of a large variety. Every individual civil lawyer cannot, therefore, develop the same expertise in handling the full gamut of civil cases, which means that the extent of business concentration would be restricted in this area.

The only way to verify these subjective reports on the state of professional monopoly at Gobindgarh District Courts was by looking through the 'diary of daily attendances' maintained by a 'munshi' for the daily conduct of the business of his lawyer-employers. We could not succeed in this as this is a well-guarded professional record and is within the reach of only two persons, the lawyer and his munshi.[4] The munshis, despite repeated persuasions, refused point blank on the plea that they will risk the wrath of their employers and their jobs if they made such records available to an outsider.

Another useful source which could possibly throw some light on this feature of lawyer's practice was the court records called the 'Cause List' which is a list of cases due for the *next*[5] day finalized by each court on the preceding evening. Even though the version of the list pasted outside the court room does not contain the names of the counsels engaged on the listed cases, those available with the court office do have this information. Since this information on the identity of counsels engaged on the specified cases is not preserved beyond sometime, compilation of information for large stretch of time was not possible. All the same, we tried to salvage whatever of this data we could lay our hands upon. We collected from various court records the information corresponding to various categories of practice for the month of March 1974, with a view to work out the number of daily appearances in respect of exclusive lawyers as a totality. The retrieval of further data for computation could not make a headway because of the mess in hitch the records were kept by the courts and also because of the fact that disparate figures kept in different courts could not be integrated together for purposes of reckoning. We are aware of the inadequacy of the evidence presented here to hazard a clear inference; however, we hope that our observations will set the tenor for deeper investigations in future along these lines.

Table 2 below also throws some further light on the problem:

Table 2

Average Daily Appearances by Practice Type for Exclusive Lawyers

Practice	*Number of Practitioners*	*Number of appearances per day for all the lawyers*	*Average number of appearances per day per lawyer*	*Range of variations in daily appearances per day among all lawyers*
Criminal	6	87	14.5	2–26
Civil	3	85	28.3	15–47
Revenue	3	79	26.3	17–38

The table shows that the average number of appearance per day per lawyer for criminal practice is the lowest and for civil practice it is the highest. This characteristic of criminal practice is understandable in view of the general fact that as a criminal lawyer rises in professional standing, i.e., as he becomes more and more in demand and is offered progressively higher fees by his clients, he concentrates more and more on serious criminal cases. He concentrates especially on the 'hurt' cases, i.e., those triable under IPC 302 and 306 which are far fewer in number compared to the total number of cognizable crimes,[6] for the obvious reason that such cases fetch a four to ten times higher fee than that charged for minor crimes.[7] The extent to which one handles serious criminal cases is also taken as a measure of one's professional standing, both by one's professional peers as well as by clients-to-be. It is this professional standing which enables a practitioner to charge higher fees from his clients than do the others who do not enjoy such professional and social esteem. It may thus be observed that this self-imposed restriction on the number of cases by an exclusive lawyer through confining himself to a specific category or sub-category of cases, does have its compensating pay-off in establishing him higher in the professional reckoning, thus commanding a higher fee from the clients.

Nearly, entire clientele of civil lawyers is urban, since the civil cases are related to urban property. As reported by some senior civil lawyers, even when a case concerning non-agricultural property comes up from village, it has usually a revenue dimension to it. In other words, such a case is invariably interconnected with some dispute about an agricultural piece of land. Since mostly a revenue lawyer handles such a case, it is classifiable as a revenue case. As far as the clientele for revenue cases is concerned, this is exclusively rural since these cases concern land located within the jurisdiction of some village or the other. However, the clientele of criminal lawyers may be of either rural or urban origin, since the practice deals with the phenomenon of criminality as such which is not specific to rural or urban background.[8]

Table 3 shows the rural-urban composition of the clientele of exclusive lawyers. Excepting one Brahman practitioner, virtually, the entire clientele of exclusive lawyers on the criminal side is drawn from rural areas. This Brahman lawyer specialized in cases of trafficking in smuggled and contraband articles from across the border of Pakistan. His clients reportedly were exclusively from Gobindgarh city.[9]

Table 3

Rural-Urban Percentage of the Clientele of Exclusive Lawyers for the Criminal Side

Caste	*Rural clientele*	*Urban clientele*
Khatri (1)	90	10
Khatri (2)	90	10
Brahmin	30	70
Jatsikh	100	—
Arora (1)	75	25
Arora (2)	99	1

Table 3 presents the caste composition of the exclusive lawyers, who are drawn from Khatri, Arora and Bania castes, and representing the mercantile syndrome. Even in the absence of necessary data, it can be generalized on the basis of the personal knowledge of the area that the Khatri-Arora-Bania nexus controls an extremely large proportion of business and commerce in Gobindgarh district.[10] The Jatsikhs, who constituted nearly 20 per cent of the District Bar, had only one member to represent them in this category of exclusive lawyers.

This is despite the fact that this caste contributes heavily towards criminal litigation in the district. The Barahman caste is also represented by a lone member in this category of lawyers. But, as reported by some senior members of the Bar, whereas a Jatsikh has rarely occupied a position of eminence at the Gobindgarh Bar, the Brahmans have quite often belonged to the top segment of the Gobindgarh Bar.

Table 4

Distribution of Exclusive Lawyers by Caste and Type of Practice

Caste	*Criminal*	*Civil*	*Revenue*	*Total*
Hindu Khatri	1	—	2	3
Sikh Khatri	1	—	—	1
Hindu Arora	2	2	—	4
Sikh Arora	—	—	—	—
Brahman	1	—	—	1
Bania	—	1	1	2
Jatsikh	1	—	—	1
Total	6	3	3	12

All the lawyers, with the exception of one Jatsikh, were drawn from urban background. They were born in big urban centres classifiable as a city, neither a town nor a village. Further, all except the Jatsikh lawyer had been living in Gobindgarh town for the last forty years or even more. The Jatsikh lawyer was born and brought up in a village in a tehsil headquarters within Gobindgarh district. It is thus observed that the entire top layer of the Bar, with the exception of one Jatsikh lawyer, is drawn from the urban centres.

All the exclusive lawyers, except the Jatsikh, were of sixty years of age or more. The Jatsikh was fifty-two. From this it appears that a minimum of twenty-five to thirty years of practice is a prerequisite for a lawyer to reach the top layer of the professional hierarchy at a District Court Bar.

Conspicuous Consumption: Living Style of the Exclusive Lawyers

A style of living marked by conspicuous consumption was the hallmark of exclusive lawyers in Gobindgarh. It was observed by a large number of both the semi-exclusive and the non-exclusive lawyers that in order to get a continuous supply of high-fee cases, it was also necessary to put up an exterior of expensive living.[11] According to them, if an exclusive lawyer allowed the impression of living in a penny-pinching style, gain ground, he was sure to come down in social as well as professional esteem. Even though no lawyer would speak of his bank balance and other assets, we could form an idea of their manner of living partly from information supplied by them, partly from our direct observation, and partly from information supplied by their colleagues.

All the twelve exclusive lawyers owned costly landed property worth between two lakhs and ten lakhs rupees.[12] All of them owned posh bungalows, six of them having constructed them on the elite outskirts of the town.

By way of an illustration, we quote below from the investigator's field diary about Mr Kapoor, an exclusive revenue lawyer, belonging to the Khatri caste:

> Kapoor lives along with his two married sons (one of them practicing with him and the other running a chemist shop) on the 'Y' road, which runs on both sides with impressive-looking bungalows of retired military officers, judges, and affluent businessmen. The house has a built area of 200 sq. yards along with two very spacious lawns, covering approximately 700 sq. yards. As one enters the bungalow from the main gate, one finds oneself flanked by the grassy, neatly mown velvety lawns. The front of the house is decorously built like a sophisticated hotel. In the spacious drawing room, there is a wide array of cushy chairs and sofa-sets along with glass top centre tables. A special care has been taken in providing the room with various modern amenities such as giant sized refrigerator, television set, radiogram, etc. Even though Kapoor maintains his office far away from his residence, yet even at his residence he keeps an adequate library with appropriate reading chairs and one easy chair. The books in the side showcases are mostly of the non-legal type, i.e., classifiable as popular classics such as *Discovery of India* or those of Bertrand Russell or S. Radha Krishnan. Kapoor admits that he has built a fortune out of his practice. Besides this house of the valuation of rupees five lakhs, Kapoor also owns an extensive agricultural farm at a distance of 10 miles from Gobindgarh, which gives him a regular income of over two thousand rupees a month. This residential complex of Mr Kapoor is far removed from his office in the commercial hub of the city at a distance of two miles.

Even though it may be hazardous to generalize on a solitary evidence, it is interesting to note that the spacious bungalow possessed by the Jatsikh exclusive lawyer, even though costly and spacious, bears a sharp architectural contrast to the residential complex of Mr Kapoor described above, and is typically in the style of a prosperous agriculturist's house in a village. Once again, the field-notes read:

> The house bears a typical pragmatic look with a single complex catering to nearly all activities of the Jatsikh lawyer while he is not attending the court. As one enters the bungalow from the main gate, one faces a little to one's right a semi-circulate porch reminiscent of buildings occupied by the British civil servants in a district headquarters in the late 19th century. Likewise, the spacious waiting room under the porch here serves as a waiting room for all visitors to the household. It opens simultaneously into three rooms (i) the library-cum-office, where the lawyer receives his clients; (ii) the drawing room where he sits and often drinks in the company of his friends and family friends. The verandah is lined with three long sitting benches often found in civil hospitals. There is no lawn in the house, with the exception of a very badly kept patch of yellowed grass and broken soil. Recently, another lawyer from his home tehsil has come to join him a partnership and has occupied a portion of this house.

It is obvious from the above that the emphasis in this rural-drawn lawyer's lifestyle is one of pragmatism and need-integration, i.e., on having one building complex comprising a residence, an office, and a consultation room for the clients. The separation between office and residence so punctiliously observed by other exclusive lawyers is absent in the case of this lawyer coming as he does from an agricultural background. He is a lawyer who seems to have grafted his rural lifestyle of a zamindar on to his urban setting.

All except one Jatsikh practitioner maintained their offices away from their place of residence.[13] The rationale for keeping apart the office and the residence, as provided nearly by all the exclusive lawyers, was that it guarded the 'health' of both the places by isolating their tensions and problems. One civil lawyer reported:

> I do not think one can remain physically and mentally healthy if one lumped office with family life. Intervals of time I spend at my residence relax me and give me a vigor to work harder and harder. I can also snatch some moments of rest and leisurely chitchat with my wife and children. They also come to feel that I do exist for them and not only for my clients and their problems. Believe me sir, whenever my clients disturb me at my residence. I feel miserable. I wish I could shut them out completely from my family life. Another reason why one should try to have separate office is that one should always keep one's domestic life private to oneself.

Another important item of personal property in the case of all the Exclusive lawyers was a car parked in the court's compound. As reported by the munshis of these lawyers and also by their juniors, display of a plush car to the clients and the clients-to-be played an important role in fostering a impression of affluence before the general comity of lawyers. The car was also used sometime in taking the clients to the court from the lawyer's residence or office where they may have come for briefing or consultations early in the day in connection with case listed for the later part of the day or the next day. When a lawyer or his junior had to represent a client at a teshil court – and this happened especially in revenue cases, the client accompanied the lawyer in his car, and it was the former who invariably paid for the petrol. A similar impression of conspicuous living was also conveyed through a lavishly furnished office with attractive array of books and journals.[14]

Semi-Exclusive Lawyers

Logically, all the lawyers other than the exclusive ones may be designated as non-exclusive, in the sense of being 'not' exclusive. However, non-exclusive practitioners may be further divided into the categories of semi-exclusive and non-exclusive. This classification is introduced to discern two different gradations of non-exclusiveness. By semi-exclusive lawyers we mean those who pursued one of the three kinds of practices predominantly and another as supplementary or secondary specialization. Non-exclusive lawyers imply those whose practice could be described as 'mixed', in the sense that they engaged themselves randomly in all the three varieties of practice. This was primarily because of the short supply of business to them so that they took up whatever case came to them.

As revealed in informal interviews, the predominant area in the case of all semi-exclusive lawyers accounted for a minimum of 80 per cent of their total practice. Table 5 classifies the 111 semi-exclusive lawyers according to predominant area of their practice. These lawyers also account for the largest of the four categories of lawyers, covering 111 out of 154 Bar members (72%). Within this category, the largest number have civil as their predominant practice area (47.8%), the smallest being engaged in revenue practice (12.6%).

Table 5

Distribution of Semi-Exclusive Lawyers by Primary Area of Practice

Primary area of practice	*Lawyer's frequency*	*Percentage*
Criminal	44	39.6
Civil	53	47.8
Revenue	14	12.6
Total	111	100.0

It is seen from Table 6 that civil and revenue practices are closer to each other than either of them is to criminal practice. Thus, while 44 out of 53 (83%) civil practitioners had revenue as their secondary area of practice, 10 out of 14 (71%) revenue practitioners had civil as their secondary area of practice. Likewise, out of 44 criminal lawyers, 29 (66%) had revenue and only 12 (27%) had civil as their secondary area of practice.

Table 6

Distribution of Semi-Exclusive Lawyers by Secondary Area of Practice

Primary area of practice	*Civil*	*Criminal*	*Revenue*	*Total*
Criminal	15	—	29	44
Civil	—	9	44	53
Revenue	10	4	—	14
Total	25	13	73	11

There may be two explanations for relatively greater interaction between civil and revenue practice than between civil and criminal practice. Firstly, both civil and revenue practices are subsumed under the same Civil Procedure Code. Therefore, a practitioner needs to master only one code to handle both civil and revenue cases. 'Parsimony of effort' may thus be advanced as the basic reason for this situation. On the other hand, pleadings for and presentation of criminal cases demand the knowledge of a different body of studies, namely, Criminal Procedure Code. This explanation by itself, however, does not adequately clarify the relatively closer fit observed between criminal and revenue than between criminal and civil practices. This particularity obviously needs further elucidation.

The clientele for revenue cases is drawn from and that for majority of criminal cases is drawn from identical social setting, i.e., the rural milieu.[15] On the other hand, clientele for criminal and civil cases is drawn from two different settings, viz., rural and urban milieu, respectively. The criminal and revenue cases emanate from the identical social base of rural setting. Naturally, therefore, a criminal lawyer who has already established his base in a village or a set of villages a large supplement of revenue cases comes from the same contacts and clients with whom he has already established a rapport during the course of his criminal practice. This substantiated from the interviews of two semi-exclusive lawyers. First, we report from a 50-year-old lawyer having revenue practice as his primary and criminal as his secondary area of practice:

> As already mentioned, the only contact I had at the time I started my practice was my father-in-law who had just retired as sub-inspector of police. He promised to help me with his contacts in police got me was regarding recovery of illicit liquor. Police party on raid had recovered a pitcher full of illicit liquor from a family. I applied all my wit and diligence and obtained a ruling from the court that the evidence furnished by police was of suspect veracity. My client got acquitted. Another case concerning another accused in the same case was going on simultaneously at another court. The defence counsel in that case happened to be the topmost criminal lawyer of Gobindgarh District Bar. He took benefit from the court's verdict on my case and consequently the court dismissed the police case against his client. News got around that topmost criminal counsel had benefited from my adept handling of the case. This spread my reputation and I started getting from the same village and its neighborhood not only criminal but also revenue cases.

The second report is from a 45-year-old semi-exclusive lawyer working primarily on the side of revenue litigation:

> People know me here of course not as a top lawyer on the revenue side, but as one in the second line. During some months, I have been netting more than even the first liners. All of us on the revenue side have suffered a setback ever since the Government brought in legislations on 'preemption' and 'declaration', according to which title on land has been clearly defined and thus the litigation arising out of this issue has gone down. Consequent upon this development, all of us have been looking for some alternative sources of income. 'X' has taken to a bit of income tax practice. 'Y' has started teaching in a local law college. I have been trying to get some criminal cases, of course not of the 'highly paid' variety such as a hurt cases because they would simply not come to me because of my modest standing in this area, but minor cases such as recovery or smuggling cases. Recently, I handled a case of sill for making illicit liquor and got my client acquitted. Once I set my mind on such cases, it is not difficult to get them since I already have my rural be through my revenue practice. But, in case I continue to get adequate supply of revenue business, I would not look out for criminal cases.

According to the characteristics of the category of semi-exclusive lawyers described earlier, these lawyers had one of the three types of practices as their main forte and either of the remaining two, as the secondary practice. The number of daily appearances of all semi-exclusive lawyers, worked out on the same lines as those of exclusive lawyers, are given in Table 7 with Table 2 for exclusive lawyers manifests certain trends.

Table 7

Average Number of Daily Appearances of Semi Exclusive Lawyers by Type of Practice

Type of practice	*Number of practitioners*	*Appearances per day for all lawyers together*	*Average number of appearances per day per lawyer*	*Range of variations in appearance per day*
Criminal	44	383	8.7	5–21
Civil	53	761	14.3	4–22
Revenue	14	159	11.3	7–27

The average number of appearances per day in both the cases follows a similar pattern. Thus, here also, the civil practice tops with 14.3 cases per day and the criminal practice comes at the bottom with 8.7 cases. The revenue practice with 11.3 cases per day retains its middle position. The explanation afforded already with respect to exclusive lawyers applies here, too.

With respect to the range of appearances per day, Tables 2 and 7 provide an interesting contrast. Whereas for civil as well as revenue practice both the highest and the lowest ranges of court appearances are higher for the exclusive than for the semi-exclusive lawyers, for criminal practice the lowest range of daily appearances for the semi-exclusive lawyers is higher than that for their exclusive counterparts. The explanation lies in the fact that while exclusive lawyers take up serious criminal cases, i.e., hurt cases, which have a high-fee potential and are comparatively scarcely available, the semi-exclusive lawyers are not able to attract many such cases and, therefore, have to do good with the criminal cases that are of common run. These cases are comparatively not only more in number but are also less remunerative. Therefore, a semi-exclusive lawyer has to take up a larger number of cases than his exclusive counterpart to earn enough for a comfortable living.

The rural-urban composition of the semi-exclusive lawyers is given in Table 8. Nearly 60 per cent of semi-exclusive lawyers came from rural background and 40 per cent from urban background. This is due to the fact that for two of the three predominant practice areas, namely, criminal and revenue, a vast majority of the clientele is drawn from rural areas. In fact, for revenue practice, it is needless to say that the entire clientele comes from rural areas. And, for criminal practice too, the majority of clients are drawn from this background. Table 3 also confirms this pattern for exclusive lawyers on the criminal side, which shows that with the exception of a solitary lawyer who specializes in customs and excise cases from Gobindgarh town, the percentage of rural clientele ranges for them from 75 per cent to 100 per cent of the total. This correspondence between the social background of the clientele and that of lawyers is conducive to the promotion of a lawyer's practice since he can conveniently cultivate his social contacts for building up professionally useful linkages and supply points. Urban clientele is predominant only in civil practice. As already remarked, civil cases are mostly related to non-agricultural property. The clientele is, therefore, bound to be confined almost exclusively to the urban areas, which, in turn, promotes the entry of urban-based lawyers.

Table 8

Rural-Urban Background and Predominant Area of Practice of Semi-Exclusive Lawyers

Predominant area of practice	*Lawyers with rural background*		*Lawyers with urban background*		*Total*
	Number	*Percentage*	*Number*	*Percentage*	
Criminal	37	84	7	15.9	44
Civil	17	32	36	67.9	53
Revenue	12	85.7	2	14.2	14
Total	66	59.4	45	40.5	111

Table 9
Distribution of Semi-Exclusive Lawyers by Age

Age	Frequency	Percentage
33–40	45	40.5
41–48	28	25.2
49–56	17	15.3
57–64	15	13.5
65–66	6	5.4
Total	111	99.9

Table 9 shows the age distribution of semi-exclusive lawyers. Granting that a lawyer must have taken nearly 14 years after the age of 5–6 years in acquiring a pre-law graduation degree, followed by another two years in law graduation, he may be considered to have been initiated into legal profession not earlier than the age of 22–23 years. Table 9 further reveals the heaviest concentration of lawyer in the youngest age group 33–40, implying that the largest single group in the category of semi-exclusive lawyers had been in the legal profession for a period ranging from 11 to 18 years. As we move towards higher age-groups, the concentration of lawyers successively decreases, so that the total number of semi-exclusive lawyers is only 5.4 per cent in the age group 65–66. This supports the tentative generalization mentioned earlier that a majority of lawyers become economically self-dependent through their earnings from legal practice by the time they complete 10 to 15 years of practice.

What about the remaining two-thirds of the semi-exclusive lawyers under the higher age groups? Is it a fact that despite their having been in practice for two or three decades, they have not moved up towards the exclusive category? The answer is in the affirmative, and the explanation for it lies in the special set of circumstances that beset the career profile of the exclusive lawyers but not the semi exclusive ones.

While none of the semi-exclusive lawyers except one had a car, all of them without exception owned a scooter. None of these lawyers had a house or a house site on the posh outskirts of Gobindgarh as is in the case of exclusive lawyers. Only 17 out of a total of 111 lived on the outskirts of the town but in localities inhabited by refugees from Pakistan. In the case of only 43 (38.7%) the office was separated from the residence, i.e., located away from the residential setting. In the rest of the cases, it formed part of the residential complex. This arrangement was usually in terms of parsimony of time, money, or effort of traveling between residence and office. Note, for example, the following typical report from a 38-year-old Hindu Khatri lawyer practising predominantly on the criminal side:

> I have started doing well only recently, i.e., for the last two years or so, which is to say that I now make around two thousand rupees a month … . Some friends suggested to me that I should take a separate office, away from my residence, but I don't think it is worthwhile. I think I can give more time to my clients if I cut on the time taken in shuffling between my office and residence. It also saves me money and besides, I can always be handy if my family needs me on some urgent business … . Let me tell you another important advantage of this arrangement. The sight of clients coming to my residence for consultation also makes me important in my own locality. People think that I am an important man both professionally and socially. This also fetches me some additional business from my locality.

Another characteristic feature of the lifestyle of semi-exclusive layers is a good deal of 'property hunt'. One often finds them floating too many enquiries for purchase of a piece of land, a housing plot or a constructed building. Such exploratory curiosity is conspicuously lacking among exclusive lawyers as well as among non-exclusive and satellite lawyers. The obvious explanation for this is that generally it is after a period of 15 to 20 years of practice that a lawyer, after meeting one's current expenditure, is able to save enough to invest in some immovable property. A typical illustration in this regard is that of a 50-year-old revenue practitioner with twenty-two years of practice, who frequently talked about his building and the various amenities provided in it. He started as a tenant in a two-storeyed building some twenty years ago and eventually bought up the whole building. Lately, he has also added two storeys to the building, so that now, as he says:

> It is the tallest building in this area, and whenever I feel depressed due to some domestic worry, a look around the house fills me with a sense of pride. This only gives me an idea, how much I have travelled professionally .... I want to show you my building one of these days. The construction of the top floor is yet on, and I am going to have a fountain on the top floor ... . Inside my building on the first floor I have my office and library having as many as five thousand volume.

Non-Exclusive Lawyers

As mentioned earlier, this category includes those lawyers who pursued 'mixed' practice. They engaged themselves in all varieties of practices depending upon what cases they could get, which usually fetched them thirty to three hundred rupees each. Further, the different types of practices did not constitute a regularly fixed quantum of their total practice per unit of time, say a week or a month. That is why, a majority of them could not assign even tentative income values to each of the three practices they were engaged in.

In all, we identified 31 lawyers under this category. Even though all of them shared the common attribute pursuing 'mixed' practice, we identified three sub-categories among them, according to the status of their practice and career. We call them (i) young strugglers, (ii) late starters, and (iii) poor performers.

For a meaningful discussion of the peculiarities of these sub-categories, we shall deviate slightly from the patter of presentation so far followed in this chapter. Instead of arranging data under such themes as practice, social background, and lifestyle, we shall present whatever material we have collected under each individual sub-category. Towards the end, however, we shall again refer to the data for all the three sub-categories together.

The numerical strength of the three sub-categories of non-exclusive lawyers is shown in Table 10.

Table 10

Distribution of Non-Exclusive Lawyers by Age

Sub Category	*Age*	*Frequency*	*Percentage*
Young strugglers	22–31	17	73.9
Late starters	48–59	3	13.0
Poor performers	68–76	3	13.0

The age composition among the three sub-categories is irregular and discontinuous. It may, however, be mentioned here that the age grouping was not resorted to as a mark of distinction between these three sub-categories. Recourse was taken to it for exposition of the lawyer's career histories, circumstances and their professional standing or position. An analysis of data about these lawyers obtained through objective data-schedule as well as unstructured interviews, marked them out as clearly belonging to the distinct three sub-categories. As the description below would show, there is ample justification for viewing them as separate sub-categories, even though they all share the common attributes of pursuing 'mixed' practice.

Young Strugglers

All 'young strugglers' could be described as fresh entrants who had not yet found their feet in the profession. They had to labour hard to eke out the barest living. As such, they could little afford to choose between one type of case or another, since they faced bleak business prospects ahead. More than half of them drew upon their family resources to keep them going. To quote a young entrant:

> Do you know that a beginner like me does not earn even a hundred rupees a day? At the same time, the moment you complete your law, every body expects you to be self-supporting. Your entire family wants it and expects it. Rather, they have a highly unrealistic image of this career and think that one starts making fat earnings as soon as one occupies a seat in the court .... But it is a hard going, a very tough going, sir. No body comes to you even for filing an application or a petition, let alone a challenging brief in the fuller sense of the term. They think you are yet a suckling baby and need to learn a lot. So, we have to grab a petty civil suit or a client looking for the registration of his land he has just acquired – anything will do. There is no room for choosing. Those who tell you they choose a case are frauds ... they are just laying and cheating you.

Let us take note of another report with a similar refrain from another practitioner of the same category:

> No use cheating you by giving false information that 'I have this brief or that brief'. I speak only for myself that I don't have enough cases. So, it does not make any sense classifying them .... I hunt and hunt around for all available touts and agents and get whatever business I can at whatever commission to these people. In fact, I treat a tout as affectionately as I would treat my new client. I want him to be happy with me this time so that he can bring me more cases next time.

Of the seventeen young strugglers, only three could ascribe precise proportions to each of the three types of practices they were engaged in. Their evaluation is presented in Table 11.

Table 11

Distribution of Practice of Three Young Non-Exclusive Lawyers by Type of Practice

Age	*Percentage of total practice*		
	Criminal	*Civil*	*Revenue*
26	10	30	60
26	50	30	20
28	10	60	30

These three lawyers were adjudged by the rest of their fellow counterparts as doing 'best of all'. This also evoked jealousy among the latter since they did not consider the trio as being more intelligent or more hard working than themselves. In several lunchroom sessions, which the investigator shared with these young lawyers, feelings of such jealousy were ventilated unreservedly and pointedly.

Each of these three lawyers had earlier worked as a junior or assistant to two or more exclusive lawyers from at least two different branches of practice at the initial stage of their practice. They also reported as having established a good rapport with their seniors, which continued even after they started their independent practice. As a result, their ex-seniors helped them with 'minor', less remunerative cases, which they were not inclined to handle themselves. To quote one of the three young successful lawyers:

> Even now 'S' supports me by sending cases without charging any touty.[16] As I told you, I left him early because I could not cope up with his sharp temperament. But I have never had any complaint about his fair deal and fair play. He told me at the time I joined him that I would get one/third of our weekly earnings. I left him not because he was dishonest, but because he flared up every now and then and even resorted to abusing. But, more important than anything, I wanted to settle on my own. He was civil lawyer, and so, in addition to some civil cases, which flowed in from him after I left him, I started acquiring some revenue and criminal cases through some touts. It was only after all these adjustments that I could get enough business to live by.

Another youngster (No. 2 in Table 11), who worked earlier as a junior to a civil lawyer and later switched over to criminal and revenue practice, benefited from contacts and connections he had cultivated during his attachment with his senior. Even after he started his independent practice, he continued to get a regular supply of business from these contacts, although on payment of higher 'touty' than charged from his senior.

Late Starters

All the three late starters struggled to eke out a living from all sorts of cases that fell to their lot. Hence, their practice was a collection of all three types of practices. Two of them had left behind varied careers of social service, active politics, teaching, and journalism. They decided to do law when they crossed the age of forty. One of them reported that during the early phase of his political career he had felt handicapped in understanding the true dynamics of political life in the country, particularly the relation between his party – Communist Party of India – and other political parties on the scene, because he had no knowledge of law. The opportunity came to him when he was appointed as executive officer of a municipal committee in nearby town through the influence of his party. He then joined law classes as a private student and graduated successfully within two years. This was at a ripe age of forty.

The second late starter retired from Military Accounts Service at the age of forty-five. With the meagre pension he received he could not support his wife and children. Therefore, immediately on his retirement, he secured his admission in law faculty as a private student and graduated in due course. At the time of interview he had been in practice for over three years.

The third later starter, of 58 years of age, was the oldest of the three. He had been in police department as prosecuting sub-inspector,[17] till about four years ago. He incurred the displeasure of his seniors and resigned from his job. Then, he enrolled himself as a member of Gobindgarh Bar and started practising.

Poor Performers

The sub-category of poor performers, as one member of the Bar described, represented the 'backwash' of the profession at Gobindgarh courts. They were all in civil practice. They had never done good business in their career. They were not much communicative with the investigator and appeared dejected and withdrawn. From whatever could be gleaned from them and about them, they seemed to have blundered their way into the profession. They had no contacts whatsoever to help them in getting business in the initial phase of their career, nor did they cultivate any contacts in the course of their career. They had none of their family connections in business, in courts, or in police. Throughout their career, they had to resort to some alternative sources of income for supporting their families, such as doing some 'side' business or doing some part-time job in a business concern.

All the three poor performers, it was reported, worked as 'touts' for other lawyers. Even when they got some case, they were not confident of handling it on their own. Of the cases they themselves handled, nearly all could be termed as 'petty suits', such as filing an application for staying the court proceedings on behalf of their clients, which brought fees from about twenty to one hundred and fifty rupees. Two of these three lawyers were from Khatri Sikh caste, and one was a Khatri Hindu.

Satellite Lawyers

The satellite practitioners are so called because they do not practise on their own, but work for their senior colleagues from whom they get a fixed amount ranging from five hundred to a thousand rupees per month. It was only rarely that such a lawyer was allowed some fixed percentage of the total income of his senior on a regular basis. They had virtually no independent practice, since nearly all the cases on which they appeared were listed in the name of their seniors for whom they worked as juniors. Nearly all the exclusive lawyers had such juniors working with them. It was very seldom that the clients agreed to a junior handling a case independently, but whenever it happened it was more because of the high professional reputation of the senior than because of his own standing. To quote a satellite lawyer, the son of an exclusive revenue lawyer:

> I do not make secret of the fact that I get cases because of my father. Frankly, some of my colleagues ten years my junior are more competent than I ... but they do not have the advantage which I have ... . The clients who let me represent them know that I have the advantage of top professional expertise at my backing. They also feel that I can have some possible access to the judges through my father.

Hence, the epithet of 'satellite' is used for these lawyers to bring out that the fact they lack the basic criteria: *autonomy of professional practice*, which, by definition, is the defining mark of every lawyer. Instead, they play instrumental, supportive or 'satellite' roles vis-à-vis other lawyers.

In all, there were nine satellite lawyers, eight of whom worked with eight exclusive lawyers in different areas of practice, and the ninth with a semi-exclusive lawyer on the criminal side (see Table 12).

Table 12

Satellite Lawyers

	Caste of senior lawyer and his satellite respectively	*Religion of the satellite lawyer*	*Area of practice*	*Category of senior colleagues*
1.	Khatri-Khatri	Hindu	Revenue	Exclusive
2.	Aggarwal-Aggarwal	Hindu	Revenue	Exclusive
3.	Khatri-Khatri	Hindu	Revenue	Exclusive
4.	Arora-Arora	Hindu	Civil	Exclusive
5.	Arora-Arora	Hindu	Civil	Exclusive
6.	Arora-Arora	Sikh	Criminal/civil	Semi-exclusive
7.	Khatri-Khatri	Hindu	Criminal	
8.	Khatri-Arora	Hindu	Criminal	Exclusive
9.	Brahman-Aggarwal	Hindu	Civil	Exclusive

As this table shows, four of the nine satellite lawyers were Arora, three Khatri and two Aggarwal by caste. Eight of the nine of them worked with their fathers, whereas the ninth (No. 8 in Table 12) worked with a lawyer on the criminal side, who virtually treated him as his own son. The said satellite lawyer (i.e., the 9th in the listing in the table) reported:

> I have been working with 'C' as his junior for the last ten years or so. He has never treated me just as an 'assistant'. He gives me a handsome share of the total income earned by both of us. He every now and then gets me a suit length or any such gifts. The only favours, I think, I do to him is to look after certain routines of his business such as settling fee with the clients, looking up relevant references from the books, briefing the clients and their witnesses, and keeping track of our work-calendar in the court, etc. But, then we do have a munshi working for us as well. I talk to my age-mates and they all say that such a nice behaviour is foreign to the mentality of a senior lawyer ... . It is no doubt a rare coincidence and a rare luck for me.

As is obvious from the above statement, a near-complete understanding between a satellite lawyer and his senior is necessary for the perpetuation of this profession – though unequal relationship between them. This is facilitated, in the case of nearly our entire sample of satellite lawyers, through the kinship bonds between the two. Objectively speaking, keeping in view the meagre compensation doled out to the junior for his assistance, the relationship may be termed as exploitative, even though not so perceived or so voiced by the satellites themselves. All the same, the relationship and its perpetuation can be appreciated in terms of cost-benefit analysis. Obviously, a son would inherit the entire professional network of his father as well as a bit of his professional repute to start ahead of his other age-mates and consequently, push faster towards the exclusive category.

As stated by the satellite lawyers, contacts and social influences multiply fast through their professional associations with the eminent lawyers. They look forward to using all these connections eventually to their own advantage on settling into independence practice. To quote the son of a semi-exclusive lawyer on criminal side (No. 6 in Table 12):

> I got a case for tehsil 'H' a few months back ... my case was the last on the fore-noon list. After the case was over and the court adjourned, I was informed by the reader of the presiding officer that the judge Sahib would like to see me in the ante-room ... . As soon as I entered his room the judge got up from his seat with a loud "hello", saying, 'why didn't you tell me that you are the some of ... . Your father was my class fellow ... . Sit down and have some tea with me'. Afterwards, he told me that if it was inconvenient for me coming to his court for the case all the way from Gobindgarh I could fix up a local counsel and just show him once ... for the rest, he said; the interest of my client would be taken care of.

Social and Cultural Construction of the Professional Hierarchy

In this section, we shall pool all the information provided in the preceding sections to argue our case – that even though, ideal-typically speaking, the basis of a professional hierarchy, like that of class hierarchy,[18] of which it is but a conceptual sub-set, is expected to be secular, in reality, however, the professional hierarchy, as revealed in our study, is heavily shaped and influenced by non-secular or particularistic factors. That is to say, rather than *de facto* performance becoming the cause and reason of where one is located in the professional stratification,[19] we find that connections, contacts and network linkages, play the determining role. But first, a few theoretical observations about hierarchy as such, and then its elucidation through the facts of the case study.

A researcher's conceptualization of hierarchy in a social group or any other structurally identifiable social grouping should correspond as closely as possible to members' own perception of it. In other words, the analytical categories employed by the researcher should bear a realistic semblance to the perceptual cognitions of the subjects themselves. In reality, however, there is rarely a close-fit between the two since the former, i.e., objective inferences are objective whereas the later are subjective influenced by predilections and at times, wishful thinking of the subjects or the cognitive impositions from outside.[20]

Indeed, there have been some attempts at integrating the subjective and objective dimensions of hierarchy – but more in the classical tradition, than contemporaneously.[21] In the account that follows, we shall first discuss the nature of stratification that emerges from the available data and then try to integrate the subjective and objective dimensions of the stratification.

Keeping in view the above elucidation, let us have another look at the fourfold classification of lawyers as identified in the discussion above. The four categories, it may be recalled, are:

(i) exclusive lawyers,
(ii) semi-exclusive lawyers,
(iii) non-exclusive lawyers, and
(iv) satellite lawyers.

Further, we have also seen that categories (i) to (iii) are arranged primarily in the decreasing order of specialization of practice or correspondingly, increasing proportion of 'mixed' practice, and also that category (iv) is atypical or residual in that the lawyers of this category do not pursue their own practice but are on the pay-roll of their senior colleagues. As such, this category does not admit of the specialization principle. The analysis that follows is confined mainly to the first three categories.

Subjective Correlates of Hierarchy

How does the lawyers at Gobindgarh District Courts generally perceive hierarchy in the Bar? Can different perceptions of hierarchy be related to specific sections of the Bar? To answer these questions we draw here extensively from the terms and nomenclatures employed by the Bar members for denoting hierarchy in the Bar without any attempt at conceptual refinement. On a perusal of some loose observations made by the Bar members, two kinds of perspectives on professional hierarchy emerge: the general and specific. While the former is common to the whole of the Bar, the later is linked to the Bar's specific sections. The hierarchies by Bar members are observed to have been induced by a variety of criteria and in more than one context.

1. The most commonly perceived hierarchy by the Bar members is only bi-polar, i.e., comprised of the 'top' and 'the rest' of the Bar. Only the former is spelt out clearly and includes all those identified by us as members of the exclusive category plus half a dozen more drawn from the semi-exclusive category of our description. The perceived hallmarks of all these lawyers are 'ability', 'experience' and 'reputation'. The consensus of opinion is that most of the practice at Gobindgarh courts is monopolized by the top, but the extent of monopoly is perceived differently by different sections of the Bar. Those included in the semi-exclusive category attributed the monopoly a lower value, 40 to 50 per cent of the total practice than those under the non-category. The latter viewed the extent of this monopoly of practice in a higher range of 55 to 80 per cent. This differential degree of monopoly – attribution to the 'top' lawyers by the semi-exclusive and non-exclusive lawyers – may be understood as a function of their relative deprivation, or as a the non-exclusive lawyers with hardly any practice to their credit perceived the gap between the 'haves' and the 'have nots' more sharply than the semi-exclusive who had comparatively rather a bit stable and up-swing practice.
2. Another term most commonly used by nearly all the Bar members was 'first choice at the courts', identifying one lawyer each from criminal, civil and revenue practice. This implied, as viewed by the respondents in question, that a certain hypothetical client looking for the best counsel at Gobindgarh court would opt for the lawyer identified by the respondent as 'first choice' in the relevant area of practice. Obviously, therefore, the core criterion in this perception is professional reputation and excellence. The twelve lawyers falling under the exclusive category and four lawyers from the semi-exclusive category were identified as 'first choices' if the responses of all Bar members are taken together. One sees, therefore, a near correspondence between the composition of the exclusive category and its popular construction as the 'first choice' by the Bar members, i.e., between the

objective and the subjective dimensions of social hierarchy. But there still remains one important difference between the two. While the researcher's or objective categorization of exclusive lawyers exists only in relation to other differentiated categories of semi-exclusive and non-exclusive lawyers, the subjective categories of 'top' and 'first choice' lawyers exist with reference to the undifferentiated mass of the rest of the Bar. In other words, in popular professional perception, the reference point for professional hierarchy is only its top summit, and the respondent does not bother to further differentiate between the rest of the Bar.

3. There is yet another professional hierarchy perceived by the Bar members, which is specific only to one section of the Bar, the semi-exclusive lawyers, as against the above mentioned perceptions which are common to the whole of the Bar. This perception divides the entire Bar into: (a) the top of the Bar or the first liners, (b) the second liners in which the semi-exclusive lawyers included themselves, and (c) the starters or the younger group.

   The first of these categories, viz., 'the top of the Bar' or 'the first liners' corresponds nearly entirely to exclusive lawyers, with the only difference that three of the twelve exclusive members – one each from each practice area – are dropped, so that only nine are identified as the first liners. The second liners are inclusive of the semi-exclusive lawyers themselves, whereas most of the rest, up to the age 39–40, are styled as 'starters' or as constituting the 'younger group'.

   The remaining, i.e., those above the age of 40 that are not covered by the above three categories, are casually mentioned by the semi-exclusives as 'unsuccessful' or 'not too serious about practice'. These lawyers, as perceived by the semi-exclusive lawyers, have not come up in profession on account of a complex of several factors: one, deficiency of professional contacts required for promotion of practice, especially in the earlier stages; two, lack of proficiency to speak persuasively; and three, lack of initiative and hard work.

As we look more closely at the three-tier division of the Bar as perceived by the semi-exclusive lawyers, we recognize an implicit recognition of the principle of practice – continuity through generations required for rising eventually to the top of the Bar. This is so because the semi-exclusive lawyers perceive themselves as second liners, i.e., immediately behind the 'top' lawyers, so that, if given time, they would naturally join the rank of the 'first liners'. By the same logic, those in the third category are styled as 'starters', i.e., those who have just started their upward professional mobility and, if given the time, are likely to gravitate towards the two higher echelons of professional hierarchy. In brief, the semi-exclusive lawyers have a more optimistic outlook towards their career than the Bar as a whole and the non-exclusive lawyers in particular. This may also be expressed by saying that they tend to universalize and extend their successful experience and career optimism to the rest of the Bar. Having successfully tidied over the teething phase of their professional career, they find no reason to feel any career uncertainty abut the future of new entrants. That is why, the categories perceived by them imply, in general, regular progression of professional career.

Objective Correlates of Hierarchy

Besides the preceding classification of the Bar hierarchy as envisaged by its various constituents, there are some other objective correlates which, in the popular perception of the professionals, go along with the highest placed lawyers at Gobindgarh. These include a variety of attributes – material, professional, and reputational. For example, nearly everybody in the Bar associated a high and a conspicuous standard of living with them. It was also felt, generally by all lawyers and particularly by the non-exclusive lawyers that the clients are unduly carried away by mistaken notions about the brilliance of the top lawyers and thereby became willing tools in their exploitative hands. Finally, the Bar had a general feeling that the top lawyers enjoyed much greater respect and consideration from the judiciary than the rest of the Bar and than they really deserved. For example, wherever the scheduled dates for hearing of their various cases conflicted with each other, the judges obliged them willingly with alternative dates to suit their convenience – a favour that they rarely extended to others, particularly to the 'starters'.

A perusal of the perceptions of hierarchy held by the Bar members and those deduced by us through objective indices of 'specialized' versus 'mixed' practice (i.e., the hierarchy split between exclusive, semi-exclusive and non-exclusive lawyers) underlines one basic contrast among the lawyers. That is, whereas we have taken into account the entire range of professionals present at the Bar for formulating a three-fold stratification of exclusive, semi-exclusive and non-exclusive, the professionals themselves perceive this hierarchy essentially in bi-polar terms – comprised of 'this and the 'rest', or 'haves' and 'have nots', thus reflecting the perception of deprivation between those who are professionally settled and those who are not. However, if we have a look at the middle category in our objective hierarchy, i.e., the semi-exclusive lawyers, a bi-polar classification of the Bar does not afford a realistic picture, because a substantial segment of the Bar can be logically placed in between the two poles of the subjective hierarchy, i.e., 'haves' and 'have nots'.

It is worthwhile to remark that the subjective categories come closest to our objective classification only through the linkage point of semi-exclusive category, i.e., through the perception of the regular progression from 'have nots' to 'haves'. Located as these professionals are at the mid-point of career process, it seems they are able to have a comprehensive overview of the Bar and the professional career profile. Keeping up a regular and continuous career progress, they are yet to reach the summit. All the same, they feel sure of achieving it in future, since they can already perceive a clear contrast between their own professional position and that of those who are still down the hill and are struggling to come up.

Keeping aside the distinctive attributes of subjective and objective hierarchies, a summation of elements from the two sets of hierarchies is attempted in Table 13.

The tabular presentation of professional hierarchy above also affords an easy interpretation.

Table 13

Integration of Subjective and Objective Elements of Professional Hierarchy

	Constituent elements of subjective and objective hierarchies					
Category of lawyers	*Degree of speciali-zation*	*High professional earnings*	*Prestigious living*	*Highly paid practice*	*Evaluation by the colleagues and also the clientele*	*Availability of kindred-based contacts in career-building*
1	2	3	4	5	6	7
Exclusive	+ +	+ +	+ +	+ +	+ +	+ +
Semi-exclusive	+ –	+ –	+ –	+ –	+ –	+ –
Non-exclusive	(–)	(–)	(–)	(–)	(–)	(–)

As we can see, columns 2, 3, 4, 5 and 7 can all be viewed as objective indicators or correlates of hierarchy. But, all these indicators are not of the equal status, or in other words all these are not objective in an identical sense. Whereas, columns 2, 3, 4 and 5 have an indisputable consensus, both among the professionals at large and the general public and have a defining significance for the category that one belongs to, column 7 constitutes the very *raison d'etre* of the professional stratification. This is because, it is on account of these kindred-based contacts[22] that top 12 lawyers classified as exclusive lawyers are able to rise to the top of the bar as it comes out copiously through their's as well as their colleagues' narrations. This variable, i.e., No. 7 thus causes and determines the top of the hierarchy, which in essence becomes the reference point for the other two categories. As we saw, though many of the semi-exclusive lawyers had put in the same number of years, the only characteristic they lacked was the benefit of kindred connections in promoting their business. The top 12 lawyers, i.e., the exclusive lawyers are thus liberally fed and furnished by their intimate kindred connections.[23]

The chief marker of the professional hierarchy, therefore, is the abundance and availability of particularistic ties and connections and not the performance-based de facto distinctions, which ought to be the case with any secular hierarchy. We may thus argue that the *gemeinschaft* character of the Indian society impinges heavily on this domain, which is supposedly universalistic and based upon rational-legality.[24] This analysis goes for various dimensions of the professional hierarchy, which can be broadly termed as *objective*. As we can see, all these dimensions, i.e., 2, 3, 4, 5 and 7 coalesce well with the other dimension, i.e., 6, which is purely attributional and *subjective*, i.e., 'evaluation by colleagues and the clientele'. The subjective and objective dimensions of the professional hierarchy are, therefore, found to be largely congruent and coterminous.

Notes

1. Pseudonym for the milieu of study located in Punjab.
2. For a discussion of the concept, see Merton (1971): 281–84, 288–89 and 295.
3. It is interesting to note that the exclusive lawyers, even when admitting of professional monopoly, attribute it to lack of initiative on the part of the rest of the Bar, especially the young lawyers, rather than to a monopolistic tendency on their part or to their reticence towards the younger lawyers.
4. *Munshi* is a traditional Urdu-Persian expression used frequently in the context of the District Courts to denote a lawyer's clerk, who looks after his business, such as the case diary and court calendar, dealings with his clients and also getting him more business – though at a separate commission.
5. That is the day after such a list is pasted on the walls outside a court room.
6. As revealed by the statistics published by the Punjab Government for the year 1975, 'hurt' cases (inclusive of 'murder' and 'culpable homicide') for the whole of Punjab numbered 807 out of a total of 12,360 'cognizable crimes', or merely 6.5 per cent of the total. The corresponding figures for Gobindgarh district for the same year are 129 out of a total of 2,180 cases of cognizable crimes, i.e., roughly 6 per cent of the total. Incidentally, the number of both 'cognizable crimes' and 'hurt' cases for Gobindgarh district is the maximum among all the districts of the state (see Statistical Abstract of Punjab, issued by the Economic Adviser to Government of Punjab, Chandigarh, 1976, p. 369).
7. For example, it was reported that for a in or cases of recovery of opium or of illicit liquor, a lawyer may charge between Rs 50, and Rs 200, while for a hurt case the fee fluctuates between Rs 500 and Rs 2,000.
8. As recognized under Indian Penal Code.
9. It was reported by lawyers practising criminal cases that nearly all the clients of Brahman lawyers worked as carriers on behalf of some rich businessmen of the town who had invested huge sums in the smuggling trade. According to a standing arrangement with their employer, whenever police caught them, their employers met all the expenditure required for their defence in a court of law and invariably engaged this Brahman lawyer as a defence counsel.
10. This is not only a feature of contemporary Gobindgarh society but was also true of this society in the beginning of the twentieth century. The Imperial Gazetteer of 1908 reports: "Khatris (34,000) and Aroras (22,000) are the chief trading castes." The Imperial Gazetteer, Oxford, Clarendon Press, 1908, p. 322. This corresponded roughly to 3 per cent and 2 per cent respectively, of the total population 1,023,828 of the district for the year 1901.
11. This corresponds to the concept of 'front' employed by Goffman (1974: 32) in his discussion of performances: "Front, then, is the expressive equipment of a standard kind intentionally or unwittingly employed by the individual during his performance". Also, it is "that part of the individual's performance which regularly functions in a general and fixed fashion to define the situation for those who observe the performance."
12. The figures pertained to late seventies' and early eighty's price indexes.
13. The maximum distance between the two settings was reported to be 3 km. The office was a place where the lawyers received their clients either when they visited them for the first time, or subsequently when they came for advice or consultation or for a formal review of the prospects of their case, or for briefing on the eve of the hearing of the case.
14. The lawyers visited their office twice a day, once before going to the court, and second time in the evening after they had finished their court work.

15. Table 4 on rural-urban composition of clientele non-exclusive criminal lawyers, which reflects that all but one criminal lawyer drew their clientele predominantly from the rural milieu, also lad's strength to this assertion.
16. A cut from the lawyer's fee (normally one-third) claimed and charged by any intermediary – including another lawyer, for supplying that business.
17. These officials are qualified lawyers on the pay role of the police department and are entrusted with the prosecution of such individuals as are charged with criminal offences against the state.
18. 'Class' being a de facto category of analysis based upon the objective criteria of material possessions.
19. Which should ensue automatically from a secular hierarchy.
20. For example, it is possible to hypothesize that among various influences working on the group members in the perception of hierarchy among them, one may be the nature of hierarchy impressed upon the group members by the outsiders.
21. See, for example, Warner's (William Lloyd Warner) studies of the American society, e.g., in the early decades of the 20th century, wherein he had examined the subjective rationales and criteria employed by members of the American community in stratifying themselves into *classes*.
22. Available to a lawyer especially in the beginning of his career, and which provides him business.
23. The sole exception being of a lawyer who was brought up by his senior virtually as his own son – since he did not have a son of his own.
24. The same thesis is re-affirmed if we consider the functioning of national polity or rather more patently, the regional polities. It is very easy to see how at the bottom of some top-level leadership at both national and regional levels, family-based ties, commitments and connections provide the very focal point for the functioning of political parties. In fact, this particularistic infusion seems to govern even the fate and destiny of several big business-houses in the country.

19 Residential Practices in the Public Sector Housing Stock of a Major Indian Metropolis

The Case of DDA Flats in Delhi

VÉRONIQUE DUPONT

For Delhi's inhabitants the *'di-di-a flats'* invoke those monotonous, perfectly identifiable, cement buildings, three to four stories high that dot the capital's urban landscape, especially on its periphery. These group housing estates, constructed by the Delhi Development Authority (DDA), from the 1960s onwards for sale to individuals, comprise apartments for different income levels. They are an example of the direct involvement of the government in real estate construction. Broadly speaking, they attest to Delhi's development within the framework of a voluntaristic urban development policy.

The analysis of this important segment of public sector housing and the residential practices of its inhabitants will enable us to address several issues pertaining to residential dynamics, such as strategies for acquiring property, keeping in mind the particular constraints imposed by the choice of locality, or even the absence of choice; the relationship between ownership and tenancy in the residential trajectories and in urban integration; strategies for investment in real estate for the purpose of enhancing income from property through rental or speculation; the householders' response to the planners' initial projects and their deficiencies. By stressing the notion of strategy, our approach is in keeping with "a line of thinking which involves restoring to the actor his share of the initiative in planning his own existence" (Godard, 1990: 9; Bonvalet and Fribourg, 1990).

In order to understand the residential practices of households and their reactions to urban policies, this study will be conducted essentially at the area level, focusing our observations on two peripheral zones where the DDA has constructed a vast number of apartment blocks: Mayur Vihar and Rohini. A presentation of these two localities will show the relevance of this choice. To begin with, we will view the public housing schemes in the context of the capital's rapid growth and the efforts at urban planning, and then try and evaluate the place of DDA flats in the total housing stock of the capital. This will involve specifying the urban structures, and painting a broad picture of the "list of 'constraints' in relation to which the potentially mobile households determine their strategies, some more explicitly and more fully, others less so, in their search for a lodging" (Rhein, 1990: 322).

The analyses presented here are based on the information on urban housing policies available in Delhi (official statistics, administrative reports, publications) and on field data collected through quantitative and qualitative methods.[1] In 1995, we undertook a socio-demographic survey of spatial mobility, employment and habitat in the Delhi metropolitan area. This study covered a sample population of 342 households in Mayur Vihar and 172 in Rohini, out of which 108 were living in DDA apartments. Additional information collected by Mriga Sidhu provides the background to each of the areas under study through the compilation of existing data and documents, direct observations and interviews (Sidhu, 1995). Besides, additional field visits in March 1997 and March 1999 also enabled us to assess the changes that had occurred towards the latter half of the decade. Lastly, in-depth interviews with residents of the DDA flats and estate agents were conducted in March and April 1999.

Urban Planning and Housing Policy in Delhi

The Challenge of Population Growth and Unchecked Urbanization

To better understand urban planning and its implementation in the case of Delhi, it is necessary to recapitulate the circumstances under which the country gained independence in 1947. Independence was won at the cost of the partition of the former British empire into India and Pakistan. The capital of the new Indian Union witnessed a massive relocation of peoples: Delhi, which at that time had a population of 9,00,000 inhabitants, had to take in 4,70,000 Hindu and Sikh refugees from West Pakistan, while 3,20,000 Muslims living here left for Pakistan. The inter-census period 1941–1951 is that of the highest demographic growth in the history of Delhi. Its population increased from 7,00,000 to 1.4 million, a growth rate of 7.5 per cent per annum, the likes of which has not been seen since. Delhi's population growth continued at an unremitting pace along with considerable spatial expansion. In 2001 the urban agglomeration[2] was home to some 12.8 million inhabitants.

At the time of independence, Delhi was in no way equipped to deal with such demographic constraints. In this critical situation, many land development schemes were undertaken by the civic authorities from 1947 to 1957, but without much heed being paid to coordination or planning (Milbert, 1998). This resulted in tremendous pressure on land, accompanied by wild speculation in property and real estate in the private sector, while slums mushroomed in the capital and unauthorized colonies in the suburbs. It then became obvious that an urban master plan to monitor Delhi's growth would have to be formulated. In 1957, the DDA was created under the auspices of the Central Government – because of Delhi's status as the national capital. This organization was entrusted with the responsibility of preparing and implementing a master plan for Delhi. Its tasks were vast. In particular, it had at its disposal a powerful instrument of land policy, the "scheme for large-scale acquisition, development and disposal of land", formulated in 1961. All lands situated within the urbanizable limits of Delhi were thus placed under the DDA's control. The Delhi Master Plan came into being in 1962. Initially, housing construction directly by the DDA was not intended as one of its functions. However, in the absence of an official construction agency, the DDA assumed this charge (Gupta, 1992; Jain, 1990).

Housing Policy and Market Segmentation of Habitat

Delhi is a prime example of the vast range of operations that the civic authorities have undertaken in relation to housing, interventions that have contributed to the physical and social structuring of urban space, a review of which will enable us to better appreciate the place occupied by the DDA flats.

The first housing schemes undertaken by the government in the capital in the aftermath of independence were for the benefit of the refugees who had come from Pakistan (rehabilitation colonies). Following British colonial tradition, from the 1950s onwards, the Central Government and other civic authorities and public enterprises also began to construct dwellings for their employees, who represented a very significant portion of the working population of the federal capital.[3]

In the early 1960s, the DDA began to develop tracts of land for the construction of individual housing, thus showing preference for a low density urban sprawl, based on the allotment of plots to individuals or housing cooperative societies. Towards the late 1960s, preference was given to a denser pattern of housing, either by the direct construction of apartment blocks by the DDA, or by leasing large plots of land to cooperatives for the construction of group housing for the middle and upper classes (Gupta, 1992; Misra et al., 1998). The plots or flats were sold, or to be precise, ceded on a 99-year lease basis. Due to this, a dual system of ownership was introduced into the property market. On the one hand, properties in the bonafide private sector localities, which existed before the new land policy was introduced, were deemed as freehold, and on the other, all lands acquired by the DDA and ceded on the basis of a long-term 99-year lease were designated as leasehold (Billand, 1990).

With regard to slum clearance policies, the alternative proposed was resettlement colonies in which their habitants were relocated. These operations, which employed coercive measures, including demolition of slums, were particularly frequent during the emergency (1975–77). About 7,00,000 persons were forcibly removed from slums in the city's centre and pericentre, and sent to semi-developed colonies situated at a distance of 10 to 20 km from the old centre. These public housing policies, however, were not able to meet the demands of a large section of the population, in particular the lower middle and working classes, that were forced to resort to informal forms of urbanization. Unauthorized colonies have thus continued to proliferate in the agricultural belt. In 1998, their population was estimated to be approximately 3 million, or more than a quarter of the population of the urban agglomeration.[4] The poorer sections have resorted to squatting on land, mainly public, in all the sectors of the capital, and to constructing makeshift dwellings, which have been consolidated with time. Despite efforts to prevent the proliferation of these slums, their population was estimated to be approximately 3 million in 2000 (or nearly 25% of Delhi's total population).[5] To complete this review of the principal forms of housing in Delhi, let us not forget the traditional sector: the compact and extremely dense habitation of the old city and the ancient villages absorbed by the advance of urbanization, that is to say about 12 per cent of the total housing stock in 1991 (Misra et al., 1998).

A Distinct Segment of Public Sector Housing: The DDA Flats

The DDA, on its internet website, claims to have 'generated' more than a million dwelling units since the inception of its building operations, either through the direct construction of apartments, or by facilitating construction through the allotment of plots to private individuals or cooperative housing societies. To confine ourselves to apartments with immediate, vacant, possession, approximately 2,76,000 dwellings were constructed from 1966–67 to 2000–01, which in 2001, housed nearly 10 per cent families of the agglomeration. In the public sector housing stock, the DDA flats represent a slightly higher share than the government employees' housing. The initial building schemes were implemented in the capital's central zones, but it is in the peripheral zones that their presence is more visible.

Until 1981, the DDA was able to satisfy only 50 per cent of the demand for its apartments (Billand, 1990). In 1990, the result was even less favourable, with only 45 per cent of the applicants satisfied (Misra et al., 1998). The extent of the unmet demand should be viewed in relation to the weight of the demographic constraints mentioned earlier. In 1999, the DDA acknowledged that there were some 48,000 applications for its apartments on the waiting list (DDA, 2002). In fact, the waiting period can extend for as much as ten years in some instances, as the case studies will show. The number of dwelling units constructed showed a marked decline in the 1990s. The DDA is now slowing down its construction activities and instead strengthening its role of 'facilitator' by favouring the intervention of the cooperative sector in the construction of housing. This evolution is in line with the economic liberalization launched by the Indian government in 1991, and espouses the principles of the new National Housing and Habitat Policy formulated in 1998 (Government of India, 2002).

The objective of the DDA's housing policy was to promote social equity through the allotment of plots and apartments to the lower income groups. The public sector housing schemes thus offer apartments for different categories of income. But all of them are for sale. This distinguishes Delhi from other experiences, which incorporate renting options, such as in Bangkok, Singapore, or Kuala Lumpur (Goldblum, 1987). According to the DDA's official statistics, nearly 60 per cent of the total number of apartments constructed are intended for lower income groups and the economically weaker sections (Table 1). But, in the last analysis, the public sector schemes for the allotment of apartments – as well as plots – benefit much more the middle and upper income groups (Pugh, 1990; Billand, 1990; Gupta, 1992; Milbert, 1998), "because the poorer people sell their housing rights for cash in order to meet the more pressing needs of food and other basic necessities" (Pugh, 1990: 1781). The target populations are often not touched, because the initial cost is too high, the access to credit too difficult and, lastly, because the market price of the plots and apartments is much higher, inducing people to sell at a profit. The misuse of public sector housing schemes is a general tendency, also seen in other Indian cities and in other developing countries (Milbert, 1986; Durand-Lasserve, 1986).

DDA apartments are generally of mediocre quality and their layout and fittings leave much to be desired. Their desirability and living standards, however, need to be seen in the context of the enormous deficit of decent housing in the capital, of the lack of amenities in the majority of dwelling units and their overcrowding. Apart from the huge number of makeshift slum dwellings, we can say that 45 per cent of the households inventoried in Delhi in 1991 lived in one-room accommodation; the average number of people per room was 2.8. The two residential pockets studied will enable us to make a more concrete assessment of DDA flats and the characteristics of their residents.

Table 1

Distribution Pattern of the Total Number of Dwelling Units Constructed by the DDA from 1966–67 to 2000–01 as per the Housing Category on the Basis of Income

Housing Category	*Numbers*	*Percentage*
Higher income groups	50,760	18.4
Middle income groups	61,846	22.4
Lower income groups	75,390	27.4
Economically weaker sections	85,770	31.1
Others	1,778	0.6
Total	275,544	100.0

Source: DDA, 2001.

Mayur Vihar and Rohini: Two Examples of Peripheral Housing

The two zones selected for the study of residential practices among the group housing stock illustrate the process of large-scale land acquisition and development of new urban extensions. The buildings constructed by the DDA in these two localities are found in great number and are adjacent to other types of dwellings, the result of diverse modes of production, the whole presenting a melange of planned and spontaneous urbanization.

Mayur Vihar[6] covers a vast area in East Delhi, approximately 12 kilometres from the Central Business District (CBD) of Connaught Place. Its population has grown at a brisk pace in the last 25 years (5% to 13.8% per annum from 1981 to 1991 in comparison with 3.9 per cent for the urban agglomeration as a whole). The original villages are now completely enclaved by the residential pockets, which have come up gradually from the 1970s onwards: unauthorized colonies, one of the biggest resettlement colonies (Trilokpuri) established during the emergency of 1975–77, numerous apartment blocks constructed from 1985 onwards by cooperative group housing societies, and lastly, in the interstices of the urban built-up areas, the ramshackle slum habitat.

These various building segments differ greatly in terms of amenities and layout. DDA apartments and the cooperative housing sector are the only ones to offer modern standards of comfort as a matter of course. Running water, electricity, in-house bathrooms and toilets and separate kitchens are elements that are not guaranteed, far from it, in the other modes of real estate production.[7] This heterogeneity of habitat directly reflects the socio-economic disparities of the population. On the basis of incomes declared in 1995, DDA flat residents are second to the residents of cooperative housing societies: 30 per cent of the working population has a monthly income equal or higher than Rs 7,500[8] (47%

in the case of workers living in apartments built by cooperative housing societies), as against only 2 per cent in the other types of habitation found in Mayur Vihar. The educational level confirms this relatively privileged status: 53 per cent DDA and 62 per cent cooperative housing society residents (aged 5 years and above) living in these apartments have studied up to the B.A. level and beyond, as against only 6 per cent in the rest of the zone covered in this study. In this context, let us clarify that the apartments constructed by the DDA in Mayur Vihar were originally meant for the lower and middle income groups. Public sector housing is not synonymous in India, as elsewhere, with 'social' housing (Milbert, 1986; Durand-Lasserve, 1986).

Rohini is situated 15–20 kilometres to the northwest of the CBD. This vast zone has diverse housing schemes constructed by the DDA, and constitutes the first development project in an urban extension, conceived like a sub-city. Started in 1980, this gigantic project was expected to accommodate 8,50,000 people in the first two phases, the construction of which has now been completed, and 1,60,000 in a third phase, which is in still underway.

The survey conducted in Rohini covered the more recently developed residential sectors, i.e., phase II, the enclaved or adjoining urban villages and interstitial slums. In 1995, the planned sectors consisted chiefly of apartment blocks constructed by the DDA and individual plots for houses, but the majority of plots were still vacant or in the process of construction. The study area was characterized by low population density (40 person per hectare in 1991) and very high demographic growth (10.3% per annum from 1981 to 1991). The residents of the Rohini DDA flats appeared to be less well-off than those of Mayur Vihar: only 4 per cent of the working population had a monthly income equal or higher than Rs 7,500. In effect, the Rohini DDA flats comprise a large portion of apartments for the lower income groups and economically weaker sections, whereas the first category is absent from the Mayur Vihar DDA flats.

Residential Practices of the Inhabitants

By focusing on the habitants of DDA flats, we will now analyse the residential strategies of households in the context of the macro-economic constraints weighing on the supply of housing.

Strategies for Acquiring Property: Two Lines of Action

There are two distinct lines of action for acquiring property from the DDA housing stock: one is the legal method, for which one has to go through a long and restrictive procedure; and the another is the more roundabout one, devised in response to the difficulties created by the official process.

According to the legal procedure, a person desirous of buying an apartment must wait for the announcement in the press for a group housing scheme. Some schemes are intended for the general public,[9] others are reserved for a specific group, for example economically weaker households, retired government employees, widows and dependants of soldiers who have died in combat, invalids, etc. (DDA, 1999–2000, 2002). As the number of applicants is always higher than the number of apartments available, a lottery system was devised to select the allotees from among the total number of people who have registered for a given scheme – a common practice in South East Asia too (Goldblum, 1987).

Apart from this luck of the draw over which the 'honest' applicant has no control, the choices are very limited. In the first place, the category of apartments that can be applied for depends directly on the postulant's income (certificate to be supplied as proof), which accordingly has direct bearing on the size of the apartment. The apartments meant for the economically weaker groups have only one room; two-room apartments are for the lower income groups, and three- or four-room apartments are meant for the middle and higher income groups. The size of the family is not taken into consideration at all. The payment modalities are also fixed by the DDA according to the category into which the apartment falls. A hire-purchase system is proposed for the lower income groups, with an initial deposit and small monthly payments spread over 20 years. For the higher income groups, this type of payment spanning a number of years is not systematically authorized. In particular, buyers who have reached retirement age have to pay the full cost of the apartment at the time of allotment in order to get possession. Lastly, in the self-financing schemes, four or five advance instalments have to be made in order to finance the construction of the apartments, sometimes even before the zone is developed or even before the procedure for the acquisition of the lands by the DDA is completed. These programmes, therefore, are meant for the highest income groups. As a result, whatever the category of apartments, most of the applicants are salaried employees with regular incomes who are able to furnish the necessary financial guarantees and have access to the various credit facilities for financing the building projects (Misra et al., 1998).

The choice of locality varies over the years from one scheme to another and according to the category of apartments. At the end of the 1960s and during the 1970s, the first schemes did not offer any choice at the time of registration. Thus, some of the allotees in Rohini had registered in the 1970s, without any idea where their homes would be located. They could never have imagined that they would one day be living in this particular locality – a zone that at that time had no urban existence and no name. The more recent schemes propose various sites, asking the applicant to list his preferences. The self-financed schemes use the same method. Once the construction is finished, however, the buyer may choose neither the block, nor the building, nor the floor. Before the delivery, another lottery is held in order to determine the exact location. As a retired government servant, who found himself in Rohini on the fourth floor without a lift despite his advanced age, put it "beggars can't be choosers".

Can we still speak of residential strategy in the face of such constraints, and without the option of choosing the location of one's home? "If the notion of strategy supposes the existence of choice, the weight of such severe constraints also supposes the use of special strategies whose aim is precisely to loosen these constraints" (Gautman, 1990: 30). As a result, in situations where a ten-year wait for a house is nothing exceptional, added to which there is a lottery system to decide one's fate, households have to come up with long-term strategies to deal with uncertainty. Moreover, the prescribed delays are often prolonged by several years, the result of which is an increase in the final cost of the apartment, borne essentially by the buyer. Once the construction of the building is complete, the delivery may again be delayed (sometimes by as much as three years and more) because the water, electricity and sewage lines have not been laid, or because of the lack of coordination between the DDA and the municipal services. Repeated scandals over the DDA's inept management of the schemes are exposed in the local press. So many 'imponderable' factors which find expression in obstacles, delays and additional costs on the road to ownership of a property. But, as we shall see, the problems do not end with gaining possession of the apartment.

Under these conditions, it is not surprising to find people resorting to indirect means of acquisition of public sector housing. This however can only come into effect in a second phase, once the DDA apartments have been allotted to the original buyers. The existing 99-year lease regime in the case of public sector housing is very restrictive. To avoid speculation, resale is not permitted for ten years. Thereafter, a prohibitive 50 per cent is deducted from the capital gains. Schemes for the conversion of leasehold into freehold exist since 1992, but there is a stiff surcharge levied by the public administration (in this case the DDA), which however does not apply to housing for the underprivileged categories. The entire system has encouraged a spate of irregular transactions on long-term leases through a unique practice known as the *power of attorney*. This procedure allows the owner of an asset to legally transfer his rights to a third person, without being alienated from his right to the property. If Indian law recognizes this deed certified by a notary public, it is generally accompanied by black money transactions, that is to say a significant portion of the money paid is not declared and so escapes taxation. Such transactions are therefore considered semilegal or irregular. In consequence, the *power of attorney* is used as a tool for getting around legal restrictions on the transfer of property. Estate agents encouraged its use as a pragmatic response guaranteeing better fluidity of the market to aspirants hoping for a "home of one's own". It makes the purchase of an apartment much easier and quicker. It also removes the restrictions with regard to the choice of locality within the urban agglomeration and the desired apartment (size, floor and exact location in the selected area).

In this less restrictive context three kinds of factors intervene in the choice of an apartment in Rohini or Mayur Vihar: financial, environmental and accessibility. In the first place, the price of property here is not as high as in the more central localities. Peripheral location is in fact seen as an advantage by agents and by some buyers, for these localities are less polluted and less congested than the central zones. In reality, the new localities are more reminiscent of concrete jungles than an ecological alternative. Lastly, if the occupants of DDA flats initially suffered from the poor bus service and connections to the rest of the city, the subsequent improvement in transportation and amenities have made these localities more attractive for new buyers.

In the last analysis, "location in the strict sense of the term only intervenes in a mediate and secondary manner: 'preferential choice of locality' [...] is in reality, and above all, the choice of the type of housing and the occupancy status, and this choice of locality implicitly depends on the spatial distribution of the housing stocks" (Rhein, 1990: 3209). Based on examples of European and North American cities, this conclusion also applies to Delhi.

Strategies for Investment in Real Estate: Income Generating and Speculative Properties

The acquisition of property as a means of providing long-term security for the family is not the only factor motivating purchasers of government-built apartments. For some, it is an investment that generates rental income. According to the 1995 survey, 17 per cent households were living in rented accommodation in the Mayur Vihar DDA flats and 15 per cent in Rohini.

For others, DDA apartments turn out to be an easy source of profit given the shortage of housing. From 'simplified' acquisitions – through indirect means – to speculative transactions is just a short step. The interviews with estate agents provide some pointers. Whereas in Mayur Vihar, now a fully developed colony, there are agents who believe that the business has come full circle, in Rohini, transactions are in full swing in the sectors still under development. Housing projects and the anticipated improvements in public amenities indicate that a fresh rise in the prices of apartments and rents is on the cards. The large number of real estate agencies is proof of the buoyancy of the market. From 1996 to 1999, it was the small one- and two-room apartments that were most in demand, and agents quoted sale prices multiplied by a factor of three for the first category and by one and a half for the second. Ground floor apartments and those facing the road are the most sought after and also the most expensive, as it is possible to build extensions to them and use them for commercial purposes. Speculators take into account the degree of development that the sector has undergone and the prospects of an increase in value in order to maximize profits.

Speculative investment and purchase of an apartment for the family to live in are not mutually exclusive practices, as Ramesh's story illustrates, which moreover resumes several key elements in the residential trajectories of public sector apartments. A former warehouse employee in a private company, Ramesh, after a 10-year waiting period, first bought a two-room apartment in 1986, through the official channels, in a locality close to Rohini. After the first instalment, which was necessary to take possession of the flat, he reneged on his monthly instalments – a practice quite frequent in the apartment categories for the economically weaker sections.[10] Since his retirement in 1990, he has opened a grocery shop and combined this activity with speculation in real estate. In 1999, he was living in his third DDA flat, having bought the last two flats through unofficial channels. His modus operandi is to sell the apartment that he is living in as soon as there is a chance of making a good profit and then buying in those sectors of Rohini which are still under development, and where the prices are the lowest and the prospects of profit the highest. He is planning to sell his current apartment as soon as an offer comes up. In shifting from one apartment to another, profit has been his principal motivation, his family's comfort rating second. Thus, his current apartment has only one room for a family of five adults and two children, but being on the ground floor it has enabled him to build an illegal extension and to open a small business.

Residential Trajectories of Varying Significance

The residential trajectories of the inhabitants edify us about the occupancy dynamics in the public sector housing stock and the integration of potential property owners into the capital. In the two zones studied in 1995, flat owners constitute a little more than four-fifths of the sample population. In Mayur Vihar, 48 per cent of the residents of DDA flats are migrants (having lived outside Delhi before this); 23 per cent have always lived in Delhi but came from another dwelling; the remaining 29 per cent have always lived in the same dwelling (these are the children of the first settlers). In Rohini, the corresponding figures are 68 per cent, 28 per cent and 4 per cent respectively (Table 2). The differences observed are partly due to the more recent construction of the Rohini DDA flats; in fact, 99 per cent of the residents have moved here in the last five years, as against only 30 per cent in the case of Mayur Vihar.

In the two localities, however, the public sector housing stock seems much more like a place of resettlement within the Delhi urban agglomeration than a place of initial reception for new migrants. Only 37 per cent of the migrants living in the Mayur Vihar DDA flats came directly from outside Delhi; in the case of Rohini, it is 11 per cent. In the category *heads of households,* whether migrants or not, 85 per cent at Mayur Vihar and 92 per cent at Rohini had lived in another lodging in Delhi before shifting to their present accommodation (Table 2). The mode of access to apartments shows that entry into this housing segment is easier for those already living in Delhi, whereas possibilities of renting, easier for the new arrivals, remain somewhat limited. Moreover, the previous accommodation can be situated in the same locality, as seen in Rohini. Renting makes it easier for the newcomer to prospect the area and seize the best options for buying through the unofficial channels.

However, ownership of a public sector housing flat is not always seen as a promotion or the "culmination of a residential itinerary" (Culturello, 1993: 126). According to the conclusion arrived at by the French studies on housing, "accession to property can be the result of a constraint", and "the ensuing stages are not necessarily part of an ascending model" (Bonvalet and Brun, 1998: 317). In Delhi, it is especially the case of retired high-ranking government officials, who have had to leave their official quarters after retirement. For them, to become the owner of a DDA apartment often means living in a smaller place, in a construction of mediocre quality, situated in an outlying suburb of lower social standing.

The case of Balram, a retired commander of the Indian Navy, is a case in point. His official residence, a spacious five-room bungalow, was situated in a posh residential zone in South Delhi. Moreover, the locality ostensibly reflected his status and rank as a government officer. Balram complied with the legal procedure to obtain his DDA apartment and four years after an initial unsuccessful attempt, he was lucky to be selected in a scheme launched in 1979 for 'immediate allotment' with three localities to choose from. Mayur Vihar seemed to him to be the best option, for it was "less congested and less polluted" than the others, all as distant from the town centre. He was able to move in three years later, but the area was still under development and the transport services inadequate. The new accommodation was smaller and in a dilapidated condition (having previously served as a warehouse for the DDA). But what Balram suffered from most in the initial years, was the poor image of this new locality, associated with the working class because of the neighbouring resettlement colony of Trilokpuri. For Balram to 'reconcile' himself with his new residence, the locality itself had to undergo transformation, subsequent to the construction of numerous blocks of flats by cooperative housing societies for the upper classes, which in turn improved the status of the zone.

Table 2

Residential Trajectories of the Inhabitants of DDA Flats in Two Peripheral Zones of the Delhi Agglomeration

Migratory Status	*Zone*			
	Mayur Vihar		*Rohini*	
	All residents	*Heads of households*	*All residents*	*Heads of households*
	Percentage distribution for each category			
Migrant (=having previously lived outside the Delhi urban agglomeration	47.8	87.2	68.1	82.6
Non-migrant:				
Having always lived in the same dwelling	28.9	0.0	4.1	0.0
Came from another dwelling in Delhi	23.2	12.8	27.8	17.4
Total	100.0	100.0	100.0	100.0
Number of cases	228	39	291	69
Place of Last Residence	*All residents*	*Heads of households*	*All residents*	*Heads of households*
	Percentage distribution for each category			
Same dwelling since birth	28.9	0.0	4.1	0.0
Within the Delhi urban agglomeration	53.5	84.6	88.7	91.3
Outside the Delhi urban agglomeration	17.5	15.4	7.2	8.7
Total	100.0	100.0	100.0	100.0
Number of cases	228	39	291	69
Place of Last Residence	*All Percentage migrants distribution in each zone*			
Inside the Delhi urban agglomeration	63.3		89.4	
Outside the Delhi urban agglomeration	36.7		10.6	
Total	100.0		100.0	
Number of cases	109		198	
Year of Arrival in the Current Dwelling	*Residents coming from another dwelling Percentage distribution in each zone*			
Before 1980	—		—	
1980–1984	27.4		—	
1985–1989	42.2		1.4	
1990–March 1995	30.4		98.6	
Total	100.0		100.0	
Number of cases	162		279	

Source: Survey-Mobility-Employment-Habitat, ORSTOM-IEG 1995.

In these residential trajectories, often, location is more important than the occupancy status in the sense that the former is considered "a symbol of social standing and as such can act as a showcase in society" (Bonvalet and Dureau, 2000: 146). But, the same locality can become more or less acceptable over the years, location in this case being reduced to "a shell without a specific content", whose content can change, "an empty shell" (Brun, 1990: 311).

Response of Households to Deficiencies in Planning

To find accommodation is not enough. Having shifted into the apartment, the residents of these DDA flats have to undertake steps to improve their day-to-day lives. In fact, the apartments are often handed over while the development of the locality is still incomplete: roads are unpaved, bus services infrequent, there are no shops or services, even drinking water connections to the buildings have not been installed. The residents are therefore forced to resort to various tactics, ranging from simple individual initiatives to the formation of residential associations, and even going as far as finding ways of getting around the regulations imposed by the civic authorities.

If there was ever a vital issue, it is water, the responsibility for which in the case of Delhi rests with the Municipal Corporation of Delhi (MCD). The DDA however has the charge of building the infrastructure within its own housing complexes and managing it for some years before transferring the responsibility to the MCD. The coordination problems spawned by this system inevitably impact on the inhabitants. In Rohini, the first tenants of a newly developed sector had to order water tankers for six months while waiting for the pumping and water treatment plants to become operational and provide them with drinking water from their taps. In some pockets, in Vasant Kunj, another vast building complex built by the DDA in South Delhi, the supply of water from tankers or temporary external reservoirs went on for two to three years after the people had moved into the apartments. Besides, no system for pumping the water to the various floors had been provided. In consequence, each household had to instal a water tank at the ground level and a booster pump to lift the water to the tanks on the roof.

The patent lack of public transport, in terms of the number of buses and frequency, or even their quasi absence, is a general problem, which the new planned extensions have to face in Delhi, and this despite the fact that many residents are entirely dependent on public transport for their everyday movements. In 1995, 58 per cent of the school children and students interviewed in the planned sectors of Rohini went to school by bus; 53 per cent workers took the bus to work; in the Mayur Vihar DDA flats, the corresponding percentage was 71 per cent school children and students and 40 per cent workers. In Rohini, for example, the residents welfare association was able to improve the situation by putting pressure on the public authorities to provide the services to which they were entitled.

Lastly, the inhabitants reacted to the lack of shopping facilities. Commercial complexes are of course included in the DDA's development plans, but they are constructed after the apartments. Moreover, the price for a commercial lease is too high and shopkeepers generally do not find it financially viable. This was the situation that prevailed, among others, in the sectors studied in Rohini where, because of the lack of commercial facilities in the initial years (with the exception of some hawkers), the residents had to make their purchases near their workplace. Moreover, the rules applicable to public sector housing complexes and neighbouring plotted colonies restrict the use to a strictly residential one. A norm of this type is nevertheless flouted. Gradually, a number of ground floor apartments as well as garages meant for two-wheelers are converted, sometimes even with illegal extensions, into shops, neighbourhood services and real estate agencies. These small shops dispersed within the residential area, ensure better accessibility to the inhabitants than the commercial complex constructed by the DDA, which is not so centrally situated.

Conclusion

The study of public sector housing in Delhi can a priori seem quite specific because of the regulatory framework that controls this real estate market segment. In spite of a highly restrictive initial context, the inhabitants nevertheless manage to carve out some room for manoeuvre, even if it is through somewhat irregular transactions, which widens the horizon of possibilities, introduces elements of choice – but also speculative practices – and ways and means of getting around rules and regulations, ill-adapted to economic realities. In the residential trajectories, the locality and the occupancy status have been weighed differently, as the trajectories aimed at the acquisition of property are not the systematic outcome of an improvement in the socio-economic standing.

As for the third important element in the residential trajectories, the type of accommodation, we have deliberately focused our observations on group housing without addressing the eventual preference for an individual house. According to the conclusions of a report on the land system and the property market in Delhi (Billand, 1990), the requirement of certain middle class sections seems to be shifting from plots for the construction of individual houses to ready-to-move-in apartments. This tendency seems to be common among full-time employees who do not have the time to devote to searching for a plot or keeping up with the long process of valorization. Moreover, in view of the price of land in Delhi, the construction of group housing complexes lowers the end cost for the buyer. Lastly, from the point of view of the planners, an ever-expanding urbaniaztion characterized by low residential density is too luxurious an option – as it gobbles up agricultural land – to be followed on a priority basis. True, the DDA's stereotyped plans allow "little flexibility to the residents to express their need for a unique identity" (Misra et al., 1998: 2008), but perhaps one should have confidence, once again, in the protagonists, this time to 'appropriate' the inner space of their apartments.

Notes

1. This study lies within the scope of a research programme on spatial mobility and residential practices of Delhi's population. This programme was financed by the *Institut de Recherche pour le Developement* (ex-ORSTOM) with supplementary funding by the CNRS in the context of *Action Concertee en Sciences Sociales ORSTOM-CNRS* and of the

Programme Interdisciplinaire de Recherche sur les Villes. In India, my project was supported by the *Centre de Sciences Humaines*, Delhi (French Ministry of Foreign Affairs) and the Institute of Economic Growth (Delhi). In these various research projects I have collaborated with Isabelle Milbert (WED, Geneva) on questions relating to urban policy (Milbert, 1998). The in-depth interviews used in this article have been conducted in collaboration with Dhananjay Tingal and Mriga Sidhu. For a more detailed presentation of the socio-demographic aspects, see Dupont and Prakash, 1999.

2. The Delhi urban agglomeration comprises the municipalities of Delhi, New Delhi, the Cantonment and adjoining urban localities.
3. In 1981, the public sector employed 28 per cent of the capital's workforce.
4. *Common Cause*, an NGO that is against the regularization of these colonies and has taken the matter to court, provided this estimate.
5. Slum and Jhuggi Jhompri Wing, Municipal Corporation of Delhi.
6. The zone covered by the study corresponds to phase I of the two phases of the Mayur Vihar development project.
7. For example, in another segment of the planned sector surveyed in 1995, 80 per cent of the dwellings in the resettlement colonies to which the inhabitants of demolished slums were sent, did not have a separate kitchen, 80 per cent did not have bathrooms, 8.5 per cent did not have toilets and 12 per cent did not have running water.
8. In 1995, the minimum official salary of an unskilled worker from the industrial sector was approximately Rs 1,500 per month.
9. Each postulant nevertheless has to fulfil certain conditions: be an Indian national; not own a plot or an apartment in Delhi (neither in his name, nor in the name of his wife or dependent children); nor be the allottee of another apartment built by the DDA or any another public body.
10. The fact that the DDA regularly opens special amnesty schemes for the regulariatzion of arrears, which are owing to it from the sale of these apartments, is an indication of the extent of this practice (DDA, 1999–2000).

References

Billand, C.J. (1990), *Delhi Case Study: Formal Serviced Land Development*, New Delhi: USAID.

Bonvalet, C. and J. Brun (1998), "Logements, mobilités et trajectories résidentielles", in M. Segaud, C. Bonvalet and I. Brun (dir.), *Logement et habitat. L'état des savoirs*, Paris: La Déouverte: 312–318.

Bonvalet, C. and F. Dureau (2000), "Les modes d'habiter: des choix sous ccontraintes", in F. Dureau et al. (dir.), *Metropoles en mouvement. Une comparaison. son* 1. Internationale, Paris, Anthropos (Coll. Villes) – IRD: 131–153.

Bonvalet, C. and A.M. Fribourg (séminaire organisé par) (1990), *Stratégies résidentielles*, Paris, INED, Plan Construction et Architecture, MELTM.

Brun, J. (1990), "Mobilités résidentielles et stratégies de localization", in *Stratégies résidentielles*, Séminaire organisé par C. Bonvalet et A.M. Fribourg, Paris INED, Plan Construction et Architecture, MELTM: 299–312.

Culturello, P. (1993), "Le poids de l'origine et la force de la parenté: la dualite familiale dans les pratiques résidentielles" in C. Bonvalet and A. Gautman (eds.), *Le logement, une affaire de famille*, Paris, L'Harmattan (Coll. Villes et Entreprises): 111–128.

DDA (1999–2000), *Annual Administration Report*, Delhi, Delhi Development Authority.

—— (2002), Delhi Development Authority, internet site: www.ddadelhi.com

Dupont, V. and J. Prakash (1999), "Enquete "Mobilites Spatiales dans I'Aire métropolitaine de Delhi", in *Biographies d'enquête*, Paris, INED-PUF/Diffusion (Coll. Methodes et savoirs): 279–315.

Durand-Lasserve, A. (1986), *L'exclusion des pauvres dans les villes du Tiers Monde. Accés au sol et au logement,* Paris, L'Harmattan (Coll. Villes et Entreprises): 198.

Goldblum, Ch. (1987), *Métropoles de I'Asie du Sud-Est. Strategies urbaines et politiques de logement,* Paris, L'Harmattan (Coll. Villes et Entreprises): 276.

Gupta, R.C. (1992), *Land Assembly in the Indian Metropolis,* New Delhi: Uppal Publishing House, p. 240.

Gautman, A. (1990), "Strategies résidentielles, stratégies de recherche", in *Strategies Residentielles* Seminaire organie par C. Bonvalet et A.M. Fribourg (Paris, 1988), INED, Plan Construction et Architecture, MELTM: 23–34.

Godard, F. (1990), "Sur le concept de strategiés", in *Strategiés résidentielles,* Séminaire organisé par C. Bonvalet et A.M. Fribourg, Paris, INED, Plan Construction et Architecture, MELTM: 9

Government of India (2002), "National Housing and Habitat Policy 1998", Ministry of Urban Development and Poverty Alleviation, internet site: www.urbanindia.nic.in

Jain, A.K. (1990), *The Making of a Metropolis.* Planning and Growth of Delhi, New Delhi: National Book Organisation, p. 283.

Milbert, I. (1986), *L'urbanisme et I'habitat et Inde,* Thése pour le doctorat d'Etat, Université de Droit, d'Economie et de Sciences Sociales de Paris (Paris II), trois tomes, p. 790.

—— (1998), *politiques urbaines a Delhi,* Genéve, IUED, p. 61.

Misra, B., R.B. Singh and A. Malik (1998), "Delhi Metropolis: Housing and Quality of Life", in R.P. Misra and K. Misra (eds.), *Millions Cities of India,* New Delhi, Sustainable Development Foundation: 196–228.

Pugh, C. (1990), *Housing and Urbanisation. A Study of India,* New Delhi: Sage Publications, p. 315.

Rhein, C. (1990), "Sens et rôle des localisations dans les stratégies résidentielles", in *Stratégies résidentielles,* Séminaire organisé par C. Bonvalet et A.M. Fribourg, Paris, INED, Plan Construction et Architecture, MELTM: 312–331.

Sidhu, M. (1995), Survey on Spatial Mobility in the Metropolitan Area of Delhi. Working Paper No 2: Residential Profile of the Studied Areas, ORSTOM-EEG, New Delhi, p. 143.

20 On Rural Transformation

RAMKRISHNA MUKHERJEE

Rural, by definition, is complementary to urban. Unlike the urban, rural is predominantly concerned with the production of agriculture and other primary goods, and the ancillary services. It complements urban in the sense that it cannot exit without urban conglomerates, and vice versa. However, changes in the rural scenario, as in the urban scenario, are taking place from time immemorial. But, transformation is not mere change.

Like transformation, change is a matter of replacement. But change is concerned with quantity and quality. Some ingredients in the inner articulation of an entity are always changing. The entity itself may change within the composite whole of entities, which defines society. In that sequence, a qualitative change is registered when the entities denoting the prime movers of society change. As a result, the society is changed irrespective of its definitional boundaries. This kind of change is trasnformation.

However, the politicians, administrators, and even a powerful segment of social scientists have used the terms change and transformation interchangeably. Upto the 1950s decade, the rural societies in India were static in the main, despite changes within their internal articulation and in a manner parallel to that in urban India. These changes, however, were in a low gear which gave rise to inconsequential concepts like sanskritization as a new phenomenon in British India and the post-Raj days.

The only form and content of change, which seemed to play counter to the static immobility of rural society, was the perennial crossing of rural-urban dichotomy. It is a powerful lever of change, but it did not transform rural India. On the contrary, it strengthened the static charactar of rural India by the investment of the rudimentary capital, obtained from services in urban India, for the purpose of buying land in the villages while being engaged in the age-old form of agricultural production.

From the 1960s decade, rural-urban dichotomy is being irrevocably replaced by rural-urban continuum in capital and labour. This has been the harbinger of rural transformation. For, within its definitional boundary, rural society became less and less analogous to urban society: it is becoming homologous. But, how do we discern this analogy and homology?

Sanskritization was mooted as the concept to detect analogy between complementary rural and urban scenarios. 'Dominant caste' was now mooted to characterize homology. But, both are inconsequential and, therefore, false concepts.

From the days the Indain society, as a composite form, emerged with the spread of organization or India, the process described as sanskritization has been taking place in urban India. This is attested to by Kautilya, Lyall, Risley, and others, namely, the statesmen, politicians and administrators. Form the British days, in particular, this process is leading to changes within society due to endogenous and exogenous forces, which are of commodity production in character, and not of subsistence. Class forces, feudal in character to begin with and colonial-capitalist later, are in operation all these years upon society of primary democracy.

The concept of 'dominant caste' underlines a breakthrough from 'sanskritization' because, truly, it does not refer to outmoded caste but to class in a distorted and diffused form. Its six attributes portend the modern capitalist class relations of society, and not of the past feudal relations of caste. Caste in 'dominant caste' is in name only and, therefore, liable to false identification and comprehension.

Despite land reform, partially successful in some and a total failure in some other states, land has lost its role as the primary means of production in agriculture. Its share in the construction of GDP today is less than one-third for agriculture. The other inputs acquiring a major role in agriculture irrigation, soil conservation, machineries, seeds, etc. Briefly, commodification of agriculture is now nearly complete, leading to qualitative change in the relations of production along with the mode of production.

Other forms of primary production in rural areas (for example, mining and quarrying) have fully attained an industrial character, with the predominant role of wage labour and capital and the concomitant class relations. Ancillary sources are following suit.

Thus, it is that the rural transformation that is taking place in India since the 1980s decade is due to the great leveller of modern capitalism and its consequent relations and mode of production. To deflect this reality by the imagery of caste and tribal relations leads to false consciousness.

Yet, there are evidence to indicate that the false consciousness assumes a pseudo-real stance in terms of the demand for tribal autonomy or independence, job reservation for the Scheduled Castes (SCs), the Scheduled Tribes (STs), and Other Backward Classes (OBCs), etc. This is a point for research.

Caste and tribe are matters of identification of a community with reference to a context. That context is jeopardized when one speaks of the SCs and the STs. These are juridical constructs, and not a matter of internal articulation of communities into society; however, cleverly, the constructs may have been drawn from the days of Ramsay Mcdonald to date. They serve the purpose of overruling polity which is evidently capitalist in character of colonial captalism before and of independent democracy presently. OBC is a more fallacious construct in this context, to suit the palate of more have-notes in a society of minority haves.

More to the point is that these constructs can easily be fed to the people because, as noted, caste and tribe are spontaneously discernible. By the same token, the concept of class can be avoided by the polity of vested interests because it is not a matter of direct identification but of indirect deduction and comprehension. Given a particular mode of production, the relations of production can be deduced and, on that base, the classes can be discerned.

Because of this difference in understanding caste-tribe and class, and the role of class in society and the consequent mode of production the society is transformed into, the latter can be avoided in the name of a harmonic society. But this anomaly cannot be pursed for ever. The class content of SCs, STs, and OBCs is becoming more and more apparent, leading to the concern with the affluent strata of these categories. Another point of research, then, is how and why the class character of the castes and tribes as fossilized classes are becoming more and more apparent with the increasing transformation of rural society as a distinctive but homologous component of the rural and urban Indian society.

From this perspective, the globalization of India within the orbit of the modern world capitalism draws one's attention. Crops in rural India have not merely turned into commodities but are in unison with the demand and supply or the world market. Agriculture is turning into an industrial enterprises, losing its age-old character or mainly the subsistence of villages. The haves and the have-notes in rural society are more and more rotating on the same axis as the haves and the haves-notes in urban society.

This is why, in those segments of society, where the feudal basis is still present, however rudimentarily (for example, in U.P. and Bihar) the class antagonism in taking the virulent forms of caste and tribal unrests in place of clear-cut class antagonism, as is found in some states of Western India and West Bengal.

The nexus is interwoven with the other deprived sections of society, which, in place of taking a clear class position is finding subterfuge in age-old synonyms like caste and tribe. The dalit is a pointer to this end, and so may be the Christian SCs, the Shiv Sena, and the communalization of Punjab. These and other synonyms are all products of unequal exchange in society in goods and services.

Briefly, the inexorable rural transformation of Indian society is thus hindered in very many ways. The point is to unravel the intricacies of this nexus.

21 Understanding Continuity in Indian Villages

PARAMJIT S. JUDGE

There has been a growing attempt to understand certain views on Indian villages as a part of the Orientalist discourse. The main argument is that the Indian villages have been continuously undergoing change and the Indian villages were never self-sufficient units, as it is found in the earlier views on the village communities. This paper is an attempt to examine the Indian villages from the perspective of classical theories of social change. The issue requires a theoretical exploration as well as an empirical examination. At the empirical level, there is a need to understand and interpret the actual situation as is available through the ethnographic and sociological studies of villages of India conducted by both the Western and Indian social anthropologists and sociologists. Accordingly, the discussion in this paper is divided into four sections. In the first section, the writings of Spencer, Marx and Durkheim have been examined in terms of their understanding of social change. The second part takes stock of the way the Indian society could be (or was) implicated in these theoretical conceptions as an exception or a counter-example. Marx was the only thinker who tried to uncover the mystery shrouding the 'unchanging' Indian society. The second part also deals with the various conceptions of Indian villages with a specific objective of how these studies have characterized the Indian village. The third part is based on the field observations, the purpose of which is to show that there is a reasonable basis to state that Marx's views on Indian villages have certain degree of validity.[1] The discussion is concluded in the fourth part.

I

Spencer, Marx and Durkheim on Social Change

In the 18th and 19th centuries the European thinkers expounded grand theories and the underlying thought among them was the common destiny of the mankind irrespective of the uneven development in the world. The societies that remained underdeveloped or were backward and primitive were soon to follow their most developed European counterparts. It may however be pointed out that though this perspective could have certain inbuilt faults due to its Eurocentric character, but such a vision appeared for the first time mainly due to the scientific development and discovery of new lands and people by the Europeans. The discovery of various lands provided the European thinkers with a paradigm of universal thinking and common destiny of mankind with a great element of teleological understanding. Much influenced by the physical sciences examining natural phenomenon, they also regarded the social phenomenon as a part of certain universal principles. Situating Europe at the centre of social and economic development provided a perspective according to which the traditional and savage societies had to attain the level of development that Europe, particularly the Western Europe, had already attained. In the specific context of 19th century during which sociology emerged and flourished as a discipline, we also witness a revolution in biological sciences. Contribution of Darwin in particular paved the way for the conceptualization of society like a living organism. This organismic analogy was virtually carried to its logical extreme by Spencer. In continuation with his conceptualization of society, Spencer also put forward his theory of social evolution, which is of a considerable significance in our understanding of change in terms of the dichotomy of evolution/revolution. For Spencer (1972: 123) the increase in population is the major factor of social evolution thus:

> Apart from social changes otherwise produced, there are social changes by simple growth. Mass is both a condition to, and a result of, organization in a society. It is clear that heterogeneity of structure is made possible by multiplicity of units. Division of labour cannot be carried for where there are but few to divide labour among them. There can be no differentiation into classes in the absence of numbers. Complex co-operations, governmental and industrial, are impossible without a population large enough to supply many kinds and gradations of agents.

Spencer's perspective is quite clear so far as the relation of population increase with social change is concerned. The increase in the size of society is a necessary condition for the emergence of a new division of labour. As the division of labour becomes more complex, society experiences more heterogeneity. As a social philosopher, Spencer did not visualize any society in the remote future that would be characterized by equality, liberty and justice – all being realized together. He made a distinction between militant and industrial societies arguing for the latter as the desirable one.

Marx's writings and activism make it clear that he did not only have different views from Spencer, but also opposite to him so far as the desirability of a good or right society is concerned. Marx thought that after the appearance of capitalism on the world scene communism had become a historical necessity. In spite of all these fundamental differences from Spencer, Marx (1976: 31–32) strongly held the view that population increase had been at the base of social change thus:

> This mode of production must not be confused simply as being the reproduction of the physical existence of the individuals. Rather it is a definite form of activity of these individuals, a definite form of expressing their life, a definite *mode of life* on their part. As individuals express their life, so they are. What they are, therefore, coincides with their production, both with *what* they produce and with *how* they produce. Hence what individuals are depends on the material conditions of their production.
>
> This production only makes its appearance with the *increase of population*. In its turn this presupposes the *intercourse* of individuals with one another. The form of this intercourse is again determined by production.

Marx has made it clear in his writings that when men started producing for others' consumption the real social dynamism began. So long as people consumed whatever they were producing, societies remained stable and unchanging. The increase in population triggered the potentialities of social and collective life in which the means of production and relations of production and the dialectical interaction between the two became the basis of the changing character of forms of division of labour as well as property.

Independent of Marx's arguments, but echoing the views of Spencer and Comte, Durkheim (1933: 262) arrived at the same conclusion when he pointed out: *The division of labour varies in direct ratio with the volume and density of societies, and, if it progresses in a continuous manner in the course of social development, it is because societies become regularly denser and generally more voluminous* (emphasis original). In a way, Durkheim's formulation is coherent and also takes stock of the possibility that increase in volume may not necessarily affect division of labour. There is also a precondition of increase in the density otherwise even if the population increases, there would be no variation in the division of labour. It is well known that for Durkheim the division of labour should be understood in terms of social solidarity and with the increasing structural differentiation and cooperation the societies develop complex division of labour. Interestingly, Comte (c.f. Durkheim, ibid.) also connects 'progressive condensation of our species' with 'more special division of labour'.

Could there be societies, which despite the density and volume, failed to have variations in their division of labour? In other words, if we think of a relatively stable society that does not change according to the increase in its population and density, then, this general explanation remains unsatisfactory. Conversely, it could be possible to keep the general explanation of population increase leading to social change intact and look for reasons that prevented change in a society. Such an approach required discursive and dialectical method and it was only Marx who put it to an effective use to solve this riddle. It is in this context that Marx's views on Indian society require an examination. What is interesting to note, as we would see in the next part, that most of the studies on Indian village communities missed this way of examination and interpretation. The next section is an attempt at knowing how the Indian village was conceptualized and empirically investigated by the social anthropologists and sociologists.

II
Various Conceptions of Indian Village

The attempt at examining various conceptions of the Indian village as found in the existing literature, however, is not exhaustive, because the main purpose of indulging in this exercise is to highlight how a different theoretical perspective and/or specific objectives of the empirical investigation may result into ignoring or overlooking – consciously or unconsciously – certain obvious facts for necessary explanation. The discussion may be started with the explication of Marx's views on Indian villages. Though Marx was not the first to write on village India as he depended on the British administrators' reports and analyses, yet his great strength lies in his ability to synthesize various views to come out with a theoretical explanation. Marx's views on India are generally understood, interpreted and commented upon in isolation from his theoretical perspective of social change in the pre-industrial societies. Broadly, Marx's views can be divided into three parts. First, he exposed the British colonialism when he extensively criticized it for causing misery to the people of India. Marx (1973:302) wrote: "There cannot, however, remain any doubt but that the misery inflicted by the British on Hindustan is of an essentially different and infinitely more intensive kind than all Hindustan had to suffer before." Second, Marx (ibid.: 307) was also of the view that "whatever may have have been the crimes of England she was the unconscious tool of history in bringing about that [social] revolution". This view of Marx situates him in the larger context of European perceptions of the Oriental societies characterized by 'oriental despotism'. These societies were considered unchanging and insulated and the European intervention was regarded as good for them, because it would break age-old structures.

We are primarily concerned with the third dimension of Marx's views that are found in his more systematic work, namely, *Capital* (Vol. I). Keeping in mind that population increase is the major factor of social change, Marx has examined the Indian village with a great degree of interest and curiosity. Marx has worked out the dialectical reverse of the explanation of social change through population increase. It is worthwhile to quote Marx (1954: 337) thus:

> Those small and extremely ancient Indian communities, some of which have continued down to this day, are based on possession in common land, on the blending of agriculture and handicrafts, and on an unalterable division of labour, when serves, whenever a new community is started, as a plan and scheme ready cut and dried.

Many of the factual observations of Marx, which were based on British sources, could be and have been questioned. Similarly, his argument that surplus produce to the market and rent to the state in kind were the only two transactions that took place out of the confines of the village political economy has not been found acceptable in the face of the empirical facts. It was, however, his attempt, which seems fairly successful, at connecting population increase with the lack of change in India that has still remained adequately and satisfactorily unattended and unexamined. Marx's (ibid.: 338) following observation requires a proper analysis, understanding and examination:

> ... If the population increases a new community is founded, on the pattern of the old one, on unoccupied land ... . The simplicity of the organization for production in these self-sufficing communities that constantly reproduce themselves in the same form, and when accidentally destroyed, spring up again on the spot and with the same name – the simplicity supplies the key to the secret of the unchangeableness of Asiatic societies, an unchangeableness in such striking contrast with the constant dissolution and refounding of Asiatic states, and the never-ceasing changes of dynasty ... .

In the above observation Marx takes into consideration two reasons for the emergence of new settlements – the first as a result of population increase and the other due to accidental destruction. What is the striking feature of this new settlement, according to him, is that it is a replica of the previous one, which signifies the unchangeable character of Indian villages. In fact, Marx makes a sweeping generaliatzion and covers all Asiatic communities. In the specific context of India, Marx's views are pertinent in the sense that it becomes possible to argue that if population increase does not bring social change, then it can safely be stated that the basic character of division of labour in the society remains unchanged. Durkheim, on the contrary, assumed that sparsely spread settlements might not experience physical density despite the population increase. One may also raise a question with regard to Marx's views that the emergence of a new settlement could only be possible if there was a space available for the purpose. As we shall see later on, Marx's arguments still hold valid in certain cases.

The sources of Marx's theory were largely the views and reports of the British administrators and scholars. One of them was Sir H.S. Maine who regarded the Indian village "marked by collective ownership, as archaic and representing the universal primitive idea of property" (Baden-Powell, 1985: 99–100). It has been argued that Marx was impressed with Maine's characterization of Indian village communities, which was quite close to the notion of primitive communism (Srinivas, 2002). Dumont (2002) pointed out that the earlier characterization of the Indian village community did not take into consideration an element of caste hierarchy, which makes it essentially inegalitarian. This fact of inequality in the village social structure rendered it ineligible for being a community. Srinivas (2002) has rejected this view of Dumont by arguing that even the communities in the West had class hierarchy.

Baden-Powell (1985: 19) has formulated the salient features of difference between two kinds of villages in India, namely, severalty or *ryotwari* village and joint village. This classification of villages on the basis of the system of revenue collection also entailed a fundamental social difference between the two types of villages. In the case of severalty village the holdings were entirely separate and the individual holder was responsible for the payment of revenue, whereas in the case of joint village all holdings were joint and the revenue liability was assessed in lump sum. It was the latter kind of villages that were common and this fact led the British to believe in common property and village community as a stable and unchanging entity to which Marx responded. Durkheim, while reviewing Baden-Powell's work, also pointed out that such kind of jointness is an ancient form of property (c.f. Dumont, 2002).

Still another feature of the village community in India, according to Srinivas (1960a: 22), "is the *panchayat* or council of elders which decided disputes between villagers, and discusses matters of common interest such as holding a festival and building a temple or road". The existence of village panchayats at the informal level was never disputed, but this is a very limited explication of the functions of the panchayat. In fact, undertaking development activities has never been the main function of these panchayats. Their main function has always been to uphold the collective consciousness of the community. Sangwan (1997) has shown that confining the informal functioning of the panchayats to the narrow confines of the village is a limited understanding of the village reality. In his study of *khap* panchayats, Sangwan has argued that the informal system of village councils has large number of villages under its jurisdiction. In another article, Srinivas (2002) has attempted to demolish the earlier conception of villages as autonomous republics. He identifies various areas of interaction of the village with the market and state. According to him, even the assumption that the village was a self-sufficient unit of production and consumption was wrong, as all villages could not have produced salt or sugar. The relative autonomy of the village community existed within the limits and confines of certain unwritten rules and conventions. So long as the king was receiving the revenue, he never bothered to temper with the social practices.

There is an underlying assumption that villages in India have tremendous similarity with each other. Baden-Powell (1985: 98) makes it clear that "the Indian village communities may differ locally in detail; they may exhibit signs of decay and change; but for purposes of comparative study they may be represented by singly typical form to which all approximate". It all depends upon the researcher's objectives according to which he/she works out his/her methodology. It may be reminded that methodology, as Wittgenstein (1967: 225e) points out, has a double meaning. Not only a physical investigation, but also a conceptual one, can be called 'methodological investigation'. If one is aimed at finding out certain common features among villages in India, then one would be able to identify some of them, because by definition village is a settlement that is based on agricultural production at the first place. However, the expression 'village India' basically characterizes Indian society as a 'nation of villages'. These common features are to be identified in terms of what constitutes the unity of a village.

The unity of the village is invariably understood as based on caste hierarchy and interdependence of castes. This interdependence is both social and economic. Essentially based on the functionalist paradigm, the elements of the village social organization are represented in such a way so as to provide a landscape of duties and obligations of each caste towards the other in a hierarchy. Similarly, the *jajmani* system further epitomizes the functional unity of the village community, which is the underlying logic of the most of villages in the country. As pointed out earlier, it is a question of objectives and subsequent choice of methods of research. One could find the elements that cause disunity, discord and conflict within the village. In fact, both are present. Village is a microcosm of the Indian rural society, but this fact must not ignore the position, relation and interdependence of the village with the surrounding villages.

Various conceptual constructions of Indian villages missed certain important facts for elaboration though these were noticed and recorded. Srinivas (1960b: 4) wrote: "There is another fact which is worthy of note. It is much more difficult for an Indian to observe his own society than it is for a non-Indian." We may raise doubts on the efficacy of this view of Srinivas. It is not a question of whether an Indian would ignore certain aspects of society or a non-Indian would be able to observe everything of significance. In fact, both of them are capable of observing all aspects of villages and neither of them may note every detail. The ethnographic method is primarily aimed at the collection of every social fact at the grassroots level. However, important thing is to interpret the data, which have been collected. For the purpose of interpretation a researcher needs a perspective of theoretical nature without which he/she may be unable to make sense of the facts. One must not sacrifice commonsense for highly logical structures as pointed out by Russell (1965) in his comparison of the philosophies of Berkeley and Locke.

In the specific context of Indian society, the inability of virtually all researchers to take cogniaznce and note of certain facts for interpretation stemmed from the lack of adequate theoretical perspective and subsequently the failure to develop appropriate methods for the study. Marx's explanation of Indian villages was never exhaustively put under investigation for which there was a need for examining a village in relation to its surrounding villages. We may thus identify certain common facts though observed by many scholars, but never examined and investigated in greater detail so as to offer some explanation for their existence and persistence. In the proceeding discussion an attempt has been made to identify and locate certain facts in some of the well-known studies for which we hardly find any attempt at analysis.

We may begin with Baden-Powell (1985: 15–16) who observed that invariably the people owning land in a village belong to one caste. In some cases, "the whole area claimed (in shares) by dominant class, who in some cases, cultivate their own holdings (e.g., the Jat villages of the Punjab), but frequently have a body of tenants under them". What Baden-Powell indicated about the villages of the 19th century India was that the predominant trend, which could be observed, was the ownership of land of a village by one caste irrespective of what kind of system of cultivation was operating, which, as his comment indicates, varied from one region to another. Still another notable expression used by Baden-Powell is 'Jat village'. Obviously, it implies that the villages could be expressed in terms of the landowning castes as if it belonged to them. This perhaps could mean that in India we had "Jat, Rajput or Brahmin villages" and so on, depending upon the members of which caste owned land. This is not to deny the existence of various castes that had been living in the village and were part of the village economic and social structure.

Still another fact that comes to light without much interpretation is regarding the founding of village, which is found in the work of Bailey (1957) and Cohn (1987). To take Cohn for illustration, he has worked out the pasts of the village Senpur in Uttar Pradesh near Benares. He (ibid.: 89) describes the village as " a Thakur-dominated agricultural village with over 2,000 residents and twenty-three different caste groups". In what sense Cohn uses the expression 'Thakur-dominated' is difficult to understand and interpret, because he is not essentially writing on the power structure. His construction of past of this village further gives us the idea that this expression has more than one meanings. It is worthwhile to quote Cohn (ibid.: 91) at length thus:

> ... The Thakurs of Senpur (with the exception of two families out of fifty-six who are related affinally) are all descendants of Ganesh Rai, a Raghubanshi Rajput who in the sixteenth century migrated to the present Jaunpur district from what is today central Uttar Pradesh. With his two sons he established suzerainty over the existing population in a region of about seventy square miles, containing today a little over a hundred villages.

Cohn has not worked out the implications of such a past. It is not in the scope of his reconstruction of the past of the village to find out whether this phenomenon of single caste-dominated villages is general or confined to a "little over hundred villages". It is less likely that all the villages were established in the 16th century. On may argue that these villages came to exist much after and might have followed the population growth of the villages originally founded by the Thakurs. There does not seem to be much difference between Baden-Powell's 'Jat villages' and Cohn's 'Thakur-dominated villages' in terms of what these expressions signify. Interestingly, Béteille (1971: 13) also observes: "*Agraharams*, or Brahmin villages, of the type which was common in the area until recently, were established extensively during the rule of the Cholas." Like Béteille, Gough (1960) also uses the expression 'Brahmin village' in the case of Tamil Nadu village. Similarly, Mukherjee (1971: 2) mentions the same pattern in his empirically-oriented work on six villages of Bengal that Rajbanshis formed one of the villages, namely, Harsahar, whereas "villages of Naopara and Amanipara are of recent origin. As stated by the local elders, these two villages are the off-shoots of the village of Hatsahar and were formed in old times when that growing village could not accommodate all its inhabitants ... ."

After going through Mukherjee's above observation one expects some reference to Marx's well-known views on Indian villages, but there is none. However, credit goes to Mukherjee by taking a cluster of villages for empirical investigation. One may raise a question with regard to the field observations of Béteille (1971), Mukherjee (1971) and even Bailey (1957) that when there is a reasonable basis to state that Brahmins, Rajbanshis and warrior castes and their villages had common identity, why the implications of such a finding were not analysed and investigated. It seems that the problem is with the theoretical and methodological paradigm, which they have used. Interestingly, Béteille (1971) based his village study on the Weberian model of stratification, but he did not pay heed to Weber's (1948) views on India where he has pointed out that with regard to the artisan production Marx was right. Since the theoretical orientation was different, the issue raised here did not figure in the list of their objectives. Srinivas is partially right in his contention that a foreign scholar may study Indian villages better than his Indian counterpart. It still is an issue of a different kind. One may ask what is the biographically determined situation of the Indian scholar? An Indian scholar may not substantially differ from his Western counterpart in terms of his perceptions of the village social structure if he has urban background. Tandon (1963) mentions that sometimes the city dwellers did not know about the village life at all. Even now, the villagers opine that the people living in cities do not know whether there is a wheat plant or tree. In this regard, the urbanized and educated Indian social anthropologist may be as fit a case to study Indian village as the Western scholar as Srinivas thinks. As a corollary to this argument, one may add that a scholar with a village background is located at a more disadvantageous position than the one mentioned earlier.

As a matter of fact as well as opinion, the issue of who is better placed than others to understand the social reality of the Indian village life is a misplaced contention. If we follow Wittgenstein's notion of language games, then it occurs to us that the possibility of multiple interpretations is always there. Whereas one researcher may be ignoring on aspect of the given reality, the other overemphasizes the same. In other words, there is not one and the only one explanation or interpretation of a given reality. Marx, Weber and Durkheim all analysed and interpreted capitalism of their times yet they differed from each other substantially. It does not imply that only one of them was right. Each of them rather used different perspectives to understand the same phenomenon. In this case, it is to be assumed that a village is to be studied from different perspectives. Placed in this context are the village studies in India, which have been having two shortcomings. First, most of the studies have been confined to the study of one village without having any perspective to see the village as a part of interconnected whole thus assuming that a village is a true representative of the rural life. Second, in the study of the village social structure, hardly any attempt has been made to probe further beyond the caste structure and economic and cultural interdependence of various castes.

At the empirical level the function of research is essentially investigating a given social reality from a theoretical perspective and accordingly a researcher sets the objectives of his/her study. In spite of the fact that each of the researchers mentioned here refers to his/her studied village as belonging to a particular caste and some of them have tried to trace the past of the village and tell us that some ancestor of that caste founded the village, we do not come across any attempt at explaining, analysing or interpreting this particular fact. It may be assumed that both the Western and the Indian scholars took this empirical fact for granted and regarded as irrelevant to the understanding of the village social structure. In the next section of the paper, an attempt has been made to understand how this dimension of village can be understood in the light of Marx's views on Indian villages which he put forward in *Capital* (Vol. I). It has already been explained that Marx's understanding of Indian villages emanates from the dominant 19th century view, which was shared by Marx, that the increase in population is the major factor of social change in society.

III
Empirical Observations

The social facts presented in this section are based on the field observations in villages of Punjab, but references to the villages in Haryana would also be made. There is a reasonable basis to infer from these facts, as we shall see, that as the villages of Punjab experienced increase in population beyond certain limits a new village came to exist, which was the replica of the original village. We may begin with the celebrated study of a Punjab village of Kessinger, which reinforces the observations of the earlier studies conducted elsewhere in India. He (1974: 34) writes: "The settlement and organization of villages in the Punjab is so much of the product of caste structure that an account of Vilyatpur's origins must start with a description of the caste which settled it." What is important in Kessinger's comment is that invariably the people of one caste established the village and he (ibid.: 34) further mentions: "Vilyatpur's founders were members of the Sahota *got* (clan or sub-caste) of the Jat *zat* (tribe or caste)." Thus, it is the people of one *got* who established the village. By definition the people of one *got* have one common ancestor. This fact is an important basis of understanding the Punjab villages. The issue of *got* has also been probed by Smith (1960: 167) thus: "In actuality, few, if any, villages are composed solely of members of one *got*. Nevertheless, villages are spoken of as being Sidhu villages, Ghil villages, etc. This refers to the fact that the village is said to have been founded by one or more Sidhus or Ghils, and that Sidhus or Ghils are the dominant group in the village, probably both numerically and in respect to the amount of land owned or farmed." Both Kessinger and Smith have dealt with the issue in a limited manner without working out the significance of one *got* in a particular village.

It is worth noting that the uniform structural pattern of villages in Punjab was disturbed by its partition in 1947 and as a result of communal riots millions of people crossed borders from one side of the state to the other. Thus, the present Punjab has two kinds of people, namely, those who are native of this part of Punjab and those who were displaced from the Western Punjab, which is now in Pakistan. The displaced people were resettled and rehabilitated at different places in Punjab. We can further classify the displaced persons who crossed the border to the Indian Punjab in 1947. In the first category may be included those Punjabis who were natives of the Western Punjab. They belonged to Sialkot, Gujrat, Lahore, Multan, Jhang, etc. districts and they hardly had any links with the Eastern Punjab. To the second category belonged the people from the canal colonies[2] who were the original inhabitants of various districts of Eastern Punjab and most of them were landowning peasants or ryots. They belonged to Lyallpur, Montgomery and Sargodha districts and at the time of their displacement they were well entrenched in their new places. They were resettled on evacuee's land, that is, land vacated by the Muslim landowners who had to go to Western Punjab due to riots. The resettlement of the refugees from Pakistan followed a pattern that depended on where the Muslim landowners had vacated the land. The resettlement and rehabilitation process in Punjab disturbed the distribution of people in terms of the region and the *got*. In the former case it may be pointed out that the present Punjab has three distinct regions known as Doaba, Majha and Malwa. After 1947, a considerable number of the farmers originally belonging to the Majha region were resettled and rehabilitated in Malwa and Doaba. A considerable portion of Majha had gone to Pakistan. For us, however, the second issue of *got* is more important. It is inseparably linked with the caste, as the former is the sub-division of the latter.

To recall the discussion in the previous section, one of the prevalent methods of characterizing the village is to identify it with the landowning caste. It seems improbable that the researcher would raise such a query. The Western researcher, contrary to what Srinivas (1960b) asserts, may never anticipate that such an overlapping between the village and the landowning caste exists in rural areas. The reason is obvious. It requires an extensive fieldwork not confined to one village but to a number of villages for which, to reiterate the same point, there is a need to have a theoretical perspective. In the discussion that follows an effort has been made to pinpoint certain dimensions of the village which may help us to make sense of what Marx said about the unchanging character of the village communities though he argued that the change is a dialectical process and inherent in the society.

When you go to a village in Punjab, you would ask a simple question, i.e., to who does this village belong? This means that which particular caste owns the land in the village. Asking this question comes natural to a rural Punjabi, because in virtually all villages only one caste is both landowning as well as dominant. The answer to the question would be that the village belongs to any among Jats, Kambohs, Sainis, Labanas, Brahmins, Mahatons, or some other caste. All these castes own land in the villages that belong to them. For example, Brahmins may be living in any village, but only that village belongs to them where they constitute the predominant landowning class. For example, village Raurian in Hoshiarpur district is a Brahmin village. Sometimes, two castes may be equally influential. For example, Matewal in Amritsar district belongs to Jats and Aroras. In some villages Jats and Sainis have the same position. However, such variations in the social composition of the villages, contrary to what Smith (1960) opines, are exceptions and thus rare.

Once a researcher comes to know the identity of the landowning caste of the village and is made aware of the kind of past of the village that has been investigated by Cohn (1987), the next query acquires a paramount importance. Following Smith's (1960) article on Punjab, if the answer to the first query has been that the village belongs to the Jats, then one may naturally, inevitably or inquisitively ask, "Which Jats"? However, it may not come naturally to many investigators. For it to occur naturally the researcher must have a stock of knowledge to ask this question for which he is expected to be having village background. However, in the case of Punjab, the issue of *got* is so powerful that when the researcher comes to know that the village belongs to Jats, he/she would inevitably, as it has happened in the case of Smith and Kessinger, inquire about the clan or the *got* of the Jats. This is irrespective of the fact whether this issue is analysed and investigated in proper perspective or not. Thus, the answer to the question is likely to be "Gill Jats or Dhillon Jats, and so on". For example, in the famous village Sur Singh in Amritsar district most of the Jats are Dhillon. What we call native villages will inevitably have the Jats belonging to one *got*. It does not imply that some families belonging to other *gots* would not be living. In fact, one will invariably find other *gots* too. Two factors have contributed to this existence of the families of other *gots* in village. One, some families might have purchased the land and settled in the village. The second and sociologically significant factor is that of what in Punjab is called *nanaka dheri*. What is meant by *nanaka dheri*"? It so happens in the case of some families that they do not have any son as a result of which the land is inherited by the daughter(s). The daughter(s) moves to her parental village along with her husband. Thus, a family of new *got* starts living in the village, but is always identified with *nanaka dheri*. In other words, when the husband settles in the village belonging to his wife due to property reasons the *nanaka dheri* come to exist.

More than anywhere else the correspondence between the village and the *got* among the Jat villages is markedly visible in Punjab. We find that the name of the village is also the *got* of the villagers. For example, the village Gill in Ludhiana district belongs to Gill Jats; Bhinder Kalan in Ferozepur district from where the well-known Sant Bhinderanwala emerged has Bhinder Jats. Similarly, we have villages Bainsan of Bains and Dhamian of Dhami (Hoshiarpur), and Tung of Tung *got* (Amritsar), and the list is quite long. One may raise an issue whether the Jats adopted the name of the village as their *got* or the founder belonged to that *got*.[3] However, there could be some villages where the Jats belonging to different *gots* reside together in such a way that no single *got* seems to be having a claim over the village. This radical change is a result of the partition of the country in 1947 and the subsequent displacement of a large population. The resettlement of the displaced people has dislocated the traditional and expected pattern of the villages.

We turn to the villages that are called as *jaddi* in Punjabi and its English equivalent 'native' may not fully denote its meanings. These villages show further sub-divisions that are called *patti*. A *patti* is a locality where all the families living except for those who belong to *nanaka dheri* are having a common ancestor from not a very distant past. To illustrate this point, we may take the village Butala in Amritsar district, which is a typical Jat village and except for few families the Jats belong to the Bal *got*. There are three *pattis* of the Jats, namely, Baba Palla, Narangpura and Rajpura. It is stated that all these *pattis* were christened in the name of three brothers. However, Baba Palla was a devout Sikh and when the sixth Guru of the Sikhs visited the village he showed reverence and attended the Guru with devotional hospitality as a result of which the Guru blessed him and told him that his successors would expand and prosper. The present prosperity and expansion of the inhabitants of the *patti* of Baba Palla is believed to be result of the blessings of the Guru.

The sociological significance of one caste and one *got* village is quite obvious in the sense that a village is predominantly inhabited by the people having a common ancestor, which implies that over a period of time their population grew to enlarge the village in area. However, the presence of a village having Jats of one *got* may not suffice to establish such a conjecture. It is only possible if we find a cluster of villages having the common *got*. Such a pattern is a reasonable basis to suggest that one among the cluster might be an original village, whereas the other sprang up due to the population increase as Mukherjee (1971) has informed in his study of six villages. There is further evidence that new villages of the same *got* came to exist after the original village experienced growth of population. For this purpose we have to enter and comprehend the anthropological constructions of the past of the village and also scan the region.

We find that the Jats of one *got* are not confined to one village, but they are living in a cluster of villages. In the case of other castes of this kind, we find they are also located in clusters. Though there are endless examples, yet let us take two *got* groups, that is, Bal and Dhillon. In the Baba Bakala tehsil of Amritsar district, there are about five villages that are contiguous and all of the Jats except for the *nanaka dheri* families living in these villages are Bal. These villages are Sathiala, Butala, Kammoke, Jhilari and Bal Sarai. Similarly, Dhillon Jats live in contiguous villages in Amritsar district, namely, Jhabal, Panjwar, Gaggobua, Padhri, Jeobala and Sur Singh. There is still another dimension of the spread of the *got* to a wide region. Most of the *gots* have their own past, which may be mythically constructed. In this construction, a particular *got* traces its origin from one village. To illustrate, Sandhus trace their origin to Sarhali in Amritsar district, whereas the Bals to Balabhgarh in Haryana, the Chahals trace it to Bhikhi Samaon in Mansa district, and Dhamis to village Dagana in Hoshiarpur district. Since the Jats have continued the practice of ancestor worship along with their conversion to other religions, particularly Sikhism in Punjab, the original village is identifiable. What is known as *jathera* in Punjabi language is an ancestor and the place where he is worshipped is called *jatherian di matti*, which is invariably located in the original village of each *got*. There is also possibility that each *got* may be having more than one place of *jatheras*. However, the affiliation of the people to a particular *jatherian di matti* is clearly defined. The contiguous spread of one *got* and subsequent formation of cluster of villages is clearly a phenomenon that is occurred as a result of population increase. The story of the villages in Haryana is not different from that of Punjab.

One may like to know the social organization of the villages, which were vacated by the Muslims and the Jats or other landowning castes have now settled there. We may take the instance the village Ajram in Hoshiarpur district (Judge, 1985). This village may be regarded as the representative of such kind of villages. There is no *patti* in this village and the Jats belong to different *gots*. The identity of each family has emerged in terms of the *jaddi* or native village. Thus, the families are known as Rajowalia, Sahriwala, Nasralia, and so on. In each case, the reference point is not the village in the canal colonies, but the village from where these families went to canal colonies. The power of the *jaddi* village lies in the fact that all of them have a common *got*.

The numerical preponderance of the Jat villages in Punjab hides the social reality of the non-Jat villages. These villages are hardly studied and empirically examined. Among the non-Jat villages we find specific castes to which these villages belong. There is also a regional specificity of the distribution of these families unlike the Jats who are widely distributed in Punjab. For example, the Mahatons have twenty contiguous villages in Jalandhar, Kapurthala and Hoshiarpur districts. The Kambohs have clusters in Amritsar and Sangrur districts. The Labanas are settled around Begowal in Kapurthala district. Sainis, on the other hand, are next to the Jats in numerical preponderance, but still have clusters of villages in Nawan Shahar, Ropar and Hoshiarpur districts. There are also Brahmin villages but they are numerically small and do not show the pattern exhibited by all other landowning castes. For example, villages Raurian, Bathian and Marhuli are contiguous and belong to Brahmins in Hoshiarpur district. The clustering of the non-Jat villages again shows that it has occurred due to the growth of population. This fact does not emerge obviously because of the small size of the castes, as it is difficult to order them along the lines of *got*.

Once we find the landowning caste to which the village belongs the presence of other castes follows a predictable pattern. Every village then has a few houses of each of the artisan castes like Kumhar, Jheer, Tarkhan, Lohar, Nai, etc. The settlement of Brahmins and Banias follows the same pattern. Next to the landowning dominant caste in numerical preponderance are invariably the landless dalit castes. In Punjab the Ad-dharmis and Balmikis are the most preponderant among the dalits. Most of them have been agricultural labourers. This fact of the existence of the service castes and their proportion in the population of village has been noted by Dirks (2002: 76) that "no village contained more than a few of these families ...".

At the first instance, there is a continuous and monotonous similarity among the villages so far as patterning of social life is concerned. This similarity is based on what Marx said about the division of labour as uninterruptedly and continuously based on the organization of various castes around the landowning caste. The uniform pattern of division of labour with a primacy of the landowners entwined with tremendous caste-class correspondence could be imagined in the pre-colonial India. The clustering of the villages having the same *got* of Jats clearly suggests that as the population of the village grew a new village came to exist. The past of the villages are the same. "When our ancestors moved from the original village they also took along all the *kamin* (artisan and working class) families that were associated with them", a Jat would tell any one interested in knowing the way his village was founded. The emergence of new settlements in Punjab is a process, which is still going on. The reason the people give is the same – the increase in population. However, the present process has undergone a qualitative change. The original village continues to be the main source of services involving artisans and labourers, whereas only the landowners move out of the village. Since the emergence of new settlement as a social unit is a long process, it is difficult to say what kind of shape such settlements will take in future.[4] Moreover, the material conditions have undergone a radical change after green revolution, and overall mobility of the dalits and artisan castes.

IV
Concluding Remarks

Varieties of conceptualizations of Indian villages and various methodologies used to study them ignored or lacked interest in examining an Indian village as a part of the totality of a large number of villages. For this purpose, they required a different way of looking at the Indian village and interestingly Marx's views on Indian village communities had elements of such a perspective to comprehend what the earlier scholars regarded as the unchanging Indian village communities. It is worthwhile to point out that even the Marxist scholars did ignore Marx's views on village India as interpolation of the prevailing perspective that an increase in population gives rise to social change. A typical instance of this is Habib (1995: 22), who has treated Marx's comments on village community in the sense of unchanging republics and seems to be defensive when he writes: "What one must remember here is that Marx is speaking of the internal conditions of the community, not of society as a whole; and even within the village community, he had noticed the existence of slavery ...". In this short defensive comment we find that Habib has missed certain basic elements of Marxist theory. For example, it should be clear that Marx's dialectical method is based on the assumption of the natural and social world as constantly changing. Secondly, in *German Ideology*,[5] which Habib mentions, Marx has made it clear that growth of population brings in change in division of labour. Inden points out that India was constructed as a country of villages though there were other countries in the east that were characterized by agrarian economies (c.f. Jodhka, 2002). From this observation it can be concluded that India essentially underwent the Oriental discourse of construction as a nation of villages. There is a principle of, what Wittgenstein says, certainty involved here. He rightly points out that the question of certainty arises only when there is an element of doubt. He (1967: 224e) comments: "But, if you are certain, isn't that you are shutting your eyes in face of doubt?" – They are shut". Thus, to say that "this is my right hand" does not come under the principle of certainty. The way the entire question of colonial construction of Indian past and history has been raised, it seems that it is almost certain that the British and other European scholars created a discourse and presented a particular kind of past history of India. There is a great scope for raising doubts on such a view. It may be reminded that the Western scholars could be seriously engaged in making sense of the reality, which to them was so different from their own. It was the interpretation of the data either textual or empirical that entailed a viewpoint in which a particular image of the village community was constructed. Marx understood and examined the implications of the lack of emergence of division of labour despite the increase in population.

The implications of the organization of cluster of villages that emerged as a consequence of the population increase and subsequent formation of a new settlement could be observed in social relations and political dynamics of the country. The clustering of a *got* of a landowning caste in both Punjab and Haryana provided tremendous solidarity along the particularistic lines. It was both a mechanism of control and maintenance of the system. In Haryana, the domination of *khap* panchayat in social affairs continues unabated. Once the landowning caste is organized and has solidarity, it could impose its will on other service castes. We know that political dynamics of the country in which the politics of numbers are central such clustering of the *got* or the caste in a region becomes the basis of the selection of a candidate in various elections. Such clusters reinforce their social domination when they get political recognition. In more than one way, India was a nation of villages that was ruptured by the British colonialism with the introduction of capitalist mode of production. The contemporary scenario of the *khap* panchayats taking decision as to vote for which candidates as well as ex-communicating a family are constant reminders that the village is still an important element in the definition of what constitutes India.

Notes

1. This paper is a result of the extensive fieldwork that the author has conducted in Punjab. See Judge (1985 and 1993) and Judge, Puri and Sekhon (1999).
2. The British established the canal colonies after the annexation of Punjab in 1849. Though the purpose of the construction of the irrigation canals was to maximize revenue collection, but in the process the peasantry of eastern Punjab benefited as it had already been marginalized. The land was allotted to any peasant who contacted the officials. In the process, cities like Lyallpur and Montgomery were established and the peasantry was settled on new and barren land that was made rich by the canal irrigation.
3. The author is grateful to his teacher Prof P.N. Pimpley for suggesting this issue.
4. The author observed the emergence of such a settlement in Hoshiarpur district near Nasrala village. The new settlement is located on the road from Nasrala to Ahrana Kalan. It is been named as Gobindgarh. In 1979, when the author conducted the fieldwork, a few houses had been constructed and looked like an extension of the nearby village. In a recent visit to that area revealed that a full-fledged locality has come to exist and it consists of various castes.
5. See Marx (1976).

References

Baden-Powell, B.H. (1985), *The Origin and Growth of Village Communities in India*, Jodhpur: Scientific Publishers.

Bailey, F.G. (1957), *Caste and the Economic Frontier*, Manchester: University of Manchester Press.

Béteille, André (1971), *Caste, Class and Power: Changing Patterns of Stratification in a Tanjore Village*, Berkeley: University of California Press.

Cohn, Bernard S. (1987), *An Anthropologist among Historians and Other Essays*, New Delhi: Oxford University Press.

Dirks, Nicholas B. (2002), *Castes of Mind: Colonialism and the Making of Modern India*, New Delhi: Permanent Black.

Dumont, Louis (2002), "The 'Village Community' from Munro to Maine", in Vandana Madan (ed.), *The Village in India*, New Delhi: Oxford University Press, pp. 31–50.

Durkheim, Emile (1933), *The Division of Labour in Society*, New York: The Free Press.

Gough, Kathleen (1960), "The Social Structure of a Tanjore Village", in M.N. Srinivas (ed.), *India's Villages*, Bombay: Asia Publishing House, pp. 90–100.

Habib, Irfan (1995), *Essays in Indian History: Towards a Marxist Perception*, New Delhi: Tulika.

Jodhka, Surinder S. (2002), "Nation and Village: Images of Rural India in Gandhi, Nehru and Ambedkar", *Economic and Political Weekly*, Vol. XXXVII (32), August 10, pp. 3343–53.

Judge, Paramjit S. (1993), "Scheduled Caste Women in Work Force in Rural Punjab", *Ambedkar Journal of Social Development and Justice*, Vol. 3, March, pp. 65–90.

—— (1985), "Class Analysis of Scheduled Castes in Ajram (a Punjab village)", in P.N. Pimpley and Satish K. Sharma (eds.), *Struggle for Status*, New Delhi: B.R. Publishing Corporation, pp. 191–216.

Kessinger, Tom G. (1974), *Vilyatpur 1848–1960: Social and Economic Change in a North Indian Village*, Berkeley: University of California Press.

Marx, Karl (1954), *Capital*, Vol I. Moscow: Progress Publishers.

—— (1973), *Surveys from Exile*, Harmondsworth: Penguin Books.

Marx, Karl and Engels, Fredrick (1976), *Collected Works*, Vol. 5. Moscow: Progress Publishers.

Mukherjee, Ramakrishna (1971), *Six Villages of Bengal*, Bombay: Popular Prakashan.

Puri, Harish K., Paramjit S. Judge and Jagrup S. Sekhon (1999), *Terrorism in Punjab: Understanding Grassroots Reality*, New Delhi: Har-Anand.

Russel, Bertrand (1965), *History of Western Philosophy and its Connection with Political and Social Circumstances from the Earliest Times to the Present Day*, New York: Simon and Schuster.

Sangwan, K.S. (1997), "Changing Aspects of Traditional Khap Panchayat", in Paramjit S. Judge and Satish K. Sharma (eds.), *Dimensions of Social Change: Essays in Honour of Professor P.N. Pimpley*, Jaipur: Rawat Publications.

Smith, Marian W. (1960), "Social Structure in the Punjab", in M.N. Srinivas (ed.), op. cit., pp. 161–179.

Spencer, Herbert (1972), *On Social Evolution*, Chicago: Chicago University Press.

Srinivas, M.N. (1960a), "The Social Structure of a Mysore Village, in M.N. Srinivas (ed.), *India's Villages*, Bombay: Asia Publishing House, pp. 21–35.

—— (1960b), "Introduction" in M.N. Srinivas (ed.), ibid., pp. 1–14.

—— (2002), "The Indian Village: Myth and Reality", in Vandana Madan (ed.), *The Village in India*, New Delhi: Oxford University Press.

Weber, Max (1948), *From Max Weber: Essays in Sociology* (tran. and ed. by H.H. Gerth and C. Wright Mills), London: Routledge and Kegan Paul.

Wittgenstein, Ludwig (1967), *Philosophical Investigations*, Oxford: Basil Blackwell.

22 Marginalization and Return

Agrarian Studies in India during the 1990s

SURINDER S. JODHKA AND PAUL D'SOUZA

I

Agrarian studies have never been a major trend or a fashion among the sociologists and social anthropologists working on Indian society. However, over the last five decades or so, the social scientists working on India have produced a substantial amount of literature on the social framework of agricultural production. Apart from extensive empirical investigations into the various aspects of changing structures of agrarian relations in context of the experience of development planning initiated by the post-independence Indian state or different movements by peasants and farmers, agrarian studies in India have also witnessed some of the most exciting debates in the Indian social sciences. These debates have been around questions such as situating the Indian experience or agrarian past in the larger schema of agrarian/economic history, interpreting the nature of contemporary changes in land and labour relations and the modes of conceptualizing these changes. Interestingly, sociologists and social anthropologists have not been the only ones who have produced this voluminous literature. On the contrary, a large proportion of this literature has been produced in the Indian context by scholars working in other social science disciplines, viz., economists, historians, and even political scientists. Furthermore, sociologists and social anthropologists focusing on some other aspects of Indian social reality have also produced rich insights on the nature of agrarian social structure and change. Most obvious example of this is that of the 'village studies' carried out by them during the decades of 1950s and 1960s.

However, beginning with 1980s the Indian society saw the rise of some 'new' social movements and the emergence of new agenda of research in social sciences (Jodhka, 2001). This trend was further expedited during 1990s with the liberalization process and a growing influence of neo-liberal ideology. An indirect effect of these shifts has been the marginalization of agriculture in the discourses on Indian society and economy. The agrarian studies also experienced a decline during this period in the social science academy.

However, notwithstanding these changes in economic philosophy or political priorities, the fact remains that nearly 70 per cent of Indian population continues to live in rural areas and more than half of India's total population still depends on agriculture for survival. In other words, the realities of village life and agrarian economy are hard to ignore. Consequently, after this marginalization for more than a decade, agriculture has once again come back to the centre stage of Indian society. The sudden and simultaneous spurt in the incidents of suicides by farmers in different parts of the country has produced a sense of 'crisis' for the Indian politics. It is this history of marginalization and return of agrarian studies in the Indian social sciences that we wish to attempt in this paper.

II
The Old Concerns

As mentioned above, though social anthropologists did not directly focus on studying the social framework of agricultural production and distribution, those who carried out 'village studies' during the 1950s and 1960s did concern themselves with questions of agrarian social structure. The foundational influence for the 'village studies' in India came from the fieldwork tradition of British social anthropology and new found interest in 'peasantry' in the western academy during the post-Second World War period (Sharma, 1997; Jodhka, 1998). The political restructuring of the world after decolonization had some important influences on the western social sciences. The most significant feature of the newly emerged 'Third World' countries was the dependence of large proportions of their populations on agriculture. The struggle for freedom from colonial rule had also made the 'masses' and the 'elites' of these societies aware of their 'backward' economic conditions and need for social transformation/development.

'Development studies' emerged as a new area of academic interest during this period. Since a large majority of the populations in Third World countries were directly dependent on agriculture, understanding the prevailing structures of agrarian relations and working out ways and means of transforming them were the most important priorities for development studies. It was around this time that the concept of 'peasantry' found currency in the discipline of social anthropology. At a time when primitive tribes were either in the process of disappearing or had already disappeared, the 'discovery' of the peasantry also provided a new lease of life to the discipline of social anthropology (Béteille, 1974). The 'village community' was identified as the social foundation of the peasant economy in Asia (Breman, 1987: 1).

It is quite easy to see this connection between the Redfieldian notion of 'peasant societies' and the Indian 'village studies'. The single most popular concept that was used frequently by the anthropologists studying the Indian village was Redfield's notion of 'little community'. Among the first works on the subject, *Village India: Studies in the Little Community* (Marriot, ed., 1955), was brought out under the direct supervision of Robert Redfield.

However, study of land relations and related questions of power and rural inequalities have not been completely alien to Indian sociology. Many of the colonial administrative reports had written on Indian countryside which offered useful insights into the institutional framework of Indian agriculture and the changes taking place in those structures after the colonial rulers introduced various reforms. Historians and economists also produced extremely valuable studies on subjects like commercialization of agriculture, peasant indebtedness and differentiation.

Though some sociologists working on village outside the dominant functionalist tradition, or those dealing with issues of nationalism or development did write on agrarian structure and change, it was only with the publication of André Béteille's *Studies in Agrarian Social Structure* in 1974 that 'agrarian studies' gained some degree of professional respectability in the disciplines of sociology and social anthropology in India (Jodhka, 2003). The decades of 1970s and 1980s saw major developments and debates on various aspects of continuities and changes in the agrarian social structure of different regions and sub-regions of India.

III

As mentioned above, beginning with 1980s, the Indian social sciences saw major shifts in its research agenda, and one of the consequences of these shifts was a marginalization of agrarian studies in the Indian academia. However, despite this marginalization of agriculture in public discourses, research on agrarian structure and village has continued. The issues and agenda have understandably changed. But, the old questions have also not completely gone away. A large number of writings and researches were published during the 1990s on subjects like land reforms, rural development, Green Revolution, farmers' mobilizations, labour, and the rural caste system.

Land Reforms and Rural Development

On the eve of India's independence from the colonial rule, the most important issue for the rural people was the issue of land rights. The policy makers also emphasized on the need of changing property relations in agriculture in order to motivate tillers of the land. It was with this dual motive of social equity and increasing productivity of land that land reform legislations were introduced during the early years of independence. While land reforms as such have become history, writings on the subject have kept coming.

The recent writings on land reforms could be divided into two categories. The first set of writings continues to focus on conventional issues, such as examining the implementations of different legislations in various states of India, and the specific strategies used by the various categories of actors involved (peasant/tenants, landowners, political elite, bureaucracy, etc.) in scuttling or facilitating the implementation of different legislations. Some of these also look at the specific trajectories of the contexts that enabled implementation of land reforms in some regions/sub-regions and their scuttling in some other regions/sub-regions (Radhakrishnan, 1989; Yugandhar and Iyer, 1993; Judge, 1999; Damle, 1993; Jha, 2002; Gill, 2001).

The second set of writings includes those that argue for continued significance and need of land reforms even today. Scholars have identified different reasons for advocating land reforms as a viable and meaningful strategy/policy of rural development. Such reforms, according to these scholars, are the best method of empowering the large rural populations of landless in Third World countries. Their success would also facilitate democratization at local level by eroding power of the traditionally dominant sections of the rural society. It is a known fact, they point out, that those who do not own agricultural land are also among the poorest in rural India. Land reforms could also be a useful policy instrument from the point of view of environmental protection. The possession of secure land titles encourages peasants to pursue sustainable practices of agricultural development (Ghimire, 2002).

Some other scholars have proposed the opposite solution. Given the increasing fragmentation of holdings, there was a case for collectivization of land through the village panchayats. Apart from making cultivation viable, such a process could help in improving agriculture. Collectively the panchayats could use the latest technology more viably and without creating class polarization and social conflict. They could also play an important role in developing small-scale industry for processing agricultural products, thus generating additional employment (Gill, 2001).

Some scholars have also pointed to the emerging new realities of agrarian relations in different regions of India. For example, in some pockets of India (such as Punjab), the nature and meaning of tenancy has completely changed with the growing popularity of what has come to be known as the 'reverse tenancy' where unlike the past, it is the bigger farmers who lease-in land from smaller landowners, who find it unviable to cultivate their small plots of land on their own. With sub-divisions within the family, their holdings have become too tiny to keep the owners of small plots of land bound to the land. So, some of them move out of agriculture, to non-farm employment, giving their lands on lease to enterprising middle and big farmers (Gill, 2001).

Green Revolution and the Changing Agrarian Relations

As was the case with land reforms, study of Green Revolution was not a major concern among scholars during the period being surveyed here. In fact, it is the petering away of the benefits of Green Revolution and the negative environmental impact of the new agricultural technology that was the concern among scholars during this period. There have been several writings on the negative consequences of Green Revolution technology, particularly its alleged role in depleting the ground water and creating environmental crisis (Shiva, 1989).

However, some scholars have also defended the Green Revolution technology. Himmat Singh, for example, argued quite passionately in defence of the Punjab experience of Green Revolution. According to him, the positive effects of new technology did not peter out after the initial successes. The state of Punjab continued to experience "sustained real per capita rise in income levels" through the decades of 1980s and 1990s. Environmentally also, agriculture-led economic growth has its positive effects. The Punjab experience shows that despite a rapid growth of its economy, the forest cover has not declined. On the contrary, the total area classified as 'forests' grew from 35,000 hectares in 1960–61 to 1,23,000 hectares in 1970–71 and further to 2,22,000 hectares by 1990–91. At the social and political plane also, the Green Revolution did not widen inequalities or lead to a 'red revolution', as was predicted by some. On the contrary, it has been a scale-neutral technology (Singh, 2001).

Though the Green Revolution technology was initially introduced in some selected pockets, over the years it has spread to other regions or states of India as well. However, the trajectory of agrarian change has not been the same everywhere and the generalizations derived from Punjab experience do not necessarily apply to other regions.

In West Bengal, for example, the Green Revolution was experienced without tractors. Irrigation, and not mechanization, was the 'leading input' in agricultural modernization. The use of HYV seeds and chemical fertilizers were introduced in a very different framework of agrarian relations. The introduction of new technology in the region was preceded by a successful implementation of land reform legislations, the 'operation barga'. As a consequence, the new technology did not accentuate social inequalities in the West Bengal countryside. However, the situation was very different in the neighbouring Bangladesh where in absence of land reforms, Green Revolution did widen social disparities (Dasgupta, 1998).

More or less, same has been the case with Bihar. Notwithstanding its popular image of being a region without any economic dynamism, the agrarian economy of Bihar has been undergoing changes. Use of tractors and other machines has grown. So is the use HYV seeds and chemical fertilizers. More importantly, the agrarian social structure has also undergone many changes. Based on a field study of a village of north Bihar, Anand Chakravarti pointed to the changes that everyday class relations had experienced in rural Bihar after the introduction of new technology. He argued that the social and economic landscape of Bihar was quite heterogeneous and the nature of stagnation and change also varied considerably within the state from one sub-region to the other. While there are some pockets in Bihar where Green Revolution technology has altered the traditional structures of agrarian relations, there are other parts of the state where industry has been a source of change (Chakravarti, 2001b).

Though the primary focus of Chakravarty's research was on the nitty-gritty of everyday class relations, he did not ignore the crucial reality of caste and its relevance for understanding the nature of changes experienced in contemporary rural north Bihar. While caste could not be used as an overarching category for explaining everything in rural India, its significance should not be underestimated. Caste defined the culture of exploitation (Chakravarty, 2001a).

Though the agrarian relations in Bihar had changed, everyone was not better off than before. Chakravarty, strongly criticizes those scholars who tended to ignore the profound negative impact that the process of capitalist development produced on lives of the underclass. The dominant landowner, the *maliks* could secure intervention of various arms of the state to advance their interests. As a consequence of the concentration of economic, coercive and social power in their hands, the *maliks* in the region were able to impose extremely rigorous working conditions on the labourers. They used unfree labour relations wherever it suited their interests (Chakravarti, 2001b).

Earlier, Tom Brass too had argued on similar lines for Haryana. He questioned the classical expectancy of the Marxist theory that the capitalist development necessarily releases labour from 'pre-capitalist' coercive relations. Brass argued that in the post-Green Revolution Haryana agriculture, farmers used the mechanism of debt and attachment to 'discipline' labour and 'decompose/recompose' labour market, which led to 'de-proletarianization' of labour. He went to the extent of saying that the indebted labourers of Haryana countryside were in fact 'bonded slaves'. Even when the recruitment itself was voluntary, in the sense that labourer willingly offered himself for work, the resultant relations of production need not be free in terms of the workers capacity to re-enter the labour market (Brass, 1990: 55; 1995).

Brass's formulation was however qualified by Surinder S. Jodhka who too had conducted fieldwork in Haryana around the time Brass carried out his study. While he disagreed with scholars like A. Rudra who had earlier argued that the attached labour in post-Green Revolution agrarian setting was more like permanent employment in the organized sector (Rudra, 1990), Jodhka also questioned Brass's assertion that 'bondage' of labourers with farmers was getting stronger and wider. Instead, he suggested that attached labour in the post-Green Revolution agriculture be viewed as "a system of labour mortgage" where the labourers, despite an acute dislike for the relationship, were compelled to accept attachment for an interest-free credit. However, their loss of freedom being temporary in nature, they could not be characterized as bonded slaves. There were many cases where the labourers after having worked as attached labourers for some time had come out of the relationship. The growing integration of the village in the broader market economy and the increasing availability of alternative sources of employment outside agriculture, along with the changing political and ideological environment of the larger social life had been leading to a process that weakened the hold of landowners over the labourers. In some cases, the developmental schemes, such as Integrated Rural Development Programme (IRDP), being run by the central government, also helped them get out of attached relations (Jodhka, 1994, 1995, 1996).

Some other students of Indian agrarian scene also participated in the debate. While Manjit Singh (1995) found Jodhka's position closer to prevailing situation in Haryana agriculture, Mohan Rao (1999) pointed to some issues that went beyond what was being debated by Jodhka and Brass. Given that capitalist relations were anyway about power and domination, the issue of 'free' and 'un-free' labour was not all that critical.

Though they did not participate directly in the debate, many other scholars working on agrarian change during this period focused on similar issues/questions. At a more general level, the evidence coming from different regions of India during this period seemed to confirm the thesis that erstwhile system of attached labour was indeed declining (Sen, 1997; Breman, 1993; 1996; da Corta and Venkateshwarlu, 1999; Lerche, 1998; 1999). However, these studies also pointed to enormous complexities and varieties of ways in which agrarian relations were changing in different parts of the country. For example, in their study of the Tamil Nadu agriculture, Venkatesh B. Athreya and D.S. Lindbery found that the ecological differences had an important role to play in determining agrarian relations. While in dry agriculture, family labour was more important, in wet agriculture it was the hired labour. A large majority of labourers in both the settings were employed on casual basis and only bigger farmers kept a small core of them as permanent farm servants to complement or substitute family labour. However, it was only in the less developed dry areas where family labour predominated that a large proportion of the attached labourers were bonded to their employers (Athreya and Lindbery, 1990). Against this, in the relatively less developed pocket of South Telangana in Andhra

Pradesh, the traditional 'vetti' system (attached/bonded labour) had nearly completely disappeared. All labour was employed on casual basis (Vaddiraju, 1999). In fact, here, it was the absence of Green Revolution technology that had weakened the hold of locally dominant castes over the labouring class. The emergence of backward castes as locally powerful groups was directly linked to this change in agrarian social structure (ibid.).

Similarly, several scholars have pointed to the fact that this process of change in labour relations also has an interesting gender dimension. While men were leaving attached labour, or in some cases even agricultural employment, women were forced to step in to fill up the space vacated by them. In other words, the employer farmers allowed male tied labourers to leave more easily if they substituted their female kin, usually their wives to work on land (Kapadia, 1997, 1999). This mobility of male labourer to casual or non-farm employment has not only led to what has been described as 'feminization of agriculture labour process' but also to some kind of 'neo-bondage' of women labour (Kapadia, 1999; Lerche, 1999; da Corta and Venkateshwarlu, 1999).

In another study of Andhra Pradesh, Priti Ramamurthy observed that though availability of employment for women had gone up after the introduction of canal irrigation and new seeds, the women she interviewed did not think that their overall economic or social situation had improved significantly that made a real difference to their everyday life. While the women labourers had to work now for longer hours, and more days of the year, there was no change in the overall value of work they did. It was still defined as 'light work' by their men (Ramamurthy, 1994).

Apart form the wider debate on the nature of changing agrarian relations in different regions of India, scholars during this period also wrote on other aspects of agricultural labour, changing patterns of their employment, forms of payment, patterns of migration, etc. Green Revolution technology has had far reaching impact on the labouring class. In this context, John Harriss has pointed to the fact that Indian agriculture is different from some other regions of the world as "poor people in India are not primarily 'small farmers' but those dependent on irregular and unreliable wage income" (Harriss, 1992). In other words, the landless labourers did not directly feel any positive impact of Green Revolution technology. Similarly, in his study of two villages in Bihar, P.K. Jha too reported that though productivity of land had increased in his study villages, there had been no corresponding increase in wage rates or increase in the availability of employment in agriculture (Jha, 1997). A little earlier Ahlawat (1988) had found a similar situation in Haryana.

Agrarian Mobilizations

In the classical notion of the peasant societies, the agrarian production is primarily geared towards consumption requirements of the peasant family or for those who are part of the local community and provide services to the cultivating households. Though peasants presumably generated surplus, the ruling elite appropriated it, generally in the form of land revenue (Shanin, 1987).

The logic of modern agriculture is however different. With the process of development and modernization a larger proportion of population begins to move to cities and gets employed in the non-farm sector. As the market grows, agriculture must also get integrated into the broader economy. Commercialization of agriculture that was enforced by the British colonial rulers in the 19th century was a step towards integration of Indian agriculture into the world market where the Indian peasants began to produce cotton for textile mills of England. This, however, was a dependent integration, which had disastrous consequences for the Indian people.

The post-independence Indian state initiated a qualitatively different process of the development and modernization. From land reforms to Green Revolution, it tried to provide incentives to the cultivators for increasing production of food grains and other crops. With the success of Green Revolution, farmers began to produce much more than what was required for the consumption of their families.

In other words, the new technology also made everyone compulsively get involved with the market. Unlike traditional agriculture, the cultivators in the post-Green Revolution agriculture had to buy all farm inputs from the market for which they often had to take credit from traders or institutional sources. In order to carry out these transactions, they had no choice but to sell the farm yield in the market even those who did not produce much surplus.

Given the precarious economic state of a large majority of them, they invariably sold their farm yield immediately after harvesting when prices were relatively low, and bought later in the year for consumption when the prices were higher. Thus, though the small farmers did take to the new technology, their resources being limited, it brought in new dependencies for them as well. On the other hand, it has definitely strengthened the economic and political position of the rich farmers (Gill, 1994; Banaji, 1994).

One of the manifestations of the growing market orientation of agrarian production was the emergence of a totally new kind of mobilization by the surplus-producing farmers who demanded a better deal for the agricultural sector. Interestingly, these 'new' farmers' movements emerged almost simultaneously virtually in all the Green Revolution areas. Though initiated in the late 1970s, these movements gained momentum during the 1980s.

Using the language of neo-populism (Dhanagare, 1994; Brass, 1994) and in some cases also invoking traditional social networks and identities of the landowning dominant castes (Gupta, 1997), its leaders argued that India was experiencing a growing division between the city and the village. While the village represented the real people of the nation, the Bharat, the city, i.e., India was alien and exploitative. The city exploited the village by manipulating terms of trade, the mechanism of 'unequal exchange'. The farmers received lesser for what they sold to the city and paid higher for what they bought from the city – the farm inputs (Omvedt, 1994). The nature of their politics was different. They initiated a new kind of rural politics – the pressure group politics. Over the years, some of them have also been tempted to join the party politics (Mukherji, 1998).

Those who led these movements were mostly the substantial landowners who had benefited most from the developmental programmes and belonged to numerically large middle level caste groups. This new 'social class' not only emerged as a dominant group at the village level, they also came to dominate the regional/state level politics in most parts of India. They had an accumulated surplus that they sought to invest in more profitable enterprises. Some of them diversified into other economic activities (Rutten, 1995) or migrated to urban areas (Upadhya, 1988, 1997) or entered agricultural trade (Harriss-White, 1996).

IV
The New Questions

The last decade of the 20th century saw several turning points and new trends, both in the Indian society and politics as also in the Indian social sciences. As mentioned above, the classical tradition of 'village studies' had, more or less, been over by 1960s or so. The agrarian studies became popular during 1970s. Though initiated by the economists, sociologists and social anthropologists also made several important contributions to this new trend. Economists also valued interaction with anthropologists in their efforts to understand complexities of the traditional structures of rural social and economic life. The dominant theoretical framework during this period was that of political economy. The 'agrarian studies' flourished for nearly two decades.

However, the 1980s and 1990s were important turning points in the Indian history. The Indian social sciences, as also the Indian society, witnessed many new trends. India witnessed the rise of several 'new' social movements during 1980s. They questioned the wisdom of developmental agenda being pursued with much enthusiasm by the post-colonial state. The following decade saw the beginning of liberalization policies and a gradual withdrawal of the state from the sphere of economy. This was an important ideological shift, a decline of Nehruvian framework of development and social transformation (Das, 1994; Jodhka, 2001).

Coupled with the changes in the geopolitics of the world following the collapse of Soviet Union, the end of Cold War, the unleashing of new technologies of telecommunications, this period also saw the beginning of new phase in the reach of the global capital. The process of 'globalization', as it has come to be known, was not confined to the economy alone. It has also influenced culture and politics everywhere and has opened up new possibilities for social interactions and networking.

The theoretical orientation and research agenda of the social sciences have also seen many changes during this period. The Indian social sciences could not have remained aloof from these processes. The gradual fading away of the older concern and a simultaneous ascendance of new modes of thinking has had some serious implication for the 'rural' and 'agrarian' studies in India. As mentioned above, virtually all shades of 'rural' and 'agrarian' studies from 1950s to 1980s were, directly or indirectly, linked to the project of 'development' and 'developmental state'. The growing influence of 'neo-liberal' economic philosophy not only led to an erosion of the 'developmental state' but also changed the priorities of development studies. There was virtually a 'paradigm shift' in the theory and practice of development.

Globalization and Agriculture

An important aspect of this paradigm shift has been to expand the reach of market and promotion of consumption culture. A direct implication of this has been the growing centrality of the middle classes and a gradual marginalization of the 'rural' and the 'agrarian' from the popular imaginations of those who mattered in countries of the Third World and in the global economy.

The new regime of globalization aspires to restructure virtually every aspect of the Third World economies including agriculture. From the system of state protection, subsidies, regulated markets and support prices, the farmers are being asked to prepare themselves for global competition. On the one hand, the farmers will have to negotiate with the new system of patented seeds, on the other, the food processing and related industries are likely to get more directly involved with the agrarian sector. One such form of involvement could be through 'contract farming'. Though, so far, the influence of the involvement of agri-business corporations is confined to only small pockets of Karnataka and Maharashtra, the trend is likely to grow in the years to come (Banaji, 1996).

The growing demand for processed food and integration of Indian agriculture into global economy could have far reaching implications for the farming communities and the rural social life. This process is still at an incipient stage and much of the discussion on the subject has been speculative, coming mostly out of the ideological predisposition of different scholars. While the neo-liberal economists and a section of the farmer unions hope that the globalization of Indian agriculture could infuse new energy and dynamism into the agrarian sector and would eventually benefit all, others, with left-wing disposition, are quite skeptical and have warned of the 'dangers' that these shifts could have for the Indian economy. Globalization, they argue, could turn out to be devastating for the Indian agriculture.

Some of the left-wing economists have, for example, argued that this kind of capitalist globalization could be harmful for the food security of India. The priorities of Indian farmers would be dictated by external factors instead of the requirements of local populace. In the new regime of market-driven production, farmers may move to production of those commercial crops that have greater demand in the global market, resulting in a shortage of food grains in the country. According to them, this is precisely what happened when the British colonial rulers forced the Indian peasants to produce cotton over food grains in order to meet the demands of Industrial Revolution in Britain during the19th century (see, for example, Patnaik, 1998). Some others have pointed to the environmental problems and a lack of sustainability of such practices. The new patent regime would lead to genetic erosion and a loss of the native varieties of seeds (Shiva et al., 1999).

However, such a view was contested by M.N. Panini, who, on the basis of his study of floriculture in Karnataka, argued that the agribusiness that has become popular in the region after globalization has injected a sense of optimism among the farmers. The farmers saw the new plant varieties and new cultivation techniques as opening the doors to economic prosperity. Their growing prosperity had also given a boost to the local economy. They were constructing new houses and spending more on education of their children. The farmers were also moving out of the smaller houses in the village to bigger farm houses, which resulted in weakening of the older caste ties and expansion of caste neutral spaces (Panini, 1999).

However, on the whole, sociologists and social anthropologists have done very little empirical work in this area as yet and one cannot say anything in conclusive terms about the possible implications that the process of globalization would have on agriculture or on the rural society of India.

Culture and Agriculture

Perhaps, the most important aspect of the 'paradigm shift' that took place in the social sciences during the 1990s was a renewed interest in culture. Culture had always been one of the core categories in the textbooks of sociology and social anthropology. Peasant societies were classically defined in terms of "a people following a specific *way of life* where land was both a source of livelihood as well as a source of identification".

Such a notion of culture was, however, widely criticized for being too general in nature. Also, it could not deal with issues such as power/domination, exclusion/inclusion. The 'new' notion of 'culture' that became popular during the 1990s drew its resources from the Marxist critical theory, post-modernism/post-colonialism and some new trends in the American anthropology. Culture, in the 1990s, came to acquire the status of a paradigm. Several scholars have written on the Indian rural scene and the peasant/agrarian economy using such a framework.

Perhaps, the first major attempt in this direction came from the discipline of history where scholars belonging to 'subaltern studies' attempted new interpretations of peasant consciousness in South Asia. Pioneered by Ranajit Guha, the subaltern historians criticized the prevailing tradition of history writing that tried to subsume peasant politics within the broader framework of the elite politics and thus erased the agency to the subaltern classes. As autonomous agents of history, they argued, peasants and workers could create their own forms of oppositional culture and identity (Guha, 1982). Though subaltern studies were initiated during the early 1980s, they continued to produce new volumes through the 1990s and their influence has been felt beyond the discipline of Indian history (Hardiman, 1996).

Another trend, which shared the notion of culture with 'subaltern studies' and appeared around the same time, though in different context, was the advocacy of looking at 'everyday forms of peasant resistance'. Initiated by James Scott (1990), the proponent of this view, argued that in absence of any organized struggle, the peasants subjected to social and cultural subordination, produce mundane and hidden ways of resisting oppression, through avoidance, ridicule and acts of petty revenge. Cumulative effect of these 'weapons of the weak' could, at times, be more effective in ameliorating their condition than organized collective action.

Using a similar critical/political notion of culture, some scholars also carried out ethnographic studies in rural India. However, their focus and arguments have been very different from the classical village studies of 1950s and 1960s. On the basis of his study of Alipur, a village in western Uttar Pradesh, Akhil Gupta (1999), for example, looked at the implications that the discourse of development has had for identities of the residents of the village. Development, according to him, was not merely a programme for social and economic change, but also an ideology and a discourse of post-colonialism. It was a body of knowledge that has been used by the new elite of the Third World countries to gain legitimacy for their rule and has shaped the everyday lives of the common people in a specific manner.

Underdevelopment, he argued, was not merely a structural location in the global community of nations; rather, it was also a form of identity, something that informed people's sense of self. Apart from the identities of caste, class, region and sexuality, the rural north Indians today have also acquired the identity of being underdeveloped, of lagging behind the West. The discourse of development made people look at things through a specific set of binary opposites, East-West, orient-occident, backward-advanced and traditional-modern. It was during the colonial period that these binaries and this language of understanding differences between the West and the 'rest' were first worked out by the colonizers. However, even after the end of direct colonial rule, the language in which the West understands the Third World and the way Third World understands it has not changed much. The continued use of 'traditional-modern' dichotomy even today is an evidence of this (ibid.).

Some scholars have also looked at the manner in which dissemination of modern agricultural methods implicates the local agricultural knowledge. The new regime of development and the intervention of external agents like the state causes re-ordering of relationship the local community has with land and the process of agricultural production. Arjun Appadurai, in his study of Maharashtra, for example, observed that the adoption and practice of modern agriculture led to differentiation of knowledge base of agriculturalists and a schism between subsistence and commercial agriculture. Such differentiation and alienation of knowledge from its original social base disintegrated the local community (Appadurai, 1989). Nandini Sundar too looked at the 'local modes of history-telling' or the meanings that people invest in or drive from their past in Bastar. These myths, she argued, may not be accurate indicators of historical events, they often form the basis on which social relations were sanctified or legitimized (Sundar, 2002: 145–46; 1997; also see Saldana, 1990).

Another interesting work in this tradition has been that A.R. Vasavi's (2000) who studied droughts in north Karnataka. Though drought had been a common occurrence in Bijapur, the response of the community has undergone a complete change with modernization of agricultural production. "In contrast to earlier forms of agriculture and agrarian life in which loss of crops were located within cosmological and social reasons, the modern production regime, based on market and scientific bases, provides no acceptance or collective framework with which persons can come to terms with loss of crops or the loss of sustenance capacities in agriculture … . Modern agriculture which provided quick and high productivity and profit provided no collective and integral frame through which loss of crop or a crisis in agriculture could be comprehended and dealt with" (Vasavi, 2000: 118–19). These studies are important as their formulation can help us understand the sudden spurt in the rise of suicides among cultivators in different parts of the country, a subject to be discussed below in the next section.

Though argued in a different mode, T.N. Madan (1994) also published a paper during this period on the network of relations between local Muslims and the Hindu Pandits that highlighted the different ways in which the two groups constructed their distinct religious identities. Through his paper, Madan underlined the significance of recognizing the fact that cultural pluralities are a common thing even at the micro level.

However, not everyone working on Indian agriculture or rural life has been equally influenced by the culturalist position. In fact, there have been some strong criticisms of these trends, particularly of 'subaltern studies' and Scott's work on 'weapons of the weak'. On the basis of his fieldwork in rural Uttar Pradesh, Dipankar Gupta argued that Scott's claim about the so-called 'everyday forms of peasant resistance' was actually based on the negative stereotypes that big landowners had spread about the poor peasants. To say that all poor peasants were cheats and liars helped the landlords justify their routine repression on the peasants. While some peasant did 'lie' and 'cheat' like everyone else, there was nothing salutary about it and these 'everyday forms of resistance' never led to any 'cumulative effect' that altered the existing structures of power and domination (Gupta, 2001). In his study of 'social power and everyday class relations' Anand Chakravarti had also argued that the low-profile strategies or the so-called 'weapons of the weak' hardly had the potential of making any substantive difference to the subordinate situation of the labouring class (Chakravarti, 2001b).

Pitching his critiques at a more general and theoretical level, Tom Brass argued that common to all those who invoke of concepts like 'moral economy', 'everyday forms of peasant resistance', 'subalterns' was the classical populist notion of undifferentiated peasantry. Post-modernism and culturalism had, in a way, revived the old 'agrarian myth' about peasant essentialism. Though they appeared radical, in reality, such writings on peasantry were conservative in nature. The ideological positions they advocated were basically hostile to any project of social emancipation informed by Enlightenment ideas and hope (Brass, 1991, 2000). On the basis of his empirical work in Rajasthan, Hira Singh also criticized the 'subaltern studies' for their symptomatic underestimation of the significance of land relations. They, he argued, worked with epistemological assumptions that were elitist (Brahmanical – bourgeois) in nature (Singh, 2002). However, notwithstanding such harsh criticism, the culturalist tradition is likely to stay, at least for some time to come.

Gender, Culture and Patriarchy

Most of the new studies using the paradigm of 'culture' were, directly or indirectly, targeted against the Marxist tradition of political economy that tried to reduce everything to class or economy. The Marxists had never been very important players in the Indian social anthropology or sociology. However, their influence on 'agrarian studies' was quite significant at the global level. The 'women' and 'gender' studies that began to gain momentum during the 1980s and 1990s questioned such frameworks of analysis where gender was not treated as a separate category of analysis. They criticized the gender-blindness of 'development studies', which included agrarian and rural studies in India. Though many of the Indian 'village studies' of 1950s and 1960s did report on the differences between men and women in the village life, they invariably presented such differences as "a natural order of things" (Jodhka, 1999). Similarly, in the famous debate on the dominant mode of production in the Indian agriculture carried out by Marxist scholars during 1970s, hardly any references were made to different ways in which men and women were subordinated in different mode of production.

Apart from pointing to the 'gender blindness' of much of the development theory and the empirical surveys on issues such as poverty and land rights of women in the region (Agarwal, 1994), students of gender and agrarian change have also shown how the new technology had a clear bias against women. It marginalized the female agricultural wage labour both in terms of work as well as earnings (Chowdhry, 1994; Kapadia, 1996).

Scholars also pointed to internal differences among women and the differential impact of change on classes or categories of women. Joan P. Mencher, for example, argued that the type of work women do depends on the social class they come from (Mencher, 1996). Among the landless, women regularly work both in fields and at home. Among the small landowners, they work on their own farms and at times even on wage. Among the bigger landowners also, apart from the household work, women did a lot of work at the cattleshed. A lot of women in these households also supervised their farms, particularly where male head was not around (ibid.).

Some scholars also commented on the status co-relates of women participation in farm labour. A study from West Bengal reported that "the relative social rank of a household was affected by the degree to which women carried out manual work. Within this, hiring out for fieldwork indicated the lowest rank, carrying out fieldwork on land owned by the household indicated the next lowest, withdrawal from fieldwork the highest. However, this was true only about caste Hindus and such a value-frame did not operate among the Santals, a tribe living in the same region" (Rogaly, 1996: 144).

Helen Lambart looked at the differential meanings of belonging and identity that men and women have in rural Rajasthan. When looked at from the perspective of women, categories like caste, kinship and village unity have different meanings. While men could live all their life in the village they are born in, women could rarely do so. They had to almost always migrate out of their native village at the time of their marriage. They, however, carry with them the identity of the village they were born in. However, in their memory of the native village, the questions of exclusion and hierarchy weighed lesser than the common identity of the native village. For example, while interacting with visitors from their parental village, the differences of caste and kinship were of relatively less significance for them as compared to men (Lambert, 1997).

Ecology and Environment

Another corollary of the decline of Nehruvian ideology during 1980s and the growing influence of post-modernist critiques of development was coming in prominence of the questions of environment. Different parts of India had also witnessed powerful mobilizations around the questions of ecology and environment during 1980s. The famous 'Chipko' movement against the felling of trees for commercial use by the local poor and the mobilizations against the displacement of tribals and peasants from their villages for the building of a dam on Narmada river acquired global visibility.

Vastly influential writings of Ramachandra Guha on the Chipko movement (Guha, 1989) and Amita Baviskar's book on Narmada Bachao Andolan (Baviskar, 1995) both appeared during the period under review. Several other scholars have also written on these movements and on the issues of rehabilitation of the displaced (Das, 1996). Some scholars also wrote on questions relating to common property resources (CPR) in rural India and how their depletion was affecting the rural poor. The poor in rural India derived part of their livelihood from CRPs. However, with Green Revolution and other changes in rural economy, these resources had been shrinking making life more difficult for the poor and the marginal (Jodha, 1995; Beck, 1994, 2000; Chakravarty-Kaul, 1999; Chopra, 2001; Didibhavi, 2000).

Apart from the writings on these two celebrated movement, several other questions of environment and ecology have also been of interest to sociologists and social anthropologists. In fact, there has been a spurt of researches on related issues. For example, the question of sustainability of the new technology and viability of the Green Revolution have become compelling issues not only for the social scientists but also for policy makers and planners. Some scholars have also raised questions about the manner in which natural resources ought to be used. What roles should the state, the market and the local communities have in their management and the regulation? How could the use of these resources be regulated? (Sundar, 2001; Baviskar, 1995, 1999; Bose, 2000; Roy, 1989).

Environment and ecology have not merely been new areas of research for sociologists and social anthropologists, the popular discourses on environment have also raised questions about the nature of Indian rurality. The discourse of environment has, in a way, revived some of the old notions of tradition and village life that tend to essentialize rural populations into homogenous communities (Baviskar, 1999; Jodhka, 2001).

V
Crises of Agriculture

The farmers' movements during the 1980s also reflected the growing discontent among the farming classes. Apart from bringing-in greater integration of agrarian economy with the larger market, the Green Revolution also raised the aspiration level of the rural populations. A small section among them has been able to diversify into other occupations, but a large majority of the landowning communities continue to be dependent on agriculture alone. However, there is very little uncultivated land available in most parts of India that can be brought under irrigation to take care of the increasing population. As a result, the holdings have been getting smaller with families dividing lands among the offspring. The growing pressure of competing in the global market and a gradual withdrawal of state has also made agriculture appear like a loosing game.

As the new agricultural practices have considerably enhanced the market orientation of the cultivators, all inputs required for cultivation have to be bought from the market. Since the smaller cultivators rarely have surpluses of their own, they invariably need to borrow for the fulfilment of such requirements. Their sources are mostly informal. At times, they have to borrow for consumption and allied requirements, such as weddings and major illnesses in the family. The only source of income being from agriculture, a crop failure could easily lead to a difficult situation for such cultivators.

Jodhka's study of three villages in a Green Revolution district of Haryana carried out during the late 1980s showed that the average outstanding debt of small and marginal farmers from informal sources was the highest even in absolute terms when compared with other categories of farmers (Jodhka, 1995: A124). Over the years this trend has continued resulting in a serious crisis in the agrarian sector leading to situations of desperation for some of them.

Beginning with the second half of 1990s media reports have been highlighting incidents of suicides by indebted farmers, virtually from all the Green Revolution pockets of India, viz., Karnataka, Andhra Pradesh, Maharashrta and even Punjab. Commentators on the subject have mostly tended to see a close link between these rural suicides and growing indebtedness of the farmers, caused in most cases by successive crop failures.

In a study of growing rural indebtedness in Punjab, Shergill (1998) locates the context of the growing indebtedness amongst the Punjab farmers in declining growth rate of agriculture, particularly during 1990s. Further, though agricultural production has been growing at a very high rate, per capita income of the farmers has not grown at the same high rate. More critically much of the additional income had been absorbed by an increase in the per capita expenditure and "rising living/consumption standards of the farming community". The growth in consumption having absorbed almost the entire increase in the real income of the agrarian population, only a few were left with any surplus of their own. As a consequence, farmers had to, regularly and routinely, borrow huge amounts to finance the modern agriculture.

Two studies of growing suicides among Punjab farmers (Kumar and Sharma, 1998; Iyer and Manick, 2000) had observed that those who committed suicide were mostly men from the landowning dominant castes. They were either small or middle farmers, owning land up to around 10 acres. Agewise, a majority of them were below the age of 30 and they had mostly killed themselves by consuming pesticides.

There was a direct link between indebtedness and suicides. The declining size of operational holdings and fragmentation of land was leading to pauperization of small and marginal farmers; growth rate had come down; and costs of input were going up. However, debt was not the only reason for suicides. The 'social factors' also played a role. The most important factors identified in this category by Kumar and Sharma were the 'family discord', followed by 'alcohol and illicit drug use'.

A general breakdown of the earlier ecological balance, disintegration of the 'community' and kinship support system in most parts of rural India and rise of some kind of individualistic orientations have also been identified among the crucial factors leading to such a crisis (Iyer and Manick, 2000; Ahalwat, 2003; Vasavi, 1999). Apparently, the Biradaris or the new institutions like panchayats and mahilla mandals were of little help to the desperate families. While in case of southern states of Karnataka and Andhra Pradesh, voluntary agencies (the NGOs) had come forward to help, in states like Punjab there were no institutions or agencies that were providing support to these families.

While in some regions the growing indebtedness of farmers was leading to increase in suicide rates, in some other region it was resulted in land transfers from owner cultivators to moneylenders. A study reported from Tamil Nadu that the local tribal peasants were loosing their lands to non-tribals. Tribals were invariably uneducated and in habit of drinking which led to their indebtedness and eventually to the loss of land. This process was pushing them further in poverty and state of marginality (Karuppaiyan, 2000).

VI
The Agrarian Studies Today: Concluding Remarks

As we have discussed earlier, the Indian society began to see qualitatively different trends during the decade of 1980s. Rise of new social movements questioned the hegemonic status of the idea of development. The collapse of Soviet Union and the ascendance of neo-liberal economic policies, globally as well as nationally, further marginalized the idea of development, as it had come to be known during the post-Second World War period. The growing reach of telecommunication technology and the resultant globalization produced a paradigm shift in the social science academy. The new language made popular by different varieties of post-modernist writings further reinforced such a shift.

The implications of this shift for rural and agrarian studies were many. The growing hegemony of the market brought the consumer middle class to the centre stage of the Indian society. The middle class grew in size, but more than its quantitative growth was the enlargement of its influence. A direct corollary of this was the marginalization of 'the rural'. Similarly, agriculture began to be talked about in terms of 'crisis'. From being the proud producers of food grains for the masses of India, the hard working farmers and rural labourers, in the new discourse of liberalization and market, began to be seen as being dependent on the state and lacking in competitive spirit. Study of agriculture and rural society was no more a fashion!

In purely economic terms also agriculture had been losing its prominence in the Indian economy for some time. Though it continued to employ more than half of India's working population, by the year 2002–03 the share of agriculture and allied sectors in the gross domestic product (GDP at factor cost) had come down to as low as 22 per cent (Khan, 2004: 3).

In the discipline of sociology/social anthropology as also in the common imagination, there has been a close relationship between agriculture and the 'rural'. One of the core defining features of the village has been the dependence of a majority of its population on the agrarian economy. However, with growth of technology and growing integration of agriculture into the broader market economy, agriculture begins to take the features of industry. In the developed countries of the West, agriculture has already been subsumed by the food processing industry. It has not yet happened in India so far but this trend is likely to pick up in India as well.

This marginalization and subsumption of agriculture obviously has far reaching implications for the agrarian economy and also for our understanding of 'the rural', in terms of its properties as a type of social and cultural reality. One of the direct implications of such a process will be that agriculture will no more be synonymous with the rural.

As the urban becomes accessible to the rural populations for employment, and for politics and leisure/entertainment, the nature of rural populations also begins to change and becomes more and more fluid. The labour moves out of village in search of better and 'secular' employment, the farmers look for opportunities beyond agriculture, leading to blurring of the boundaries between 'rural' and 'urban' (Racine, 1997; Rutten, 1995; Varshney, 1995; Sharma and Gupta, 1991).

Though, in India, demographically, rural population has not yet seen any decline, village has certainly begun to disintegrate as a social, economic and cultural unit. Though this process is not evident to the same extent in different regions of India, village is changing everywhere. When a village in Punjab attracts labour from eastern Uttar Pradesh or Bihar, its effects are felt not only in the village where the migrants replace the local labour, the rural life in less developed pockets from where the labour migrates also undergoes considerable changes. Mass media and growing communication is also playing some role in this process of social, cultural and political transformation of rural life (Dwarakanath, 1998; Kapadia, 1997; Johnson, 2000).

Village today means different things to different scholars. Similarly, when we think of agriculture, we no longer think of toiling peasants of a subsistence economy, living in a traditional and closed set-up. The agriculture is now integrated with the market. Even those areas where Green Revolution technology had not been introduced initially are catching up. The growing integration of agriculture into the market economy also means growing vulnerability of agricultural sector.

However, despite this 'disintegration' of the rural and a gradual decline in the significance of agriculture in the Indian economy, the logic of demographics works against any attempts at ignoring these areas of research. Despite a considerable increase in the absolute size of urban population, a large majority of Indian population continues to live in rural settlements and remains dependent on agriculture for its survival. Even when the urban population has been growing in proportional terms, there has not yet been any decline in the absolute size of rural population. Neglect of 'agriculture' and 'rural populations' could thus be socially and politically perilous. As is evident from the volume of research, after a decline of interest for nearly a decade, agrarian studies have picked up once again.

References

Agarwal, Bina (1994), *A Field of One's Own: Gender and Land Rights in South Asia*, Cambridge: Cambridge University Press.

Ahlawat, S.R. (1988), *Green Revolution and Agricultural Labour*, New Delhi: Deep and Deep.

—— (2003), 'Sociology of Agrarian Crises: Peasant Suicide and Emerging Challenges', *Man and Development*, September: 97–110.

Appadurai, Arjun (1989), 'Transformations in the Culture of Agriculture', in Borden Carla (ed.), *Contemporary Indian Tradition: Voices on Culture, Nature and the Challenge of Change*, Washington: Smithsonian Institution Press.

Athreya, Venkatesh B. and Lindberg, D.S. (1990), *Barriers Broken: Production Relations and Agrarian Change in Tamil Nadu*, New Delhi: Sage Publications.

Banaji, Jairus (1994), 'The Farmers' Movement: A Critique of Conservative Rural Coalitions', *Journal of Peasant Studies*, Vol. 21, No. 3 and 4: 228–45.

Baviskar, Amita (1995), *In the Belly of the River: Tribal Conflict Over Development in the Narmada Valley*, Delhi: Oxford University Press.

—— (1999), 'Participating in Ecodevelopment: The Case of the Great Himalayan National Park', in Roger J. and N. Sundar (eds.), *A New Moral Economy of India's Forests? Discourses of Community and Participation*, New Delhi: Sage Publications.

Beck, Tony (1994), 'Common Property Resources Access by Poor and Class Conflict in West Bengal', *Economic and Political Weekly*, 29 (4): 187–197.

—— and Madan G. Ghose (2000), 'Common Property Resources and the Poor: Findings from West Bengal', *Economic and Political Weekly*, 35 (3): 147–53.

Béteille, A. (1974), *Studies in Agrarian Social Structure*, Delhi: Oxford University Press.

Bose, Ashish (2000), 'Ecology, Economy and Society in Himalayan Villages', *Economic and Political Weekly*, 35 (31): 2707–09.

Brass, Tom (1990), 'Class Struggle and the Deproletarianisation of Agricultural Labour in Haryana (India)', *Journal of Peasant Studies*, 8 (1): 36–67.

—— (1991), 'Moral Economists, Subalterns, New Social Movements, and the (Re-) Emergence of a (Post-) Modernised (Middle) Peasant', *Journal of Peasant Studies*, 18 (2): 173–205.

—— (1994), 'The Politics of Gender, Nature and Nation in the Discourse of the New Farmers' Movement', *Journal of Peasant Studies*, 21 (3 and 4): 27–71.

—— (1995), 'Unfree Labour and Agrarian Change: A Different View', *Economic and Political Weekly*, 30 (13): 697–99.

—— (2000), *Peasants, Populism and Postmodernism: The Return of the Agrarian Myth*, London: Frank Cass.

Breman, J. (1987), *The Shattered Image: Construction and Deconstruction of the Village in Colonial Asia*, Amsterdam: Comparative Asian Studies.

—— (1993), *Beyond Patronage and Exploitation: Changing Agrarian Relations in South Gujarat*, New Delhi: Oxford University Press.

—— (1996), *Footloose Labour: Working in India's Informal Economy*, Cambridge: Cambridge University Press.

Chakravarti, Anand (2001a), 'Caste and Agrarian Class: A View from Bihar', *Economic and Political Weekly*, 36 (17): 1449–62.

—— (2001b), *Social Power and Everyday Class Relations: Agrarian Transformation in North Bihar*, New Delhi: Sage Publications.

Chakravarty-Kaul, Minoti (1999), 'Market Success or Community Failure? Common Property Resources in Colonial North India and a Case Illustration from a Cluster', *Indian Economic and Social History Review*, 36 (3): 355–88.

Chopra, Kanchan (2001), 'Wastelands and Common Property Land Resources', *Seminar*, 499 (24–31).

Chowdhry, Prem (1994), *The Veiled Women: Shifting, Gender Equations in Rural Haryana, 1880–1990*, New Delhi: Oxford University Press.

da Corta, Lucia and Davuluri, Venkateshwarlu (1999), 'Unfree Relations and the Feminisation of Agricultural Labour in Andhra Pradesh, 1970–95', *Journal of Peasant Studies*, 26 (2 and 3): 71–139.

Damle, C.B. (1993), *Land Reform and Changing Agrarian Relations*, Jaipur: Rawat Publications.

Das, Arvind N. (1996), *Changel: The Biography of a Village*, New Delhi: Penguin.

Das, V. (1994), *Mirrors of Violence: Communities, Riots and Survivors in South Asia*, Delhi: Oxford University Press.

Dasgupta, Abhijit (1998), *The New Technology and Agrarian Change in Bengal*, Delhi: Manohar Publishers.

Dhanagare, D.N. (1994), 'The Class Character and Politics of the Farmers' Movement in Maharashtra during the 1980s', *Journal of Peasant Studies*, Vol. 21, No. 3 and 4: 72–94.

Didibhavi, R.V. (2000), 'Management of Common Property Resources: A Review and Some Policy Issues', *Journal of Rural Development*, 19 (2): 199–217.

Dwarakanath, H.D. (1998), 'Mass Media: An Instrument for Rural Development and Social Change: An Overview', *Social Action*, 48 (3): 302–13.

Ghimire, K.B. (ed.) (2002), *Land Reforms and Peasant Livelihoods: The Social Dynamics of Rural Poverty and Agrarian Reforms in Developing Countries*, London: ITDG Publishing.

Gill, Sucha Singh (1994), 'The Farmers' Movement and Agrarian Change in the Green Revolution Belt of North-West India', *Journal of Peasant Studies*, 21 (3 and 4): 195–211.

Gill, S.S. (ed.) (2001), *Land Reforms in India: Intervention for Agrarian Capitalist Transformation in Punjab and Haryana*, New Delhi: Sage Publications.

Guha, Ramachandra (1989), *The Unquiet Woods: Ecological Change and Peasant Resistance in the Himalaya*, Delhi: Oxford University Press.

Guha, Ranajit (1982), *Subaltern Studies–I: Writings on South Asian History and Society*, Delhi: Oxford University Press.

Gupta, Akhil (1999), *Postcolonial Developments: Agriculture in the Making of Modern India*, New Delhi: Oxford University Press.

Gupta, Dipankar (1997), *Rivalry and Brotherhood: Politics in the Life of Farmers in Northern India*, New Delhi: Oxford University Press.

—— (2001), 'Everyday Resistance or Routine Repression? Exaggeration as Stratagem in Agrarian Conflict', *Journal of Peasant Studies*, Vol. 29 (1).

Hardiman, David (1996), *Feeding the Baniya: Peasants and Usurers in Western India*, New Delhi: Oxford University Press.

Harriss, John (1992), 'Does the 'Depressor' Still Work? Agrarian Structure and Development in India: A Review of Evidence and Argument', *Journal of Peasant Studies*, 19 (2): 189–227.

Harriss-White, Barbara (1996), *A Political Economy of Agricultural Markets in South India: Masters of the Countryside*, New Delhi: Sage Publications.

Iyer, Gopal K. and Manick Mehar Singh (2000), *Indebtedness, Impoverishment and Suicides in Rural Punjab*, Delhi: Indian Publishers Distributors.

Jha, P.K. (1997), *Agricultural Labour in India*, New Delhi: Vikas Publications.

Jha, P. (2002), *Land Reforms in India: Issues of Equity in Rural Madhya Pradesh*, New Delhi: Sage Publications.

Jodha, N.S. (1995), 'Common Property Resources and the Environmental Context: Role of Biophysical versus Social Stresses', *Economic and Political Weekly*, 30 (51): 3278–83.

Jodhka, Surinder S. (1994), 'Agrarian Changes and Attached Labour: Emerging Patterns in Haryana Agriculture', *Economic and Political Weekly*, 29 (39): A102–A106.

—— (1995), *Debt, Dependence and Agrarian Change*, Jaipur: Rawat Publications.

—— (1996), 'Interpreting Attached Labour in Contemporary Haryana', *Economic and Political Weekly*, 31 (29).

—— (1998), 'From 'Book-View' to 'Field-View': Social Anthropological: Constructions of the Indian Village', *Oxford Development Studies*, 26 (3): 311–31.

—— (1999), 'Patriarchy as a 'Natural Order': Constructions of Caste and Gender in the Indian 'Village Studies''. *Studies in Humanities and Social Sciences*, 6 (2, Winter): 119–39.

—— (2001), 'Marginalisation of Punjab', *Seminar*, Annual (497): 69–74.

—— (2003), 'Agrarian Structures and their Transformations', in Veena Das (ed.), *Oxford India Companion to Sociology and Social Anthropology*, Delhi: Oxford University Press.

Johnson, Kirk (2000), *Television and Social Change in Rural India*, New Delhi: Sage Publications.

Judge, P.S. (1999), *Social Change through Land Reforms*, Jaipur: Rawat Publications.

Kapadia, Karin (1996), *Siva and Her Sisters: Gender, Caste and Class in Rural South India*, Delhi: Oxford University Press.

—— (1997), 'Mediating the Meaning of Market Opportunities: Gender, Caste and Class in Rural South India', *Economic and Political Weekly*, 32 (52): 3329–35.

—— (1999), 'Gender Ideologies and the Formation of Rural Industrial Classes in South India Today', *Contributions to Indian Sociology*, 33 (1 and 2): 329–52.

Karuppaiyan, E. (2000), 'Alienation of Tribal Lands in Tamil Nadu: Panel Data Analysis', *Economic and Political Weekly*, 35 (37): 3343–50.

Khan, A.R. (2004), *Highlights Economic Survey 2003–04*, Delhi: V.P.G. Books.

Kumar, P. and S.L. Sharma (1998), *Suicides in Rural Punjab*, Chandigarh: IDC.

Lambert, H. (1997), 'Caste, Gender and Locality in Rural Rajasthan', in C.J. Fuller (ed.), *Caste Today*, Delhi: Oxford University Press.

Lerche, Jens (1998), 'Agricultural Labourers, the State and Agrarian Transition in Uttar Pradesh', *Economic and Political Weekly*, 33 (13): A29–35.

—— (1999), 'Politics of the Poor: Agricultural Labourers and Political Transformation in North India', *Journal of Peasant Studies*, 26 (2 and 3): 182–241.

Madan, T.N. (1994), 'The Social Construction of Cultural Identities in Rural Kashmir', in T.N. Madan (ed.), *Pathways: Approaches to the Study of Society in India*, Delhi: Oxford University Press.

Marriot, Mckim (1955), *Village India: Studies in the Little Community*, Chicago: The University of Chicago Press.

Mencher, Joan P. (1996), 'South Indian Female Cultivators: Who they are and what they do?', in A.M. Shah, B.S. Baviskar and E.A. Ramaswamy (eds.), *Social Structure and Change: Women in Indian Society*, Vol. 2, New Delhi: Sage Publications.

Mukherji, Partha Nath (1998), 'The Farmers' Movement in Punjab: Politics of Pressure Groups and Pressure of Party Politics', *Economic and Political Weekly*, 33 (18): 1043–48.

Omvedt, Gail (1994), 'We Want the Return for Our Sweat: The New Peasant Movement in India and the Formation of a National Agricultural Policy', *Journal of Peasant Studies*, 21 (3 and 4): 126–64.

Panini, M.N. (1999), 'Trends in Cultural Globalisation: Farm Agriculture to Agribusiness in Karnataka', *Economic and Political Weekly*, 34 (31): 2168–73.

Patnaik, Utsa (1998), 'Scenario in Developing Countries and India: Export-Oriented Agriculture and Food Security', *The Great Grain Drain*, Bangalore: Books for Change.

Racine, Jean-Luc (ed.) (1997), *Peasant Moorings: Village Ties and Mobility Rationales in South India*, New Delhi: Sage Publications.

Radhakrishnan, P. (1989), *Peasant Struggles, Land Reforms and Changes in Social Structure in Kerala*, Delhi: Sage Publications.

Ramamurthy, Priti (1994), 'Patriarchy and the Process of Agricultural Intensification in South India', in A.W. Clark (ed.), *Gender and Political Economy of Asian Systems*, Delhi: Oxford University Press.

Rao, J. Mohan (1999), 'Agrarian Power and Unfree Labour', *Journal of Peasant Studies*, 26 (2 and 3): 242–62.

Rogaly, Ben (1996), 'Agricultural Growth and the Structure of 'Casual' Labour-Hiring in Rural West Bengal', *Journal of Peasant Studies*, 23 (4): 141–65.

Roy Burman, B.K.,(1989), 'Society, Ecology and Land Reform in Tribal India', *The Indian Journal of Public Administration*, 35 (1): 41–48.

Rudra, A. (1990), 'Labour Relations in Agriculture: A Study in Contrast', in Utsa Patnaik (ed.), *Agrarian Relations and Accumulation of the Mode of Production Debate in India*, Bombay: Oxford University Press.

Rutten, M.A.F. (1995), *Farms and Factories: Social Profile of Large Farmers and Rural Industrialists in West India*, New Delhi: Oxford University Press.

Saldana, Indra Munshi (1990), 'The Political Ecology of Traditional Farming Practices in Thana District, Maharashtra (India)', *Journal of Peasant Studies*, 17 (3): 433–43.

Scott, James C. (1990), *Weapons of the Weak: Everyday Forms of Peasant Resistance*, Delhi: Oxford University Press.

Sen, Abhijit (1997), 'Structural Adjustment and Rural Poverty: Variables that Really Matter', in G.K. Chadha and A.K. Sharma (eds.), *Growth Employment and Poverty: Change and Continuity in Rural India*, New Delhi: ILO-ARTEP.

Shanin, Theodor (1987), *Peasants and Peasant Societies*, London: Blackwell.

Sharma, K.L. (1997), *Rural Society in India*, Jaipur: Rawat Publications.

—— and Dipankar Gupta (eds.) (1991), *Country-Town Nexus: Studies in Social Transformation in Contemporary India*, Jaipur: Rawat Publications.

Shergill, H.S. (1998), *Rural Credit and Indebtedness in Punjab*, Chandigarh: IDC.

Shiva, Vandana (1989), *The Violence of the Green Revolution: Ecological Degradation and Political Violence in Punjab*, Dehradun.

Shiva, Vandana, Ashok Emani and Afsar H. Jafri (1999), 'Globalisation and Threat to Seed Security: Case of Transgenic Cotton Trials in India', *Economic and Political Weekly*, 34 (10): 601–13.

Singh, Himmat (2001), *Green Revolution Reconsidered: The Rural World of Contemporary Punjab*, New Delhi: Oxford University Press.

Singh, Hira (2002), 'Caste, Class and Peasant Agency in Subaltern Studies Discourse: Revisionist Historiography, Elite Ideology', *Journal of Peasant Studies*, 30 (1): 91–134.

Singh, Manjit (1995), 'Capitalist Agriculture and Freedom of Labour', *Economic and Political Weekly*, 30 (52): 3390–92.

—— (1995), *Uneven Development in Agriculture and Labour Migration: A Case of Bihar and Punjab*, Shimla: Indian Institute of Advanced Study.

Sundar, Nandini (1997), *Subalterns and Sovereigns: An Anthropological History of Bastar 1854–1996*, Delhi: Oxford University Press.

—— (2002), 'Village Histories: Coalescing the Past and Present', in Partha Chatterjee and Anjan Ghosh (eds.), *History and the Present*, Delhi: Permanent Black.

Sundar, Nandini, Roger Jeffery and Neil Thin (2001), *Branching Out: Joint Forest Management in India*, New Delhi: Oxford University Press.

Upadhya, Carol Boyack (1988), 'The Farmer-Capitalists of Coastal Andhra Pradesh', *Economic and Political Weekly*, July 2, 1376–42.

—— (1997), 'Social and Cultural Strategies of Class Formation in Coastal Andhra Pradesh', *Contributions to Indian Sociology*, 31 (2): 169–93.

Vaddiraju, Anil Kumar (1999), 'Emergence of Backward Castes in Southern Telangana: Agrarian Change and Grass Roots Politics', *Economic and Political Weekly*, 34 (7): 425–430.

Varshney, Ashutosh (1995), *Democracy, Development and the Countryside*, Cambridge: Cambridge University Press.

Vasavi, A.R. (1999), 'Agrarian Distress in Bidar: Market, State and Suicides', *Economic and Political Weekly*, 34 (32): 2263–68.

—— (2000), *Harbingers of Rain: Land and Life in South Asia*, Delhi: Oxford University Press.

Yugandhar, B.N. and K. Gopal Iyer (1993), *Land Reforms in India*, New Delhi: Sage Publications.

23 Factionalism and District Level Politics in Rajasthan

A Sociological Study of Factional Politics in Udaipur District from 1954 to 1971

B.K. NAGLA

In this paper, we will discuss some of the studies on factionalism at district level in India which could be relevant referent points for our analysis. To begin with, we would take up Paul Brass' study: *Factional Politics in an Indian State,* which is based on factionalism in five districts of Uttar Pradesh, namely, Gonda, Aligarh, Dheoria, Meerut and Kanpur (Brass, 1965).

According to Brass, factional conflict at the district level has enhanced in an atmosphere of ideological consensus. Ideology is less important in district politics than at the state level. Most leaders are connected with more pragmatic questions of "how to get things done for followers and constituents". Thus, a faction becomes an interest configuration and not an ideology in philosophical or intellectual sense (ibid.). Factional conflict is part of the indigenous social and political order. The leader-follower relationship in a faction represents India's social and political structure. Loyalty to a faction could be compared with loyalty to a lineage group, to a caste, to a village or a region (Weiner, 1957). There are three varieties of factional system in India as observed by Brass: (1) dominance of a single faction at local level in the party for a long period; (2) the multi-factional system; and (3) the bi-factional system (op. cit.). These patterns of factional system referred to the concentration and the dispersal of political power in the Congress party in the districts studied by Brass. The important bases for factional formation are: ability of a leader to distribute material benefits to his followers, "including private economic resources", the lawyer-client relationship, control over a local institution of self-government, and cooperation and community support (ibid.). As such, according to Brass, a faction, is a vertical structure of power, which cuts across caste and class divisions; a faction is in this sense, like a political party. The ties between a leader and his followers, and economic patron and his dependents, and a lawyer and his clients are vertical ties. These ties go beyond the traditional loyalties and relationships. Most factions are based on a combination of traditional loyalties and relationships. They are based on a combination of traditional loyalties and individual interests. Faction leaders combine power, prestige and politics in their personality, and one could find various ramifications or combination of these three, namely, power, prestige and politics (ibid.).

District is the real political arena to see the operation of factionalism in different political parties. At the state level, factionalism gets diffused in terms of its social-structural base, and at the village level factionalism is predominated by primordial considerations, such as caste, clan and kinship. However, at the district level, political stratification and political alliances could be understood in terms of both the considerations, namely, social-structural and ideological. A district is an intermediate unit between the village and the state having an amalgamation of the characteristics of both levels. Brass, while analysing a high degree of instability of alliances, observes that the factional character of internal Congress politics in Uttar Pradesh tends to produce patternless politics (ibid.).

Anthony Carter's observation regarding factionalism is different from that of Paul R. Brass. He distinguishes between two types of political alliances, viz., vertical and horizontal. "Vertical alliances are those between elite leaders and members of political class generally, on the one hand, and their followers outside the political class, on the other. Horizontal alliances are those between one elite leader or political class member and another" (Carter, 1974). Carter further says: "Vertical alliances occur primarily within village arenas, and are most often tied on economic dependence. Horizontal alliances are found in all political arenas. Ties of caste and kinship sometimes influence them, but purely factional considerations are of much greater importance. Vertical alliances are relatively stable, while horizontal alliances are relatively unstable" (ibid.). Carter, while agreeing with Barth's distinction between description of 'pattern of regularity' and 'explanation of the processes', observes that studies of factions by Brass, Barth, Bailey, Mayer and his own analysis of alliances in rural Maharashtra[1] are attempts at explanatory generative model. They are all studies of dynamics of social organizations. In order to use 'generative model' in this manner, however, we need to know (1) how structural framework is interconnected, (2) how organizational decisions are influenced by structural framework, and (3) how organizational decisions, in turn, affect structural framework" (ibid.). In other words, the application of generative model refers to relationship between caste, class, kinship and class (structural framework) on the one hand, and political parties and factional alliances (organizational decisions), on the other.

Anthropological studies of factions explain connections between structural framework, namely, caste, clan, kinship, class, etc., and the studies by political scientists explain connections between parties, political alliances and factional coalitions. Both these types of studies are limited in their significance as the structural frameworks do not explain organizational decisions, and the latter do not explain how they affect structural framework. Analysis of district level factions and factionalism does not indicate patterns of regularity as it is found at village level, nor can it be a pattern of unstable alliances as it could be at the state and national levels.

We have another study of four districts of Maharashtra, namely, Ratnagiri, Poona, Aurangabad and Akola by Carras (1972). Like Brass, Carras also observes that factions do not emerge suddenly, they have roots in the past as well as in the present conditions and have ramifications at higher levels. It is a study of factionalism in Zila Parishads of the above districts, which are dominated by the Congress party. Factionalism, according to Carras, is determined by: (a) the characteristics of political actors, socio-economic and political environment; (b) a political actor's involvement in the power structure; (c) economic background of a political actor; (d) the nature of certain emotional commitments and attitudes towards the Congress party; and (e) particular combination of these factors (ibid.). Thus, Carras opines that certain hypotheses regarding explanation of Indian politics, such as personal or primordial loyalties, ministerial and organizational factional conflict and cultural or historical antecedents regarding domineering communities are not adequate enough to explain power politics and nature of Indian society. Carras says that factional behaviour of a political actor in India is 'rational' in the sense that it is predictable to a certain extent, given a certain configuration of environmental and individual factors (ibid.).

Factionalism in Maharashtra underlies some other conflict situations as well, which are perceived as distinct and isolated phenomena. The right and the left split represents basic divisions reaching down to local level politics at the district level. These two levels of factionalism make Indian politics rational and predictable. The element of conscious reasoning is also not entirely lacking in Indian political behaviour. However, awareness may be more prevalent in one segment of political elite than other. There are levels of political actors and of awareness, and these should be taken into account in underlying the dynamics of factional phenomena. Basically, relationship between political actors is a hierarchical one. However, to say that economic interests are rational or calculable is one thing and to say that primordial and personal loyalties are emotional or irrational is another, and further to say that they go against economic interest, is still a different thing. A number of studies of entrepreneurs, factory workers and industries indicate that primordial loyalties have not come in the way of fulfilment of economic interests and adoption of new ideas, innovations and technologies.

Factionalism is a complex phenomenon. Factional controversies and shifts in factional alliances at the local level are not automatically transposed into differences or oneness at state level and vice versa (Shrader, 1968). Sometimes the state leaders allow considerable factional controversies at local level and even encourage them while maintaining considerable unity at the state level. There is generally a hiatus between what the factional leaders actually want and what they do in reality. Therefore, there are several permutations and combinations in factionalism of personal, traditional, regional, ideological and strategic or contingent factors. Factionalism is not an organic process, affecting state, district, block and village in the same way. The differences can be seen in terms of the nature of conflicts and their manifestations, and also in terms of the contingent factors at different levels.

Now, we would discuss factions and factionalism in Udaipur district of Rajasthan based on our study conducted in the mid-seventies.

Caste Composition

Caste composition in Udaipur district is distinct from that of the other regions of Rajasthan. Dangi is the main agricultural caste (with the exception the Bhil tribe). The other important caste groups are: Rajput, Mahajan and Brahman. The higher castes never had a challenge to their dominant position. They have maintained their dominance even after independence. The Bhils, who are a numerically preponderant group, were outside the caste-fold, could not challenge, due to their socio-cultural and economic backwardness, the caste Hindus in electoral politics. Such a situation did not prevail in other regions of the state, where agricultural castes had numerical preponderance, as they were organically a part of the caste hierarchy.

Historical Background

Factions and factionalism in Udaipur district were not cut off from feudalism and caste system. We will reflect here upon historical background of the Mewar region, Praja Mandals and political dynamics to analyse factionalism at district level to understand factionalism at this juncture.

The evolution of legislature in the princely state of Udaipur was an outcome of cumulative effects of political consciousness, role of political leaders, and constitutional provisions in British India, especially in the post-war period. Political consciousness created realization for rights and soared spirit to fight for them. The religious and social reform movements of Swami Dayanand Saraswati and Vivekanand, the Bijolia movement led by Vijay Singh Pathik, and the Kisan (peasant) movements against *begar* (forced labour) and *lagan* (land revenue) encouraged people for non-payment of taxes.[2] The Civil Liberty Movement of 1938–39 and the Quit India Movement of 1942, under the influence of Gandhian ideology, played a vital role in creating political awakening in the state of Rajasthan.

Praja Mandal and Politics in Udaipur District

In the late thirties, Praja Mandal[3] emerged as a political weapon but its establishment was not welcomed by the princely states. The authorities of the princely states turned down the Praja Mandal as lawful associations.[4] Such adverse attitude on the part of the authorities compelled the political leaders to launch a movement to have recognition and registration of the Praja Mandals as lawful associations for civil liberties. The Mewar Praja Mandal was established in 1938. The Government of Udaipur declared it as illegal. The leaders of the Praja Mandal made peaceful efforts to persuade the state authorities to withdraw the order but the government did not relent. Left with no alternative, the Praja Mandal launched a Civil Disobedience Movement on 4th October, 1938. The movement spread all over the Mewar region and continued for six months despite the government's efforts to suppress it in a ruthless manner. A total of 288 persons were arrested, of which 35 were sentenced to imprisonment. On the advice of Mahatma Gandhi, the *satyagrah* was suspended on 3rd March, 1939, though the ban on Praja Mandals continued till April 1941.

The year 1942 was unique in the political history of India. Mahatma Gandhi gave the two-word slogan – *Quit India* – that stirred the whole nation and revolutionary fire began to blaze in every corner of India. In Mewar too, the movement was launched on 21st August, 1942. Citizens as well as students organized demonstrations and processions. Many leaders were arrested. Gradually, the movement engulfed all the towns and villages of the Mewar state, e.g., Nathdwara, Bhilwara, Chittorgarh, Chhoti-Sadari, Bhinder, Kenera, Bijolian, Rishabhdev, Rajnagar, Kapasan and Jahazpur. Resultantly, some five hundred persons including seven women were arrested.

The leaders of calibre like Vijay Singh Pathik,[5] Manik Lal Verma,[6] Prem Narain Mathur and Janardan Rai Nagar[7] played a leading role in political awakening and constitutional process in the state. Prem Narain Mathur, a scholar and politician, guided the activities of the Mewar Praja Mandal during the year of trial. He played a leading role in negotiating the constitutional reforms to be introduced in the state. Bhawani Shankar Vaidya, Vaidya Amrit Lal,[8] Dayashankar Shoktriya, Bhuralal Baya, Balwant Singh Mehta, K.L. Bordiya, the first generation leaders, and also Parasram Trivedi, Mohan Lal Sukhadia,[9] Nandlal Haster, Roshan Lal Sevak, Udailal Bordia, Shankar Bharti, Bhawani Shankar Nandwana, who were the second generation leaders, played active role in creating political awakening among the masses. It may be recalled here that activities of the people during this period were more or less of an agitational nature, with little or no emphasis on the constructive actions.

Against this background, the leaders realized that to create a healthy political awakening among the masses, education was the most effective instrument. This, they thought, will not only sensitize them but also enable them to understand many other serious problems, especially prevailing in the backward region of Dungarpur-Banswara. In this connection, the role played by Mohan Singh Mehta deserves a mention here. During this period, Rajasthan Seva Sangh was established in Dungarpur-Banswara region of the Mewar state with the cooperation of workers like Bhogilal Pandya, Jagannath Upadhyay and Chandubhai Trivedi. Several schools and hostels were opened by the Seva Sangh in the areas which had no educational institutions earlier. For this, effective guidance came from Delhi Lok Rajya Parishad, which had Haribhau Upadhyay as its organizer. This organization did a lot of work for mass awakening in the tribal areas. While these activities were going on, a significant development took place in the region. A movement, popularly known as 'Tejawat Revolution', took place in Dungarpur. It was a revolt against the oppressive exploitation of Bhils by the feudal authorities. Motilal Tajawat not only succeeded in raising the level of discontentment among the villagers against the state feudal rulers but also directed the activities of the oppressed people.

But this could not persist for a long time as Thikanedars and Jagirdars organized a counter-*morcha* to safeguard their own interests. It may be recalled here that that feudalism element was a strong phenomenon in Mewar throughout the 19th and the 20th centuries. Thakurs and Jagirdars wielded great influence on the ruler. Thakur Gopal Singh of Badnor and Rao Manohar Singh of Bedla were very close to Maharana Bhupal Singh of Udaipur. Having such advantages, the Thakurs and Jagirdars organized themselves into a political organization in 1945 known as Kshatriya Parishad. The Kshatriya Parishad played an important role in bringing some constitutional reforms in the state. In 1945, All India State People's Conference was held at Udaipur by the Mewar

Praja Mandal. Pandit Jawahar Lal Nehru presided over the meeting. The conference created a sense of confidence among the people. There was a great enthusiasm to effect political reforms. Obviously, the state authorities were vexed to find out some solution, as they had no other way out. It is important to mention here that the changing political situation in the country and the persistent demands of the people compelled the Maharana for introducing some reforms. However, the Praja Mandal rejected the proposed reforms, as they did not fulfil the demands.

In March 1947, Rao Manohar Singh of Bedla was appointed as the acting Dewan of the state in place of Sir T. Vijay Ragvacharya.[10] On the advice of Manohar Singh, the Maharana appointed K.M. Munshi as his constitutional advisor. He drafted new schemes of reforms and the same were promulgated by the Maharana on 23rd May, 1947. The leaders of the Mewar Praja Mandal also vehemently opposed the new constitution. H.L. Verma, condemning the constitution, declared that "Munshi's suggestions are not in the interest of the ruler of Mewar. Vijay Ragvacharya prepared two constitutions for Mewar. The constitution drafted by Munshi was also rejected. The Mewar Praja Mandal adopted a resolution in its meeting held on 11th June, 1947 and expressed strong disapproval of the constitution. S.V. Ramamurthi, a newly appointed Dewan, advised the Maharana to amend the Munshi Constitution in the light of public demands. Consequently, Dr Mohan Singh Mehta[11] was appointed to suggest amendments to the Munshi Constitution and the Maharana approved the same on 11th January, 1947.

The Mewar Praja Mandal decided to contest Legislative Assembly elections as recommended by Munshi. Twenty-three candidates belonging to Praja Mandal were elected unanimously. It is interesting to note that only two parties, namely, Praja Mandal and Kshatriya Parishad, contested. The first round of elections started in Udaipur on 4th April, 1948. When the polling was half way in the city of Udaipur, the Praja Mandal[12] decided to boycott the elections because of the alleged irregularities in the polling. This resulted in a strike in the city on 5th April, 1948. The Praja Mandal organized meetings and held processions and also went on strike. The Kshatirya Parishad supporters tried to break the strike. Several hundered people gathered at the Ghanta Ghar (Clock Tower). The Praja Mandal people removed the Kshatriya Parishad flag[13] from a truck and hoisted Tiranga (National Flag). In the meanwhile, students of B.N. College[14] appeared on the scene. Trouble flared up. The district collector and police intervened. But, the situation could not be controlled. Eventually, the police opened fire on the huge procession near Kotwali (city police station), in which two students, named, Anandi and Shanti died. Few persons were injured, including Gulab Singh Shaktawat,[15] Parasram Trivedi, Roshanlal Chordiya and a few others. The incident of unwarranted firing provoked two leaders of Praja Mandal to register their protests. Consequently, M.L. Sukhadia resigned from the Executive Council. The elections were postponed, the constitution was withdrawn and the establishment of interim cabinet was shelved. Thus, the efforts for the formation of a responsible government in Mewar came to an end. This incident gave a setback to Maharana, who wrote a letter to the Government of India for taking over of the state by the government. This was the last episode relating to the political movement in Mewar. Soon after, rapid political changes occurring on the Indian horizon resulted into the merger of Mewar along with other princely states into the newly envisaged state of Rajputana, which was renamed as Rajasthan later on. Maharana Bhupal Singh was appointed as the Maharaj Pramukh and M.L. Verma was appointed as the Prime Minister. The formation of Rajasthan was formally inaugurated on 7th April, 1949, by Sardar Vallabhbhai Patel, the Home Minister of India.[16] Patel impressed upon the masses in his inaugural speech that they should be above the ideology of regionalism/parochialism. Later on, the leaders of the Praja Mandal, namely, Verma and Sukhadia also agreed to Patel's advice to accept Jaipur as the capital of Rajasthan.[17]

Factionalism in Udaipur District since Independence

So far we have discussed the role of Praja Mandals, leadership and feudalism in politics and factionalism in Udaipur region during the pre-independence era. Now, an attempt will be made to understand factionalism and politics since independence. Our analysis shows that the nature of politics and factionalism in Udaipur district has been much different from the rest of Rajasthan and particularly from the rest of Marwar region. Generally, factions have been antagonistic within the Congress party in Rajasthan. However, factionalism has been by and large non-antagonistic in the Congress party in Udaipur district (Nagla, 1984). No common pattern of factionalism could be discerned in Rajasthan. A multiplicity of factors, such as events and issues, political awareness, and external factors such as factionalism at the higher levels determine the nature of factionalism and politics in a given region. We would analyse factionalism in Udaipur district in relation to state level politics and the role of Udaipur faction, feudalism and particularly the role of Maharana of Udaipur and other Jagirdars. We would also examine elections, sub-regionalism, and social background of the district leaders in the dynamics of politics and factionalism.

State Level Politics and the Udaipur Faction

The state level faction percolated down up to the district level politics immediately after independence. There were two factions in the early 1950s, one led by M.L. Verma and Jai Narain Vyas, and the other by Hiralal Shastri. These factions were replica of factions at the national level led by Jawaharlal Nehru and Sardar Vallabhbhai Patel respectively. The rivals at the state level had their followers at the district level. Such a rivalry motivated the respective followers to have offices in each and every district belonging to both factions. Udaipur district was also under the spell of factional fighting. Even academic institutions like Vidyapeeth and Mahila Mandal had factions parallel to political factions. In the PCC election the Shastri faction lost against the Verma-Vyas alliance. The Verma-Vyas faction had more credibility among the masses. Shastri was considered as an imposition by Patel although none opposed so long Shastri as Patel was there. Later on, all the three (Verma, Vyas, Bhatt) expressed their unwillingness to accept the leadership of Shastri in the PCC meetings. Knowing the mood of the people, the Vyas-Verma faction mobilized opinion in its favour in the Congress party. This faction did not have matching resources to counter the move of Verma-Vyas faction. Moreover, Nehru supported Verma-Vyas faction in the power game of Rajasthan.

In Udaipur the institutions like Mahila Mandal supported the Shastri faction whereas the Vidyapeeth had two groups – one supported the Shastri faction and the other Verma-Vyas faction. The Vice Chancellor of Vidyapeeth, Janardanrai Nagar supported the Verma-Vyas faction along with Prem Narain Mathur. This dissension divided the district leaders into two factions on the same pattern. There was an impression in the minds of the people that Shastri ruled like a 'dictator' since he had Patel's support. After the death of Patel, Shastri faction could not sustain and had to recede. Consequently, some members of the Shastri faction joined the Socialist Party and some who remained in the Congress had only a marginal status. Eventually, some leaders switched to the Sukhadia camp, as they visualized this group to remain at the helm of political affairs for years to come. This assessment proved to be true as Sukhadia dislodged Jai Narayan Vyas from chief ministership in 1954 and remained as the Chief Minister of Rajasthan for 17 years.

As a politician, Sukhadia understood the intrigues of factional politics and started casting his net wide. He functioned as a leader of the Verma-Vyas faction at the district level and worked against Vyas at the state level. With his political acumen he dislodged Vyas and became Chief Minister with the blessings of Prime Minister Jawaharlal Nehru. Several leaders shifted their loyalty to Sukhadia. Those who did not accept Sukhadia's leadership were isolated. Gulab Singh Shaktawat was the only person who was appointed as minister, not based on merit, but because of the support of the Rajput lobby. Shaktawat had supported Kshatriya Parishad and the Shastri faction. At Udaipur district level those who were incorporated in Sukhadia group too had internal bickerings, however, the same did not surface openly.

Mohanlal Sukhadia and his mentor Manik Lal Verma were the leaders of the Udaipur faction at the state level. The Udaipur faction drew its support from the Mewar region. The Sukhadia faction was quite cohesive. Sukhadia had the ability to accommodate diverse groups and individuals. He could ensure maximum benefits for the Udaipur region by adopting the policy of accommodation and adjustment. He was quite successful in winning over the dominant Jat leaders of Bikaner and Shekhawati regions, including Kumbha Ram Arya, Nathu Ram Mirdha, Ram Niwas Mirdha and Sardar Har Lal Singh. The Rajput leaders were also not away from Sukhadia's hold. By initiating a process of recruiting Rajputs into Congress party, Sukhadia won their confidence and support.

When Sukhadia became the Chief Minister of Rajasthan in 1954, he did not enjoy reputation of a state level leader and his political stature was low compared to that of Manik Lal Verma, Jai Narain Vyas, Heera Lal Shastri, Tika Ram Paliwal and Master Adityendra. Jai Narain Vyas was higher than all the leaders, and therefore, none of them could muster courage to contest against Vyas for chief minstership. No one stood openly against Vyas. They agreed for Sukhadia to contest for the leadership of Congress Legislature Party. In 1954, the Udaipur faction with the strength of 20 MLAs supported Sukhadia. Sixteen Jat MLAs under the leadership of Kumbha Ram Arya, also supported Sukhadia because they felt that the new leadership would be light-weight and short-lived, and this would pause a way for ascendance of the Kumbha Ram Arya group in state politics by supporting Sukhadia as their leader. The anti-Vyas faction, which included almost all top leaders of the state, not only from Udaipur region but also from other regions, made promises for giving ministerial positions to some of the close supporters of Vyas. However, Vyas refused to give such allurements and temptations either to his own supporters or to the supporters of the opposite camp.

Those who opposed Vyas in state politics included regional factions, and most important among them were the Udaipur faction and the Jat faction. After the defeat of Vyas for leadership of the Congress Legislative Party (CLP), many of his opponents turned to his side, including Tika Ram Paliwal, and some of the supporters of Vyas shifted their loyalties to the Sukhadia camp after he became Chief Minister.

Sukhadia consolidated his position by accommodating representatives of various regional factions, which had supported him in the leadership contest. He created an impression that there was no discontinuity, and he continued with the tradition adorned by his predecessors, particularly Jai Narain Vyas. But, in fact, Sukhadia tried to satisfy all those who supported him in the political game.

Thus, Sukhadia, by the time of the second general elections held in 1957, was quite successful in establishing his leadership. Such political credentials helped him in gaining complete support of the leaders of the Udaipur region. The Pradesh Congress Committee (PCC) was, however, under the control of Vyas faction as Vyas was the PCC chief. Several supporters of Sukhadia and Arya were denied party tickets. Those who stood solidly behind Sukhadia included Manik Lal Verma, Mathura Das Mathur, Punam Chand Vishnoi and Manik Chand Kothari. However, Sukhadia was successful in getting tickets for his supporters with the exception of one or two candidates.

In 1958, out of 119 members of the CLP, 15 were with Sukhadia, 45 supported Vyas, and 23 supported Arya. Arya again supported Sukhadia. The Arya group did not have any support from Bikaner region, while Vyas had support from all the regions including Udaipur. However, Sukhadia had maximum support from his own region, but Vyas had almost negligible support from his own region Jodhpur. He had maximum support from Matsya, Jaipur, Kota and Shekhawati regions. The Arya faction had maximum support from Bikaner, Jodhpur and Shekhawati regions.

Sukhadia became an unquestioned leader of the Udaipur region in 1962 when the charges made by Jai Narain Vyas against him were declared unfounded by Jawaharlal Nehru. Thus, the weakening of the influence of Vyas in state politics enhanced the hold of Sukhadia in his region and consolidated his position as Chief Minister in the state. The decline of Vyas in state politics did not contribute correspondingly to the rise of the Arya faction. Sukhadia did not give due attention to Arya's supporters. And, Sukhadia's position was not that of a solid and monolithic leader in his own region. Several of his own supporters, including some from Jodhpur division, opposed him and supported Vyas in the 1962 elections. They included Jugal Kishore Chaturvedi, Phul Chand Bafna, Bhure Lal Baya, Jai Singh Ranawat, Gopi Lal Yadav and Gokul Lal Asawa. Sukhadia had a sense of political insecurity after 1962 general elections. In 1957 elections, Jai Narain Vyas was supported by Jawaharlal Nehru, but Nehru's public denigration of Vyas at the time of 1962 elections created a sense of confidence and security in the Sukhadia faction. This was the time when Sukhadia emerged as a state level leader though he had been Chief Minister by that time for seven years.

It is interesting to note that when Sukhadia's position got consolidated at state level, he did not bother much about the Udaipur-based contingent of supporters. Because he had supporters from other regions of the state. During 1963–65, he had support from all the regions of the state. Thus, after 1962, Sukhadia extended his political base to other regions of the state where he did not have much support, and this he could do by creating cleavages within the existing factions. Such a tactic he adopted in the case of the Arya faction too. He offered ministerial positions to some of them, and consequently, they shifted to Sukhadia's side. Nathu Ram Mirdha, Mathura Das Mathur and others were cured by Sukhadia. Thus, in 1963, with the exception of Jodhpur and Shekhawati regions, Sukhadia had maximum support in the PCC from all other regions of the state.

Sukhadia had also maximum support of Brahmans and Mahajans from 1958 onwards, whereas Jai Narain Vyas had maximum support of these two castes up to 1956. Sukhadia had more support of Jats than Vyas, and Vyas had more support of Rajputs than Sukhadia. But, the fact is that these two castes had maximum representation in the CLP and the PCC. Kumbha Ram Arya's faction had no support of Rajputs till 1965, and he had always support of nearly 70 per cent of Jats. During 1948–50, all the Jats supported him. He had negligible support of Brahmans and Mahajans. In terms of representation in the PCC, Brahmans had maximum members. Mahajans occupied the second rank. The number of Rajputs up to 1956 was not significant, as there were not many Rajputs in the Congress party. The Jats occupied the third rank in the PCC up to 1956. The number of Rajput representation increased from 1958.

Thus, Sukhadia as a leader had support of diametrically opposed elements, namely, feudal and democratic. The Maharana of Udaipur bestowed his blessings on Sukhadia, and in return Sukhadia paid respectful tributes to the Maharana. The two supported each other without interfering in their respective affairs. Sukhadia had also support of his political mentor Manik Lal Verma, who even spearheaded a political battle against a stalwart like Jai Narain Vyas for his disciple, and ultimately succeeded in defeating Vyas to help Sukhadia to become Chief Minister of Rajasthan. Sukhadia did not have opposition from Jats as they were not strong in the Udaipur region as they were in Jodhpur, Bikaner and Shekhawati regions.

Political Participation

Elections

In the first general elections in 1952, there were ten assembly constituencies in Udaipur district. In all, 28.3 per cent voters exercised their right of franchise. The highest percentage of polling (37.9%) took place in the Udaipur City constituency, and the lowest was in the Kumbhalgarh constituency where only 20.4 per cent votes were polled. In all, four seats were captured by the Congress party candidates, and one each by Jan Sangh and Krishikar Lok Party (KLP). A separate seat for Lok Sabha election was allotted to the Udaipur constituency by clubbing up of six assembly constituencies. This seat was won by the Congress party candidate. The remaining four assembly constituencies were merged with another parliamentary constituency.

In the second general elections held in 1957, the number of assembly constituencies was raised to 11 and two were made double-member constituencies. In all, 35.2 per cent voters exercised their right of franchise. The highest percentage of polling was 58.7 per cent in Bhim constituency, and the lowest was in Gogunda constituency where only 25.8 per cent votes were polled. The Congress won 12 seats and one went to an independent candidate. The Congress party also won the Udaipur seat in 1957 Lok Sabha election too.

In the third general election held in 1962, the Congress party could win only five out of 13 seats, and the rest of the eight seats went to opposition parties, namely, Swatantra (5) and Jan Sangh (3). A total of 41.4 per cent voters cast their votes. Along with the Congress, Jan Sangh and Swatantra Party also contested the 1962 Lok Sabha elections. The Udaipur constituency was reserved for the scheduled tribes. The Congress party won the Lok Sabha election in 1962 as well.

In 1967, there were 13 Vidhan Sabha constituencies including six reserved. The Lok Sabha seat was also an ST reserved seat in 1967. The highest percentage of polling was 68.29 in the Udaipur constituency and the lowest was in Gogunda where 50.88 per cent votes were polled. Congress captured 11 seats and of the remaining two, one each went to Swatantra Party and to an independent candidate. The percentage of votes polled for major political parties, namely, Congress, Swatantra Party and Jan Sangh was 56.41, 17.01 and 18.14, respectively. The Congress candidate won the Lok Sabha election again in 1967.

Both the Congress and the Swatantra Party also contested the mid-term election for the Lok Sabha in 1971 from the Udaipur constituency. Thus, there was a direct contest between the Congress and the Swatantra Party. The Congress was defeated. The Congress captured 11 seats for Vidhan Sabha in the fifth general elections held in 1972. The Jan Sangh candidate won the elections for the first time from the Udaipur City constituency. One seat went to an independent candidate.

Political Process: Political Parties

There were 13 Vidhan Sabha constituencies in Udaipur district, of which five were reserved for the scheduled tribes and one was for the scheduled castes. A number of political parties functioned in Udaipur. The parties were Congress, Jan Sangh, Swatantra Party, Praja Socialist Party (PSP), Communist, Krashikar Lok Party (KLP), Ram Rajya Parishad (RRP), Kisan Janata Sanyukta Party (KJSP) and Sanyukta Socialist Party (SSP). The Congress remained in substantial strength from 1952 to 1972. It also won all the parliamentary elections from the Udaipur constituency except one in 1971.

Table 1

Seats Won by Various Political Parties from Udaipur District in Assembly Elections Since 1952 to 1972

Year of Election	*Congress*	*Jan Sangh*	*Swatantra*	*Krashikar Lok Party*	*Independent*	*Total*
1952	7	4	—	1	1	13
1957	12	—	—	—	1	13
1962	5	3	5	—	—	13
1967	11	—	1	—	1	13
1972	11	1	—	—	1	13

In the 1952 general elections, a lot of tussle was there between the princes and Jagirdars and the Congress party. A former Jagirdar Rao Manohar Singh contested assembly election against Mohanlal Sukhadia. Sukhadia however won. The Communist leader, Hukum Singh Mehta initially sided with Rao Manohar Singh, but ultimately retired in favour of Sukhadia. Hukum Singh Mehta and Shanta Trivedi, an independent candidate, secured only 2,608 and 493 votes, respectively.

In 1952, Jan Sangh and Kshatriya Mahasabha were formed. Jan Sangh and Congress had a straight fight. Though the Congress was defeated in many assembly constituencies in Udaipur division against the Jan Sangh, both the seats of the Udaipur Lok Sabha went to Congress. CPI also took part in the elections but its performance was very poor. In a way, the 1952 general elections reveal two things. First, they were against the feudal lords as the masses still perceived the Rajas and Maharajas to be their rulers or leaders. Secondly, the masses were not so conscious about the new political set-up of the country and its norms. The former feudals knew well such perceptions of the masses and, therefore, they jumped into the politics.

The disappearance of several local parties ensured victory to the Congress in the 1957 elections with thumping majority as many Jagirdars had joined the Congress, except Vijay Singh Jhala, who joined the Jan Sangh and contested as its nominee, but lost. Sukhadia virtually enjoined almost everybody into the Congress who aspired for power, and by this he strengthened his own position and that of his faction in the party.

The former Maharana Bhagat Singh of Udaipur extended support to the Jan Sangh, which gave a big shock to the Congress. There were a number of leaders who were not happy with Sukhadia's functioning, particularly on the eve of the general elections in 1962. This impelled the Congress to give a serious thought to the evident conflicts within the party. The Congress party was fully aware that such internal conflicts would weaken its position and the chances of its victory in 1962 elections would be very dim. Therefore, some Congress leaders realized that they should form a few groups and the positions therein should be rotated among the Congressmen in order to avoid internal dissensions and heart-burning. But, the differences were so acute that could not realize the plan. The result was that as many as eight Congress candidates out of 13 lost, including Gulab Singh Shaktawat, Janardan Rai Nagar, Kishan Lal, Master Roshan Lal and Heera Lal Devpura. Swantantra Party nominees defeated some of the Congress contestants and one Congress candidate was defeated by a Jan Sangh candidate in reserved constituency.

Sukhadia started fresh efforts to reconsolidate his position in the district after the defeat of 1962 general elections. Sukhadia joined hands with Manik Lal Verma for a common strategy but this did not work. Verma voiced that government was corrupt and was leaning towards Communist ideology. After this confrontation, he got alienated from the state politics. In the 1967 elections, the Congress did not have majority in the state, but in Udaipur district, with the exception of one ST candidate, the Congress won all the seats from the district. But, for Sukhadia himself, it was a very close fight. Despite his intensive campaigning, he won by a margin of, 3431 votes only. It is interesting to note that Sukhadia won all the four elections, but the declining margin of votes during the subsequent elections is not an indication of Sukhadia's receding popularity. It was reflection of the simmering personal and factional politics among Sukhadia's second-line leaders. Consequently, voters turned towards Jan Sangh, because their top brass as well as rank and file were close to their select supporters. However, Sukhadia had full support of Amrit Lal Vaidya, founder of Ayurved Sevashram at Udaipur, who was also Treasurer of the local Congress unit. He was instrumental in formulation of the strategies for the 1952, 1957 and 1962 assembly elections.

Former Maharana Bhagat Singh and Sukhadia both had retired from politics before the 1972 elections. During the 1972 general elections the All India Congress Committee (AICC) appointed K.N. Singh as observer to ascertain the position of the party in Udaipur district in the absence of Sukhadia. Singh got no indication whatsoever that Congress might get defeated. In these elections, which were held just after Sukhadia's retirement from politics, Congress lost two seats, one of these being the constituency from which Sukhadia was elected previously. Generally, the 'Indira wave' helped the Congress candidates to sweep the polls. In Udaipur, Sukhadia's successor, Prakash Atur, a university teacher, got defeated by 933 votes due to dissensions in the party ranks. Atur was not a member of the Congress party. The ticket was given to him as Sukhadia expressed his desire in his favour. Thus, most of the old Congress workers got annoyed and formed another group within the party. The dissidents nominated their own candidate, who after the intervention of the Congress High Command retired from the contest. For the first time, two Vohra Muslims contested who had earlier supported the Congress. These two Muslim candidates and the dissidents took away only 939 votes. These votes should have gone in all probability to the Congress candidates. Moreover, alliance was formed between Jan Sangh and Swatantra Party to contest the 1971 Lok Sabha and the 1972 assembly elections. However, such a pact could not be arranged between the parties for the municipal elections.

In the 1972 assembly elections, the other Udaipur seat went to an independent candidate Niranjan Nath Acharya[18] from Mavali constituency. Earlier, he was in the Congress, and on failing to get ticket from the Congress party, he contested the elections as an independent candidate. The Congress candidate against Acharya was not only defeated but he also lost his security deposit.

Leadership and Party

After independence, the Praja Mandal leaders, namely, Manik Lal Verma and Bhogi Lal Pandya, could not sustain their position in the new setup. In Mewar, Udaipur, Banswara and Kushalgarh were strongholds of the socialist ideology. The Congress smashed the socialist elements due to their failure to formulate a clear policy. But, the Banswara-Dungarpur region, even today, has some known socialists like Mama Baleshwar Dayal. Thought the Socialist Party had a band of enthusiastic workers, it could never become strong as there had been maximum splits and divisions in the party more than any other party in India. Communist parties were not so active and strong in Udaipur region. Hukumraj Mehta worked alone for sometime on the Communist front. His comrades were Kuber Kant Paneri, Bhagavat Bhandari, Pratap Singh Mahayariya and Madan Lal. The Communist leaders like Bhogilal contested the assembly elections against the Congress and Jan Sangh, but without success. Later on, Kuber Kant Paneri joined the Congress party.

Jan Sangh flourished in the Mewar region as a counter-force to the Congress. The leaders of Jan Sangh blamed Congress as an anti-Hindu party. Such a call attracted some Punjabis and Sindhis to the Jan Sangh as the partition of India horrified them. The landowning class did not support the policies of the Congress, especially relating to the land reforms, and they also joined the Jan Sangh. In the beginning, Lal Singh Shakatwat, Narendra Singh Lakheri, Madan Lal Dhpad, Sampat Bohra, Jodh Singh Chouhan and Jagat Singh Jhala were active Jan Sangh workers. The Kshatiryas, also supported Jan Sangh. Thus, the Jan Sangh was a party of the upper castes namely, Brahmins, Rajputs, Mahajans and Jains. Besides the support of higher castes, the Jan Sangh also enjoyed substantial support of tribals and some other lower communities.

However, on the whole, the Congress was the only dominant party in Udaipur district up to 1977. The leadership of the district remained with upper caste leaders, namely, Mohan Lal Sukhadia, Gulab Singh, Niranjan Nath Acharya, Roshan Lal Nagda, Kishan Lal Sharma and Manohar Lal Kothari. Amrit Lal Yadav was an exception, who belonged to a scheduled caste. None of the scheduled tribe leaders occupied a significant position of power in the state. However, Bhika Bhai, a scheduled tribe leader from Dungarpur district, was a minister in Sukhadia's cabinet for a long time. It is difficult, however, to claim that he represented the tribals of the entire region. He did not carry enough political weight to challenge the upper caste leadership in the region.

Factionalism and Bickerings in the Udaipur District since 1971

We have discussed above factionalism in Udaipur district in relation to state-level politics. Now, we would analyse the latent conflicts, which became manifest after Sukhadia's retirement from politics. During Sukhadia's stewardship of the party, different political parties and their leaders and factions were subdued. After Sukhadia's retirement, both inter- and intra-party factionalism aggravated. Before Sukhadia's retirement from politics, it may be pointed out here that factional politics was simmering in the Congress party, though it could not come out because of towering personality of Sukhadia. But, after his retirement, factions started surfacing as no other leader of his stature could replace him.

Three factions[19] emerged in Congress party in Udaipur district. One comprised of the leaders of the Udaipur City Youth Congress and some members of the District Congress. They included Kuber Kant Paneri, Sheshmal Pagaria and Heera Lal Devpura, who was a minister in the Hari Deo Joshi's cabinet. The second faction comprised of the leaders of the Udaipur Municipal Council and some trusted followers of Sukhadia, such as Roop Kumar Khurana and Prakash Atur. At the state level, they aligned with Mohan Changani and Paras Ram Maderana, who were also ministers in the Joshi government. The third faction comprised of professionals, including some doctors, advocates, journalists and school teachers. The leaders of this faction were Atam Prakash, Fateh Lal Nagori (an advocate), Chandresh Vyas (a freedom fighter) and Shanta Trivedi (a teacher). At the state level this faction had links with Gulab Singh Shakatwat Minister of State in the Joshi government.

The three factions became visible at the time of the election of the President of Udaipur City Congress. All the three nominated their respective candidates. Kuber Kant Paneri, a candidate of his faction, was connected with Heera Lal Devpura, who was in a dominant position, and he was elected with an overwhelming majority. He secured 70 per cent of the total votes. Devpura came into prominence after Sukhadia's retirement from politics in 1971. Prominent supporters of Devpura faction included Paneri, Master Kishan Lal, Sheshmal Pagariya, Hanuman Prabhakar and Bhai Bhagwan. The other two factions were not very strong, but nevertheless they opposed the Devpura faction, at least symbolically, in various Congress fora such as the District Congress Committee, Youth Congress, City Congress Committee, and the Mahila Wing of Congress.

The Shaktawat faction had its hold in the Zila Parishad. Bhanwar Lal Kothari, the Pramukh of the Zila Parishad and Roshan Lal Nagda, ex-president of the District Rural Congress Committee, were among his supporters. The leaders of the third faction, viz., Girdhari Lal Sharma, Roop Kumar Khurana and Prakash Atur, were also close to the Shaktawat faction.

In contrast to Manik Lal Verma and Mohan Lal Sukhadia, the new factional leaders had very little support at the grassroots level. The leaders of the factions had narrow support of their respective castes on casteism to a large extent. Devpura favoured the Mahajans, and Shaktawat was for the Rajputs. Shakatwat's supporters were from the Panchayat Samitis of the district, where they were in power. The only exception was the Kumbhalgarh Panchayat Samiti from where Devpura hailed. However, at the state level, Devpura was a cabinet minister whereas Shaktawat was only a minister of state. Devpura was polished in politics interpersonal relations while Shaktawat had a martial background being a Rajput, and therefore, lacked social grace. In spite of the limitations in his style of functioning, Shaktawat was more popular both in the District Rural Congress as well as in the Panchayat Samitis. In 1975, both factions fielded candidates for the office of the President of the District Rural Congress. The Devpura faction asked Hanuman Prabhakar to contest against Bheru Lal Verma of the Shaktawat faction. Shaktawat's candidate, Bheru Lal Verma, was elected securing more than three-fourth votes. Prabhakar was quite popular as a Congress worker of the district, but due to inept temperament and acute factionalism he could not get elected. It is worth noting that this was the first election for President of the District Congress or the Dehat Zila Congress Committee.

Conclusion

The pre-independence movement aimed at political awakening among the masses. A new wave of political mobilization started through Praja Mandals. The Praja Mandals emerged in the 1930s and 1940s, which were influenced by the ideology and philosophy of Mahatma Gandhi, and provided a forum for launching protest movements against the atrocities of feudal rule in Rajasthan. Thus, the Praja Mandals represented the ideas and goals of the Indian National Congress in Rajasthan.

In 1945, the Praja Mandals were merged into Rajputana Sabha, which functioned as a provincial unit of the All India State People's Congress. Subsequently, in 1948, the Rajputana Krantiya Sabha transformed itself into the Rajputana Pradesh Congress Committee, and finally, merged into the Congress party.

Udaipur played a prominent role in pre-independence political activities. The Praja Mandal leaders in Udaipur state came largely from towns, a large number of them came from Nathdwara – an important temple town. Participation in the Praja Mandals in several sub-divisions of the Udaipur region, where the scheduled castes constituted the vast majority of the population, was low and the leadership came from the highly educated Brahmans and Mahajans. The leaders of the Praja Mandals were the first generation leaders of the Congress party.

The Congress, and formerly the Jan Sangh, and now the Bhartiya Janata Party (BJP), have survived as main political actors. Though Congress has been dominant in Udaipur region, but it could not secure a majority of seats from the district in all the assembly elections, from 1952 to 1972. The loss could be mainly attributed to the simmering personal and factional politics in Udaipur district.

The above analysis of factionalism centres around factionalism within the Congress party. Factionalism in Udaipur district has been examined in relation to the state-level politics and the Udaipur faction, and intra-party factionalism in the Congress in Udaipur district. Udaipur faction dominated the state politics, as M.L. Sukhadia from Udaipur was Chief Minister of the state for 17 years. There was, however, latent factionalism which surfaced clearly in the district after Sukhadia's retirement from state politics in 1971.

Notes

1. See Paul Brass (1965); Fredrick Barth (1959a), *Political Leadership among the Swat Pathans*, London: LSE Monographs on Social Anthropology, No. 19, and also (1959b), 'Segmentary Opposition and the Theory of Games', *Journal of the Royal Anthropological*

Institute, 89:5–22; Bailey, F.G. (1968), 'Networks and Political Process' in *Local Level Politics* (Marc S. Swartz, ed.), Chicago: Aldine Publishing Co.; Mayer, Adrain C. (1966), 'The Significance of Quasi-groups in the Study of Complex Societies' in *The Social Anthropology of Complex Societies,* ASA Monograph 4, London: Tavistock Publications.

2. In 1918, tribal people of Sirohi, Mewar and Marwar started the non-payment of land revenue movement under the leadership of Moti Lal Tejawat.
3. The movement in Udaipur started first in rural towns but eventually its activities spread in the capital cities. The Praja Mandal leaders in the state came largely from district towns, and in Udaipur, political protest commenced a large proportion of people from the temple town of Nathdwara, an important centre of religious pilgrimage (R. Sision, *The Congress Party in Rajasthan,* 1972, 48n, 43n, 61n). In terms of ideology, the Praja Mandals were influenced by Gandhi. Violent techniques were used to achieve their goals by the Praja Mandals (L. Shrader "Rajasthan" in *State Politics in India*), Princeton: Princeton University Press.
4. The reasons were advanced by the authorities of the states of Rajasthan for non-recognition of Mandals.
5. The activities of Vijay Singh Pathik and his co-workers in the villages of Mewar inspired the masses in the political awakening.
6. Verma encouraged the masses since 1918 Bijolia Movement, then shifted to Bhilwara and Udaipur from Bijolia and later on centred all political activities at Udaipur, the capital Mewar.
7. He was Vice Chancellor of Rajasthan Vidyapeeth (an educational institution) which was established by him.
8. Founder of Ayurvedic Sevashram Udaipur, Varanasi and Hyderabad.
9. Sukhadia has been Rajasthan's most successful Chief Minister.
10. Sir T. Vijaya Ragwacharya resigned on account of ill health.
11. Sir T. Vijay Ragwacharya, Dr Mohan Singh Mehta and K.M. Munshi played a significant role in the constitutional reforms introduced in the state. It was all due to Dr Mehta's political insight and diplomatic reforms in the Mewar state was and an agreement on the amendments to the constitution of the Legislative Assembly was arrived at in the state (R.S. Darda (1971), *From Feudalism to Democracy,* New Delhi: S. Chand and Company, pp. 74–75; R.S. Darda (1970), "Struggle for Democratic Government in Mewar", in D.L. Paliwal (ed.), *Mewar Through the Ages,* Udaipur: Sahitya Sansthan, Rajasthan Vidypeeth.
12. Some bad elements threw the national flag (Tiranga Jhanda) in the well near Barisadri ki Haveli (name of the building called Barisadri building). This incident motivated to Praja Mandal people to boycott the elections.
13. It was the symbol of Kshatriya Parishad Party.
14. B.N. College was a Rajput College and Kshatriya Parishad was the faction of Rajput.
15. Shaktawat was a Rajput student and had a affiliation with Kshatriya Parishad, later on he joined the Congress party and also became the Home Minister of Rajasthan.
16. Prior to the merger, Mewar had joined name princely states of Rajasthan to form the state of Rajasthan Union which was inaugurated on the 15th April, 1948 by late Jawaharlal Nehru.
17. It may be recalled here that it was once decided to merge all the states with Udaipur which should be the capital of entire Rajasthan.
18. He was a lawyer, middle class talented person, having Communist ideology. Verma took him into his confidence and made his personal assistant. Later on, he became the secretary of the Chief Minister Mohan Lal Sukhadia. Acharya selected Rajsamand constituency for assembly election which was later on converted into reserved constituency so he had to shift to Mavali. He being a writer and also a social worker in his own way rose in the party as a state leader. Though he has been always controversial being as

a Congressman. Congress leaders never accepted Acharya as a true Congress candidate even when he was in the party but he was given Congress ticket. Acharya used to contest elections on the Congress ticket but he never accepted him as a Congressman. Conversely, Manohar Kothari, a Congress was the Congress President at Rajsamand who had always tried for contesting elections from Congress. How can he deny that he was not a Congressman?

19. The description for three factions here is extracted from the study, *Factionalism, Politics and Social Structure* (1984), by B.K. Nagla, Jaipur: Rawat Publications, pp. 161–64.

References

Brass, Paul R., (1965), *Factional Politics in an Indian State: The Congress Party in Uttar Pradesh,* Berkeley: University of California Press.

Carter, Anthony (1974), *Elite Politics in Rural India,* Bombay: Vikas Publishing House Pvt. Ltd.

Nagla, B.K. (1984), *Factionalism, Politics and Social Structure,* Jaipur: Rawat Publications.

Shrader, Lawrence L. (1968), "Rajasthan", in Myron Weiner (ed.), *State Politics in India,* Princeton: Princeton University Press.

Sisson, Richard (1965), *The Congress Party in Rajasthan,* Delhi: Oxford University Press.

Sukhadia, M.L. (ed.), *Mewar Praja Mandals* (1938–45), pp. 1–3 and B.D. Kalla, pp. 240–241.

Surana, Pushpendra (1983), *Social Movements and Social Structure: A Study of Princely State of Mewar,* New Delhi: Manohar Publications.

Weiner, Myron (1957), *Party Politics in India,* Princeton: Princeton University Press.

24 Brahmin, Widow and Businesswoman

GÉRARD FUSSMAN

Prof K.L. Sharma and I are working closely together since 1989. Without his hard work, dedication and acumen, the Chanderi project, in every of its aspects, would have been a failure. Whatever we achieved in Chanderi bears the stamp of Professor Sharma. During these years I learned to see India also through his eyes and experience of Indian life. I owe him much of my present knowledge of present-day Indian reality. Although I am mainly a historian of ancient India, i.e., of societies and polities which do not exist any more for centuries, the knowledge of today's Indian way of life is nevertheless essential for my work. How could I write about village life, for instance, in ancient India, without knowing any Indian village, not from the outside – as any tourist can do – but as an insider, i.e., somebody born and bred there, who knows by personal experience how people feel and talk, how they behave, how they marry, etc. Not being an insider, I am fortunate to have a good colleague who was not only an insider, but also a good sociologist, able to see beyond the mere facts of everyday life. This colleague was Prof K.L. Sharma.

But the historian of ancient India is also faced with the risk of anachronism: how can he be sure that his vision of the past, which he often gets by implicit analogy or avowed reference to his knowledge of today or 19th century India, is true to the fact? Most of the historians of ancient India use as corrective evidence the 'dharmasastras' and the 'nitisastras', especially the Kautiliya's *Arthasastra*. But these are a disputable evidence: the date of the early core of the text is usually unsure, the distinction between core and later accretions is difficult, if not impossible, and the relation of the juridical or political assertions they contain to the true state of facts is unknown. Most scholars today believe that sastras are more theoretical than practical, a kind of ideal which people and institutions were not always able or willing to attain. The only way to check their accuracy at such a place in such a time is to confront them with contemporary independent evidence, viz., archives or inscriptions. Royal or official archives, if often very informative, are not always the most trustworthy because kings and administrators always tend to present themselves as acting according to eternal laws and practices. They know how to present facts in the most favourable light. Private documents, which are not intended to be made public and are known only by the handful of people who have to deal with them, are more straightforward. They show that if the name of legal categories may not have changed for centuries, the juridical limitations or capacities of these categories may be very different and henceforth the relationship between persons belonging to these categories may have been quite different in the past from what it is today although the vocabulary is the same. Here is an instance coming from the core of Hindu Madhyadesa, Mathura.

It is a three-line stone inscription discovered in 1988 nearby Mathura, now in the Mathura Museum, which probably did not buy it: it does not come from the antiquities market. This is one of the key elements which proves its authenticity, although fakes are now many in the market. Although broken in the middle, the inscription is entire, without any lacuna. Its script is well and careful engraved Brahmi, an Indian script easy to decipher. Its language is reasonably correct Sanskrit, simple enough for the translation to be almost sure. The date may be disputed. Let us say the stone was engraved between 70 BC and 40 AD.[1] The text is the following.

1. *Yavanarajasya sodasuttare varsasate 100 + 10 + 16 hematamase 4 divasa 30 etaye purvaye*
2. *brahmanasya maitreyasagotrasya Ghosadatta-putrasya sarthavahasya Vairabalasya matu Rahoganaiya udapana*
3. *puskirini saha putrena Vairabalena vadhye Bhaguriye pautrehi ca Suradattena Rsabhadevena Viradattena ca punyam vardhatu*

"In the 116th year of the Greek Kingdom, during the 4th winter month, in the 30th day (of this month), that very day Rahogana, mother of Vairabala, Brahmana of the Mitrayu gotra, a caravan-leader son of Ghosadatta (ordered the making of this) well (and) pond. The merit (resulting from this act) should grow and benefit also her son Vairabala and Bhaguri, his wife, and her grandsons Suradatta, Rsabhadeva, and Viradatta."

Whoever has ever walked through a North Indian village or qasba as we so often did in Chanderi together with Professor Sharma will easily understand the facts this record alludes to. Rahogana commissioned the digging (or the building of a dam) of an artificial pond (*talab*) where cattle would come to drink or bathe and also the digging of the nearby well where people come to draw pure water. She did not do it for financial gain, e.g., for irrigating fields which thus could provide her with more revenue. Her intent was altruistic. This new water resource was meant for villagers, passers-by, travellers and thirsty cattle. Rahogana also hoped to derive some religious merit from her altruistic action, part of which she offered to her only son, his wife and their three sons. Many Indian Hindus, Buddhists, Jains and Moslems still behave like that.

To be sure that the ensuing merit would go to her and her family, Rahogana wanted to have this record engraved on stone, i.e., for ever. These stone records are usually placed inside the well (if so, as the stone is flat, the well would have been square in shape) or on its margin. Nobody but archaeologists usually care to decipher them. They are records made by people for their own intent. But they cannot lie: not only is there the risk that somebody (a neighbour, a relative, a state officer) takes the fancy to read the inscription and then tell everybody the donor is telling lies, but the personal merit, which is the main purpose of the commissioning of this water work, would be nil. So that we can be sure that Rahogana is telling the truth.

She belongs to an orthodox Brahmin family. Her son (and so, her husband) belongs to a Bhargava (Mitrayu) gotra, her daughter-in-law wore a name well-known in Brahmin families. Her son is a caravan leader, which is not a trade usually ascribed to Brahmins. But we know for long that some Brahmins used to be successful traders. There is even evidence of some of them being skilled generals, i.e., leaders of men. Vairabala was only leader of caravans. At this early date, there was no shame in proclaiming it. Rahogana was proud to record the professional activity of her son, which probably was the same as his father's. Indeed, the money for digging the pond probably came from the wealth gained by the family from merchandise transport, either in bullock-carts or on pack-animals. But historians now should be very cautious when interpreting names ending in *datta* found in early Indian records. For the names of his Brahmin father of Vairabala and his Brahmin sons did not end with *sarma* or *deva,* as one would expect after a perusal of every sastra, but with *datta,* an ending usually assigned by these same sastras to Vaisyas. Around the beginning of the Common Era, Vaisyas did not have a monopoly on long distance trade nor on *datta* names!

More surprising is the fact that Ghosadatta is obviously dead: if otherwise, the record would have been made in his name if the money came from him, or some part of the religious merit would have been assigned to him if the money came from Rahogana's personal dowry or property. So, Rahogana is either divorced or widowed. There is no doubt she is a widow, with one living adult son, father of three male sons. But, she has personal resources she owns in full, with which she can do whatever she wants, without asking any permission from her sons or relatives. Indeed, she is probably the head of the family and the sole owner of the family property. It is even possible that she is the acting manager of her late husband's business. Quite unusual for Brahmin widows and Brahmin families if we trust they followed the prescriptions of dharmasastras as we read them now ! Quite usual when we have a look at Buddhist donations in Ajanta, Nasik, Sanchi or Mathura: many of the donors the names of which are recorded are women, not only queens or kings'daughters, but also humbler people.

This small inscription thus shows the very high juridical status of women in ancient India. But we should also read out what is not engraved. Can we surmise that Vairabala begot from his wife Bhaguri only sons? Or should we think that their daughter(s), if any, are not mentioned in the inscription and not assigned any merit accruing from this altruistic use of the family money because she was no more, or even never, part of Ghosadatta's family? If we refer to most sastras and to 19th century North Indian customs, we should opt for the second hypothesis and deduce that already at that time, Indian daughters, being given to their groom, were no more part of their biological family, and receiving a dowry, had no more right in their father's inheritance. But beware: among the many inscriptions lying unedited in the drawings and cupboards of the Epigraphical Survey of India, there may exist a small record which would point that this was not an universal North Indian custom.

Note

1. For more details, see G. Fussman, *Annuaire du Collège de France 1990–1991*, pp. 665–68 and *Journal Asiatique* 1993, pp. 111–17. There are some minor differences with the decipherment and translation by P. Thakurel and B.N. Mukherjee, *Bulletin of Museums and Archaeology in Uttar Pradesh*, No. 41–42, 1988, pp. 103–9.

25 Gender and Disability Management in Rural Haryana

NILIKA MEHROTRA

The paper elucidates the problem of disability from an anthropological perspective by locating it in the social context of rural Haryana. It is argued here that disability should be understood as a cultural construct as people attribute meanings to certain conditions that construe persons as 'abled' or 'disabled' Inherent here is the notion of 'normalcy' and 'ability' Implications of disability for women who constitute almost 50 per cent of the agrarian class are significant both in terms of the kind of social lives they lead and their participation in the development process. Since a large number of disabled live in rural areas, the absence of accurate information on the magnitude of the problem has hampered planning of realistic policies and services for them. Thus, a culture-centred, gender-sensitive, holistic approach has been adopted to explore the social context of disabled women, and traditional support mechanisms that carry implications for state policy.

The paper is divided into three sections. Firstly, it looks at the cultural conceptions of disability and expounds the relevance of social factors in understanding disability. The second section profiles the social life of physically disabled women, and describes the community and the family strategies in supporting them in negotiating family, work, economy and society. It is argued here that physical disabilities of various forms further worsen their situation as they act as additional disadvantages to their otherwise subordinate position. Finally, in the third section, implications are explored for state policy on disability in rural Haryana.

There are several approaches in understanding disability. The *medical model* views disability as a personal tragedy. Disability, such as the impairment of limb, organ or function, has traumatic physical and psychological effects on a disabled person. Disabled people, in this model, are regarded as people with limitations who cannot ensure a reasonable quality of life because of their impairment. The *medical model* expects individuals to find ways of adapting to society. It puts the

---

This paper is based on an intensive fieldwork carried out in villages of Rewari district of Haryana in the months of May-June 2002 as part of a larger study titled Disabled Women in Rural Haryana, sponsored by Ministry of Social Justice and Empowerment, Government of India. Some other versions have appeared as articles elsewhere see, Mehrotra, 2004a, and 2004b.

duty of adjusting and adapting to their environment and to the society on the disabled people.

The *social model,* on the other hand, presents disability as a consequence of oppression, prejudice and discrimination by the society against disabled people. It is the society that constructs economic, social, health, architectural, legal, cultural and other barriers in order to deliberately prevent people with impairments to enjoy full benefits of the society. The social model shifts the emphasis from a disabled individual to the society and its disabling attitudes and environment.

These approaches adequately raise the point that disability has remained an obstruction in attaining the full potential of an individual which surfaces against the cultural backdrop. Adopting a culture-centred approach, it is argued here that disability locates the individual in a compromised position which is not only a function of biology but also product of a complex interaction among non-biological factors like gender, caste, class, neighbourhood relations and the nature of kinship and family structures.

In an urban context, the disabled are recognized as a social category for their special needs. There are attempts to integrate the people with disability into the mainstream of society through promoting technical assistance in a formally institutionalized set-up like a special school or a training centre, to ensure that the individuals make optimal utilization of their available faculties. The situation is quite different in a rural context. Here disability does not contribute to the formation of any socially recognized group. In order to understand how people define disability in a rural culture, it is important to recognize its social fabric, work-related requirements, cultural notions and the structure of gender relations. No policy can work here unless these factors are properly understood and policies be framed accordingly.

I
Cultural Conceptions of Disability

In the Indian context, Hindu scriptures explain causes of human sufferings through the theory of *karma,* i.e., if one has committed misdeeds in the previous births, he/she has to inevitably bear the consequences. Illness and disability are understood to be a punishment for the sins of previous births and one is called upon to accept it as divine retribution. Belief in the theory of *karma* has very often led to a ready acceptance of disability, with little effort in the direction of improving the life conditions. Srivastava (2002) writes that Indians pay far less attention to mental illness than to physical illness. It is argued that the acceptance of disability as *karma* (or due to cosmic causation) give people some explanation of their suffering, which cannot be justified otherwise. As noted by Paranjpe, the belief in *karma* keeps the faith in a just world alive, even under adverse conditions it reinforces hopes that good deeds will ultimately lead to a good outcome (cf. Dalal, 2002). The positive role of religion cannot be dismissed here. Srivastava (2002) also points out that traditional belief systems are 'hope generating.'

Against a generalized conception of disability in Indian society, in this section, we examine the cultural conceptions and social stereotypes regarding physical disabilities with construction of folk etiology and taxonomy in Haryana.

Disability in most academic approaches is understood as the deviance from normalcy; however, in Haryana, it is, for theoretical purposes, explained as the 'dependency' of an individual on others in the community, i.e., *aashrit*. In addition to this, in the neighbouring state of Rajasthan, it is also understood in terms of *kasar*, a 'fault' (lack, lag) in the individual. The definition of disability remains ambiguous here and is often made synonymous with limb deformities. Haryana, being an extensively agricultural state, depends heavily on manual labour in the fields. For this the sturdiness and robustness of physique in people are highly valued. Thus, the question of disability is understood as *viklangta* or *apangta*, i.e., in terms of locomotory disorders. Also, a locomotory disorder is visually more prominent. Thus, the society ideally maintains that people with limb deformities are the ones who are dependent on others.

The severity of the condition in case of limb deformities is not taken into consideration and on pointing out that the people with minor limb deformity might actually be well capable of looking after themselves, villagers quietly accept this, but such individuals remained in the category of disabled. The blind or deaf and dumb are placed in separate categories of *andhe* and *goonge-behre* respectively. The enquiry as to how a blind individual can be considered as self-sufficient is responded to by conveniently shifting the category of blind into that of disabled, but there is a constant debate on whether or not people with hearing and speech impairment should be included into the category of disabled. More so because they are physically able to perform all kinds of laborious tasks and the family of the individual concerned develops a fair amount of communication skills with him or her. The mentally challenged individuals were not included into the category of disabled. They were often referred to as *bhola* or *bholi*, i.e., innocent. In case of a mentally slow male, the individual was assigned work that was essentially identified with a woman, *aurato ke kam*, like fetching water, weeding in the field, etc. Thus, a male with reduced mental faculty was supposed to be able to perform the tasks of a woman. When the case of a mentally challenged individual is coupled with the other physical disability, the individual is included into the category of disability. Disabled are often stereotyped as incomplete persons who are aggressive and have low sexual prowess.

Causation

The causation of disability is understood based on a number of different variables. These could be recognized as either mutually exclusive categories or in combination with each other. What remains true to all these causes is the supervening reality of fate. An individual's condition is essentially understood in terms of his or her fate or *kismat*, which is all-pervasive in nature. Besides, there are many magico-religious beliefs and rituals performed by the villagers to evade such calamities. The various parameters responsible for disability in an individual form a mutual cause and effect relationship with fate. The biomedical system of cure is highly sought after leaving the people vulnerable to scams by quacks and other non-professionals. Going by local conceptions of disability, all possible resources are availed to find the cure for disability. The effort is towards finding a cure and not rehabilitation. Disability might be totally ignored lest it comes in way of smoothly discharging the work in everyday life.

II
Women, Work and Disability

Historically, Haryana has been notorious in terms of high rates of female infanticide and of late misuse of sex selection technologies leading to large number of foeticides. Clinics performing such tests and consequent abortions are mushrooming in all the towns here (George and Dahiya, 1998). Since 1981 Census, lowering sex ratios have become a serious concern. Large-scale dowries, anti-women attitudes and strong male preference are often cited reasons for this. Strong patriarchal traditions, *purdah*, rigid gender segregation, widespread prevalence of the dowry system, devaluation of women and the life-long liability of girl's family to endow her with gifts throughout her life, after her marriage, connote the girl as a burden. Women largely remain unwanted as evidenced in the skewed sex ratio.

Scholars have pointed at prevalence of anti-women attitudes in Haryanavi society, expressed through abuses, folk tales and stereotypes (Chaudhry, 1994). Nevertheless, women's contribution to economy is significant as every woman is expected to participate in agricultural and household activities. Socially, this contribution goes unrecognized and is often devalued. Girl children and women remain discriminated in terms of food distribution and access to health care. It can thus be easily assumed that a girl, with a disability, would be totally unwanted. The case studies clearly reflect initial neglect in the case of a disabled girl child, where in a number of situations the parents actually admitted their eager anticipation of the child loosing its life. But, what is significant is the fact that when the child is able to cope up, fighting all odds in spite of neglect, the family comes together to support it. This neglect of providing basic health care to women of all ages is due to both gender discrimination and financial difficulties. Among the scheduled castes, economic hardships were mainly found to be working against the survival of the girl child. Women across all castes are socialized to take their health less seriously.

Young girls are socialized in traditional gender roles as capacity to work is the key deciding factor for her marriage and future. Some concessions may be made to disabled as not expecting heavy work, etc. They are also being sent to school; however, not much value is attached to education. In the management of disability role of family is significant. Mother and other female relatives look after the child and make the early diagnosis.

A woman's destiny and social security is still being conceived in terms of marriage. The dearth of women in the society, due to male preference, actually acts to a disabled woman's advantage. The most professed support that a woman can get is the sharing of her responsibilities with her sisters. For this the disabled girl is often married into the same household as her sister, usually with a consecutive brother and at times to the same man as her sister. This type of marriage practice often comes to aid to a disabled woman. Other variable associated with the marriage of a disabled woman is that she is usually married to a disabled man, a widower, in a household whose economic condition is lower than her natal home, or to a man who cannot find a spouse for some reason or the other (illiteracy, low income, caste endogamy, etc.). There were also reports of heavy dowries paid by parents of disabled girls. A spouse is found for almost every disabled girl.

A disabled woman in the reproductive age group could be seen to be most vulnerable as she is pushed towards performing work like any normal individual in the society. This is explained in terms of rigid division of labour and indispensability of the woman's work, both within the domestic as well as agricultural sphere, especially after her marriage. No special concessions are made with the disability in mind (i.e., redesigning of house, exempting her from work), a girl child is initiated into all possible responsibilities. She may have a problem in fetching water, as she cannot use earthen pots over her head and she has to carry buckets. She could have a problem in performing agricultural labour too. No special care is extended in terms of their specific physical/mental disability. Rural society does not perceive disabled as people with any special requirements. It is truer in case of women. Their traditional gender roles as worker and reproducer are strictly enforced as in case of any non-disabled.

The women of the family, usually the mother and the sisters and other female relatives, distribute the household chores to best accommodate the disabled individual. Efforts are made to ensure that the disabled individual is accompanied at all times. Though she is made to do all possible jobs, there might be a relaxation in the amount of load she carries, or the time she takes to perform a particular task. Work might also be distributed in a manner that in terms of the disabled sharing a greater load of the household chores while the others pursue agricultural labour. She often gets lot of support in her natal home, but in her marital home she is expected to do all the household chores.

The Brahman women enjoy a slight advantage because they are not expected to contribute in agricultural labour, unless the household is in a dire economic condition. The Jat and Yadav women face a greater strain because tending to the animals is also taken to be a part of the household chores. Most of the disabled women continue to perform almost all the household chores, including fetching water from the well, cutting fodder, cooking, cleaning up, etc., stretching their maximum bodily limits.

New technology like fodder machines often work to the disadvantage of women as we found a number of cases of amputation due to their use. And, a number of them also reported domestic strain and violence on this account.

The condition of a disabled woman changes with her age and status. In the childhood she enjoys parental care and support but is socialized into her duties of a woman. After marriage she is rigorously put to task, this physical and mental exertion is the most strenuous phase of her life. With age, she gains more social and moral authority in household affairs. With the expansion of the family, there are more supporting hands in terms of sons, daughters, daughters-in-law and grandchildren for her social and physical support.

The foregoing analysis clearly reveals that disability is not the primary disadvantage of women in rural Haryana; rather it becomes an additional burden to her marginalized gender position. Disability is engendered in specific ways. Disabled women are stereotyped to be incomplete, however, they are expected to fulfil all the gendered duties and primarily taken to be working members of the society. We clearly see here that apart from extending support and help in their work, families do not necessarily create special opportunities for them in order to cope better. Management of disability in the context of a community is often related to a crisis situation and it does not take a permanent order. The more permanent form of rehabilitation is centred in the household where a disabled lives and with help of several social mechanisms learns to cope with her state. No professional help is sought in most cases.

III
State Policy on Disability: A Critique

A comprehensive legislation known as Persons with Disabilities (Equal Opportunities, Protection of Rights and Full Participation) Act, 1995 (Act 1 of 1996), was unanimously passed by both the houses of Parliament on 22nd December, 1995 that provides a broad framework and directions for the state governments to make positive strategies for the disabled. The Act, however, treats the individual as a unit of analysis; it ignores gendered realities of everyday lives of disabled, situated in families and communities. Though there are provisions for providing rural infrastructure, they remain in the papers. Haryana policy paper in fact talks mainly of concessions, scholarships and job reservations.

State provides meagre pension of Rs 200 to the disabled whose information is usually disseminated through announcements by the Panchayat, *chowkidar* and women's informal networks. Health camps are usually held in easily accessible places. This pension is made available for those whose disability is 70 per cent or more. People with lesser disabilities said that that they had to face a lot of problems as well and should be given at least half the concession. People also complained of pension money to be very meagre. More importantly, there is no provision for children and those below eighteen years of age as the State government expects families to fend for them.

The criteria of assessing disability are entirely based on bio-medical practice. Srivastava (2002) points out that there is hardly any relationship between the traditional healing system and formal health care system in India. Thomas and Thomas (2000) opine that CBR planners give little respect to these factors during policy development and planning, risking failure of their projects. Hence, CBR policies require a greater understanding of the 'needs' of the community. Rehabilitation is a gradual and long process that cannot escape the influences of local cultural factors.

Women's education is a highly neglected area, as dropout rate of girl children after primary level is alarmingly high. Girl children among the scheduled castes virtually do not receive any education. Devaluation of women's education in general is one of important reasons why a disabled woman in a rural context cannot able to become self-dependent. Nowadays younger girls are sent to school. Very few complete it. Women's work outside the family is still not taken as a viable option. They hardly ever pursue higher education and professional jobs, though there is now an awareness building. Despite legal rights in the property, patriliny ensures that they remain dependent on men of the family. Land rights are rarely given to the woman virtually rendering her resourceless.

Whether or not the disability pension and other facilities have been able to enforce empowerment remains a point of reference, especially in a society, which is ruled by the norms of patriarchy. In most cases it simply gets absorbed in the household without recognizing it as a concession to the disabled. In this area, due to low literacy rate of women, concessions provided by the state are hardly relevant largely due to heavy bias of the policy in favour of the urban educated middle society. Since needs of rural disabled women find no place in the policy framework, they remain marginalized in their relationship to the State. Role of State agencies like state department of social welfare is also limited to disbursing of the pension, whereas panchayat and other village level government officials merely help disabled to get information and access to limited concessions by the state. NGOs' initiatives are almost negligent in this area.

In conclusion, it may be stated that unless state policies are informed by micro level realities, the desired goals will remain distant.

References

Chowdhry, Prem (1994), *The Veiled Women: Shifting Gender Equations in Rural Haryana 1880*, New Delhi: Oxford University Press.

Dalal, Ajit K. (2002), 'Disability Rehabilitation in a Traditional Indian Society', *Asia Pacific Disability Rehabilitation Journal.*

Dube, Leela (1998), 'Trends in Kinship and Gender Relations in South Asia', in Carla Risseeuw and Kamla Ganesh (eds.) (1996), *Negotiation and Social Space: A Gendered Analysis of Changing Kin and Security Networks in South Asia*, New Delhi: Sage Publications.

George, Sabu M. and Ranbir S. Dahiya (1998), 'Female Foeticide in Rural Haryana', *Economic and Political Weekly*, August 33(32): 2191–97.

Mehrotra, Nilika (2002), *A Study of the Disabled Women in Rural Haryana*. Unpublished Report submitted to Ministry of Social Justice and Empowerment (PREM Division), Government of India.

—— (2004a), 'Understanding Cultural Conceptions of Disability in Rural India: A Case from Haryana', *The Journal of Anthropological Society*, 39: 33–45.

—— (2004b), 'Disability, Women and the Social Support in Rural Haryana', *Economic and Political Weekly*, Vol. XXXIX, No. 52.

Palriwala, Rajni and Carla Risseeuw (eds.) (1996), *Shifting Circles of Support: Contexualising Kinship and Gender in South Asia and Sub Saharan Africa*, New Delhi: Sage Publications.

Risseeuw, Carla and Kamla Ganesh (eds.) (1998), *Negotiation and Social Space: A Gendered Analysis of Changing Kin and Security Networks in South Asia*, New Delhi: Sage Publications.

Srivastava, V.K. (2002), 'Some Thoughts on the Anthropology of Mental Health and Illness with Special Reference to India', *Anthropos*, 97: 529–54.

Thomas, Maya and M.J. Thomas (eds.) (2002), 'Status of Women with Disabilities in South Asia', *Asia Pacific Disability Rehabilitation Journal.*

26 Young Women

An Emerging Force in India

RENUKA SINGH

Young women in India are emerging as a vanguard of new sensibility during the present socio-economic, cultural and political transition. What sort of alternative do they offer to cope up with the resultant changes? Today, young women are consciously in pursuit of success, opportunities and power, and are globally longing for their commitment and confidence to take control of their lives and achieve their cherished goals. Market, educational institutions, magazines and books and cyber space are used to highlight the nature and direction of their choices and their new way of *being*. Such new values become a means of re-socialization and regulation in order to create productive members in a given society.

During the last few decades, there has been an intensified flow of people, commodities, ideas and images on a global scale. Modern communication technology contributes in two ways to the disengaging of certain cultural phenomena from their given space. First, a multitude of new phenomena, including certain aspects of 'youth culture', notions of prestige, commodities from Colas to Jeans or CDs, popular films and the environmental shift to dilemmas exist both globally and locally simultaneously. Second, the increased mobility of people and communication with people (at least, in principle) anywhere in the world at any time through the telephone, fax or Internet is quite feasible these days. Space can no longer be said to create a clear barrier between 'cultures'.

It is obvious that both politics and economics are integrated in an abstract, anonymous and globally connected network of investments, exchange and migration. No single person can affect this system in decisive ways, and events taking place at one point in the system can have ramifications in other parts of the world. The creation of agencies and NGOs with a worldwide scope also indicates the importance of globalization. The UN and organizations, such as the Red Cross and Amnesty International as well as the Third World networks, have contributed to the development of the discourse about morality and politics. So, today, there are many cultural phenomena that are global in the sense that they are not located in a particular place; and at the same time, they are local as they are generally perceived and interpreted locally.

Young women today face greater challenges in terms of possibilities and anxieties regarding their new identities as the present times are characterized by dislocation, change and globalization that demand more versatility, flexibility and self-realization. In post-modern times, the concepts of risk and individualization would become central to the understanding of the world inhabited by young people representing the future.

A. Furlong and F. Cartmel assert: "Young people today are growing up is different world to that experienced by previous generations – changes which are significant enough to merit a re-conceptualization of youth transitions and processes of social reproduction."[1] The previous era of modernity was characterized by a system of industrial capitalism built around formation of strong centralized government, enduring social ties based on shared identifications with community, class and place, and in the post-war era, was known for the development of both liberal welfare states and robust social justice movements. A. Harris distinguishes this previous era from the late modernity by focusing on the complex, global capitalist economies and a shift from state support and welfare to the private provision of services. The key feature of the late modern economy is de-industrialization – the contraction of large-scale manufacturing, and the expansion of global communications, technology and service industries. Part-time, casual, temporary and short-term contract work has replaced full-time ongoing employment and production, distribution and consumption are increasingly globalized. This process has been accompanied by the information revolution, the capacity to move capital and information instantaneously and changes in national regulations about trade, ownership, movement of capital, and offshore production.[2]

Apparently, the economic impact of these conditions can be seen in an increased pauperization process and in a greater polarization between the rich and the poor. The resultant insecurity, fragmentation and discontinuity within communities have, however, produced a new brand of competitive individualism, whereby people are expected to somehow make a success of their lives. Anthony Giddens mentions about a new sense of danger replacing the idea of predictability[3] whereas U. Beck talks about the 'risk society' wherein global insecurities and economic unpredictability are combined with weakening collective ties and identities. Further, Beck observes that today, one witnesses mass movements of migrants and refugees; the visibility of civil, religious and ethnic conflicts; worldwide health threats; and global human security concerns in the wake of terrorism.[4]

Thus, the sign of our times is negotiating risks on an individual level. This process of individualization creates opportunities for developing autonomy, exercising freedom and making personal choice without the traditional patterns of support structures. The young people, therefore, try to forge their futures by mastering the anxieties, uncertainties and insecurities conjured up by these unpredictable times. The media theorist Marshall Mcluhan introduced the concept of the global village.[5] This notion was intended to account for the new cultural situation in the world, following the spread of modern mass media. The world has become one place, and he called this place a global village. The central paradox of globalization is perhaps that the world has become both larger and smaller at the same time. It has become smaller in the sense that one can reach any corner of this world within a day and enjoy the same lifestyle anywhere. On the other hand, it has become larger in the sense that we have been exposed to remote and exotic places, and thus more easily recognize our mutual differences. Hence, one does not dare to stress cultural homogenization and undermine the cultural variation among the of young people.

The main questions are: How do young women react to the process of globalization? To what extent they are exposed to the news about the Olympics in Greece, to wage work and to the concept of human rights? What is the global cultural melting pot? How is the local appropriation of the global processes taking place?

Recently, I visited Kashmir after a gap of sixteen years. My visit to Kashmir has convinced me of the indegenization of modernity taking place there. As one approached the interior villages of the area surrounding Pahalgam, the visibility of young boys and more so of girls was quite impressive. Most of the boys had the latest hair styles and were clad in jeans and T-shirts, whereas girls were dressed up in the traditional salwar-kameez, but tailored with the city-flair and in fashionable styles, i.e., with long slits on the side. However, as far as one remembers, the Gujjar women always had those long slits, which they have retained till today. On my way to Chandanwari, a glacier on the way to Amarnath, I saw the Gujjar women camping, cooking and herding their sheep, but they did not have any schooling. The village girls, at least, had a school to go to and would often be seen going to school in groups. They carried a look of confidence and the impact of radio, TV and newspapers was clearly visible as one overheard them singing the latest film songs, discussing about the enquiry into the latest bomb blasts in the Pahalgam bazaar or in Anantnag, or sporting designer shoes. The youth camps organized in Pahalgam give a clue to the way the young people there plan to counter the disruptive forces and form solidarity in order to move towards a more productive and successful future for themselves.

At the same time, however, as observed by A.A. Khan, "Pain and suffering cannot be dissociated from even the great Kashmiri poetesses like Habba Khatoon, Lalla Aarifa and Aarrimaal when one tries to glorify them. In today's Kashmiri context, still the financial, legal, psychological, moral and social aspects of women's lives remain pertinent for the developmental issues. Although the young women are educated, they are not given the social space to express themselves, are unaware of their legal rights, and women's psychology is tamed by the ruthless moral and social order that does not allow them to break the shackles of tradition and invisible walls of culture built around them by the social milieu."[6] Nonetheless, he does not end with a pessimistic note. Hopes that young women like Naheed Hamdani, who decided to work at Kupwara with Medicines Without Frontiers (MSF) away from Srinagar, Aasiya Jeelani, who laid her life for the cause of human rights, or a woman like Taufiq Rashid, who works as a journalist in Delhi, and yet has not given up her Kashmiri attire, and, not to forget, Seema Tahir, Asifa Ali, and Sameena who are contributing in a constructive way to the mass media,[7] are the young representatives of Kashmiri women spelling a bright future for the Kashmir society.

In the present context, changing conditions, combined with the feminist achievements, have created new possibilities for young women. Expansion of girls' education and employment have coincided with a restructured global economy that tries to take young women's labour seriously, and new ideology relating to personal responsibilities and choices also encourages young women to take charge of their lives and available opportunities. Earlier, a comfortable middle class status was attained or sustained through marriage but today there is no such guarantee. Moreover, the intense connection between consumption and middle class status requires more than one working man to sustain a family's appropriate class lifestyle. Thus, young women must become successful and financially independent, and this implies a good academic and professional record. The private world of relationships, marriage, divorce, reproduction and sexuality, harassment, and violence is no longer seen as the realm of a personal domain. Feminism has helped young women to become more assertive, as they now enjoy new freedom and opportunities without the unstinting support of their families, male members or institutions in general.

Today, urban young women are encouraged to become achievers, and are perceived as powerful. The popular belief is that girls as a whole are a hope for the future as they are excelling in every field. Educated, professional women with glamorous lifestyles can be seen all over the world, including India. It is actually the idea and image which gives the impression of the new urban powerful women. To make this idea more effective, the consequences of the sexual and economic exploitation of young women need to be confronted. It is projected as a failure owing to bad choices and irresponsible support system. Thus, the well-packaged image of the young women as winners in rapidly changing societies needs to be questioned as the situation is more complex. The struggles, disappointments and obstacles are very much a part of their social reality as are inequalities produced by the factors of class, caste, education, and family background.

Within feminism a generational contest is occurring. Social scientists may be interested to study the implications of entry of young women into professions vis-à-vis changing family patterns. Besides this, violence against girls, their health care and discourses related to their educational performance have preoccupied policy makers. At the same time, behaviour of low achievers is also becoming a matter of concern for parents and educationists. Depression and eating disorders are manifest in consumerist lifestyle and exceptional commitment shown by ambitious women. Hence, young women become a site of either new possibilities or problems that make them confident and optimistic or leave them alienated and lost. It is this shifting market, economic and cultural globalization, educational expansion, the notions of changing female identity, the family, citizenship and state that create new choices for young women.

As Harris recounts that in the Western countries there is an intense interest in young women, and specifically, the new depiction of girls, as either can-do or at-risk, suggests that what it means to prevail or lose out has become bound up with how we understand girlhood. Their public presence indicates that they have come to stand for a number of hopes and concerns about the late modernity.[8] So, clearly, it is in the context of work, consumption and motherhood that young women today are quite able to enact the reality of the late modernity.

It is argued that flexibility and self-actualization are now expected of young women because they are perceived as most confident, resilient and empowered of all the social groups affected by risk.[9] In Delhi, the can-do girls are notable for their high ambitions with regard to their employment and their commitment to planning for success in their careers. In fact, boys on campus seem to complain about their sole determination to make it at the expense of the loss of interest in gender relationships. With the help of family, friends and teachers, young women ensure the realization of their professional ambitions. The visibility of young women in the 'new meritocracy' clearly indicates how success is being valued in the context of work. Even in the West, asserts A. MeRobbie, "With the stripping away of gender-based barriers to participation in education and labour market and the development of a more open, meritocratic system, young women are perceived to have risen quickly to the top in terms of educational attainment, aspirations, and job prospects. The signs of their success are glamorous careers and luxurious lifestyles, financial independence, and high standards of physical beauty and grooming."[10] She suggests that political, media and advertising interests have converged in the construction of young women as standard bearers for the new economy as the creators of wealth. However, while media and advertising have always focused on feminine success in relation to body and appearance, what is new is that this is now connected to success at work. The processes of working on self and competing with others, especially other women, to be perfect in self-presentation have been extended so that improving oneself is necessary to success in labour and consumer markets.

Success at the workplace, therefore, is associated with the display of a consumerist lifestyle. With the emergence of young women as those most likely to be successful in the new economy, it also entails that they would form the key consumer group. The purchasing power of young women enhances their image of successful and individualized womanhood. Of course, young and attractive women have always been engaged in selling of products, and marketing by women has always been a matter of constructing the new femininity. So, many websites for young women are being supported by advertisers, and successful young women are seen having purchasing power and influence over family consumption and lifestyle patterns.[11]

Success and femininity of young women are connected through notions of choice, versatility, beauty and cleverness. The notion of Campus Babes in Delhi colleges suggests that young intellectual women are being seen as both smart and attractive which they do not hesitate to display through consumption. The labour market accomplishments and a glamourous consumerist lifestyle are based on the idea of an unencumbered individual who can devote herself to a full-time paid work. Part of the package of the *can-do experience* is thus the delaying of motherhood. Young women in Delhi with professional prospects are not only putting off marriage but also having children into their thirties, choosing to have only one or two children, or opting for childlessness altogether. Certainly, this has given rise to a lot of tension within family, but it is also reshaping traditional family values around mothering to accept the new image of a young woman as high-status worker. This can also be looked at as the regulation of female sexuality in the middle class as it is a part of a wider regulation of women's goals and achievements. However, the traditional prescription for women to have children at some point still comes to bear on these young women. Thus, motherhood has been repackaged as an emotionally profitable choice for the new career women in their thirties. Even, the career women from Neena Gupta to Madonna have accepted motherhood to be part and parcel of their glamorous world. It is seen as something feasible without forfeiting beauty, fun and work.

In contrast to the upcoming successful lot, *at-risk women* are those who are victims of their circumstances in terms of poverty, unstable families, violence and crime-ridden social environment and lack of access to education. These structural disadvantages are recast as poor personal choices, laziness and incompetent family practices, points out Harris.[12] They always seem to be treated as an underclass, but it must be kept in mind that it starts with the connivance of social processes and social institutions.

To conclude, one needs to monitor both these groups of young women achievers and the non-attainers as the achievers who are at times unable to cope up with the pressures of achieving, whereas the non-attainers can be pathologized and even punished. However, what cannot be denied today is the potential power centre in these young women at both local and global levels.

Acknowledgement

I have had the privilege of being the pioneer student in Gender Studies in the mid-seventies to have worked under the guidance of Prof K.L. Sharma at the Centre for the Study of Social Systems, Jawaharlal Nehru University for both my M.Phil and doctoral dissertations. During my association with him for over a quarter of a century, I have gradually learnt to appreciate his scholarship, simplicity, humaneness and openness of mind in equal measure. Today, I rejoice that a volume is being brought out in his honour. Through this humble contribution of mine, I would like to express my gratitude to him for chiseling out the sociologist in me.

Notes

1. Andy Furlong and Fred Cartmel (1997), *Young People and Social Change: Individualization and Risk in Late Modernity*, Maidenhead: Open University Press, p. 6.
2. Anita Harris (2004), *Future Girl*, New York: Routledge, pp. 3–4.
3. Anthony Giddens (1991), *Modernity and Self-Identity: Self and Society in the Late Modern Age*, Cambridge: Polity Press.
4. Ulrich Beck (1992), *Risk Society: Towards a New Modernity*, trans. Mark Ritter, London: Sage Publications, p. 135.
5. Marshall Mcluhan (1964), *Understanding Media*, New York: McGraw Hill.
6. A.A. Khan (2004), 'The Phenomenon of Womencipation' *Greater Kashmir*, June 11.
7. Ibid.
8. A. Harris, op. cit., p. 14.
9. See Walkerdine, Lucey and Melody (2001), *Growing up Girl: Psycho-Social Explorations of Gender and Class*, London: Palgrave.
10. Angela McRobbie (2001), "Good Girls, Bad Girls? Female Success and New Meritocracy" (unpublished paper).
11. Catherine Nikas (1998), "The Power of Girls", *Ragtrader*, April 3–16, pp. 20–21.
12. A. Harris, op. cit., p. 25.

27 Crystallization of the Traditional Pattern of Stratification in India

SHRIRAMA AND INDRA DEVA

The seeds of the traditional hierarchical structure lie in India's ancient past. In around 1500 BC, hordes of Aryans, a light complexioned people, began to enter the Indian subcontinent. These people were not only well equipped with arms but were also more robust and militant than the earlier settlers. The hymns of the *Rgveda*, which portray the events of this invasion so well, were composed by different poets over a long period of time during which the Aryan hordes were coming and settling in India. The Aryans were disdainful of the ethnic characteristics of the pre-Aryan settlers. In such circumstances conflict was inevitable. But, gradually, a pattern of social adjustment was evolved.

Rgveda: The Establishment of Aryan Supremacy

The *Rgveda* portrays the Aryans primarily as warriors. We do find some priest-cum-poets but these poets did not form an exclusive class. The sons of these poets could take the profession of warrior; and the son of a warrior could become a priest if he so chose. As the Aryans moved eastwards, the threat of losing their identity became real. They strove hard to save their racial and cultural heritage, creating a sacerdotal class which performed the function of preserving the Aryan-lore, primarily the *Rgveda.* Gradually, this priestly grouping was transformed into the Brahmana class for whom the Aryan and non-Aryan kings and traders provided a good clientele. The process of racial segregation that was reflected in the hymns of *Rgveda* flourished during the period of the later *Samhitas* and the *Brahmanas*, finally crystallizing into a rigid caste system. These castes were hereditary. The priestly caste secured the highest position and constituted the elite stratum of society. The other castes followed the norms set by these elites.

In many ancient civilizations, we find ranks based on birth and occupation. The ancient Greeks and Persians, distant cousins of Rgvedic Aryans, had similar categories. But these ranks never acquired the rigidity and complexity that we find in the Indian caste system.

In the *Rgveda,* the word 'varna' means colour. In some hymns this is used to indicate the colour of skin of the people of two different races, the Aryan varna and Krsna varna. But, nowhere is the word 'varna' used for caste in the *Rgveda.* Though the two classes – Brahmana and Ksatriya – mentioned often, the word 'varna' is not used to denote them. Even, in the *Purusa Sukta,* where the origin of the four classes is described, the word 'varna' does not occur. The words Rajanya, Vaisya and Sudra are also found only in the *Purusas Sukta* of *Rgveda,* which is a late composition.

These Aryan hordes were quite conscious of their cultural and ethnic identity and looked down upon the dark complexioned earlier settlers. The latter are referred to in the *Rgveda* as Dasas and Panis, both being described as dark complexioned (Krsna varna).

The word 'Dasa' seems to be connected with the Iranian word 'Dahae' which means countrymen. The Aryans of *Rgveda* called the local population Dasa whom they subjugated as slaves. Later on, the word 'Dasa' came to be used for slaves in the *Rgveda* itself.[1] In the *Valakhilya Sukta,* a latter part of the *Rgveda,* we find a prayer to Indra: "Give me one hundred asses, one hundred sheep, and one hundred Dasas."[2] The Aryans considered the Dasas not only inferior beings but also their enemies. One of *Rgveda's* poets says: "Indra, the killer of enemy, destroyer of cities, destroyed armies of the black. He has given earth and water to mankind." The Dasas lived in cities. They were militant people and gave a tough fight to the Aryans. Finally, however, they were vanquished and were either absorbed in the lower rungs of society or driven away from their dwellings and had to take shelter in dense forests and other inhospitable regions. In the *Rgveda,* a poet says: "Indra kills Dasas and increases the might of the Aryans."[3] At another place, it is said: "Indra slew the Dasa Sambara of the mountain for the sake of king Divodasa." It appears that the Aryans were militant and well armed and they massacred the simple peace-loving people at will. The Aryan god-hero Indra is credited with demolition of ninety-nine cities of the Dasa king Sambara: "And Indra for the sake of king Divodasa demolished Sambara's ninety-nine cities."[4] The disdain of the Aryans towards the Dasas, because of different racial features, was so great that they were considered non-human or Amanusya.[5] And, since the Dasas were considered non-humans all inhuman behaviour towards them was justified in the eyes of the Aryans. This attitude is by no means confined to the victorious Aryans of those days. It is a common attitude towards vanquished people. In a hymn of *Rgveda,* we find: "You (Indra) subdued Pipru and powerful Mrgayu for Rjisvan, the son of Vidathin; you smote down fifty thousand darks, you shattered cities, as old age shatters good looks."[6] Fire was the most effective and powerful weapon of the Aryans. They used it liberally against the Dasas.

> O Fire due to thy fear forth led the dark races,
> Scattered abroad deserting their possessions,
> O glowing Vaisvanara when for Puru,
> You burn up and rend their cities.[7]

Thus, the Dasas had to leave their settlements in utter despair. Similarly, at another place, it is asserted that "fire drove Dasas and brought light to Aryans".[8]

The Aryans thus acquired the vast fertile lands of north-western India but they badly needed manpower. For them, the Dasas were the most suitable source of labour. The Dasas were captured and compelled to work for them. The *Rgveda* says: "Indra binds hundred and ten Dasas."[9] Many Dasas accepted this slavery. In a hymn of *Rgveda* it is said: "An Aryan leads away a Dasa at his will."[10] While other Dasas, who were more self-respecting and rebellious, ran away. But Aryans hounded them from place to place: "The dark coloured Dasas were driven away by Indra from place to place."[11] From this hymn it becomes quite clear that the settlements of Dasas were demolished more than once. Ultimately, the Dasas took shelter in dark caves and dense forests: "Indra made Dasa varna low and dweller of caves."[12] It is stated that "Dasas lived in darkness".[13] The word 'Dasa' is used for slave even in the *Rgveda*. In later times also, Dasa has been used as the most common word for slave.

Another people mentioned in the *Rgveda* are Panis. Probably, these were a commercial people. Panis are often connected with the ancient Phoenicians. Phoenicia is the ancient name of the coastal part of Syria. Panis are portrayed as rich cattle-breeders and traders. Culturally, the Panis seem to be akin to the civilized Mediterraneans but by the time of the Aryan invasion, racially, they seem to have become predominantly proto-Austroloid. This is, by and large, true also of the people of the Indus valley civilization, who probably belonged to the category of Panis of the *Rgveda*. The wealth of the Panis greatly lured the Aryans. The Panis did not want to share their wealth with the Aryans. This tendency of Panis always to expect something in exchange, seemed absurd to the pastoral Aryans. Commercial values do not seem to have taken root by that time among the Aryans, and they considered this tendency reprehensible.

In the tenth Mandala of *Rgveda*, we find a whole sukta in which the she-god of hero-god Indra came to find out the hidden treasure comprising cows, horses and riches is well stored in the mountain castle and those Panis who are excellent guards guard it well.[14] But, the Aryans found out that concealed Panis treasure and appropriated it. "Searching out everywhere, they have obtained the great treasure of Panis hidden in the cave."[15] Fire was employed by the Aryans against the Panis also:

> Agni, the hero, kills his enemy;
> The poet takes away the riches of Panis[16]

The poet praises fire because through its help the Aryans were able to open the doors of Panis: "The fire is the wisest god who opens the doors of Panis forcefully."[17]

In due course it seems that the Panis were absorbed among the Vis or the Aryan countrymen. The commercial terminology in the Indo-Aryan languages of India owes a great deal to the Panis. Terms such as 'Apana' or the market; 'Panana' or to sell; 'Panya' or commodity; 'Papa' or coin and 'Vanik' or the trader are among those derived from them. In the word 'Vanik' the sound of 'Pa' changed to 'Va', which is not uncommon in the evolution of languages. It is common to add the letter 'ka' for making diminutives in the Avestan as well as in the Sanskrit languages. The word 'Vanijya' or trade is derived from the word 'Vanik'.

In the Indo-Aryan social structure, this whole class was given the third position – lower than the priests and militarymen. In the *Purusa Sukta,* this class is called Vaisya or "the sons of Vis". In the *Rgveda* the word 'Vis' is used for people. In the Zend-Avesta the word 'Vis' means many families or a village.[18]

Priests and Warriors

In the earliest hymns of *Rgveda* the word varna means colour. The two colours refer to fair and dark complexioned people. The Aryans were fair complexioned people whereas the Dasas were dark complexioned. The composer Agastya is described in *Rgveda* as one who belonged to both varnas: "The fierce sage cherished both varnas."[19] His brother is Vasistha. Both of these poets are sons of the gods Varuna and Mitra from Urvasi – the famous nymph. Though both these poets belong to Dasa varna from their mother's side, they are considered established perceivers of hymns. Vasistha was the most prolific among the composers of hymns. He was also a known military strategist and priest:

> Bharatas were like scattered infants;
> The way cows are controlled by rod,
> When Vasisthan became their leader;
> The people of Trtsus stood out.[20]

In the *Rgveda,* we find a society in which any individual of Aryan origin had the right to choose his profession according to his abilities and achievements. He could become a priest or a warrior, or an ordinary man. The word 'Brahma' means hymn and also the power inherent in the hymn. Thus, Brahmana is one who is the repository of hymns. Like all ancient civilizations, in the ancient *Rgvedic* civilization too, priesthood was considered the noblest profession. A priest had precedence even over the king. But becoming a successful priest was not easy. The priest was expected to compose such hymns as would lull wealthy enemies to sleep and swollen rivers to lower their level so that armies would cross them without difficulty. Moreover, he had also to be a master strategist and an excellent warrior himself. Naturally, there was a competition among various priests for the patronage of powerful kings. King Sudaṣa replaced Vasistha by Visvamitra as his priest. Many of the composers of hymns seem to be priests of one king or the other. Some of their sons became composers of hymns while some others found the profession of warrior more suitable. A poet vividly describes that everybody has to do some work or the other to earn his livelihood:

> I am a poet, my father is a physician,
> My mother grinds corns with stone;
> Striving for wealth,
> We follow different occupations.[21]

However, as stated earlier, composing hymns was not an easy task. Mere knowledge of language was not considered enough to become a good poet. A poet compares speech with a fond wife who exposes her beauty only to her husband:

> A man though knows speech, does not know her;
> Though he hears her yet not bears.
> Like a fond well-dressed wife,
> She exposes her beauty to her master.[22]

Entry into the rank of warriors was also quite difficult. One who failed to be a good poet could hardly be a success in the battlefield:

> Wandering in illusion gainlessly;
> The speech heard by him bears neither

blossom nor fruit.
Dull in friendship he is called a laggard;
Nobody expects him to perform deeds of valour.[23]

The fierce scene of battlefield is vividly portrayed in the *Rgveda:*

With their banners raised where heroes fight, where nothing is pleasing.

Where anything that one perceives is terrifying, O Indra and Varuna may you comfort us there.

Darkened with dust were seen the boundaries of earth. The shouts went up to heaven.

The enemies of our people have come near, you who heard the calls come to us with help.[24]

Vis was the third rank. Nowhere in the *Rgveda* do we find a hymn in which a poet aspires to be a Vis or a common man. Obviously, those who could not get entry into the two higher professions remained Vis. The Vis are described as those who give taxes to the king.[25] These were cattle breeders and agriculturists. The poet compares the earth with a cow from whom he milks a rich harvest year after year:

May Indra press the furrow down,
May Pusan guide its course aright
May she be rich in milk
For milking year by year,
Happily let the shares turn up the land.
Happily the plougher go with the oxen,
With honey and milk Parjanya make us happy.
O Suna and Sira may you grant us prosperity.[26]

The Fourfold Hierarchy: Organic Analogy

Thus, there were three ranks in the ancient *Rgvedic* society. The occupations of all the three were well demarcated. The first two ranks – the Brahmanas and the Ksatriyas – were considered higher and nobler. All young Aryans aspired to get entry into these ranks. Those who could neither become Brahmanas nor Ksatriyas automatically went to the third rank of Vis. In the *Rgveda* we do not find the mention of the Sudra except in the *Purusa Sukta*, which is considered to be of a later origin. The *Purusa Sukta* contains a myth about the origin of the four-fold social structure. Here, all the four ranks are mentioned together. In this hymn it is asserted that all the four ranks originated from the great sacrificed Purusa. The occupations of the four ranks are related symbolically to the parts of the body of the Purusa. Obviously, it is an organic analogy between man and society, legitimizing the varying ranks and functions of different groups. The words 'Rajanya', 'Vaisya' and 'Sudra' occur only in the *Purusa Sukta:*

The Brahmana was his mouth,
The Rajanya was made of his two arms;
His thighs became the Vaisya,
From his feet was produced the Sudra.[27]

The Brahmana has been called the mouth of Purusa. He is placed highest in the society and his special function pertains to speech. Being a priest, invoking gods is his privilege. The second rank – Rajanya – is born of the arms of Purusa and has the privilege of wielding arms. The thighs of Purusa became Vaisya. The occupation of Vaisya is agriculture and trade. From his feet were produced the Sudras. Just as the feet are the lowest in the body, Sudras are the lowest in society.

Royal Weiler's statement[28] that the Rajanyas were later called Ksatriyas or rulers is not correct. The sequence is just the opposite. In the *Rgveda* the word 'Rajanya' occurs nowhere except in the *Purusa Sukta* while the word 'Ksatriya' is used in many hymns. Thus, the earlier word is Ksatriya, and Rajanya is definitely later. The *Purusa Sukta* appears to be the composition of an era when the Aryans had already settled down in the Indian sub-continent. The Vis or the common masses of Aryans required agricultural labour, so they employed the Dasas. Gradually, the Dasas were given the generic name of Sudra. Both these words are of Iranian origin. The word 'Dasa' is the transformation of the Iranian word 'Dahae' or common man. The word 'Sudra' seems to be a transformed version of 'Khurda', a pre-Aryan Iranian tribe still living in Iran. In the Persian language the word 'Khurd' means small. The Sanskrit word 'Ksudra' which also means small seems to be a variant of Khurd which means small.

In the *Rgveda* itself we find a tendency of considereing the professions of priest and warrior higher, and the profession of the agriculturist lower. The people who were employed as agricultural labourers or slaves naturally had to occupy the lowest position in the society. The Sudra class comprises artisans, craftsmen, artists, dancers and musicians, besides manual labourers.

The composition of the *Purusa Sukta* and its inclusion in the *Rgveda* was probably the first attempt to justify and legitimize the systematic exploitation of non-Aryan massess by the Aryans. The easiest way was to find some divine basis. This tendency of imputing divine sanction is a characteristic of the period of later *Samhitas* and *Brahmanas*. We do not find this tendency in the earlier parts of the *Rgveda*. In those parts of the *Rgveda* the non-Aryans were considered 'Amnusya' or non-humans and the descendents of Manu, the primeval father. Therefore, their subjugation was considered natural. The Vis Aryans, or the agriculturists, employed non-Aryan labour – for agricultural society requires a vast though periodic labour force. In due course, with their shrewd farsightedness the Aryan elite evolved an institutionalied zarrangement which provided cheap labour as a matter of course. Sudras formed the lowest class of Aryan society. The inclusion of this hymn in the *Rgveda* sanctified this arrangement as natural and God-given. The society was conceived as a single whole and all the classes formed its parts. Later on, in order to preserve the privileges enjoyed by the upper classes, and to avoid racial admixture, it was necessary to give a more clear-cut character to various classes. Consideration of heredity replaced those of individual achievement. And, the classes crystallized into castes.

In the *Avesta,* the land of seven rivers is mentioned as a settlement of Aryans. In this land the leader of Aryan migration, Yim, married a demoness and gave his sister Yimuk to a demon. The issues born of these unions have been referred to as 'abnormal' in the *Avesta* and as monkeys and bears in the Pahlavi texts. These descriptions allude to the racial admixture which took place in the early era. To avoid deformity, Yim married his sister Yimuk and thus preserved racial purity. Form this myth it is quite clear that during the earliest era of settlement the Aryans married indigenous women, but when the children born of such unions had dark complexions and snub noses, such marriages were avoided. In ancient Iran, where the racial features of victorious Aryans and the subjugated people did not differ much, ranks did not crystallize into endogamous groups as happened in India. In Iran, the rank of priest was hereditary first and marriages in direct order were permissible. But, in course of time, castes crystallized into hereditary as well as endogamous units.

Theoretically, though the non-Aryans were included into the Aryan pale through the pronouncement of the *Purusa Sukta,* distinction is often made to separate Sudras from the higher varnas in the later *Samhitas.* The higher castes are referred to as Aryans while Sudras are mentioned separately.

Later *Samhitas* and *Brahmanas:* The Rise of Ritualism

In the later *Samhitas* hypergamy is permissible. Thus, the Aryans or men of the upper varna could have Sudra wives. We find a reference in the *Taittriya Samhita* that Aryans used to establish illicit relations with Sudra women: "If a Sudra woman has an Aryan paramour she does not expect wealth for maintenance".[29] A Sudra could never think of marrying an Aryan woman legally. We find a number of justifications for the low status of Sudras in the later *Samhitas* and *Brahmanas.* In the *Taittiriya Samhita* of the black Yajurveda, we find: "Among men Sudra has the same position as the horse has among animals. These two, the horse and the Sudra, are conveyances of the beings (Aryans); therefore, the Sudras could not participate in a sacrifice."[30]

On the basis of the *Purusa Sukta,* the *Tandyamaha Brahmanga* propounds: "Therefore, even if a Sudra has a lot of cattle, he is not entitled to perform a sacrifice, as he is without god, no god was created after him, since he was created from the feet, he should not do anything but wash the feet (of the three higher varnas)."[31] The *Aitareya Brahmana* puts forth another mythical justification: "He crated the Brahmana with Gayatri, the Rajanya with Tristubh and the Vaisya with Jagati, but he did not create the Sudra with any meter."[32] In the *Satapatha Brahmana,* a Sudra is simply declared: 'toil'.[33]

At another place, Sudra, woman, dog and crow are called the untruth itself, that is, personification of falsehood, and it is suggested that a teacher while teaching should not look at them.[34] The *Aitareya Brahmana* ordains that the Sudra is to be ordered about by the others (three varnas), he can be made to rise to will, he can be executed at will.[35] Thus, the Sudras were given the lowest position in society. The social elite maintained a strict vigil to ensure that they were excluded from Aryan society. Their inclusion in the fourfold hierarchy is granted only because of the service that they perform for the higher varnas. They can in no way be counted as among them. To serve the three higher varnas was the sole duty of the Sudra class. This relationship is asserted time and again in all the works, including those of later periods.

By the time of the later *Samhitas* and *Brahmanas,* the doctrine of four varnas was broadly accepted by all members of the society as god given. We can perceive the change of the ethos in this period from the period when the hymns of *Rgveda* were composed. In the later *Samhitas* the struggle with non-Aryans did not exist anymore. The non-Aryans, now the Sudras, accepted the superiority of the Aryans and considered serving the latter as their sacred duty. Consequently, the old militant spirit of the Aryans declined. For acquiring the comforts of life, they did not have to fight anymore. Since priesthood was the most remunerative and respected occupation, the bulk of The Aryan people became Brahmana or priest. Simple and human sacrifices were made elaborate and expensive. The priest now was neither a military strategist nor a poet; his sole job was to preserve the hymns and employ them in various complex sacrifices which were to be performed for the fulfilment of different wishes. The character of the gods changed too. The militant gods lost their heroic spirit and vigour. The Aryans had by now settled down in the Indo-Gangetic plains. For the settled agricultural way of life such gods were needed no more. The gods now were expected to fulfil their mundande wishes and solve their day-to-day problems. The centres of the civilization shifted further east and the land of seven rivers is not mentioned anymore. Now, the land of Kuru and Panchala became the seat of Aryan culture. The river Saraswati in the west and the river Drasadvati in the east form its boundary. Broadly speaking, this land comprises the modern states of Haryana and Uttar Pradesh. The secure and comfortable life of the plains made the priests self-assured and complacent. Probably, there existed neither competition nor criticism and as a result the literature composed in this era is of a poor quality as compared to the Rgvedic hymns.

The priestly elites preserved the highest position for themselves. There are many assertions in the later *Samhitas* which are meant to establish their supreme position. It appears that the priestly elites themselves were not quite sure of their superiority, so that it was necessary for them to make repeated assertions. In all the texts of the later Vedic era, we find glorification of priestly elites, for instance, the *Taittiriya Samhita* declares them "the gods on earth".[36]

The sacrament of initiation – Yajnopavita – played an important part in rationaliinzg and strengthening the varna system. The first three varnas acquired a privileged position for themselves. Though studentship is mentioned in the *Rgveda,* we do not find any mention of initiation. In the *Atharvaveda,* for the first time, we get the description of initiation where the poet conceives the sun as the child who is to be initiated into studentship by his teacher. This seems to be a forced analogy and there remain a number of incongruities. In this hymn, studentship is called a second birth.

Gradually, the sacrament of initiation became much more elaborate. The *Taittiriya Aranyaka* prescribes that a Brahmana should wear a Yajnopavita of antilope skin or of cloth. It asserts that the sacrifice which is performed while wearing a Yajnopavita is spread out, or becomes successful, whereas the sacrifices of the one who does not wear a Yajnopavita would not spread.[37] And, in due course, Yajnopavita became the most essential part of initiation. In the *Dharma Sutras* we find that the sacred cord is introduced as an option. The *Apastamba Dharma Sutras* prescribe that a householder should always wear an upper garment, or in its place he may wear the sacred thread.[38]

By the time the *Brahmana* texts were composed the sacerdotal class had become quite leisurely self-assured. The *Brahmana* texts are not very systematic and articulate in their style. We find lengthy passages for it appears that the composers did not take any pains to make them concise or complete. Some parts of the sacrificial procedure are dealt with at great length while some others are left out without even a mention. In fact, at times, some rather insignificant rites are explained in great detail while the main sacrifice is altogether ignored in rationalizing insignificant sacrificial activities, myths are created which are often left incomplete.

In the *Satapatha Brahmana,* the Brahmana and Ksatriya varnas are identified with the twin gods, Mitra and Varuna: "Mitra is priesthood and Varuna is nobility; and the priesthood is the conceiver, and the nobility is the doer." It is asserted that Mitra (priest) could stand without Varuna (nobility), but not Varuna nobility, without Mitra. It is concluded, "therefore a Ksatriya who wants to do something should seek guidance from a Brahmana, for he verily succeeds only when he is guided by a Brahmana".[39]

Upanisads: Revolt against Ritualism and Brahmanic Supremacy

Gradually, the three varnas other than the Brahmana developed a kind of apathy for the ritualistic way of life and a new school of thought appeared formulating its philosophy in the *Aranyakas* and *Upanisads.* In these texts it is asserted that expensive, cumbersome and prolonged grand sacrifices do not lead to real knowledge. It was a challenge against the supremacy of the Brahmanas, and signified loss of faith in the sacerdotal science inherent in it. People began to doubt the efficacy of these sacrifices. Another interesting feature of the *Upanisads* is that contrary to tradition, the newer thought was marked by contributions primarily from Ksatriyas, lower varnas and women.

The Upanisadic thought is quite different in its spirit from the Vedas. As a matter of fact, it was implicit revolt against the varna hierarchy. The teachings of the *Upanisads* are in simple language; therefore, they became highly popular among the people. The younger generation of the priestly class took active interest in it. In this era, the importance of family and varna also diminshed. *Upanisads* contain the seeds of the systems of metaphysics which evolved later on. We come across many instances where Brahmana teachers went to learn the ultimate truth from Ksatriyas. 'Brahma' which means only prayer in *Rgveda,* assumed a new mystical meaning in the *Upanisads*. Now, this term stood for the Ultimate Reality.

In this era, the Brahmanic supremacy was challenged in various overt and covert ways. In the *Chandogya Upanisad,* we find a story in which a procession of white dogs is depicted as the Brahmanas. These white dogs come one after another, each holding the tail of the preceding dog in his mouth just as priests do when they go to sing the Vahisapavamana hymn. (In this ceremony priests have to walk in a procession, each priest holding the gown of the preceding priest). When all the dogs settled down, they began to recite, "Om, let us eat; Om, let us drink; Om, may the divine Varuna, Prajapati, Savitri bring us food; Lord of food bring hither food, bring it, Om."[40]

Another interesting feature of the *Upanisads* is their dynamic approach towards life. Nearly all the teachers of the *Upanisads* are householder. They perceived life as a continuous process. Each individual is expected to make persistent effort to achieve something which is yet to be achieved: "Caraiveti, Caraiveti" or "proceed on, proceed on".

Many established teachers approached kings to acquire the ultimate knowledge. Pravahana Jaivali, king of Panchala, instructed Gautama and claimed that "Brahmanas do not have this knowledge, only the Ksatriyas possess it".[41] We also find glorification of Ksatriyas in the *Brhadaranyaka Upanisad* also: "The Brahmana being not strong enough, the most excellent power or Ksatriyas was created therefore (at the Rajasuya sacrifice) the Brahmana sits down below the Ksatriya. He confers that glory on the Ksatra alone."[42] At another place, we find that five great householders and theologians approached king Asvapati of Kekaya carrying fuel in their hands like students to get the knowledge of Self.[43]

Even the kings sometimes approached persons of lower classes to get knowledge of Self. Jansruti Pautrayana approached a cartman named Raikva for instruction.

Before the *Upanisads* were composed, a great deal of racial admixture must have taken place. In the Vedic tradition persons of dark complexion were considered as non-humans or 'Amanusya'. Due to the strong patriarchal values, the birth of a daughter also was considered a misfortune. In the *Upanisads,* we perceive a peculiar change in the general ethos, which is totally absent in the literature composed both before and after the *Upanisads.* In the Upanisadic literature a dark complexion is not considered necessarily bad. The *Brahmanyaka Upanisad* mentions rituals for having a dark-complexioned son together with that for a blind son. We find a ritual even for the birth of a daughter which is very uncommon for the Indian elite tradition.[44]

The *Upanisads* mark a new epoch in the history of Indian thought. The ideas found in them are in marked contrast to the traditional way of thinking which always looks back for the golden past. The *Upanisads,* on the other hand, are refreshingly forward-looking. Instead of expecting people to stick to the beaten path of the past, they exhort them to move on and on, hoping that each new generation will be better than the older ones. In the *Brhadranyaka Upanisad,* the father blesses his new-born son and wishes him to be more assertive than his father and his grandfather.

In the *Upanisads,* for the first time, the concept of rebirth is introduced. As a matter of fact, it is not in consonance with the Aryan tradition. In the *Rgveda,* as well as the *Avesta,* the dead go to live with their forefathers in heaven. It is possible that the concept of rebirth has an Assyrian origin, though the idea of souls taking another birth is found in a rudimentary form in Austric tribal cultures also. As recorded by Arrian, Assyrians invaded India and ruled over its north-western part. Through continuous cultural interaction many Assyrian beliefs entered the Indian tradition, the idea of transmigration of souls and rebirth, seemingly, being one of them. This was further developed in the classical Indian systems of metaphysics, specially in the Samkhya Yoga and Vedanta. It crystallized into the theory of 'karma', which rationaliezd and provided the rockbed to the system of varna hierarchy for thousands of years.

The *Upanisads* marked a revolt against the Brahmanic supremacy. This wave of liberalization must have led to the adoption of ideas from non-Aryan sources. However, it is ironic that this new idea of transmigration of souls was itself turned into the most effective instrument to justify inequality based on birth. The doctrine is that one is born as a Brahmana or a Sudra entirely on the basis of his own deeds in the earlier lives; in his present life he should pursue steadfastly the duties of his own varna in order to better his prospects in subsequent lives. Not only was this doctrine propagated by the Brahmanas as self-evident truth, but it was accepted and internalized by the most underprivileged and exploited sections also. The doctrine provided perfect justification for gross inequality based on birth.

Sutras: The First Attempt towards Revival

During the Upanisadic era, the varna hierarchy and the strong patriarchal order that constituted the foundation of the ancient Indian social structure was badly undermined. The *Grhya Sutras* seem to mark the systematic and concerted efforts on the part of the priestly elites to re-establish their supremacy and resuscitate the social order in which they would have an unrivalled position. The hierarchy could no longer be established on the basis of race as there had already been a great deal of racial admixture. Because of this, it seems that the criteria of ritual admixture. Because of this, it seems that the criteria of ritual purity were introduced by the *Grhya Sutras* to take the place of racial purity.

In the *Grhya Sutras*, for first time, a number of 'sanskaras' or sacraments were explicitly codified. These sanskaras are to begin before the birth of a child and this process lasts for many years even after the death of an individual. It is expected from each individual to offer oblations to his father, grandfather and great-grandfather. A professional priest has to officiate at these sacraments. All the individuals of the higher varnas, who wanted to establish themselves, had to get these sacraments performed. Non-performance of these sacraments could result even in ex-communication from the community.

During the era of Aryan invasion, the victorious Aryans had to marry women belonging to the subjugated people. But, there is no evidence that they gave their own women in marriage to the non-Aryanas. Thus, a sort of hypergamy was established. However, during the Upanisadic period, some kings gave their daughters in marriage to persons belonging to a lower order in gratitude for the esoteric knowledge received from them. It seems that the Brahmanical revival marked by the *Sutras* sought to reverse this trend. The *Grhya Sutras* laid down that marriages should be hypergamous, that is, in the direct order of varnas.

As far as the varna of the progeny is concerned, there seems to be two types of tradition which are divergent. According to one, the progeny belong to the varna of their father irrespective of the varna of the mother. This seems to be the earlier practice when the Aryans had no option but to marry women from amongst the non-Aryan people. The other set of norms, which is already in evidence in the *Sutras*, and is vigorously asserted in the *Smrtis*, insists that both the parents should belong to the same varna.

This is in sharp contrast to the practice of bestowing sonhood on children acquired in various ways. The *Gautama Dharma Sutra* recognizes twelve types of sons which include besides the real son even the sons which had no biological relationship with the father or the mother. Even those whose parents are unknown have been included. The sons of all these types were given the class name which would imply also their inclusion in the varna of their social father. It would be reasonable to surmise that such a son had to be of a fair complexion.

The *Dharma Sutras* introduced many new rules about not taking food from the house of persons of lower varnas. In the early Vedic texts, we do not find such rules. The *Baudhayana Dharma Sutra,* which because of its archaic language seems to be the earliest among the *Dharma Sutras,* does not contain any rules about taking food in the houses of lower varnas. Gautama introduced such restrictions in a liberal way. It is interesting to note that Gautama allows a Brahmana student to take food from the house of all the three higher varnas;[45] but after completing his studentship he should not take food from the house of Ksatriya and Vaisya varna. He was expected to take food only at the house of a Brahmana householder. Apastamba further propounds that even among Brahmana householders, one should eat only in the house of a true Brahman.[46]

It appears that the society in that era was not prepared for the imposition of such rigid norms and many elites took objection to this. Apastamba refers to the opinions of 'some' who allow a Brahmana to take food in the houses of Ksatriya nad Vaisya householders. In times of distress a Brahmana could eat food prepared in the houses of a Sudra who was under his protection for the sake of spiritual merit. Gautama says that during distress a Brahmana may take food from a Sudra.[47]

In the Upanisadic era Ksatriyas enjoyed a position at least equal if not higher to that of Brahmanas. But, in the *Dhrama Sutras,* the priestly elites made it a point to assign a lower position to Ksatriyas. It is provided that even a king should make way for a Brahmana on the road. The gap between the two higher varnas definitely widened. A Brahmana of ten years and a Ksatriya of a hundred years stand to each other in the relation of father and son: among these the Brahmana is the father.[48]

Sudras constituted the fourth varna. Apastamba and Vasistha refer to the Sudras and outcastes as burial ground.[49] Apastamba, Gautama and Vasistha provide that serving the three higher varnas is his sole occupation. The higher the varna he serves, the greater merit he earns.[50] Gautama provides that for serving the three higher varnas, he would get remnants of their food, cast off shoes, umbrellas, garments and mats. When a Sudra servant is unable to serve his Aryan employer due to old age or illness, the Aryan employer was expected to support him. Similarly, if the employer fell into distress, the servant was expected to maintain his master. It is ordained that the savings of the servant could be used by the master.

Baudhayana and Apastamba both provide that a Sudra can cook under the superintendence of the first three varnas. The cooks should daily have their hair-cut, shave the beards and cut their nails before cooking.[51]

During the Upanisadic era, Sudras too participated in metaphysical discussions. In the revivalist era the priestly elites scrupulously forbade them even the listening to recitation of the Vedas if a Sudra intentionally listens to the recitation of the Vedas, his ears shall be filled with molten lead or lac. If he recites Vedic texts, his tongue shall be cut off; if he remembers them, his body shall be split into two.[52] Apastamba and Gautama provide that if a Sudra tries to converse with an Aryan on an equal footing, walks on the road side by side with him or sits on the same couch, he should be given corporal punishment. The tongue of a Sudra who speaks evil of a virtuous person belonging to one of the first three varnas shall be cut out.[53] In case a Sudra commits homicide or theft, appropriates land, or commits similar crimes, his property shall be confiscated and he himself shall suffer capital punishment.[54] It seems that the priestly elites were quite aware of the fact that the Sudras were as capable of learning and propagating knowledge as any member of the three higher varnas. They did not want to share the privileged position which they enjoyed on grounds of possessing sacred knowledge even with the Ksatriya and Vaisya varnas, and not at all with the Sudras. All the members of the Brahmana varna were expected to maintain a close vigil over the Sudras to prevent them even from listening to a Vedic recitation. Any kind of self-assertion on the part of a Sudra amounted to a crime according to the *Dharma Sutras.*

Though it is provided that a Sudra can cook the food of a Brahmana, Apastamba and Baudhayana both provide that food brought by an impure Sudra must not be eaten.[55]

The value of the life of a Sudra is assessed quite low. Apastamba provides the same penance for killing a Sudra as he provides for killing a crow, a chameleon, a peacock, a Brahmani duck, a swan, frog, a mongoose, a musk-rat, or a dog.[56]

Buddhism: Challenge to the Brahmanical Order

In the eastern parts of India, however, there developed a parallel non-orthodx stream of culture through the emergence of *Upanisads* and Buddhist literature. Gradually, this became a challenge to the Vedic-Brahmanical tradition in the beginning rather covertly, but later quite openly.

In these movements we find a unique synthesis of different ethno-culture streams. Because of the complex interweaving of the varied strands, it is not easy to identify and isolate the contribution made by various cultures. Among the prominent ethno-cultural streams are the Aryan, the Mediterranean civilization, the Australoid, and the Mongoloid. In the early Rgvedic times, though, there existed the notion of superiority based on race, the division of society was not as rigid and elaborate as found in the post-Rgvedic treatises. In Buddhist literature, on the whole, the people described are highly commercial, liberal, affluent and happy. It appears that in the north-eastern parts of India which became the seat of the *Upanisads* and Buddhism, trade and commerce flourished extensively and liberal ideas developed among the elites of that region. Perhaps it was these ideas that found expression in the two revolts against Brahmanical orthodoxy. A strong plea was made for equality and fraternity in that early era of civilization both in the monarchical and republican states of that region. The predominant position of Brahmanas on the basis, of birth was challenged. This, in a way, was also a challenge to the Aryan supremacy.

Though the *Upanisads* cite many respectable teachers as belonging to the lower varnas, they do not directly criticize the varna hierarchy. The Buddha openly declared the varna system unreasonable and reprehensible, as all human beings belong to a common human species, whatever be the colour of their skin. He refuted the Vedic myth of the origin of the varna hierarchy and declared it to be false.

The social structure depicted in the Buddhist texts is not very different from the structure that actually existed in recent pre-modern times. We find in the Buddhist texts descriptions of proud kings and warriors, Brahmanas who were well versed in the three Vedas, Vaisyas or rich Sresthis who liberally made gifts to the newly founded religion, and skilful craftsmen.

In the Buddhist texts, the supremacy of the Brahmanas was openly challenged. The Buddha declared that one cannot be considered superior just because or birth of lineage. He declares:

> By mere birth no one becomes a Brahmana,
> By mere birth no one becomes on outcaste.
> By deeds one becomes a Brahmana,
> By deeds one becomes an outcaste.[57]

During a discussion with a young Brahmana, Buddha systematically argued that all varnas, whether white or black, belong to one human race.

Buddhist literature bears witness to the earlier phases of an industrial and commercial society in India when artisans organized into strong guilds, produced beautiful things. There were traders who used to take long sea voyages to sell silks, muslins, brocades, drugs, ivory and ivory work, perfumes, jewellery and gold.[58] Thus came into existence a rich, liberal middle class mainly comprising artisans and Vaisyas. It is remarkable that in the Buddhist texts we find norms and values of the rising puritanical middle class. These values promoted activism and the formation of capital. The advice given to traders in the *Digha Niksya* brings out the commercial spirit of the Buddhist era:

> Making money like the bee,
> Who does not hurt the flower;
> Such a man makes pile,
> An ant hill gradually.
> The man grown wealthy,
> Thus, can help his family,
> And firmly bind his friends to himself.
> He should divide his money into four parts,
> On one part he should live,
> With two expand his trade,
> And the fourth he should save
> Against *a rainy day*.[59]

These values promoted accumulation of capital which was necessary for industry and commerce.

Smritis and the Brahmanical Revival

Buddhism was the greatest challenge to the priestly elites, for it gained great popularity among the masses. Many kings and Sresthis found Buddhism more suitable and they contributed to its spread in India and abroad. The religion of the pre-Aryans, too, reasserted itself among people. The priestly elites were quite conscious of all these forces. It was clear to them that the ancient Vedic religion could not be revived in its earlier form. Many old Aryan practices were rejected and non-Aryan customs found entry into the revived religion. The *Smritis* came into being for restoring the varna hierarchy, the backbone of the traditional Indian social structure. During the first revival of the Sutra period, many ancient Indo-European rituals and customs were consolidated into aphorisms or Sutras. We do not find much about the 'sanskaras' (Indian rites of passage) in the *Rgveda*. The sanskaras were introduced in an effective manner primarily by the *Sutras*. It seems that when racial purity was compromised beyond the point of retrieval, ritual purity was substituted for it. And ritual purity itself became the hallmark of higher varna. It was all the more necessary because during the Buddhist era inter-marriages with the lower varnas had not remained taboo anymore. In the *Jataka* we find many such instances.

Since the *Smaritis* belong to the revivalist era, all the authors of *Smrtis* adopted the names of Vedic seers to get themselves established. *Manu Smriti* is the first attempt of the priestly elites in the direction. Therefore, it was perhaps natural to attribute this *Smriti* to the primogenitor, Manu. Armed with the ancient myth of creation and various sacraments, together with the doctrine of karma, Manu tried to revive the bygone golden age by re-establishing the ancient system of varna hierarchy. In this process, women and Sudras were the greatest losers. The social justice they had found during the Buddhist period was taken away with a vengeance. Manu tried to assign each and every ethnic group, whether Indian or foreign, a specific place in the varna system according to his own criteria. Broadly, Manu followed the guidelines laid down by the *Dharma Sutras*. Yajnavalkya, Brhaspati, Narada and Katyayana followed the institutes of Manu.

Manu Smriti reflects the strong resentment of the Brahmanical elites against the levelling influence of Buddhism. It has been categorically asserted that the dominance of priestly elites and the hierarchy based on varna must be re-established not only through religious prescriptions but by the full might of the king and the state. The use of arms to restore their supremacy is openly commended. Manu calls, "punishment, the son of the creator". The king is enjoined to establish varna hierarchy through the power of punishment. Other twice-born people too are exhorted to resort to arms if they are in any way hindered in carrying out the duties prescribed for their particular varnas.[60] It is obvious from these ardent exhortations and ruthless prescriptions that Manu was conscious that re-establishing the supremacy of Brahmanas was no easy task – its attainment required all the power at their command, physical as well as moral.

In the *Smriti* era, once again, the Brahmanas ensured an unquestionably supreme position for themselves. Manu declares that "the Brahmana from the very birth is an eternal incarnation of the sacred law". Manu calls the Brahmana a great god just like fire, be he ignorant or learned. Just as the fire does not get contaminated, so also a Brahmana, although he may follow even a low occupation should always be honoured and should be considered a great deity.[61]

This is a marked contrast to the theory of equality proclaimed by the Buddha. Birth in a particular varna was considered enough for securing all sorts of privileges. It appears that by the time *Manu Smriti* was composed, norms of ritual purity had to substitute those of racial purity. Manu declared that the Brahmana is the lord of all varnas because of his superiority of birth and observance of rituals and sacraments.[62] He says that a non-Aryan may have Aryan appearance, therefore, one must judge person by his acts and not by his physical appearance.[63]

The Sudras are considered lowest of all varnas because no sacrament is prescribed for them. Following Apastamba and Baudhayana, Manu too justified the low status of Sudras. The sacrament of initation is not permissible for the

Sudras. Initiation is like a second birth because through initiation the boy becomes a full member of the Aryan society. Since the Sudras are not entitled to have initiation, they have only one birth. Manu has emphasized that their sole occupation is to serve the twice-born. Brahmanas belong to the highest varna; serving them would be most meritorious. Manu took no cognizance of the doctrine forwarded by Buddha that the people of all the varnas belong to one human species as all of them are biologically similar. To justify the low position of the Sudras, Manu refers to the ancient divine myth of the self-existent Brahmana, since the mouth is the purest part of the body, the Brahmanas are the lords of this whole creation.[64] The Sudras were produced from the feet of the self-existent; the service of Brahmana alone is declared to be an excellent occupation for the Sudras. In return, the Sudras are entitled to receive the remnants of food, old clothes, the refuge of grain and old household furniture. Since the Sudra has only one birth (he is not a twice-born) no sin would cause loss of varna to him.[65] Brhaspati provides that in case a Sudra cannot serve the twice-born he may pursue the artisan's occupations and handicrafts.[66] In any case a Sudra must not be allowed to possess wealth. Obviously, if a Sudra became rich, he would no longer serve a Brahmana or any other twice-born. Manu explicity declared that the existence of a wealthy Sudra is painful for the Brahmanas.[67] According to commentators, this is so because by accumulating wealth Sudras become proud and do not want to serve. In the Buddhist era people of all the varnas were free to follow the occupations that they liked without attracting any social disapproval.

The fact that Manu assigns a low position to the Vaisyas and Sudras does not mean that he was not aware of their functional utility. In fact, he enjoins the king to ensure that the people of the Vaisya and Sudra varnas continue to perform the work prescribed for them. Because if castes "swerved from their duties, the world would be thrown into confusion."[68]

The varna hierarchy influenced the legal system a great deal. Since Brahmanas are placed highest in the social structure, they enjoyed the highest privileges. The life of a Brahmana is given the highest esteem while that of the Sudras the lowest. The provisions are not based on any faith in equality before law for all.[69] The traditional Indian legal system clearly discriminates between persons belonging to different varnas. It is particularly harsh towards the Sudras. This system of law seems to have its roots in the ancient confrontation between the fair-complexioned Aryan hordes and the dark-skinned snub-nosed earlier settlers whom they vanquished and subjugated. In course of time, the criteria of racial purity had to be substituted by that of ritual purity, but the attitude of disdain persisted. Though this traditional system of law may not be enforced by the state today, its norms even now underlie the patterns of behaviour and attitudes of a large portion of the people of India. The dicta of the *Dharma Sutras* and *Smritis* still form the basis of traditional institutions and values.

Notes

1. *Rgveda*, I. CIII. 3.

2. *Rgveda*, II. 19.6.
3. *Rgveda*, X. 22.8.
4. *Rgveda*, II. 19.6.
5. *Rgveda*, X. 22.8.
6. *Rgveda*, IV. XVI. 13.
7. *Rgveda*, VII. V.3.
8. *Rgveda*, VIII. V.6.
9. Ibid.
10. *Rgveda*, V. XXXIV. 6.
11. *Rgveda*, IV. XLVII. 21.
12. *Rgveda*, II. XII. 4.
13. *Rgveda*, II. XX. 7.
14. *Rgveda*, X. 108.
15. *Rgveda*, II. XXIV. 6.
16. *Rgveda*, VI. 13.3.
17. *Rgveda*, VII. IX. 2.
18. Even in the present-day northern India, among the Agrawals (one of the prominent Vaisyas), we find two sub-castes, Bise and Dasre. The origin of these two words seems to be Vis and Dasa. The people belonging to the Bise sub-cast often use the Brahmanical gotras or family names such as Garga and Varsney and consider themselves superior. Traditionally, these sub-castes were endogamous groups. For a Bisa sub-caste person, taking food from a person of the Dasre sub-caste was forbidden. The famous author Bhartendu Harishchandra was expelled from his caste for staying and taking food with a Dasre Agrawal who was his friend.
19. *Rgveda*, I. CLXXIV. 6.
20. *Rgveda*, VII. 0–11.
21. *Rgveda*, IX. CXII. 3.
22. *Rgveda*, CXII. 3.
23. *Rgveda*, X. LXXI. 5.
24. *Rgveda*, VIII. LXXXIII. 3.4.
25. *Rgveda*, X. CLXXIII. 6.
26. *Rgveda*, IV. LVII. 7.8.
27. *Rgveda*, X.XC. 12.
28. Royal Weiler, 'The Vedic Hymns' (*Sources of Indian Tradition*, ed. Theodore de Bary), Motilal Banarasidas, Delhi, 1963, p. 15.
29. *Taittiriya Samhita*, VII. 4.19.3.
30. *Taittiriya Samhita*, VII. 1.1.6.
31. *Tandyamaha-Brahmana*,, VI. 1.11.
32. *Aitareya Brahmana*, V. 11.
33. *Satapatha Brahmana*, V.XIII. 6.2.10.
34. *Satapatha Brahmana*, V. XIV. 1.2.31.
35. *Tandyamaha Brahmana*, V. 5.14.
36. *Taittiriya Samhita*, 1.7.3.1.
37. *Taittiriya Aranyaka*, II. 1.
38. *Apastambna Dharma Sutra*, II. 2.4.22–24.
39. *Satpatha Brahmana*, IV. 1.4.1–6.
40. *Chandoga Upanisad*,, I. 12.1–5.
41. *Chandogya Upanisad*,, V. 3.7.
42. *Brhadaranyaka Upanisad*, I. 4.41.11.
43. *Chandogya Upanisad*, V. 11.7.

44. *Brhadaranyaka Upanisad*, VI. 4.14–17.
45. *Gautama Dharma Sutra*, XVII. I.
46. *Apastamba Dharma Sutra*, 1.6.18.9–10.
47. *Aspastamba Dharma Surta*, 1.6. *Gautama Dharma Sutra*, XVII.5.
48. *Aspastamba Dharma Surta*, II. 5.11. 5.6; I.4.14.25.
49. *Aspastamba Dharma Surta*, I. 3.3.9.9.
50. *Aspastamba Dharma Surta*, I.I.I. 7–8; *Gautma Sutra*, X. 56; *Vasistha Dharma Sutra*, II.20.
51. *Aspastamba Dharma Surta*, II.10.27.15.
52. *Gautama Dharma Sutra*, XII. 7.
53. *Aspastamba Dharma Surta*, II.10.27.14; *Gautma Dharma Sutra*, XII. 1.
54. *Aspastamba Dharma Surta*, 1.5.16.22; *Baudhayana Dharma Sutra*, II. 2.1.
55. *Aspastamba Dharma Surta*, I.5.16.22; *Baudhayana Dharma Sutra*, II. 2.1.
56. *Aspastamba Dharma Surta*, I.9.25 13
57. *Suta Nipata*, 135.
58. *Digha Niksya*, 3.180.ff.
59. *Jataka*, I. 108.
60. *Manu Smriti*, VII. 14;VIII. 346.
61. *Manu Smriti*, I.98.
62. *Manu Smriti*, X.3.
63. *Manu Smriti*, X.57.
64. *Manu Smriti*, I. 92–94.
65. *Manu Smriti*, X. 123–126.
66. *Manu Smriti*, X. 99–100, *Brhaspati Smrti*, Sanskara Kand I. 530.
67. *Manu Smriti*, X. 129.
68. *Manu Smriti*, VIII. 417–418.
69. For a more detailed analysis of the evolution of the dual system of traditional law, see Indra Dava and Shrirama, *Growth of Legal System in Indian Society*, New Delhi, ICSSR/Allied Publishers, 1980.

28 Caste in Contemporary India[1]

ANDRÉ BÉTEILLE

Meaning and Legitimacy of Caste

Caste has been a subject of continuous interest to ethnographers, historians and sociologists for the last hundred years, and attempts have been made to identify its fundamental structure, either in terms of a set of enduring groups and the enduring relations between them (Mayer, 1960; Berreman, 1963), or in terms of some principle of opposition, for instance, between purity and pollution (Dumont, 1966; Marriott, 1990). 1 have myself written on the subject from time to time (Béteille, 1969a, 1991), opposing some views and supporting others, but I will not enter into an extended discussion here of the social morphology of caste or the cultural oppositions on which it is based.

My primary concern will be with questions of meaning and legitimacy. What does it mean in India today for a person to belong to a particular caste or subcaste? What demands can it make on him or her and in what contexts, and to what extent is he or she prepared to meet those demands? We know very well that individuals do not always meet the demands made on them, that they are subjected to contradictory pulls and pressures, and that they sometimes subordinate social obligation to personal interest. We also know that there are sanctions of various kinds against the violation of prescribed or generally accepted codes of conduct What are the sanctions available to the caste or subcaste today to ensure the conformity of the individual with the codes prescribed or acknowledged by it?

It is quite obvious that being a member of a caste or subcaste does not have the same meaning today for all individuals everywhere, if it ever did in the past, nor do caste sanctions operate with the same force in all sections of Indian society. I shall not attempt to provide a key to the understanding of caste as a whole or as a 'total social system' in either the past or the present, being mindful of the fact that such attempts have usually come to grief. I shall confine myself largely to urban Indians in what may be described as modem occupations, leaving aside, except for occasional comments, the large majority of Indians who inhabit the rural areas and derive their livelihood from agriculture and allied occupations. This does not mean that my argument does not have some implications for the latter, but those implications are not as yet fully clear.

I do not wish to circumscribe too narrowly the class or section of society on which I seek to focus attention. It may be referred to loosely as the 'urban middle class' or even the 'urban middle classes'. More recently, the terms 'intelligentsia', 'professionals' and 'service class' have been employed to refer to roughly the same category of persons (Rudra, 1989; Bardhan, 1984; Béteille, 1989). These terms are useful, not because they are accurate, but because they draw attention to the growing importance of this class or stratum in contemporary India. Here numbers are important but not necessarily decisive. If we adopt a narrow definition and take into account only civil servants, managers and higher professionals, we will still be dealing with a population that runs into hundreds of thousands. If we extend the conception to include school teachers, clerks and other white-collar workers, as some are inclined to do, we will have a much larger category, numbering 50–75 million persons or more. Of course, these distinctions have to be made much more carefully if we are to achieve precision, but I am not now in a position to do so.

There is a reason why it is necessary to have some sense of the numbers involved even when it is not possible to give precise numbers. It is sometimes said that the underlying structure of caste remains what it was, and that if there are changes in caste practice, they are superficial and confined to a handful of urban, or educated, or westernized individuals who are in any case not truly representative of Indian society and culture. I wish to emphasize that the class or stratum that I am talking about, whether conceived broadly or narrowly, does not comprise a mere handful of individuals, and that socially, if not demographically, it is a very important part of contemporary India.

Again, I am anxious to avoid the impression of making too large a claim for my argument. What needs to be stressed as much as the social significance of the class or section in question is its great social diversity in terms of language, region and religion – and, what is as important, in terms of wealth, occupation, and education. Limiting ourselves only to the professionals, there is all the difference in the world between a senior member of the Calcutta or Bombay bar and a small-town advocate, or between the research scientist in the Indian Institute of Science and the science teacher in a mofussil college. The stratum as a whole is so large and so diverse that any statement made about it could be either wholly true or wholly false for at least some of its individual members. Caste cannot possibly have the same meaning or the same legitimacy for all the individual members of such a large and diverse population, but that in a sense is the point I wish to make against those who would represent it as a kind of uniform medium that constrains all individuals in the same way.

Growing Ambivalence of Upper Strata

In viewing the section or stratum of society referred to above, whether narrowly or broadly conceived, we observe a characteristic ambivalence in the orientation to caste as it exists today. It is very marked among academics – sociologists, political scientists, historians, economists, and so on – but may be noted also among judges, lawyers, journalists and others, and is probably very widespread and extends beyond the section of society with which I am particularly concerned. The ambivalence is easy to recognize and not difficult to describe, but it has not received the scholarly attention it deserves. It can lead the same individual to deny any significance to caste at one time and to give it exaggerated importance at another.

European and American visitors to India often remark that when they ask educated Indians about caste, they are told that it does not exist anymore. It would be a mistake to think that this is always an act of conscious deception. There is certainly an element of self-deception here, and we must ask why this form of self-deception is so commonly encountered. Of course, educated Indians know that caste exists, but they are unclear and troubled about what it means for them as members of a society that is a part of the modem world. No one can say that it is easy to give a clear and consistent account of the meaning and significance of caste in India today.

In a presidential address of 1957, entitled 'Caste in Modern India', M.N. Srinivas (1962: 15–41) drew attention to the continuing if not increasing importance of caste in public life. *The Times of India* of 21 January 1957, commenting editorially, said that the role of caste had been greatly exaggerated in the address. It was pointed out that caste barriers were falling, both in ordinary interchanges among persons and in ceremonial life. However, the same newspaper reported shortly afterwards that caste loyalties were being extensively used for mobilizing political support in the second general election that followed in a few weeks.

Facts on the ground aside, Srinivas' view of caste was not in tune with the general intellectual climate in India in the wake of independence. I may say on the basis of personal experience in both Calcutta and Delhi, that the intelligentsia in general then had its mind on other things than caste. The preoccupation of the social anthropologist with the subject was on the whole viewed with disfavour by all those who believed that India was on the move, and that the eye should be to the future and not upon the past.

At the time of independence, most reflective Indians felt that they had come to a watershed on the other side of which were many new possibilities which it was up to them to seize and turn to the country's advantage. They had a new Constitution, a new Five-Year Plan, and they felt that, given the will-power, they could do many things to bring about justice, equality, growth and well-being for the people of India. Certain things needed to be put out of the way in order to achieve these objectives: poverty, hunger, malnutrition, illiteracy ignorance and superstition. The caste system too was counted among the obstacles in the way of progress. Certainly, it would be fair to say that those who fashioned the Constitution and the plans did not wish to give a new lease of life to caste.

Caste proved to be much more obdurate than it was judged to be. Perhaps, the will-power was not adequate to the task of its removal or containment. But we can also say now, with the advantage of hindsight, that there was a basic misperception of its strength among Indian intellectuals. It is important for us today to examine, honestly and with the maximum possible detachment, the reasons behind this misperception.

We have to go back to the period immediately preceding independence in order to form an idea of the different perceptions of caste and the changes in those perceptions. Caste had become a subject of debate and discussion before independence, and more than one view was formed regarding its pervasiveness and strength. At the risk of some oversimplification, I will pick out two among them that were in many ways the opposites of each other. There was the view of the colonial government and its many able administrators that caste was not only the pre-eminent institution of India, but that it permeated every area of life, and the idea that caste could be dispensed with was wishful thinking. As against this was what I may call the nationalist view, to which Indian intellectuals by and large then subscribed, that the importance of caste had been greatly exaggerated by the colonial administration, that it was clearly on its way out, and that its decline would be greatly hastened once India became independent. Here, I must point out that a change in the orientation to caste had come about in the course of the nationalist movement itself. Indian intellectuals did not condemn caste as widely a hundred years before independence as they were ready to do when independence came.

The Indian perception of caste at the time of independence had been shaped, at least to some extent, by the dialectic between the colonial and the nationalist views regarding its place in the present and future society of India. For the Indian intellectual, it had become a matter of pride to confute the colonial view that, however eloquently they might talk about democracy and development, Indians were and would remain under the grip of caste with its exclusiveness, its hierarchy, and its ineluctable fragmentation of civil society.

But, the misperception of caste among Indian intellectuals was not based solely on national pride; it had another more tangible, if not more credible, basis. Indians could use the evidence the colonial administrators themselves provided to argue, with some plausibility, that caste was definitely and irreversibly in decline. The predominant western view was that caste was basically a matter of religion and ritual, and educated Indians could see that that side of caste was withering before their eyes.

Religious Definition of Caste

The centrality of caste in Indian society and the religious definition of it became a part of the conventional wisdom of comparative sociology, so that social stratificationor, – if one prefers, social hierarchyw – as perceived as being essentially a religious phenomenon, emanating somehow from the very nature of Hinduism. This became the predominant view of Indian society among those who were specialists on India and also among those who were not. Nirad C. Chaudhuri (1979: 7) has written bitingly about the 'Western legend of Hindu spirituality', and argued that many educated Indians found it convenient to acquiesce in the legend and even to promote it. It gave them a kind of comfort in the face of India's manifest economic and political inferiority to the West to feel that they were, spiritually superior. Chaudhuri's own erudite work on Hinduism pays very little attention to caste.

Emile Senart, who published an influential book on caste at the end of the nineteenth century, wrote, "Hindu society is regulated by religious custom, and the law books are essentially collections of religious precepts" (1930: 91). Henry Maine (1950: 14–17), writing in the second half of the nineteenth century, had found it difficult to detach Hindu law from Hindu religion, and the belief became widely established that Hindu society was unchangeable because it was rooted in immutable religious observance.

Max Weber, perhaps the most outstanding comparative sociologist of all time, clearly defined the social identity of the Hindu in terms of caste, and of caste in terms of ritual. "Caste, that is, the ritual rights and duties it gives and imposes, and the position of the Brahmans, is the fundamental institution of Hinduism. Before everything else, without caste there is no Hindu" (Weber, 1958: 29). Even those who would broadly accept this view might point to significant exceptions: Hinduism always had a place for the renouncer, and the *sannyasi* might still be considered a Hindu, although without caste or clan.

Like Weber, C. Bouglé too was an outsider to Indian studies for he had not done fieldwork in India or learnt any of its classical or modern languages. Yet his work on caste has had great influence among scholars. Pointing to the remarkable historical continuity of the system, he wrote: "The caste system allows all regimes to pass over its head; it alone remains" (Bouglé, 1971: 65). He drew attention repeatedly to the inseparability of caste and Hinduism. "All observers are agreed on this: caste is basically a religious institution" (ibid.). And again, "Hinduism is defined more by the observance of caste rules than by fidelity to some precise dogma" (ibid.: 66). Louis Dumont (1966) has carried Bouglé's perspective further forward and greatly enriched it by his mastery of Indian ethnography as well as his knowledge of Indian languages, both classical and modern.

The assumption about Hinduism in much of the early sociological writing is that in it religion and social structure are inseparable so that Hinduism stands not only for a particular religion but also for a particular social structure, that structure being caste. Western writers on religion, including sociologists, rarely make such an assumption about Christianity, for they see quite clearly that Christianity as a system of beliefs and practices has a certain autonomy in the sense that it can be transferred, more or less easily, from one social or historical context to another. On the other hand, we are shown a somewhat peculiar feature of Hinduism that makes it appear quite different from Christianity, Islam, or Buddhism. This poses an intriguing problem for the sociologist of religion. To be sure, there is everywhere some relationship between religion and social morphology, but why should the two be inseparable in only one particular case? This assumption of inseparability leads directly to the question whether Hinduism is at all a religion in the true sense of the term.

The 'Western legend of Hindu spirituality' was more a creation of nineteenth century Orientalists and Indologists than of twentieth century ethnographers and sociologists. By the time ethnographic studies came into their own in the early decades of the twentieth century, the legend of Hindu spirituality had largely evaporated. It was displaced by a view in which ritual observances of every conceivable kind were given pride of place. The view of Hinduism that dominates the ethnography of the late nineteenth and early twentieth centuries may be best summed up in the words of Herbert Risley (1969: 233) as "magic tempered with metaphysics". Today's anthropologists have learnt to become more circumspect than the civil servants and missionaries who were their predecessors, but if we look closely into their accounts of Hinduism, we will encounter Risley's ghost at many places.

The evidence on which anthropological accounts of caste and Hinduism were based was impressive. The British had built an administrative system in India which was remarkable in its own way. One of its permanent achievements was the decennial census, now more than a hundred years old, and the massive apparatus associated with the ethnographic mapping of the country. From the end of the nineteenth century onwards, a voluminous body of literature began to be built up which described extensively and in detail the castes and tribes in the different parts of the country (Risley, 1892; Thurston, 1909; Enthoven, 1920–2). The official accounts of the civil servants were supplemented by accounts by missionaries. This whole body of literature is an invaluable record of the customs, usages and practices of the people of India.

The ICS ethnographers, if the phrase be permitted, included men of considerable scholarship such as Ibbetson (1916), Risley (1969), Gait (1913), Blunt (1931), O'Malley (1932), Hutton (1946), and many others. They were in India not merely to collect taxes and maintain law and order, but also to observe, describe and interpret, with patience and care, and not always without sympathy, the new social world they had come to inhabit. In addition to the detailed descriptions of particular castes and tribes, they provided a number of general accounts of caste as the framework of Indian society.

These detailed and voluminous accounts repeatedly bring caste to our attention, and do so in their own distinctive way. There is a continued emphasis on the religious basis of caste, so that the system appears to be pervaded by a general aura of ritual and ceremony. Even when such subjects as endogamy, exogamy, division of labour, occupational specialization, craft practices and so on are being discussed, we are never far away from the world of religion, magic, and superstition.

Description and analysis are saturated with accounts of purity and pollution, and the manifold taboos or interdictions associated with them. These struck the attention of administrators, missionaries and others in the nineteenth century, and every successive generation of ICS ethnographers tried to dig a little deeper in order to get to their roots. Most of them gave a central place to the rules relating to food and drink in their accounts of caste. These rules were so elaborate and so complex that one could fill volumes merely by listing them. Another favourite topic was the maintenance of distance and the avoidance of physical contact between members of different castes and subcastes.

Since many of the ICS ethnographers had antiquarian interests, their accounts of caste, apart from the general stress on ritual, purity, pollution, taboos, interdictions and so on, carried a certain archaic flavour. Now, educated Indians in the 1930s and 1940s naturally felt that if this was the essence of caste – kacca food and pakka food, 36 paces between Tiyan and Nambutiri, 12 paces between Tiyan and Nair, and so on – then, going by their own experience and observation, caste was clearly in retreat. These manifold customs which had been practised in the past, though perhaps not exactly as described in the ethnography, were rapidly losing their meaning and significance among educated Indians, and those who continued to practise them, at school or at work, were sometimes ridiculed by those who did not. Dwelling mainly on the ritual side of caste, it did not appear too implausible to maintain that it was irretrievably in decline.

Thus, the misperception of caste common among the Indian intelligentsia at the time of independence was due partly to the misplaced emphasis on ritual in accounts of it by civil servants and others in the preceding decades. Was there a misperception among the latter as well, and how can we account for it? Whatever place religion may have had in it in the past, the future of caste lay not with religion but with politics. I think that on the whole – for different reasons, and with notable exceptions – both sides failed to read the signs of the future. The ICS ethnographers like Hutton failed to read them because, before independence, they were themselves too closely involved in preparing the very ground on which caste was taking its place in politics. And if, immediately after independence, the Indian intelligentsia failed by and large to dwell on the future role of caste in politics, wishful thinking had something to do with it. They knew that it was there, but hoped that it could be made to wither away – through rapid economic development, through the spread of education, and through science and technology.

Erosion of Legitimacy

The concentration in the anthropological (as against the Indological) literature on Hinduism, as I have shown, has been on ritual, purity pollution, taboos, interdictions, and so on – what pertains largely to magic rather than religion in the proper sense of the term. There is also another side of religion, concerned with morality, that has received rather less attention. It is characteristic of educated Indians today that they find it difficult to acknowledge, not only before outsiders but also among themselves, that caste might have had something to do with morality. N.K. Bose (1967, 1975) was one of the few anthropologists who, despite his deep antipathy to caste, tried to understand and interpret its moral and ethical basis in the traditional social order. But he also pointed out that basis was being irrevocably undermined.

Indians have not always been shy of writing about the moral basis of caste. It was expounded in the nineteenth century by such men as Bankimchandra (1961); and as late as in the 1930s, Gandhi (1962) wrote in support of the morality of caste, at least in the form of *vama*. Gandhi favoured *varnadharma* to the extent that it stressed the community rather than the individual, cooperation as against conflict, and duties rather than rights. His conception of *varnadharma* was somewhat remote from reality as it did not take into account considerations of superior and inferior rank.

The student of comparative sociology, on the other hand, views caste society as above all a hierarchical society, in fact the prototype of all such societies. There social distinctions of certain kinds not only exist, but are widely acknowledged as right, proper and desirable. Law, religion and morality all serve to strengthen and reinforce the subordination of the individual to the group and the ranking of groups as superior and inferior (Lingat, 1973). In such a society, the individual has certain obligations to the group of which he is a member by birth, and the group as a whole to other groups according to their respective ranks.

It is true that religious reformers from Buddha to Chaitanya and after have questioned the significance of these distinctions, and have asked what meaning they have for man's dignity and worth, and for his inner life (Bose, 1975: 116–36). There were continuous fluctuations in the force and significance of caste and it was not the inflexible, invariant and unchanging system it has often been made out to be. Nevertheless and despite these fluctuations, it retained for many centuries a very distinctive character. There is no other way to account for the correspondence between representations of caste in the ethnographic record of the late nineteenth and early twentieth centuries, and in the record of classical Indology (Bose, 1975; Dumont, 1966).

The point to stress here is that when we first encounter caste in the writings of nineteenth century observers and scholars, we encounter it as a more or less complete system. We encounter not only the existential order of caste, as something that might be observed on the ground from the outside, but also its normative order, as something regarded by its individual members as both meaningful and morally binding. This is not to say that there was perfect consensus regarding the values of caste, but that caste distinctions were considered significant and legitimate by most members of society, and particularly by those belonging to the upper castes whose descendants in contemporary India are precisely the ones who are most ambivalent and troubled about its meaning and legitimacy today.

Since the Indian intelligentsia is today most troubled about the hierarchical distinctions of caste, it needs to be emphasized that in the past and up to the middle of the nineteenth century, those distinctions were, at least among the Hindus, acknowledged, upheld and reinforced by law, religion and morality. Things began to change thereafter, as a result of the British presence as well as the Indian response to it. It would be seriously to misrepresent the dialectics of that change if we were to attribute it solely to the colonial intervention and ignore the nationalist response to it (Ganguli, 1975). As I have noted elsewhere, Indians probably learnt more about equality from the colonial practice of inequality than from the British theory of equality (Béteille, 1979).

Caste undoubtedly exists in contemporary India, and I shall speak in a while of its continuing influence in marriage and its marked, if not increasing, presence in politics. It does not, however, exist as a complete system anymore, but – if the phrase be permitted – as a truncated system. The first and most decisive casualty has been the legal basis of caste (Sivaramayya, 1984). No two texts can be more divergent in their orientation to cast than the *Manusmriti,* which we may take as the charter of traditional Hindu law, and the Constitution of India, which may be regarded as the charter of contemporary Indian law. As we have seen, comparative sociologists from Weber to Dumont have dwelt on the intimate connection between caste and Hinduism, regarding it as the social expression of the Hindu religion. But many of the modern proponents of Hinduism, such as Vivekananda, have attacked caste instead of defending it. There are very few contemporary proponents of Hinduism who would be prepared to argue that caste has to be saved in order to strengthen the Hindu religion.

The question of caste morality is more difficult to dispose of briefly, for the evidence is often unclear and sometimes contradictory. One of its principal components was the sense of obligation that the individual carried towards the caste into which he was born, to abide by its customs, to adhere to its style of life, and to pursue the occupation allotted to it. Perhaps that sense of obligation, though not easily articulated, is still quite strong among cultivators, artisans and others in the rural areas. But it has weakened considerably in the urban areas and among those sections of contemporary Indian society to which I said I would largely confine this discussion. The compulsions of occupation operate rather differently in the different sectors of the Indian economy. Among engineers, doctors, scientists, civil servants and managers, the obligation to one's occupation exists independently of the obligation to one's caste and to some extent displaces it. The school teacher, the clerk, or the electrician no longer feels very strongly that he has a duty to encourage his offspring to persevere in his own occupation or the occupation of his forefathers as the village blacksmith, carpenter, or potter might have felt in the past.

Nothing could be more mistaken than to believe that caste was something that for two thousand years Indians merely lived by, without giving thought to its meaning or its rightness, that it existed merely as practice and not as theory. We must not lose sight of the intellectual tradition of India in which theoretical reflection and dialectical skill were used for describing, explaining, and justifying the distinctions of caste by generations of intellectuals. Dumont (1966: 56) was right in drawing attention to the systematic thinking on which caste observances were based, but he was plainly wrong in suggesting that "Hindus of today and of past times" think about caste in the same systematic way. Until the nineteenth century, Hindu intellectuals could argue with force and conviction about the significance and value of caste. Their counterparts of today, who are still mainly of upper caste, have lost the capacity not only to explain and justify caste, but even to describe it coherently.

Endogamy and Reproduction of Identity

It is often said that no matter how loudly Hindus might proclaim their indifference or even hostility to caste, when it comes to marriage, all of them – educated and uneducated, urban and rural, professional and peasant – turn to caste. Many have in fact maintained that the regulation of marriage and the social exclusiveness associated with it – something akin to a sense of race – are what make caste what it is. Risley stressed this aspect of caste far more than religion: "Race dominates religion; sect is weaker than caste" (1969: 80). Obviously, we cannot associate caste with race as a biological fact, as Risley was inclined to do, but only with a sense of race more or less widely felt in society.

It will be of little avail to argue about the decline in the legal, religious and moral basis of caste if it turns out that on such an important issue as marriage, nothing has changed at all. One hears both kinds of arguments among the intelligentsia today: some say that intercaste marriages are now quite common while others maintain that they are rare and exceptional. Sometimes one hears a person argue vehemently that intercaste marriages are impossible in Indian society, only to learn that he himself has married outside his caste. More common perhaps is the man who declares himself passionately against caste in every form, but nonetheless opposes strenuously the marriage of his children outside his caste.

Some changes are in fact taking place in marriage rules and practices among educated Indians in the higher occupational strata, but we are hindered in our assessment of them by the paucity of systematic data. People frequently take recourse to casual empiricism, selecting one or another set of examples to argue for and against the same proposition. No clear conclusion can be reached in the absence of statistical data that tell us something about rates and frequencies. But rates and frequencies are not enough; for where it concerns marriage, we have to attend not only to practices but also to rules and to enquire whether these rules continue to carry the same sanctions and the same meanings as before.

In an interview with the editor of the *Times of India*, M.N. Srinivas noted the changing role of caste in marriage. "Equally significant as regards pan-Hinduism, Professor Srinivas says, is the diminishing importance of caste in marriage. Intercaste, interregional and even interreligious marriages are on the rise" (Padgaonkar, 1993). What is remarkable about the observation is not that Srinivas is India's leading sociologist, but that he has repeatedly cautioned the Indian intelligentsia against underrating the strength and resilience of caste.

Similar observations were made thirty years earlier by C.T. Kannan in the only satisfactory full-length study of intercaste marriage:

> Just twenty-five years ago the instances of intercaste marriages were very few; and those individuals who dared to marry outside the caste had to undergo truly great hardships. Today, the situation is altogether different. Not only has the prevalence of intercaste marriage become considerable, but even the difficulties the intercaste marriage couples have to face have become comparatively quite mild. (Kannan, 1963: vii)

Kannan limited himself to 200 couples formed by intercaste unions (and 50 others formed by intercommunity unions), and therefore his study cannot tell us very much about rates and frequencies that are statistically significant. At the same time, it does draw attention to significant social processes that had been set in motion at least a decade or two before his study was published.

In discussing these questions we must remember that not all intercaste marriages are of the same kind. A marriage across two sub-subcastes of Smarta Brahmans would be an intercaste marriage in some sense, but it would be very different from a marriage between any Brahman and an Adi-Dravida. In an earlier paper (Béteille, 1966), I had suggested that there are ambiguities in the very idea of intercaste marriage. There I had drawn attention to the slow and gradual way in which even for arranged marriages, the horizons of endogamy were being extended from sub-subcaste to subcaste, and then to caste among the Tamil Brahmans. I am not suggesting that there never was any ambiguity in the past, but the ambiguity over what constitutes the unit of endogamy has almost certainly become more pervasive now, particularly among the upper castes.

It is possible that a more permissive attitude towards caste in the selection of spouses is being accompanied by a greater attention to other restrictions such as those relating to education, occupation and income. Many different criteria are taken into account in the selection of a spouse, and in the case of someone who is highly desirable on a number of important counts, one may overlook the traditional restrictions of caste if the person belongs to a different subcaste of the same caste or even to a different but cognate caste. It is only rarely that caste considerations are ignored altogether.

One can get a good sense of the diversity of the categories at play by looking at the matrimonial advertisements in the Sunday papers. These advertisements are classified, but not according to any single or consistent plan. The categories of caste are very prominent, but those of religion, such as Sunni, Sikh and Muslim, and of language, such as Sindhi, Bengali and Tamil, are also found. Cheek by jowl with these are categories belonging to other sets, such as 'doctors', 'engineers', 'MBA/CA', 'postgraduate', and 'cosmopolitan'. One should not be misled, however, because caste is frequently indicated, directly or indirectly, even under 'cosmopolitan'. But then again someone may indicate his own caste, in case the other party finds it relevant, even if he writes, "Caste, dowry no bar", to show that he does not regard it as relevant for himself.

To be sure, even in the past, people took many factors into account in addition to caste, but those factors were taken into account after keeping caste constant. One always looked for an appropriate family in seeking a match, but one took it for granted that such a family would be of one's own caste. An advertisement in the *Sunday Times* of 19 December 1993 reads: "32/167, C.K.P. well-settled businessman from educated family seeks alliance from good-looking, cultured girls with good family background. Caste no bar." (The man was 32 years old, 167 cm in height and of the Chandraseniya Kayastha Prabhu subcaste.) I have been much struck by the insistence on 'good family', 'cultured family' or 'status family' even in advertisements that do not give any specification as to caste.

I would like to return very briefly to the traditional rules of marriage through which the identities of caste, subcaste and sub-subcaste were maintained and reproduced. As is well known, there was not one single rule, there were several rules. Of these, two are of particular significance, the rule; of endogamy and the rule of hypergamy. The rule of hypergamy not only distinguishes between castes (or subcastes) but also ranks them, and on that ground it has sometimes been regarded as even more distinctive of caste than the rule of endogamy (Dumont, 1966: 152–61). It should be pointed out that the rule of hypergamy (or *anuloma*) was not universally or even extensively observed in all places in all times (Karve, 1968: 16), aithough it was clearly acknowledged by the Shastras (scriptures) whereas its opposite or *pratiloma* was universally condemned.

Where intercaste marriages do take place among the intelligentsia, ignoring for the moment the question of frequency, such marriages are in general as likely to be of the *anuloma* (or sanctioned) as of the *pratiloma* (or unsanctioned) type. More than that, in some areas where hypergamy was widely prevalent, the rule appears to have lapsed altogether. I can say from personal knowledge that many Bengali Brahmans, of both the Rarhi and the Barendra castes, well-known until the middle of the nineteenth century for the observance of hypergamy (associated with the notorious system known as Kulinism), have now little or no knowledge of the traditional rule and its implications. The attack on Kulinism in nineteenth century Bengal and its gradual disappearance throw an interesting light on the relationship between caste, hierarchy and marriage rules.

It seems clear to me that Kannan's assessment of the weakening of collective sanctions against intercaste unions in urban India was on the whole the right one. His data show that the collective pressure of the caste or the subcaste against intercaste unions among the urban middle classes is neither very strong nor very effective. In risking a wrong alliance, the primary focus of anxiety is the family or perhaps the 'kindred of cooperation' (Mayer, 1960), itself more restricted in the city than in the village, whereas caste figures only dimly in the background. There are of course exceptions, and these must be noted. Newspapers sometimes report instances of brutal violence in small towns or villages against certain unions, typically where the woman is of a high caste and the man a Harijan or a Muslim. These acts are reminiscent of the lynchings that took place in the American South until forty or fifty years ago when a black male sought union with a white female. Otherwise, intercaste marriages in metropolitan cities are not accompanied by any significant public violence, although there is no lack of urban violence in contemporary India.

Political Uses of Caste

I mentioned earlier that in the 1950s, most Indian intellectuals believed that caste was on the way out, while only a few said that it was there to stay. Even those who said that it was gaining a new lease of life could point to evidence from only a single domain, that of politics, to support their argument. No one could seriously maintain that, to use the language of J.H. Hutton (1946), the strictures and sanctions of caste were becoming stronger; or that the many ritual injunctions and interdictions relating to food and physical contact were gaining in strength; or that the association between caste and occupation was growing closer; or even that the rules of endogamy were being more strictly defined and observed. In all these domains, caste was growing weaker, very slowly, almost imperceptibly in some cases, more clearly and noticeably in others.

It is only when we turn to politics that we get a very different picture. When Srinivas argued in his 1957 address that caste was getting a new lease of life, all of the evidence that he provided, or almost all of it, came from the domain of politics. But only a few years earlier, Radcliffe-Brown (1952: x), reflecting the views till then common among anthropologists, had observed as follows in his foreword to Srinivas' book on the Coorgs: "A caste is in its essence a religious group, membership of which entails certain ritual observances. The rules of caste behaviour are rules of religion." Clearly, some changes were under way which had not come to the attention of Radcliffe-Brown, although he had registered his interest in political anthropology as early as in 1940.

Caste did not enter politics all at once with independence, but it made its presence strongly felt in the first general election, and increasingly with each successive election. Although the subject of caste and politics was initially of interest to only a handful of social anthropologists, it soon attracted the attention of political scientists and others (Kothari, 1970; Frankel and Rao, 1989–90), and there is now a large literature on it. Even after the subject had been taken up by scholars in various disciplines in the 1960s and 1970s, some differences remained between the social scientists who saw and stressed the importance of caste in politics, and what are called 'left intellectuals' who were inclined to treat it lightly. Today, many more scholars, both Marxists and non-Marxists, acknowledge the importance of caste in politics, although they draw different policy conclusions from it (Centre for Social Studies, 1985; Béteille, 1992).

It will not be possible for me in the brief space remaining to review or even summarize the principal findings of the very large literature that we now have on caste and politics. I will only draw attention to certain processes that are known to be quite widespread, and indicate very briefly how those processes are viewed, explained and justified by some of the principal actors who participate in and give shape to them.

In an essay written more than 30 years ago (Béteille, 1969a: 152–69), I had, after making a distinction between problems of distribution and problems of process, tried to identify the basic processes through which caste becomes involved in politics. The loyalties of caste are used for the mobilization of political support in a number of ways: by a generalized appeal to caste sentiment, by activating networks of kinship and marriage, and by the organized activities of caste associations. Studies conducted in the last 30 years have shown the extensive use of caste for the mobilization of political support during elections and in between elections, although there are significant regional variations.

As Srinivas showed, caste came to be used in the electoral process from the first general election, and indeed it had entered the political arena even before. But, the question is not simply of the extent of the use of caste in electoral politics, but also of its meaning and legitimacy for the different sections of Indian society. Clearly, those who yielded to the appeal of caste loyalty and voted for candidates of their own caste, could not have all thought that it was a bad thing to vote according to caste. By and large, the intelligentsia showed an ambivalent attitude. They were troubled by 'casteism' in politics even though they might support someone from their own caste. They were inclined to treat this kind of caste preference more as an aspect of realpolitik than of political morality.

In the 1950s and 1960s, the leaders of all political parties condemned in public the use of caste in politics. Politicians freely acknowledged that caste was being extensively used in the politics of post-independence India, but they said that it was being used by other parties, not their own. When it was shown that their party too was using caste, their reply was that they did not start the process but were being forced to accommodate caste in order to survive, for in politics, or at least in Indian politics, one could not afford to be too idealistic if one wished to remain in business. In other words, they sought to defend the use of caste (unlike, for instance, the use of class) on tactical rather than ethical grounds.

A change in the orientation of political leaders, and with them of other members of the intelligentsia, appears to have started in the 1970s when the politics of backwardness took a new turn with the installation of the first non-Congress government in New Delhi in 1977. It began to be argued that caste needed to be given a place in public life not so much on grounds of realpolitik as on grounds of social justice. The lower castes had been stigmatized and exploited in the past, and they should be given special protection through extensive quotas in every domain of public life. The argument was not new; it had been an important component of colonial policy in the decades preceding independence (Irschick, 1969; Béteille, 1992). What was new was its increasing appeal to social justice and its increasing vehemence.

Again, I cannot enter into a discussion of the principal features of the politics of backwardness on which I and others have written extensively, but would like to point out that it has acquired a markedly ideological tone since 1990. The ideological tone was given a new articulation when the left parties decided to join hands with V.P. Singh's Janata Dal in pressing for the extension of caste quotas in the cause of social justice. This made it in effect impossible for any party openly to oppose caste quotas, so that caste has, at least for the time being, strengthened its grip over politics. But it still is an unsteady grip for neither the supporters nor the opponents of caste quotas say that caste itself should be revitalized. In fact, the strongest supporters of caste quotas are, paradoxically, also the strongest opponents of caste as a hierarchical system.

Ethnicity and the Metaphor of Caste

Those who are given to moralizing sometimes observe that democracy has been debased in India by the pernicious influence of caste. The issue for the moment is not how caste has altered politics, but how politics is altering caste. Leach (1960: 6–7) had already asked more than fifty years ago whether castes cease to be castes when they compete with each other for political power. My view then (Béteille, 1969b) was that there were obvious and significant continuities between the castes of the present and those of the past; something so complex and deeply entrenched as caste does not cease to be itself as soon as one or even a few of its basic characteristics change. I would now like to examine some of the shifts that are taking place in the ways in which caste identities are defined.

As is well known, conventionally, caste has had at least two distinct (though related) meanings, *varna* and *jati*. While it is true that most Indians recognize both meanings of caste, they now think of it more as *jati* than as *varna*; that would be consistent with the shift in emphasis from religion to politics in matters relating to caste. In an influential paper, Srinivas (1962: 63–69) had drawn attention to the distinction, and argued that caste has been frequently misrepresented as *varna*. Srinivas' own argument was perhaps one-sided, but it was timely, for it came at a moment when educated Indians were probably beginning to think of caste less as *varna* than as *jati*. They probably thought of it as *varna* much more commonly until after independence when the role of caste became increasingly prominent in politics. A few years before the publication of Srinivas' paper, the historian Niharranjan Ray (1945) wrote a book on caste in Bengali which he entitled *Bangali hindur barnabhed,*[2] meaning distinctions of *varna* among Bengali Hindus. He was following a well-established usage for the representation of caste – a usage which was, however, changing.

There are other ambiguities besides those that might arise from the confusion of *varna* and *jati*, for there are collective identities that are not identities of caste in the strict anthropological sense, but are nevertheless represented as such. Though most frequently paired with *varna* in the ethnographic (and Indological) literature, the term *jati* (or the more colloquial *jat)* has other associations as well. It is commonly used to cover a series of identities of increasing degrees of inclusiveness from sub-subcaste through caste to religion and language.

Those who use data from large-scale censuses and surveys have often to deal with lists of castes (or *jatis*) that are very heterogeneous indeed. While conducting a survey in 1958 for the Indian Statistical Institute in Giridih town and its surrounding villages in Bihar, I encountered in the entries under 'caste', in addition to the names of castes in the restricted sense, such terms as 'Marwari', 'Oriya', 'Jain' and 'Muslim'. Later, in 1963 and 1964, in the villages in Burdwan district in West Bengal, I was told that the inhabitants included Brahmans, Baidyas, Sadgopes, Aghuris, Bagdis, Santals and Muslims.

We have moved some distance away from caste as *varna* when we are dealing on the same plane with such disparate groups and categories as Baidyas, Sadgopes, Telis, Bagdis, Santals, Oriyas and Muslims. The disparate assemblage of clans, sects, castes, tribes, religious communities, and linguistic groups that can all, according to context and situation, pass as *jatis* fits at best awkwardly into the clear and symmetrical design of the four *varnas*. It would be unwise to declare that these modes of representation are all new, without any roots in past social experience and practice. At the same time, new perceptions of collective identities are forced upon people by the political process which uses the distinctions of language, religion and caste in the same way for the mobilization of political support.

The operation of caste along with language and religion in the political arena has led some to speak in a rather inclusive sense of 'ethnic groups', 'ethnic identities' and 'ethnic loyalties'. This is to signal a shift in the meaning of caste brought about by its increasing role in a new field of activity. Srinivas has recently been quoted as saying, "In the future, too, caste will remain a predominant feature of Indian life. But it will be conceived more in terms of ethnicity" (Padgaonkar, 1993).

The movement from caste as *varna* to caste as ethnic group has been seen by some as the 'substantialisation of caste' (Dumont, 1966: 280; Deliége, 1993: 107–10). This may be somewhat misleading insofar as the notion of substance conveys a sense of homogeneity, whereas in fact each caste is becoming progressively differentiated in terms of occupation, education and income. Clearly, some shifts are taking place in the meanings that people assign to caste. When journalists and political commentators refer to castes as ethnic groups, they have in mind not so much hierarchical distinctions of status as differences in bargaining power and in life chances in general.

Few will deny that caste has become increasingly salient in the political arena, or that in that arena hierarchical distinctions of status count for less than differences in life chances. Does that mean that distinctions of status are losing their meaning and significance for Indians? it would be rash indeed to answer that question categorically in the affirmative. For one thing, we cannot say for certain what meaning and significance the innumerable ritual restrictions of the past had for distinctions of status among persons; the ethnographers have tried mainly to explain either the origins of those restrictions or their formal structure, but rarely asked what they meant for those who applied them or to whom they were applied. For another, distinctions of status continue to enjoy a luxuriant life among all social strata in contemporary India.

Some of the best accounts of distinctions of status and their meaning (or lack of meaning) in contemporary Indian life are to be found in literary as against ethnographic writing. V.S. Naipaul has left a memorable account of his encounter with rank and status in settings that are characteristic of modern

India. Naipaul's *An Area of Darkness* (1964) caused much resentment among educated Indians, no doubt in part because many of them found something of themselves in his account.

Contemporary Indian life provides numerous occasions for the play of status in the factory, in the office, in hospitals, in laboratories, and in banks; in work and outside work; and in both public and private places. I am speaking now simply of the distinctions of rank that are an inherent feature of every modern association, institution and organization, but of patterns of deference and invidious distinction that grow within and around them in great and sometimes unexpected profusion. It is this luxuriance of status distinctions that some are inclined to regard as the characteristically Indian part of modern Indian life. They point out that all the professions of equality in the Constitution and the laws are but words in the face of the Indian's undying preoccupation with hierarchy, rank and status.

It is natural to ask about this preoccupation with rank and status in contemporary Indian life whether it is anything more than a new manifestation of the old hierarchy of caste. The concept of caste has always been elastic, and the concept of status even more so. It is of course possible to speak of caste both literally and metaphorically, and in the latter case to describe every form of invidious distinction and social exclusion as a form of caste. But then one must be careful to note when one is speaking of caste in the restricted sense of distinctions of status based on specific ideas of purity and pollution, of birth and inherited bodily substance, and when one is speaking of it in the broad and general sense of rigid and elaborate social distinctions.

Even when an Indian is acutely conscious of his own caste and also of his status, he may not make distinctions of status among others solely or even mainly according to their caste. The social world of the professional, the civil servant, and the executive in the large metropolitan city is different from the social world of the village or even the small town. It would be rash to declare that the city is less animated by a concern for status than the village, and, indeed, from the villager's point of view, the case may appear to be the opposite. That apart, the definition of status, its symbolic form, and its social expression are not the same for the two. There are innumerable tales of persons from the village or small town being bewildered by the intricate conventions of status among their upper class relatives in the metropolitan city.

In addition to caste, the things that count for status in the sections of society about which I am writing are education, occupation and income, and the subcultures of the profession, the office and the association. The latter are by no means unrelated to caste in the traditional sense, but they can hardly be regarded merely as aspects or expressions of it. The social world created by education, occupation and income, the office, the firm, the law court and the laboratory cuts across the social world of caste. The social circle of the Brahman judge, diplomat, engineer, civil servant, or manager is not the same as that of the Brahman clerk, school teacher, or cook. Particularly among the higher occupational strata, many relationships are formed that cut across caste, as may be easily seen from the patterns of residence in large metropolitan cities where housing goes directly with occupation and income, and only indirectly with caste.

There are, to be sure, many continuities and linkages between the new status distinctions prominent among the intelligentsia and the old ones based largely on considerations of purity and pollution. Different criteria of status, different symbols of distinction and different strategies of exclusion now coexist in various sectors of Indian society. It is clear that they do not all fit neatly into a single, unified hierarchical design; whether and to what extent they did so in the past are questions that cannot be addressed here.

If we are to reach a proper understanding of variation and change in contemporary Indian society, we have to be on our guard against the unreflective switch from the literal use of the term caste to its metaphorical use as, for instance, in the phrase that the Boston Brahmans are an acutely caste-conscious set. It is of course well known that western writers from Alexis de Tocqueville (1956) to Michael Young (1961) have used the metaphor of caste while commenting on their own societies. No great confusion or misunderstanding is likely to result from the metaphorical use of caste to describe status, the sense of distinction, or the strategies of exclusion in western societies; few readers are likely to think that the court of Louis XVI or the playing fields of Eton were teeming with Brahmans of different kind, carefully calculating what kinds of boiled vegetables they might share and with whom without serious risk to the purity of their bodily substance. Yet such misunderstanding repeatedly arises when the metaphorical use of caste is extended to contexts in contemporary India where caste in the traditional sense has ceased to have its old significance.

Conclusion: Imputed Meaning and Actor's Meaning

I began by pointing to the highly ambivalent attitude to caste among certain influential sections of Indian society, and some will no doubt object that I have ended by trying to show that caste no longer has any legitimacy at all. How can certain identities remain so manifestly durable if they have no meaning and no legitimacy for their bearers?

I would like to state clearly and firmly in conclusion that I do not believe that caste has disappeared or is likely to disappear from even the sections of society about which I have written; but I do believe that shifts are taking place in the meaning and legitimacy of social relationships and social activities among many members of it. We are likely to miss the significance of those shifts if we continue to think of caste – or, indeed, Indian society – in the old way, relying mainly on the ethnographic record of village studies or the Indological record of the classical texts. The problem in the past has been that anthropologists often came to India in search of the eternal, and that is why so many of them were drawn, instinctively as it were, to the remote village and the classical text. I have tried to redress the balance somewhat, but there is always the danger of going to the opposite extreme and, by focusing attention on a relatively small though very influential section of society, losing sight of the larger body of people.

The exercise I have undertaken above has to be seen primarily as an effort to redress the balance among anthropologists. To draw attention to the growing ambivalence towards caste is not to say that caste has become or is becoming meaningless, but to indicate that there are now both positive and negative components of evaluation that sit uneasily together. The negative components of evaluation have not in my view received sufficient attention from social anthropologists who study caste, and that is why I have dwelt on them at some length. It is of course true that meanings do not always lie on the surface but may be latent or hidden, and meanings that appear inconsistent on the surface may in fact be resolved at a deeper level. Psychoanalysis and some forms of structural analysis deal with these latent or hidden or imputed meanings, whereas my concern has been more with the empirical or observed meanings (Kolakowski, 1982), or the meanings that actors themselves assign to their actions (Weber, 1978). All that I can say is that if caste today has a single or homogeneous meaning, I have failed to discover it either in my own observation and experience or in the writings of other anthropologists.

It would be strange if something that occupied such a central place in society were to lose all positive significance for its members simply because they have changed their laws, or acquired a different system of education, or taken to new occupations. Evidence of some positive attachment to caste may be found in almost every sector of Indian society among doctors, lawyers and scientists, not to speak of administrators, managers and businessmen. I said at the very beginning that the statement from educated Indians that caste does not exist anymore should not be taken at face value. The attachment to caste may lie very deep indeed, so that a person may not even be fully aware of it; but then it might find expression suddenly and unexpectedly when, for instance, a daughter declares that she wants to marry a man from a very low caste, or when a man of a different caste boasts about the achievements of that caste. Much patience and care are required for collecting such evidence in a systematic way, and going back to the village or the classical texts cannot be a substitute for it.

It is easy enough to show that caste has both a positive and a negative significance for many members of contemporary Indian society. What is difficult is to weigh and measure these different components. Where the evidence is contradictory and points in different, even opposite, directions, the sociologist is very likely to draw on it in accordance with his own bias, and that bias may lead him either to exaggerate or to underrate the contemporary significance of caste. For the last twenty-five years, I have been told by anthropologists in London, Cambridge and Chicago that I ignore evidence of the significance of caste in contemporary India, and by scientists, economists, and others in Calcutta and Delhi that I exaggerate it, and, indeed, that as a sociologist I am paid to do so.

In 1990, Indian intellectuals became deeply divided over the significance of caste in contemporary Indian society. The division was over an issue of policy, that of caste quotas in education and employment (Béteille, 1990; Guhan et al., 1990). It has been said that those who opposed quotas minimized the significance of caste, sometimes deliberately. But it must not be assumed that those who supported quotas thought that caste was a good thing which ought to be strengthened; on the contrary, they said that caste was an evil but believed that the best way of doing away with it in the long run was by having quotas in the short run. No doubt, personal interest played some part in this, but it would hardly be reasonable to suppose that Indian intellectuals are unique in the world in supporting or opposing policies solely on the basis of personal interest. At any rate, those who supported the quotas belonged to diverse castes, and Indian intellectuals, who are predominantly of upper caste, both supported and opposed the quotas.

If among the intelligentsia, individuals differ in their perception of caste or in the significance they give to it, it may well be that these differences have some relationship to the differences in their positions in the hierarchy of caste. Where some individual mobility is possible, the burden of caste may weigh more heavily on the lower than on the upper caste person. In certain contexts, caste might matter more for Harijan than for Brahman intellectuals as race seems to do more for black than for white intellectuals in the United States (Carter, 1991; West, 1993). But this again would be a kind of reversal of the traditional order where caste matters were ultimately the responsibility of the upper and not the lower castes. That at least is my reading of the literature relating to village India and to classical India. If we are to understand what is happening to caste in contemporary India, we will have to look for new types of data, devise new concepts, and, above all, approach the subject with a more open mind that does not seek either to ignore the distinctive features of Indian society or to maximize the difference (Molund, 1991) between India and the West.

Notes

1. A first, very preliminary version of this essay was presented as a lecture at the, University of California, Berkeley, in April 1992 where Professor G.D. Berreman, who was in the chair, made a number of observations from which I have greatly benefited. I am grateful also for the many helpful comments I received when it was presented in London in July 1993, and would like in particular to thank Professor Jonathan Parry and Dr C.J. Fuller for their comprehensive written comments which have helped me in making extensive revisions.
2. In transliterating Bengali words, I have gone by the sounds of spoken Bengali, and not followed any consistent scheme. Thus, I have written 'Barendra' and not 'Varendra', and hence 'barna' and not 'varna' which is the more common North Indian form and also closer to Sanskrit.

References

Bankimchandra (1961), 'Dharmatattva', in *Bankimrachanabali,* Calcutta: Sahitya Samsad, Vol. 2, pp. 584–679.

Bardhan, P. (1984), *Political Economy of Development in India,* Oxford: Basil Blackwell.

Berreman, G.D. (1963), *Hindus of the Himalayas,* Berkeley: University of California Press.

Béteille, A. (1966), 'Closed and Open Social Stratification in India', *European Journal of Sociology,* Vol. 7, pp. 224–46.

—— (1969a), *Castes: Old and New,* Bombay: Asia Publishing House.

—— (1969b), 'The Politics of 'Non-Antagonistic' Strata', *Contributions to Indian Sociology* (N.S.), Vol. 3, No. 1, pp. 17–31.

—— (1979), 'Homo Hierarchicus, Homo Equalis', *Modern Asian Studies,* Vol. 13, No. 4, pp. 529–48.

—— (1989), 'Are the Intelligentsia a Ruling Class?', *Economic and Political Weekly,* Vol. 24, No. 3, pp. 151–55.

—— (1990), 'Caste and Reservations', *The Hindu,* 20 October.

—— (1991), *Society and Politics in India,* London: Athlone Press.

—— (1992), *The Backward Classes in Contemporary India,* Delhi: Oxford University Press.

Blunt, E.A.H. (1931), *The Caste System of Northern India,* London: Oxford University Press.

Bose, N.K. (1967), *Culture and Society in India,* Bombay: Asia Publishing House.

—— (1975), *The Structure of Hindu Society (Hindu Samajer Garan,* 1949, translated from the Bengali with an introduction and notes by A. Béteille). Delhi: Orient Longmans.

Bouglé, C. (1971), *Essays on the Caste System,* Cambridge: Cambridge University Press.

Carter, S.C. (1991), *Reflections of an Affirmative Action Baby,* New York: Basic Books.

Centre for Social Studies (1985), *Caste, Caste Conflict and Reservation,* Delhi: Ajanta.

Chaudhuri, N.C. (1979), *Hinduism,* London: Chatto and Windus.

Deliége, R. (1993), *Le systeme des castes,* Paris: Presses Universitaires de France.

Dumont, L. (1966), *Homo Hierarchicus,* Paris: Gallimard.

Enthoven, R.E. (1920–2), *The Tribes and Castes of Bombay,* Bombay: Government Central Press (3 Vols.).

Frankel, F.R. and M.S.A. Rao (eds.) (1989–90), *Dominance and State Power in Modern India,* Delhi: Oxford University Press (2 Vols.).

Gait, E.A. (1913), *Report on the Census of India,* Calcutta: Government Printing.

Gandhi, M.K. (1962), *Varanashramadharma,* Ahmedabad: Navajivan.

Ganguli, B.N. (1975), *Concept of Equality,* Shimla: Indian Institute of Advanced Study.

Guhan, S. et al. (1990), 'South India and Reservations: A Reply to André Béteille', *The Hindu,* 27 October.

Hutton, J.H. (1946), *Caste in India,* Cambridge: Cambridge University Press.

Ibbetson, D. (1916), *Punjab Castes,* Lahore: Government Press.

Irschick, E.F. (1969), *Politics and Social Conflict in South India,* Berkeley: University of California Press.

Kannan, C.T. (1963), *Intercaste and Inter-community Marriage in India,* Bombay: Allied Publishers.

Karve, I. (1968), *Hindu Society: An Interpretation,* Poona: Deshmukh Prakashan.

Kolakowski, L. (1982), *Religion,* London: Fontana.

Kothari, R. (ed.) (1970), *Caste in Indian Politics,* Delhi: Orient Longmans.

Leach, E.R. (ed.) (1960), *Aspects of Caste in South India, Ceylon and North-West Pakistan,* Cambridge: Cambridge University Press.

Lingat, R. (1973), *The Classical Law of India,* Berkeley: University of California Press.

Maine, H.S. (1950), *Ancient Law,* London: Oxford University Press.

Marriott, M. (ed.) (1990), *India Through Hindu Categories,* New Delhi: Sage Publications.

Mayer, A.C. (1960), *Caste and Kinship in Central India,* London: Routledge and Kegan Paul.

Molund, S. (1991), 'Sociology as Critical Understanding: An Interview with André Béteille', *Antropologiska Studier,* 48, pp. 31–47,

Naipaul, V.S. (1964), *An Area of Darkness,* London: Andre Deutsch.

O'Malley, L.S.S. (1932), *Indian Caste Customs,* Cambridge: Cambridge University Press.

Padgaonkar, D. (1993), 'In Conversation with M.N. Srinivas', *Sunday Times of India,* 12 December.

Radcliffe-Brown, A.R. (1952), 'Foreword', in M.N. Srinivas, *Religion and Society among the Coorgs of South India,* Oxford: Clarendon Press.

Ray, N. (1945), *Bangali Hindur Barnabhed,* Calcutta: Vishvabharati Granthalaya.

Risley, H.H. (1892), *The Tribes and Castes of Bengal,* Calcutta: Bengal Secretariat Press.

—— (1969), *The People of India,* New Delhi: Oriental Books.

Rudra, A. (1989), 'The Intelligentsia as a Ruling Class', *Economic and Political Weekly,* Vol. 24, No. 3, pp. 142–50.

Senart, E. (1930), *Caste in India,* London: Methuen.

Sivaramayya, B. (1984), *Inequalities and the Law,* Lucknow: Eastern Book Company.
Srinivas, M.N. (1962), *Caste in Modern India and Other Essays,* Bombay: Asia Publishing House.
Thurston, E. (1909), *Castes and Tribes of Southern India,* Madras: Government Press (7 Vols.).
Tocqueville, A. de (1956), *Democracy in America,* New York: Alfred Knopf (2 Vols.).
Weber, M. (1958), *The Religion of India,* New York: Free Press.
—— (1978), *Economy and Society,* Berkeley: University of California Press (2 Vols.).
West, C. (1993), *Race Matters,* Boston: Beacon Press.
Young, M. (1961), *The Rise of Meritocracy,* London: Thames and Hudson.

29 Occupational Mobility among Backward Castes

SUNANDA PANDE

India has traditionally limitations and restrictions on occupational choices, and the caste system has been the chief mechanism in this regard. Occupational ranking coincided with caste hierarchy. The present study attempts to examine the extent to which a backward caste, namely, Padmasali of Hyderabad, Andhra Pradesh, still adheres to traditional occupation of weaving. Four generations (grandfathers, fathers, sons and grandsons) have been studied for analysing occupational mobility. Inter-generational occupational mobility between the four generations has been studied at two levels, that is, deviation from caste occupation and deviation from parental occupation. Class position, education and migration have been treated as independent variables and impact of these variables on occupational mobility among Padmasalis has also been studied. Findings of the study will be discussed in the present paper.

Significance of the Study

Social stratification and mobility have emerged as key areas of sociological enquiry both in rural and urban settings. Mobility depends upon a number of social factors, such as social stratification, size of community, nature of family, education, degree of technological and industrial growth, power structure, economic opportunities, etc. These social factors, along with motivations and aspirations of the people, create the conditions which chiefly account for the nature of social mobility. The pre-industrial social system, where rural and urban communities were socially isolated from each other, offered limited scope for an individual's aspirations and opportunities for social climbing compared to the modern industrial society.

Migration of people from villages and towns to cities makes it almost inevitable that they follow occupational careers different from that of their parents. Even for for the families living in cities for two or more generations, the deviation from parental occupations is a normal feature. While there are numerous traditional occupations for members of various castes and religious groups, The occupational diversity in the city provides a considerable range of choices. The present-day urban occupational structure necessitates some departure from parental occupations. As lower caste members become better educated and acquire superior occupational skills, they tend to give up the low-skilled and manual occupations of their fathers for claiming higher social status.

The present study aims to understand and analyse nature and direction of occupational mobility. An attempt has been made to know the nature of departure from the traditional occupation among the Padmasalis. The respondents include most of the migrant Padmasalies from the nearby villages, working in Hyderabad.

Objectives of the Study

Migration from rural to urban areas brings occupational mobility. An attempt has been made in this study to know the extent to which Padmasalis have acquired higher occupational status vis-à-vis their occupation of weaving. The aim is to see how caste and occupation are related to each other. The objectives of the present study are:

1. To understand and analyse the trends of occupational mobility among Padmasalis (weavers' caste) of Hyderabad in order to investigate inter-generationally mobility among the migrants.
2. To know whether or not rural to urban migration has helped the Padmasalis in improving their status.

An attempt has also been made to study the occupational differences between the migrants and the non-migrants. The role of traditional occupation, i.e., weaving, as an in occupational mobility obstacle, has been analysed along with the above objectives.

Methodology

Sampling

For census information on ward-wise distribution of various castes, the present study suffered from certain sampling problems. Thus, it was difficult to assess the size of Padmasali population within the city as well as in the localities from where the data have been collected. The selection of these four localities has been done only on the basis of certain assumed economic differences. Thus, based on the general assessment of the size of the population in each locality, 122 respondents have been selected and interviewed. While 75.72 per cent of the respondents have been picked from Karvan area, 19.67 per cent of them come from Hussaini-alam area, 16.39 per cent from Padma Nagar colony (Nallakunta), and lastly 8.19 per cent belong to Sultan Bazar area.

Interview Schedule

Data for the present study have been collected with the help of interview schedules. These schedules include questions pertaining to the personal profile of respondents, family size and particulars regarding sex, age, marital status of family members, educational background of respondents' grandfathers, fathers, children, wives and also other members in case of joint families. Different categories of education have been framed for the said purpose. Some of the other factors included are particulars regarding occupational backgrounds of respondents and other generations, before and after migration. Income, as a separate factor, has also been compared. Questions pertaining to the impact of urban values on occupational choice have been included to study whether caste occupation creates any hindrance in the process of occupational mobility, even after migration.

Ecological Distribution

As far as the distribution of Padmasali families is concerned, it has been found that they generally tend to live together, though sometimes separated by other caste inhabitants. Some of the localities to be mentioned are Karvan, Gazibanda, Laldarwaza, Hussainialam, Goulipura, Gouliguda, Sultan Bazar, Nallakunta, Amberpet, Musheerabad and Ramnagar. The distance between these localities and the central business district (Abids and Residency) ranges between 5–7 kilometres. In Nallakunta area, they have a separate colony called 'Padmanagar'. In all the localities, Reddy, Marwadi, Marathi and Telugu-speaking Brahmins co-exist with Padmasalis.

Findings of the Study

Deviation from Caste Occupation

The present section of the study deals with the rate of deviation from caste occupation, i.e., weaving, among Padmasalis. The idea behind the present discussion is that, since weaving is an occupation which pays them definite rewards, therefore, as hypothesized, it would encourage Padmasalis to retain the same instead of moving into other occupations with indefinite incomes. It is also hypothesized that less educated may tend to live with weaving-oriented occupations instead of moving into occupations with lesser and insecure incomes. People having professional education can be able to secure higher occupational positions. In order to study this, an attempt has been made to measure the rate of occupational deviation in all the four generations under consideration, from caste as well as parental occupation.

Table 1

Deviations from Caste Occupation among Grandfathers, Fathers, Respondents and their Sons

Occupational Category	*Grandfathers*	*Fathers*	*Respondents*	*Sons*
1. *Professionals*				
Doctors	—	—	1.64	—
Engineers	—	—	0.8	3.92
Lawyers	—	—	0.8	—
2. *Semi-professionals*				
University teachers	—	—	0.8	—
College teachers	—	—	0.8	1.96
School teachers	0.8	—	4.09	—
Accountants	—	—	—	1.96
Photographers	—	—	0.8	—

Cont'd...

Cont'd...

Social workers	—	0.8	0.8	—
Other professions	6.67	2.45	—	—
3. *Business owners*				
Owners of small business	4.09	6.67	11.48	3.92
Owners of medium business	—	—	5.73	15.69
Owners of large business	—	—	3.27	3.92
4. *Clerks*				
UDCs	—	—	2.45	—
LDCs	—	—	3.27	—
Typists	—	—	0.8	1.96
Other non-gazetted officials	—	—	1.64	3.92
5. *Skilled workers*				
Compounders	—	—	0.8	—
Technicians	—	—	1.64	3.92
Compositors	—	—	0.8	—
Binders	—	—	1.64	3.92
Other occupations	—	—	—	—
6. *Semi-skilled workers*				
Weavers	85.82	77.87	32.78	21.57
Tailors	—	—	4.09	9.80
Carpenters	0.8	1.64	1.64	3.92
Masons	1.64	1.64	1.64	—
Cloth printers	—	—	0.8	—
Other occupations	—	—	—	5.88
7. *Unskilled workers*				
Helpers	—	—	1.64	7.84
Labourers	—	—	2.45	—
Watchmen	—	—	1.64	—
Attendees	—	—	1.64	—
8. *Farming*				
Farm tenant or farm workers	—	—	—	—
Tenant with paid help	—	—	—	—
Owner or manager with paid help	—	—	—	—
Farm owner without paid help	3.27	8.19	—	—
9. *Other occupations*				
Military	—	—	0.8	—
Government service	—	—	6.67	5.99
Other occupations	—	—	—	—

From the data as cited in Table 1, it is evident that in the first category of occupations, which includes professions like, doctors, engineers and lawyers, there are/were no grandfathers and fathers engaged in the said professions. There are only 1.64 per cent of respondents who are doctors. No son has been found engaged in this profession. In the engineering profession only 0.8 per cent of respondents are included. There are 3.92 per cent sons engaged in the profession of engineering. In the category of lawyers only 0.8 per cent of respondents are included.

In the second category of occupations, which includes semi-professionals, there are 0.8 per cent of respondents who are university as well as college teachers each. The percentage of sons who are engaged in the same profession is 1.96. These two categories do not include any father or grandfather. In the same category of semi-professionals, there were 0.8 per cent of grandfathers who were school teachers, and there are 4.09 per cent of respondents who are also teachers by profession. There are no fathers and sons found engaged in the said profession. There are 1.96 per cent of sons who are accountants. There are 0.8 per cent of respondents who are photographers. There are 0.8 per cent of fathers and 0.8 per cent of respondents who are social workers by profession. There were 6.67 per cent of grandfathers and 2.45 fathers who practised Indian medicine. No respondent or son has been found engaged in the said profession.

In the next category of business owners, there were 4.09 per cent of grandfathers and 6.67 per cent of fathers who owned small business. There are 11.48 per cent of respondents and 3.92 per cent of sons who are also engaged in the same type of business. There are 5.73 per cent of respondents and 15.69 per cent of sons who are engaged in medium type of business. No grandfather or father has been found engaged in the medium type of business. There are 3.27 per cent of respondents and 3.92 per cent of sons who own large type of business.

In the category of clerks, among respondents, there are 2.45 per cent UDCs, 3.27 per cent of LDCs and 0.8 per cent typists. In the sub-category of typists, 1.96 per cent sons are also included. Besides, there are 0.8 per cent of fathers, 1.64 per cent of respondents and 3.92 per cent of sons, who are engaged in non-gazetted positions as storekeepers.

In the next category of skilled workers, there are 0.8 per cent of respondents who are compounders, whereas 1.64 per cent of respondents and 3.92 per cent of sons are technicians. A total of 0.8 per cent of respondents work as compositors and there are 1.64 per cent of respondents and 3.92 per cent of sons who are binders.

In the category of semi-skilled workers, there are 85.82 per cent of grandfathers and 77.87 per cent of fathers who were engaged in their caste occupation, i.e., weaving. Similarly, there are 32.78 per cent of respondents and 21.57 per cent of sons who still practise weaving. There are 4.09 per cent of respondents and 9.80 per cent of sons who are tailors. A total of 0.8 per cent of grandfathers and 1.64 per cent of fathers were carpenters and the percentage of respondents sons who are also engaged in the same occupation is 1.64 and 3.92 respectively. The same category includes 1.64 per cent of grandfathers, 1.64 per cent of fathers and 1.64 per cent respondents who were/are masions. Finally, there are 0.8 per cent of respondents who work as clothprinters, whereas 5.88 per cent of sons are engaged in beedi-making.

The next category of unskilled workers includes 1.64 per cent of respondents and 7.84 per cent of sons who work as helpers, 2.45 respondents as labourers and 1.64 per cent as watchmen.

In the category of farming there are 3.27 per cent of grandfathers and 8.19 per cent of fathers who were farm owners without paid help.

The last category includes other occupations, which are not fit into the preceding categories. Thus, the present category includes 0.8 per cent of respondents who are in military services. There are 6.67 per cent of respondents and 5.88 per cent of sons who are engaged in some of the government services.

From the data furnished in Table 1, it is evident that there were 17.27 per cent of grandfathers who had left their caste occupation (weaving) and deviated into occupations such as teaching, business, carpentry, construction work and farming, etc. There were/are 22.13 per cent of fathers who have also deviated from the weaving and have taken up business, social work, carpentry, construction work and farming, etc. At the level of the third generation, there are 66.67 per cent of the respondents who have deviated from their caste occupation. They have, thus, moved into occupations like medicine, engineering, photography, social work, clerical jobs, business, and some of them work as technicians, tailors, and unskilled workers like helpers, watchmen and attenders, etc. Likewise, there are 78.43 per cent of sons who have moved from their caste occupation and are engineers, college teachers and accountants. Some of them are also engaged in business, there are others who are engaged in clerical jobs, and some of them work as skilled workers and semi-skilled workers (other than weaving) as tailors, carpenters and beedi-makers. Some of them also work as helpers. A few of them are government servants.

Thus, it is clear that there is gradual deviation from caste occupation from one generation to the other. Thus, when compared to grandfathers (first generation) majority of sons (fourth generation) have deviated from their caste occupation.

Deviation from Parental Occupation

After studying the deviation from caste occupation among four generations of Padmasalis, an attempt has been made to trace the deviation from parental occupation. The occupational background of grandfathers has been treated as the point of departure for other three generations under consideration. Since deviation from the caste occupation (weaving) has been studied separately, it has not been included in the present analysis.

It has been already discussed that out of (17.27%) grandfathers, who have deviated from their caste occupation, i.e., weaving, 0.8 per cent have been found engaged in teaching, followed by Indian medicine (6.67%), small business (4.09%), carpentry (0.8%), construction work (1.64%), farming (3.27%), etc.

Fathers (22.13%), who have deviated from the caste occupation, were found engaged in social work (0.8%), Indian medicine (2.45%), small business (6.67%), godown-keeping (0.8%), carpenting (1.64%), masonry (1.64%) and farming (8.19%). Therefore, the data reveal that not many of fathers have moved into occupations different from that of grandfathers.

Out of the (66.67%) respondents, who have deviated from their caste occupation and have moved into professional occupations, are doctors (1.64%), engineers (0.8%) and lawyers (0.8%). There are (7.37%) respondents who are engaged in various semi-professional jobs as university teachers (0.8%), college teachers (0.8%), school teachers (4.09%), photographers (0.8%) and social workers (0.8%). There are 20.49 per cent respondents who are engaged in business. Out of these respondents, there are small business owners (11.48%), medium business owners (5.73%), and large business owners (3.27%). Besides, among the respondents 3.27 per cent work as UDCs, and 0.80 per cent each as LDCs and typists. There are also respondents (4.91%) who are engaged in skilled occupations as compounders (0.8%), technicians (0.8%), compositors (1.64%) and binders (1.64%).

Some (8.19%) of the respondents are semi-skilled workers (other than weaving). Thus, there are respondents who are helpers (1.64%), labourers (2.45%), watchmen (1.64%) and attenders (1.64%). None of the respondents has been found engaged in farming (parental occupation). There are also respondents found engaged in military and government services (7.37%).

Thus, from the above, it is evident that when compared to fathers, respondents proved to be more mobile with regard to their occupational choice, i.e., more number of respondents have been found to be mobile from their parental occupations (where the parental occupation is other than weaving or caste occupation).

Coming to the deviation at fourth generation level, it is found that out of sons (78.43%), who have deviated from their caste occupations, there are 3.92 per cent who are in professional jobs as engineers against 3.27 per cent of respondents who are also in the professional fields as doctors, engineers and lawyers.

In the category of semi-professionals, there are 3.92 per cent of sons engaged in teaching at college level and work as accountants. In the same category, there are 7.37 per cent of respondents who are also engaged in teaching at university, college and school levels. Others are photographers and social workers.

There are 23.5 per cent of sons against 20.49 per cent respondents who are engaged in business (small, medium and large type).

There are 5.88 per cent of sons against 8.10 per cent of respondents who are engaged in various clerical jobs.

In the category of skilled workers, there are 7.84 per cent of sons against 4.91 per cent of respondents working as technicians, binders, compounders, compositors, etc.

In the category of semi-skilled workers, there are 41.17 per cent of sons against 42.26 per cent of respondents found engaged in various occupations, viz., tailoring, carpentry, construction, cloth printing, etc.

In the category of unskilled workers, there are 7.84 per cent of sons who work as helpers, against 7.37 per cent of respondents who work as helpers, labourers, watchmen and attendees.

No son or respondent has been found engaged in farming.

There are 5.88 per cent of sons against 7.37 per cent of respondents who are engaged in military and other government services.

From the data, it is evident that out of 78.43 per cent sons who have deviated from their caste occupation, i.e., weaving only 5.88 per cent of them have deviated from their parental occupations (other than weaving). The minor deviation from parental occupations among sons can be attributed to the better placement of the respondents in various jobs, which naturally prevented them from moving from the same.

Keeping in view all the four generations, the general trend of deviation from parental occupation has been found to be gradual from one generation to that of the other, upto the third generation level of respondents. At the level of fourth generation, mobility has been found to be almost none. Thus, in a nutshell, more number of respondents have proved to be mobile, when compared to their fathers and sons.

Direction of Mobility

Since Padmasalis belong to an occupational caste (weaver's caste), weaving in the present study has been treated as a constant factor and trends of occupational mobility from the same have been traced between four generations of grandfathers, fathers, respondents and their sons. For the purpose of the analysis, occupations have been divided into the following nine categories: (1) professional jobs (doctors, engineers and lawyers); (2) semi-professional jobs (university teachers, college teachers, school teachers, accountants, photographers, social workers, etc.); (3) business owners (small, medium and large business); (4) clerks; (5) skilled workers (compositors, technicians, binders, etc.); (6) semi-skilled workers (weavers, tailors, carpenters, masons, cloth printers, etc.); (7) unskilled workers (helpers, labourers, watchmen, attenders, etc.); (8) farming (farm tenant or farm worker, tenant with paid help, farm owner without paid help, owner or manager with paid help, etc.); and (9) the final category includes some of the occupations which have not been included in any of the above categories, e.g., military and other government services.

The term 'occupational mobility' in the present study is concerned with the mobility of the occupations and individual movement from one occupation to another. Mobility may, therefore, involve changes in locus, function, income, prestige, power independence, or other occupational attributes. The process of mobility can occur in two different directions, viz., horizontal and vertical. By horizontal mobility or shifting is meant the transition of an individual from one social group to another situated on the same level, for example, transition of an individual from one citizenship to another, from one family to another, and from one factory to another, in the same occupational status. By vertical mobility is meant the relations involved in a transition of an individual from one social stratum to another. According to the transition, there are two types of vertical mobility, viz., upward and downward. Inter-generational trends form an important part in the process of going up and coming down of individuals in various occupations. According to the nature of the stratification, there are upward and downward currents of occupational mobility.

In the present study, the concept of occupational mobility refers to changes in vocational affiliation between four generations. Thus, for the purpose of analysis, all the Padmasalis, who have moved into occupations on par with their caste occupation (weaving) like tailoring, carpentry, construction and cloth printing, etc. (including in the 6th category of semi-skilled occupations) along with those who have taken up to farming (included in the category of occupations) have been considered mobile in the horizontal direction.

Padmasalis, who have moved into occupations included under professional, semi-professional, business, clerical jobs, skilled jobs, etc., have been treated as vertically mobile into upward direction and those who have moved into occupations included under the category of unskilled occupations have been treated as downwardly mobile.

Table 2

Direction of Occupational Mobility in Four Generations

(in percentage)

Type	*Grandfathers movement*	*Fathers*	*Respondents*	*Sons*
Horizontal	5.73	11.48	8.19	19.60
Vertical				
(a) Upward	11.48	10.65	41.64	50.98
(b) Downward	—	—	7.37	7.84
Total	17.27	22.13	66.67	78.43

Thus, from the viewpoint of the classification of various occupations as indicated in Table 2, it has been found that out of 17.27 per cent of grandfathers, who have deviated from their caste occupation, 5.73 per cent have moved horizontally into occupations which are on par with their caste occupation, i.e., weaving. There are 11.48 per cent of them who have moved vertically in an upward direction. No grandfather has been found mobile in the downward direction.

Further, out of 22.13 per cent of fathers who have left their caste occupation, 11.48 per cent have moved horizontally into occupations such as tailoring, carpentry, construction and farming, etc. There are 10.65 per cent of them who have moved vertically in an upward direction into various occupations, placed at the higher levels when compared to their caste occupation, viz., social work, Indian medicine, business, etc. No downward mobility has been traced among fathers.

Out of 66.67 per cent of the respondents, who have deviated from their caste occupation, 8.19 per cent have moved horizontally. And, of the respondents who have moved vertically, 41.64 per cent of them experienced upward mobility and 7.37 per cent downward.

Similarly, out of 78.43 per cent of sons, who have moved from their caste occupation, 19.60 per cent have moved in the horizontal direction, whereas 50.98 per cent of them have moved vertically in the upward direction and 7.84 per cent in the downward direction.

When viewed in terms of four generations under consideration, gradual mobility with regard to occupational attainment has been traced, from one generation to the other. Thus, as indicated from the available data, there were 17.27 per cent of grandfathers, 22.13 per cent of fathers, 66.67 per cent of the respondents and 78.43 per cent of sons, who have deviated from their caste occupation, i.e., weaving. In a nutshell, mobility among all the four generations is favourable in the sense that, compared to grandfathers (first generations), majority of sons (fourth generation) have entered into new occupations.

Conclusion

The occupational mobility trends among Padmasalis in the light of the correlation between traditional caste hierarchy and the new western occupational hierarchy, as suggested by Srinivas, it has been found that irrespective of their caste position, Padmasalis in general could move upwardly with regard to their occupational position when compared with their forefathers. As has already been stated, respondents and their sons could move from their caste occupation, i.e., weaving in particular and their parental occupations in general, owing to their educational attainment and migration. As the result of migration, respondents in general have realized the value of education of modern times. This awareness has been the key factor in understanding the trends of occupational mobility among them.

References

Gist, N.P. (1960), *Industrial Relations in India*, Bombay, p. 92.

Salz, Arthur (1944), 'Occupations: Theory and History', *Encyclopedia of the Social Sciences* VI, New York: The Macmillan Co.

Sorokin, P.A. (1959), *Social and Cultural Mobility*, Glencoe: The Free Press, p. 133.

Srinivas, M.N. (1972), *Social Change in Modern India*, Bombay: Orient Longman.

30 Social Inequalities in Health and Nutrition among Children of Haryana

MADHU NAGLA

Inequality in health status is perhaps the most serious and unacceptable of all inequalities, related as it is to matters of life and death. Persistent inequalities between the health of populations in developing and industrialized countries have been a cause of grave concern in recent years. Wide gap between the rich and the poor has always been a matter of concern in India. It is now widely accepted that the issue is just not confined to economic inequalities; the wider issue that needs to be addressed is the 'inequality of opportunities' (Gopal, 1983). This dimension has assumed special significance recently in the context of economic reforms. There is a fear that inequalities will be further intensified as the poor and weak are likely to be marginalized in this process because the expanded economic opportunities are difficult to be used if a person is handicapped by ill-health or illiteracy. Education and health are recognized to be the two distinct influences which can promote the freedom and capability of individuals to make use of available opportunities (Dreze and Sen, 1995).

India is committed to the goal 'health for all' and in the last five decades, a wide network of primary health centres (PHCs) and sub-centres has been created. Yet most of the states in India are far away from this goal. Many surveys as well as NFHS-1 and NFHS-2 have provided ample evidence to show that either the services do not reach the disadvantaged sections of the society or people from those sections do not utilize the available services. Apart from economic condition, the social hierarchy or the system of social stratification existing in the society is likely to influence the health behaviour of individuals. Social stratification system determines the living conditions, privileges, obligations and cultural traditions surrounding the life of a person which in turn affect his perception regarding health, knowledge of health care and accessibility to health resources (Kopparty, 1994). Food consumption pattern of an individual is an important determinant of his/her nutritional status of a person but it is also affected by child rearing practices. In India, the caste represents the traditional ascriptive framework of life conditions, values and social choices. Class and achievable social status are represented by education, occupation and economic status, but often there is a strong overlap between caste and class (Roy, Kulkarni and Vaidehi, 2004).

Haryana provides an ideal situation for exploring social inequalities in health and nutrition among the children of the state. It is fairly a well-developed state with third highest per capita income in India (Government of India, 2001). The National Family Health Survey-2 (Haryana), which provides data on a variety of health and nutritional indicators by caste, education and standard of living, sex, nativity, offers ample opportunities to examine the social inequalities in health and nutrition among children in the above context. This paper attempts to assess the extent of inequalities in health care and nutritional status among children in the Haryana state. It also examines patterns of inequalities among children in terms of health outcomes, including disease incidence, use of preventive health care services and nutritional status. The focus on health outcomes for children is mainly for the reason that these outcomes, such as child morbidity, are relatively less influenced by choices of children themselves but potentially more indicative of parents' socio-economic background and hence may indicate more clearly the social inequality among children. Specifically, the paper addresses the following questions: Are socio-economically well-off children more likely to have complete vaccination than poor children? Are children from poor socio-economic background suffer more from different diseases? Are socio-economically better off children more likely to receive 'better' care than children of poor socio-economic background? Are children from poor socio-economic background more likely to be undernourished and malnourished than children from higher socio-economic background? If so, does the extent of health inequality depend on various socio-economic factors? A knowledge of levels and patterns of social inequality in health, utilization of health care services, and nutrition and food consumption is important for policy makers and programme managers to ensure equitable access to service utilization and also avoid any adverse impact of social inequality among children.

Data regarding rates of mortality and morbidity pattern among the children have been taken into account to examine the health of the children in Haryana. Use of preventive measures by people in terms of consumption of iodized salt and iron content shows the health of the individual. Immunization intervention is also considered as a preventive measure and results in good health of the child. Nutritional status of children is calculated on the basis of anthropometric indices. Breast feeding and weaning practices also account for the nutritional status of children.

The Government of India has repeatedly taken steps to strengthen maternal and child health (MCH) services in India, started during the First and Second Five-Year Plans (1951–56 and 1956–61) under the Ministry of Health, and continuing with the Minimum Needs Programme initiated during the Fifth Five-Year Plan (1974–79). More recently, efforts to improve MCH have been enhanced by activities of the Family Welfare Programme and by introduction of the Child Survival and Safe Motherhood Programme (Ministry of Health and Family Welfare, 1992). The Ministry of Health and Family Welfare has also sponsored special projects under the Maternal and Child Health Programme, including the Oral Rehydration Therapy (ORT) Programme, the establishment of Regional Institutes of Maternal and Child Health in states where infant mortality rates are high, the Universal Immunization Programme, and the Maternal and Child Health Supplemental Programme within the Postpartum Programme (Ministry of Health and Family Welfare, 1992). These programmes are now integrated into the Reproductive and Child Health Programme that was launched in 1996.

MCH services in rural areas of India are delivered mainly by government-run PHCs and sub-centres. In urban areas, such services are available mainly through government or municipal hospitals, urban health posts, hospitals and nursing homes operated by non-governmental organizations (NGOs), private nursing homes, and maternity homes.

Data and Methods

This study utilizes data from NFHS-2 (Haryana) the large-scale survey on demography and health conducted in Haryana. The NFHS-2, conducted in 1998–99, collected information from a state representative sample of 2,841 households and interviewed 2,908 ever-married women. In addition, the survey collected information on 1,060 children born to eligible women.

According to 2001 Census, about 71 per cent of the population lives in rural areas. The age distribution is typical of populations that have recently experienced a fertility decline, with relatively low proportion in the younger and old age groups: 11.1 per cent of the population is below age 5 and 5.5 per cent is 65 and above. The *de facto* sex ratio in Haryana is only 861 females per 1,000 males. About 20.5 per cent of households belong to scheduled caste and another 21.6 per cent to other backward classes and 57.8 per cent to general castes category. The literacy rate in Haryana is 68.59 per cent as a whole; for males it is 79.25 per cent and for females it is 56.31 per cent (IIPS, 2001).

Health Status of Children

Health status of children has been analysed in terms of infant and child mortality and child morbidity.

Infant and Child Mortality

Infant and child mortality reflects a country's level of socio-economic development and quality of life and data pertaining to it are used for monitoring and evaluating population and health programmes and policies. Data regarding the early neonatal deaths have not been seriously underreported in Haryana, since the ratios of deaths under seven days to all neonatal deaths are consistently high (between 67% and 72%) for the different time periods preceding the survey (a ratio of less than 25% is often used as a guideline to indicate underreporting of early neonatal deaths). The ratios of infant deaths that occurred during the neonatal period are also consistently high (between 54% and 64%) for the different time periods preceding the survey (IIPS, 2001).

Infant mortality in Haryana declined from 74 deaths per 1,000 live births during 1984–88 (10–14 years before the survey) to 57 deaths per 1,000 live births during 1994–98 (0–4 years before the survey) – an average rate of decline of 1.7 infant deaths per 1,000 live births per year.

Rural mortality rates are considerably higher than urban mortality rates. Infant mortality rate (IMR) is 48 per cent higher in rural areas than in urban areas. The much higher IMR in rural areas is mainly due to a much higher post-neonatal mortality rate in rural areas (26) than in urban areas (9). Neonatal and child mortality rates are only slightly higher in rural areas than in urban areas. Overall, the under-five mortality rate is 36 per cent higher in rural areas than in urban areas (Table 1).

Table 1

Infant, Child and Under-five Mortality in Haryana, 1998–99

Years preceding the survey	*Neonatal mortality*	*Post-neonatal mortality*	*Infant mortality*	*Child mortality*	*Under-five mortality*
			Urban		
0–4	32.6	9.1	41.6	19.6	60.4
5–9	28.2	28.2	56.4	11.9	67.6
10–14	34.0	18.4	52.3	16.8	68.3
			Rural		
0–4	35.6	25.9	61.5	21.7	81.9
5–9	34.9	27.6	62.5	25.0	85.9
10–14	41.4	40.2	81.6	31.7	110.7
			Total		
0–4	34.9	21.9	56.8	21.2	76.8
5–9	33.2	27.7	60.9	21.6	81.2
10–14	39.4	34.3	73.6	27.5	99.1

Source: NFHS-2 (Haryana) 1998–99.

The probability of dying in early childhood is higher in some population groups than in others. Table 2 presents inequality in infant and child mortality rates according to socio-economic differentials. Children in rural areas of Haryana experience a 30 per cent higher probability of dying before their fifth birthday than urban children.

Table 2

Neonatal, Postnatal, Infant, Child, and Under-Five Mortality Rates According to Socio-Economic Background in Haryana, 1998–99

Residence					
Urban	30.1	19.6	49.7	15.5	64.4
Rural	35.2	26.8	62.0	23.4	84.0
Mother's Education					
Illiterate	38.7	31.6	70.3	26.2	94.6
Literate<middle complete	34.2	14.5	48.8	19.0	66.9
Middle school complete	17.5	11.4	29.0	20.8	49.2
High school complete and above	23.1	16.7	39.8	2.8	42.5
Caste					
Scheduled Caste	36.8	30.6	67.5	26.4	92.1
Other Backward Class	30.3	25.0	55.3	20.5	74.7
General Caste*	34.3	22.2	56.5	19.4	74.8
Standard of Living					
Low	59.8	41.0	100.8	49.5	145.3
Medium	35.8	26.4	62.2	23.4	84.2
High	21.4	16.0	37.4	7.7	44.8
Total	34.0	25.0	59.0	21.4	79.1

* Not belonging to scheduled caste or any other backward class.

Source: NFHS-2 (Haryana) 1998–99.

The overall IMR declines sharply with increasing education of mothers, from 70 deaths per 1,000 live births for illiterate mothers to 40 deaths per 1,000 live births for mothers, who have at least completed high school. Other mortality indicators shown in the table vary similarly with the education of the mother.

The under-five mortality rate ranges from 90 among Muslims to 80 among Hindus and 61 among Sikhs. Mortality differentials by religion presumably reflect influences other than religion alone (for example, a larger proportion of Muslims than Hindus in Haryana live in rural areas, where mortality rates are generally high). This is confirmed by a study based on NFHS-1 data, which noted that the difference in infant and child mortality rates between Hindu and Muslim children is reduced considerably when other demographic and socio-economic variables are controlled statistically (Pandey et al., 1998).

Children of women belonging to scheduled castes have higher rates of infant and child mortality than children of women belonging to other backward classes. All indicators of infant and child mortality decline substantially with increases in the household standard of living. For example, for children in households with a high standard of living, the under-five mortality rate is 45 deaths per 1,000 live births; the corresponding rate for children in households with a low standard of living (145) is more than three times as high. The child mortality rate is more than six times higher in households with a low standard of living than in households with a higher standard of living.

Child Morbidity

Acute respiratory infection (ARI), primary pneumonia, is a major cause of illness among infants and children and also the leading cause of childhood mortality throughout the world (Murray and Lopez, 1996). Early diagnosis and treatment with antibiotics can prevent a large proportion of ARI/pneumonia deaths. The data reveals that 12 per cent of children under age three in Haryana suffered from ARI (cough accompanied by short, rapid breathing). Table 3 shows that the prevalence of ARI does not vary by sex of child or by urban-rural residence. ARI was somewhat more common among children of 12–23 months of age, of birth order four or higher, of illiterate mothers, children from other backward classes and from low standard of living households. The relatively small variations in the prevalence of ARI by most socio-economic characteristics indicate that respiratory infections are widespread and affect children of all strata in the state. Eighty-eight per cent of children received advice or treatment from a health facility or health provider when ill with ARI. The results indicate that treatment seeking for ARI is universally high (80% or more) across all socio-economic groups for which estimates are shown in the Table 3.

Fever is the most common of the three conditions examined in Table 3, with 24 per cent of children suffering from it. The prevalence of fever does not vary much by most background characteristics. As with ARI infection, fever tends to strike young children irrespective of their demographic and socio-economic background. Diarrhoea is the second most important killer of children under age five worldwide, following acute respiratory infection. Deaths from acute diarrhoea are most often caused by dehydration due to loss of water

Table 3

Prevalence of Acute Respiratory Infection, Fever and Diarrhoea according to Background Characteristics

Socio-economic background	*Acute respiratory infection*	*Fever*	*Diarrhoea*	*Per cent with ARI taken to a health facility or health provider*
		Age of Child		
1–5 months	8.9	21.6	15.6	—
6–11 months	10.7	23.5	16.4	—
12–23 months	14.9	28.4	16.5	80.0
24–35 months	10.6	20.1	9.2	94.3
		Sex of Child		
Male	11.9	23.5	12.9	87.8
Female	11.6	23.9	15.1	88.0
		Birth Order		
1	10.2	26.9	14.7	96.5
2	11.6	19.8	13.3	82.4
3	9.1	22.6	10.4	—
4+	15.8	25.4	15.9	84.2
		Residence		
Urban	11.6	25.9	12.7	92.8
Rural	11.9	23.0	14.2	86.4
		Mother's Education		
Illiterate	13.2	24.8	12.6	87.6
Literate<middle complete	8.7	23.9	15.4	—
Middle school complete	12.1	24.0	14.3	—
High school complete and above	11.4	20.7	15.3	
		Caste		
Scheduled Caste	12.0	27.0	15.4	86.2
Other Backward Class	14.8	25.1	12.8	91.4
General Caste*	10.3	21.3	13.7	86.5
		Standard of Living		
Low	15.0	28.7	16.9	—
Medium	13.6	24.8	13.7	90.9
High	8.5	20.9	12.8	80.7
		Source of Drinking Water		
Piped water	13.8	23.0	14.7	85.6
Handpump	10.4	23.7	13.3	91.5
Well water	10.5	25.6	13.6	—
Total	11.8	23.7	13.9	87.9

* Not belonging to scheduled caste or any other backward class.

Source: NFHS-2 (Haryana) 1998–99.

and electrolytes. Nearly all dehydration-related deaths can be prevented by prompt administration of rehydration solutions. The Government of India has launched the Oral Rehydration Therapy Programme as one of its priority activities for child survival. One of the major goals of this programme is to increase awareness among mothers and communities about the causes and treatment of diarrhoea. Among children between the age of 1–35 months, those with age of 24–35 months are least susceptible to diarrhoea. Boys (13%) are somewhat less likely to have suffered from diarrhoea than girls (15%). Differentials by birth order, place of residence, mother's education and caste background are generally small. As expected, the prevalence of diarrhoea is negatively related to household standard of living. Contrary to expectations, however, diarrhoea is slightly more prevalent among children living in households that use water from a handpump or well for drinking.

Utilization of Health Care Services

Utilization of health services can be worked out by understanding preventive measures taken for immunization of children.

Preventive Care: Child Immunization

The vaccination of children against six serious but preventable diseases (viz., tuberculosis, deptheria, pertussis, tetanus, poliomyelitis, and measles) has been a cornerstone of the child health care system in India. As a part of the National Health Policy, the National Immunization Programme is being implemented on a priority basis. The Expanded Programme on Immunization (EPI) was initiated by the Government of India in 1978 with the objective of reducing morbidity, mortality and disabilities from these six diseases by making free vaccination services easily available to all eligible children. Immunization against poliomyelitis was introduced in 1979–80, and tetanus toxoid for school children was added in 1980–81. Immunization against tuberculosis (BCG) was brought under the EPI in 1981–82. In 1985–86, immunization against measles was added to the programme (Ministry of Health and Family Welfare, 1991). The Universal Immunization Programme (UIP) was introduced in 1985–86 with the aim to cover 85 per cent of all infants against the six vaccine preventable diseases by 1990 and to achieve self-sufficiency in vaccine production and the manufacture of cold-chain equipment (Ministry of Health and Family Welfare, 1991). Pulse Polio immunization campaigns began in December 1995 as a part of major national effort to eliminate polio.

The analysis of vaccine-specific data indicates higher coverage for each type of vaccine in urban areas than in rural areas. Seventy-seven per cent of children aged 12–23 months in urban areas had received all the recommended vaccinations at the time of the survey, compared with 58 per cent in rural areas (see Table 4). Boys and girls in Haryana are about equally likely to be fully vaccinated. However, girls are less likely to have received each of the individual vaccinations except measles. Vaccination coverage has a strong positive relationship with mother's education and household standard of living.

Table 4
Childhood (12–23 months) Vaccinations by Background Characteristics

Background characteristics	*Percentage vaccinated from all**	*Percentage who did receive any vaccination*
	Sex of Child	
Male	62.4	9.2
Female	63.2	10.8
	Birth Order	
1	74.0	2.2
2	66.6	7.6
3	55.7	10.8
4+	50.8	20.0
	Residence	
Urban	76.5	7.3
Rural	58.2	10.7
	Mother's Education	
Illiterate	50.8	17.4
Literate < middle school complete	67.8	6.5
Middle school complete	65.0	2.7
High school complete and above	83.6	0.0
	Caste Background	
Scheduled Caste	56.4	14.7
Other Backward Class	59.8	11.6
General Caste**	67.7	6.3
	Standard of Living Index	
Low	33.4	25.3
Medium	61.8	9.1
High	74.8	5.3
Total	62.7	9.9

* BCG, measles, and three doses each of DPT and polio vaccines (excluding oral dose of polio).
** Not belonging to scheduled caste or any other backward class.
Source: NFHS-2 (Haryana) 1998–99.

Source of Childhood Vaccination

Table 5 gives the per cent distribution of children under age three years who have received any vaccinations by the source of most of the vaccinations, according to selected background characteristics.

Table 5

Source of Childhood Vaccination According to Socio-economic Background

Background characteristics	*Source of vaccination*			*Total per cent*
	Public medical sector	*Private medical sector*	*Other*	
	Sex of Child			
Male	92.3	7.5	0.2	100.0
Female	93.3	5.9	0.8	100.0
	Birth Order			
1	88.7	10.9	0.4	100.0
2	94.0	6.0	0.0	100.0
3	96.4	3.6	0.0	100.0
4+	93.9	4.4	1.7	100.0
	Residence			
Urban	80.4	18.1	1.6	100.0
Rural	96.6	3.3	0.2	100.0
	Mother's Education			
Illiterate	95.6	3.6	0.8	100.0
Literate, <middle school complete	97.7	1.7	0.6	100.0
High school complete	90.7	9.3	0.0	100.0
High school complete and above	83.1	16.9	0.0	100.0
	Caste			
Scheduled Caste	96.0	3.5	0.5	100.0
Other Backward Class	92.4	6.5	1.0	100.0
General Caste*	91.4	8.4	0.2	100.0
	Standard of Living Index			
Low	92.3	5.4	2.2	100.0
Medium	97.0	2.5	0.5	100.0
High	87.5	12.5	0.0	100.0
Total	92.7	6.8	0.5	100.0

* Not belonging to scheduled caste or any other backward class.

Source: NFHS-2 (Haryana) 1998–99.

The public sector is the primary provider of childhood vaccinations in Haryana. Ninety-three per cent of all children, who received vaccinations received most of them from a public sector source and only 7 per cent received them from a private medical source. The percentage of vaccinated children receiving vaccinations from the private medical sector is much higher in urban areas (18%), where private sector services tend to be concentrated, than in rural areas (3%). Even in urban areas, however, 80 per cent of children received most of their vaccinations from the public sector. Children of more educated mothers and those belonging to households with a high standard of living are more likely than other children to receive vaccinations from the private medical sector. Likewise, children from scheduled castes are much less likely than other children to receive vaccinations from the private medical sector. Boys, younger children and lower birth order children are more likely to receive vaccinations from the private medical sector than other children (see Table 5).

Nutritional Status of Children

Undernutrition among children is a major problem in every part of India. Overall, nearly half of young children in the country are underweight (47%) and stunted (46%), and one in six children wasted (16%). The prevalence of undernutrition is among the highest levels found in any country in the world. Similarly, about half of children are stunted in Haryana. The main reasons for the low nutritional status of children in the state are anaemia among children and deficiency of iodine in salt.

Nutritional status is the major determinant of the health and well-being of children. Inadequate or unbalanced diets and chronic illness are associated with poor nutrition among children. To assess the nutritional status of children, measurement of weight and height/length has been obtained by NFHS-2 for Haryana. Each of these indices provide somewhat different information about the nutritional status of children. Weight-for-age is a composite measure, which takes into account both chronic and acute undernutrition. Children who are more than two standard deviations below the reference median on this index are considered to be underweight. The height-for-age index measures linear growth retardation. Children who are more than two standard deviations below the median of the reference population in terms of height-for-age are considered short for their age or stunted. The percentage in this category indicates the prevalence of chronic undernutrition, which often results from a failure to receive adequate nutrition over a long period of time or from chronic or recurrent diarrhoea. Height-for-age, therefore, does not vary appreciably by the season in which data are collected by NFHS. The weight-for-height index examines body mass in relation to body length. Children who are more than two standard deviations below the median of the reference population in terms of weight-for-height are considered too thin or wasted. The percentage in this category indicates the prevalence of acute undernutrition.

Table 6 shows the percentage of children classified as undernourished by socio-economic and demographic variables. More than one-third (35%) of children under three years of age are underweight and one-half (50%) are stunted. Corresponding estimates at the national level are 47 per cent and 46 per cent, respectively. The proportion of children, who are severely undernourished, is also very high, i.e., 10 per cent according to weight-for-age and 24 per cent according to height-for-age. In addition, wasting is also evident in Haryana, affecting 5 per cent of children under three years of age, although this percentage is much lower than the national estimate of 16 per cent. The proportion of children under three years of age who are underweight remained at 35 per cent between NFHS-1 and NFHS-2, but the proportion of severely underweight increased from 8 per cent to 10 per cent. The prevalence of wasting also remained at about the same level between the two surveys. The prevalence of stunting increased from 43 per cent in NFHS-1 to 50 per cent in NFHS-2 and the prevalence of severe stunting increased from 16 per cent in NFHS-1 to 24 per cent in NFHS-2 (IIPS, 2001).

The proportion of undernourished children increases steadily with the child's age. During the first six months of life, when most babies are breastfed, 3.16 per cent of children are undernourished, according to the three nutritional indices. It is notable that at age 24–35 months, when most children have been weaned from breast milk, 30 per cent are severely stunted and 11 per cent are severely underweight. Overall girls are more likely than boys to be underweight and stunted, whereas boys are slightly more likely to be wasted. Undernutrition generally increases with increasing birth order. Young children in families with six or more children are nutritionally the most disadvantaged. First births have lower than average levels of undernutrition on all three measures. Children born after a short birth interval (<24 months) are more likely than other children to be underweight and stunted (IIPS, 2001).

Table 6 also shows the nutritional status of children by socio-economic background. Children in rural areas are more likely to be stunted and underweight than children in urban areas. Even in urban areas, however, two-fifths (40%) of children are stunted and about one-third (31%) are underweight. Children whose mothers are illiterate are twice as likely to be stunted as children whose mothers have at least completed high school. The proportion of underweight children also declines sharply with an increasing level of mother's education. Children belonging to scheduled castes or other backward classes have considerably higher levels of undernutrition according to weight-for-age and height-for-age than other children. The proportions of underweight and stunted do not vary much by mother's work status, but the proportion of wasted is much higher for children of mothers working in a family farm or business house than for children of mothers employed by someone else or children of mothers who did not work. The nutritional status of children is also strongly related to maternal nutritional status. Undernutrition is more common for children of mothers whose height is less than 145 cm or whose body mass index is below 18.5 kg/m^2 than for other children. The proportions of underweight and stunted are strongly negatively associated with the standard of living of the household. Children from households with a low standard of living are more than one and a half times as likely to be stunted or underweight as children from households with a high standard of living. The association between the household standard of living and the proportion of severely underweight or stunted is even stronger.

Table 6

Nutritional Status of Children According to Socio-economic Characteristics

Background characteristics	*Weight-for-age*		*Height-for-age*		*Weight-for-height*	
	Percent-age below 3 SD	*Percent-age below 2 SD*	*Percent-age below-SD*	*Percent-age below 2 SD*	*Percent-age below 3 SD*	*Percent-age below 2 SD*
			Residence			
Urban	7.6	31.3	18.1	40.3	1.0	5.5
Rural	10.9	35.6	26.2	53.0	0.7	5.3
			Mother's Education			
Illiterate	15.4	43.4	33.6	59.6	0.9	5.3
Literate <middle school complete	7.3	29.5	17.7	47.1	0.0	4.0
High school complete	8.0	33.5	18.3	50.7	1.2	6.9
High school complete and above	1.6	19.6	11.9	30.3	1.2	6.0
			Caste			
Scheduled Caste	12.8	40.3	29.6	56.3	0.5	3.9
Other Backward Class	11.5	42.8	28.3	55.3	0.4	5.8
General Caste*	8.2	28.0	19.9	44.6	1.1	5.7
			Mother's Work Status			
Working in family farm/business	15.8	40.6	15.8	51.5	7.7	15.6
Employed by someone else	11.8	33.3	23.9	55.6	0.0	2.6
Not worked in past 12 months	9.9	34.5	24.7	49.8	0.6	5.0
			Mother's Height			
< 145 cm	15.2	53.2	43.8	64.5	1.8	7.5
145 cm	9.8	33.4	23.0	49.1	0.7	5.2
			Mother's Body Mass Index			
< 18.5 kg/m2	13.1	45.6	26.5	52.0	1.0	5.9
18.5 kg/m2	8.7	29.4	23.2	49.0	0.7	5.0
			Standard of Living			
Low	14.6	42.8	32.9	59.8	0.0	4.6
Medium	13.2	40.8	27.7	55.6	1.1	5.7
High	4.0	23.5	16.3	38.8	0.6	4.9
Total	10.1	34.6	24.3	50.0	0.8	5.3

* Not belonging to scheduled caste or any other backward class.

Source: NFHS-2 (Haryana) 1998–99.

Anaemia among Children

Anaemia is a serious concern for young children because it can result in impaired cognitive performance, behavioural and motor development, coordination, language development, and scholastic achievement, as well as increased morbidity from infectious diseases (Seshadri, 1997). One of the most vulnerable groups is children between age of 6–24 months (Stoltzfus and Dreyfuss, 1998). Overall, more than four-fifths (84%) of children have some level of anaemia, including 18 per cent who are mildly anaemic (10.0–10.9 g/dl), 59 per cent who are moderately anaemic (7.0–9.9 g/dl), and 7 per cent who are severely anaemic (less than 7.0 g/dl). Notably, a much larger proportion of children than women are anaemic, and the difference is particularly pronounced for moderate to severe anaemia.

Several groups of children have particularly high levels of moderate to severe anaemia. These include children aged 12–35 months (an age at which children are often being weaned), boys, rural children, scheduled caste children, and children from poor families. The prevalence of moderate to severe anaemia is lower among children whose mothers have at least completed high school education than among children whose mothers are illiterate or have less than a high school education. As expected, there is a strong positive relationship between the prevalence of anaemia among children and the prevalence of moderate to severe anaemia among mothers. Despite these differentials, anaemia is very widespread in Haryana. More than 74 per cent of children in every group are anaemic, and more than 48 per cent in every group are moderately to severely anaemic (IIPS, 2001).

Iodine in Salt

Iodine is an important micro-nutrient. Lack of iodine in diet can lead to iodine deficiency disorders (IDDs), which, according to the WHO, can cause miscarriages, brain disorders, cretinism, and retard psychomotor development. Iodine deficiency is the single most important and preventable cause of mental retardation worldwide. It has been estimated that 200 million people in India are exposed to the risk of iodine deficiency and 70 million suffer from goiter and other IDDs (IDD and Nutrition Cell, 1998). In addition, about one-fifth of pregnant women are at considerable risk of giving birth to children who will not reach their optimum physical and mental potential because of maternal iodine deficiency (Vir, 1995). Overall 7, out of 10 households in Haryana (71%), use cooking salt that is iodized at the recommended level of 15 ppm or more (much higher than the national average of 49%). However, this level is low in light of the government regulations on salt iodization. One, out of five households (20%), use salt that is not iodized at all and 9 per cent use salt that is inadequately iodized (less than 15 ppm). Differentials in salt iodization by background characteristics are pronounced. More than 9 out of 10 households in small cities and towns use salt with 15 ppm or more of iodine, compared with 62 per cent of households in rural areas. The use of adequately iodized salt (15 ppm or more) is relatively low in households headed by persons from scheduled castes or other backward classes, compared with households headed by general castes. The widest differentials are observed for the standard of living index. Eighty-four per cent of households with a high standard of living use adequately iodized salt, compared with only 53 per cent of households with a low standard of living (IIPS, 2001).

Food Consumption

Over half of the children under age of five years in India are moderately or severely malnourished, 30 per cent of new-born children are significant underweight and nearly 60 per cent of women are anaemic. This is despite the country has gained self-sufficiency in food production for well over a decade, with mounting public food stock at its commands. The food security at the national level has not percolated to poor households. The prevalence of undernutrition – a condition resulting from inadequate of food or essential nutrient resulting in deterioration of physical growth and health is widespread. Protein/energy among malnutrition is the most common form of malnutrition among children in age-group of 0–4 years. Iron deficiency anaemia is quite common in children as well as women, particularly pregnant women. A critical consequence of widespread incidence of malnutrition is the impact it has on cognitive development and learning achievements, reducing the capacity to work and productivity among adults and enhancing mortality and morbidity among children.

The NNMB reports provide malnutrition estimates based on Gomez classification for children. The NNMB data show that the incidence of undernutrition among rural children, even though slowly declining, was alarmingly high and their incidence at 47.7 per cent in 2000–2001 was substantially higher than that of income poverty (NNMB, 2003). NFHS data also show that in 1998–99, in rural areas, 20.3 per cent of the children were severely malnourished, another 30.2 per cent were moderately malnourished and 50.5 per cent were malnourished (moderate and severe), whereas in urban areas 12 per cent were severely malnourished, 27 per cent were moderately malnourished and 39 per cent were malnourished (severe and moderate). About half of the children suffered from severe malnutirition (NNMB, 2003). Hence, half of the children of India might not have reached their physical or mental potential and about one-fifth of the children might be functionally impaired.* India faces the problem of child malnutrition despite progress in food production, disease control and economic and social development. Recent estimates show that about 40 per cent of undernourished children in the world are in India although India accounts for less than 20 per cent of the children in the world.

Intake of Calories

At the national level, the inequality in consumption expenditure has declined in rural areas from 0.298 in 1983 to 0.258 in 1999–2000. In Haryana the consumption expenditure is below national average despite its fifth rank in

*Seckler (1982) observes that severe malnutrition is caused by nutrient intake deficiency and mild to moderate malnutrition is due to environmental factors. He argues that the former problem calls for nutrition intervention and the latter for environmental intervention. There is as yet, not much empirical basis for his proposition relating to cause of malnutrition.

Human Development Index (NHDR, 2001). Distribution of consumption expenditure between food and non-food items also reflects the economic well-being of the population. In general, poor households are expected to spend substantially more on food items as against the non-food. One expects the proportion of expenditure on food to decline with development and economic disparities. At the national level, the share of expenditure on food declined from 65.6 per cent in 1983 to 59.4 per cent in 1999–2000 in rural areas. There was a corresponding increase in expenditure on non-food items from 34.4 per cent to 40.6 per cent during this period. The share of expenditure on food items among scheduled castes and scheduled tribes is consistently higher than that for the total population in both rural and urban areas in 1983 for which the data is available.

It is also noteworthy that in spite of higher per capita income, calorie intake level in Haryana has gone down drastically, which in turn also affects children and partly explains the high incidence of malnutrition among children. In the rural areas of Haryana average calorie intake fell by more than 600 kcal per person per day. It is more significant because the decline in nutritional intake was steepest whereas at the initial level it was highest in India. The data on urban areas also shows a sharp reduction in nutritional intake in Haryana. On the other side, despite low calorie consumption, malnutrition among children was low in Kerala and Tamil Nadu. The nutrition status at comparatively lower level of consumption of food energy could be due to better health care and nutritional intervention programmes. Surprisingly, in Orissa and West Bengal, children consume comparatively higher levels of calorie intake. Yet, their malnutrition level was higher in 1991–92 (NNMB, 1993). This could be due to their deficiencies in health care and environmental hygiene and weak intervention programmes.

Infant Feeding Practices

Infant feeding practices have significant effects on both mother and children. Mothers are affected through the influence of breastfeeding on the period of postpartum infertility, and hence on fertility levels and the length of birth interval. These effects vary by both the duration and intensity of breastfeeding. Proper infant feeding, starting from the time of birth, is important for the physical and mental development of the child. Breastfeeding improves the nutritional status of young children and reduces morbidity and mortality. The timing and type of supplementary foods introduced in an infant's diet also have significant effects on the child's nutritional status.

The WHO and UNICEF recommended that infants should be given only breast milk for about the first six months of their life. Under the Reproductive and Child Health Programme, the Government of India recommends that infants should be exclusively breastfed from birth for at least four months. Most babies do not require any other foods or liquids during this period. By age seven months, adequate and appropriate complementary foods should be added to the infant's diet in order to provide sufficient nutrients for optimal growth. It is recommended that breastfeeding should continue, along with complementary foods, through the second year of his life or beyond. It is further recommended that a feeding bottle with a nipple should not be used at any age, for reasons related mainly to sanitation and the prevention of infections.

Initiation of breastfeeding immediately after childbirth is important because it benefits both the mother and the child. As soon as the infant starts suckling at the breast, the hormone oxytocin is released, resulting in uterine contractions that facilitate expulsion of the placenta and reduce the risk of postpartum haemorrhage. It is also recommended that the first breast milk (colostrums) should be given to the child rather than squeezed from the breast and discarded, because it contains colostrums which provide natural immunity to child.

Table 7 shows the percentage of children who are breastfed within one hour and one day of birth. It also gives the percentage of children whose mothers squeezed the first milk from the breast before breastfeeding, which is not recommended. Although breastfeeding is nearly universal in Haryana, the very few children are put to the breast feed immediately after birth. Only 12 per cent of

Table 7

Initiation of Breastfeeding According to Socio-economic Background (in%)

Background Characteristic	*Breastfeeding within one hour of birth*	*Breastfeeding within one day of birth*	*Mothers squeezed first milk from breast*
	Residence		
Urban	13.4	39.0	77.8
Rural	11.2	28.7	76.1
	Mother's Education		
Illiterate	12.1	28.3	79.1
Literate <middle school complete	11.6	31.5	72.4
High school complete	14.8	37.0	72.9
High school complete and above	9.2	34.9	75.4
	Caste		
Scheduled Caste	9.0	24.3	78.5
Other Backward Class	14.8	35.2	75.5
General Caste*	11.6	32.6	75.9
	Mother's Work Status		
Working in family farm/business	16.4	32.9	73.0
Employed by someone else	14.5	30.8	66.0
Not worked in past 12 months	11.5	31.1	77.1
	Standard of Living Index		
Low	6.5	25.4	71.9
Medium	11.1	30.2	78.0
High	14.6	34.2	76.1
Total	11.7	31.1	76.5

* Not belonging to scheduled caste or any other backward class.

Source: NFHS-2 (Haryana) 1998–99.

children begin breastfeeding within one hour of birth, and only 31 per cent begin breastfeeding within one day of birth. Three out of every four women (77%) who gave birth to children squeezed the first milk from the breast before they began breastfeeding. No more than 21 per cent of children in any group shown in the table are put to breastfeeding within one hour of birth and, with the notable exception of births that took place in a public health facility, no more than 39 per cent started breastfeeding within one day of birth. For births that occurred in public health facilities, a substantially higher proportion of children are put to breastfeeding within one day of birth. Urban women, literate women, women from backward classes, and women from higher standard of living households are more likely than other women to start breastfeeding their children early. Initiation of breastfeeding does not depend much on type of assistance at the time of delivery.

Weaning Practices

A contributing factor to infant malnutrition is prolonged breastfeeding without appropriate and timely introduction of complementary feeding. Weaning can be defined as a systematic process of introduction of suitable food at the right time in addition to the mother's milk to provide needed nutrients to the infant. Too early an introduction of weaning food involves the risk of infection and adverse effect on lactation. Too late an introduction would be harmful to the infant's growth and development arising from insufficient quantity of breast milk. A WHO study of weaning practices by rural mothers in India showed that by 6–7 months only 12 per cent of mothers gave complementary feeds. Many of them started weaning foods at one year or later, resulting in protein energy malnutrition of the child (UNICEF, 1984).

Mothers of children are asked if the child has been given plain water, other liquids, or solid or mushy (semi-solid) food at any time during the day or night. Children who received nothing but breast milk during that period are defined as being exclusively breastfed. The introduction of supplementary food before four months of age may put infants at risk of malnutrition because other liquids and solid foods are nutritionally inferior to breast milk. Consumption of liquids and solid or mushy foods at an early age also increases children's exposure to pathogens and consequently puts them at a greater risk of getting diarrhoea. However, a recent study based on findings from NFHS-1 concluded that breastfeeding with supplements is more beneficial than exclusive breastfeeding. From about six months of age, the introduction of complementary food is critical for meeting the protein, energy and micro-nutrient needs of children. However, in Haryana, the introduction of complementary food is delayed for a substantial proportion of children. Less than one-third (29%) of breastfeeding children consume solid or mushy foods at 6–7 months of age. This proportion rises to more than 75 per cent at age 10–35 months. Only 43 per cent of such children aged 6–9 months receive solid or mushy foods, as recommended, compared with 35 per cent for India as a whole (NFHS-2, Haryana, 1998–99: 160).

Table 8 shows that the median duration of breastfeeding is two months shorter for girls than for boys. This pattern is often observed in societies where son preference is strong, because the parents may stop breastfeeding a girl at a younger age to increase their chances of having another child earlier (with the hope that the next child will be a boy). The median length of breastfeeding is also slighter shorter in urban areas than in rural areas. In both the urban and rural areas, children are exclusively breastfed for a very short median period of about one month.

Table 8

Median Duration of Breastfeeding

Background characteristics	*Median duration in month*		
	Any breastfeeding	*Exclusive breastfeeding*	*Exclusively breastfeeding or breastfeeding plus water only*
Sex of Child			
Male	25.8	1.0	3.5
Female	23.5	1.4	4.8
Residence			
Urban	24.0	1.1	3.1
Rural	24.4	1.2	4.1
Mean duration (months)	25.1	2.9	5.3

Source: NFHS-2 (Haryana) 1998–99.

Conclusion

Analysis of inequality among children in Haryana, presented in this paper, has brought out the effect of social stratification on utilization of health care programmes and nutritional status. It brings out that differentials between SC, OBC and general categories show the differential pattern of infant mortality, morbidity and nutritional pattern among children. Differentials in terms of rural-urban residence, level of literacy, standard of living index and educational level form the basis of inequality among children for health and nutritional intake. Despite fifth in Human Development Index at the national level, and continuously increasing food stocks, food and nutritional security at the household level continues to be a distant dream for a substantial section of population in Haryana. With all the resources, trained manpower and even a reasonable health infrastructure at its command, a large part of the state suffers from mortality, morbidity and malnutrition among children.

References

Basu, Alaka Malwade (1989), 'Is Discrimination in Food Really Necessary for Explaining Sex Differentials in Childhood Mortality?', *Population Studies*, 43(2): 193–210.

Das Gupta, Monica (1987), 'Selective Discrimination Against Female Children in Rural Punjab, India', *Population and Development Review*, 13(1): 77–100.

Dreze, J. and A. Sen (1995), *India's Economic Development and Social Opportunity*, Delhi: Oxford University Press.

Gopal, S. (1983), *Jawaharlal Nehru: An Anthology*, Delhi: Oxford University Press.

Government of India (2001), *Economic Survey*, New Delhi: Central Statistical Organization.

IDD and Nutrition Cell (1998), *Policy Guidelines on National Iodine Deficiency Disorders Control Programme*, New Delhi: DGHS, Ministry of Health and Family Welfare.

International Institute of Population Sciences (IIPS) (1995), *National Family Health Survey, Haryana, 1992–93*, Bombay.

—— (2001), *National Family Health Survey, Haryana, 1998–99*, Bombay.

Kopparty, S.N.M. (1994), *Social Inequality and Health Care*, New Delhi: Northern Book Centre.

Ministry of Health and Family Welfare (MOHFW) (1991), *Family Welfare Programme in India: Year Book, 1989–90*, New Delhi, Department of Health and Family Welfare.

—— (1992), *Family Welfare Programme in India: Year Book, 1990–91*, New Delhi: Department of Health and Family Welfare.

Murray, Christopher J.L. and Alan D. Lopez (1996), *The Global Burden of Disease*, Cambridge-Massachusetts: Harvard University Press.

National Human Development Report (2001), Planning Commission: Government of India, Oxford University Press.

National Nutrition Monitoring Bureau (1993), *Report for the Year 1991*, Hyderabad: National Institute of Nutrition.

—— (2003), *Report for the NNMB Repeat Surveys*, Hyderabad: National Institute of Nutrition.

Pandey, Arvind et al. (1998), 'Infant and Child Mortality in India', *National Family Health Welfare Subject Reports No.11*. Mumbai: International Institute for Population Sciences and Honolulu, East West Center.

Retherford, Robert D. et al. (1989), 'To What Extent does Breastfeeding Explain Birth-interval Effects of Early Childhood Mortality?' *Demography*, 26(3): 439–50.

Roy, T.K. Sumati Kulkarni and Y.Vaidehi (2004), 'Social Inequalities in Health and Nutrition in Selected States', *Economic and Political Weekly*, Vol. XXXIX, No. 7, February 14–20, 677–83.

Seshadri, S. (1997), *Change in Prevalence of Anaemia in Urban Low Income Pre-School Children in Vadodara*, Personal Communication.

Stolzfus, Rebecca J. and Michele L. Dreyfyss (1998), *Guidelines for the Use of Iron Supplements to Prevent and Treat Iron Deficiency Anemia*, International Nutritional Anemia Consultative Group, Washington, DC: International Life Sciences Institute Press.

UNICEF (1984), *An Analysis of the Situation of Children in India*, New Delhi: UNICEF.

Vir, Sheila (1995), 'Iodine Deficiency in India', *Indian Journal of Public Health*, 39(4): 132–34.

31 Religious Violence in South Asia

Limits of Majoritarian Nation-building in a Syncretic Civilizational Complex

ANAND KUMAR

South Asia is a region of great diversities. There are cultural cleavages due to plurality of religions and languages. There are regional differences due to the variations in the topography, demography, economy and political history. Unity in diversity has been the quest of South Asian peoples and countries. As a result, it has been always very difficult to make general observations about any problem or aspect of culture and society. But, social violence, particularly religious violence, is one of the major features of socio-cultural profile of the peoples and nation-states of South Asia for quite some time. It has been there, as a marginal phenomenon in the pre-colonial past. It became very pronounced in the later part of the colonial period. Now, in the post-colonial period, it is not only surviving but gaining strength, particularly in the era of liberalization-privatization-globalization. The last two decades have been much worse in terms of the socio-political implications of religious violence. There is a visible drift towards regimes which are marked by 'low legitimacy' and 'low efficacy' in the context of management and elimination of religious violence.

Any form of social violence is an indicator of institutional crisis in the context of the inter-group relations in the contemporary societies. The institutional frameworks are a response to the needs of the society and the South Asian societies have been engaged in nation-building with democracy as the lode star since the end of the Second World War. But, the imperatives of nation-building and democratization have not been necessarily conducive for each other in the region. It is true that the principles, institutions and processes of democratization are not always accelerating 'centre formation' for nation-building in a multi-religious setting because they tend to create pressures of majoritarianism and fears of minoritization. Furthermore, the political systems in South Asia, whether it is parliamentary democracy or authoritarian or military rule, lack built-in mechanisms to accommodate aspirations of the minority groups. It is so important for the South Asian states to have such a mechanism for protecting the rights of the minorities and to provide them a life based on justice and dignity not only for internal peace but also to maintain a relation of peaceful co-existence with the neighbouring nation-states. Because, one country's internal minorities may be the majority in the bordering country. But it is not a peculiar problem of the region because almost all nation-states of the modern world system have one or more minority groups.

It becomes a problem when there is growth of 'majoritarianism' beyond 'public interest' and 'imperatives of citizenship' and the state becomes an instrument of discrimination and manipulation in favour of the majority group at the cost of the minorities. Such a setting creates settings of inter-group violence on communitarian lines like religion, language, ethnicity, etc.

In case of democratic response, there are institutional arrangements for preventing 'majoritarianism' through institutional permutations and combinations between fundamental rights, protective discriminations, enhanced representation, federalization, decentralization and autonomy. The process is akin to social and political engineering. But, in the authoritarian settings, social violence, including religious violence, is generally controlled through a different methodology. It ranges from benign neglect to brutal repression. In such regimes, when the 'concern for justice' is ignored, then, the seeds are sown for group violence. It ranges from group migration and terrorism to internal war, which mostly creates decline in the 'nation-ness' and sometimes may lead towards nation-destruction through secessionism.

The South Asian region offers us good examples of both kinds of responses to social violence: (a) democratic institutional reforms, and (b) authoritarian repression and internal wars. The examples are related to group conflicts and violence around mostly the issue of linguistic cleavages, where the other divisive factors were present only in minor or negligible proportions. The democratic response caused re-drawing of the map of India through states' reorganization. But, authoritarian response created mass migration in Bhutan and split of nation-state in Pakistan (and gave birth to Bangladesh). The Sri Lankan example is presently in between the two extremes as the country is facing an internal war.

II

Most of the nation-states of South Asia are marked by religious plurality. They have the presence of a dominant religious group at the national level and at least one or more significant minority religious groups with pockets of dominance and influence in the regions except Pakistan and Nepal. All these countries are going through a historical transformation in the political character in the direction of democratization around the imperatives of nation-building through modernization. At the same time, it should not be overlooked that the polities of most of the nation-states of South Asia are found to be oscillating between secular democracies and regimes based on patronage to a particular religion.

Pakistan, Sri Lanka, Nepal, Bhutan and Bangladesh each give state patronage to a particular religion. India was engaged in the construction of secular democracy till the end of the seventies. Then, it also started drifting from the early eighties towards politicization of religions by the national political parties in search of 'vote banks'. Earlier, the central government in India was dominated by a political party which believed in making a departure from the prevailing model of secular democracy (which has been criticized by them as 'pseudo-secularism' and is only a facade for the appeasement of the minorities) and the party had started pushing in non-coalition situations like Gujarat for a thrust towards a new pattern of state-religions relationship on the basis of promoting dominance of political Hinduism in the name of cultural nationalism or Hindutva.

Religion-based social violence in South Asia is identified as 'communal violence' perpetuated by communalist forces that are organized on the basis of a mix of fear and hatred about the other religions and arrogance and pride about their own religion. Such persons, forces and organizations have more focus on the political dimensions of religious identities and have little to do with philosophical, sociological and spiritual aspects of the religions.

This form of social violence is mostly inter-religious in the cases of India, Sri Lanka, Bangladesh, Bhutan and Maldives. It is inter-religious as well as intra-religious in Pakistan and Bangladesh. It ranges from socio-political discrimination to absolute cultural decimation through destructions of the places of worship and residential areas. A wave of communalism, accompanied by majoritarianist thrust, is overwhelming the state apparatus and civil society. Democratic institutions and processes have become marginal, and sometimes suspended, in the context of promoting 'common interest', enlarging 'public sphere' and protecting the 'minorities'. It seems that religious plurality has become a cause of crisis for the project of 'nation-building and citizenship' in each one of these countries – whether democratic, semi-democratic, or authoritarian. The political community is getting drifted due to the acceleration of the process of minoritization. There is increasing marginality of the minorities in the discourse of power.

The processes of 'harmonization' and 'integration' are getting replaced by the pressures for homogenization and consequential conflicts and clashes. It is also obvious that there is a rapid growth of cult of violence around the 'fear of the others' within each religious community. It is generating an unprecedented number of 'internal refugees' from Colombo to Kashmir, Karachi, Kolkata and Kathmandu. There is decline in the legitimacy of the state and rise in the problem of governability. The commitment to eliminate various forms, including emancipation of women, eradication of diseases and elimination of poverty, is getting diluted.

As a consequence, the global community is forced to ask about what is happening to the peoples, communities, political parties, social movements and the governments in South Asia who are inheritors of the legacy of Gautam Buddha and Gandhi, Ashoka and Akbar, and who led the post-colonial countries towards the path of humane social order through decolonization and democratization?

This large question needs following complementary questions:

(a) Was it always like this or there can be identification of events, factors and forces, which have emerged in the post-colonial polity, economy and society? For example, what has been the role of democratic political processes, particularly the imperatives of electoral equations? What is relation between decline in the employment, intensification of poverty, liberalization and communalism? What is the impact of modernization upon the principles of social inequalities, and group identity, including the religious identity, in urban complexes of South Asia?

(b) What are the linkages between the local, national, regional and global aspects of the problem of religious violence in South Asian countries? For example, the role of religious diaspora, resource centres for promoting religious following, foreign governments, international organizations, etc.
(c) What are the consequences of recurring religious violence for the nation-states and the region of South Asia? For example, what is their impact upon governance system, citizenship building and 'nation-ness'? What is their role the context of the efforts of regional networking and institutions of regional cooperation?
(d) Is there a future beyond the cycles of religious violence? Is there any lesson about it from the other contexts of social violence in South Asian region, i.e., linguistic, ethnic, and class violence? Or, the South Asian region is condemned to hand over the responsibility of looking after its religious heritage to the forces of lumpenization and violence?

These questions are often discussed in the media, parliament, NGO's workshops, and other important forums. So, we leave any direct response to them in this discussion.

III

Historically speaking, religious violence is not a new phenomenon in South Asia. It has been associated with communitarian competitions arid conflicts as well as a wide variety of state systems in the pre-colonial and colonial discourses of power. Similarly, religion has not been the only source of social violence in the contemporary South Asian history. The nation-states of South Asia have witnessed cycles of violence around linguistic, ethnic, regional and caste-class conflicts in the post-colonial era.

In other words, collective violence has been an integral part of the contemporary political culture of South Asia. But, the increase in the frequency and intensity of religious violence gives it a new face. There is also anxiety about it because of decreasing efficacy of the civil society to contain it. But it is most alarming that there is a declining role of the state in controlling it.

If we take a look at the historicity of religious violence in various countries of South Asia, India, Pakistan and Bangladesh of today share pre-colonial and colonial legacies of religious violence. The pre-colonial memories have prominence of the instances of religious discrimination and destruction by the Hindu kings (of the indigenous faiths, the Buddhists and the Jains) and Muslim rulers (of the Hindus, the Jains and the Sikhs).

The religious violence of the colonial era was linked with (a) the 'divide and rule' policy and benign neglect of the atrocities of the Christian groups by the foreign rule, (b) fear of future among the elite of the minorities (particularly the Muslims, the Anglo-Indians and the Sikhs) of British India, (c) the dominance of Hindu-oriented approach in the leadership of the Indian National Congress, and (d) the cultural crisis of new cities in South Asian region. It culminated into communal partition preceded by a decade of low and high intensity violent clashes between Hindus and Muslims and Sikhs and Muslims between 1937 and 1947. The subcontinent was divided on the eve of freedom in a brutal manner with hundreds of thousands dead and millions uprooted forever.

The partition-related violence created enlargement of the communities that have faith in the necessity of religious conflicts. Such communities and groups have found uses of the memories of pre-colonial and colonial discriminations, competitions and conflicts as fuel for new mobilizations. It has proved contradictory for nurturing the ideal of secular democratic citizenship, which was adopted as the creed of the new state and new rulers of post-colonial India and Pakistan.

In case of Sri Lanka, the history is full of memories of recurring attempts to protect Buddhism from external incursions. The self-conscious ethnic groups of Sri Lanka are differentiated by religion, language and racial cleavages. There are three major cleavages of religion, language and race (which are mutually reinforcing each other) between the three major communities – Sinhalese (above 73 per cent), Tamils (nearly 18%), and Moors (about 7%).

The Chola invasion of the 11th century AD from South India is associated with large-scale devastation and pushing of the Sinhalese people to the central and southern parts of Sri Lanka. Even today, many Sinhalese believe that the decline and fall of the great Sinhalese civilization was caused by the Tamils. During the rule of the first two of the colonial powers, the Portuguese (1597–1658) and the Dutch (1658–1796), new elements of diversity were introduced by way of proselytization by Christian missionary organizations. The British continued the patronage till the end of their rule in 1948. Buddhism and Hinduism suffered due to the loss of state patronage.

As a response, the Buddhist priests resisted the expansion of missionary activities in Sri Lanka. The Tamils were more receptive of the missionary schools, etc. and beneficiary of the colonial process of modernization. After independence, the ethnic divides were reinforced by the politicization of the religious and linguistic distinctions.

Bhutan and Nepal were never colonized by any of the western powers. They also never experienced large-scale foreign invasion or incursion which may be associated with prevailing patterns of inter-religious violence in Bhutan and intra-religious strain in Nepal.

Bhutan has been living peacefully with the togetherness of the Buddhists and the Hindus for last two centuries. It has no pre-colonial or colonial heritage of religious violence. But, in the last decade, the differences of political-cultural orientations between the Buddhist and non-Buddhist communities (which gets reinforced by the differences of language, region, as well as insider-outsider categories) became so explosive that the entire non-Buddhist section (nearly 20 per cent of the population) was pushed out by the royal administration of Bhutan. They are living in refugee camps in Nepal under the supervision of the UNO.

Nepal escaped colonization and has no pre-colonial memories of religious violence. But it has been experiencing strain due to intra-religious differences between the majority hill people and the minority plains people ('Tarai' people are 37% of the total population). The differences are in terms of languages, cultural roots, economic power and political capacity. The differences became more pronounced during the democratic regime of the 1990s. But it is safe to suggest that Nepal has not offered any evidence of explicit religious violence so far. In fact, it is going through a phase of class violence.

The story of political destabilization through military coup and communal conflicts in Maldives became the headlines of the South Asian media in the last few years. It has been found to be associated with the changing power relations between the Hindu, Muslim and indigenous communities after the introduction of voting rights and multi-party system.

IV

This synoptic view of the pre-colonial, colonial and non-colonial contexts of the use of religion as a basis for social violence needs to be supplemented by a glance at the contemporary transformations going on in the region. There are three primary processes of social transformation and consequential changes in the principles of group formations and inter-group relation: (i) modernization, (ii) decolonization, and (iii) legitimaton crisis of the state. Modernization through industrialization, urbanization and democracy has been the essence of the social changes in South Asia since the end of the Second World War. At the same time, neither modernization nor democratization has been found to be always conducive for the political and economic elite of the countries of the region. It is also true that the principles, institutions and processes of secular democracy are not always found to be cohesive and integrative in a multi-religious society with high degree of economic and cultural unevenness (or inequalities and discriminations) between and within groups, communities and regions. Often, democratization tends to create pressures of majoritarianism and fears of minoritization. The situation becomes more complicated due to the presence of long and dark shadows of the pre-colonial and colonial pasts. Politics of vote bank creates temptations for communal mobilization. In such a situation the marginal groups do not get any space for institutional competition in a just manner and look for survival through a complex choice making between protracted conflict and ultimate exit.

At the same time, it is interesting to note that cultural diversity (particularly religious plurality) was turned into an advantage in Indian experiment with democracy as the presence of significant minority religious groups enhanced the stability of political formations in favour of secular democracy. On the other hand, absence of significant minority religious groups has been found to be no guarantee to social peace, political freedom and economic betterment in Pakistan, Bhutan and Nepal.

Decolonization of identities is another major process which is often associated with non-modern components of political and cultural mobilizations in South Asia. There are oblique relations between this process and the processes of (a) policization of religions, and (b) communalization of politics. It emerges in the post-colonial societies in the context of the relationship between the state, the communities and their collective action patterns.

The communities have been uncomfortable with the colonial state's engagement in the supervision of their 'sacred spaces', 'cultural identity' and 'social practices'. They expect decolonization of the relationship and withdrawal of the state from the domains of culture.

On the other side, the post-colonial state assumes the responsibility of secular nation-building as it is constitutionally empowered to actively promote secular citizenship and progressive social order through necessary investments and reforms. The post-colonial state prefers to ignore the community and promote the citizen. But, there is an irreducible role of 'communitarian cultural bonds' in the everyday life of all citizens. They will not like to barter their age-old group cultural identity for a handful of new individual rights. They will like to have both and engage in a voluntary reformation through a creative dialogue between them. This gap of perception is available for short-term exploitation by the vested interests in the name of group rights and imperatives of survival and protection. If it gets a place in the agenda of a political party, then, there is long-term mobilization, including religious violence to reform the state-community relations in the direction of decolonization. Religion and language are two most sensitive domains of culture and the post-colonial states have not proved efficient in addressing either of them in South Asia.

Legitimation crisis of the post-colonial state is linked with the incapacity of the state in engaging with the communities in a constructive partnership despite decolonization of the discourse of power. The challenges of mass illiteracy and poverty, women's emancipation, class and caste exploitation, regional disparities, uneven development and socio-cultural progress have remained insufficiently resolved despite more than half century's rule by the native elite. The internal disparities have been increasing and a class of neo-rich has effectively manipulated the state apparatus to maximize its advantages at the cost of common good and public interest. A self-perpetuating nexus of power elite (composed of political managers, big industrialists, big farmers, senior bureaucrats and military officers) has become instrumental in devaluation of the democratic agenda through corruption at high places and criminalization of politics. The process got more complex with the arrival of religious leaders in the political arena with new legitimacy due to the wave of communalization of politics. The crisis of legitimacy has become more acute since the promotion of liberalization and capitalist globalization, which has limited the economic and welfare roles of the state in the context of common citizens. There is widespread belief that the international financial forces and institutions have eliminated the economic sovereignty of the young nation-states of South Asia with the connivance of the power elite.

In the context of the instances of cycles of religious violence, it is an extremely critical aspect for a holistic comprehension of the phenomenon. Because in case of contest between the 'nascent nation-state' and 'age-old religion' for the loyalty of the citizens and communities, there is no match because the religions are not only older but wider (trans-national), more durable, and more integral to the people beings. It also contributes towards politicization of religions and communalization of political competitions.

V

What are the consequences of the cycles of religious violence in South Asia?

First of all, it is proving to be an indicator of the failures of the modern statecraft and limits of majoritarianist nation-building. The urgency of reforms in both spheres is underlined by the recurrence of religious violence. The political incarnations of all the major religions in South Asia is creating the threat of 'state within state' and it needs institutional response to prevent the collapse the project of modernization-based nation-building. It is also exposing the parochialism of the proponents of religious violence who are proving to be ignorant of the reach of their own religion in the civilizational framework of South Asia and the rest of the world.

Secondly, it is promoting the process of regionalization of religious communities, the civil society and political culture around the issues of human rights, religious freedom, cultural identity and social justice. A system of interrelation and cooperation is getting encouraged militants of different countries of South Asia. On the other hand, a network of citizen groups, NGOs and media is taking shape in response to the challenges from the forces of communalism in the subcontinent. The process of regionlization is also growing through the chain reactions to communal violence in the form of revenge with innocent local communities, refugee problem and media focus. The examples of the consequences of incidents like mass killing of Sikhs in 1984, the Shia-Sunni violence in Pakistan, the demolition of Babri Masjid in 1992, the mass migration of the Hindus from Kashmir, Bhutan and Bangladesh and crisis of Chakma refugees are some of the major examples of it.

Thirdly, there is a sense of crisis of faith among the followers of various religions due to appropriation of the religious space by the politically motivated persons and organizations. It is putting at least Hinduism on trial in India, Islam in Pakistan and Bangladesh, and Buddhism in Sri Lanka and Bhutan. A debate about the essentials of a particular religion and the need of inter-faith dialogues has been getting emphasized. There is new enthusiasm about interrogating religions in the context of their functions to meet the needs of an ethical and dignified life for men and women in their normal life settings. It is putting focus on the urgency of reforming the religious orders to provide justice to women, lower caste groups and the other weaker sections. This is creating a new receptivity for the spiritual voices belonging to Bhakti and Sufi tradition. There is re-discovery of Kabir and Gandhi by the anti-communal forces, spiritual communities, social reform groups and the secular activists.

Fourthly, there is a new role of media as the watchdog for the civil society and supervisor of the state in the context of religious violence. It has learned to function as the resource of relief and instrument of self-defence by the victims of religious militants and their attacks.

Finally, the paralysis of political parties and the partisan role of the bureaucracy and police has provided new significance to the military forces in the context of controlling religious violence. It is not healthy for a democratic future as it underlines the insignificance of the political instruments and significance of forces of violence. It is also promoting 'cult of violence' in the context of self-defence imperatives. It may cause 'u-turn' from democratization to militarization.

Contributors

Ajit K. Pandey, Professor, Department of Sociology, Banaras Hindu University, Varanasi.

Anand Kumar, Professor of Sociology, Centre for the Study of Social Systems, School of Social Sciences, Jawaharlal Nehru University, New Delhi.

Ananta Kumar Giri, Madras Institute of Development Studies, Chennai.

André Béteille, Emeritus Professor of Sociology, Delhi School of Economics, University of Delhi, New Delhi.

Arvind Kumar Agrawal, Head, Department of Sociology, University of Rajasthan, Jaipur.

B.K. Nagla, formerly Professor of Sociology, Maharshi Dayanand University, Rohtak.

D. Sundaram, formerly Professor of Sociology, University of Madras, Chennai.

Dipankar Gupta, Professor, Centre for the Study of Social Systems, School of Social Sciences, Jawaharlal Nehru University, New Delhi.

Gérard Fussman, Professor of Indian Civilization, Collège de France, Paris.

Heinz Werner Wessler, Bonn University, Germany.

Indra Deva, Emeritus Professor of Sociology, Ravishankar University, Raipur.

J.S. Gandhi, formerly Professor of Sociology, Jawaharlal Nehru University, New Delhi.

Madhu Nagla, Reader, Department of Sociology, Maharshi Dayanand University, Rohtak.

Nilika Mehrotra, Associate Professor, Centre for the Study of Social Systems, School of Social Sciences, Jawaharlal Nehru University, New Delhi.

P.C. Jain, Professor, Rajasthan Vidyapeeth, Udaipur.

Paramjit S. Judge, Professor of Sociology and currently Dean, Faculty of Arts and Social Sciences, Guru Nanak Dev University, Amritsar.

Paul D'Souza S.J., Director, St. Xavier's Social Service Society, Ahmedabad.

Rajiv Gupta, Associate Professor, Department of Sociology, University of Rajasthan, Jaipur.

Ramkrishna Mukherjee, formerly Director, Indian Statistical Institute, Kolkata.

Ranjita Mohanty, Head, Research and Academic Linkage Programme, Society for Participatory Research in Asia (PRIA), New Delhi.

Ravindra K. Jain, National Fellow, Indian Council of Social Science Research, New Delhi.

Renuka Singh, Associate Professor, Centre for the Study of Social Systems, School of Social Sciences, Jawaharlal Nehru University, New Delhi.

S.L. Doshi, formerly Professor of Sociology, M.L. Sukhadia University, Udaipur.

S.M. Dahiwale, formerly Professor of Sociology, University of Pune, Pune.

S.M. Michael, Professor, Department of Sociology, Mumbai University, Mumbai and Director, Institute of Indian Culture, Mumbai.

Sanjay Mishra, Associate Professor of Sociology, Rajasthan Vidyapeeth, Udaipur.

Shrirama, formerly Professor of Sociology, Ravishankar University, Raipur.

Shyamlal, Vice Chancellor, Patna University, Patna.

Sunanda Pande, Professor of Sociology, Osmania University, Hyderabad.

Surinder S. Jodhka, Professor of Sociology, Centre for the Study of Social Systems, School of Social Sciences, Jawaharlal Nehru University, New Delhi.

Véronique Dupont, Senior Research Fellow in Economic-Demography, Institute of Research for Development (IRD), Paris.

Vinay Kumar Srivastava, Professor, Department of Anthropology, University of Delhi, Delhi.

Yogendra Singh, Emeritus Professor of Sociology, Centre for the Study of Social Systems, School of Social Sciences, Jawaharlal Nehru University, New Delhi.

Index